100 Years of Science and Technology in Texas

A Sigma Xi Centennial
Volume

100 YEARS OF SCIENCE AND TECHNOLOGY IN TEXAS

A Sigma Xi Centennial Volume

Edited by

Leo J. Klosterman, C.S.B.,

Loyd S. Swenson, Jr., and

Sylvia Rose

Rice University Press

Houston, Texas

Printed in the United States of America

First Edition, 1986

Requests for permission to reproduce material
from this work should be addressed to:
Rice University Press
Rice University
Post Office Box 1892
Houston, Texas, 77251

Library of Congress Cataloging-in-Publication Data

100 years of science and technology in Texas.

   Bibliography: p.
   Includes index.
   1. Science—Texas—History.   2. Engineering—
Texas—History.   3. Technology—Texas—History.
I. Klosterman, Leo J., 1927–   II. Swenson,
Loyd S.   III. Rose, Sylvia.   IV. Title: One
hundred years of science and technology in Texas.
Q127.U6A616   1986   509.764   86-61306
ISBN 0-89263-262-3

To the memory of the
Challenger *seven, who lost their*
lives in the pursuit of
research in space

Contents

List of Illustrations

Acknowledgments

THE author of the History of Sigma Xi in Texas acknowledges with gratitude the assistance of the presidents of the Texas chapters and clubs and their delegates who graciously responded to a questionnaire formulated by him. Without their help, and that of Evan Ferguson of the National Office of Sigma Xi, this chapter could not have been written. He also wishes to thank several local members who provided information in private conversations.

The author of Part 1 acknowledges, with gratitude, information obtained from several authors of chapters in Part 2 of this work. Their contribution is specified in his endnotes. He would also like to thank the staff of the Barker Texas History Center, where the archives of the University of Texas are located, for their assistance.

The author of Chapter 1 wishes to thank Mary W. McBride, research associate of the Bureau of Economic Geology in Austin for forwarding necessary reference materials, and the staff of the University of Houston–Clear Lake for their generous assistance. She also wishes to express her gratitude to Richard Bishop of Exxon Corporation for helpful suggestions made in many discussions on the topic.

Significant contributions to various portions of Chapter 2 describing activities of pertinent divisions of the University of Texas system involving oceanography were prepared by Loyd Hampton, Arthur Maxwell, and Carl Oppenheimer.

The authors are pleased to acknowledge the assistance of the following people who provided much of the information contained in Chapter 3: Douglas L. Davis, National Weather Service, Fort Worth; Mickey Flynn, National Weather Service, College Station; John C. Freeman, Jr., University of St. Thomas, Houston; Norman K. Wagner, The University of Texas at Austin; Donald R. Haragan, Texas Tech University, Lubbock; Robert R. Riggio, Texas Water Commission, Austin; Jay Sheehan, Dow Chemical Company, Freeport; and the faculty of the Meteorology Department at Texas A&M University, College Station.

Chapter 5 was produced in the performance of NASA contract NAS9-16646. The United States government has a royalty-free license to exercise all rights under copyright claimed herein.

The author of Chapter 6 wishes to acknowledge the following persons, whose contributions comprise almost all the material presented: Narayan Bhat, Charles Coppin, R. E. Greenwood, H. E. Lacey, Patrick Odell, D. E. Owen, H. C. Parrish, Paul Pfeiffer, George Reddien, Charles Robinson, Howard Rolf, W. B. Smith, Dalton Tarwater, R. O. Wells, Jr., Bennie Williams, and J. N. Younglove. The author regrets that he is not able to give adequate recognition to the many persons involved in mathematical research who are not mentioned in this chapter.

For Chapter 8, the following individuals are gratefully acknowledged for their guidance and their assistance in obtaining key information from obscure written and verbal sources: W. Shive, W. H. Wade, D. Zeigler, S. Simonsen, J. Whitsell, and N. Hackerman, all at the University of Texas at Austin; N. Dittrich at the Welch Foundation; John Files and JoAnn Hendrick at the Merichem Company; A. D. Cyphers, Jr., at E. I. Dupont de Nemours and Company, Inc.; C. P. White of Texas Gulf Chemicals Company; G. Tromblee of Monsanto Chemical Company, Inc.; Gloria Millsap at Dow Chemical U.S.A.; and H. P. Whitworth at the Texas Chemical Council.

Chapter 10 was written with principal assistance from Herbert H. Woodson, the University of Texas at Austin; William L. Fisher, the University of Texas at Austin; Alvin F. Hildebrandt, the University of Houston–University Park; and Marion O. Hagler, Texas Tech University.

The author of Chapter 11 wishes to acknowledge with gratitude the financial support of the Texas section of the American Society of Civil Engineers in honor of distinguished engineers John A. Focht, Joe J. Rady, and I. W. Santry.

For assistance in the research for Chapter 13, the author thanks his colleagues who provided information about their institutions. Marian McCarley and other members of his family provided editorial support. Cathy Stewart prepared the manuscript, and George Diggs gave technical help and advice. Members of his 1985 ecology class provided lists of Texas ecological publications. Austin College provided time to finish the manuscript. He also appreciates the efforts of the many editors and contributors responsible for the 1954–80 newsletter, SWANEWS, of The Southwestern Association of Naturalists.

The author of Chapter 14 gratefully acknowledges the generous cooperation of many scientists. They provided recollections, materials from their files, and reprints. Special assistance came from Dean Sam Curl, Texas Tech University, Raymond Loan of the College of Veterinary Medicine at Texas A&M University, and Bruce Miles, director of the Texas Forest Service. The oral histories developed by Irvin May for the Texas Agricultural Experiment Station were a special source of information.

For superior assistance with some of the research for Chapter 16, Chester Burns is most grateful to Megan Seaholm.

The author of Chapter 17 wishes to acknowledge information obtained during discussions with Dee Ann Story, T. N. Campbell, and Carolyn Spock of the University of Texas.

For Chapter 18 Rand Evans would like to thank the following individuals for supplying him with their knowledge and memories of psychology in Texas: E. H. Kemp, William Howell, and Robert Young.

The author wishes to acknowledge with gratitude all those who contributed material for Chapter 19, especially those mentioned in his endnotes.

The author of Chapter 20 wishes to thank the officials of the many Texas foundations, museums, and scientific societies who responded to letters of inquiry, provided annual reports, and responded graciously to telephone calls; she also thanks Donald Richter and other staff members of the library for their time-consuming and helpful service.

The editors are grateful to all of the authors who have contributed to this work and provided indexes, the Texas Timeline, and the illustrations that accompany their contribution. Additional illustrations were obtained, with permission of the editor, from *Discovery: Research and Scholarship at the University of Texas*, Centennial Issue, 1983.

Publication of this work and its distribution to university, high school, and public libraries has been assisted by the generosity of the following:

PATRONS
Harris County Medical Society
Houston Academy of Medicine
M. W. Kellogg Chapter of Sigma Xi
M. W. Kellogg Company
Michel T. Halbouty Energy Company
Shell Development Company (Division of Shell Oil Company)

SPONSORS
C. T. Wells Investment
Pharmacia Company
Rice University/Texas Medical Center Chapter of Sigma Xi
Sara E. Huggins
Schlumberger Well Services
Skatron, Inc.
Texas A&M Chapter of Sigma Xi
Texas Academy for the Advancement of Life Sciences
Union Exploration Partners, Ltd.
University of Houston Chapter of Sigma Xi
University of Texas Medical Branch, Galveston Chapter of Sigma Xi

In addition, gratitude is due to the nine member chapters of the Southeast Texas Sigma Xi Council who assisted in this enterprise by donating their share of funds provided by the National Office of Sigma Xi for the Centennial Celebration.

The History of Sigma Xi in Texas

Leo J. Klosterman, C.S.B.

ALTHOUGH honor societies such as Phi Beta Kappa were already well established in the humanities by 1886, no comparable institution was in place for those interested in the sciences. That year, however, some students doing graduate-level research conceived the idea of forming such a society, and with the help of Frank Van Vleck, a member of the faculty at Cornell University in Ithaca, New York, they organized the first chapter of Sigma Xi: The Scientific Research Society. From these modest beginnings, the society has grown to include 120,000 members at this writing, and has elected over 350,000 members during the period covered by this centennial volume.

Sigma Xi was born at a time when scientists and engineers were still trying to establish their rightful place in the academic community. Though some scientists of the time wrote disparagingly of the state of their profession,[1] American science in the late nineteenth century was far from being the "intellectual backwater" that they suggested it was.[2] There were about five hundred serious researchers in the country in 1880, publishing in all of the major scientific disciplines.

Increasingly, these scientists were becoming more committed to professionalism, teaching and doing research in a university atmosphere. Though scientific activity may have been largely localized, national groups had begun to appear. Members could share their findings at meetings of the American Association for the Advancement of Science (AAAS), and the American Chemical Society (ACS), for example.[3] Journals published by these organizations provided alternatives to publication in the European journals, even though the latter were more prestigious.

Attaining status in the academic community was not easy for scientists, yet it was important for young people who were entering the profession. It was essential that they have expertise in their field, but it was equally important that they be accepted with honor in the community in which they lived and worked. Even more, young scientists needed the companionship, encouragement, and cooperation of like-minded peers and older researchers who shared the desire to open new frontiers in the world of ideas.

These were the needs that led the eight young men at Cornell to organize The Society of Sigma Xi and to choose that name to identify the unique group. The Greek letters Sigma Xi (ΣΞ) represent the motto of the group, *Spoudon Xynones*, "Companions in Zealous Research." Within a year they had established in a general way the characteristics that have been associated with the society ever since. As early as 1888 women were elected to membership, and new groups had been organized at Rensselaer Polytechnic Institute and Union College. Within a few years there were chapters at many of the prestigious universities along the Atlantic seaboard, in the Midwest, and in California.

Over the years many young men and women with doctorates who had been elected to membership in Sigma Xi at one of these institutions found themselves on the faculties of colleges or universities that had no chapter. They became members-at-large. As the number of members at a particular university increased, they would often meet informally to share their interests. Eventually a university committed to a research program would draw enough members of Sigma Xi to the campus to make a petition for chapter status a possibility. Then all that was needed was a catalyst.

The University of Texas at Austin Chapter

In 1908 John T. Patterson (see fig. 1) came to the University of Texas at Austin (UT-Austin) from the University of Chicago, where he had acquired a doctorate in embryology and membership in Sigma Xi. Three years later, when he had become chairman of the Zoology Department, Patterson began to investigate the possibility of forming a chapter. By this time a gradu-

Figure 1. John T. Patterson, first president of the University of Texas Sigma Xi chapter, the first one in the state.

ate school had been organized at the university, accompanied by a corresponding increase in laboratory and library facilities. An informal census of the science departments in 1913 showed that fifteen of the younger faculty had already been elected to membership in Sigma Xi, certainly a sufficient number. But were they ready to petition for a chapter? Did they meet the criteria that had been decided upon?

The criteria used in 1913 differ somewhat from those given in the current bylaws of Sigma Xi, but the spirit is the same:

> close attention shall be paid to the following: the roster of personnel, the technical competence and achievement of the petitioners, their teaching loads and the time allowed for research, salary schedules and fringe benefits, retirement programs, opportunities for advancement and encouragement of original research in science and technology, record of prior publications, research in progress, the courses of study offered at the location, facilities and financial structure of the institution, equipment available for research, and the attitudes of the administration towards research and towards the establishment of a chapter. Of considerable importance are evidences of official commitments to the development of the institution in the immediate and long-range future.[4]

A preliminary examination of the qualifications of the faculty and university, the quality of courses offered, student accomplishment, and graduate achievement suggested that they were ready. A committee was chosen, with Patterson as chairman, to prepare the formal application for membership.

The petition, endorsed by the president of UT-Austin and the Board of Regents of the university, bears the names of those listed in Table 1.[5] Copies were made to be sent to the twenty-nine existing chapters, as well as to the National Council;[6] a representative of the Council was sent to inspect the facilities and qualifications of the university; the inspector reported favorably; and agreement of a majority of the chapters was received. A charter was granted to the Texas chapter of the Society of Sigma Xi on December 28, 1914.

Patterson was elected president at the second meeting of the group. Frederic W. Simonds became vice-president and I. M. Lewis corresponding secretary. Edward L. Dodd, who had worked untiringly with Patterson to prepare the petition, was chosen for the office of recording secretary. Installation of the chapter took

Table 1

List of Petitioners for a Chapter of Sigma Xi at UT-Austin

Name	Research Area	Chapter Affiliation
Bantel, E. C. H.	Civil Engineering	Rensselaer Polytechnic Institute
Brown, N. H.	Electrical Engineering	Cornell University
Brown, S. Leroy	Physics	University of California, Berkeley
Casteel, Dana B.	Zoology	University of Pennsylvania
Dodd, Edward L.	Mathematics	University of Iowa
Hunter, W. S.	Philosophy	University of Chicago
Kuehne, John H.	Physics	University of Chicago
Lewis, I. M.	Botany	Indiana University
McAllister, Frederick	Botany	University of Wisconsin
Patterson, John T.	Zoology	University of Chicago
Porter, Milton B.	Mathematics	Yale University
Schoch, Eugene P.	Physical Chemistry	NA
Simonds, Frederick W.	Geology	Cornell University
Whitney, F. L.	Geology	Cornell University
Yoakum, Clarence	Philosophy	University of Chicago
Young, Mary S.	Botany	University of Chicago

place on May 17, 1915, following a banquet at the University Club. After introductory remarks were made by Patterson, the charter was presented by S. W. Williston, paleontologist from the University of Chicago, who then addressed the group. Patterson accepted the charter, and the acting president of UT-Austin, William J. Battle, spoke on behalf of the university.[7]

Nearly twenty-five years passed before a second chapter was organized. This may be attributed to several factors. Despite the promise in 1914 of a strong research program at UT-Austin, few departments were able to meet Sigma Xi's high expectations. Some of the difficulties involved have been pointed out recently:

The plain truth is that the conditions did not foster quantity research and publication. The amount of teaching required (the "teaching load"), the lack of advanced graduate students (in 1930 the University had 494 graduate students but awarded only 19 Ph.D. degrees), and the lack of financial support for research were limitations on the teacher's ability "to produce." Unlike many other universities, The University of Texas did not provide sabbatical leaves or any equivalent. It is probably true that a majority of professors in the 1930s were, as I, not given one penny of research assistance from the University. The one great aid that the University

offered was a strong library—thirteenth in those days in size among academic libraries.[8]

The author went on to describe the problem of isolation in terms of the great distances to the centers of research, conventions, consultation service to either government or industry, and conference or committee work. It was two days and nights to Washington or New York by train, for example.

There were, of course, exceptions: departments such as mathematics (see Chapter 6) and zoology (see Chapter 15), were strong. This may be attributed to gifted personnel, but there were probably financial reasons as well. Little additional outlay was required for genetics research; microscopes were needed for teaching and fruit flies were not only abundant but relatively easy to breed. At the time, no expensive laboratory equipment was required to teach mathematics.

But for most departments, the difficulties were real if not insurmountable. And the practical bent of Texans added to them. In the Atlantic states, the Midwest, and California, changes in attitudes toward academic knowledge and its relationship to the practicalities of daily living had come slowly, but they had come. Texans would not see such a change until the advent of World War II. The dictum more generally accepted was: "Those who could, did; those who couldn't, taught." There was little financial support available for research in the universities, either from industry or for government. And there was very little research being done elsewhere.

Other Sigma Xi Chapters in Texas

Rice Institute was founded in 1912 as a private liberal arts institution of higher education with a strong science and engineering component. Despite the attitudes discussed in the previous section, these departments had grown in stature, and by 1938 Rice was able to meet the standards laid down by Sigma Xi. G. Holmes Richter accepted a research grant from Cornell University soon after receiving his doctorate from Rice in 1929. At Cornell he became a member of Sigma Xi, and when he returned to his alma mater two years later to teach organic chemistry, Richter suggested that a chapter of Sigma Xi be organized at the university. Little happened, however, until Edgar Odell Lovett, president of Rice, invited Richter to do what-

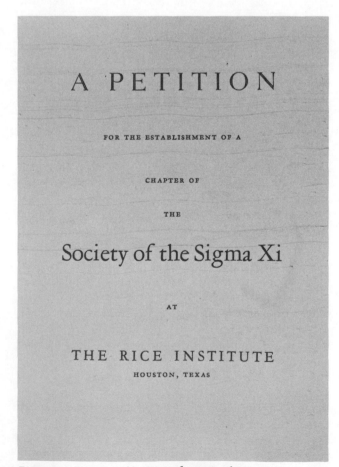

Figure 2. Petition for Rice chapter of Sigma Xi.

ever was necessary to establish a chapter at the university. When the petition was finally prepared (see fig. 2)[9], twenty-two members of the science and engineering faculties signed (Table 2). Many of them, like their counterparts at UT-Austin, have found their place in the pages of *100 Years of Science and Technology in Texas.*

George Baitsell, professor of zoology at Yale University, gave the chapter its charter in a ceremony held on March 23, 1938. President Lovett spoke on behalf of the Institute.[10] Seven of the petitioners were accepted as members that day: Beckenbach, Bonner, Bray, Garrison, Lovett, Milligan, and Pattie.[11] Chandler was elected president of the new chapter; Richter, secretary; and Pound, treasurer. In March 1940 four new members and seventeen associate members were elected.

As World War II came to a close, science and technology assumed a growing importance in Texas. With it came a concomitant increase in research at other universities, and many more chapters were founded. A complete list of chapters and clubs in Texas that are active at this writing is given in Table 3. Table 4 gives the first officers of these chapters and clubs and Table 5 those who held office in 1986. At the time of founding, chapters and clubs normally elected three officers: president, secretary, and treasurer; or president, vice-president, and secretary-treasurer. Mature chapters usually had four officers.

Sigma Xi Clubs in Texas

In the early years of Sigma Xi, the only group affiliate was the chapter. By 1921 the number of requests for affiliation was increasing rapidly and the decision was made to raise the standards of the society by strengthening the requirements for affiliation and inspecting the qualifications of the petitioning group more carefully. Not wishing to discourage formation of groups, however, the Executive Council introduced a new type of organization, the club. Requirements and procedures for affiliation as a club were basically the same as those for a chapter, and members had all of the same privileges, but with one important exception. Clubs could elect associate members, but not members.

Clubs were given sequential numbers according to date of affiliation, beginning at 400. When they were accepted as chapters, they received new numbers according to their date of charter as a chapter. Thus, as a rule, club status was considered to be the first step to-

Table 2

List of Petitioners for a Chapter of Sigma Xi at Rice University

Name	Research Area	Chapter Affiliation
Altenburg, Edgar	Biology	Columbia University
Beckenbach, Edwin F.	Mathematics	New member
Bonner, Tom W.	Physics	New member
Bray, Hubert E.	Mathematics	New member
Burr, Arthur H.	Mechanical Engineering	Worcester Polytechnic Institute
Chandler, Asa C.	Biology	University of California, Berkeley
Cramer, Raymond H.	Mathematics	University of Rochester
Ford, Lester R.	Mathematics	University of Missouri, Columbia
Garrison, Allen D.	Physical Chemistry	New member
Heaps, Claude W.	Physics	Northwestern University
Kitchin, Irwin C.	Biology	Yale University
Lovett, Edgar O.	Mathematics	New member
Milligan, Winfred O.	Chemistry	New member
Mott-Smith, Lewis M.	Physics	California Institute of Technology
Nicholas, Henry O.	Chemistry	Yale University
Pattie, Franklin A.	Psychology	New member
Pipes, Louis A.	Electrical Engineering	California Institute of Technology
Pound, Joseph H.	Mechanical Engineering	University of Missouri, Columbia
Richter, G. Holmes	Organic Chemistry	Cornell University
Ulrich, Floyd E.	Mathematics	Union College
Weiser, Harry B.	Chemistry	Ohio State University
Wilson, Harold A.	Physics	NA

ward having a chapter. This rule has been codified in a recent bylaw: "In general . . . any group wishing to obtain chapter status will have first had a successful period of operation as a club."[12]

The first club in Texas was organized at Texas Technological College (later Texas Tech University) on May 26, 1931. Seventeen members of Sigma Xi were present for the charter meeting.[13] TTU remained a club for nearly thirty years before members applied for and received chapter status during the presidency of Wesley W. Wendlandt. The second club was founded at Texas A&M University, but fewer than five years passed before its petition for chapter status was made and approved. The University of Houston applied for club status soon after the university was founded in 1927 but did not obtain a chapter until 1966, when research began to be taken more seriously by the administration.

One of the most active chapters, the University of Texas Medical Branch (UTMB), was organized as a club in 1949 despite some opposition. It has the most complete archival records of any chapter in Texas, perhaps in the country, due to the untiring efforts of Glenn Russell, who was deeply involved in the activities of Sigma Xi at both the local and national levels. It is a tribute to the UTMB chapter that members continued to be involved in Sigma Xi centennial preparations despite Russell's untimely death in October 1985. Further information about the UTMB chapter will be found in chapter 16 of this book.

For various reasons, a club or a chapter may find it necessary or desirable to change its name. Uncontroversial name changes can be made by the executive director of Sigma Xi, and a new charter is issued without a change in number. The University of Texas Health Science Center at Dallas was founded as the Southwestern Medical College, and the club organized in 1945 was the Southwestern Medical College Club. The current name was given with the new charter on April 22, 1978.

Table 3

Names and Locations of Texas Chapters and Clubs of Sigma Xi in Order of Their Number

NAME AND LOCATION	SIGMA XI NUMBER	DATE OF CHARTER Club	DATE OF CHARTER Chapter	NO. OF MEMBERS At Founding	NO. OF MEMBERS At Present
Chapters					
University of Texas at Austin	30	—	28 Dec. 1914	17	700
The Rice University–Texas Medical Center, Houston	73	—	23 Mar. 1938[a]	22	740
Texas A&M University, College Station	109	1945	9 May 1951	200	594
University of Texas Medical Branch, Galveston	121	28 Oct. 1949	3 June 1954	33	234
Texas Tech University, Lubbock	136	26 May 1931	22 Apr. 1960	23	120
University of Houston-University Park	157	1 Dec. 1949	2 June 1966	21	334
Texas Christian University, Fort Worth	159	6 Jan. 1961	8 May 1967	45	107
Baylor University, Waco	167	21 Jan. 1955	4 May 1968	43	91
The University of Texas at Arlington	182	21 Feb. 1964	23 Mar. 1972	23	120
The University of Texas at El Paso	194	20 Nov. 1958	1 Oct. 1975	43	170
Southern Methodist University, Dallas	197	16 Apr. 1970	20 Apr. 1976	75	336
Alamo, San Antonio	208	—	31 May 1974[b]	150	208
M. W. Kellogg, Houston	214	25 Feb. 1953	1 Jan. 1974[b]	58	141
Clubs					
Stephen F. Austin State University, Nacogdoches	424	1 Feb. 1965		14	80
Lamar University, Beaumont	432	29 Jan. 1954		22	66
North Texas State University, Denton	445	13 Oct. 1955		NA	50
Texas Woman's University, Denton	446	17 May 1956		16	56
University of Texas Health Science Center, Dallas	465	10 Oct. 1945[a]		NA	NA
Sam Houston State University, Huntsville	530	29 Dec. 1963		12	32
East Texas State University, Commerce	538	26 Apr. 1965		NA	—
West Texas State University, Canyon	549	22 Apr. 1966		17	35
Prairie View A&M University, Prairie View	670	23 Jan. 1970		19	38
Central Texas Research Society, Temple	718	21 June 1964		29	56
University of Texas at Dallas, Richardson	776	28 Sept. 1983		70	95

[a]Names changed.
[b]Founded as RESA chapters. See text under that subheading.

Table 4

First Officers of Texas Chapters and Clubs of Sigma Xi

	PRESIDENT	VICE-PRESIDENT	SECRETARY AND TREASURER
Alamo	Harold Murray	—	ST–John Burke
BU	Sol Haberman	Virgil L. Tweedie	ST–Jack G. Bishop
CTRS	Mary Preston Clapp	Earl Burnett	S–Walker A. Lea
			T–Ralph J. Hervey
ETSU	Daude N. Griffin	Dev R. Chopra	S–W. Frank Jenkins
			T–W. Farrin Hoover
LU-B	Lloyd Cherry	H. J. Kaplan	ST–H. E. Alexander
MWK	Joseph F. Skelly	—	NA
NTSU	David M. Morris	—	ST–E. H. Hanson
PVAMU	R. N. S. Rao	Thomas P. Dooley	S–Sam Daravalla
			T–L. C. Collins
Rice-TMC	Asa C. Chandler	—	S–G. Holmes Richter
			T–Joseph H. Pound
SHSU	Everett D. Wilson	W. M. Harding	ST–James D. Long
SMU	Lee McAlester	—	ST–George Salita
SFASU	P. A. Wooder	N. T. Sampson	ST–A. R. Machel
TAMU	Arthur W. Mellon	James E. Adams	S–Edward A. Hiler
			T–George M. Watson
TCU	Arthur Ehlmann	William Watson, Jr.	ST–W. H. Manning
TTU	L. T. Patton	E. F. George	ST–R. A. Studhalter
TWU	Dixie Young	J. C. Sherrill	S–J. C. Sherrill
			T–Helen A. Ludeman
UH-UP	G. W. Drake (Chairman)	—	ST–N. Catherine Cominsky
UT-Arl	J. W. Dalley	Tom Kennerly, Jr.	ST–Scott Poage
UT-Aus	J. T. Patterson	Frederick W. Simonds	Corr.S–I. M. Lewis
			Rec.S–E. L. Dodd
			T–NA
UT-Dal	R. P. Lutz	—	S–J. Hoffman
			T–R. Marsh
UT-E1	E. James Landers	Charles L. Darby	S–Eugene W. Lewis
			T–Charles H. Gladman
UTHSC-Dal	William F. Mengert	Donald Slaughter	ST–Herbert C. Tidwell
UTMB	John George Sinclair	—	ST–Joy B. Cross
WTSU	Gerald E. Schultz	—	S–Dero Brooks
			T–William A. Hooper

The Scientific Research Society of America

During the years before World War II, Sigma Xi gradually grew until it occupied a position of influence in most major universities, especially those having engineering departments. But no provision was made for grouping members who had gone into industrial research laboratories. These had proliferated during the war until there were thousands of members who were no longer affiliated with university chapters, who were graduates of universities where there had been no chapter, or who had become capable researchers after leaving their alma mater.

The Executive Committee of Sigma Xi, increasingly

Table 5

Current Officers of Texas Chapters and Clubs of Sigma Xi

	PRESIDENT	PRESIDENT-ELECT	SECRETARY AND TREASURER
Alamo	Helen Oujesky	Mary Pat Moyer	S–Gloria Lyle T–Milton Marshall
BU	Loy W. Frazier, Jr.	Robert S. Baldridge	ST–Samuel E. Taylor
CTRS	Hyrum B. Johnson	Nancy D. Mabry	S–Paul E. Boldt T–Harold E. Beaty
ETSU	Kenneth R. Ashley	James McFeeley	ST–Charles E. King
LU-B	Michael A. Laidacker	Richard G. Marriott	ST–John T. Sullivan
MWK	Harry P. Leftin	I–Robert E. Templeton II–Paul S. Chan	S–Una M. Gourlay T–Calvin F. Spencer
NTSU	John H. Rodgers, Jr.	NA	S–Barney J. Venables
PVAMU	Jewel E. Berry	Larry L. Cole	S–R. N. S. Rao T–Edward W. Martin
RU-TMC	Millicent C. Goldschmidt	John L. Margrave	S–Elizabeth A. Smith T–Roy Hopfer
SFASU	David L. Kulhavy	Donald Hay	S–Kenneth G. Watterston T–Wayne Procter
SHSU	Michael Warnock	Rowland Miller	ST–Harold F. Foerster
SMU	Edward R. Biehl	David Matula	S–John Maguire T–Bijan Mohraz
TAMU	Greta A. Fryxell	Marvin K. Harris	S–Edward A. Hiler T–Robert D. Baker
TCU	William Graham	Steven Cole	ST–Victor A. Belfi
TTU	Joseph E. Minor	Richard E. Peterson	ST–Gary Elbow
TWU	Robert E. Collier	Donald Walsh	ST–James Hardcastle
UH-UP	Stuart Feldman	Garret Etgen	S–Sara Huggins T–Lorin Vant-Hull
UT-Arl	Louis Rayburn	Robert Francis	S–Robert Neill T–David Lou
UT-Aus	Bassett Maguire	Beth Gillham	S–Otto M. Friedrich T–T. Bassett Maguire
UT-Dal	Austin J. Cunningham	—	S–Gary Myers T–G. Moushegian
UT-El	Lillian F. Mayberry	Richard A. Marston	S–Harmon N. Hosch T–Joanne T. Ellzey
UTHSC-Dal	Carole R. Mendelson	George Ordway	ST–Marc Mumby
UTMB	Harvey S. Levin	Michael A. Lett-Brown	ST–Gordon Mills
WTSU	Ted Montgomery	Gerald E. Schultz	ST–Larry Higgins

aware of the need to resolve this anomaly, permitted clubs to be established in some of these laboratories as a stopgap measure. Finally in 1947, they made the decision to form an entirely new society, The Scientific Research Society of America (RESA) for members of Sigma Xi who worked in industrial research laboratories.[14] The committee invited representatives from about fifty industrial research organizations to a meeting in New York in June 1948 to outline the reasons for founding RESA, its purposes, and the plans for its future. Sigma Xi drew up a constitution for the new society patterned after its own.

Initially interest was high, and within a few months there were nearly seven hundred members. Several prominent research laboratories were represented. among the branches or clubs that affiliated at the time. Members elected a Board of Governors as well as national officers. Among the former was W. V. Houston, president of Rice University. Unfortunately seeds of discontent were sown early by insistence that Sigma Xi be well represented in the administration and that the chairman of RESA (equivalent to the president of Sigma Xi) be from a university. Furthermore, several of the industrial clubs that had been accepted into Sigma Xi would not change their allegiance. Though the concept was good, putting it into practice was neither very easy nor very successfully accomplished.

For two decades RESA continued to grow, but the reasons for distinguishing between the two organizations seemed less apparent. While the more narrowly focused branches of RESA flourished, those that were more diffuse suffered. By 1973 it became evident that there was no further need for separate societies. Sigma Xi had created RESA in 1947; its continued existence was in the hands of the parent organization. On January 1, 1974, RESA ceased to exist. And what happened to the clubs and branches? What was done in Texas probably represents what happened in the other states.

The first Texas branch of RESA, the Southwest Research Institute (SRI), was founded in San Antonio on December 20, 1951. An active group, it elected to enter Sigma Xi as a chapter when the Research Society of America met its demise. While SRI grew stronger, its neighbor in San Antonio, the Trinity University Club, organized in 1966, grew weaker. On May 31, 1978, the two groups agreed to merge with a new name, the Alamo Chapter of Sigma Xi, keeping the same number used by the Southwest Research Institute.

The M. W. Kellogg Company (MWK) petitioned for branch status on June 2, 1952, and was chartered on February 25, 1953. Narrowly focused, it has always been active. MWK applied for and received chapter status when RESA ceased to exist. On the other hand, a group in Houston led by Ellis Strick of the Shell Research Laboratory and Elmer Eisner was more diffuse. Its members were drawn from several oil and oil-related companies as well as from the Medical Center. Chartered in April 1959, the Houston branch started well. Members still remember lectures by the NASA planning group, Carl Savit describing his visit to Russia, and traffic engineer Bill Hinch discussing Houston plans for the future. Yet the meetings soon became irregular, and in 1974 this branch disappeared along with RESA. Members joined one of the local Sigma

Xi chapters. Many of the Medical Center members joined the Rice chapter. By 1974 this component had become so large that the group requested a change of name to the Rice University–Texas Medical Center chapter.

Another group that succeeded was the Central Texas Research Society (CTRS) in Temple. Organized in 1964 as a RESA club, CTRS was virtually unaffected by RESA's disappearance. CTRS entered Sigma Xi but changed neither its name nor its number. It had been a club, and it remained a club. The Mobil Dallas Club was less fortunate. Its number, 739, suggests that it was formed in the early 1970s, but that is the only piece of information remaining about the club. Its existence must have been very short-lived.

Activities of the Sigma Xi Chapters and Clubs in Texas

Certain activities are associated with the national office: provision of national lecturers; research grants to encourage scientists at an early stage; national awards (the William Proctor Prize for Scientific Achievement, the Monie A. Ferst Award for promoting research through teaching and supervision, and the Common Wealth Awards of Distinguished Service in science and invention); and publication of the journal *American Scientist.*

Unlike some honor societies, Sigma Xi expects its members to maintain their commitment to the society's goals by taking part in local chapter activities.[15] These vary somewhat from one group to another but have two components: service to the members and service to the public.

The primary service to members is the local meeting. Since most chapters are associated with universities, meetings are generally held during the fall and spring semesters of the school calendar. Within this framework, some groups meet as frequently as once a month, others quarterly or semiannually. Speakers for these meetings are drawn from the local, regional, national, or occasionally international communities. For example, lectures were given at UT-Arlington in 1972 by the eminent historian of technology Melvin Kranzberg, and in 1975 by Nobel laureate in physics E. T. S. Walton, codeveloper with Sir John Cockroft of the first particle accelerator. The national office maintains a list of names of scientists who are available during the current year to speak on request to chapters about their specialities. Most Texas chapters avail

Table 6

Schedule of Events for the PVAMU Sigma Xi Club, 1984

DATE		TYPE	ATTENDANCE
Sept. 17	"Treatment of Cancer with Antibody. Toxin Magic Bullets," by Keith A. Krolick, Professor of Microbiology, University of Texas Health Science Center San Antonio, Tx.	Seminar	35
Oct. 4	"Approaches and Solutions to Industrial Problems," by Roy J. Jackson, Research Chemist, Shell Development Company, Houston, Tx.	Seminar	30
Nov. 7	"Overview of Drug Pharmacokinetics," by Winfred J. Sanders, Animal Health Products Department. Smithkline Beckman. Westchester, Penn.	Seminar	35
Dec. 4	"A Review of Program for Excellence in Science and Applied Science 'Education,'" by Ronald Sheehy, Dean of Benjamin Bannaker College, Prairie View A&M University	Christmas luncheon program	60
Mar. 19	"Mission Analysis and Radar Conceptual Design," by Lawrence S. Wunk	Seminar	50
June 26	Business meeting	Business	10
June 27	"Science and Religion," by the Rev. Andrew Mepham, Vicar, Saint Francis Episcopal Church, Prairie View, Tx.	Annual initiation banquet	23

themselves of this resource once a year or every two years.

Local lectures are usually followed by lively, sometimes heated discussions which contribute to a better understanding of the topic, sometimes by the speaker as well as those attending. Occasionally the seriousness of the presentation is disguised by a humorous title. One of the SMU lectures was titled: "Giant Armadillos, Glyptodonts, and Rudyard Kipling: Just So Stories from the Pleistocene of North America." (Glyptodonts were like armadillos, but similar in size and shape to a Volkswagen Beetle, it was noted.) The Prairie View A&M list of events for 1984–85 (Table 6) is a good example of an annual schedule of events for a club. Numbers of those attending are generally larger for chapters, particularly for the installation meeting.

One meeting each year is set aside for installation of new members and associate members. Since the founding of Sigma Xi, this meeting has generally been preceded by a banquet, and this tradition is honored in nearly all Texas chapters. Since this meeting is open to guests, the lecture given is usually less sophisticated. Table 7 gives an example of the components of an installation meeting. Members sometimes take part in field trips to natural or industrial sites. Although meeting notices are sent by all chapters, none publishes a newsletter or journal. The Stephen F. Austin State University Club has assisted its members by making a study in 1965–66 of research handicaps at the university.

Though Sigma Xi is dedicated to serving its members in the ways indicated, some efforts are also expended in giving the general public, and such specific elements of it as high school teachers and students, a better understanding of the sciences and a greater interest in them. This is done at the local level by public lectures. An example is provided in the efforts of James A. Cooke and Ulrich Herrmann of UT-Arlington in 1973. After showing a feature-length film, "The Violent Universe," they discussed in layman's terms the nature and origin of our world and beyond. An auditorium that holds four hundred was more than full.

Some chapters gives lectures for high school students. The Rice–Medical Center chapter has a High School Enrichment Lecture Program (HELP) in which

Table 7

Program for the UT-Dallas Annual Spring Banquet, 1984

SIGMA XI CLUB OF
THE UNIVERSITY OF TEXAS AT DALLAS
ANNUAL SPRING BANQUET

Wednesday, May 2, 1984
Texas Room—Founders North Building—UTD
7:00 PM Social Hour
7:30 PM Dinner
8:30 PM Program

1. Initiation of new members. [Names listed]
2. Introduction of new officers. [Names listed]
3. Address:
   "Maintaining Antarctic as an International Research Laboratory"
   by Robert H. Rutford, President, The University of Texas at Dallas
4. Remarks by Jay Chivian—President

graduate students from Rice and UH-University Park go to high schools to speak on topics related to their research. Members of nearly all chapters and clubs serve as judges for high school science fairs, but the Sigma Xi contribution as a chapter activity is not as clear since individual members are contacted directly by science fair personnel.

At the local level, encouragement to do research has been given through award programs. Several Texas chapters have given grants-in-aid for beginning researchers. Awards for outstanding teaching, usually at the high school level, have been given by others. Some have given awards for research at the high school level through science fairs. Texas Woman's University (TWU), for example, gives awards each year for an outstanding teacher of the Denton Independent School District; outstanding supporters of research at TWU; outstanding science professor of the year at TWU; and the research scientist of the year at TWU.

To carry out the activities described in the last section, financial support is required. Most chapters and clubs take advantage of the funds supplied by the national office from members dues, but this is not always sufficient. Some chapters have local dues as a supplement; in particular situations a few have made special assessments. Some programs are limited because of lack of funds, but generally this is not an obstacle to carrying out those programs that are less ambitious.

Since chapters are expected to send members to the national convention, the delegate receives in whole or in part the funds needed for this purpose from the chapter.

Table 8

Delegates to the Southeast Texas Sigma Xi Council (SETSXC), 1984–86

CHAPTERS	DELEGATE
M. W. Kellogg	Martin Fankhanel
Rice University–Texas Medical Center	Joseph L. Goldman
Texas A&M University	Greta Fryxell
University of Houston-University Park	Sara E. Huggins
University of Texas Medical Branch, Galveston	Michael A. Lett-Brown
CLUBS	
Lamar University	Michael Warren
Prairie View A&M University	R. N. S. Rao
Sam Houston State University	Harold F. Foerster
Stephen F. Austin State University	Kenneth D. Mace

The Southeast Texas Sigma Xi Council (SETSXC)

In the Spring of 1984 the nine chapters and clubs of Sigma Xi that are located in southeast Texas decided that a major effort should be made to commemorate the centennial of Sigma Xi, because, coincidentally, the year 1986 is also the sesquicentennial of the state of Texas and the city of Houston. Delegates (Table 8) from each of the chapters and clubs attended an organizational meeting on February 25, 1984, at which officers were elected: Martin Fankhanel, M. W. Kellogg chapter, chairman; Joseph Goldman, Rice–Medical Center chapter, co-chairman; Sara Huggins, UH-University Park, secretary; and Millicent Goldschmidt, Rice–Medical Center, treasurer.

Among the activities planned for 1986 were publication of a commemorative volume, a series of open houses in the home locations of the various chapters and clubs, a joint public program with the Smithsonian Institution, and a public program memorial lecture by one of Sigma Xi's Centennial Lecturers, Herbert A. Simon, Nobel laureate in economic sciences, in the Cullen Auditorium of UH-University Park on the process of scientific discovery. Committees were formed to oversee the various activities. The principal editor of this volume was invited to be chairman of the Centennial Volume Committee, which decided on the nature and general content of the volume.

SETSXC will continue to be active after the celebration of the centennial, coordinating activities for its chapters and clubs on a regional basis.

Notes

1. One of the most prominent was the physicist Henry A. Rowland, vice-president of AAAS in 1983. See Rowland, 1883, 242.

2. Kevles, et al., 1980.

3. Kohlstedt, 1985. This chapter includes a good bibliography of works on these and other institutions organized in the nineteenth century.

4. *Manual of Procedure, 1985*, pp. 40–41.

5. Ward and Ellery, 1936, pp. 702–703.

6. The current petitioning process varies in detail. At this writing, only five copies are required by the national office, which then notifies all chapters and requests their comments.

7. Ward and Ellery, 1936, p. 703. The procedure varies little from that used at this writing.

8. Emmette S. Redford in *Discovery*, 1983, p. 8.

9. A copy of the petition, a pamphlet, is in the Woodson Research Center, Rice University Library.

10. *Edgar O. Lovett Personal Papers.*

11. There is no record that Wilson, a distinguished professor from England, ever became a member of Sigma Xi.

12. *Manual of Procedure, 1985*, p. 98. At Rice University a chapter was founded directly in 1938, an exception to this rule.

13. Three members were known to be absent and three others were on leave for the year. Five years later membership had risen to twenty-eight. Ibid., p. 931.

14. RESA is "designed primarily to meet the needs of research workers in industrial laboratories." *The Society of Sigma Xi*, 1949, p. 26.

15. To avoid complexity, the term "chapter" will be the normal one used in the rest of this history of Sigma Xi, but most of what is written applies also to clubs.

Bibliography

Discovery: Research and Scholarship at the University of Texas at Austin, 7 (1983), No. 3. This was the centennial issue.

Edgar O. Lovett Personal Papers and Speeches, 1937–1940. Unpublished speech at the installation of the Rice University chapter of Sigma Xi, Woodson Research Center, Rice University Library.

Kevles, Daniel J., Jeffrey L. Sturchio, and P. Thomas Carroll. "The Sciences in America Circa 1880," *Science*, 209 (1980), 27–32.

Kohlstedt, Sally Gregory. "Institutional History," in *Osiris*, Ser. II, 1 (1985), 17–36.

Manual of Procedure, 1985, for Chapters and Club Officers of Sigma Xi, The Scientific Research Society. Private publication.

Rowland, H. A. "A Plea for Pure Science," *Science*, 2 (1883), 242.

The Society of Sigma Xi, Private publication, 1949. Pamphlet-newsnote of the society.

Ward, Henry Baldwin, and Edward Ellery. *Sigma Xi Half Century Record and History 1886–1936.*

Introduction. A Century of Science and Technology in Texas and of Texans in Science and Technology

Loyd S. Swenson, Jr.

TEXAS IN 1886 was only fifty years removed from Mexican sovereignty and only forty years old as one of the United States of America. The Confederate, Civil War, and Reconstruction periods had ended only a decade earlier. Cowboys with six-shooters had eclipsed Comanches in West Texas by that time, but soon barbed-wire fencing and windmills for water were closing in the open range. Many if not most of the myths and legends that characterize Texas in its first century (1836–1936) after the Alamo and San Jacinto obscure our understanding of the intellectual leadership of the state in its formative years.

Recent historical scholarship, however, is recovering an appreciation for the life of the mind in Texas, especially during the last two-thirds of the current sesquicentennial period. From 1886 to 1986 there can be traced an enormous socio-economic and intellectual evolution, so broad and deep that the changes might almost be characterized as revolutionary. Yet the cultural roots from which these changes grew provide an intertwined network so continuous and overlapping that Darwin's "tangled bank" makes a better analogy. Repeated floods of immigrants into Texas refertilized the banks of the mainstreams so that every year witnessed some luxuriant growth. Newcomers to Texas have long been greeted by old-timers with a friendly welcome and an assurance that if they settled down for seven years, they might consider themselves "natives." One outgrowth of San Antonio's 1968 HemisFair, the Institute for Texan Cultures, beautifully illustrates the overlays and interpenetrations of this rich mixture of heritages. Yet, pure and applied science were not well-represented there in breadth or depth.

Science and technology have been important in the shaping of twentieth-century Texas and will become increasingly more important in shaping its future. Whether or not the "fifth-generation" supercomputer comes out of Texas-based research, or whether a super Grand Unified Theory for synthesizing elementary particles and intergalactic cosmology emerges from the Texas Symposia on Relativistic Astrophysics, the fact that such real possibilities exist today in this state means that historians have some explaining to do. How did this state of affairs, state of mind, and state of events come to characterize the State of Texas? Hence, this introduction will aim at three goals: 1) to describe the book's purpose and frame its focus in context with regional, national, and international cultures; 2) to set this work within the context of the larger literatures of the history of science and technology; and 3) to explain the form of this book and the selection of its contents.

Perhaps a brief look at the human geography of Texas, not specifically treated elsewhere in this book, might give us some perspective. Essentially, Texas consists of a complex of about eight subcultural regions. Clockwise around a central area called the Hill Country, these regions might be listed as North Central, East Texas, Southeast Texas, South Central, the Valley, West Texas, and the High Plains or the Panhandle. Climatological differences and very diverse flora and fauna give each region a distinctive character. Settlers of different ethnic stock soon hybridized these lands. Thus the state of Texas exhibits as much diversity of culture and economics as of climate and environment. Nature and nurture have reinforced the people's diversity, ranging from the heritage of Tennessee in East Texas or of the Old South in the southeastern part of the state to the ranching culture of the West; from the hard-scrabble farmers of the North to the urban-industrial complexes of Houston, Dallas–Fort Worth, and San Antonio–Austin, complete with home-grown but world-class opera companies, symphony orchestras, and art museums. Scattered among the manorial palaces of the cattle barons, metropolitan skyscrapers, and the sharecroppers' shanties are the tidy towns of early German, later Scotch-Irish, Scandinavian, and other European colonies of immigrants, who settled in ethnic enclaves. Native Mexicans as well as other ambitious Latin American and Asian peoples of all economic and social backgrounds have crossed over the Texas borders—ranging from migrant workers to aristocratic entrepreneurs. Against this variegated background—both historical and human—the scientific and technological enterprises of Texans should be seen as part of the global processes of modernization, westernization, urbanization, and industrialization.

This book is a contribution to several birthyear parties. It is a festschrift celebrating the centennial of the Scientific Research Society, Sigma Xi, as well as the sesquicentennial of the state of Texas and of the city of Houston. The book was planned only in late 1984 to be published concurrently with these three anniversaries. It was supposed to be a sampler set of essays reviewing the history of various types of scientific and engineering research done in Texas or by Texans. It is, we now know, less than comprehensive but far more than merely celebratory. As a collection of retrospective essays on the state of twenty professional specialities in Texas, this book may serve as a unique reference work, for a while at least, to the origins and growth of pure and applied research and development in this state.

In 1975 the Texas State Historical Association devoted one session at its annual meeting in Austin to the history of natural science in Texas. Poor attendance and the very limited scope of presentations indicated that there was little interest and a lack of studies on the pure and applied sciences in Texas history. Now, a decade later, the histories of science and technology in Texas have not grown much but interest certainly has, and so we may expect more local and regional studies to parallel the last decades' growth of interest in national histories of science and technology. This book is a step toward that goal.

The cross-fertilization of different disciplines provided by the juxtaposition of these chapters afforded for the editors a liberal education and will give our readers the opportunity to become acquainted with a larger context of relevant literature both in Texana and in history of science and technology. Indeed, in the past, so superspecialized have been most academics as research experts that they hardly know each others' specialties, much less personalities. But now societies such as Sigma Xi, journals like the *American Scientist*, and books like this exist to help bridge such gaps.

There is an extraordinary centennial literature for science and technology in the older states back east. New England, New York, Pennsylvania, Virginia, and the Carolinas have innumerable local and regional celebratory books honoring one hundred years of personal achievements by local heroes. One example that fairly closely parallels our own anthology was published in San Francisco in 1955 in celebration of the centennial of the California Academy of Sciences: *A Century of Progress in the Natural Sciences, 1853–1953*, edited by Edward L. Kessel. That massive work on natural history contains primarily chapters on the progress in systematic entomology but also several which aim at a broader audience of Californians interested in the intellectual history of the West Coast.

A proposal for a multi-volume history of technology in Texas is under consideration in Austin. The essays gathered here might also stimulate the production of a multi-volume history of the sciences in Texas, if not soon then at least by the bicentennial to follow. We hope this book will serve as an invitation to build on this beginning.

The history of science grew out of intellectual history early in the twentieth century. The history of technology, evolving a generation later, grew out of economic and business history as well as the history of science. We are fortunate in the 1980s to benefit from a large and growing body of literature about these subjects. But relevant local and regional historical literature is much more limited. Very few histories of statewide activities in science and technology, for instance, could be found for models to be followed. Universities, colleges, departments, societies, academies, and other institutions often have been the locus of celebratory historical accounts. But the intellectual life of a whole state has not often attracted such treatment. One reason certainly must be the difficulty of determining what and who might be considered relevant in the artificial world of the state.

Are primary criteria the professions and achievements of scientists and engineers in Texas, or of Texans at work in science and technology? How should attention be focused on accidental affiliations? Are the accomplishments of native Texans elsewhere of equal interest as those of famous retirees who happen to die in Texas? How much of the work, initial or major, of people associated in some sense with Texas should be claimed as central to the concerns of this overview? To these and other such self-centered questions we have not tried to provide answers. Rather, we have sought to stimulate the asking of such questions.

Shakespeare may be paraphrased during the Texas Sesquicentennial to the effect that some folks are born Texan, some achieve Texanhood, and some have Texanhood thrust upon them. But however measured, say by James Michener's *Texas* or by the TV series "Dallas," or however much exaggerated by Texas braggadocio, the mind and spirit of the patch on planet Earth that all the world thinks it knows as Texas is bigger still, for its sons and daughters both native and naturalized have ranged far and wide imaginatively in all human endeavors. Our focus in this book is on activities in Texas and by Texans attempting to understand and to control Nature.

No doubt, the spirit of the times of the mid–1980s celebrating Texas' and Houston's sesquicentennials and a nationwide centennial for Sigma Xi have colored the contents of this book. Quite likely also, this work would have looked far different if done from the Dallas–Fort Worth area, or by industrial scientists primarily, or with a different set of editors, or another publisher. Subtle variations in perspectives are to be expected for a host of reasons, but none are more important in this case than each author's individual appreciation of his or her experience. Although there has been a vast outpouring of contextual literature from historians of science and technology during the past decade or so, the essays presented here (with but a few exceptions) are by practitioners—scientists and engineers—rather than by historians. Therefore, the

annual critical bibliographies from the leading journals, such as *Isis* for the History of Science Society and *Technology and Culture* for the Society for the History of Technology, have not contributed much as background for these essays. We refer the reader to these aids for further contextual study. Reference should also be made to the elaborate series of bibliographies on the *History of Science and Technology* published by Garland under the general editorship of Robert P. Multhauf and Ellen B. Wells. Most appropriate from that series for this purpose would be Marc Rothenberg, *The History of Science and Technology in the United States: A Selective and Critical Bibliography* (New York: 1982).

Most useful of all, however, is the revived annual *Osiris*, a companion to *Isis* and a research journal devoted to the history of science and its cultural influences, Second Series, Volume 1, 1985. In fact, that work suggests an alternate title for this one: "Historical Memoirs on Texas Science." Therein are seventeen review articles describing *Historical Writing on American Science*, edited by Sally G. Kohlstedt and Margaret W. Rossiter. They explain the field, describe its classic themes, review six of its older main specialties and four newer areas, and give a guide to the sources.

So much has been accomplished fairly recently, for instance in the history of geology, astronomy, chemistry, biology, physics, and the social sciences in the United States alone, that the magnitude of incorporating it all into this book would have delayed it indefinitely. We would have missed the centennial and sesquicentennial that are its inspiration and would have perhaps also distracted from its purpose: to celebrate Texas and Texans specifically. Historical perspectives will come later and will be built largely on such monographs as are presented here.

In this regard we must also mention the sizeable outpouring of periodical literature related to the Texas and Houston Sesquicentennial (e.g., March 2, 1986, Sunday supplements to all major newspapers in the state and special issues of magazines like *Texas Monthly*, *The Texas Humanist*, and others). One of the best prepared anthologies was developed and edited by Donald W. Whisenhunt, *Texas: A Sesquicentennial Celebration* (Austin: Eakin Press, 1984), which set forth twenty scholarly chapters (eight by periods, twelve by topics) giving fresh interpretations by historians of Texana. Eldon S. Branda's Supplement (or Volume III) to the *Handbook of Texas* (1976) has served us well, but the whole *Handbook* is under major revision, with primary attention to scientific and technological topics, as perhaps a seven-volume encyclopedia (but not to be expected before 1995).

Another facet of the context in which this book has been composed is the growing but incompletely sampled body of university, college, and departmental histories that now exist. Because the coordinating board of the Texas College and University System lists a total of 155 institutions of higher education in Texas for 1985–86, we found it necessary to devise an appendix (Appendix B) for acronyms, information retrieval, and systemic relations. Thirty-nine public universities, seven public medical schools and health science centers, two independent medical and dental schools, and thirty-eight independent senior colleges and universities are the primary sites for most sponsored research in science and technology in Texas. But the sixty-three public community colleges, four public technical institutes, and three independent junior colleges may also be staffed by ambitious researchers doing their best work independently as part of the hopeful cohort of young men and women with doctorates.

Obviously, institutional pride and public relations needs for both industrial and governmental as well as academic research centers have produced a large and growing body of historical or quasi-historical information about research activities. No systematic search of this literature, even for the major public universities mentioned above, has been attempted here. But it should be done! Compare, for instance, the centennial histories of Texas A&M University that appeared around 1976 (by H. C. Dethloff, C. W. Crawford, and others) with earlier "Aggie" histories; then contrast those with the University of Texas centennial histories published around 1983 (see entries in R. McCaslin's bibliography). Such studies of the two oldest state centers of higher education alone could provide even more of the context for the intellectual life of science and technology in Texas. The 1983 centennial issue (vol. 7, no. 3) of *Discovery* magazine, describing research, scholarly, and creative activities at UT–Austin, carried seventeen articles, for example, directly pertinent to this study. Less direct, but more relevant to the new social approach to all human history, would be the comparison of such impressionistic histories as those by Joe B. Frantz for UT–Austin, *The Forty-Acre Follies* (1984), Fredericka Meiners' *A History of Rice University: The Institute Years, 1907–1963* (1983), and Patrick J. Nicholson's *In Time: An Anecdotal History of the First Fifty Years of the University of Houston* (1977).

Finally, a few words of linkage to Klosterman's account of Sigma Xi in Texas may be helpful. All six issues of *American Scientist* during 1986 are carrying special articles for this centennial year, but the September–October issue will be specially edited by Melvin Kranzberg, former president of Sigma Xi as well as the doyen for *Technology and Culture.* In addition, Michael M. Sokal has researched and written an extensive centennial-year history of the national Sigma Xi organization from its founding and first years at Cornell (until 1893) to its merger with The Scientific Research Society of America (RESA) and further programmatic growth since 1970. Like most professional organizations with scholarly, scientific, or technical publishing as a primary purpose for existence, Sigma Xi became both a cause and an effect of an improved climate for scientific research in Texas, but it really had to struggle to survive.

Now let us turn to the composition of this book and the organization of its contents. Dividing the history of science and technology in Texas into two parts, before and after the end of World War II, was of course somewhat arbitrary, but 1945 as a dividing line seemed appropriate for several reasons. Most of our authors we knew would be active professionals of senior status in their fields who would be most comfortable in recounting the changes they had experienced during the last forty years. Although Texas has a few historians or other scholars with professional training in the humanistic or social studies of science and technology, (the 1983 *Isis Guide* lists thirty-four subscribers in Texas), our numbers are too few and our own interests too specialized to grasp this target of opportunity properly. However, we were very fortunate to identify early the advanced young scholar Richard McCaslin to provide the synoptic overview that makes Part One, "Science and Technology in Texas before World War II," such a delight. McCaslin's historical sense for combining unique details to illustrate broad trends in Texas history serves well to frame the background for each subsequent chapter in Part Two. Although there are a few overlapping allusions, especially in the earth and space sciences section, McCaslin's narrative gives a solid feeling for the six-decade progression (1886–1945) of Texas from a frontier society through a rural culture and into an urban-industrial matrix. He begins and ends with the triple incarnation of the Texas Academy of Science, but it is no accident that central ingredients of his story are centered around the histories of the two oldest public universities in the state, Texas A&M (est. 1876) at College Station and the University of Texas (est. 1883) at Austin.

While Part One is written and conceived as more of a "pure history," Part Two, the rest of the book, takes on a different cast. It is a set of memoirs of the scientists and engineers who not only witnessed the changes they chronicled but participated in them in many cases. Consequently, this book will not be the last word for historians of science and technology by any means, but should be of significant use to future historians who may then synthesize the scientific and technological experience in Texas as a whole—perhaps for the first Sigma Xi sesquicentennial. In other words, Part Two of this book provides what may be termed as near-contemporary, almost eyewitness accounts of certain changes within each of the disciplines, written by those closest to them and eminent experts in their own fields.

Naturally, the historical bias of two editors had to be modified as the authors' research and writing progressed. Originally hoping for more of a "pure history" of the development of science and technology in Texas, we found that the book was developing into a work of a different but equally significant character. We had hoped to alternate chapters of "pure" science with chapters of "application" in some form of technology. For example, genetics and molecular biology would be followed by biomedicine, ecology, agriculture, and so on. For several reasons this plan proved to be unworkable when we received the actual articles.

In some cases, chapters like "Mathematics and Computers" and "Meteorology and Oceanography" were too big to handle together and so have now been split for separate treatments. We were delighted that certain others, like the studies of geology and astronomy in Texas, turned out to have chronicled so much more activity than we had suspected in Texas and to be so interesting in their relation to the other sciences that we discarded our original plan and let the material shape itself naturally, according to its content, as we saw it. Hence, the final organization reflects disciplinary more than historical desiderata. We were influenced also to some extent, but not slavishly so, by the organization of disciplines and bibliographies in Sigma Xi's *American Scientist*.

Ultimately, we have placed the contributed chapters in sections that reflect the chronological as well as logical ordering of their emphases. Cross-references and the chronological timeline in Appendix A should help the assiduous reader to make more historical sense out of the separate articles. But, as editors, we assume that most of our initial readers will be concentrating on their own disciplines first, then on their own institutions, and finally on their own acquaintances. We believe that this large-scale map of the territory, so to speak, will become an invaluable tool for orientation to and exploration of the history of the research professions in science and technology in Texas.

One

Science and Technology in Texas before World War II

Richard B. McCaslin

The Awakening Giant

Texas in 1886 slumbered at the dawn of a great era of scientific and technological progress, stagnating within the dominant cotton culture of the post–Reconstruction South. Speaking before the Texas Academy of Science scarcely a half dozen years later, Edgar Everhart, professor of chemistry at the University of Texas, lamented, "It needs but a cursory glance at America to discover that the South is behind every other portion of the country in progress and prosperity." Just as in the long years before the Civil War, in Texas "everything which requires expert knowledge for its completion seeks its experts elsewhere."[1] Cotton, cattle, corn, and raw timber exports dominated the state economy at the turn of the century. The value of Texas manufactures was negligible; profits from cotton alone exceeded those for all finished goods in 1900. Texas, like the rest of the South, found itself integrated into the United States economy on a colonial basis, exporting raw material and importing industrial products despite a great wealth of human and natural resources.[2]

The sleepy facade of a thoroughly agrarian state, however, masked the first stages of a dramatic economic evolution. Agricultural production did continue to increase sharply through the next few decades, but by the beginning of the twentieth century a "complex and growing superstructure of industry had firmly attached itself to the agricultural base."[3] Farmers themselves changed their habits, growing more for the market and less for subsistence, subtly opening themselves to the influence of those who argued for scientific agriculture to further boost productivity and profit. Lumber companies matured, shipping from Texas less raw timber and more wood products with an increasing amount of value added by manufacture. Finally, the oil industry awakened, slowly at first, then with an explosive roar from a barren mound near Beaumont. "The door of agricultural leadership in Texas was sealed at Spindletop," and oil conglomerates soon outstripped in capital even the most avaricious lumberman's efforts.[4] In 1921, paced by the petroleum industry, the annual value of Texas manufactures exceeded agricultural production for the first time, setting the pattern for the future.[5]

The development of science and technology in Texas before World War II was inextricably tied to this economic shift. Research primarily concentrated on uncovering and providing for the most efficient exploitation of the resources of Texas. To Everhart and numerous others, the key to the South's lack of progress was painfully clear: a lack of the "spirit of scientific research and scientific training." Without it, the region would "never leave the ruts worn by years of false doctrines and misconceptions." Progress began with the effort of talented amateurs and makeshift state organizations, but, as Everhart predicted, the institutions of higher education in Texas led the way to development through greater professionalization.[6] Former Governor Lawrence S. Ross, president of Texas A&M College (as it was called at the time) and director of the Texas Academy of Science in 1897, foresaw even then that "the prizes of the future [would] be found upon the highway of scientific education."[7] Recognition that progress depended upon science and technology permeated every level of the Texas economy, from agriculture to industry, leading to a proliferation of state and private universities and colleges and a growth in professional organizations before World War II.

A strong element of romanticism persisted in the early technical efforts, but did not impede progress. Texas scientists in the period were probably even more romantic than the most starstruck latter-day dreamer, for they lived close to the mythology of the Old South. In 1905 Thomas H. Montgomery, professor of zoology at the University of Texas, devoted his presidential address before the Texas Academy of Science to "The Aesthetic Element in Scientific Thought," insisting scientists "properly belong closer to the artists and far from the technologists."[8] He declared that a true man of science conducted research "without any ulterior motive except the pleasure of the work itself" and the eternal hope of discovery.[9] Scientific disciplines without a direct impact on economic productivity, however, actually developed slowly in Texas, but by the eve of World War II the groundwork for many advances had been laid. George B. Halsted, a renowned mathematician who began his career at the University of Texas, expressed it best when he wrote, "to extend the limits of science is really to work for the progress of humanity."[10] Men and women of science in Texas embraced that ideal through research in many disciplines.

Agriculture

Agricultural science facilitated and amplified the cotton boom in Texas before World War II. While farmers initially suspected and resisted innovation, organization and education effected a great change.[11] The Patrons of Husbandry, or the Grange as they became known, initiated the first effective movement to establish scientific agricultural education in Texas. Organized in Salado County by 1873, they spread rapidly, holding their first state meeting that fall and electing W. W. Lang, a college-educated farmer, as the first Worthy Master. They stressed from the very beginning that coursework on the "natural sciences" should be taught in public schools, especially "agricultural chemistry," or "the constituent properties of the different soils, the means of change and improvement, the mechanical or chemical agencies, the organic constitution of cereals, and the physiology of vegetation." The members made plans to build more elementary schools, and avidly supported measures for establishing Texas A&M College.[12]

As the Grange disintegrated, the Farmers' Alliance became its spiritual and political successor. Organized in 1875 in Lampasas County, Texas, the Alliance made little headway until 1885, when it exploded across North Texas as a rural response to worsening economic conditions, expanding debts, and farmers' loss of faith in the cooperative ideal. The turning point in its growth came when a schism developed during the state meeting at Cleburne in August 1886; the division had disappeared by the next convention, and the revitalized organization, led by Charles W. Macune, spread outside of Texas.[13] Alliance members campaigned in favor of increasing production through scientific farming as the only way to insure profit in an uncertain cotton market, and clearly found support among the farmers of Texas.[14]

The Farmers' Alliance had effectively spent itself by 1890, but the cause of scientific agriculture was taken up by the Farmers' Educational and Cooperative Union of America in 1902. Organized in Rains County by Isaac N. Gresham, an early initiate into the Farmers' Alliance and a sometime Populist, the Texas Union seceded from the national organization in 1906 and charted an independent course through at least another decade. Members pledged "to labor for the education of the agricultural classes in the science of crop diversification and scientific agriculture," and that simple promise developed into the consuming purpose of the organization. The primary technique was "mixing education with the seed," working in the field with fellow farmers to teach better methods for crop diversification, insect control, animal husbandry, and veterinary care, establishing a precedent for the county agent system. Real success did not come until the establishment of a sound agricultural education program at Texas A&M College which was able to support broad extension work.[15]

Texas A&M College, established under the aegis of the Morrill Act, which sponsored "land grant" schools in each state, offered great promise as it opened in 1876. Speaking at its inauguration that fall, Governor Richard Coke boasted that the new institution offered "all that is necessary to a complete and liberal, literary, and scientific education, which shall be, as regards agriculture and the mechanic arts, thorough in practical application and experiment as well as in theory."[16] The new president of A&M, Thomas S. Gathwright, assured listeners that his administration would soon begin an experimental farm and, "if means will justify," purchase or construct "all those appliances and appointments that will illustrate the subject of scientific agriculture." Such brave words must have cheered the expectant farmers and pleased the officials of the Grange who had worked so hard to establish an agricultural college.[17]

Carlisle P. B. Martin served as the first professor of practical agriculture, chemistry, and natural sciences. Martin, a Doctor of Divinity, had made his living as a minister and worked his small farm only part-time. He offered courses in agriculture to seniors only, and most of them shied away from his curriculum, which remained primarily vocational in nature. His dismissal as part of a general housecleaning in 1880 occasioned little regret from either students or administration. Charles C. Gorgeson replaced Martin; although he did initiate classes on veterinary anatomy and horticulture as part of a full four-year curriculum, he persisted in teaching agriculture as a vocation with little or no foundation in science.[18] Most students enrolled in other curricula, seeing little to attract them in the agricultural courses as they were listed in the catalog.

Farmers' organizations grew impatient with A&M; Worthy Master Lang in 1880 railed against the "willfull perversion" of the college from the purpose for which it was designed.[19] George W. Curtis replaced Gorgeson, who departed in 1883. Curtis updated the curriculum and in 1888 published one of the earliest texts on animal husbandry, *Horses, Cattle, Sheep, and Swine*, when he was unable to find a book suitable for his classes. The students, having found a professor who taught truly scientific agriculture, flocked to Curtis' classes in droves.[20] His success paved the way for the establishment of a School of Agriculture early in the next century, which provided the leadership in scientific farming anticipated from the first. At Prairie View A&M College, founded as an adjunct to Texas A&M in 1876, "Professor Ferguson" taught vocational agriculture courses for Negro students,

but they were no more eager than their white counterparts for simplistic job training. The legislature converted Prairie View into a normal school when enrollment did not reach the level anticipated by the supporters of the Negro education program.[21]

Almost all agricultural research in Texas before World War II originated with the Agricultural Experiment Station at A&M (AES) or its branches scattered across the state.[22] Created under the Hatch Act of 1887, the AES used federal and state funds to conduct original research and to verify earlier studies on plant and animal physiology, diseases, soil chemistry, and other vital scientific inquiries. Like its sister operations in other states, it cooperated with the U.S. Department of Agriculture (USDA), but disseminated its results as an extension of A&M. Its timely publications "inspired thoughtful farmers with a zeal to learn scientific truth and to profit by its application."[23] Efforts expanded as demand increased for more productive farming; sixteen branches of the AES were open across Texas in 1930, searching for solutions to each region's particular problems.[24]

In 1914, following passage of the Smith-Lever Act, which provided additional funding, the AES initiated an extension service to aid farmers in the field and to free researchers from the demands of those who dropped by nearly every day for a quick answer to their complex questions. Extension work amplified the benefits already accomplished through agricultural education by county agents. Seaman A. Knapp from the USDA, who became a national leader in the extension movement as he traveled the country, had organized the first extension work in Texas in 1903. The USDA gave $40,000 to develop the program in Texas, where it was called Farmers' Cooperative Demonstration Work. The first agents were appointed in 1903, initially by regions, then by counties. The legislature formally adopted the system in 1908, retaining a few of these pioneers. County agents, along with the A&M Extension Service, were crucial in Texas' success in meeting the increased agricultural needs of the United States during World War I. By assuming the responsibility for scientific instruction from AES researchers, the extension service freed them to explore new topics and to contribute to the development of a sound agricultural economy through innovation.[25]

Agricultural experiment station research enhanced the ability of cotton farmers to return a profit. The boll weevil crossed the Rio Grande into Texas in 1893 and spread quickly, infesting "the most important cotton-producing division" of the state, from the Sabine River on the east to San Saba County on the west, and north to Hopkins and Franklin counties. The Agricultural Bureau of the Texas Department of Agriculture, Fisheries, Statistics, and History, established in September 1887, formed a "Boll Weevil Commission," which offered a $50,000 bounty for a remedy, but to no avail. Entomologists at A&M later made the first breakthrough in controlling the pests by poisoning, leading to development of the calcium arsenate dusting process successfully carried out by the USDA. Meanwhile, Knapp and others demonstrated planting methods for returning a profit in weevil-infested areas, and new plant varieties were introduced for the arid Panhandle region.[26]

Texas agricultural experiment stations also contributed to crop diversification. Chillicothe Station researchers originated and propagated the valuable dwarf milo, a hardy hybrid, as well as other varieties of grain sorghum after protracted experiments to find a feed grain crop that would thrive in central and western Texas. By the early 1930s almost all of the grain sorghum crop in Texas came from varieties developed by agricultural experiment stations. Sudan grass was established first as a hay crop, then gained widespread popularity as grazing cover. Worth $10 million in 1919, the annual crop had increased to many times that value by 1935. Other improvements were made through new strains of wheat and workable methods for water conservation.[27]

Some of the most outstanding agricultural experiment station accomplishments came in veterinary medicine. Early research in this field by the AES focused primarily on eradicating "Texas Fever," a common malady known by a variety of names and almost invariably fatal to cattle who had not developed an immunity to it. Although the disease had been noted since the beginning of the nineteenth century in southern states along the Atlantic seaboard, the dominance of Texas cattle in the markets after the Civil War attracted attention, as northern stock sickened rapidly and died. Many livestock dealers in other parts of the country boycotted Texas ranchers; estimates of the total cost of this scourge to the state's cattle industry through deaths and loss of revenue ranged as high as $23 million annually. The cause of Texas Fever, a parasitic protozoa carried by ticks, was uncovered by the USDA's Bureau of Animal Industry in 1887, the first time ever that an arthropod host was shown to be the carrier of a pathogen. A quarantine line from the North Carolina coast to a point on Texas' border with Mexico was established in 1890. Within ten years all of Texas was south of the quarantine line and remained there until 1906.[28]

Mark Francis, a graduate of Ohio State University, joined the staff of the AES shortly after its establishment. He worked with cattleman Richard J. Kleberg to perfect a dip that would kill the culprit, the Southern cattle tick or *Boophilus Bovis*, without harming the stock. Along with researchers from the Department of Agriculture, he devised a solution of oil combined with flowers of sulphur for a complete immersion of the cattle, which totally exterminated the pesky ticks on each animal. Francis also developed the blood serum inoculation to immunize cattle from the disease, by taking blood from native cattle, who developed an immunity while young, and injecting it into stock imported into the state, which soon reduced their previously high mortality rate to negligible levels.[29]

Francis' invaluable contributions to the eradication of Texas Fever highlight a career remarkable for its importance to the development of modern veterinary care in the state. Through his efforts, the Texas Livestock Sanitary Commission, established in 1893, was able to slowly reduce the quarantined area, until by 1946 the only regions still affected were small portions of eight counties along the Rio Grande. Francis took over the veterinary medicine courses from George W. Curtis, further developed the program, and served as dean of the School of Veterinary Medicine from its establishment in 1916 until his death in 1936. He became the first president of the Texas Veterinary Association, organized in 1903, and remained active in experiment station projects that reduced the instance of loin disease in cattle and sore mouth in sheep, both often fatal before remedies were developed.[30]

Verminous disease in livestock remained the province of patent medicine peddlers until the introduction of more advanced preparations after World War II. Government experts were often stumped for solutions when a few years of wet weather would bring an epidemic of listless cattle, horses, and sheep that often died. A researcher from the USDA in 1905 recommended gasoline to kill stomach worms after experimenting with chloroform, turpentine, creosote, thymol, and oil of cloves. He reported that he was able to give a horse seven ounces of gasoline in an hour, but one uncooperative yearling steer expired after only an ounce and a half. Other remedies of the era, carefully listed in books sold for the edification of stockmen, contained similar ingredients, adding a little sage or tartar emetic with linseed oil as a tonic. The increasingly common use of wire fencing and the introduction of infected new stock from out of state made the menace of stomach and lung worms an important economic factor by the end of the 1920s, but a study of available commercial preparations by the Texas Livestock Sanitary Commission in 1927 concluded they had little if any effect on the parasites.[31]

Demands of the marketplace along with the educational efforts of the agricultural experiment stations effected the employment of scientific methods in stock breeding. In 1884 over 3.9 million Longhorns were sold in Northern markets, but their number soon declined dramatically, due in part to the Texas Fever scare but also attributable to the increasing availability of improved breeds of beef cattle. Texas cattlemen imported several varieties as breeding stock by the turn of the century, but the most popular was the English Shorthorn, which by 1888 outnumbered all other improved breeds by four to one. Because inoculation against Texas Fever was not uniformly successful until this century, most of the cattle that were brought into the state were actually "grade bulls," having at least three-fourths pure blood and costing less than half of pedigreed stock. Herefords supplanted Shorthorns after 1900, and the bloodlines of imported breeds improved as the threat of Texas Fever diminished. Brahmans came into Texas through a number of channels, most notably from Brazil by way of Mexico, and were well established by World War II primarily as breeding stock to further improve native herds. Similar improvements were initiated by breeders of swine, as evidenced by the warning of H. E. Singleton to the Swine Breeders' Association in 1903 that "breeding should be more scientific" to emphasize important qualities such as good digestion, not appearance.[32]

Researchers in the Texas agricultural experiment stations were by no means infallible. The problem of wind erosion went unsolved for many years; as late as 1934 the USDA in its yearly report on soil depletion ignored wind erosion as a factor. The dust bowl crisis, which began in 1932, finally brought attention from scientific agencies, including the U.S. Weather Bureau and the A&M agricultural experiment stations. The huge storm of May 12, 1934, which dumped dust on the nation's capital, prompted the federal government to build a single station between Dalhart and Conlen, Texas, to study the problem within the five-state area. H. H. Finnell, formerly director of the experiment station at Panhandle A&M College, where he studied timber windbreaks, soil evaporation, and terraces, was assigned to supervise the project.[33]

Soil conservation, however, lagged far behind other phases of agricultural science, and the dust bowl residents paid dearly for years of neglect. At best, the federal soil conservation program was a mixed blessing. Trees planted by the U.S. Soil Conservation Service as shelterbelts would not grow or were too scattered to be of much use. The plowing of rows along the contour of the land and other methods advocated by federal agents were better suited for more humid areas, where they were developed to control water erosion. Persistent employment of such techniques became a costly folly. The technological innovations of the farmers themselves saved their topsoil from the swirling winds. Machines were designed to lay earthen rows across the path of the wind while plowing, and disk harrows were modified to dig small pits for conserving water as they turned a field. The agricultural experiment stations and national programs, however, did provide subsidies to encourage Texas farmers to remain and to employ more conservative practices, thereby granting an indirect benefit by instilling the desire for more scientific agriculture.[34]

Horticulture, too, got its primary impetus through individual efforts. The Experiment Station Council of A&M established a branch at Prairie View under the supervision of the United States Experimental Section of Texas. The primary focus of the Prairie View station became horticulture, but the program received little support. The most famous Texas proponent of horticulture became Thomas V. Munson, a Denton resident who created a classification system later adopted by American horticulture authorities with few subsequent changes. In 1885 Munson's botanical arrangement and herbarium, the result of fifty thousand miles of travel in forty states, were displayed at the New Orleans Exposition. His greatest achievements, however, came with grapes. Experts hailed Munson's display of grape species and genera at the Columbian Exposition in 1893 as the most complete collection ever assembled. He bred some three hundred grape species and introduced many hybrids into commercial production by the end of World War II. A prolific writer, his often technical articles appeared in American, French, and German trade journals. In 1911 the French Republic sent a delegation to Denton to confer on him the Legion of Honor for salvaging their vineyards after a disastrous blight. He was only the second American ever to receive that prestigious award. The research of Joseph W. Stubenrauch, although not of the exemplary caliber of Munson, produced several commercially valuable peach hybrids, which earned him a commendation from the USDA in 1937.[35]

The broadest effect of the agricultural experiment stations was an increasing awareness of the opportunity afforded by scientific agriculture. The difference in farmers' attitudes became apparent after the turn of the century, as their organizations grew more devoted to the development of scientific methods. The Texas Industrial Congress, formed in December 1909 by Colonel Ike Pryor and others in San Antonio, led the way for a number of years. Created as a lobbying organization, within its first year it became a service association committed to the improvement of agriculture in Texas. It submitted only one direct recommendation for a law, which the legislature approved, allowing county commissioners to pay part of farm demonstration agents' salaries, and contributing to the evolution of county agents. The first state meeting of the Texas Industrial Congress was held in April 1910 in San Antonio, but the scope of the organization quickly outgrew regional boundaries, attracting adherents from all over the state.[36]

Much of the development of the Texas Industrial Congress as a force for agricultural progress can be directly attributed to the flamboyant Colonel Henry Exall, elected president in November 1910. He began competitive crop contests, issued a series of educational bulletins, and spoke incessantly on soil conservation and fertility. Colonel Exall used the press extensively in his effort to popularize scientific farming, creating a larger-than-life image of himself as "no cold, unemotional scientific investigator, but the very evangelist of the soil, preaching the doctrine of conservation as wholeheartedly as ever [a] missionary spread the gospel among the heathen." In 1911, true to form, he offered $10,000 in gold for the best crops grown in Texas without irrigation.[37]

Colonel Exall realized the limits of Texas' water resources and advocated soil conservation through natural fertilization as the only remedy. He anticipated the future when he wrote in 1910, "the sewage of cities and towns, a large part of their garbage, dead animals, etc., should be converted into fertilizers by scientific methods, and returned to the soil, instead of being allowed to pollute the streams and poison the atmosphere." Other scientific topics addressed in his publications included seed selection and cross breeding, crop rotation, with an emphasis on planting legumes and other "restorative" crops, and dry farming. He died in December 1913, but his contributions were immortalized in print the next year by his associates: "Texas fields . . . now yield two stalks of corn where only one grew before he preached the doctrine of scientific farming."[38]

A&M sponsored a less dramatic but no less important movement for widespread incorporation of classes on scientific agriculture in public school curriculums. The Texas Farmers' Congress, which convened at College Station in 1903, coordinated the influence of fifteen agricultural organizations to initiate a call for better instruction, pointing out that "many . . . vital questions will soon be attacked by the educated minds of bright boys and girls upon our farms," and insisting that, "these minds must be trained to scientific observation and to reach scientific conclusions." The assembled representatives agreed that if the children were given the ability to "observe with scientific accuracy," the benefits would be tremendous.[39]

The Texas legislature answered in 1907, requiring that elementary agriculture be taught in all schools. The statute also dictated minimum requirements for students in the state normal schools: prospective teachers had to take at least twelve weeks of classes on agriculture, and those who wished to specialize in the subject had to enroll in three years of coursework. In 1914 the Texas Department of Education, in conjunction with both A&M and the University of Texas, prescribed a curriculum for public secondary schools that included simple animal husbandry, soil chemistry, horticulture, zoology, botany, and entomology. Although it would be several years before such work could be implemented in many Texas schools, the public education movement exposed farmers and their children to new ideas, advancing the cause of scientific agriculture. The Texas Department of Education continued to emphasize science in all curricula, from the first grade, with a definite stress on the applicability of such education in all vocations, including farming as it evolved in the state.[40]

The movement for scientific agricultural education in public schools reached a climax with the establishment of the Texas Association of Future Farmers of America in 1928. The assembly began in Virginia under the leadership of Henry C. Groseclose in 1926 and spread quickly across the United States. Their first national congress was held on November 20, 1928, in Kansas City. In July of that year, organizers in Texas initiated efforts for their own chapter, and a state charter was granted on February 28, 1929. The first annual state meeting was held in College Station on April 22, 1929, and a constitution was adopted which pledged the delegates "to develop an agriculture lighted by science."[41] To publicize its efforts, the Texas Association printed a monthly magazine, the *Future Farmer News*. Later, as their clientele matured, the publishers changed the title to *Lone Star Farmer*, but retained their emphasis on scientific methods.

Agricultural experiment stations also provided

Texas farmers and the national government with a dependable source of information on meteorology in the region for the first time. Previously, such data had come from volunteer weather observers who often worked for the Smithsonian Institution. Some of them were quite good, such as Lum Woodruff, who published some of his observations on Bexar County weather in the *American Meteorological Journal* between 1885 and 1888. With the establishment of the AES, the professor of physics at A&M was designated as a meteorological observer, completing a network of observation posts across Texas reporting directly to the United States Signal Service.[42]

A series of severe hurricanes, including the storm which totally obliterated the port of Indianola, prompted a reorganization of the Texas Weather Service, which was placed under the aegis of the United States Weather Bureau, a division of the USDA. The earliest recorded educational activity in meteorology in Texas occurred in 1918 when three hundred enlisted men attended the School of Meteorology at A&M, which was organized and maintained under the supervision of the U.S. Army Signal Corps. The camaraderie developed within this small group led to the organization of the American Meteorological Society at A&M the following year.[43]

Forestry

Texas industrial production outpaced agriculture in the second decade of the twentieth century, a shift initiated by the lumber companies. In 1907 they reported cutting over 2.2 billion board feet, making Texas third among the United States in production of lumber. Corporations developed tremendous plants to process timber, including substantial camps in the woodlots; roads and railroads to transport the cut trees to the sawmills; kilns, drying yards, and planing mills to quickly produce marketable products; and large warehouses to store the finished goods until sold. Sawmill technology progressed in response to demand; the standard became the double band rig, capable of cutting 100,000 board feet a day. Each mill employed a work force of two to five hundred men, a boon for the East Texas economy.[44]

In the second decade of this century the lumber industry appeared well established and ready for another thirty years of development. Prosperity, however, told only part of the story; in truth, little had been done to provide for the future. The lumber industry had reached the zenith of its unfettered develop-

ment in Texas by 1917. Companies boasted of a third annual production of over two billion board feet in 1913, but four years later the last big sawmill opened in East Texas. The *Texas Almanac* for 1904 estimated that the state then contained sixty-seven billion board feet of standing pine, but in 1912 the editors reduced the figure to twenty-five billion. By 1930, when less than a million of the fourteen to eighteen million acres of woodlands which originally covered East Texas survived, most of the large national lumber companies had shut down their Texas operations and moved on, many to the West Coast. The lumber industry bottomed in 1932 when production fell to about four million board feet, its lowest level since 1880 when the boom began.[45]

As Robert Maxwell, one of the foremost students of forestry in Texas observed, "The conservation of natural resources ordinarily is undertaken only when those resources are nearly exhausted."[46] The Texas state government received warnings from its citizens somewhat earlier than its neighbors, but failed to act due to a laissez-faire attitude fostered by the "cut-out-and-get-out" mentality of the majority of lumbermen, who for years held more political power than those concerned with conservation. Only the actions of a few civic-minded patriots, the renewed awareness sparked by an accelerated national forestry program, and the great recuperative powers of the loblolly and shortleaf pines in Texas insured there was anything to conserve when the legislature moved at last to enact effective measures for timber conservation.[47]

The first alarm was sounded as early as 1882 by H. C. Schmidt, a civil engineer from Austin, who reported as "Statistician of the Forestry" in 1882. The greatest demand for Texas timber at that time came from the railroad companies that denuded vast expanses of land to provide crossties. Schmidt estimated over 10 million crossties were in place in 1882, when railroad mileage in the state totaled less than 5,000 miles. Just to maintain the existing system required 2.6 million crossties annually. He could hardly have anticipated the demand for crossties in the next century, when railroad mileage peaked at 16,900 miles in 1930, but he correctly predicted a growing problem. His solution was just as prophetic: he called for the establishment of a state agency charged with conservation of timber resources and "judicious replanting" of treeless regions, and recommended construction of experimental farms to investigate quick-growing varieties of trees which could withstand the Texas climate, such as pines. Schmidt wooed legislators by emphasizing the economic benefit of forests, insisting "Agriculture depends on the forestry, sanitary and climatic effects of woodlands," but his report apparently received little notice.[48]

The second official warning came from William Bray, an agent of the Bureau of Forestry within the USDA. He found that, although Texas' "merchantable forest" covered only 10 percent of its surface area in 1904, "125,000 acres are cut annually, and cut in such a way that the land will not grow valuable forests again." Other timberlands, of vital importance as protection for agriculture and a valuable water supply, were "burned and destroyed without regard for their great usefulness." Bray concluded sadly that "under present methods the exhaustion of a great economic resource is taking place," that the public interest was not being protected, and that conditions were "rapidly changing for the worse." His solution echoed the words of Schmidt twenty years before: establish a state agency charged with real responsibility for forest management, including fire protection, replanting, and policing of the lumber industry to implement conservative practices. Bray believed the best hope for the future lay with the private operators, as they controlled 95 percent of the timberland in Texas.[49]

Bray's more detailed assessment of Texas timberlands painted an even bleaker picture of the future for the lumber industry than Schmidt's report. Longleaf pine furnished four-fifths of all Texas pine marketed each year, yet tracts were small and rapidly diminishing, and Bray predicted that within fifteen years all virgin stands would be gone. Continuing through his extensive catalog of commercially valuable species, he pessimistically estimated, "Of pure shortleaf forest not enough remains uncut to make the question of conservative management important." He reported in favor of creating a state forest board to formulate a definite policy to aid private owners with proper conservation measures, but stopped short of recommending the establishment of state forests, although he admitted the value of woodland reservations for agriculture and other interests.[50]

The credit for initiating effective forest conservation measures should go to one man, W. Goodrich Jones. He had studied "forest science" as a youth in Germany while traveling with his parents in the 1870s and had earned the nickname "Tree Crank" for his later campaign to plant trees in and around Temple, where he was a successful businessman. Active in establishing "Arbor Day" for Texas in 1889, within a year he was serving as secretary of the newly organized Texas Arbor Day and Forestry Association, which worked to foster "the conservation, management, and renewal of forests, the collection of forest statistics

and the advancement of educational and legislative tree knowledge." At the request of Bernard E. Fernow, chief of the Bureau of Forestry, Jones sent a pessimistic report to Washington in 1900 on the Texas forest industry, urging a mandatory planned cutting program.[51]

The federal government balked at implementing strict regulation of the lumber industry, and Jones realized the companies would not police themselves. He was encouraged by the organization of the Forest Service in the USDA, combining the duties of the forestry offices there and in the Department of the Interior. The Forest Service hailed Jones as the "leading conservationist and advocate of scientific forestry in the Lone Star State" at a conference of governors on conservation called by President Theodore Roosevelt in 1908, but offered no material support. Undaunted, Jones returned home and established the Conservation Association of Texas in 1910 to replace the then defunct Texas Arbor Day and Forestry Association. The new assembly united representatives from state government and the lumber industry with professional conservationists and concerned citizens for "development and conservation of all the natural resources of this state."[52]

The Conservation Association became virtually extinct by 1914, but J. Lewis Thompson, president of the Yellow Pine Association, who had been active in the organization, continued to fight for state reforestation and protection. He became an important ally for Jones, who in November 1914 established yet a third organization, the Texas Forestry Association, which led the fight for a state agency. A&M threw its support behind the new movement, as did the Bureau of Economic Geology and Technology being formed at the University of Texas. Governor James E. Ferguson spoke in favor of forestry needs in his inaugural address and signed the bill drafted by the Texas Forestry Association establishing the Texas Department of Forestry in March 1915.[53]

John H. Foster, who held a Master of Forestry from Yale, became the first state forester. He received matching funds under the Weeks Law from the national government for fire protection, and in one year had 7.5 million acres under fire protection, with six fire patrolmen stationed at Lufkin, Longview, Livingston, Linden, Jasper, and Tenaha. Foster also served as chief of the Division of Forestry created within the AES and taught forestry at A&M. The initial years were rocky because the legislature appropriated few funds for the Texas Department of Forestry and the new Division of Forestry. Governor William P. Hobby, a native of East

Texas, reversed the situation in 1920 by establishing a state task force on forestry, which reported in favor of increasing their budgets and won press support for the fledgling programs. The Texas Forestry Association survived and developed alongside its bureaucratic offspring.[54]

Foster did not weather the lean years; he quit at the end of his first year and was replaced by Eric O. Siecke, who remained until 1942. Under Siecke, appropriations for the Department of Forestry increased from $18,000 in 1918 to a peak of $64,000 in 1932. The A&M Board of Directors created a separate Texas Forest Service in 1926 and appointed Siecke as Director. Because it "tended to be the step-child of the College's main effort in agriculture and engineering" through the eve of World War II, the Texas Forest Service under Siecke grew ever more autonomous, substantially enlarging its operations in cooperation with his other charge, the Texas Department of Forestry. The results were remarkable, especially in fire protection for East Texas, where a supplemented police force succeeded in reducing the annual number of acres burned by two-thirds in twenty years.[55]

Research by the Texas Forest Service before World War II spanned a broad spectrum of activities. Along with the Soil Conservation Service, investigators developed more effective patterns of preserving or recreating "protection forests," indispensable in combating erosion in East Texas. Improved fire protection and the systematic replanting of young trees brought cutover forests back to production again; in 1939, 90 percent of East Texas woodlands were second growth and were producing both hardwoods and pines. Reproduction remained poor on only 222,300 of the more than 10.5 million wooded acres in the region, a little over 2 percent of the total. Reforestation seemed to be working well when private owners retained ownership of almost all of the timberland, in keeping with Bray's recommendation. Research efforts centered on the southern pine, the preferred stock for replanting, as well as on the effects of pruning and thinning on all species. State forest nurseries for seedlings operated near Kirbyville and Conroe in East Texas, in the heart of the commercial forests, which absorbed most of the attention of the Texas Forest Service staff.[56]

The Department of Forestry established the first state forest in 1924. Embracing 1,720 acres of cutover land in Newton County, the park was renamed in honor of Eric O. Siecke in 1951. Several more state forests were created before World War II, including 1,725 acres in Montgomery County, designated W. Goodrich Jones State Forest in 1949. Jones was present at the dedication of the reserve named for him. He graciously accepted the accolades bestowed upon him as the "Father of Forestry in Texas." The Texas Forest Service later constructed a tree nursery at Jones State Forest, an appropriate tribute to the pioneer conservationist. In 1934 the federal government began purchasing forestland in Texas under the provisions of special legislation passed by the state in 1933, acquiring over 630,000 acres for reserves by 1940. Most of it, too, was cutover land in East Texas, which the lumber companies were only too glad to sell, but all of it was soon restored as productive woodlots by the Civilian Conservation Corps.[57]

The restoration of East Texas timberlands made possible the birth of pulpwood enterprise in Texas. The state engaged in the pulp and paper industry rather tardily, coming at the end of a general pattern of migration from east to west across the South which did not reach Texas until the late 1930s. Champion Paper and Fiber Company opened a plant at Pasadena on the Houston Ship Channel in 1937 to produce bleached sulfate pulp, which it shipped to its Ohio paper mill until 1940, when the company completed a facility nearby to produce a variety of high-grade papers. That same year Champion also began shipping pulp to the Southland Paper Mill in Lufkin. In a great gamble that paid for itself many times over, the Southland plant used a new process perfected by Charles H. Hertz, a Georgia chemist with a Harvard doctorate, to make newsprint from southern yellow pine pulp for the first time.[58]

Natural History and Ecology

Much of the impetus for forest conservation came from the more general concern for the natural history of Texas. That field originally belonged almost entirely to a talented phalanx of amateurs. Julien Reverchon, a French-American, came with his father to the Fourieristic Colony of La Reunion near Dallas in 1858, and remained there after the failure of that utopian enterprise. An amateur botanist, he was inspired by his friendship with Jacob Boll, a Swiss naturalist who traveled to the Dallas area shortly after the Civil War on a collection trip for Harvard University. At Reverchon's death, his collection of almost 20,000 specimens, representing 2,600 species of Texas flora gathered on exploratory trips into the northern and western regions of the state, was the best in existence.[59] Frank B. Armstrong, a native of Canada, toured the Southwest and Mexico as a young man in the 1880s. He settled in Brownsville, and earned an international reputation as a tropical ornithologist for the collections he sent to museums in Europe and the United States, including the Field Museum in Chicago and the Smithsonian Institution.[60] Joseph D. Mitchell, one of the first native Texan naturalists and a gifted amateur student, joined the U.S. Bureau of Entomology at the turn of the century, but published much of his work for the Texas Academy of Science.[61] Rudolph Menger, from San Antonio, had a medical degree from Leipzig, but turned his microscope on the environment surrounding his home and published his classic *Texas Nature Observations and Reminiscences* in 1913.[62]

The impending extinction of many bird and animal species brought professional conservationists to the forefront in Texas and in many other states. Improvements in firearms contributed to the large-scale slaughter of many wildlife species to be sold as meat in urban centers. This and the hunting of birds for plumage took a frightful toll, along with reduction of suitable habitat and with competition from domestic livestock. By the end of the century, herons, egrets, and other attractive wild species were becoming quite rare in Texas, if not extinct. Settlement along the shores of waterways and bays also took an increasing toll on the native fishes and other aquatic life in the waterways and bays of Texas. The first agent of the Texas Fish Commission, Joseph H. Dinkins, appointed by Governor Oran Milo Roberts in 1879, found himself almost helpless to enforce state regulations on fishing, and the agency expired in 1885. Resurrected in 1895 as the Fish and Oyster Commission with the energetic I. B. Kibbe as Commissioner, the organization enjoyed far greater success. Kibbe stumped the coastal counties urging conservative methods for oyster harvesting and wrote increasingly dour reports on the prospects for Texas wildlife during a hectic eleven years in office.[63]

The turn of the century brought better news for conservationists and naturalists in Texas. The new state chapter of the Audubon Society, organized in March 1899, became active in 1903 when Henry P. Attwater, an agent for the Southern Pacific Railroad, and others began pushing for enforceable game laws. Attwater served on both the bird protection committee of the American Ornithologists' Union and the advisory council of the National Association of Audubon Societies. He later authored several intriguing tracts, including an argument for the use of birds to control boll weevils, which did not earn him the $50,000 bounty from the state. The legislature, how-

ever, listened to him this time and in 1903 declared a five-year closed season on pronghorn antelope and bighorn sheep, made it illegal to sell, purchase, or possess nongame species of birds, and prohibited commerce in waterfowl and game mammals. Captain M. B. Davis, secretary of the Texas Audubon Society from 1905 to his death in 1912, organized more than one hundred chapters of the Audubon Society in Texas and campaigned for stricter enforcement of game laws with the aid of Attwater and Thomas P. Montgomery, the romantic zoologist from the University of Texas, who was also a member of the National Audubon Advisory Council.[64]

In 1907 the legislature renewed and amplified the provisions of the 1903 statutes, adding a game division to the Fish and Oyster Commission and employing deputy commissioners, or game wardens, for the first time. Despite low morale and high turnover for more than two decades, the Commission did initiate efforts to repopulate the wildlife of the state, with limited success in freshwater fish, oysters, deer, quail, turkey, and antelope. A statute approved in 1925 provided funds for game reserves; in the first year, the state established thirty-three reservations, totaling more than a million acres. In its heyday in the 1930s, the system grew to fifty-three reserves enclosing 2.7 million acres. The Game, Fish, and Oyster Commission in 1929 became a six-man board whose first executive secretary, William J. Tucker, served for fifteen years, a record unmatched by any of his predecessors. His reforms brought national attention, and Texas became one of nine states selected to take part in the USDA's Biological Survey, which was completed shortly before World War II. This capped fifty years of federally-sponsored field studies in Texas.[65]

The Texas Audubon Society forged an active alliance with the Texas Farmers' Congress to sponsor surveys of the wildlife in the state and to work for the creation of reserves. The combined effort led to the leasing of Big Bird Island, Little Bird Island, and Green Island in the Laguna Madre, important seabird nesting sites, to the National Audubon Society without charge for fifty years beginning in 1921. The resident warden there continued to receive aid from scientists George Simmons and B. L. Tharp of the University of Texas. Many local organizations contributed greatly to these achievements, one of the most important being the Central Texas Audubon group formed in 1914 by H. Tullsen of Taylor, with the assistance of Attwater, George F. Simmons, and W. S. Taylor from A&M. In 1930 the Texas Wildlife Agency was reconstituted as a six-member commission which instituted more significant steps for managing the state's flora and fauna, indicating an awakening interest by the state government in the idea of wildlife preservation. The first federal wildlife refuge in Texas, the Aransas National Wildlife Refuge, opened in 1937, giving promise of support for the future.[66]

In addition to the literature referred to earlier, many of these early naturalists completed important works on the flora and fauna of Texas. Harry C. Oberholser began a survey of the birdlife in the Big Bend region in 1903 for the Bureau of Biological Survey, a task which became a life's obsession. He retired in 1941 without having published his work, and was still not satisfied that he had sufficiently discussed all aspects of Texas ornithology when he surrendered an almost twelve-thousand-page typescript to an editor in 1962. Published after Oberholser's death by the University of Texas Press in 1974, the volumes were hailed as *"the major publication of this generation on aspects of the flora and fauna of Texas."*[67] Not nearly as monumental, but no less meticulous, is *Adventures with a Texas Naturalist* by Roy Bedichek. The result of thirty years' study, it is both a poet's reflections and the observations of a scientific mind, blurring the distinction between a naturalist and a natural historian. Bedichek, with the "arduous, painstaking method of the scientist," chronicled the migration patterns of robins, recorded the northward extension of the range of the vermilion flycatcher during this century, and documented other minute detail with "the controlled and objective zeal of the scientific spirit."[68] The work of Oberholser and Bedichek represent the diversity of scientific writing on natural history before World War II.

A number of museums and publications fostered the study of natural history during the period. In 1866 Ashbel Smith, revered as one of the founding lights of Texas, helped charter the Houston Scientific Institute, which started a museum of Texas natural history in 1888. The Houston Museum of Natural Sciences opened shortly after the city, prodded by the Houston Museum and Scientific Society, acquired Attwater's personal collections in 1922. George H. Kalteyer, a noted amateur paleontologist and geologist, became the first director of the Museum of Natural History at San Pedro Springs in San Antonio in 1885. That city also hosted the Scientific Society of San Antonio, which published a journal featuring articles by naturalists such as Attwater. Austin boasted *The Naturalist: A Monthly Magazine Devoted to Natural Science*, edited by Herbert Sterzing, but it was printed for only a few years in the 1890s. Baylor University Mu-

seum offered a series of offprints on natural history, beginning with John K. Strecker's addendum to an earlier list of butterflies in Waco. The Texas Memorial Museum, completed on the University of Texas campus in 1939, became the flagship of the state museum system. It promoted scholarship in the fields of history, geology, natural history, paleontology, anthropology, and archaeology under Elias N. Sellards, its first director and a nationally recognized geologist in his own right.[69]

Petroleum Technology

Petroleum revolutionized industry in Texas and brought science and technology to the forefront in the rush for greater profits and progress in the twentieth century. In 1886 the Petroleum Prospecting Company, founded by B. F. Hitchcock and Edgar H. Farrar with a capital stock of only $100,000, drilled the first commercially successful oil well at Oil Springs in Nacogdoches County. Using simple machinery and operators hired from the Pennsylvania fields, they struck oil at seventy feet and were soon taking nearly three hundred barrels a week from the ground. The company drilled over forty wells, twenty of which were still productive in 1890, but the boom played out shortly thereafter. Oil and gas were also produced in small quantities near San Antonio after George Dullnig hit oil at about three hundred feet while drilling a water well in 1886. Although never a true "gusher," Dullnig's discovery placed Texas for the first time in the reports of the United States Geological Survey (USGS) as an oil and gas producer when four Bexar County wells squeezed out forty-eight barrels of oil and $1,728 in natural gas, its value determined by the coal and wood it replaced.[70]

The next bonanza came when a company hired by Corsicana officials to dig three water wells hit oil at a little over a thousand feet on June 9, 1894. Farsighted local businessmen convinced the company to abandon the attempt to drill for water on the site, then chartered the Corsicana Oil Development Corporation and began leasing mineral rights. Two well-known Pennsylvania operators and wildcatters, John H. Galey and James M. Guffey, bought a half interest in the concern in 1895. Galey and Guffey had drilled profitably in Pennsylvania, the Indian Territory, and Kansas; smelling success once more, they agreed to sink five holes. Their efforts yielded 1,450 barrels in 1896, sparking a frenzied boom that produced 65,975 barrels from forty-seven wells during the next year and 2,300 barrels a day in 1898 from 287 new enterprises crowded into the tiny field, barely five miles long and two miles wide. Eager prospectors scoured the surrounding area, investigating reports of surface oil in Sour Lake, Menardville, and Powell.[71]

The greatest discovery came in the most unlikely place. Patillo Higgins had long insisted that a mound near Sour Spring held oil, despite the emphatic contrary opinion of prominent geologists such as William Kennedy. In 1892 Higgins established the Gladys City Oil, Gas, and Manufacturing Company with $54,000 in capital from George W. Carroll and George W. O'Brien. Gladys City was a nonexistent town named in honor of a little girl in Higgins' Sunday school class. After seven years and several dry holes, the corporation almost dissolved, but instead switched tactics and advertised for someone to take out a lease with an option-to-sell contract. The only reply came from Anthony F. Lucas, a mining engineer of Dalmatian birth, who had graduated from the Polytechnic Institute at Graz in 1877 and the Naval Academy of Fiume and Pola in 1878. Lucas probably knew more about salt domes, the correct terminology for the barren mound, than any other man in the United States, having prospected a number of successful finds since 1893 as chief engineer for a salt company near New Iberia, Louisiana. His first test wells came up dry, but urged on by geologist William B. Phillips of the University of Texas, Lucas persisted, with financial assistance and drillers from Guffey and Galey. On January 10, 1901, "Spindletop" blew in at 1,020 feet, spewing 75,000 to 100,000 barrels of oil a day into the air. A daily production of fifty barrels had been considered a "whopper" for the Corsicana field, which at its peak in 1900 produced less than a million barrels annually.[72] (See figs. 1, 2, and 3.)

For Galey, Spindletop "constituted a fitting climax to the most illustrious career of wildcatting in the annals of the industry." Lucas was overwhelmed; the gusher completely destroyed his tiny derrick and inundated the countryside with a swelling tide of foul-smelling crude oil. He hired farmers who built levies and reservoirs in nearby fields with gangplows, but was not able to cap the discovery well until nine days after striking paydirt, when an estimated 800,000 gallons of oil stood in pools upon the surrounding countryside. Fearing fire, Lucas ordered his crew to construct a large iron standpipe to encase the wellhead; when the inevitable happened on March 3, ignited by sparks from a passing locomotive, that innovation protected his primary investment, but the oil lake, which covered several hundred acres, burned with an unprecedented intensity. Despite more disasters and

Figure 1. Spindletop blows in on January 10, 1901, spewing 75,000 to 100,000 barrels of oil a day into the air.

Figure 2. The Keith Ward District on Spindletop in 1902, whose "Boiler Avenue" proudly boasted the "densest drilling in Texas."

Figure 3. Drillers watch helplessly as an oil well fire rages out of control at Spindletop in 1902.

waste, the Spindletop field produced over 1.7 million barrels in 1901, a greater capacity than production in the rest of the world combined.[73]

New prospectors flocked to the region around Beaumont, and great oil conglomerates were born almost overnight. Guffey, with funds secured from Andrew W. Mellon and Richard B. Mellon, partners in the Pittsburgh banking house of T. Mellon & Sons—later the Mellon National Bank and Trust Company—recapitalized his company in May 1901, releasing Galey and Lucas and forming the James M. Guffey Petroleum Company with stock worth $15 million. On November 26, 1901, Texas chartered Gulf Refining Company, a subsidiary owned by Guffey, the Mellons, and other influential investors such as Charles Schwab, who would later found Bethlehem Steel. Another reorganization in January 1907 created the Gulf Oil Corporation, a combination of the earlier two firms with Andrew Mellon, who bought out Guffey for $3 million, as president. Texas Company, or Texaco, founded by Joseph S. Cullinan, Sun Oil Company, and numerous independent operators began at Spindletop.[74]

Wildcatters and corporate prospectors alike scattered across Texas looking for more "black gold." Tiny coastal towns such as Batson, Saratoga, Dayton, and Humble exploded overnight into boom towns as drillers tapped into sizable oil deposits, often in the center of town. Humble Oil Company, now known as Exxon, took its name from the field where it originated, before it grew to be the largest domestic producer of crude oil during World War II. The first West Texas gusher came in at Electra in January 1911, where Producers Oil Company, a subsidiary of Texaco, had leased most of William T. Waggoner's ranchland after a few small strikes. The Electra field produced a million barrels in 1911, then ballooned to over 8.2 million in 1914, the biggest single discovery since Spindletop. Like the coastal rigs, most of the wells were quite shallow, few going as deep as 1,900 feet. Successive booms in Ranger, Sour Lake, Saratoga, Desdemona, Breckenridge, Burkburnett, and Mexia flooded the market—Mexia alone produced 35 million barrels in 1922—but prices continued to rise, bringing great wealth into a state until recently dominated by the production of corn and cotton.[75]

A modest well gushed in Mitchell County in June 1920, heralding the opening of the fabulous Permian Basin, followed by the famous Santa Rita Number One on May 28, 1923, which uncovered the Big Lake Field and enriched the Permanent Fund of the University of Texas. Santa Rita Number One pioneered a new oil horizon. Before 1920 no producing well had gone below three thousand feet, but University Number 1–B in the Big Lake field came in at 8,525 feet in 1928, the deepest in the world at that time; and within five years sixteen more had been drilled as deep

Figure 4. Over 100,000 barrels of oil go up in smoke in an open sump fire at Sour Lake. The caption boasts that "Texas has oil to burn" and asserts their famous Searchlight brand is "homemade and unsurpassed for brilliancy."

Figure 5. Another oil tank is rushed into place during the East Texas oil boom, the last to use steam rigs, wooden derricks, and mule teams.

or deeper, with the largest, University Number 8–B, flowing at over 14,000 barrels per day. The Permian Basin fields hit rock bottom in 1932, slowed by poor markets and low prices, after producing over 440 million barrels between 1920 and 1930, but recovered to end the second decade on a positive note as ten fields in the area held over three hundred producing wells each in 1940.[76]

Meanwhile in East Texas, the years between 1926 and 1935 were a golden age of discovery. Columbus M. Joiner, a shoestring wildcatter nicknamed "Dad," brought in the biggest oil well known to man at that time from the Woodbine sand near Henderson on September 5, 1930, at 3,536 feet. By the first of the year the East Texas Woodbine field held 3,612 producing wells, and within seven years 25,987 rigs stood in an area forty-two miles long and four to eight miles wide. Towns such as Kilgore and Longview swelled to ten times their previous population in the last great Texas oil boom. Coming at the lowest point of the Depres-

sion, the new discoveries glutted the market, driving down petroleum prices and increasing the severity of the lean years for Texas corporations and their employees. With unbeatable optimism, however, the oil industry rebounded within a few years, providing a seemingly limitless supply for the war effort in the next decade.[77]

Texas oil producers quickly realized the value of natural gas, although its development as a natural resource was delayed by the abundance of crude oil. Natural gas in commercial quantities was first discovered in Washington County in 1888 when two wells produced a total of 725 cubic feet per minute from a depth of 145 feet. The Henrietta field in Clay County, which spawned the boom town of Petrolia, peaked at an annual production of two million barrels of oil in 1914, but also yielded ten billion cubic feet of gas that year. The year 1906 marked a watershed for the natural gas industry at Petrolia when 702 domestic users and one industry converted to using it as fuel. Lone Star Gas Company, chartered in 1909, began piping gas to Fort Worth and Dallas from Clay County, and within a decade fifty-nine Petrolia wells supplied gas to 14,719 domestic consumers and 133 industries in Texas. The largest single producing gas field in the world opened in the Panhandle during December 1918, piping ten million cubic feet of gas daily to Amarillo. Texas ranked first among the United States in natural gas production by 1935, when 102 companies supplied nearly 550,000 gas meters through 12,000 miles of pipelines to 657 towns across the state. A well in Mitchell County blew out in 1922 with a gas that would not burn, and the Panhandle got its first natural gasoline plant. Natural gas also fostered other industries, such as a government plant to extract helium, which opened in 1929 near Amarillo, and forty carbon black plants, producing 82 percent of the national consumption in 1937.[78]

A revolution in petroleum technology facilitated the Texas oil and gas boom. The Petroleum Prospecting Company drilled its wells in Nacogdoches County with a cable-tool rig, the standard device used since E. L. Drake sank the first oil well in Pennsylvania in 1859. It worked like a vertically positioned sledgehammer, using the percussion principle by repeatedly dropping a heavy drill bit with a cutting edge on rock formations to break them up as the well deepened. Power was supplied through a motor attached to a walking beam. Although such rigs proved unsuitable to dig through the loose sand at Spindletop—no cable-tool outfit ever finished a well in that field—they remained dominant in Texas due to their financial and technical advantages in many media until the 1930s, when rotary drills triumphed at last. Operators drilled most of the wells in the Panhandle before World War II, including the pioneer deep well University Number 1–B, with cable tools before greater depths made such devices impractical.[79]

In the 1890s the Corsicana field witnessed the first widespread use of rotary drilling platforms, devised in 1882 by C. E. and M. C. Baker in South Dakota for boring water wells. They brought the rig to Corsicana for oil exploration, where it was perfected with the aid of H. G. Johnston, a local machinist. Using a gear-driven turntable which gripped a hollow pipe—or "kelly"—the fishtail rotary bit loosened and dislodged rock rather than pounding it. Water flowed through the pipe to reduce friction and to flush out well cuttings. The Bakers could sink a hole in six to eight days, which had taken cable tools two or three months to complete. The first rotary rigs employed mules or horses, but by 1898 steam and gasoline engines were being used to turn the bit and to pump the wells. J. G. Hamill, business manager for Guffey and Galey, sank the first successful well at Spindletop with a rotary rig which employed a sturdy drive block to turn a fishtail bit on an eight-inch pipe. As outfits grew more complex, the drill bit became a handicap because machinists followed the designs developed for cable-tool rigs. John S. Wynn built the first cone rock bit in his shop in 1908. He sold his working model to Walter B. Sharp, who pioneered the use of rotary rigs at Corsicana and Spindletop, and to Howard R. Hughes. The pair took out a patent on an improved model and established the remarkable Hughes Tool Company of Houston. They also bought the rights to the first cross-roller rock bit, devised by G. A. Humason, in 1917.[80]

Oil technology developed in a number of other areas also. Steel derricks had supplanted wooden ones in West Texas by 1926. Engines were employed very early to pump wells, replacing the galvanized bailing buckets—ten to fifteen feet in length—used in Nacogdoches County. As wells went deeper, electric motors replaced steam and gasoline power plants. Operators encased wells with iron pipe to prevent collapse, but at Corsicana they put only clear water through their drilling pipes until Sharp used colloidal mud, a simple breakthrough with far-reaching impact. Spindletop, with its loose sand, defied the drillers until the Hamills drove cattle into the water pit and pumped the gumbo into the well, a trick they had learned in Corsicana. Nitroglycerine charges blasted oil from porous strata or from pulverized formations that resisted drill bits.

Companies recovered additional crude oil by mining the producing sands at Electra, and poured hydrochloric acid into the Breckenridge wells to dissolve calcareous material. Fire was an ever present threat, but drillers built batteries of multiple steam boilers to combat the inevitable blowout. Texas offshore production began in 1918 at Goose Creek, where the oil field extended under Tabbs Bay.[81] East Texas became the last of the mule-drawn oil booms, coming in the "twilight of steam rigs and wooden derricks."[82] Oil production by 1940 had matured, establishing patterns that would persist for decades to come.

The new Texas oil was black and heavy with sulfur, not clear like Pennsylvania crude. Its asphalt base convinced many that it could not be refined into "sweet-burning kerosene," admirably suited for illumination, the primary use for fuel oil at the turn of the century.[83] The development of the internal combustion engine and the advent of the automobile and other motorized vehicles for work and transportation completely reversed the demands of the marketplace. The use of oil and gas for power and heat in the United States rose from 8 percent of the total requirement in 1900 to 44 percent by 1940. The number of passenger cars rose from 23,000 in 1902 to over 27.5 million in 1940, while trucks, not built in 1902, increased to more than 6.8 million in the same period. Only 4 percent of the world's merchant tonnage and navies burned oil in 1914; by 1944, 75 percent did. In 1899, 57.7 percent of each barrel of crude became kerosene, 15.5 percent fuel oil, and 12.7 percent gasoline; forty years later, only 5.5 percent was refined into kerosene, 37.8 percent into fuel oil, and 45 percent into gasoline, indicating the shift in demand from illumination to fuel. About 142,000 barrels a day were distilled nationwide in 1899; four decades later the figure was almost 3.4 million.[84]

Lubricating Oil Company, the Petroleum Prospecting Company's biggest rival in Nacogdoches County, refined the first oil in Texas. John C. Fibinger served as its president, but actual management of the company was left to Pennsylvania oilmen D. C. and H. H. Criswell. Situated along Bayou Vistador, about four miles northeast of Oil Springs, their plant included five storage tanks, a receiving tank, an iron evaporating pan three feet by twenty feet with a steam chest underneath it, a steam filter pump, a boiler and steam engine, an iron shipping tank, and drums for transport of the finished product. Operators drew crude oil from the ground with bailing buckets and emptied it into a separating tank with two bungs, one for drawing off oil, the other water. The crude was then carried in barrels to the receiving tank on a hillside above the storage house, where it was fed by gravity through pipes to the evaporating pan. There, heat from the steam chest vaporized the remaining water and the small amount of naptha before the hot oil was filtered by steam pressure through a specially woven cloth to remove particles of grit. Discharged into the shipping tank, the oil was tapped into drums fitted with wrought iron wheels and shipped to Nacogdoches by wagon for rail shipment.[85] This small-scale activity ceased with the demise of the Nacogdoches field after 1890.

Sharp built the first small refinery at Corsicana for the Trinity Lubricating Oil Company of Dallas, producing eight grades of oil until his plant burned in 1898. Pennsylvania oilman Joseph S. Cullinan, the "Father of the Texas Oil Industry," contracted to build a refinery for the Corsicana field in 1897. He founded J. S. Cullinan and Company, a predecessor of Magnolia Petroleum Company, and constructed a plant with six crude stills capable of processing one thousand barrels a day. He fired his boilers on Christmas Day, 1898; within a year the value of Texas petroleum doubled. Seeking to expand their market, he and his brother devised a mechanism for burning oil in locomotives. The Houston and Texas Central converted all of its stock beginning in 1901; fifty years later, over 5,500 oil-burning locomotives traveled the nation's rails along with nearly 11,000 diesel electric units.[86]

Spindletop brought many competitors for Cullinan. The coastal area around Beaumont became the center for petroleum refining in Texas, beginning with a plant started in Port Arthur in 1901 and acquired the next year by Gulf Refining Company. Capable of processing 11,000 barrels daily, the Port Arthur refinery also experimented with producing gasoline by catalytic cracking soon after its completion, and paved the streets with asphalt, a byproduct, as early as 1904. Cullinan's Texas Company built a refinery at Port Arthur in 1902, and Magnolia opened a plant in Beaumont in that same year. Within ten years, the state had eleven refineries with a total daily capacity of 100,000 barrels. As its operations expanded, Gulf established refineries at Fort Worth in 1911 and Sweetwater in 1928. In 1919 Humble Oil Company built its Baytown refinery with a daily capacity of 260,000 barrels and a second one, which produced 12,000 barrels daily, at Ingleside, near Corpus Christi, in 1928. The Rio Grande Oil Company built a refinery at El Paso in 1919, the first of twenty-two West Texas refineries by 1929, of which eighteen were operational with a daily capacity of 92,200 barrels. As of March 1, 1938, 112 refineries operated in Texas, processing

over a million barrels of crude daily. Larger but fewer plants were built after 1935; by 1947 Texas held only eighty-four refineries.[87]

A growing network of pipelines fed the refineries. As a pioneer in the phenomena of Texas oil booms, the Petroleum Prospecting Company also established the first pipelines for petroleum. They built a two-thousand-gallon tank on Aaron's Hill in Nacogdoches, to which a three-inch pipeline brought crude oil from the wood and iron receiving vats by the wells 14.5 miles away. A small steam engine maintained pressure in the system. Most of the coastal fields were too close to the refineries to require pipelines of any length, but after several years of declining Texas production, Gulf Pipeline Company built an eight-inch pipeline from the Glenn Pool field in Oklahoma to its Port Arthur refinery in 1907. Texas Pipeline Company also completed an eight-inch line from Oklahoma to the Gulf Coast, building a refinery at West Dallas.[88]

Until 1920 the only pipelines lay in East Texas, with a single extension to the Ranger field. The introduction of welded joints to replace the leaky screw couplings allowed companies to expand their network into previously untapped regions. Seven trunklines extended into the Permian Basin during the 1930s. Economy begat innovation: Texas Pipe Line Company saved over a half million dollars on the construction of its pipeline from Monohans in Ward County, Texas, to Houston by mapping nearly half of its 573-mile length with aerial photography in 1929. At the end of the line, a growing fleet waited to transport Texas oil to an eager world. The first full tanker sailed from the Gulf Refining Company wharf in 1902. In response to the demands of the petroleum industry, the Houston Ship Channel opened to deepwater traffic in 1914. That same year, the Texaco fleet totaled ninety-four vessels, a far cry from the single wooden barge it owned just ten years earlier. Houston became the largest city in Texas by 1930, when nine refineries lined the Channel, and continued growth made it the nation's third busiest port by World War II.[89]

A growing concern for conservation accompanied the expanding oil economy. Spindletop spawned the first organized effort in Texas, if not the world, to control oil and gas wastage. Operators and company representatives met on August 30, 1901, and established a committee to enforce a series of ad hoc regulations. They also were bound by the state's first oil conservation laws adopted in 1899 as a response to wasteful practices in Corsicana, mandating the casing of active wells, the plugging of abandoned holes, and the restriction of wasteful natural gas flaring.[90] Despite these early efforts, criminally negligent practices continued. Drillers crowded their rigs into tiny lots, increasing the risk of fire and reducing the possibility for economical recovery. Spindletop's "Boiler Avenue" in 1903 proudly boasted the "densest drilling in Texas," and the pattern was repeated in other fields across the state for many years. Operators drilled under the persistent "Rule of Capture," a legal precedent established by the courts in Pennsylvania, which allowed companies to keep any oil that came through their wells, regardless of its origin. The wasteful effect of the overcrowding is indicated by the fact that 90 percent of the wells at Spindletop never produced. Furthermore, officials estimated half of the potential yield of the tremendous Desdemona field was lost through ignorance or disregard of conservation methods.[91]

The legislature finally codified the Texas Railroad Commission's implied authority over oil and gas. A law of February 20, 1917, declared pipelines to be common carriers, placing them under the jurisdiction of the Commission. Legislation in June 1920 extended this authority over natural gas. The Oil and Gas Division of the Railroad Commission originated on June 18, 1919, under a statute which became the fundamental conservation law of the state. On July 26, the Commission issued thirty-eight permanent regulations for oil and gas conservation, including provisions for regulating the production of all wells and penalties for wasteful practices such as flooding abandoned fields and flaring natural gas. Rule Number 37 regulated the economical spacing of wells and was upheld by Texas courts as a conservation measure against the rule of capture. The Commission quickly showed it meant business: the first shutdown, in the Burkburnett area, came on July 11, 1919, and the first proration was declared for the same region on July 18. Governor Pat Neff imposed martial law over the Mexia field in January 1922 to enforce the quotas imposed there in the face of concerted resistance.[92]

The Railroad Commission weathered its most severe legal tests in the East Texas imbroglio of the 1930s. Governor Ross Sterling, confronted with plummeting oil prices and corporate defiance of the Commission's orders to restrict their production, declared martial law, shut down the wells, and sent in the National Guard to keep order. A Federal Court of Appeals declared his actions unconstitutional in December 1932, but not until after a year of enforcement marked by violent resistance. "Hot Oil"—that which was produced in excess of decreed limits—continued to flood the petroleum market until 1935, when the

national government passed new regulations in favor of proration. By that time Texas had signed the Interstate Oil Compact along with five other states, agreeing to cooperate for effective enforcement of conservative petroleum and natural gas recovery practices. Texas became the third state to completely outlaw the flaring of all natural gas from producing wells, curtailing what Secretary of the Interior Harold Ickes denounced as "cruel and devilish waste" in an impassioned speech before a meeting of the American Petroleum Institute at Dallas in 1934.[93]

The Texas petroleum industry on the eve of World War II dominated the world market after only forty years of remarkable progress. The state in 1896 contained no successful oil wells of note and shipped only a thousand barrels of oil. Elsewhere in the United States some 54,319 wells pumped almost 7.7 million barrels that same year. Spindletop began a revolution, quadrupling Texas oil profits in one year, but the accelerating change in scale did not become readily apparent until after World War I. Texas between 1919 and 1920 nearly doubled its rig count, from 6,900 to 12,900, initiating a boom that would reach a pre–World War II plateau of 78,385 in 1937. Its proportion of productive wells in the United States increased from 1.4 percent in 1901 to 22.3 percent in 1937, pumping 5.1 billion barrels of crude oil, over 25.7 percent of the national total. Thanks to the persistence of Texas wildcatters, the United States' pre-eminent share of the world market increased after the turn of the century, growing from 53 percent in 1896 to 63 percent in 1937.[94] Oil enabled Texas to redefine its position in the national economy, shedding much of the colonial role imposed through agriculture and investing in a diverse spectrum of technical industry for the future.

Geology

Geology became the major scientific activity in Texas during the period before World War II because of its importance in the ongoing search for exploitable mineral and agricultural resources. Efforts to establish a state geologic survey were shaped by many factors. From a scientific point of view, one of the most important factors was the climatic diversity of Texas: the majority of the population lived in the eastern portion of the state, which received plenty of rainfall and did not share the concern for water resources of the farmers and ranchers in semi-arid West Texas. The belief that Texas had great surface deposits of valuable minerals spurred the creation of three surveys during the pre–World War II period, but they reported truthfully that the solid fossil fuel and sedimentary metallic ore deposits in the state were very low grade and that extraction was not economically feasible. Only oil finally vindicated the true believers.[95]

Professional geologists stressed the need for a geologic survey of Texas in the 1880s, and two events finally stirred public support: a movement for land reform, and an extended drought in 1886. The state government overextended its land grants, awarding by 1882 six million more acres than were in the public domain, mostly to large corporations and speculators. Concern mounted for the proper disposition of tracts reserved for the support of public schools and the University of Texas. The passage of the Land Reform Act of 1883 was a triumph for the vigorous popular movement in favor of responsible accounting. The Farmers' Alliance meeting at Cleburne in 1886 issued a series of demands for additional federal and state legislation, indicating the extent of public outrage and precipitating the Land Act of 1887, which placed supervision of reserved lands in the General Land Office. The harrowing drought of 1886–1887 impoverished some thirty thousand people in the Trans-Balcones counties and sent hundreds more reeling back from the frontier. The forces agitating for land reform allied with the angry farmers of West Texas in demanding a scientific study to find both the actual value of the public domain and relief for parched crops.[96]

At the same time, a national land reform movement led by Major John W. Powell, director of the United States Geological Survey (USGS), which was created in 1879, got underway. One of the most active groups in the state in demanding the formation of a third survey was the Texas State Geological and Scientific Association of Houston, newly founded in 1884 by Edwin T. Dumble, an amateur geologist who operated a chemical laboratory. When Powell sent Robert T. Hill to Texas to lobby for a state survey he found a good deal of interest, already astir and Dumble, a prime candidate for director, already active in the field. Ironically, the Farmers' Alliance proved to be the strongest opponent of a revitalized survey. Although farmers from the drought-stricken area supported the motion, the "parsimonious and suspicious extremists" of the Alliance believed that such action would benefit only railroads, corporations, and land speculators. The vote on the bill, which finally established the survey in May 1888, reflected the same split: a humid, prosperous East still opposed it, while the arid West supported the measure.[97]

Major Powell, in selecting Hill, sent both the best and the worst man to press for the creation of a survey. As a teenager Hill had settled in Comanche, Texas, where he fell in love with the unique topography of his adopted state. He earned international recognition not only as a geologist, but also as a geographer, explorer, historian, and writer, before his death in 1941. With a degree from Cornell, Hill first explored the Texas Cretaceous, the focus of his life's work, as a surveyor for the USGS in 1886. He discovered the Comanche Cretaceous Series the following year, then mapped the full extent of that strata, subdividing the Lower Cretaceous into the groups which have become standard. Hill also conducted the first scientific probe down the Rio Grande through the Big Bend region, delineated and named the Balcones Fault Zone, and discovered the westerly belt of faulting now known as the Texas Lineament while working for several state and national geological surveys in Texas.[98] However, because of his short physical stature he had developed a "persecution complex, which had given him a grating personality that often offset his scientific accomplishments."[99] Hill lost important positions with several organizations, including the University of Texas, due to his mercurial temper.[100] Such episodes do not detract from his contributions as a geologist, but do serve to emphasize the accomplishment of the people of Texas in 1888 when they succeeded in bringing about the creation of a geological survey to which Hill contributed so much despite continual controversy.

Lafayette L. Foster, Commissioner of Agriculture, Insurance, Statistics, and History, said about Dumble when he appointed him to lead the state survey, "Mr. Dumble already possesses a more thorough and scientific knowledge of the geology of Texas than could be acquired by any new man by close application and hard study for several years." The legislators actually chose Dumble because he was a Texan, but he did have a good background and did do a good job, maintaining a concern for proper scientific inquiry against mounting political and economic pressure. The enormous amount of research accomplished by the Dumble Survey in its four years of active existence "dwarfed all previous geological explorations in Texas in both quantity and quality."[101] Dumble initiated the first sophisticated stratigraphic studies of the Permian deposits of the Texas region in 1889 with the assistance of USGS paleontologist Charles A. White, who worked with William F. Cummins of the Texas organization. Cummins and Noah F. Drake uncovered the complex interfingerings of marine and terrestrial sediments that characterize the Osage Plains, work that was later amplified by the Texas Mineral Survey, although it was not until the extensive petroleum discoveries of the 1920s that definite stratigraphic correlation with surrounding regions was proven. Researchers under Dumble also pioneered a study of the Gulf Coastal Plain, a unique Southern geological formation, in Texas. Dumble looked into the iron ore and lignite deposits of East Texas, but did not explore the region's potential for petroleum because he believed lignite to be the fossil fuel of the future for the state, to his later chagrin.[102]

Governor James S. Hogg, as a response to political pressure for economy in state government, vetoed the survey appropriation for 1894, despite scattered Populist support from West Texas for its water and soils studies. Dumble continued as state geologist to conduct water and mineral studies under contract for individuals and to maintain the correspondence of the survey until 1899. In 1901 the legislature officially terminated the organization and transferred its laboratory, library, and specimen collections to the University of Texas, headquarters of a new mineral survey. Dumble, although not academically trained as a geologist, chose to continue in that discipline, organizing the first geological department devoted to petroleum exploration in 1897 for the Southern Pacific Railroad Company. His research staff at the Rio Bravo Oil Company became the first to apply micropaleontology in the exploration of subsurface structures in 1920. In all, Dumble published seventy scientific papers in his adopted field.[103]

George W. Brackenridge and his fellow regents, prompted by the ubiquitous Hill, requested an appropriation from the state legislature in 1900 for an organization to "devote itself to questions of industrial progress rather than to those of a more purely scientific nature." Governor Joseph D. Sayers' speech to the legislature in favor of the proposal on January 10, 1901, came on the very day that Spindletop blew in, reviving interest in a survey by the state of its mineral resources. William B. Phillips, who held a doctorate from the University of North Carolina and had done postgraduate work in the mining district of Freiberg, Germany, was promoted from instructor to professor of field and economic geology and appointed director of the University of Texas Mineral Survey in May 1901. Phillips enjoyed wide recognition for his work as a proficient chemist, geologist, mining engineer, mineralogist, and metallurgist in several Southern states. He authored about three hundred articles and books before his death in 1918. He received very ca-

pable support from Frederick W. Simonds, an associate professor of geology with a doctorate from Syracuse who became a member of the Geological Society of America, a fellow of the American Association for the Advancement of Science, and a noted writer during a career with the University of Texas that spanned five decades, beginning in 1890.[104]

The scope of the University of Texas Mineral Survey included private as well as public lands, but its research effort focused primarily on the Trans-Pecos region because almost all public lands were there, including the university reserve. Discovery of commercially valuable deposits of quicksilver ore near Terlingua stimulated other official inquiries into this region. Hill, the USGS man on the spot, earned his national reputation as "one of the foremost American reconnaissance geologists" in West Texas. Federal effort complemented Phillips' research when the USGS surveyed and printed topographical maps and funded Hill's broad sweeps while the state geologists conducted more detailed economic studies. Benjamin F. Hill performed very ably as assistant director of the Mineral Survey and Phillips' man in the field when the latter had to return to his teaching duties. B. F. Hill resigned in 1903, however, to become a full-time instructor in petrology and mineralogy at the University of Texas. Phillips forged a more durable association with Johan A. Udden, professor of geology and biology at Augustana College in Illinois, who worked with the survey for several summers and made significant observations on the formation and value of the mercury deposits at Terlingua. The University of Texas Mineral Survey succeeded in its geological work, mapping and detailing many important formations in the Trans-Pecos, but it failed politically because the geologists did not satisfactorily identify the potential mineral-bearing lands, largely due to the dearth of financial and administrative support from the state. After four years of substantial work, the Mineral Survey expired, the victim again of a contracting state budget, East Texas apathy, and personal politics.[105]

The resumption of subsurface stratigraphic studies came with the creation of the Bureau of Economic Geology and Technology (BEGT) at the University of Texas in 1909, which also resumed systematic exploration of the mineral resources under university and public school lands in the Trans-Pecos. Phillips, who had left Texas after the collapse of the Mineral Survey, returned as director of the new organization and convinced Udden to join him as the first field geologist employcd by the BEGT. Phillips served as director for only four years before accepting a position as president of the Colorado School of Mines, but his "strong dedication that bordered on being aggressive and abusive" left an indelible stamp, immortalizing Phillips as the "Father of the Bureau of Economic Geology."[106]

Udden became director in 1915 and brought scientific respect to the BEGT by establishing durable models for scientific inquiry at the University of Texas. As a research institution, the BEGT lent more to the development of the natural resources in Texas than any of its predecessors. Udden's staff effected the final unraveling of the geosynclinal history of the coastal plain in the 1930s. Udden tailored the research with an eye for practical application; for example, he introduced the micropaleontology techniques to Texas that would later be used by his students under Dumble at Rio Bravo Oil Company to facilitate oil exploration. The activities of the BEGT became increasingly diverse until in 1915 Udden reorganized it into three divisions which later became independent bureaus—Industrial Chemistry, Engineering Research, and Economic Geology—allowing the geologists to concentrate on Texas mineralogy, particularly petroleum. Udden reported on the existence of oil under UT lands in 1916, but his advice was not heeded until seven years later. The laboratory founded by the BEGT at Big Lake field became a model for geologists and oilmen alike, especially in deep well research. Previously, oil exploration depended almost entirely on surface geology, but new techniques brought a greater reliance on subsurface data obtained from well logs and core samples. Udden's many accomplishments earned him wide recognition from numerous professional organizations as well as the Order of the North Star from the king of his native land, Sweden. He stepped down as active head of the Bureau in 1925, but research progressed apace under his capable successor, Elias H. Sellards.[107]

Professional and amateur geologists came together in a number of organizations to advance the practice of their chosen vocation or hobby. San Angelo Geological Society convened in 1926 to further the study of oil exploration. When the center of the petroleum industry shifted to Midland, the West Texas Geological Society, primarily composed of petroleum geologists, emerged to become the dominant assembly in the region. Robert T. Hill presided over the first annual convention of the Southwestern Geological Society, organized in 1918 to pool the expertise of geologists

employed in the oil industry. The Society disbanded in 1924, but the Dallas section continued as the Dallas Geological Society, allied with the American Association of Petroleum Geologists to foster the development of subsurface research, including the greater use of seismological equipment. The first notable discovery of an oil field by reflection seismograph came in East Texas in October 1933, when a crew from Geophysical Services, owned by two members of the Dallas Geological Society, located the Long Lake Field in Anderson County.[108]

The geological surveys failed to uncover any significant mineral deposits other than petroleum. Commercial coal mining began in Texas during the 1880s, producing 125,000 tons in 1884. The oil boom crippled the industry. Coal production peaked at about 2.4 million tons in 1913, but rapidly shrank to 18,169 tons by 1950. Mining operations remained small, selling coal primarily within Texas. Tools were few and rather primitive, and most of the work was done by hand. Railroads, the primary customers, found the quality of Texas coal poor and used it only sparingly. The abundance of oil and natural gas also curtailed lignite production. Small quantities, however, were burned in homes for heat, converted into briquettes as fuel for generating steam power, or reduced to activated carbon used as a clarifying agent in sugar refining. But development of an electric power distribution nctwork eliminated smaller stations which burned lignite or coal in favor of large steam plants powered by natural gas, thus reducing even further the demand for solid fuels. Engineers at the University of Texas continued research into the utility of lignite, and its new steam plant, designed by Professor Hal C. Weaver in 1927, used lignite exclusively. East Texas iron production, initiated in the late nineteenth century, employed furnaces fired with charcoal. New Birmingham and Pittsburgh contained probably a score of these operations in their heyday, but the industry died out by 1910, the victim of a shift in technology from charcoal to coke, which smelted harder iron but could not be found in any great quantity in Texas. World War I brought a brief revival through Texas Steel Company, a minor producer at Rusk.

The Freeport Sulphur Company mined sulfur, beginning in 1913, by pumping superheated water into deep wells and pumping the liquefied sulfur out.[109] This process, invented by Herman Frasch and first used successfully in Louisiana in 1901, was made feasible by the presence—at the nearby Spindletop field—of the cheap fuel needed to heat the vast quantities of superheated water required. During the war, Texas Gulf Sulphur Company organized and opened the Big Hill sulfur dome in Matagorda County.

Chemical Technology

Texas chemists turned their talents to creating useful substances from the resources at hand, primarily for use in the petroleum industry. Two chemists worked for the Dumble survey: J. H. Herndon at the University of Texas, and P. S. Tilson at Texas A&M. Herndon later served as state chemist, conducting a spirited feud with Dumble over the focus of mineralogical research. Because study failed to reveal anything of use to existing industries, lime and gypsum remained the principal chemical products of Texas until after the turn of the century. Texas Chemical Company, a joint venture of the Pacific Bone Coal Company and Stauffer Chemical, incorporated in 1916 and built a bone coal, fertilizer, and ammonia plant in Houston. By 1919 it produced thirty tons of sulfuric acid daily for use in the petroleum industry. Southern Acid Company also made sulfuric acid for the refineries in Port Arthur beginning in 1917. As part of the Olin Corporation, the present site began production in 1928. Gulf Oil Corporation opened the largest electrolytic chlorine and caustic plant in the United States at Port Arthur in 1925, producing the chlorine for their own aluminum chloride catalyst plant.[110]

The depression briefly slowed down the Texas chemical industry but the advent of war brought renewed vigor. Southern Alkali, jointly owned by the Pittsburgh Plate Glass and American Cyanamid corporations, established a plant to produce soda ash, caustic, and chlorine at Corpus Christi in 1934, the first of its kind in the state, built at a cost of $7.5 million. By 1940, Dow Chemical Corporation's facility at Freeport produced caustic, chlorine, magnesium, ethylene, and ethylene glycol. Soon after Dow commenced operations in Freeport, Union Carbide and Carbon built a plant at Texas City to make ethanol and isopropanol, while Humble Oil produced butyl rubber and toluene for the war effort at Baytown. On the eve of the nation's entry into World War II, Shell Oil brought its first butadiene plant on stream in September 1941, and Ethyl Corporation cooperated with Dow to establish an ethylene dibromide plant in Freeport.[111]

Engineering

Texas engineers participated in the development of all sectors of industry in the state and built a sprawling infrastructure to expedite growth. The first state engineering school, Texas A&M College, opened in 1876. Major Robert P. W. Morris, whose discipline was actually applied mathematics, taught civil engineering—naturally with an emphasis on military applications. In 1886 the departments of Mechanical and Civil Engineering were established, the latter combining with physics under John H. Kinealy the following year. James C. Nagle became the director of the Department of Civil Engineering in 1890 and first dean of the School of Engineering in 1911. Physics separated from civil engineering in 1899 but enjoyed only a few years of independence before becoming part of the Department of Physics and Electrical Engineering from 1903 to 1909. A&M offered a curriculum of chemical engineering in 1907 but did not establish a department separate from chemistry until 1940. The creation of the departments of Agricultural Engineering in 1908, Architecture and Architectural Engineering in 1909, Sanitary and Municipal Engineering in 1926, Geological Engineering in 1933, Industrial Engineering in 1939, and Aeronautical Engineering in 1940 completed a full selection of courses. David W. Spence succeeded Nagle as dean, but Nagle returned to serve another term when Spence died unexpectedly. Francis C. Bolton, dean from 1922 to 1931, initiated the transition from an older style of engineering to a highly technical aspect, which was continued by his successor Gibb Gilchrist.[112]

The Texas Engineering Experiment Station originated in 1914 at A&M. Created to foster industrial development by investigating engineering problems and disseminating technical information, its efforts focused primarily on the use of Texas' natural resources. Much early work focused on highway construction; faculty members such as Robert J. Potts and his successor Robert J. Morrison campaigned actively for good roads, spurring the creation of the Texas Highway Department in 1917. Under Frederick E. Giesecke, an A&M graduate, research in the Engineering Experiment Station matured to include topics as diverse as municipal sanitation, under noted engineer Ernest W. Steel, and air conditioning in response to the increasingly complex demands of a developing state.[113]

One early publication of the Engineering Experiment Station is of particular interest because it focuses on the cotton textile industry in Texas. A&M,

like many land grant colleges, offered coursework on textile engineering and even organized a department in 1905. Although by the second decade of this century Texas had long led the nation in cotton production, it manufactured less than 2 percent of its crop into textiles each year, while the nation as a whole spun almost half its cotton into cloth. Of twenty-one mills in the state, only one, Miller Cotton Mills in Waco, held as much as a million dollars in capital; eight were valued at less than $100,000. During the 1920s, investors increased the number of plants to twenty-seven, but output never exceeded 1.13 percent of the national total, and by the close of World War II cotton textiles were a "stagnating industry." Most of the graduates of A&M's textile engineering program had to leave the state to find work, and the department was abolished in 1938. If it is true that cotton textiles were the predominant industry of the "New South," then Texas did not follow the pattern which reinforced the region's colonial role in the national economy.[114]

The University of Texas opened its doors in 1883, advertising a full selection of courses for those wishing a degree in civil engineering. Actually, the coursework depended heavily on John W. Mallet, an industrial chemist and a member of the Royal Society in London. Mallet's sudden departure at the end of the first year caused some consternation, but Alvin V. Lane filled the position admirably, broadening the simple curriculum. Thomas U. Taylor replaced Lane in 1888, remaining in charge of engineering at the university through the next five decades. Taylor was originally employed to teach applied mathematics but received a master's degree in civil engineering from Cornell and assumed direction of the nascent Department of Engineering in 1895, becoming dean in 1906. The first additional school within the department was mining engineering, established under Phillips' direction in 1900 and discontinued thirteen years later when the School of Mines and Metallurgy opened at El Paso. Electrical engineering began in 1903, followed by architectural engineering in 1906, architecture in 1909, mechanical engineering in 1914, petroleum engineering in 1929 under Sellards and Frederick B. Plummer, both noted geologists, and aerospace engineering in 1942, after a false start in 1926. Eugene P. Schoch, revered as the "Father of Industrial Chemistry for the Southwest" for his work as director of the Bureau of Industrial Chemistry, established a Department of Chemical Engineering in 1917, which separated from the Department of Chemistry in 1938. Willis R. Woolrich succeeded Taylor as dean in 1936; he accentuated the emphasis on research in the engi-

neering program, which was upgraded to the College of Engineering in 1922.[115]

Engineering research at the University of Texas centered in the Bureau of Engineering Research (BER), created in 1915 by Udden's reorganization of the Bureau of Economic Geology and Technology. Giesecke served as director until he returned to A&M in 1927; then the bureau became the responsibility of the dean. Studies prior to establishment of the BER were primarily conducted by Dean Taylor, including his investigations of stream flows while serving as state hydrologist for the USGS at the turn of the century and as a consultant for the dams at Austin. Like A&M, early work within the BER focused on road construction. R. G. Tyler's studies on municipal sanitation, however, predate the work of Steel, who in 1950 moved from A&M to the University of Texas. Giesecke produced his own work on the friction of water in pipes and fittings. Dean Woolrich initiated research in air conditioning just before World War II, aided by Byron E. Short, who conducted some of the first inquiries on heat transfer. Schoch continued his work in the analysis of Texas minerals in the Bureau of Industrial Chemistry after his department joined the College of Engineering in 1938, pioneering the conversion of methane into acetylene through electrical discharge during World War II.[116]

The University of Texas became one of six institutions in the country chosen by the Army Signal Corps to host a ground school in 1917. Although there had been virtually no air activity in the state before World War I, flying fields were soon built all over Texas, including Kelly and Brooks at San Antonio, Ellington at Houston, and Richfield at Waco. Training was in full swing by the end of 1917; the faculty in Austin, primarily engineers, graduated 4,600 cadets before the war's end. Lethargy returned with peacetime before research and development funding increased. The aviation branch of the Signal Corps, reorganized as the "Air Service," reactivated its programs in Texas, and the state became the primary center for initial and advanced training. Texas programs produced many noted pilots such as Charles A. Lindbergh, who trained at Brooks and Kelly fields; Randolph field became known as the "West Point of the Air." Texas researchers tested several new designs, including twin engine bombers and models with armor plating. Commercial aviation in Texas began with airmail service between Dallas and Chicago in 1926, and Austin's Mueller Airport supported three airlines—Braniff, Bowen, and American—by 1935. No aeronautical industry of note originated in Texas until World War II, but the state contributed personnel and facilities to the ongoing attempt at modernization between the great wars.[117]

On the ground, Texas engineering accomplishments were even more remarkable. Railroads increased from 3,244 miles in 1880 to a peak of 16,900 miles in 1930. The year 1900 marked the beginning of a flurry of interurban railroad construction; the state borders eventually contained almost five hundred miles of electric railways. The largest system was the Texas Electric, whose 226 miles centered on Dallas made it the longest interurban rail system west of the Mississippi River. Electric railway mileage declined rapidly in the United States after 1920 due to the increase in motorized traffic, and by 1950 nearly all of the tracks in Texas were abolished or converted to roads and highways. Automobiles traveled over 20,789 miles of roads in Texas in 1936, of which 87 percent were paved, thanks largely to the efforts of Gibb Gilchrist, a graduate of the University of Texas who doubled the paved road mileage in Texas as director of the State Highway Department. (In 1937 Gilchrist turned his talents to revitalizing the curriculum at A&M as dean of Engineering, later as president, and finally as chancellor of the A&M system in 1948.) Public health advanced through the construction of 405 enclosed sewer systems in 575 incorporated towns. Beginning with the first central electric station at Galveston in 1882, more than 18,000 miles of high-tension lines crisscrossed Texas by 1936. Austin completed the first successful hydroelectric plant in 1937 when its third dam in less than fifty years, named for former Mayor Tom Miller, passed inspection. Buchanan and Inks dams on the Colorado River also provided power before World War II. Galveston claimed the honor of the first telephone in Texas when a line was strung from the home of Colonel A. H. Belo to the editorial room of his paper, the *Galveston News*. Less than sixty years later, 392 firms serviced over a half million telephones in the state. There was still a long way to go, but technology had reached most of the population by 1940, when the census revealed for the first time that over half of the people in Texas lived in urban centers.[118]

Physics

The travails of the physics curriculum at Texas A&M unfortunately seem all too typical of the neglect accorded the subject during this period. Not until 1911 was it given independent recognition as a separate department by the college administration. Its equipment remained very crude and hard to obtain. Some confusion attended the use of the terms "physic" and "physics." For years, people came to the faculty for medical treatment or even veterinary problems. Legend says Governor Oscar H. Colquitt blue-penciled the physics appropriation in the 1915 budget with the remark: "Let them go to the Medical School in Galveston." In 1916 Oscar W. Silvey became the first chairman of physics at A&M who was not a graduate in engineering, although all of the staff were engineers. A building for physics was completed in 1920, and the department moved out of the civil engineering building at last. Following World War I, increased enrollment allowed advanced courses in physics, but no one chose physics as a major field of study until after the establishment of the School of Arts and Sciences in 1924. Through World War II the department remained primarily a service discipline for technical fields such as engineering.[119]

The Department of Physics at the University of Texas benefited from greater administrative and financial support. Its move to a new building in 1932 facilitated advanced research, which included the development of an early analog computer before the end of the decade by S. Leroy Brown, who called it a "mechanical multiharmonograph," and the construction of a seismograph machine by Arnold Romberg. The latter, together with his student Lucien J. B. LaCoste, improved the design of the machine and used it in the construction of a more reliable gravity meter, the LaCoste-Romberg gravity meter. Before World War II, Charles P. Boner initiated the research in acoustics which would bring him international recognition in the postwar technological boom, and Brown directed studies in electronics which laid the groundwork for developments in computer engineering.[120]

Mathematics

Texas mathematicians made important contributions to the growth of knowledge as well as their applications in state development through engineering. George B. Halsted of the University of Texas was a student under J. J. Sylvester at Johns Hopkins, one of the greatest mathematicians of the nineteenth century. Halsted introduced non-Euclidean geometry to the English-speaking world through his own translations, which remain the standard English interpretation of the key works in this field. Robert L. Moore, Halsted's most distinguished student, became the best-known mathematician in twentieth-century

Texas. A native of Texas, he earned his doctorate at the University of Chicago and returned to his first alma mater, the University of Texas, in 1920, initiating research on point-set topology, which brought him some of the United States mathematical community's highest honors, including election to the National Academy of Sciences in 1931. Another one of Halsted's students, Milton B. Porter, preceded Moore as the dominant personality in the Department of Pure Mathematics from about 1903 to 1930. In 1915 the university began to make its mathematical developments available to teachers all over Texas in a bulletin published for several decades.[121]

Health Sciences

The medical profession of Texas, charged with responsibility for the human resources of the state, embraced the spirit of progress which infected every other facet of society. After the American Medical Association reorganized in 1903, integrating each state chapter as a unit within a national whole, membership in the State Medical Association of Texas increased nearly tenfold in one year as doctors rushed to cement professional unity. The practically useless district boards of medical examiners had been abolished in 1901 in favor of a stricter system for central regulation of medical licenses; but continued agitation, especially against those fields outside the mainstream of medical practice, brought additional restrictions in 1907. President S. C. Red of the association stated its views quite clearly in 1903 when he said, "I think osteopathy should be struck with the jaw bone of an ass," and dismissed Mary Baker Eddy, founder of Christian Science, as "an hysterical woman of limited intelligence."[122] The "One Board Medical Practice Act" signed by Governor Thomas M. Campbell on April 17, 1907, made only the "scientific branches of medicine" eligible for certification, but the board originally included allopaths, eclectics, homeopaths, an osteopath, and a physiomedical practitioner who eschewed the use of drugs. The general intention soon became clear, however; in 1930 Texas supported as many as 11,000 allopaths—or regular physicians— and only a few hundred each from the eclectic, homeopathic, and osteopathic schools. A law adopted in 1907 created a similar review council for pharmacists, initiating efforts to eliminate patent medicine sellers and other dangerous hoaxsters.[123]

Higher standards reduced the number of medical schools in Texas, as it did throughout the United States. In 1900 there were three recognized medical schools in the state: the University of Texas Medical Branch in Galveston, the Fort Worth School of Medicine (a department of the nonexistent University of Fort Worth), and the University of Dallas Medical Department, organized in 1900 as a division of another school which never made it past the drawing board. North Texas endured a proliferation of medical schools in the next decade, ten in the Dallas–Fort Worth area. Only one, the Baylor University College of Medicine, survived the accreditation review of the American Medical Association by combining two other operations, the Medical Department of Texas Christian University and the University of Dallas Medical Department, into one sound institution, which included schools of pharmacy, dentistry, and nursing by 1918. Texas Baptist Memorial Sanitarium, completed in 1909, became Baylor University Hospital in 1920, completing a fine facility for medical study in North Texas. The University of Texas Medical Branch, located in Galveston after long and heated arguments, set the pace for medical progress in the state, and within months of its establishment in 1891, the faculty began introducing new techniques and medicines to their colleagues. The records of John Sealy Hospital, their institution for teaching and research, reveal the magnitude of their contributions: while splenectomies, hysterectomies, and transfusions were almost invariably fatal in 1886, according to a survey of Texas doctors, by 1939 the instance of death from surgery at John Sealy was only 3 percent, including cases involving serious head trauma, cancer, and pneumonia.[124]

Public health in Texas, as in other southwestern states, did not easily progress due to the lingering effect of a medical fad of the nineteenth century. The science of climatology, advocated by the American Climatological Association for over fifty years, convinced doctors "back East" to send patients suffering from a variety of maladies to enjoy the healing weather of the region. Texas became a favorite of migrant invalids, especially those suffering from tuberculosis—the "white plague"—for which there was no certain cure. Some survived to a ripe old age, like Edmund D. Montgomery, the eccentric scientific philosopher who retired to Texas from Europe with tuberculosis and wrote some of his most brilliant work at Liendo, the scenic farm he shared with artist Elisabeth Ney near Hempstead. Meanwhile, San Antonio, the center of at least a dozen resorts, earned distinction as the "Sanitarium of the West" and endured an inflated death rate as tubercular travelers, exhausted by their trek, settled to die in Texas. Citizens in the area welcomed the tourists at first, but discovery of the communicable tubercle bacillus turned thoughts of profit into a growing demand for isolation and public hygiene. W. M. Brumby, state health officer, declared Texas off limits to consumptives in the 1909 edition of the *Journal of the American Medical Association*, but the flow of invalids did not slacken greatly until twenty years later, with the final demise of the American Climatological Association and its unwelcome pseudoscience.[125]

The Texas Medical Association realized the need for an effective public health program quite early. Q. C. Smith regaled his excited and receptive audience in 1885 with a diatribe against the state government for failing to act, asking rhetorically what could be expected "when the mercenary harlot, politics, with bayonet power, captured white-robed science and forced her into most unholy prostitution, for the sensual gratification of her avaricious, dissolute masters?"[126] After years of agitation, the legislature finally created a State Board of Health in 1909. Although the state had appointed a health officer since 1879, not until 1927 was the Board of Health allowed to select its own candidate, removing the position from the realm of political patronage. John W. Brown became the first state health officer who had professional training in 1932. A special committee of the Association brought about the construction of the Carlsbad Sanatorium for tuberculars, opened in 1912.[127]

Men of science combated epidemic disease through a number of methods, some of them quite unique. Charles A. R. Campbell's plan to construct roosts from bats that would eat mosquitoes and reduce the instance of malaria gained widespread acceptance and brought a Nobel Prize nomination for the San Antonio naturalist. Proponents of public health in Texas did make some headway before World War II; I. L. McGlasson reported in 1926 that the yellow fever epidemic, with its accompanying hysteria, had become a threat of the past. Patrick I. Nixon fought to improve public health in San Antonio as a member of the city health board for twenty years, but the area still had the highest infant death toll in the country in 1936. Tuberculosis deaths totaled 145 per 100,000, twice the national average of 69.5 during 1936. The Mexican barrios posed the greatest problem, prompting Nixon to exclaim, "A perfect solution of it would be a beneficent fire that would spare the land and the people and consume the squalid shacks of rapacious landlords."[128] Nixon was no arsonist, and the problem remained unsolved for years to come.

Psychology and Psychiatry

Progress in the care of the mentally ill in Texas paralleled that of the nation as a whole, developing little in the period before World War II. The Austin State Lunatic Asylum opened in 1861, but before 1896, no supervisor remained more than five years. W. W. Reeves, superintendent of the asylum, was shot down in 1892 by a recently discharged patient. Overcrowding necessitated the establishment of the North Texas Lunatic Asylum, later the Hospital for the Insane, at Terrell in 1885, and the Southwestern Insane Asylum at San Antonio in 1891. H. A. West later described conditions within the institutions at the turn of the century as "abhorrent in the extreme."[129] As elsewhere in the United States, treatment consisted of rest, diet, massage, hydrotherapy, and electric shock. Charles W. Castner, who served as a staff physician at Terrell in 1915, recalled that recovery rates rarely exceeded 12 percent; as superintendent of the institution at Rusk in 1963, after years of reform, he proudly reported success with 75 percent of admitted patients, drawing a vivid contrast. A separate epileptic colony opened in 1904, accepting patients from asylums all over Texas and providing specialized care for the first time.[130]

Improvement began with the establishment of a central board for administering the state hospitals in 1920, consolidating the authority of twenty-one agencies. The old state penitentiary buildings at Rusk became the East Texas Hospital for the Insane in 1919, Wichita Falls State Hospital opened in 1922, and Big Spring State Hospital began as a model program for the future in 1938 for West Texas. By 1940, methods centered on diagnosis and treatment rather than custodial care, but Texas still spent far less than the national average on mental health care. The state government did resist movements for regressive laws such as mandatory sterilization of all state hospital patients, adopted by twenty-nine states and upheld by the Supreme Court in 1934, remaining an island of stability in a stream of public opinion that would make "insanity, imbecility, and idiocy" a crime.[131]

The University of Texas led the way in scientific education for mental health care in the Southwest. Hugh Blodgett, a graduate of the University of California at Berkeley, joined the faculty of the Department of Psychology in 1928, continuing research which questioned many of the basic assumptions of the behavior theorists then in vogue. Titus H. Harris, a Texas native, attended the University of Texas Medical Branch in Galveston and the New York Neurological Institute before becoming chairman of the Department of Neurology and Psychiatry at the former. He was a pioneer in the field of psychiatry, and by his retirement in 1962 had made his organization one of the largest and most highly acclaimed in the nation. The state established a psychopathic hospital in connection with the University of Texas at Galveston in 1931 to treat conditions which did not come within the strict legal definition of insane. For good or bad, researchers at the Medical Branch followed every trend in treating mental illness. Just five years after Ludwig von Meduna of Budapest used metrazol as shock therapy for his patients, John L. Otto in Galveston reported success with the treatment, although the convulsions caused cracked vertebrae in four of his seventeen subjects. The Hogg Foundation, begun on the Austin campus under Robert L. Sutherland, advocated a pluralistic concept of mental health, relating all the factors in an individual's environment to proper personality growth. The University also aided the Texas Society for Mental Hygiene, founded in 1934 to humanize the care of both the mentally ill and the handicapped in the state. In 1937 the Division of Mental Hygiene of the State Department of Health was established through their efforts.[132]

Genetics

The University of Texas also pioneered in the field of genetics. Herman J. Muller, who had studied under T. H. Morgan at Columbia University, came to the university in 1927. He continued research initiated in New York, tying together the loose ends of cytology, taxonomy, and genetics into an experimental study of inheritance. His new compatriots included Theophilus S. Painter, a cytologist, and John T. Patterson, an embryologist. "Muller's genius was born out of elbow grease," expended for over twenty years in the study of *Drosophila Melanogaster*, or vinegar flies. "He had studied them, bred them, murdered them, quartered them, lived with them night and day." Indeed, a companion wrote, "Muller had acquired such an emotional attachment to the genetical eccentricities of the little beasts that, had he failed to produce his results, one would have been more impressed than with his actual achievement." Muller's major breakthrough was in the production of mutations with x-rays, a "spectacular contribution," as it compressed thousands of years of random change into a manageable timeframe. His work was "anathema for the anti-evolutionists for it shattered their hyperphysical play-

houses, and drained all the psychic juice out of their ecclesiastical squirt-guns."[133]

Others soon reproduced Muller's results, and he was hailed as a champion. Patterson produced mutations in somatic cells as opposed to Muller's germ cells, leading to new knowledge about cancer. Painter led the way to new plateaus, successfully mapping the chromosomes themselves in cells from the salivary glands of the ubiquitous vinegar flies. All three men— Muller, Patterson, and Painter—were elected to the National Academy of Sciences, along with fellow researchers Carl G. Hartman, who in 1915 became the first person to receive a doctorate from the University of Texas, Wilson S. Stone, later an eminent professor of zoology for the university, and Elmer J. Lund, who founded the university's Marine Science Laboratory at Port Aransas in 1941. Muller enjoyed the highest recognition of his contributions when he received the Nobel Prize for his research at the University of Texas. Painter was later hailed as "one of America's foremost geneticists" and in 1938 was awarded the Daniel Giroud Elliot Medal by his fellow members of the Academy. Through their efforts, the University of Texas earned an international reputation for excellence in scientific research.[134]

Anthropology and Archaeology

Anthropology, the comparative study of the biology and cultures of human groups, began slowly in Texas. The publication of systematic research into the diverse societies of historic and prehistoric times, such as A. S. Gatschet's reconstruction of Karankawa culture in 1891, was rare in the nineteenth century. At the beginning of the twentieth century the wealth of archival material on Indian life in Texas was only just beginning to be exploited, most notably by historian Herbert Bolton, who compiled information on a number of Indian groups for the encyclopedic *Handbook of North American Indians*, published by F. W. Hodge in 1907 and 1910. At the same time, archaeological interest in the desert Southwest was attracting a few researchers, such as J. W. Fewkes and Charles Peabody, into the far western part of the state, and a scattering of notes appeared in print about the new archaeological materials unearthed in the Panhandle and northeast Texas.[135]

Despite the record of meager interest, one of the earliest departments of anthropology founded in the United States, preceding those in many other states by as much as thirty years, was established at the University of Texas in 1919, building upon an earlier program called institutional history. The founder, James E. Pearce, a Texan trained in anthropology at the universities of Chicago and Paris, was soon joined by George C. Engerrand, a colorful French anthropologist and geologist, who had spent most of his career in Mexico. This pair taught all the branches of anthropology in the department for many years.[136]

Engerrand conducted the first field work in cultural anthropology in Texas, a study of the descendants of the Wend colonists in the state. At Texas Technological College, W. C. Holden, a historian and anthropologist, began cultural anthropological research in the thirties among the Yaqui Indians of Sonora, Mexico. It was archaeological research, however, that dominated anthropology in Texas in the two decades preceding World War II. Although most of the field work was initiated by Pearce and his students at the University of Texas, many other institutions in the state also sponsored archaeological excavations in the 1930s. In the middle and late part of the Depression, field work increased sharply when federal relief projects poured funds into archaeological research because it provided work for laborers. At the University of Texas, physical anthropological studies of skeletal material from the archaeological field work were also instituted.[137]

In addition, systematic amateur archaeology, as contrasted with simple digging for relics, which destroys the site, began to contribute to the study of Texas prehistory. Many individuals and local societies became active; of particular note is the Texas Archaeological and Paleontological Society, formed in 1928 at Abilene by Cyrus N. Ray, an osteopathic surgeon. The annual meetings of the Society provided the principal opportunity for Texas archaeologists, professional and amateur, to come together. Its yearly bulletin, which first appeared in 1929, soon became nationally known and was for many years almost the sole outlet in the state for publication of archaeological reports. Other groups also contributed to the development of archaeology in Texas: the El Paso Archaeological Society formed in 1922, and Dallas began its own organization in 1936. The Texas Society, however, was the primary forum. Ray, "crusty but indomitable," remained as president and editor of the bulletin until 1940, when W. C. Holden became editor.[138]

Archaeologists in Texas also established an organization for professional development in the prewar period. The Council of Texas Archaeologists formed at the November 1939 meeting of the Texas Archaeological and Paleontological Society. Pearce had died, but his successor, J. Gilbert McAllister, continued the dominance of the University of Texas by serving as president, with fellow faculty members A. T. Jackson as vice-president and Thomas N. Campbell as secretary. They published a few issues of a newsletter, but professional archaeology came to a halt during World War II. Although the group existed only a short time, their work is vital because "the chronological and the cultural frameworks within which the interpretation of Texas archaeology still functions were established during this period."[139] The legacies of Pearce's reign also include the Texas Memorial Museum, which he helped to establish on the Austin campus.[140]

The archaeological field work resulted in the accumulation of a very large body of important information. However, archaeologists in Texas during this period did not take advantage of great developments elsewhere in the country, where crucial progress was made in techniques for data collection and analysis. Most of the material from the field work of the thirties would have to wait until after World War II for sophisticated analysis. Some change began after 1938 when McAllister, a Texas native with a doctorate from the University of Chicago, took charge of anthropology at the University of Texas, imported trained archaeologists from outside the state, and saw to it that the final work before the war was on a par with much of that in the rest of the United States. In 1940 Campbell and J. Charles Kelley, Texans who had worked in the Big Bend as Harvard graduate students, published the state's first up-to-date archaeological monograph.[141] These achievements indicate that the foundation had been laid for the growth of modern anthropology in Texas after the war.

Astronomy

Similar to some of the other scientific disciplines, astronomy in Texas benefited from a union of amateurs and professionals before World War II. The majority of the early professional astronomical research was conducted by visitors from out of state. Professor William Harkness of the United States Naval Observatory arrived in May 1878 to observe a transit of Mercury across the face of the sun, a somewhat rare event which allowed nineteenth-century astronomers the opportunity to measure the linear dimensions of the planet by determining the precise instant at which it was seen to impinge upon and depart from the solar

Figure 6. Assembled observers of the 1878 total eclipse at Fort Worth (from Waldo's book).

disk (fig. 6). In his reports from Austin, Harkness remarked upon a bright spot which appeared between him and the planet during the transit; he could not know that he was recording early evidence of the refraction of light around a circular obstacle. Harkness was also one of the first to report the distortion of the image of the smaller body as it approached the solar disk, much to his dismay. A total eclipse of the sun later that same year (fig. 7) brought more expeditions from northern institutions, including one from Thomas A. Edison's laboratory.[142]

A transit of Venus, an extremely rare celestial event, drew a new flood of scientific observers to Texas in 1882. Previous ones had occurred in 1761, 1769, and 1874, with the next one expected in 2004. Its importance lies in the fact that Venus is relatively close to the earth, about twenty-six million miles, so that from different stations the tracks of the planet across the solar disk are quite dissimilar, permitting measurements for an accurate calculation of the earth's distance from the sun, a largely unknown quantity in the nineteenth century. The event prompted the first

overseas scientific expedition by Belgians, who established observation posts in Chile and in San Antonio, Texas, the best site in North America. The Belgian research team was led by the director of the Royal Observatory at Brussels, Jean-Charles Houzeau de Lahaie, whose exploits from a very young age on had attracted international attention. He had been expelled from his native Belgium for his republican writings in 1848 and later settled in Uvalde and San Antonio, from whence Houzeau was hounded out of Texas for his antislavery views at the outbreak of the Civil War. He returned to San Antonio in triumph in 1882, establishing his headquarters at a house on Government Hill about four miles from town. The event took on many of the trappings of a carnival as curious amateurs and earnest professionals jostled for attention from the attendant crowd of newspaper reporters, but the reports published from the observations made in San Antonio provided new grist for academic mills for many years to come.

Precious little professional astronomy was undertaken in Texas for the balance of the period before

World War II. Isolated amateurs contributed in some measure to the continued interest in the field during these doldrums. H. S. Moore of McKinney was an independent discoverer of the bright supernova in the Andromeda galaxy in 1885, using a four-inch refracting telescope on August 30 of that year. S. H. Huntington of Kerrville sent over three hundred observations to the American Association of Variable Star Observers from 1913 to 1915. Oscar W. Monnig outdid Huntington: he contributed over twelve hundred astronomical observations to the association between 1929 and 1945, using a five-inch telescope and a Schmidt camera. Monnig also distributed a monthly "Texas Observer's Bulletin" for fifteen years, founded a small private observatory outside his native Fort Worth, and built an unusual collection of meteorites. He received the ultimate recognition when Minor Planet Number 2870 was named in his honor.

Academic astronomers also remained active in Texas during this period. Father John Joseph Lesage of the order of St. Vincent de Paul at Holy Trinity College in Dallas, where he taught science courses which included astronomy, made systematic observations of Halley's Comet in 1910. John L. Boon, a teacher and a member of the Dallas Astronomical Society who often wrote for *Field and Laboratory*, published by Southern Methodist University, helped to bridge the gap by disseminating information, but his writing reflected little original research. The MacDonald Observatory, founded as a cooperative venture between the University of Texas and the University of Chicago in 1937, established advanced astronomical inquiry in this state, providing new insight into age-old questions about the heavens.[143]

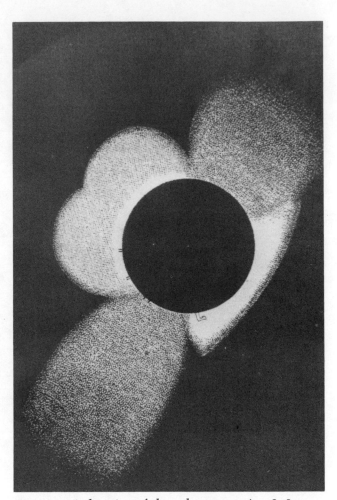

Figure 7. A drawing of the solar corona in 1878.

The Texas Academy of Science

Samuel W. Geiser, the finest early historian of science in Texas, said fifty years ago, "The history of scientific progress offers a confusing, kaleidoscopic succession of viewpoints associated with personalities."[144] Two state associations have tried to organize the tremendous diversity of scientists and technologists in the state. The first Academy of Science of Texas endured from 1880 to 1886 under the direction of S. B. Buckley and Franklin L. Yoakum. The academy's presence must have been missed, because in 1892 fourteen men of science reorganized it at the University of Texas. Dedicated to the promotion of both the natural and exact sciences, with membership open to all disciplines, the assembly quadrupled in size during its first year. The remarkable growth in the state economy effected by the members soon overtook them, however, and the academy dissolved once more in 1912 as other interests drew its adherents into distant fields. Again, its demise must have been mourned, for the academy revived in 1928 with a new resolve to stimulate scientific research and promote fraternal relationships among all scientists, which has lasted to the present.[145]

The intermittent existence of the Texas Academy of Science does not indicate a lack of interest in scientific progress in Texas before World War II. Rather, it illustrates the integrations of science and technology into every aspect of a rapidly evolving economy. Technical knowledge raced forward during the period, par-

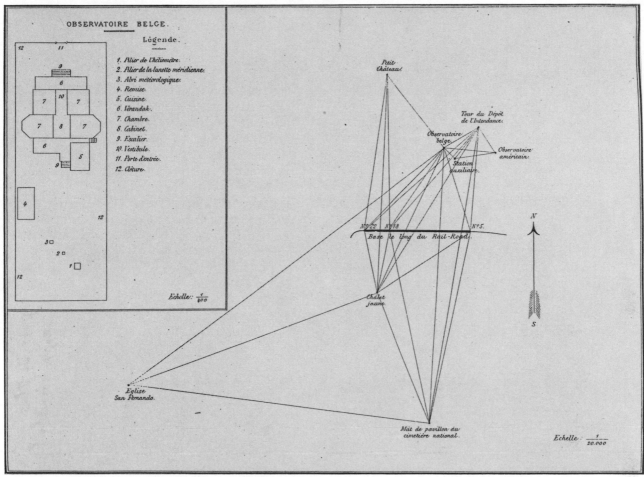

Houzeau's plan showing the location of the Venus transit observers in San Antonio in 1882 (from Annales of the Brussels Observatory).

alleling material progress and even pulling it along in the rush to escape the colonial role imposed by a predominately agrarian culture. Scientists and technologists were simply too busy to convene as often as an organization such as the academy required. Scientific publication did not slacken significantly in the interregnum; frequently, local or corporate societies met in the field near the site of another big oil strike, at a sprawling industrial facility, or at an important archaeological or geological discovery to exchange ideas in the flush of new research and development. The excitement infected every level of life in Texas, spurring popular movements for more scientific education within each sector of the workforce. As enterprise matured and academic departments developed, the need for established forums became more apparent and the academy revived. Its members continued to work for the future, completing the groundwork that made Texas a model for scientific research and economic prosperity in the post–World War II world.

Notes

1. Everhart, 1892, pp. 26–27.
2. Caldwell, 1965, p. 405.
3. Spratt, 1971, p. 277.
4. Ibid., p. 285.
5. Caldwell, 1965, p. 407.
6. Everhart, 1892, p. 30.
7. Ross, 1898, p. 19.
8. Montgomery, T. H., 1905, p. 10.
9. Ibid., p. 5.
10. Halsted, 1895, p. 204.

11. Calvert, 1970, p. 512.

12. Hunt, 1953, pp. 7–8, 11.

13. Ibid., p. 27, 29–36.

14. Farmers' State Alliance of Texas, 1887, pp. 8–9; Woodward, 1951, pp. 188–193.

15. Hunt, 1953, pp. 41, 83, 100, 130–131; Woodward, 1951, pp. 413–416.

16. *Inauguration*, 1951, p. 5.

17. Ibid., p. 10.

18. Dethloff, 1976, 1:pp. 32, 57, 71, 74; Ousley, 1935, pp. 45, 52.

19. Hunt, 1953, pp. 12–15.

20. Dethloff, 1976, 1:pp. 74, 99, 217.

21. Woolfolk, 1962, p. 103; Dethloff, 1976, 1:p. 81.

22. Texas A&M University. AES, 196–, passim.

23. Ousley, 1935, p. 17.

24. Hunt, 1953, p. 15; *Proceedings*, 1891, p. 18; Dethloff, 1976, 1:pp. 219–223.

25. Dethloff, 1976, 1:p. 220; Ousley, 1935, pp. 22–25, 31; Woodward, 1951, pp. 409–411.

26. Clay, 1904, pp. 520–521; Foster, 1889, p. ix; Ousley, 1935, pp. 23–24; Texas A&M University. AES, 196–, passim; Woodward, 1951, pp. 410–411.

27. Ousley, 1935, pp. 111–117; Texas A&M University. AES, 196–, passim.

28. Schmidt, H., 1958, p. 2; Havins, 1948, pp. 147–150, 158–159; Welborn, 1908, pp. 249–250.

29. Schmidt, H., 1958, pp. 2, 4, 6, 36; Havins, 1948, pp. 160–161.

30. Havins, 1948, pp. 159, 162; Texas Livestock Sanitary Commission, 1946, passim; Schmidt, H., 1958, p. 8; Ousley, 1935, pp. 93, 118–124.

31. Woolfolk, 1962, p. 104; Webb, W. P., and Carroll, 1953, 2:p. 250; Geiser, 1939, p. 48.

32. Stiles, 1902, pp. 356–371; Lowrey, 1902, p. 68; LeGear, 1897, passim; Texas Livestock Sanitary Commission, 1927, passim.

33. Havins, 1952, pp. 52–53; Schreiner, 1949, pp. 432–434; Texas Swine Breeders' Association, 1903, p. 170.

34. Bonnifield, 1979, pp. 153–154.

35. Bonnifield, 1979, pp. 155–157, 160–161.

36. Texas Industrial Congress, 1914, p. 11.

37. Texas Industrial Congress, 1914, pp. 13–14, frontispiece; Texas Industrial Congress, 1911, passim.

38. Texas Industrial Congress, 1911, passim; Texas Industrial Congress, 1914, p. 19.

39. Texas Farmers' Congress, 1903, pp. 153–155.

40. Yarbrough, no date, passim; "Courses," 1914, passim; Woods, 1938, passim.

41. Texas Association of Future Farmers of America, 1937, passim.

42. Geiser, 1939, p. 34; Geiser, 1942, p. 284; Dethloff, 1976, 1:p. 222; Texas A&M University. AES, 1889, p. 75.

43. The author is indebted to John F. Griffiths, Professor of Meteorology at Texas A&M University and Texas State Climatologist, for his invaluable aid in completing this passage on the seminal era of meteorology in Texas.

44. Hyman, 1948, p. 19; Maxwell, 1974, p. 360.

45. Maxwell, 1974, pp. 355, 359; Maxwell and Baker, 1983, pp. 169, 195, 201; Hyman, 1948, p. 18.

46. Maxwell and Baker, 1983, p. 168.

47. Ibid., p. 168.

48. Schmidt, H. C., 1882, pp. 1, 4, 5, 7–9; Jonah, 1936, p. 57.

49. Bray, 1904, pp. 36–37.

50. Ibid., pp. 37, 39, 44, 45, 50–51.

51. Maxwell and Baker, 1983, pp. 169, 171.

52. Hyman, 1948, p. 9; Maxwell and Baker, 1983, pp. 170–172.

53. Maxwell and Baker, 1983, pp. 171–174.

54. Maxwell and Baker, 1983, pp. 174–175; Texas Forestry Association, 1922, pp. 4–7.

55. Maxwell and Baker, 1983, p. 175; Dethloff, 1976, 2:pp. 361, 371–372.

56. Texas A&M University. Texas Forest Service, 1939, pp. 3, 5, 7, 14; Texas A&M University. Texas Forest Service, 1936, p. 11.

57. Maxwell, 1974, p. 379; Maxwell and Baker, 1983, pp. 179, 208–209; Texas A&M University. Texas Forest Service, 1939, p. 14; Hyman, 1948, pp. 18, 24–29.

58. Caldwell, 1965, p. 411; Maxwell and Baker, 1983, pp. 209–212.

59. Geiser, 1948, pp. 218–223, 271.

60. Branda, 1976, p. 39.

61. Geiser, 1948, pp. 278–279.

62. Ibid., p. 278.

63. Doughty, 1984, pp. 99–101, 107–108, 155–157, 160–164.

64. Ibid., pp. 165–168; Attwater, 1903, passim.

65. Doughty, 1984, pp. 175–180; Oberholser, 1974, 1:pp. 5–6.

66. Ibid., pp. 169–172, 181.

67. Webster, 1975, pp. 32, 40, 46; Branda, 1976, p. 664; Oberholser, 1974, 1:pp. xi–xii.

68. Adkins, 1948, pp. 275–276.

69. Geiser, 1939, p. 47; Branda, 1976, pp. 411, 985; Geiser, 1948, p. 276; Attwater, 1917, pp. 47–60; Strecker, 1925, passim; Ferguson, 1981, pp. 297–299.

70. Gard, 1966, pp. 7–8.

71. Clark, 1958, p. 130; Gard, 1966, pp. 9–12.

72. Clark and Halbouty, 1952, pp. 12–13, 25, 37–38; Gard, 1966, pp. 11–13; Branda, 1976, pp. 389–390; Webb and Carroll, 1953, 2:p. 91; Phillips, 1901, passim; Woodward, 1951, pp. 302–303.

73. Clark and Halbouty, 1952, p. 133; Gard, 1966, pp. 13–14; Woodward, 1951, pp. 302–303.

74. Thompson, 1951, pp. 12–14, 23; Webb and Carroll, 1953, 1:pp. 747–748; Gard, 1966, p. 14; Woodward, 1951, pp. 303–304.

75. Gard, 1966, pp. 14, 16–19, 21; Webb and Carroll, 1953, 1:p. 863.

76. Myres, 1973, pp. 155, 194, 216, 250, 253, 565; Gard, 1966, p. 22; Myres, 1977, pp. 6–7, 16–19.

77. Presley, 1981, pp. 81–82; Gard, 1966, pp. 24–26.

78. Warner, 1939, p. 11; Gard, 1966, pp. 14, 16, 20–21, 23–24, 29; Myres, 1973, p. 56; Thomas, 1936, pp. 98–99.

79. Clark and Halbouty, 1952, p. 101; Myres, 1973, pp. 61–62, 251; Rundell, 1977, p. 217.

80. Gard, 1966, pp. 11–12; Myres, 1973, pp. 61, 66–68; Clark, 1958, p. 131; Webb and Carroll, 1953, 1:p. 860, 2:p. 597; Warner, 1939, pp. 20, 85.

81. Myres, 1973, pp. 267–268; Gard, 1966, pp. 7, 22; Warner, 1939, pp. 12, 14–15, 36–37; Webb and Carroll, 1953, 2:p. 597; Rundell, 1977, pp. 51, 119–120, 126–130, 158, 167, 172.

82. Presley, 1981, pp. 85, 93, 100, 105, 115.

83. Thompson, 1951, p. 15.

84. Clark, 1958, pp. 124–125, 127.

85. Gard, 1966, p. 7.

86. Warner, 1939, pp. 22–23, 83–84; Rundell, 1977, p. 21; Webb and Carroll, 1953, 1:p. 444; Gard, 1966, p. 11; Clark, 1958, p. 131.

87. Gard, 1966, pp. 14, 17, 20; Thompson, 1951, p. 45; Rundell, 1977, p. 58; Warner, 1939, p. 117; Webb and Carroll, 1953, 1:pp. 747–748, 2:pp. 306, 736–737; West Texas Oil Scouts Association, 1929, p. 97.

88. Gard, 1966, pp. 7, 16; Webb and Carroll, 1953, 1:pp. 747–748.

89. Myres, 1973, p. 74; Rundell, 1977, p. 240; Myres, 1977, p. 19; Stevenson, 1930, pp. 4–5; Gard, 1966, p. 14; Webb and Carroll, 1953, 3:p. 413; Thompson, 1914, p. 9.

90. Warner, 1946, p. 8; Warner, 1939, pp. 33–34.

91. Rundell, 1977, pp. 43–45, 74–75, 84, 207; Clark, 1958, p. 97; Clark and Halbouty, 1952, p. 102; Gard, 1966, p. 19.

92. Warner, 1946, pp. 11–12; Gard, 1966, p. 20; Texas Railroad Commission, 1919, passim; Hart, 1941, pp. 309–310.

93. Hart, 1941, pp. 313–320; Gard, 1966, pp. 26–28; Myres, 1977, pp. 14–15; Clark, 1958, p. 177, pp. 198–199.

94. Thompson, E. O., pp. 3–6, 9–12; Webb and Carroll, 1953, 2:p. 305.

95. Ferguson, 1969, pp. vii–viii; Deussen, 1935, pp. 37–38, 41.

96. Ferguson, 1969, pp. 74–77.

97. Ibid., pp. 77–81, 83–84, 87.

98. Alexander, 1976, pp. ix–x, 17, 54, 57, 68–82.

99. Ferguson, 1969, p. 82.

100. Alexander, 1976, pp. 68–81.

101. Ferguson, 1969, pp. 90, 93.

102. Ferguson, 1969, pp. 137–138, 140, 145–147; Deussen, 1935, pp. 38–39.

103. Ferguson, 1969, pp. 94–96; Underwood, 1964, pp. 53, 71–72.

104. Ferguson, 1969, pp. 115–118; Webb and Carroll, 1953, 2:pp. 373, 613; "William Battle Phillips," 1935, p. 10.

105. Ferguson, 1969, pp. 118–119, 124–128, 130–131; Deussen, 1935, p. 47.

106. Ferguson, 1981, pp. 3–4, 10; Heiman, 1963, pp. 46–47; Webb and Carroll, 1953, 2:p. 373.

107. Ferguson, 1969, pp. 150, 159; Heiman, 1963, pp. 61, 64; Myres, 1973, pp. 82–85, 265–267, 567; Webb and Carroll, 1953, 2:p. 816; Ferguson, 1981, pp. 4–6, 13, 298, 301.

108. Myres, 1973, pp. 589–591; *First Annual Proceedings*, 1920, pp. 8–10; Wilson, 1974, pp. 1, 9.

109. The University of Texas at Austin. Mineral Survey. *Coal*, 1902, pp. v–vi; Branda, 1976, p. 179; Eckhardt, 1938, pp. 14, 38; Dahl, 1931, p. 9; Coleman, 1900, passim; Caldwell, 1965, p. 423; McClure, 1983, p. 18; Cunningham, 1931, p. 26; Tindall, 1967, pp. 57, 60.

110. Underwood, 1964, pp. 60, 62; McClure, 1983, pp. 17–18.

111. Columbia-Southern, 1954, pp. 1–2, 10–11, 15; Caldwell, 1965, pp. 413–414; McClure, 1983, pp. 18–20.

112. Crawford, 1976, pp. 16, 22, 31, 35–36, 38, 51–52, 58–59, 245; Dethloff, 1976, 1:pp. 243, 252–253.

113. Webb and Carroll, 1953, 2:pp. 738–739; Crawford, 1976, pp. 38–39; Morrison, 1915, passim; Coghlan, 1915, p. 7; Potts, 1917, passim; Coghlan, 1916, p. 6; Steel and Zeller, 1928; Branda, 1976,

p. 751; Steel and Zeller, 1930, passim; *Papers,* 1939, passim.

114. Crawford, 1976, pp. 30–31, 35, 46, 57; Bagley, 1922, pp. 9–11; Caldwell, 1965, p. 409; Woodward, 1951, p. 308.

115. "John William Mallett," 1913, p. 17; Woolrich, 1964, pp. 20–22, 48, 72–73, 83, 91–93, 108–110, 126–127, 130–132, 149–150, 161; *Faculty Report,* 1888, pp. 5, 17; Taylor, 1938, pp. 92–93, 378–380; Battle, 1951, p. 411; Eckhardt, 1978, pp. 80–81.

116. The University of Texas at Austin. Bureau of Engineering, 1953, passim.

117. Giles, 1950, pp. 150–151, 153, 157; Tillotson, 1978, pp. 167–188; Lockwood, 1976, p. 5; Long, 1962, p. 26; Udden, 1935, p. 87.

118. Jonah, 1936, p. 57; Grant, 1980, pp. 30, 48; Branda, 1976, pp. 338, 773; Gilchrist, 1936, p. 107; Montgomery, J., 1936, p. 89; Thomas, 1936, pp. 99–101; Long, 1956, pp. 90, 95; Lockwood, 1976, pp. 4ff; White, 1938, p. 3.

119. Silvey, 1953, pp. 69–74.

120. Horton, 1983, pp. 23–25; Lacoste, 1983, pp. 28–30; Horton, 1983, pp. 26–27.

121. Halsted, 1897. frontispiece; Halsted, 1895, pp. 204–206; Halstead, 1896, pp. 12–13; Branda, 1976, p. 610; "Salutatory," 1915, p. 5; Greenwood, 1983, pp. 18–20; Lewis, 1976, pp. 123–129; Traylor, 1972, passim. The author is indebted to Professor Albert C. Lewis of McMaster University, Hamilton, Canada, for his comments on this passage. Halsted's students, and their students, are discussed at greater length in Chapter 6.

122. Nixon, 1953, pp. 185, 194, 222–224, 234–235, 237.

123. Nixon, 1953, pp. 255, 259, 346; Needham, 1908, pp. 6–8; Branda, 1976, p. 728.

124. Moursand, 1956, pp. 3–5, 7, 19, 26, 37, 48, 51, 62, 66, 69, 73; Nixon, 1953, pp. 94, 130, 183; Brady, 1939, pp. 134–136.

125. Jones, 1967, pp. 108–112, 124–126, 133–134, 148–149, 169–171, 174–176, 190–191; Webb and Carroll, 1953, 2:pp. 225–226.

126. Nixon, 1953, pp. 88, 119–120.

127. Nixon, 1953, pp. 217, 267, 337, 367.

128. Campbell, 1925, passim; Branda, 1976, p. 140; MacCormack, 1985, p. 39; McGlasson, 1926, p. 6; Nixon, 1979, pp. 220–222; Nixon, 1936, pp. 156–157, 309–310.

129. Nixon, 1953, pp. 172, 216; Clay, 1904, pp. 188–189, 191; Evans, 1964, pp. 17, 20.

130. Nixon, 1953, p. 195; Evans, 1964, p. 25; Clay, 1904, p. 188.

131. Evans, 1964, pp. 28, 32–34; Webb and Carroll, 1953, 2:pp. 886–887.

132. Jeffress, 1983, pp. 31–32; Branda, 1976, pp. 377, 400; Nixon, 1953, p. 319; Evans, 1964, p. 13; Otto, 1939, pp. 85–88; Manuel, 1936, p. 36; Hincks, 1936, p. 5; Smith, 1938, p. 5.

133. Cumley, 1935, pp. 948–951.

134. Cumley, 1935, pp. 951–953; Branda, 1976, pp. 687; Oliver, 1983, pp. 13–17.

135. This paragraph and the ones which follow on the subjects of anthropology and archaeology are largely the work of Professor E. Mott Davis of the University of Texas. Any additions will be clearly noted. For further information, see Kingston, 1985, p. 51; Wendorf, 1978, p. 8; Gatschet, 1891, passim; Fewkes, 1902, pp. 57–75; Hodge, 1907 and 1910, passim; Peabody, 1909, pp. 202–216; Moore, 1912, pp. 453–644; Eyerly, 1912, pp. 1–5.

136. For further information, see Pearce, 1932, pp. 47–48, 51; Pearce, 1935, p. 5; Kingston, 1985, p. 52; Webb and Carroll, 1953, 2:p. 350.

137. In addition, the reader might wish to consult Kingston, 1985, p. 52; Davis, 1980, pp. 166–175; Engerrand, 1934, passim; Holden, et al., 1936, passim; Goldstein, 1940, pp. 312–313.

138. For more information on Ray and his organization, see Kingston, 1985, p. 51; Wendorf, 1978, p. 9; Branda, 1976, p. 971; Davis, 1980, pp. 159–176; Wetherington, 1978, p. 15; Webb, 1978, p. 28.

139. Wendorf, 1978, pp. 10–11; Kingston, 1985, p. 52; Webb, 1978, p. 30; Texas Council of Archaeologists, 1940, passim.

140. "Obituary," 1939, p. 256.

141. Kingston, 1985, pp. 52–53; Davis, 1980, pp. 174–175; Kelley, Campbell, and Lehmer, 1940, passim.

142. Most of the information contained in this and the next three paragraphs has been graciously supplied by Professor David S. Evans of the University of Texas. It has been condensed, so the errors of omission and brevity are those of the author alone.

143. In addition to the information given by Professor Evans, the reader might also want to consult Mayfield and Batchelder, 1940, pp. 9–10; Struve, 1940, pp. 11, 13, 15; Boon, no date, passim.

144. Geiser, 1936, p. 41.

145. Webb and Carroll, 1953, 2:p. 731.

Bibliography

Adkins, Mary Grace Muse. "Review of *Adventures with a Texas Naturalist,* by Roy Bedichek." *South-*

western Historical Quarterly, LI (January 1948), pp. 275–277.

Alexander, Nancy. *Father of Texas Geology, Robert T. Hill*. Dallas: Southern Methodist University Press, 1976.

Attwater, Henry P. *Boll Weevils and Birds*. Houston: Southern Pacific Passenger Department, 1903.

——. "The Disappearance of Wildlife." *Bulletin of the Scientific Society of San Antonio*, I (January 1917), pp. 47–60.

Bagley, J. B. *Cotton Mill Development in Texas*. Texas A&M College Bulletin, 3d Series, VIII (September 1922).

Battle, William J. "A Concise History of the University of Texas 1883–1950." *Southwestern Historical Quarterly*, LIV (April 1951), pp. 391–411.

Bonnifield, Paul. *The Dust Bowl: Men, Dirt, and Depression*. Albuquerque: University of New Mexico Press, 1979.

Boon, Joseph L. "The Collected Writings of John L. Boon, A Texas Scientist." Photocopy in the Barker Texas History Center, University of Texas at Austin.

Brady, R. J. "Report of the Cause of Death in John Sealy Hospital, Year 1938–1939." *Bulletin of the John Sealy Hospital*, I (December 1939), pp. 134–136.

Branda, Eldon Stephen, ed. *The Handbook of Texas, Volume III: A Supplement*. Austin: Texas State Historical Association, 1976.

Bray, William L. *Forest Resources of Texas*. United States Department of Agriculture, Bureau of Forestry Bulletin, No. 47. Washington, D.C.: Government Printing Office, 1904.

Caldwell, Edwin L. "Highlights of the Development of Manufacturing in Texas 1900–1960." *Southwestern Historical Quarterly*, LXVIII (April 1965), 405–431.

Calvert, Robert A. "Nineteenth Century Farmers, Cotton, and Prosperity." *Southwestern Historical Quarterly*, LXXIII (April 1970), 509–538.

Campbell, Charles A. R. *Bats, Mosquitoes, and Dollars*. Boston: Stratford Company, 1925.

Clark, James L., and Michel T. Halbouty. *Spindletop*. New York: Random House, 1952.

Clark, Joseph Stanley. *The Oil Century: From the Drake Well to the Conservation Era*. Norman: University of Oklahoma Press, 1958.

Clay, W. J. *Statistical Report, Department of Agriculture, Insurance, Statistics, and History, 1904*. Austin: Von Boeckmann-Jones Company, 1904.

Coghlan, B. K. *Highway Bridges and Culverts*. Texas A&M College Bulletin, 3d Series, I (May 1915).

——. *Highway Engineering at the A. and M. College of Texas*. Texas A&M College Bulletin, 3d Series, I (July 1915).

——. *The Organization of a State Highway Department*. Texas A&M College Bulletin, 3d Series, II (November 1916).

Coleman, Richard L. *The New Birmingham, Texas, Iron Properties*. Privately published, 1900.

Columbia–Southern Chemical Corporation. *20-Year Story, 1934–1954*. Corpus Christi: Columbia–Southern Chemical Corporation, 1954.

Courses in Agriculture for the Secondary Schools of Texas. The State Department of Education, The University of Texas, and The A&M College of Texas Joint Bulletin, No. 1 (1914). Austin: Von Boeckmann-Jones Company.

Crawford, Charles W. *One Hundred Years of Engineering at Texas A&M, 1876–1976*. Privately published, 1976.

Cumley, Russell W. "The Story of the Gene." *School Science and Mathematics*, XX (December 1935), pp. 946–953.

Cunningham, William C. "Sulphur Mining in Texas." *The University of Texas Engineer*, I (January 1931), pp. 26–27.

Dahl, George L. "Power Plant for an Educational Institution." *The University of Texas Engineer*, I (January 1931), p. 9.

Davis, E. Mott. "The First Quarter Century of the Texas Archaeological Society." *Bulletin of the Texas Archaeological Society*, L (1980), pp. 159–194.

Dethloff, Henry C. *A Centennial History of Texas A&M University 1876–1976*. 2 volumes. College Station: Texas A&M University Press, 1976.

Deussen, Alexander. "Thirty Five Years of Progress in the Knowledge of the Geology of Texas," in *Quarter-Centennial Memorial Volume of the Division of Natural Resources*, Bulletin of The University of Texas, No. 3501 (January 1, 1935), pp. 37–57.

Doughty, Robin W. *Wildlife and Man in Texas*. College Station: Texas A&M University Press, 1984.

Eckhardt, Carl J. *Fifty Stars in the University Firmament*. Privately published, 1978.

——. "Texas Fuels—Yesterday, Today, and Tomorrow." *The University of Texas Engineer*, I (September 1938), pp. 14, 38.

Engerrand, George C. *The So-Called Wends of Germany and Their Colonies in Texas and Australia*. Bulletin of The University of Texas at Austin, No. 3417 (1934).

Evans, James Leroy. "The Care of the Mentally Ill in Texas." Master's thesis, University of Texas at Austin, 1964.

Everhart, Edgar. "The Educational Need of the South." *Transactions of the Texas Academy of Science*, I (1892), pp. 25–31.

Eyerly, T. L. "The Buried City of the Panhandle." *Archaeological Bulletin*, III (1912), pp. 1–5.

Faculty Report of the University of Texas 1887–1888. Austin, 1888.

Farmers' State Alliance of Texas. *To the Farmers of Texas*. Pottsboro, Texas: Farmers' Alliance of Texas, 1887.

Ferguson, Walter Keene. *Geology and Politics in Frontier Texas 1845–1909*. Austin: University of Texas Press, 1969.

———. *History of the Bureau of Economic Geology 1909–1960*. Austin: Bureau of Economic Geology, 1981.

Fewkes, J. W. "Pueblo Settlements Near El Paso, Texas." *American Anthropologist*, IV (1902), pp. 57–75.

First Annual Proceedings. Bulletin of the Southwestern Geological Society, No. 1 (December 1920). Dallas: Southwestern Geological Society.

Foster, Lafayette L. *First Annual Report of the Agricultural Bureau of the Department of Agriculture, Fisheries, Statistics, and History, 1887–1888*. Austin, 1889.

Gard, Wayne. *The First 100 Years of Texas Oil & Gas*. Dallas: Mid-Continent Oil and Gas Company, 1966.

Gatschet, A. S. "The Karankawa Indians: The Coast People of Texas." *Papers of the Peabody Museum, Harvard University*, I (1891), No. 2.

Geisecke, Frederick E., H. R. Thomas, and G. A. Parkinson. *Progress Report of the Engineering Research Division of the Bureau of Economic Geology and Technology*. Bulletin of The University of Texas, No. 2215 (April 1922).

Geiser, Samuel W. "A Century of Scientific Exploration in Texas, Part I: 1820–1880." *Field and Laboratory*, IV (April 1936), pp. 41–55.

———. "A Century of Scientific Exploration in Texas, Part ib: 1820–1860." *Field and Laboratory*, VII (January 1939), pp. 28–51.

———. *Naturalists of the Frontier*. 2d ed. Dallas: Southern Methodist University Press, 1948.

———. "Texas Collection: Lum Woodruff," *Southwestern Historical Quarterly*, XLV (January 1942), p. 284.

Gilchrist, Gibb. "History of Highway Development in Texas." *The Texas Engineer*, VI (December 1936), pp. 104–107.

Giles, Barney. "Early Military Aviation Activities in Texas." *Southwestern Historical Quarterly*, LIV (October 1950), pp. 143–158.

Goldstein, Marcus S. "Cranial Deformation Among Texas Indians." *American Journal of Physical Anthropology*, XXVII (1940), pp. 312–313.

Grant, H. Roger, "'Interurbans are the Wave of the Future:' Electric Railway Promotion in Texas." *Southwestern Historical Quarterly*, LXXXIV (July 1980), pp. 29–48.

Greenwood, Robert E. "Mathematics." *Discovery*, VII (Fall 1983), pp. 18–22.

Halsted, George B. "Original Research and Creative Authorship the Essence of University Teaching." *Science*, I (February 22, 1895), pp. 203–206.

———. "The Culture Given by Science." *Science*, IV (July 3, 1896), pp. 12–13.

———. *Mathematical Works by George Bruce Halsted*. Austin: Privately published, 1897.

Hart, James P. "Oil, the Courts, and the Railroad Commission," *Southwestern Historical Quarterly*, XLIV (January 1941), pp. 303–320.

Havins, T. R. "The Passing of the Longhorns." *Southwestern Historical Quarterly*, LVI (July 1952), pp. 51–58.

———. "Texas Fever." *Southwestern Historical Quarterly*, LII (July 1948), pp. 147–162.

Heiman, Monica. *A Pioneer Geologist: Johan August Udden, A Biography*. Kerrville, Texas: Privately published, 1963.

Hincks, Clarence M. "Organized Mental Hygiene Work." *Mental Hygiene and the Texas Society for Mental Hygiene, 1935, A Yearbook*. Bulletin of The University of Texas, No. 3617 (May 1, 1936), pp. 5–7.

Hodge, F. W., ed. "Handbook of North American Indians." 2 vols. *Bulletin of the Bureau of American Anthropology*, No. 30 (1907, 1910).

Holden, W. C., et al. *Studies of the Yaqui Indians of Sonora, Mexico*. Lubbock: Texas Technological College, 1936.

Horton, Claude W. "Physics." *Discovery*, VII (Fall 1983), pp. 23–25.

———. "Mechanical Multiharmonograph." *Discovery*, VII (Fall 1983), pp. 26–27.

Hunt, Robert Lee. *A History of Farmer Movements in the Southwest 1873–1925*. College Station: Texas A&M University Press, 1953.

Hyman, Carolyn F. "A History of the Texas National Forests." Master's thesis, University of Texas at Austin, 1948.

Inauguration of the State Agricultural and Mechanical College of Texas, Bryan, October 4th, 1876. Bryan: Appeal and Post Book and Job Print Establishment, 1876. [Reprinted by A&M College Press, 1951.]

Jackson, A. D. "Subject List of Texas Agricultural Experiment Station Publications as of September 1, 1933—For Use by Libraries and Station Workers." Typescript in the Barker Texas History Center, University of Texas at Austin.

Jeffress, Lloyd. "Psychology." *Discovery*, VII (Fall 1983), pp. 31–34.

"John William Mallet, A.B., Ph.D., M.D., LL.D., F.R.S, F.R.C." *Alcalde*, I (April–August 1913), p. 17.

Jonah, Colonel F. G. "The Development of Railways in Texas." *The Texas Engineer*, VI (December 1936), p. 57.

Jones, Billy M. *Health Seekers in the Southwest, 1817–1900.* Norman: University of Oklahoma Press, 1967.

Kelley, J. Charles, Thomas N. Campbell, and Donald J. Lehmer, "The Association of Archaeological Materials with Geological Deposits in the Big Bend Region of Texas." *West Texas Historical and Scientific Society Publications*, X (1940), pp. 9–173.

Kingston, Mike. "Archaeology: A Slow Start in Texas," in *Texas Almanac and Industrial Guide, 1984–1985*, Mike Kingston, ed. Dallas: A. H. Belo Corporation, 1985.

LaCoste, Lucien J. B. "Gravity Meter." *Discovery*, VII (Fall 1983), pp. 28–30.

LeGear, Louis D., and Newton G. LeGear. *Dr. Le-Gear's Stock Book.* Austin: Privately published, 1897.

Lewis, Albert C. "George Bruce Halsted and the Development of American Mathematics," in *Men and Institutions in American Mathematics*, Graduate Studies, Texas Technological University, No. 13 (1976), pp. 123–129.

Lockwood, Robert M. "The Last Hundred Years." *Texas Business Review*, L (January 1976), pp. 4–5.

Long, Walter E. *Flood to Faucet.* Austin: Steck Company, 1956.

———. *Wings Over Austin.* Austin: Privately published, 1962.

Lowrey, David J. *Private Prescriptions and Lectures.* Weatherford, Texas: Democrat Publishing Company, 1902.

MacCormack, John. "Flying Tribute to First Bat Man." *Dallas Times Herald*, October 27, 1985.

Mackensen, Bernard. "Report on the Excavation of Mastodon Remains Undertaken by a Committee of the Scientific Society of San Antonio." *Bulletin of the Scientific Society of San Antonio*, I (January 1905), pp. 3–10.

Manuel, H. T. "The Texas Society for Mental Hygiene: A Statement." *Mental Hygiene and the Texas Society for Mental Hygiene, 1935, A Yearbook.* Bulletin of The University of Texas, No. 3617 (May 1, 1936), pp. 35–36.

Maxwell, Robert S. "One Man's Legacy: W. Goodrich Jones and Texas Conservation." *Southwestern Historical Quarterly*, LXXVII (January 1974), pp. 355–380.

Maxwell, Robert S., and Robert D. Baker. *Sawdust Empires. The Texas Lumber Industry 1830–1940.* College Station: Texas A&M University Press, 1983.

Mayfield, Mamie Birge, and Paul M. Batchelder. "William Johnson MacDonald." *Contributions from the MacDonald Observatory*, I (1940), pp. 1–10.

McClure, H. H. "The Chemical Industry in Texas." *Proceedings of the Symposium on the Development and the Future of the Chemical Industry in Texas, Held at the University of Texas, May 6–7, 1983.* Austin, 1983.

McGlasson, I. L. "The Romance of Medicine." *Texas State Journal of Medicine*, XXI (June 1926), pp. 6–15.

McNew, J. T. L. *Proceedings of the Fourth Annual Short Course in Highway Engineering.* Texas A&M College Bulletin, 3d Series, XIV (July 1928).

Menger, Rudolph. "Original Observations, with Photographic Illustrations, on Reptiles and Insects of Texas." *Bulletin of the Scientific Society of San Antonio*, I (January 1905), pp. 11–31.

———. *Texas Nature Observations and Reminiscences.* San Antonio: Guessaz and Ferlet Company, 1913.

Montgomery, Julian. "The Development of Municipal Engineering in Texas." *The Texas Engineer*, VI (December 1936), pp. 82–93.

Montgomery, Thomas H., Jr., "The Aesthetic Element in Scientific Thought," *Scientific Quarterly*, VIII (1905), pp. 5–10.

Moore, Clarence B. "Some Aboriginal Sites on Red River." *Journal of the Academy of Natural Sciences of Philadelphia*, XIV (1912), pp. 453–644.

Morrison, R. L. *Earth Roads.* Texas A&M College Bulletin, 3d Series, I (February 1915).

Moursand, Walter H. *A History of Baylor University College of Medicine 1900–1953.* Houston: Gulf Publishing Company, 1956.

Myres, Samuel D. *The Permian Basin, Petroleum Empire of the Southwest: Era of Discovery, From the Beginning to the Depression.* El Paso: Permian Press, 1973.

——. *The Permian Basin, Petroleum Empire of the Southwest: Era of Advancement, From the Depression to the Present.* El Paso: Permian Press, 1977.

Needham, R. H. "Advance in Pharmacy." *The Microbe,* I (November 1908), pp. 6–8.

Nixon, Pat Ireland. *A Century of Medicine in San Antonio: The Story of Medicine in Bexar County, Texas.* San Antonio: Privately published, 1936.

——. *A History of the Texas Medical Association 1853–1953.* Austin: University of Texas Press, 1953.

——. *Pat Nixon of Texas: Autobiography of a Doctor by Pat Ireland Nixon,* Herbert H. Lang., ed. College Station: Texas A&M University Press, 1979.

Oberholser, Harry C. *The Bird Life of Texas.* 2 vols. Austin: University of Texas Press, 1974.

"Obituary of Dr. J. E. Pearce," *Bulletin of the Texas Archaeological and Paleontological Society,* XI (September 1939), p. 256.

Oliver, C. P. "Zoology." *Discovery,* VII (Fall 1983), pp. 13–17.

Otto, John L. "The Treatment of Non-Schizophrenic Reaction States with Metrazol." *Bulletin of the John Sealy Hospital,* I (January 1939), pp. 85–88.

Ousley, Clarence. *History of the Agricultural and Mechanical College of Texas.* Texas A&M College Bulletin, 4th Series, VI (December 1935).

Papers Presented at the First Annual Air Conditioning Short Course, August 17, 18, and 19, 1939. Texas A&M College Bulletin, 4th Series, X (December 1939).

Peabody, Charles. "A Reconnaisance Trip in Western Texas." *American Anthropologist,* XI (1909), pp. 202–216.

Pearce, James E. "The Present Status of Texas Archaeology." *Bulletin of the Texas Archaeological and Paleontological Society,* IV (September 1932), pp. 47–51.

——. *Tales That Dead Men Tell.* Bulletin of The University of Texas, No. 3567 (October 1, 1935).

Phillips, William B. *Texas Petroleum.* Bulletin of The University of Texas, No. 5 (July 1901).

Potts, Robert J. *The Benefit of Good Roads.* Texas A&M College Bulletin, 3d Series, III (July 1917).

Presley, James. *Never in Doubt: A History of Delta Drilling Company.* Houston: Gulf Publishing Company, 1981.

Proceedings of the 11th Regular Annual Meeting of the Farmers' Alliance, August 19, 1890. Dallas: Robert T. Bibb, 1891.

Ross, Lawrence S. "An Address to the Texas Academy of Science, December 22, 1897." *Transactions of the Texas Academy of Science,* II (1898), pp. 19–22.

Rundell, Walter, Jr. *Early Texas Oil: A Photographic History 1886–1936.* College Station: Texas A&M University Press, 1977.

"Salutatory." Bulletin of The University of Texas, No. 44 (August 5, 1915), p. 5.

Schmidt, H. C. *Treatise on Forestry in Texas.* Austin: Privately published, 1882.

Schmidt, Hubert. *Eighty Years of Veterinary Medicine at the Agricultural and Mechanical College of Texas.* College Station: Texas A&M University Press, 1958.

Schreiner, Charles, III. "The Background and Development of Brahman Cattle in Texas." *Southwestern Historical Quarterly,* LII (April 1949), pp. 427–443.

Silvey, Oscar William. "A History of the Physics Department, Texas A. and M. College, 1876–1952," in *Fragments of Early History of Texas A. and M. College,* David Brooks Cofer, ed. College Station: Texas A&M University Press, 1953.

Smith, W. Arthur. "Mental Hygiene in the State Board of Health." *Mental Hygiene in Action: Second Yearbook of the Texas Society of Mental Hygiene.* Bulletin of The University of Texas, No. 3832 (August 22, 1938), p. 5.

Spratt, John S. *The Road to Spindletop: Economic Change in Texas 1875–1901.* Austin: University of Texas Press, 1970.

Steel, E. W., and P. J. A. Zeller. *The Dunbar Sewage Filter.* Texas A&M College Bulletin, 3d Series, XIV (September 1928).

——. *The Treatment of Dairy Wastes.* Texas A&M College Bulletin, 4th Series, I (May 1930).

Stevenson, B. D. "Aerial Photography is Aid to Oil Men." *Petroleum Reporter,* II (July 1930), pp. 4–5.

Stiles, Charles W. *Verminous Diseases of Cattle, Sheep, and Goats in Texas.* Washington, D.C.: Government Printing Office, 1902.

Strecker, John K. "Additions to a List of the Diurnal Lepidoptera of the Vicinity of Waco, Texas." *Con-*

tributions from Baylor University Museum, No. 1 (December 15, 1925).

Struve, O. "The Organization of the Observatory." *Contributions from the MacDonald Observatory*, I (1940), pp. 11–15.

Taylor, Thomas Ulvan. *Fifty Years on Forty Acres.* Kingsport, Tennessee: Kingsport Press, 1938.

———. "The Engineering Department." *The University Record*, IV (July 1902), pp. 378–380.

Texas A&M University. Agricultural Experiment Station. *First Annual Report of the Texas Agricultural Experiment Station, For the Year 1888.* Houston: J. J. Pastoriza, 1889.

———. *Agricultural Research: Its Story.* College Station, 196–.

Texas A&M University. Texas Forest Service. *Texas Forestry.* Texas Forest Service Circular, No. 8 (Revised 1939).

———. *Texas Forestry and Forest Products, Centennial Edition.* Texas Forest Service Circular, No. 8 (1936).

Texas Association of Future Farmers of America. *Constitution and By-laws of the Texas Association of Future Farmers of America 1936–1937.* Austin: Privately published, 1937.

Texas Council of Archaeologists, *Texas Archaeological News*, No. 1 (March 1940).

———. *Texas Archaeological News*, No. 2 (December 1940).

Texas Farmers' Congress. *Annual Address of President Cornell of the Texas Farmers' Congress, at College Station, Texas, July 7, 1903.* Privately published, 1903.

Texas Industrial Congress. *$10,000 in Gold to be Given Free to the Farmers of Texas for the Best Yields of Corn and Cotton.* Dallas: Texas Industrial Congress, 1911.

———. *Modern Agricultural Methods: The Henry Exall Farm Book.* Dallas: Exline-Reimers Company, 1914.

Texas Livestock Sanitary Commission. *Rules and Regulations and Sanitary Laws.* Austin, 1946.

———. *Test for Efficiency of Various Remedies for Stomach Worms, Conducted at San Angelo, Texas, June 27, 1927, to August 3, 1927.* Austin, 1927.

Texas Railroad Commission. *Rules and Regulations Promulgated by the Railroad Commission of Texas.* Dallas: Mid-Continent Oil and Gas Association, 1919.

Texas Swine Breeders' Association. *Science in Breeding Hogs: Speech to the Texas Swine Breeders'*

Association by H. E. Singleton at College Station, July 7–10, 1903. Privately published, 1903.

Thomas, Julian. "Public Utilities in Texas During the Last Century." *The University of Texas Engineer*, VI (December 1936), pp. 98–101.

Thompson, Craig. *Since Spindletop: A Human Story of Gulf's First Half Century.* Pittsburg: Privately published, 1951.

Thompson, Ernest O. "The Function of Geological and Engineering Science in the Conservation Movement: A Statistical Supplement." Typescript in the Barker Texas History Center, University of Texas at Austin.

Thompson, W. A., Jr. "The Texas Company Marine." *Texaco Star*, I (January 1914), pp. 7–14.

Thornton, M. K. *The Comparative Value of Fuels.* Texas A&M College Bulletin, 3d Series, I (April 1915).

Tillotson, Stephen L. *Remnant of an Era: The History of the Little Campus Site 1859–1977.* Austin: 1978.

Tindall, George B. *The Emergence of the New South 1913–1945.* Baton Rouge: Louisiana State University Press, 1967.

Traylor, D. Reginald. *Creative Teaching: Heritage of R. L. Moore.* Houston: University of Houston Press, 1972.

Udden, S. M. "Electrical Development in Texas During the Past Twenty-Five Years," in *Quarter-Centennial Memorial Volume of the Division of Natural Resources*, Bulletin of The University of Texas, No. 3501 (January 1, 1935), pp. 87–95.

Underwood, James R., Jr. "Edwin Theodore Dumble." *Southwestern Historical Quarterly*, LXVIII (July 1964), pp. 53–78.

The University of Texas at Austin. Bureau of Engineering. "Publications, May 1953." Typescript in the Barker Texas History Center, University of Texas at Austin.

The University of Texas at Austin. Mineral Survey. *Coal, Lignite, and Asphalt Rocks.* Bulletin of The University of Texas, No. 15 (May 1902).

Warner, C. A. *Texas Oil and Gas Since 1543.* Houston: Gulf Publishing Company, 1939.

———. "Texas and the Oil Industry," *Southwestern Historical Qaurterly*, L (July 1946), pp. 1–24.

Webb, Clarence. "Changing Archaeological Methods and Theory in the Transmississippi South," in *Texas Archaeology: Essays Honoring R. King Harris*, Kurt D. House, ed. Dallas: Southern Methodist University Press, 1978.

Webb, Walter Prescott, and H. Bailey Carroll, eds. *The*

Handbook of Texas. 2 Volumes. Austin: Texas State Historical Association, 1953.

Webster, Fred S. "The Bird Life of Texas: A Review." *Southwestern Historical Quarterly,* LXXIX (July 1975), pp. 31–54.

Welborn, W. C. *Elements of Agriculture, Southern and Western.* New York: MacMillan Company, 1908.

Wendorf, Fred. "The Changing Roles of Amateurs and Professionals in Texas Archaeology," in *Texas Archaeology: Essays Honoring R. King Harris,* Kurt D. House, ed. Dallas: Southern Methodist University Press, 1978.

West Texas Oil Scouts Association. *General Report and Summary Review of Operations, West Texas–New Mexico District tô November 1, 1929.* San Angelo: Angelo Printing Company, 1929.

Wetherington, Ronald. "Anthropological Perspectives in Texas Archaeology," in *Texas Archaeology: Essays Honoring R. King Harris,* Kurt D. House, ed. Dallas: Southern Methodist University Press, 1978.

White, Ross. "The Marshall Ford Dam." *Journal of Architecture, Engineering, and Industry,* I (September 1938), p. 3.

"William Battle Phillips," in *Quarter-Centennial Memorial Volume of the Division of Natural Resources,* Bulletin of The University of Texas, No. 3501 (January 1, 1935), p. 10.

Wilson, Joseph M. *A History of the Dallas Geological Society.* Dallas: Dallas Geological Society, 1974.

Woods, L. A. *Teaching Science in Junior and Senior Schools of Texas.* Texas State Department of Education Bulletin, No. 14 (March 1938).

Woodward, C. Vann. *Origins of the New South, 1877–1913.* Baton Rouge: Louisiana State University Press, 1951.

Woolfolk, George Ruble. *Prairie View: A Study in Public Conscience 1878–1946.* New York: Pageant Press, 1962.

Woolrich, Willis R. *Men of Ingenuity From Beneath the Orange Tower, 1884–1964: The College of Engineering of The University of Texas.* Austin: Engineering Foundation of the College of Engineering, 1964.

Yarbrough, Joseph U. "The Status of Agricultural Education in Texas." Typescript in the Barker Texas History Center, University of Texas at Austin.

Two

Science and Technology in Texas from World War II to the Present

Earth and Space Sciences

1

Geology

Margaret S. Bishop

THE RECORD OF breakthroughs in geology in Texas is different from that of most sciences. Progress in understanding the earth is not the story of a few brilliant scientists, but instead is the record of governmental bodies, scientific organizations, corporations, and people, all with the goal of acquiring and interpreting a body of data in an efficient manner.

Within the confines of this paper, it is impossible to cover all the avenues of research that have been pursued or all the successes achieved in understanding Texas geology. Where Texas geology is considered unique, that will be emphasized, but it should be remembered that geological conditions do not stop at state boundaries, and many of the geologists involved worked across state borderlines. Louisiana has its salt domes; Oklahoma its buried hills. New Mexico is a part of the Permian Basin, as are Oklahoma and Kansas. Emphasis on Texas solutions and research does not imply unawareness of bordering states' contributions to Texas solutions. Another author possibly would have chosen different topics to detail but he or she still would have had to make a selection. For those who wish to pursue Texas geology in greater detail, books by Ferguson[1] and Owen[2] are highly recommended.

In the early nineteenth century geology gradually emerged from its European natural history origin and became a true science. In America geologists of this early period seldom had academic training in geology but instead were chemists or physicians who became interested in rocks and minerals through their interest in nature. Often physicians became paleontologists and chemists became mineralogists through their pursuit of field work. A few then went to Scottish, English, or German academies to further their knowledge of geology. However, by 1835 geology was being taught in universities along the Atlantic coast, and states there were beginning to use geologists to determine the extent of their resources. During field survey work the geologists learned to produce scientific descriptions of rocks, minerals, and fossils. Thus, they laid the foundations for future exploitation of resources and also built up a body of scientific data from which to interpret geologic processes.

The land now called Texas once was claimed to be a border province of Spain and Mexico, but in 1836 this frontier country became an independent entity. In 1845 it joined the United States. The size of the area, diversity of its geological features and climate, and its unsettled nature made the unraveling of Texas geology a difficult challenge. To meet the challenge, however, geologists came from abroad, from the Atlantic coast, and from the heartland of America. Some were sent by foreign organizations looking for land and mineral resources, many were sent by the U.S. government to survey the new territory; others were individuals seeking their fortunes, probably lured by tales of Spanish gold.

Contributions to the geology of Texas include data and interpretations from federal, state, academic, and oil industry sources. All have provided information on the structure, stratigraphy, paleontology, and geologic history of the land, as well as the extent and distribution of resources.

Even before Texas joined the Union the federal government began reconnaissance along its borders. In 1820 President Monroe sent an expedition to the frontier area along the Louisiana Territory boundary (interpreted as anything west of the Mississippi River). The geologist Edwin James, who accompanied the expedition, sketched the rock types encountered on the trip down the Canadian River through the Panhandle of Texas. He quickly recognized that these western rocks did not fit the classical Wernerian system of stratigraphy and that a new rock classification was needed.[3]

After Texas became a state, federal expeditions were sent west to establish supply and communication routes for the military and to find the best route for a proposed railroad between the east and west coasts. These expeditions frequently were accompanied by participants who could sketch the territory covered by the survey and describe the rocks and minerals encountered. The Red River expedition of the federal government in 1852 included George Shumard as both physician and geologist.[4] Shumard collected fossils, later studied by Edward D. Cope, vertebrate paleontologist of Philadelphia,[5] and provided the first information about the geology of the Osage Plain of West Texas from Fort Belknap on the Brazos River to the Llano Estacado on the high plains of the Panhandle.[6] (Seé fig. 1.) On another expedition Shumard described rock samples gathered during the drilling of two wells, attempted to assure an adequate water supply for a possible railroad route through Texas.[7] The support of Congress for the reconnaissance surveys of the western United States territories was important, not only for the mapping and information on soil, water, and mineral resources, but for the training provided to a growing number of young men who became the geologists of the following decade. A further contribution of the federal government to the opening of the country was the establishment of the Coast and Geodetic Survey. This government bureau developed the pri-

mary base line net along the coast of the United States; from these points of departure, local surveys could be tied into established elevations and geographic positions. Thus, accurate topographic and geologic base maps were a possibility even in frontier Texas.

The first trained geologist to publish a report on Texas geology came from Germany. Ferdinand von Roemer from the Berlin Academy was sent to Texas by the *Adelsverein*, a group of German nobles interested in obtaining and settling a land grant lying between the Llano and Colorado Rivers. Roemer's survey began along the Balcones scarp, but in 1846 he also explored the Central Llano Uplift where he hoped to find the rumored Spanish mines. No minerals of economic importance were found, but of scientific interest were the Carboniferous rocks bordering the granite of Central Texas. Roemer also reported finding numerous trilobite fossils in beds of limestone (Ordovician age) surrounding the granites of the San Saba River. (Table 1 places geologic periods in perspective.)

Roemer recognized faulting along the Balcones scarp in the New Braunfels area, but he attributed the

Table 1

Geologic Time Scale

Eras	Period[a] (System)[b]	Years Before the Present
Cenozoic	Quaternary	
	Tertiary	65,000,000
Mesozoic	Cretaceous	
	Jurassic	
	Triassic	275,000,000
Paleozoic	Permian	
	Carboniferous	
	Pennsylvanian	
	Mississippian	
	Devonian	
	Silurian	
	Ordovician	
	Cambrian	575,000,000
Precambrian		4,600,000,000

[a]Period refers to a time unit.
[b]System refers to rock units belonging to a time unit.

whole exposed section on the Edwards Plateau to Upper Cretaceous. This interpretation proved to be incorrect. Roemer's two articles for the *American Journal of Science* were the first scientific reports on Texas geology.[8]

With the coming of statehood in 1845, both state and federal legislators began to consider the advantages of encouraging immigration. To this end they needed to know more about the resources of the state, and in 1858 they appointed a state geologist to survey the public lands and to determine its assets in minerals, soil, and water. Legislators would have preferred to appoint a native Texan but none was as well trained as B. F. Shumard (born in St. Louis, Missouri, April 4, 1869), who received the appointment.

Shumard's formal education, like that of his brother George, was pursued first at Miami University of Ohio, then in medicine at the Jefferson Medical Institute of Louisville, Kentucky. Shumard practiced medicine for about a year before he joined the David Dale Owen survey of the Northwest territories. Shumard learned his geology from Owen in the field and later assisted J. Evans in the Oregon territory survey. In 1853 Shumard became Missouri state geologist, and then in 1858 he agreed to come to Texas where he quickly began field work. He made a reconnaissance survey of Central Texas and examined the iron ores of East Texas as well as the coal beds on the Brazos River. His brother, of the Red River expedition, and W. P. Riddel helped set up plans for the detailed surveys to follow. Politics interfered with these plans, so Shumard returned to Missouri where he practiced medicine and became a private consultant on geological problems. Eventually, his notes were turned over to a later survey and printed in 1886.

The state survey, turned over to men without geological background, went out of existence as the Civil War began in 1861. A second survey was set up under William Buckley, but he failed to produce any results; this survey also lapsed in 1875. In 1888 a third survey was organized under E. T. Dumble, who became a major figure in Texas geology and left a legacy of excellent scientific work.

Robert T. Hill was an assistant under Dumble during which time he produced a major work on the Cretaceous stratigraphy; another assistant, W. F. Cummins, worked on the Permian stratigraphy of northwest Texas, and N. F. Drake worked on both Triassic and Permian stratigraphy. The Dumble survey lasted until 1894 when funds were depleted. Even after the survey officially ceased to exist, Dumble continued to make water supply reports for individuals and to an-

swer the correspondence of the survey. In the meantime Dumble was hired by the Santa Fe railroad to head their research efforts, and he became one of the leading figures in the developing science of petroleum geology.

In 1901 William B. Phillips began another survey effort. This time, the Mineral Survey, as it was named, was authorized by the state to evaluate only university-owned lands. Eventually, its duties were enlarged to include all public lands and finally all Texas mineral lands. Because Phillips also had teaching duties at the University of Texas at Austin, the survey was active only during vacations. He and his assistants began a detailed survey of university lands in the Trans-Pecos region and also arranged for the United States Geological Survey (USGS) to make a topographic map of the same area.

During this time the USGS was engaged in a broad reconnaissance of the entire Trans-Pecos area (fig. 1). The results were published by Robert Hill, by this time working for the federal survey.[9] The Phillips Mineral Survey was terminated when the legislature provided for a new method of protecting public mineral lands, but in 1909 a new bureau was established as a research entity within the university, with Phillips as its director. This Bureau of Economic Geology is the equivalent of a state geological survey with its director a member of the Association of State Geologists. Funding from the legislature comes through UT-Austin. The following scientists have served as directors for

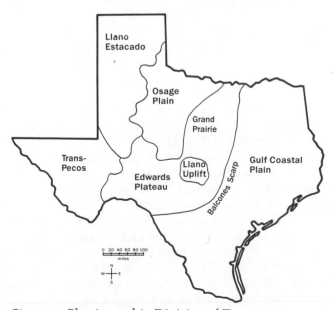

Figure 1. Physiographic Division of Texas

the Bureau since its beginning: William Battle Phillips, 1909–15; Johan August Udden, 1915–32; Elias Howard Sellards, 1932–45; John Tipton Lonsdale, 1945–60; Peter T. Flawn, 1960–70; and William L. Fisher, its current director.

Members of the Dumble Survey made the earliest major contributions to Texas geological concepts. Robert Hill working for the state and Wayland Vaughan of the USGS studied the Cretaceous stratigraphy of the Edwards Plateau and the underground water system.[10] Hill later made a detailed study of the Cretaceous System of the Black and Grand Prairies.[11] In this work Hill correctly interpreted Cretaceous events and relationships over a large geographic area.

The Cretaceous sea advanced across Texas from the south and southeast depositing extensive beds of limestone across an eroded surface that ranged in age from Precambrian to Jurassic. Texas has an almost complete Cretaceous sequence and provides an excellent section with a break between the Lower and Upper Cretaceous.

As a result of uplift and tilting that accompanied the movement along the Rocky Mountain front, the Cretaceous rocks are buried by Cenozoic deposits on the Coastal Plain, but they outcrop over a wide area of Central Texas, where they are on the uplifted block west and northwest of the Balcones fault (fig. 1). Cretaceous rocks also occur in scattered outcrops in the Trans-Pecos region, across the southern half of the Llano Estacado, and around some interior salt domes of East Texas.

The uplift and tilting toward the Gulf of Mexico occurred in Late Paleozoic and again during Miocene time. Hill's study of the Cretaceous led to the correct interpretation of age relationships along the Balcones fault and refuted the earlier interpretation by Shumard and Roemer. Hill found Upper Cretaceous outcrops on the downthrown side and Lower Cretaceous beds on the upthrown block of the Edwards Plateau. Jules Marcu, a French geologist working for the Pacific Railroad survey in 1853, had recognized the correct Cretaceous relationship also, but his work was ignored by earlier workers.

The Texas Cretaceous rocks are noted for their abundant fossils, which include rudistids, corals, sponges, ammonites, oysters, and dinosaur bones. The Late Cretaceous sea was the last extensive oceanic invasion of the North American continent, reaching as it did into the Rocky Mountain states on the west and across to Florida on the east and south. The sea withdrew by stages, and by the end of the Mesozoic era, the continent emerged. In the coastal region several embayments were formed during the Cretaceous Period, recognized by thickening of beds in the basins and thinning over the positive areas. In East Texas erosion occurred along the Sabine uplift where Cretaceous beds were removed from the top of the structure but remained undisturbed on the flanks.

During the Rocky Mountain uplift drainage was reversed, and since then rivers have carried surface waters eastward toward the Gulf of Mexico, instead of westward. The crustal uplift was accompanied by intrusions and extrusions of molten rock along the inner coastal belt adjacent to the Balcones fault, where movement continued into Cenozoic time. The publications on Cretaceous structure and stratigraphy represent the first major scientific contribution of the Bureau of Economic Geology.

Along another front, Texas paleontology had an early breakthrough when B. F. Shumard, in 1858, learned that Permian fossils had been identified in Kansas. Shumard quickly examined fossils that had been gathered from the Osage Plain and Guadalupe Mountains in former reconnaissance surveys. He found that some of the fossils were identical with the Kansas species; others correlated with Russian and English Permian forms. For the first time Texas geologists became aware that the marine limestones overlying Carboniferous beds belonged to the Permian system.

The Permian system was first recognized and named in 1841 for its great extent in the Perm province of Russia where an unconformity separates the Permian from underlying Carboniferous beds. In some areas of Texas, however, transition between the two systems is very gradual, with many fossils common to both. A detailed study of Permian structure and stratigraphy was not possible for another decade because correlations between outcrops could not be made without information from rocks buried in the intervening basins. Meanwhile, however, the Permian Red Beds became famous for the variety and abundance of their vertebrate fossils. These fossils included fishes, amphibians, and reptiles many of which were new forms not found elsewhere. The late nineteenth century was a time when fossil collecting was an exciting hobby for many and of tremendous interest for museums across the country.

John Boll, a paleontologist trained in Switzerland, came to Texas in 1869 to collect fossils for the Harvard Museum of Comparative Zoology. After several years of field work Boll discovered the first Permian vertebrate fauna found in North America. In 1877 Edward D. Cope of Philadelphia, an authority on the backboned animals, also came to Texas to collect. Cope was associated with the Academy of Natural Sciences of Philadelphia but on this trip was collecting for the USGS. Cope persuaded Boll to collect for him, and based on their collections Cope gave the first professional description of the Permian vertebrate fauna of Texas.[12] Following Cope's paper, Boll also published on his discoveries of petrified fossils, which included ferns, vegetables, fishes, and reptiles from along the Wichita River.[13]

Next to join the rush to collect vertebrate fossils was Ermine C. Case, in 1896. He collected principally for the American Museum of Natural History in New York City, but some of his collections are now in the University of Michigan museum. The American Museum of Natural History also supported James W. Gidley in the field for three summers. Based on their field work Case concluded that the Permian Red Beds had been deposited during a period of emergence that probably began in Late Carboniferous and continued into Triassic time. By this time a wealth of Permian fossils had been described but a detailed study of the stratigraphy was just beginning. Meanwhile, interest switched to the coastal region as oil discoveries came into the limelight.

The various state and federal surveys of the late 1800s were mostly involved with the reconnaissance of West Texas where they expected to find minerals of economic importance. Three reports of the Texas Geological Survey under Dumble, however, and a number of other USGS bulletins and papers were concerned with discussing the Interior Domes of East Texas.[14] Topographically the Interior Domes were visible, and they were of definite interest economically as a source for salt. Eventually some of the domes were mined, but the domes of the lower coast that produced oil were the ones of greatest importance.

Texas' first oil field, discovered in 1886, was located near Nacogdoches. The well was drilled near a gas seepage, and production came from a depth of seventy feet. The field never became very important, but it did encourage drilling in the nearby Corsicana area, where production was so good that a refinery was needed by 1898.

Encouraged by the presence of oil near the coast, Anthony Lucas began his investigation of the Spindletop mound about four miles south of Beaumont, Texas. Lucas, a graduate in mining engineering from Austria, had supervised an exploratory drilling program in Louisiana. He was familiar with the characteristics of salt domes and believed that they might produce oil because of their anticlinal structure.

Phillips, professor and later director of the University of Texas Mineral Survey, agreed with Lucas and suggested possible investors in the project.

Lucas drilled a well that gushed oil on January 10, 1901, and changed the future of Texas geology and economics. The Lucas well produced an estimated 75,000 barrels from the cap rock the first day. Because owners were unprepared for anything like the production they found, the oil blew out and covered a large area around the bore hole making an exact gage of the amount of oil impossible. The well caught fire a few days later and had to be abandoned, but other gushers soon followed, and for years Spindletop has continued to produce oil.

The dramatic discovery at Spindletop led to the rapid development of all known or suspected domes in the coastal plains of Texas and Louisiana. Mostly, the search for oil was conducted by wildcatters with no geological background, but they learned to look for gas seepages, sulfur water, saline springs, and any evidence of a topographically higher dome-shaped area. Few domes are more than ten to twenty feet above their surroundings, and some have no surface expression, so many were overlooked during the first wave of drilling. Eventually, geophysical surveys brought about a second wave of discovery in the mid-1920s.

The discovery of oil at Spindletop had many unforeseen consequences for geology and the Texas economy. Production of petroleum became a dominant factor in the growth of the state economy. The search for new fields expanded to include anticlines, faults, stratigraphic traps, reefs, igneous intrusions, and various combinations of these features. The dependence on field work gradually gave way to dependence on the interpretation of data derived from well cuttings, electric logs, paleontology, airborne and satellite (Landsat) photos, as well as the important geophysical surveys. Corporations now support research staffs to study the state's structures and stratigraphy, formerly just a function of the state survey. On the other hand, corporations have funded many research projects carried out by the Bureau of Economic Geology, and they have contributed data to supplement that of the bureau geologists. Ultimately, the working relationship between industry and the Bureau has furthered geologic knowledge and the interests of both.

Another important step toward a mature science was the formation of societies like the American Association of Petroleum Geologists (AAPG). A characteristic of all geologists is a desire to discuss their questions and problems with other professionals. Modern geologists have a number of such opportunities because in 1916 a group of like-minded geologists from the southwestern states got together to form some kind of organization for the promotion of geology. The first meeting of the group was held in Norman, Oklahoma, in 1916. A committee was appointed to make plans for a meeting in Tulsa in the following year. At the 1917 convention a constitution was adopted, and plans were worked out for the publication of papers presented at this and subsequent meetings. The purpose of the society was the promotion of the science of geology among men engaged in finding oil and natural gas.

Charles Gould, then state geologist for Oklahoma but also a worker in the Texas Panhandle, bemoaned the number of scientists who had labored in the southwest without ever publishing their findings. He looked upon the new society as a place for petroleum geologists to communicate their views. So many papers were submitted that in time groups of specialized interests formed affiliate societies such as the Society of Economic Paleontologists and Mineralogists and the Society of Exploration Geophysicists. Each society increases the opportunities for geologists to publish, and publish they do. Numerous local societies also have been formed under the wings of the AAPG; today no one complains of a lack of publishing opportunity.

Not only was publishing encouraged by the society, but many problems were discussed to advantage at the yearly conventions. As problems were brought forward within the industry, solutions often were found by cooperative action. For example, as geologists worked with well cuttings instead of outcrops, they had to learn new techniques in order to interpret the stratigraphy. Earliest drilling was with cable tools that emptied the bailer at intervals, and the samples represented a mixture of whatever was encountered within that interval. As long as the intervals were limited, usually to five feet, the problem of delineating the character of the rock being drilled was not insurmountable. Then came rotary drilling, which meant that mud was introduced into the bore hole, and the rock being drilled came up to the surface in a continuous stream of well cuttings (ground up rock) mixed with mud from outside the hole. The geologist found it difficult to recognize the true character of various layers from this mixture and to recognize the boundaries between different beds.

Faced with the need for more sophisticated subsurface studies if they were to solve the coastal stratigraphy, many speakers at the 1919 meeting of the AAPG suggested the possibilities of using micropaleontology in sample examination. When brought to the attention of management, several Houston-based oil companies were persuaded to establish micropaleontology laboratories in the following year. The Rio Bravo Company, with Esther Richards (later Mrs. Paul Applin), Humble Oil Company (now Exxon), with Alva C. Ellisor, and the Texas Company, with Hedwig Kniker, were among the first to make micropaleontology a successful tool. Many other companies followed this lead to micropaleontology, but perhaps Dumble with Rio Bravo was the most effective. Dumble examined well cuttings for all independents who brought him their samples. Consequently his expertise was extended over most of the drilling area. In the meantime, both the method of catching well cuttings, and the coring tools had been improved, so that samples reached the laboratory in somewhat more usable condition.

In 1925 Applin, Ellisor, and Kniker collaborated in publishing a summary of the subsurface stratigraphy of the Coastal Plain based on their work in micropaleontology.[15] In this summary they were able to define zones by their diagnostic foraminifera. They identified three zones within the Jackson, Eocene; three in the Oligocene; and larger divisions within the Lower, Middle, and Upper Miocene. Diagnostic fauna, their range, and geographic occurrences were listed and made available to the petroleum industry.

The center of activity concerned with foraminifera identification was in Houston, although paleontological studies were widespread throughout the oil industry by 1925. The Bureau supported studies by Helen Plummer, Dorothy Carsey, and Julia Gardner from time to time. In fact, Gardner's stratigraphic and paleontologic studies represented the most effective cooperation of the federal and state bureaus. This work involved a careful examination of the Midway group in which Gardner also was aided by maps and fossils provided by the oil industry.

During the initial stages of the micropaleontologic research, most workers were too busy to publish their results, but by 1928 the *Journal of Paleontology* published large numbers of papers originating with oil company employees. These paleontologists were now able to identify the position of samples within the geologic section, recognize the character of reservoir and source rocks, and often predict the character of rocks still to be encountered at greater depths.

In the 1930s with the introduction of the electric log, which could be used to identify changing lithologies with greater precision than from rotary samples, the economic use of micropaleontology became less important. Research, however, continued making contributions to science.

During the 1920s Joseph A. Cushman, who had

worked in Texas and Mexico for the oil industry, built a laboratory for foraminiferal research in Sharon, Massachusetts. The laboratory served as a center for identification, and as a result it acquired immense collections of fossils, which were bequeathed to the Smithsonian Institution.

Now that geologists of the Gulf Coast had better tools with which to attack the problem of salt dome origin, and a place to publish their ideas, they made progress toward understanding this type of feature. American salt domes occur throughout the Louisiana to Mexican Gulf Coast. Characteristically, they are roughly circular masses of salt frequently capped by limestone, gypsum-anhydrite, and possibly sulfur. The salt has either domed up the overlying sedimentary layers, or it has pierced them and sealed the truncated edges. The Gulf Coast domes are in an area where no major compressive forces are apparent, and consequently, determining the source of the force that started the upward movement has been a major problem. The geologic section through which the salt has penetrated ranges from Cretaceous through Holocene. Production ranges in age from Eocene to Pleistocene. Oil may be produced from the cap rock, as at Spindletop, from sedimentary beds arched over the dome, or from the steeply dipping beds sealed against the flanks of the salt. Oil also may be trapped against faults radiating outward from the dome.

Because the outline of a salt dome resembles that of a volcano, many early geologists believed that there was an association between volcanoes and salt domes. Over the years, beginning with the first meeting of the AAPG in 1917, various hypotheses have been suggested as to what the relationship between volcanoes and salt might be. Edgar Owen summarized the various "notions" proposed to explain the origin of the salt intrusions.[16] It was not until about 1936, however, that an acceptable theory of salt dome origin was proposed by Donald Barton, chief geologist of Rycade Oil Corporation.[17]

Barton had traveled to the German and Rumanian salt deposits to study their characteristics. The German deposits were in the process of being mined, and consequently, their structural features could be examined and their deformation traced from bedded layers through gentle anticlines, to sharp ridges where the salt had broken through the apex, to salt plugs pushing vertically through the overlying beds. As a result of this investigation, Barton was convinced that plastic deformation and upthrust of sedimentary beds accounted for the American domes. American domes differed from the German domes in their geologic setting. Whereas lateral dynamic movement was evident

in the German salt fields, the Gulf Coastal Plains had no such apparent orogenic activity. Barton described the American dome-forming process as "downbuilding" due to the static weight of the sediments compared to the weight of the salt.

Barton[18] and Nettleton[19] fairly well summarized what had been learned about the structure and stratigraphic characteristics of salt domes since the discovery at Spindletop. Nettleton accounted for salt dome origin based on the density difference between salt and surrounding sediments, but his model suggested movement similar to fluid flow, rather than the plastic deformation and upthrust suggested by Barton. Both theories, however, ruled out the need for lateral thrusting as a necessary component of uplift.

Today, the sedimentary load of a prograding delta as it reaches the continental slope is believed to be the triggering mechanism that mobilizes salt movement. Both salt and shale diapirism commonly is associated with thick delta and slope sedimentary prisms in the modern continental shelf and slope environment.[20] (See fig.2-b,c.)

As geologists worked on the specific problems of salt dome oil fields they felt the need to understand the stratigraphy and structure of the whole coastal area. Through the use of micropaleontology and electric logs,[21] they were able to work out correlations of stratigraphic sections and to recognize the broad structural features of the Sabine Uplift, the East Texas Syncline, and the Rio Grande Embayment.

The presence of old ocean crust in the Gulf of Mexico was established during several ocean research projects including coring and seismic surveys. This basin was tectonically stable except for gradual regional subsidence following the Laramide uplift, which changed the drainage pattern from west to east. After the uplift a flood of debris carried by the Mississippi and Rio Grande drainage systems, as well as a number of lesser rivers, buried the old ocean crust. About sixteen thousand feet of sediment accumulated near the basin center; sixty-nine thousand feet collected along the Texas and Louisiana coasts near the northwestern margin of the basin. Sediments were deposited in deltas that migrated laterally back and forth across the shelf.

The earliest deposits on the Texas shelf adjacent to the coast were Jurassic, which included bedded salt of Louann age, source of the salt domes throughout the coastal plain. Cretaceous platform carbonates overlie the Jurassic, and over the Cretaceous beds the Tertiary fluvial delta and slope systems filled the basin with sands and shales. Basin filling was controlled by the rate of subsidence compared to the rate of compaction

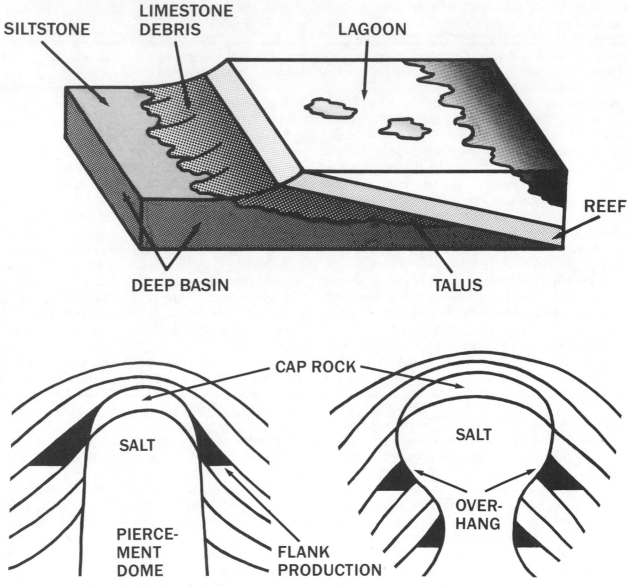

Figure 2. *Diagrams of a Reef and a Salt Dome*

and the abundance of debris. Depositional wedges accumulated primarily on the continental shelf where slope ranges were from one to five degrees. Beyond the shelf, on the continental slope, loading caused mud slides, growth faults, and diapirism. Today, both salt and shale diapirs are forming in the Pliocene and Pleistocene sediments offshore from the Mississippi delta.

The search for oil led geologists from the upper coast into the province of South Texas, where they found other types of fields in addition to salt domes. Most of the fields south from Corpus Christi were re-

lated to pinchouts of shore line sands or traps formed by reservoir rock sealed by impervious beds across a fault. Geologists soon came to the conclusion that all of the Cenozoic deposits of the Gulf Coast had potential for oil accumulation some place along the Coastal Plain. Some beds had marine components that contained productive sands downdip, but that were unfavorable in the updip zone. Other beds had production further updip, but had only barren shales in the downdip extension of the unit. More emphasis on stratigraphic relationships was necessary.

As exploration moved westward from the coast,

production was discovered along the Balcones structural zone, which forms the inland margin of the Coastal Plain. The Balcones fault is downthrown to the south and southeast for the most part, but some of the minor faults are upthrown on the gulfward side. The Mexia fault zone is roughly parallel to the Balcones zone, but downthrown to the west except for a few of the minor faults. Thus a graben is present between the Balcones and Mexia faults. Production along the Mexia-Powell fault is found where the reservoir sands are sealed across the fault by an impervious layer.

Associated with the fault zone, some production comes from weathered igneous rock, which is structurally higher than the adjacent intruded beds. The reservoir rock is porous serpentine altered from original basic rock intruded into Upper Cretaceous rocks.

After salt domes, probably the most unique geologic problem confronting Texas geologists was identifying the structural characteristics and stratigraphic history of the Permian Basin of West Texas. The Permian Basin stretches from the Pecos River valley through Texas and New Mexico into western Oklahoma, central Kansas, and Nebraska.

The Permian sea spread northward from the Trans-Pecos region and separated into two branches. One branch passed around a structural uplift in Eastern New Mexico and reached into Arizona. The other branch transgressed through Oklahoma, Kansas, and Nebraska. The Trans-Pecos Permian deposits are marine, but when the sea regressed southward from Kansas, the deep basin in Texas became landlocked and filled with thick beds of evaporites and terrestrial sediments. The Texas section of Permian is the most complete in North America; it includes deep marine to shallow water sediments as well as continental deposits.

The stratigraphy of the marine Permian outcrops in the Guadalupe Mountains was studied in 1901 by George Girty, a USGS paleontologist who worked with Robert Hill's reconnaissance party.[22] Hill's work was supported by the state. In 1903 John Udden of the State Mineral Survey and George Richardson of the USGS extended Girty's fossil correlations to the Chinati and Glass Mountain outcrops. By 1917 Udden had detailed the relationships of the Glass Mountain fauna and subdivided this complete marine section into formational units.

In 1889 Dumble persuaded the USGS to send their paleontologist Charles A. White to assist W. F. Cummins of the state survey in working out the Permian stratigraphy of the Osage Plains. White identified marine invertebrate fossils of Permian age in the gypsum beds, which conformably overlie the Pennsylvanian beds. On the basis of White's fossil identification and his studies of the lithology, Cummins separated this Permian section into three major units representing the transgressive and regressive aspects of the sediments. As the sea withdrew, it left great thicknesses of evaporites behind.

Also working in the Osage Plains was George Adams of the USGS. He was there in 1902 to study water resources when he observed a delta that extended from Texas into Oklahoma and cut across the marine limestones that thinned toward the red beds of the delta with complex interfingering of deposits.

By the late nineteenth century the Permian outcrops of both the Osage Plain and the Trans-Pecos region had been studied by federal and state geologists, but relationships among the different segments of the basin still were not clear. Well data, geophysical surveys, and imagination were still needed to resolve the geologic history of this complex region. Many years were required to unravel the stratigraphy and structure of the Texas Permian Basin, but Owen believes it now is the best understood reef province in the world.[23] The solution to the correlation and structural problems of this area constitute a major contribution to petroleum geology.

The Permian Basin contains a variety of structural and stratigraphic traps unmatched outside the Ural region of Russia. Even for Texas the production was phenomenal, but the problems also were immense. Geological science served the petroleum industry well in unraveling the habitat of this western oil. Possibly geologists were unusually effective in this province because cooperation was encouraged by the various oil companies. The drilling density provided an abundance of high quality data with a relatively rapid exchange of information and ideas.

One example of the cooperation in the province was the establishment of a laboratory in which heavy mineral residues were prepared for twenty participating companies. The Ellenberger (Ordovician) did not contain microfossils usable for correlation, and the heavy minerals proved to be the most efficient method of identifying position within the geologic section. Exploration proceeded at the most orderly, systematic pace of any oil province in North America because petroleum geologists worked together in the Permian Basin.

The Permian Basin of West Texas originated during the Late Paleozoic era when mountains were formed to the north in the Red River, Wichita-Amarillo

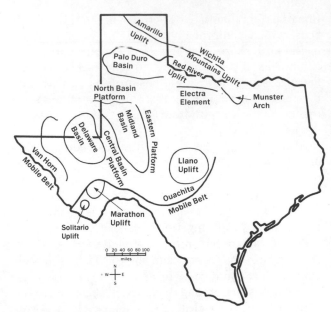

Figure 3. Texas Structural Units

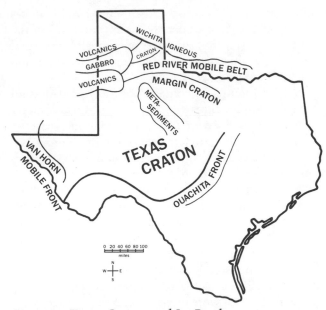

Figure 4. Texas Craton and Its Borders

mobile area, and to the south and east in the Ouachita mobile belt. These mountain belts surrounded the Texas Precambrian craton (Fig. 3), which was involved in the tectonic movements but to a lesser degree than in the mobile fronts.

The mountain complex on the southwest, including the Guadalupe, Delaware, and Glass Mountains, was a part of the Laramide orogeny. The Ouachita and

Rocky mountain uplifts met in the vicinity of the Marathon and Solitario domes (fig. 4). As a result of the surrounding tectonic activity, several basins were formed in the craton adjacent to the mountains. The basins were surrounded by shelf areas, or platforms, that to a large extent determined the pattern of sedimentation within the deep basins. The farthest west of these features is the Diablo Platform. In sequence toward the east lie the Delaware Basin, the Central Basin Platform, the Midland Basin, and the Eastern Shelf. The Northwest Shelf is the northern boundary of both the Delaware and Midland basins.

Following uplift and prior to Permian deposition, erosion removed much of the Paleozoic deposition from the foothills and block fault mountains that were parallel to the higher Central Basin Platform. During transgression of these features by the Permian sea, some remained islands, and fringing reefs were built up around their flanks. Some became atolls with their lagoons surrounded by limestone highs. All were buried beneath Permian sediments and were not apparent from the surface. About two hundred miles of relatively featureless plains lay between the Osage Plains outcrops and those of the Trans-Pecos region. About three hundred miles lay between the Trans-Pecos exposures and those of the Canadian River.

The first commercial production in the Permian Basin occurred in 1920 in Mitchell County. Early discoveries were made without benefit of much geological evidence, but by 1925 there were twenty-six major fields on the Central Basin Platform. Then, in 1925, the USGS published a general guide to the geology of the Permian Basin which proved to be *the* guide for most future exploration.[24] By 1929 drilling had defined the position of the Capitan Reef rimming the Delaware Basin and outlined fairly well the Central Basin Platform.

The Capitan is a barrier reef, the largest reef in the Permian complex. It borders the Delaware Basin on the north and follows the Central Basin Platform to the south, where it outcrops in the Guadalupe, Delaware, and Glass mountains. This extensive reef separated the Permian evaporite basin from open sea on the southeast, and it determined the sequence of sedimentation within the Delaware and Midland basins.

The reef (fig. 2-a) is a massive, structureless rock mass of calcareous algae and sponges, with minor amounts of other shells such as corals and brachiopods. On the lagoonal side, back of the reef, interfingering lenses of shales and sandstones merge with red beds, gypsum, salt, and anhydrite. From deep basin to reef, deposits are fine-grained lime, sandy lime, and talus or lime rubble with steep dips. The steep dips result when debris worn from the reef is carried basinward by the waves and down the slope area by mud slides. Oil production on the Central Basin Platform is associated with the reef bordering the platform, with lagoonal lenses of sand, and with buried uplifts truncated to the Ellenberger layer, prior to Permian deposition.

The Midland Basin, lying to the east of the Central Basin Platform, was filled by prograding during Late Mississippian and Early Pennsylvanian periods. Fans and fan-deltas border the eastern shore, and furnished debris eroded from the Eastern Shelf highlands. On the western shore, adjacent to the Central Basin Platform, carbonates predominated. By the Late Pennsylvanian period deposits were mostly fluvial delta debris, and the rate of filling from the east was more rapid than the rate of subsidence. Off-lapping wedges of deep water deposits merge rather abruptly with deposits from the western flank of the basin where carbonates still dominate. The relationship between delta filling and limestone suggests the starved basin facies in which the center of the basin is too far from the clastic source and too deep for limestone build-up to occur.

The Permian Basin has enormous oil reserves from both structural and stratigraphic traps. Most production has come from the Central Platform and the Midland Basin, but all units of the major basin produce. Reefs, lagoonal deposits, and pre-Permian structures such as buried ridges contain oil in a variety of traps. Some of the fields have unusual characteristics, such as the Scurry Reef, a Pennsylvanian atoll eighty miles in diameter. This reef is partly in the Midland Basin and partly beneath the Eastern Platform. It was built on a very minor regional shelf, where it continued to grow into Early Permian until it was covered by younger beds that left no surface indication of its presence.

Sprayberry, the most extensive field of the Midland Basin, covers 700,000 acres. Its production is surprising because of its low porosity and permeability, which makes secondary recovery methods necessary. Production comes from a fine-grained siltstone with apparently micro-fracture porosity, unrelated to structure.

The Panhandle of Texas belongs to the Permian Basin as it extends into Oklahoma and Kansas. The buried Amarillo Mountains, which extend east and west across the district, separate the Anadarko Basin on the northeast from the Permian Basin complex on the southwest.

Gas was discovered in Texas in 1918, in Oklahoma in 1922, and in Kansas first in 1922 but productively not until 1927. Based on the similarity among the wells, it appears that they defined the extent of an immense gas field, not separate fields as at first expected. The productive gas area is more than two hundred miles long and ranges from five to forty miles across, probably the most important gas discovery to the present. Gas occurs in both the Permian and the Pennsylvanian basins from the southwest flank of the Anadarko Basin and the north flank of Amarillo Mountains. Producing formations overlap against the granite core of the mountain and consist of dolomite, limestone, sandstone, and arkose or granite wash. In the Texas Panhandle within the defined gas areas, the number of dry holes is negligible, which makes this a unique area in which to drill. Some oil occurs in the upper portions of the anticlinal fold beneath the gas and above the water level with the amount of production dependent on local porosity. The sheer size of this gas field makes its inclusion in a report on Texas production imperative.

During the 1930s most of the more easily found structural pools had been discovered, so finding a new kind of trap was important to the petroleum industry. The East Texas field that reached oil on October 3, 1930, gave geologists a new tool in their search for production. This field, however, was not found through the application of geology. Instead, a rank wildcat led to the concepts of facies studies in basin analysis. East Texas is considered a classic example of oil accumulation determined by stratigraphic relationships. A stratigraphic trap is one that is bounded on one or more sides by nonporous beds, unless the nonporosity is due to local structural deformation. If the edge of porosity results from overlap or lateral lensing of a reservoir layer, it is considered to be a stratigraphic trap.

The East Texas oil field is immense; stretching across portions of five counties, it covers over 130,000 acres. Although wells were drilled by a "wildcatter," geologists monitored them; when enough oil was discovered, a number of oil companies were ready to begin leasing. In this field the oil is trapped in a westward dipping homocline between the Sabine Uplift on the east and the East Texas syncline on the west. Reservoir rocks are sands and conglomerates rather loosely held together by siliceous and calcareous cement. An uncomfortable overlap of Austin chalk across the Eagleford-Woodbine reservoir rock, and onto the underlying Washita bed, forms the porosity seal necessary to trap the oil. The unconformity at the base of the Austin chalk is a major erosional event that truncated beds inclined against the western flank of the Sabine Uplift. Inclined beds then were covered by a veneer of conglomerate, following which deposition of the Austin chalk closed the reservoir on the east. The position of the water layer on the downdip side determined the extent of production on the west. Late Cretaceous and Tertiary movements increased uplift of the Sabine high but buried the East Texas field with these younger deposits.

The East Texas oil field is not the only important resource of East Texas. Large quantities of lignite have been known to be present in the area since the first state survey activity. Following the discovery of oil at Spindletop, however, the production of oil had been paramount until the energy crisis of the 1970s.

The early geologists who mapped the lignite deposits of East Texas had prepared the state for exploitation of this resource long before it was economically feasible. Today lignite, or brown coal, is being strip mined, but the Bureau is preparing for the future when deep surface mining to a depth of at least three hundred feet may be necessary. The Bureau also expects that some tonnages of fuel will be recovered by underground gasification.

Mining of the Wilcox Group, Eocene-age lignite is of some concern with regard to the groundwater resources. For this reason the Bureau has made a detailed study of both the ground water pathways and their special characteristics. The geology of the Carrizo sand and its interconnectedness with the Wilcox aquifer appears to be such that the Carrizo may be in danger of environmental damage northeast of the Brazos River where thick lignites will be mined eventually. Computer software for simulation of conditions is being developed to try to anticipate and test a means of protecting the aquifers.

Three regions of Texas contain lignite of sufficiently thick seams to be considered mineable. These regions include the east-central, between the Colorado and Trinity Rivers; northeast Texas, north of the Trinity River to Texarkana; and the Sabine Uplift, or East Texas province.

In addition to its concern for water resources, the Bureau also is conducting research to determine the suitability of salt domes as containers, or storage caverns, for chemical waste products. Not all chemical waste degrades in time, so it is imperative that these chemicals do not leak. If it can be determined that salt domes are leak-proof, they can be solution mined, and the space filled with waste products can be sealed to prevent contaminating the biosphere.

The Basin and Range province of the Rocky Mountain area is being studied by the USGS with the help of the states within the province. The Texas Trans-Pecos region lies in the area being evaluated as a possible host for high-level radioactive wastes (fig. 1). The Bureau of Economic Geology annual report for 1984 discusses the geological and hydrological characteristics of the province. Mineral resources, distribution of various rock types, regional groundwater flow systems, and tectonic conditions will be considered in a final report to appear as a USGS professional paper.

The legacy of John Udden's pioneering efforts in the laboratory study of well cuttings is demonstrated in several of the current Bureau projects. The geological characteristics of Texas oil reservoir rocks, both carbonate and clastic, are studied using cores where available, geophysical logs, and core analyses and some thin sections. Thickness maps and cross sections have been used to identify the facies distribution as well as to recognize wave-dominated versus barrier strand plain reservoirs. A major objective of this study is to understand the relation of production characteristics to reservoir conditions.

A somewhat similar project is focused on the Miocene and Frio facies distribution on the Texas portion of the continental shelf and the upper slope. Well logs, paleontologic reports, scout tickets, and production records have been used to extend what is known of the onshore sections across the shelf. Dip sections and strike sections as well as reports and maps are used to illustrate the interpretation of the projection of facies assemblages into offshore areas.

Among the most useful of the Bureau projects is the series of atlases being printed. A geologic map of Texas on a scale of 1:500,000 replaces the outdated USGS 1937 map. The new map is based on a series of thirty-eight sheets at a scale of 1:250,000 covering all of Texas. These sheets show the distribution of outcrops each covering an area within one degree of latitude and two degrees of longitude.

Other maps include the tectonic map, which will replace the 1940 edition. The new map brings up to date both surface and subsurface information and uses new techniques to illustrate structural events for Texas and the surrounding area. Gravity and magnetic maps also are planned as computer reprocessing of various federal surveys becomes available.

Environmental concerns have led to the publication of a new type of map, the Environmental Geologic Atlas of the Texas Coastal Zone, which represents the distribution of sediment, benthic macro-invertebrates, trace elements, and wetlands. This new look at submerged lands from the shoreline seaward for about ten statute miles includes a study of the bay-estuary-lagoon system from the Rio Grande to Sabine Lake.

Of great interest to geologists is the study of the Texas Bay shore showing major changes during the last one hundred or so years. Based on old topographic maps from the late 1800s and on aerial photographs from 1929, it is apparent that progressive erosion of the shoreline has occurred. The erosion rate ranged from about one to five feet per year, but even higher rates were noted on unprotected shores where vegetation is lacking. The rate of recovery of the vegetation line following hurricanes will help establish legal property boundaries where these are in question.

In its seventy-seven years since being established officially as the Bureau of Economic Geology, emphasis has changed to include responsibility for environmental problems such as toxic waste disposal, land reclamation, and future resource needs and potentials. Studies in stratigraphy, structure, and geologic mapping, however, are still the major interests of the Bureau.

But what of the new "revolution" in earth science? Was Texas involved? Like geologists everywhere Texans were interested in finding a theoretical framework to synthesize the subsurface and surface data that were being accumulated at such a rapid rate. Although most oil companies have their headquarters in Texas, their interests are global, and their research necessarily must be on a worldwide scale. The 1960s brought many distinguished lecturers to the university campuses and to oil company auditoriums. Texas geologists also conducted their research abroad and brought back new information concerning such areas as the Afar Triangle of Africa and the Red Sea. Whenever possible, results of such research were shared with the local Texas community of geologists, the largest such group in the western world. During this period of ferment, continental drift became respectable!

In 1928 the American Association of Petroleum Geologists had sponsored a symposium on continental drift and published the discussion in their second bulletin. Although at the time the mechanism for movement of continents was still a major problem, this group had not buried the idea of drift. The AAPG also sponsored J. Tuzo Wilson's talk on drifting continents at their convention in Calgary, Alberta, Canada in 1970. The acoustics were poor and the lecture room too small, but by this time there were many believers as Wilson pictured the movement of plates throughout geologic time.

In 1957–58 the geophysical community worldwide inaugurated the Geophysical Year. This project initiated research concentrated on planetary geophysical problems. Of course, the work was only begun during the official "year"; in fact, it still continues along many lines. Exploration of the ocean floor began during this period, and it revealed a relatively unknown area, especially in the Pacific. A most significant discovery was the presence of the mid-ocean ridge, which extends through the Pacific ocean and around the globe to join the Mid-Atlantic ridge. The ridge is bordered by symmetrical magnetic anomalies on either side, suggesting that the ridges pull apart and allow new lava flows to form new ocean floor from time to time. Flows increase in age with distance from the central ridge, but match in age and polarity with flows on the other side of the ridge.

On the basis of these observations Robert Dietz, of Arizona State University, Tempe, suggested that sea floor spreading accounted for the movement of continents. The late Harry Hess (Princeton University) took the idea one step further and suggested the framework of global change, now known as plate tectonics. Hess suggested convection currents rising in the vicinity of the mid-ocean ridges brought new additions from the aesthenosphere to add basaltic material to the ocean floor. As the convection currents moved horizontally away from the central ridge, they carried crustal plates to new positions. When ocean plates encountered continental plates, the convection currents carried the more dense ocean plate downward beneath the lighter continental plate. These downward currents formed subduction zones, which account for the presence of volcanic action along the continents, as ocean crust is melted and as new mountains are forced upward by the converging plates. Some convergence is between two continental plates, or in other cases between two oceanic plates. Divergent margins also are found on continental as well as oceanic crustal plates.

One of the important aspects of the plate tectonic theory is the new look it has given to basin analysis, as well as to the geologic history of each continent. Basin analysis has become a better way of evaluating oil prospects as basins around the world are compared for their hydrocarbon content and their geologic patterns of deposition and tectonic origin. A global classification system for basins of the world has been worked out by Kingston, Dishroon, and Williams.[25] According to these authors most hydrocarbons found to date occur in one of four major types of basins associated with continental crust. This classification system also suggests a model for a new look at geologic history. For the most part, theories of a contracting earth, isostasy, an expanding earth, or drifting continents were part of a geologist's collection of ideas for interesting arguments at geologic meetings, but they were not significant to the business of mapping the data at hand, or studying the minerals or fossils of his immediate assignment. The theories did not impinge upon the serious business of identifying bones, shells, rocks, or finding oil. Identification of the materials of geology, however, are extremely important to determining where the bits and pieces of crust have come from. The study of ocean basins has led to a greater understanding of the earth's crust and its long history of being reworked, buried, and uplifted.

In 1960 Time-Life published a map of the ocean floors based on the work of Bruce Heezen, M. Tharp, and M. Ewing, of the Lamont Geological Observatory. This map provided an overview of the ocean bottom, its trenches, and displacements, and proved important in the acceptance of the concept of continental drift. In similar fashion, images provided by the Landsat program of the National Aeronautics and Space Administration (NASA) have given us a better understanding of the continents. Eduard Suess, in his attempt to provide a global synthesis for earth science, had asked his readers to observe the world from the mountain tops, or as a celestial visitor looking down from great height. NASA has provided earth photographs beginning with its Gemini III program in 1967, but the Landsat images have provided outstanding views of the world.

Landsat, originally known as Earth Resources Technology Satellite, is a program based on remote sensing from space. Data provided by the program are useful in many disciplines, but perhaps geology benefits the most. Features of structural significance can be recognized better from the overview images than from the ground, and geologic mapping can be speeded up immeasurably. Landsat data also have been useful in mineral and petroleum exploration, and in finding water resources. Mountain ranges, depositional landforms, and volcanic fields are readily recognized from the images, as are drainage systems, glacial features, and coastal areas. Industry has made good use of the program, and the layman also will find publications such as "Mission to Earth" informative.

Because of the Johnson Space Center's location near Houston, perhaps, Texans have a special interest in the information emanating from the Lunar and Planetary Science Conference hosted each year by the Lunar Planetary Institute. This annual meeting is attended by specialists in petrology, geochemistry, geophysics, geology, and astronomy. Early meetings concentrated

on analyses of the moon rocks, but by now it is agreed generally that the moon rocks are similar to Earth's mantle material. Basalts, such as are found on the ocean floor or in Hawaiian flows, have a chemical composition very much like that of moon rocks except that moon rocks are depleted of some volatile elements present in Earth's rocks.

Now argument has passed from moon materials to moon origin. Hypotheses of the past, such as fission from Earth, capture of the moon by Earth, and the moon as part of a binary planet system are no longer in favor and have been supplanted by a new hypothesis. The latest concept suggests that Earth was impacted by a large body, possibly the size of Mars. Proponents of this idea suggest that as a result of impact, hot and perhaps partly vaporized mantle material was ejected from primordial Earth. The impact, theoretically, would heat Earth's mantle to the point at which large amounts of volatiles would be lost. If impact occurred after the core of Earth had formed, the difference in iron content between Earth and the moon could be accounted for, as the surface mantle material would be most likely to enter orbit.

Another hypothesis dependent on the impact of an extraterrestrial body is the extinction theory suggested in 1980 by Walter Alvarez (University of California at Berkeley). According to this idea, the widespread extinctions evident in the fossil record at the boundary between Cretaceous and Tertiary periods resulted from impact of an exceptionally large body. This suggestion has initiated a wave of research and discussion with respect to the general topic of extinctions as a basis for divisions of geologic time. Peter Vail (Exxon Research, Houston) suggests that seismic stratigraphic data that record both global sea level changes and global tectonic events are better bases for correlation than extinction events.[26] Research by Thor Hansen (University of Texas at Austin), however, relates extinctions in the Gulf Coastal region to thermal changes, rather than sea level. More discussion and research along this line, and an increased interest in Earth history are anticipated.

From Roemer's first report on the geology of Texas in 1846[27] to the present, geologists have been publishing on the various aspects of Texas structure, stratigraphy, and geologic history. They have contributed a large body of knowledge to science won through the dedicated efforts of both state and oil company geologists, as well as scientists from the United States Geological Survey.

John Udden, then director of the Bureau of Economic Geology, began the microscopic examination of well samples when he published a paper recording the lithology of a deep boring at Spur in the Permian Basin. This was the first look at the stratigraphy of the basin sediments beyond the area of outcrops. From this meager beginning the history of what happens to a growing reef through time, as seas transgress and retreat, gradually was worked out. The study of modern reefs, supplemented by data from the facies changes in the vertical direction, gave geologists the clues needed to understand the geological history of complex reef environments. The Permian Basin is cited in historical geology and stratigraphy texts as the classic example of the ancient reef environment.

The discovery of oil at Spindletop led to research in micro-paleontology, a study of deltas and the continental slope deposits, as well as an investigation of all aspects of salt dome development. The question of salt dome formation finally was solved through a study of sedimentation on the Coastal Plain. The concept of density differences between salt and sediments as the cause of upward movement of salt led to theoretical explanations, but a detailed study of the modern delta environment proved sediment loading of the continental slope to be the triggering action that initiated salt uplift.

The study of modern deltas and their progressive growth across the shelf shows distribution of fluvial sediments in the lateral direction until debris reaches the slope, when movement is downward, mostly through mud slides. The rapid dumping of the massive load of rivers like the Mississippi not only causes salt and shale diapirs, but also is responsible for faulting in the slope environment.

An increased appreciation for the importance of the facies concept led to increased research into sedimentation processes. Facies may be defined as different but contemporaneous rocks and faunas reflecting the environment in which each is deposited. Research into wave-dominated features such as barrier islands and beaches, compared to the distribution of delta deposits, has proved important in identifying variations in sedimentary structures of coastal deposits. Studies of lateral change in sedimentary structures and stratigraphy together with research on vertical changes determined from well data have led to an understanding of coastal history. Without the wealth of information derived from well cuttings and electric logs, understanding of Texas geologic history would be far behind its present status.

Discovery of oil in 1918 and 1919 in the Red River Valley brought about litigation to determine the boundary between Texas and Oklahoma. E. H. Sellards and R. T. Hill helped to establish Texas' claim through their studies of river valley sedimentation. However, because the Red River geology is not unique to Texas, but activity along this area belongs both to Oklahoma and Texas, we have not tried to include details of the Red River-Wichita zone of uplift. Much of the history of the Ouachita uplift in Texas similarly begins in Arkansas, extends across Oklahoma, follows around the Llano Uplift to the south, and eventually turns westward to reach the Solitario and Marathon uplifts. These orogenic movements affected sedimentation over much of Texas, and they were an important part of geologic history.

Texas geology is varied and complex, but it has been served well by its numerous practitioners. They have discovered oil fields so numerous and varied that most any type of accumulation can be illustrated by one of the state's pools. They also have published a vast literature covering a developing science for which they never lose their enthusiasm.

In the Texas sesquicentennial year we find that Texas, through its petroleum industry, academia, and Bureau of Economic Geology, has accumulated a vast body of data from which to understand the structure and stratigraphy of the state. Not all problems have been solved, nor all oil discovered, but the broad questions of local geology are fairly well answered. Texas geologists have steadily progressed from concentration on local data gathering to participation in seeking global syntheses to explain the observed facts that they have accumulated.

Early workers believed that studying mountain structure was the key to understanding Earth origin and development. Ongoing research indicates that oceanographic studies reveal global links among many observed phenomena. Landsat and probes of Earth's sister planets show that other planets can tell us much about Earth history in spite of differences between them. In the next one hundred fifty years we anticipate that most of the current questions about plate tectonics, mass extinctions, mountain origin, and vulcanism will have been solved along with questions not yet asked.

Notes

1. Ferguson, 1969, 1981.
2. Owen, 1975.
3. Ferguson, 1969, p. 7.
4. Southwestern Association of Petroleum Geologists, 1917, p. 28.
5. Cope, 1875, 1884.
6. Ferguson, 1969, p. 16.
7. Ferguson, 1969, p. 19.

8. Roemer, 1846, 1848.
9. Hill, 1900.
10. Hill and Vaughan, 1898.
11. Hill, 1901.
12. Cope, 1878.
13. Boll, 1879.
14. Dumble, 1890, 1891, 1918.
15. Applin, Ellisor, and Kniker, 1925.
16. Owen, 1975, p. 204.
17. Barton, 1936, pp. 20–79.
18. Barton, 1936, pp. 20–79.
19. Nettleton, 1936, pp. 79–109.
20. *Diapirism* is the process during which a mobile core injects brittle overlying rock, forming an anticline pierced by the mobile salt, or shale.
21. *Electric logs* are obtained by lowering electrodes into an open bore hole and measuring various electrical properties of the formations encountered. The two basic parameters continuously recorded are the spontaneous potential and the electrical resistivity of the rock layers. The pattern recorded determines the exact boundaries of various sedimentary layers as well as the kind of fluid present in porous rock. Additional physical parameters currently are in use in the more modern sophisticated logs.
22. Girty, 1908.
23. Owen, 1975, p. 904.
24. Hoots, 1925.
25. Kingston, Dishroon, and Williams, 1983, p. 2175.
26. Vail, 1977.
27. Roemer, 1846.

Bibliography

Adams, George, *Oil and Gas Fields of the West Interior and North Texas Coal Measurers and of the Upper Cretaceous and Tertiary of the West Gulf Coast*, Bulletin 184, Washington, D.C.: U.S. Government Printing Office, 1901.

Albritton, C. C., Jr., "Stratigraphy and Structure of the Malone Mountains, Texas," *Geological Society of America Bulletin* 49(1938): 1757.

Applin, Esther, Alva E. Ellisor, and Hedwig T. Kniker, "Subsurface Stratigraphy of the Coastal Plains of Texas and Louisiana," *American Association of Petroleum Geologists Bulletin* 9(1925): 79–122.

Baker, C. L., Discussion of Permian Symposium, *American Association of Petroleum Geologists Bulletin* 13(1929): 1057–63.

———. "Formation of Coral Reefs and Atolls," *Pan American Geology* 60(1933): 15–24.

Barton, Donald C., "Natural History of the Gulf Coast Crude." In *Problems of Petroleum Geology*, 109, American Association of Petroleum Geologists, 1934.

———. "Mechanics of Formation of Salt Domes with Special Reference to Gulf Coast Salt Domes of Texas and Louisiana." In *Gulf Coast Oil Fields*, edited by Donald C. Barton and George Sawtelle, American Association of Petroleum Geologists Symposium, 1936.

Bauer, C. M. "Oil and Gas Fields of the Texas Panhandle," *American Association of Petroleum Geologists Bulletin* 10(1926): 742–43.

Blanchard, W. G., Jr., "Permian Stratigraphy and Structure," *American Association of Petroleum Geologists Bulletin* 13(1929): 975–94.

Boll, Jacob, "Texas in Its Geognostic and Agricultural Aspect," *American Naturalist* 13(June 1879): 375–84.

Brown, L. F., and W. L. Fisher, "Seismic Stratigraphic Interpretation of Depositional Systems," In *Seismic Stratigraphy*, 213–49, American Association of Petroleum Geologists, Memoir 26 (1977).

Bybee, H. P., *Major Structures in West Texas*, University of Texas at Austin, Bulletin 3101(1931): 26.

Cannon, R. L., "Structure and Stratigraphy of South Permian Basin," *American Association of Petroleum Geologists Bulletin* 16(1932): 189–208.

Carsey, J. Ben, "Basin Geology of the Gulf Coastal Area and the Continental Shelf," *Oil and Gas Journal* 47(8): 246–51, 266–67(1948).

Cheney, M. G., "Geology of North Central Texas," *American Association of Petroleum Geologists Bulletin* 24(1940): 89.

Clark, F. R., "Origin and Accumulation of Oil." In *Problems of Petroleum Geology*, 309–35, American Association of Petroleum Geologists, 1934.

Cook, Harold James, "Geological Evidence of Early Man," *Geological Society of America Bulletin* 42(1931): 326.

Cope, Edward Drinker, *The Vertebrata of the Cretaceous Formations of the West*, Report of the U.S. Geological and Geographic Survey of the Territories (Hayden Survey), Vol. II, Washington, D.C.: U.S. Government Printing Office, 1875.

———. "Extinct Batrachia and Reptilia from the Permian of Texas." In *Proceedings of the American Philosophical Society*, Vol. 17, 505–30, April 1878.

———. *The Vertebrata of the Tertiary Formations of the West*, Report of the U.S. Geological and Geographic Survey of the Territories (Hayden Survey),

Vol. III, Washington, D.C.: U.S. Government Printing Office, 1884.

Cotner, Victor, and H. E. Crum, "Geology of Natural Gas in the Hugoton District." In *Geology of Natural Gas*, 385, American Association of Petroleum Geologists, 1935.

Darton, N. H., and J. B. Reeside, Jr., "Guadalupe Group," *Geological Society of America Bulletin* 37(1926):413–28.

DeFord, R. K., The Permian System of the United States West of the Mississippi River," *American Association of Petroleum Geologists Bulletin* 24(1940):10–11.

———. "Correlation of the Permian Formation of North America," *Geological Society of America Bulletin* 71(1960):1763–1805.

DeGolyer, E., "Origin of North American Salt Domes." In *Geology of Salt Dome Oil Fields*, edited by Raymond C. Moore, 1045, American Association of Petroleum Geologists Symposium, 1926.

Dickinson, W. R., *Plate Tectonics and Sedimentation*, Society of Economic Paleontologists and Mineralogists, Special Publication 22(1974):1–27.

Dietz, Robert, "Continents and Ocean Basin Evolution by Spreading of the Sea Floor," *Nature* 190(1961):854–57.

Dumble, E. T., First Annual Report of the Texas Geological Survey, 1890.

———. Second Annual Report of the Texas Geological Survey, 1891.

———. *The Geology of East Texas*, University of Texas at Austin, Bulletin 1869(1918).

Dunbar, C. O., "Permian Fauna: A Study in Facies," *Geological Society of America Bulletin* 52(1941):323–25.

Ellisor, A. C., "Coral Reefs in Oligocene of Texas," *American Association of Petroleum Geologists Bulletin* 10(1926):976–85.

———. "Anahuac Formation," *American Association of Petroleum Geologists Bulletin* 28(1944):1357.

Faul, Henry, and Carol Faul, *It Began with a Stone*, New York: John Wiley & Sons, 1983, p. 230.

Feldman, Rodney M., "Extinction Hypotheses Gave a Focus in 1984," *Geotimes* 30(4):12–15(1985).

Ferguson, Walter K., *Geology and Politics in Frontier Texas, 1845–1909*, Austin: Univ. of Texas Press, 1969.

———. *History of the Bureau of Economic Geology, 1909–1960*, University of Texas at Austin, 1981.

Flawn, Peter T., *Basement Rocks of Texas and Southeastern New Mexico*, University of Texas at Austin, Bureau of Economic Geology, Publication 5605(1956).

Friedman, Gerald, and Sharon Poissant, "Petroleum Geology in the United States," *Journal of Geological Education*, 33 (September 1985).

Garrison, L. E., and R. G. Martin, "Geologic Structures in the Gulf of Mexico Basin," *American Association of Petroleum Geologists Bulletin* 59(1975):838–55.

Girty, G. H., "Guadalupian Fauna," United States Geological Survey, Professional Paper 58(1908).

Gould, H. R., "Sedimentary Facies and Their Importance in Oil," *American Association of Petroleum Geologists Bulletin* 51(1967).

Greene, Mott T., *Geology in the 19th Century*, Ithaca: Cornell Univ. Press, 1982.

Greenman, Norman, and Rufus LeBlanc, "Recent Marine Sediments and Environments of the Northwestern Gulf of Mexico," *American Association of Petroleum Geologists Bulletin* 40(1956).

Halbouty, M. T., *Salt Domes, Gulf Region, United States, and Mexico*, Houston: Gulf Publishing, 1979.

Halbouty, M. T., et al., Part I, American Association of Petroleum Geologists, Memoir 14(1970a):502–28.

———. Part II, American Association of Petroleum Geologists, Memoir 14(1970b):528–55.

Halbouty, M. T., and G. C. Hardin, Jr., "Trends in Petroleum Geology of the Gulf Coast," *Oil Weekly* 125(5):32–35; 125(6):42–44; 125(7):40–43(1947).

Halbouty, M. T., and B. T. Simmons, "Hitchcock Field, Galveston Co., Texas." In *Stratigraphic Type Oil Fields*, A. I. Levorsen, ed., 641–60, American Association of Petroleum Geologists, 1941.

Hanna, Marcus A., "Geology of Gulf Coast Salt Domes." In *Problems of Petroleum Geology*, 629–79, American Association of Petroleum Geologists, 1934.

Hartman, W. K., "Giant Impact on Earth Seen as Moon's Origin," *Geotimes* 30(6), 1985.

Heezen, B. C., M. Tharp, and M. Ewing, *The Floors of the Oceans: I. The North Atlantic*, Geological Society of America, 1959.

Hess, Harry, "History of the Ocean Basins." In *Petrological Studies*, A. E. J. Engel, ed., 1962.

Hill, Robert T., "Physical Geography of the Texas Region." In *Topographic Atlas of the United States*, No. 3, United States Geological Survey, 1900.

———. "Geography and Geology of the Black and Grand Prairies, Texas," United States Geological Survey, Annual Report 21, Part VII, 1901.

———. "The Beaumont Oil Field," American Institute of Mining and Metallurgical Engineers, *Transactions* 33(1903): 363–405.

Hill, R. T., and T. W. Vaughan, "The Geology of the Edwards Plateau and Rio Grande Plain Adjacent to Austin and San Antonio, Texas," United States Geological Survey, Annual Report 18, 1898.

Hills, J. M., "Rhythm of Permian Seas," *American Association of Petroleum Geologists Bulletin* 26(1942): 250–551.

Hoots, Harold W., *Guide to the Geology of the Permian Basin*, United States Geological Survey, Bulletin 780(1925).

Keyes, C. R., "Guadalupan Reef Theory," *Pan American Geology* 52(1929): 41–60.

King, P. B. "Permian Reefs in Van Horn Region," *American Journal of Science*, Fifth Series, 24(1930): 337–54.

———. "Geology of the Marathon Region, Texas," United States Geological Survey, Professional Paper 187(1938): 92–109.

———. "Permian of West Texas and Southeastern New Mexico," *American Association of Petroleum Geologists Bulletin* 26(1942): 535–763.

———. "Geology of the Southern Guadalupe Mountains," United States Geological Survey, Professional Paper 215(1948): 76–88.

Kingston, D. R., C. P. Dishroon, and P. A. Williams, "Global Basin Classification Systems," *American Association of Petroleum Geologists Bulletin* 67(1983): 2175–93.

———. "Hydrocarbon Plays and Global Classification," *American Association of Petroleum Geologists Bulletin* 67(1983): 2194–98.

Ladd, H. S. "Recent Reefs," *American Association of Petroleum Geologists Bulletin* 13(1929(: 645–58.

Lloyd, E. R., "Capital Limestone," *American Association of Petroleum Geologists Bulletin* 13(1929): 645–58.

Lonsdale, J. T., *Igneous Rocks of the Balcones Fault Region of Texas*, University of Texas at Austin, Bulletin 1744(1927).

Lucas, Anthony F., "The Great Oil Well Near Beaumont, Texas," American Institute of Mining and Metallurgical Engineers, *Transactions* 31(1902).

Lurife, Edward, and Jules Marcou, *Dictionary of Scientific Biography*, Vol. 9, pp. 99–101, 1974.

Merrill, George P., *The First One Hundred Years of American Geology*, New Haven, Conn.: Yale Univ. Press, Reprint, Hafner, 1969.

Moore, Raymond, "Pennsylvanian Stratigraphy and Fauna," *Pan American Geologists* 49(1928): 227–28.

———. "Stratigraphy-Geology, 1888–1938," Geological Society of America, Fifteenth Anniversary Edition, 1941, pp. 179–220.

Morley, Harold T., "A History of the American Association of Petroleum Geologists; The First 50 Years," *American Association of Petroleum Geologists Bulletin* 50, no. 4(1966).

Myer, Samuel, *The Permian Basin: Petroleum Empire of the Southwest*, El Paso, Texas: Permian Basin Press.

Nelson, Clifford, "Facies in Stratigraphy: From Terrains to Terranes," *Journal of Geological Education* 33, no. 3(1985).

Nettleton, L. L., "Fluid Mechanics of Salt Domes." In *Gulf Coast Oil Fields*, 79–109, American Association of Petroleum Geologists, 1936.

Newell, N. D., et al., *The Permian Reef Complex of the Guadalupe Mountains Region, Texas and New Mexico*, W. H. Freeman & Co., 1953, p. 236.

———. "Depositional Fabric in Permian Reef Limestone," *Journal of Geology* 63(1955): 301–9.

———. "The Evolution of Reefs," *Scientific American* June(1972): 113–25.

Owen, E. W., "Trek of the Oil Finders: A History of Exploration for Petroleum," American Association of Petroleum Geologists, Memoir 6(1975).

Plummer, F. B., *Stratigraphy of Lower Pennsylvanian Coral Bearing Strata of Texas*, University of Texas at Austin, Bulletin 4401(1945): 63–76.

Plummer, F. B., and R. C. Moore, *Stratigraphy of the Pennsylvanian Formations of North Central Texas*, University of Texas, Bulletin 2132(1921): 98.

Pyne, Steve, "From the Grand Canyon to the Mariana Trench." In *Earth Sciences After Darwin; The Sciences in the American Context*, edited by Nathan Reingold, 165–93, Smithsonian Institution Press, 1979.

Rainwater, E. H., "The Environmental Control of Oil and Gas Occurrence in Terrigenous Clastic Rocks," Gulf Coast Association of Geological Societies, *Transactions* 13(1963): 79–94.

Reed, R. D., "Microscopic Subsurface Work in Oil Fields of the United States," *American Association of Petroleum Geologists Bulletin* 15(1931): 731–54.

Richardson, C. B., "Regional Aspects of Pennsylvanian Reefs of Texas," *Oil and Gas Journal* 48, no. 51(1950).

Rister, Carl C., *Oil! Titan of the Southwest*, Norman: Univ. of Oklahoma Press, 1949.

Roemer, Ferdinand, "A Sketch of the Geology of

Texas," *American Journal of Science,* Second Series II, November(1846):358–65.

———. "Contributions to the Geology of Texas," *American Journal of Science,* Second Series VI, November(1848):21–28.

———. Mit besonderer Rücksicht auf deutsche Auswanderung, und die physischen Verhältnisse des Landes nach eigener Beobachtung geschildert, n.p., n.d.

———. Mit einem naturwissenschaftlichen Anhange und einer topographisch-geognostischen Karte von Texas; Die Kreidebildungen von Texas und ihre organischen Einschlüsse, n.p., n.d.

Rundell, Walter, Jr., *Early Texas Oil,* College Station: Texas A&M Univ. Press, 1977.

Sellards, E. H., *The Geology of Texas, Vol. I, Stratigraphy,* University of Texas at Austin, Bulletin 3232(1932a).

———. "Oil in Igneous Rocks in Coastal Plain of Texas," *American Association of Petroleum Geologists* 16(1932b):741–68.

———. *The Geology of Texas, Vol. II, Structural and Economic Geology,* University of Texas at Austin, Bulletin 3401(1934).

Short, Nicholas, P. D. Lowman, Jr., S. C. Freden, and W. A. Finch, Jr., *Mission to Earth: Landsat Views the World,* National Aeronautics and Space Administration, 1976.

Southwestern Association of Petroleum Geologists Bulletin 1(1917).

Stephenson, L. W., "Cretaceous," United States Geological Survey, Professional Paper 81(1914):77.

———. "Cretaceous Eocene Contact," United States Geological Survey, Professional Paper 90(1915):155–82.

Stuart, Charles J., and Charles A. Caughey, "Seismic Facies and Sedimentology of Terrigenous Pleistocene Deposits in Northwest and Central Gulf of Mexico." In *Seismic Stratigraphy,* American Association of Petroleum Geologists, Memoir 26(1977).

Seuss, Eduard, *The Face of the Earth,* 5 vols., Oxford: Clarendon Press, 1904–24.

Suter, John, and Henry L. Berryhill, Jr., "Late Quaternary Shelf Margin Deltas, Northwest Gulf of Mex-ico," *American Association of Petroleum Geologists Bulletin* 69(1985):77.

Taylor, G. J., "Lunar Meeting Favors Impact Theory," *Geotimes* 30, no. 4(1985).

Teichert, Curt, "Concept of Facies," *American Association of Petroleum Geologists Bulletin* 42 (1958):2718–44.

Thompson, W. C., "The Geologic Section in Texas," *American Association of Petroleum Geologists Bulletin* 21(1937).

Trowbridge, A. C., "A Geologic Reconnaissance in the Gulf Coastal Plain of Texas Near the Rio Grande," United States Geological Survey, Professional Paper 131d(1923).

———. "Tertiary and Quartenary Geology of the Lower Rio Grande Region of Texas," United States Geological Survey, Bulletin 837(1932).

Udden, J. A., *Notes on the Geology of the Glass Mountains,* University of Texas at Austin, Bulletin 1753(1918):3–59.

Udden, J. A., C. L. Baker, and Emil Bose, *Review of the Geology of Texas,* University of Texas at Austin, Bulletin 44(1916).

Udden, J. A., and H. P. Bybee, *The Thrall Oil Field,* University of Texas at Austin, Bulletin 66(1916).

Vail, P. R., et al., "Seismic Stratigraphy and Global Change in Sea Level," American Association of Petroleum Geologists, Memoir 26(1977):49–83.

Vaughan, T. W., "Corals of the Trinity Group," *Journal of Paleontology* 6(1932):225–27.

Warner, C. Q., "General Geology of Edwards Plateau, Balcones Fault, and the Gulf Coastal Plains," *Oil and Gas Journal* 31(4):50–54(1932).

———. *Texas Oil and Gas Since 1543,* Houston: Gulf Publishing, 1939.

White, Charles A., and W. F. Cummins, *The Texas Permian and its Mesozoic Types of Fossils,* Bulletin 77(1891), Washington, D.C.: Government Printing Office.

Wilson, J. T., "Some Rules for Continental Drift," Royal Society of Canada, Special Publication 9(1966a):3–17.

———. "Did the Atlantic Close and Then Re-open?" *Nature* 211(5050):676–81(1966b).

2

Oceanography

Richard A. Geyer

Introduction

The definition of oceanography ranges from the naive, which includes such terms as "snorkling" and "SCUBA diving," to marine biology and the more accurate description: "a multidisciplinary science dedicated to the study of all scientific aspects of the environment *ocean* in both *space* and *time*." The three emphasized terms characterize the academic and economic problems which are unique to the study of this discipline and which will be discussed later. They also give rise to such questions as (1) What constitutes an oceanographer? and (2) What is the source of funds necessary to provide ships and a wide variety of expensive platforms needed to obtain the data from the astronomic volume (1.35×10^9 kms^3) of water in the world oceans that cover 70 percent of the earth's surface? Research in oceanography involves taking samples, which must be done repeatedly with respect to time and place, now and in the future.

Since the collected samples are studied from many interdisciplinary viewpoints. As a result, several fields quickly developed: biological, chemical, geological, geophysical, and physical oceanography. Each of these is an umbrella for several subspecialties. Studies of the boundary between the ocean and the atmosphere lie within the domains of both meteorology and oceanography.

After World War II the use and importance of oceanography increased dramatically in the academic, industrial, and governmental sectors for a wide variety of reasons. Initially, the public became aware that the ocean could and would play an important role as a source of food, raw materials, recreation, and energy. Later it became more and more apparent that the ocean would become a source of worldwide pollution problems, but that it could also provide some solutions for these and similar problems.

A rapid and major growth of interest in oceanography was also reflected in the proliferation of degree-granting programs in the academic sector, when it became obvious that there would be an ever-increasing demand for personnel to staff marine operations as well as research programs, a need that first occurred in the governmental sector, then in industry.

Some oceanographic research was already undertaken in a very limited and uncoordinated manner during expeditions to various sectors of the world's oceans and occasionally on circumnavigations. This era began in the late 1800s, when monarchs from a few seafaring nations with a special interest supplied the necessary funds. During these expeditions, the emphasis was generally on marine biological aspects, with minor attention to chemical and physical oceanography. Marine fisheries research was an exception, for governmental agencies of several maritime nations conducted ocean surveys before the turn of the century, resulting in the rapid development of the sciences of fisheries and biological oceanography.

Before World War II, only three oceanographic institutions existed in the United States: the Scripps Institute of Oceanography, founded at La Jolla, California, in 1924; the group of University of Washington scientists who gathered at the Friday Harbor Marine Laboratory; and the Woods Hole Oceanographic Institute in Massachusetts, founded in 1931 with funds from the Rockefeller Foundation.[1] Degrees in oceanography were not offered at Woods Hole until many years later.

Coordinated efforts to formally train oceanographers as they are known today did not exist in Texas before World War II. However, both federal and state agencies funded laboratories which were primarily involved in the study of marine fisheries and shellfish in the state. The U.S. Fish Commission regularly conducted research cruises in the Gulf of Mexico as early as the 1880s. Even the private sector was involved in these activities. The eminent Louis Agassiz described the research results of many cruises of the vessel *Blake*.[2] Findings made by scientists from Yale University laboratories during a cruise of the *Mabel Taylor* in 1932 were described by Alfred Parr.[3]

The history of oceanography in Texas is reflected in the activities that occurred during the time when four separate marine laboratories and institutes were founded and developed in the state: the University of Texas Marine Laboratory at Port Aransas, the Department of Oceanography at Texas A&M University, the Applied Research Laboratories of the University of Texas, and the Marine Science Institute of the University of Texas. Interwoven with the activities and developments at these academic institutions, which will be discussed in the following sections, were the oceanographic research and studies carried out or sponsored by government agencies and industrial concerns.

The Oyster Mortality Program

One of the incidents which may have triggered a change in attitude toward oceanographic education in Texas was the sudden death of masses of oysters in 1940. Mass mortality of oysters along the Gulf of Mexico had been recorded and studied in detail as early as the late 1800s. However, in 1940 a group of oyster growers along the Gulf brought suits against several oil companies, claiming that oil operations were responsible for a wave of recurrent mortalities that were severely endangering the oyster industry. These were landmark suits, not only legally but also scientifically.

In an effort to discover the actual cause or causes of the deaths, the oil companies involved—with the exception of the Gulf Oil Corporation—formed a consortium to provide adequate funds for a detailed study of the problem. A major research contract was awarded to the Texas A&M Research Foundation to conduct the necessary studies.

The multimillion dollar project was coordinated by A. Jakkula, the Director of the Foundation. The bulk of the research on the project was conducted by the faculty and staff of various departments of the Texas Agricultural and Mechanical College with emphasis on biological and chemical aspects. But the college also contracted the help of other laboratories and universities as well as individual consultants throughout the states of Texas, Louisiana, and Mississippi. A wide variety of scientific disciplines, including biology, geology, chemistry, and physics, played a role in this program. Charles C. Doak, John G. Mackin, Sewell H. Hopkins, and Charles C. Hancock spearheaded the studies. In addition, Mackin was responsible for the organization and operation of the special laboratory established at Grand Isle, Louisiana. The laboratory facilities of Louisiana State University and, to a lesser extent, laboratory facilities in Mississippi were used as well. William Hewitt of Texas Christian University at Fort Worth was responsible for the study—extensive both in area and time—of salinity and temperature variations in Barataria Bay and contiguous areas. The Marine Laboratory of the University of Texas, established at Port Aransas in 1941, also played a leading role, especially when laboratory and field studies were required. E. J. Lund was the director of the Marine Laboratory, but many projects were run by Gordon Gunter, who later became the director of the laboratory at Gulfport, Mississippi.

This study was carried out between 1945 and 1948 and was the first example of an extensive interdisciplinary cooperative research program conducted in this region. Involving a half dozen universities and laboratories, the program was the forerunner of many other cooperative ventures during the ensuing decades as oceanography in Texas matured. Most of the scientists involved arrived at a consensus about the cause or causes of this oyster mortality wave. However, the cases were settled out of court, and the findings of the scientists were never subjected to a legal test. The scientific results and the conclusion drawn from them are buried in the extensive literature that was compiled during the investigation. Unfortunately, no review of that literature has ever been published due to the extremely interdisciplinary nature of the subject and the immense number of detailed reports and monographs that were prepared and distributed to the various participants in the program.

There was, however, one tangible outcome of the program. The State of Texas established the Texas Game, Fish, and Oyster Commission, which in turn supported a new research laboratory at Rockport: the Texas Fish and Wildlife Laboratory, a state agency founded in 1948 (fig. 1). Currently under the direction of Tom Heffernan, it supports a professional and technical staff of twenty-one persons. Boats for research activity include a 45-foot shrimper and auxiliary shallow-water craft. Research activities emphasize the solution to shallow-water marine, bay, and estuarine environmental problems.

The University of Texas Marine Laboratory

Soon after the University of Texas was established in 1876, the Department of Zoology recognized that the natural resources of the state included a shore environment of approximately 4 percent of the total area of the state. Most of the fresh-water fish and upland game had been exhausted by the settler's need for food. The use of explosives and nets across the passes

Figure 1. Texas Fish and Wildlife Laboratory at Rockport, Texas.

into the bays and estuaries had considerably reduced marine fisheries' resources because the fish were being caught while they migrated during their spawning activities.

The first report of the Texas Fish Commissioner for the year 1880 described the loss of wildlife in both the fresh and marine waters. Over the next ten years many fish were imported for seeding, and hatcheries were developed. At the turn of the century a marine fish hatchery at Galveston was proposed. Fish from other areas were introduced, including carp and eel from Europe, but there was a need to understand the shoreline environment.

This need was first expressed in 1892 in an exhibit attached to a report by the Board of Regents of the University of Texas to Governor James S. Hogg:

> The Coast of the great State of Texas, washed up by the tides and currents of that magnificent inland sea, the Gulf of Mexico, offers at the very door of the State University an unrivaled opportunity for the establishment of a marine station. Strange animals and plants, of a fauna and a flora little known, invite the research of the student and investigator.[4]

This statement was made at a time when marine science was an important topic of conversation around the world. The Zoological Station of Anton Dohrn was under development in Naples, Italy, and a treaty for the international exploitation of the North Sea was under consideration.

Because funds were not available and the coast was plagued with major storms, the dream of a marine laboratory was not realized until fifty years later and after several unsuccessful starts. As early as September 15, 1892, the UT Board of Regents had recommended the establishment of a marine facility on the site of the old Galveston quarantine station, and had requested an appropriation of $5,000 for equipment. But the twenty-third Texas legislature did not even consider the bill introduced, and awarding of the funds was precluded. Shortly thereafter, the first University of Texas field study was begun on Bimini Island in the Bahamas.

In May of 1900 the board appropriated $300 to establish a marine laboratory at the UT Medical School in Galveston (now the University of Texas, Medical Branch). The first class of five students enrolled to study the littoral and shallow water in the vicinity of Galveston Bay and the shoreline. In the same year, a University of Texas regent, G. W. Brackenridge, donated a steam launch for research purposes as well as $300 for its conversion, but the terrible tropical storm that year all but destroyed the vessel. Fifteen years later he donated the *Navidad*, a 114-foot schooner, for the same purpose; it too was so badly damaged by a tropical storm that year that it was never repaired.

No further attempt was made until 1941, when the efforts of E. J. Lund of the Department of Zoology to establish a small marine laboratory finally met with success. With others, he had worked to demonstrate the uniqueness of the area and the need for public education and research in this vital section of the state. Moreover, Lund had interested several persons within the University of Texas in plans to construct a sizable marine laboratory on the coast. He discussed these plans with W. Boone Walker, then mayor of Port Aransas, who reacted by offering the university in 1940 a ten-acre tract of his own property for the site. In addition, Lund purchased twelve acres from the Corps of Engineers, Department of the Army, and donated it to the university.

Through Lund's efforts, the UT Development Board obtained an initial grant of $25,000 a year toward constructing and outfitting the proposed laboratory. Early in its history, funds were provided to buy books and periodicals, not only for the laboratory but also for the main library on the Austin campus. Currently, over 200 periodicals are available at Port Aransas; and the UT-Austin geology library has two copies of the *Challenger* reports and the activities of the *Blake* expedition.

Between 1948 and 1956 the laboratory at Port Aransas served primarily as a biological field station, usually with two residents. The number of buildings on the site had grown to six, including the pier laboratory used for experiments requiring running sea water. During this period, Gordon Gunter and Henry Hildebrand served as director and acting director, respectively.

Under the direction of H. T. Odum (1956–61), five scientists were added—a chemist, a zoologist, a geologist, a botanist, and a microbiologist. The small buildings were converted into laboratories, and the library was significantly enlarged both through purchases and gifts. During this period the academic activities of the laboratory staff were served through the respective science departments in Austin. Staff members held the position of lecturer in the Departments of Chemistry, Botany, Zoology, and Microbiology. In 1968 these positions were upgraded to professorships.

The staff continued to hold joint appointments at the Austin campus and at the Marine Laboratory. Class activities involving both upper division and

Figure 2. Longhorn, *Institute of Marine Science, University of Texas at Port Aransas, Texas.*

graduate school participation were catalogued in the Department of Marine Studies, with many classes cross-listed. During this period other departments organized marine-related programs in the fields of engineering, aerospace, architecture, and education. Unfortunately, no attempt was made to consolidate these into a total interdisciplinary marine program which would provide the student with a good education relating to the oceanic environment.

For many years the Laboratory used the eighty-foot steel-hulled vessel *Longhorn* (fig. 2) for research. During the expansion period under Odum's direction, new facilities were added using matching funds obtained from the U.S. Public Health Service, the National Science Foundation (NSF), and the Atomic Energy Commission. A new 25,000 square foot building provided space for an expanding library of 2,000 books and a commensurate number of bound periodicals, temperature rooms, and a one-pass air-conditioning system. However, running sea water was still only available at the pier laboratory. During the expansion period from 1961 to 1965, Patrick Parker served as acting director and then director.

In 1965 Donald E. Wohlschlag, who had been active in Antarctic programs and fish physiology at Stanford University, became director. No major changes were made until his successor, Carl Oppenheimer from Florida, initiated a program in marine microbiology. Oppenheimer and Parker had both served under Odum but had left the UT Marine Laboratory only to return later to the magnetically attractive environment of Port Aransas.

In 1968 the university acquired forty-nine acres of adjacent land from the government. Appropriation of $3,000,000 funded construction of a building system

Figure 3. Laboratory at Port Aransas of the Institute of Marine Science, UT-Austin.

Figure 4. National Marine Fisheries Laboratory at Port Aransas, Texas.

that included 60,000 square feet in a new two-story laboratory building (fig. 3). This laboratory was also used by John Mackin of Texas A&M University (TAMU) for research on the basic physiology of oysters and the impact of hydrocarbons on their growth and reproduction. When the facilities of the National Marine Fisheries Laboratory at Port Aransas (fig. 4) became available, UT–Austin obtained a lease for its use jointly with TAMU and the Texas Park and Wildlife Service.

Among the first specific projects undertaken after the red tide research[5] were studies conducted by Lund and Gunter on the distribution, life histories, and relative abundance of the marine fishes of Texas.[6] During this time, Lund also carried out experiments in

biophysics and physiology. In the period before the Marine Laboratory became part of the Marine Science Institute of the University of Texas in 1974, eighty-four advanced degrees—thirty-seven doctorates and the others at the master's level—were awarded in such diverse areas as zoology, biology, chemistry, geology, and microbiology.[7]

Early industrial research

Prior to World War II, industry showed little interest in the science of oceanography other than research and studies concerning finfish and shellfish. One major exception was the Dow Chemical Company, which had established a plant in North Carolina but was attracted to the Gulf Coast by the availability of cheap energy. In the late 1930s the company built a processing plant in Freeport, Texas, to produce magnesium and bromine from sea water. William McIlhenny was responsible for coordinating the oceanographic and meteorological aspects of this operation for many years.

Industrial interest increased dramatically after the war when the oil companies began looking to the Gulf of Mexico for oil, gas, and even sulfur. A broad spectrum of oceanographic problems had to be solved to provide safe and successful discovery, production, and transport of these substances—a task that required a detailed knowledge of oceanography. Originally, industry conducted the necessary research primarily through contracts with the faculties and staffs of several universities and private consulting companies in Texas and elsewhere in the United States. Very few companies maintained an extensive in-house capability for this purpose. In 1948 the pioneering Humble Oil & Refining Company established the first commercial oceanographic research group in the industry, headed by the author. Subsequently, this group expanded considerably under the Exxon banner and is still in the forefront in 1986. Shell, Gulf, and Conoco quickly followed in Humble's footsteps.

Emphasis during the early years was on research directed toward a better understanding of the effect of wave forces on offshore production platforms and on submerged pipe lines. During the past ten to fifteen years, industry has also conducted extensive research directed toward solving pollution and other ecological problems, using both in-house capabilities and contracting out to consulting companies.

A number of the early graduates of the oceanography department of TAMU founded oceanographic consulting companies. These provided information to various types of offshore industries. One of the earliest, A. H. Glenn & Associates with offices in New Orleans, Louisiana, and Houston, Texas, was founded in 1948. One of the partners, Charles C. Bates, had received the first doctorate granted by the oceanography department at TAMU. Another, Randolph Blumberg, who had offices in Houston for a number of years, provided the oceanographic data needed to design a platform that would withstand the strongest forces of wind and wave that might be expected.

The Department of Oceanography at TAMU

Although UT–Austin was involved in oceanographic activities through the Marine Laboratory at Port Aransas, it did not develop a major sea-going capability until 1972. About that time other state colleges and universities began to offer courses in oceanography as part of their science curriculum. The emphasis generally was placed on biological and geological aspects. A similar trend, but on a much more restricted scale, occurred in the private universities in Texas such as Rice University in Houston.

The Department of Oceanography at TAMU had gotten its start much earlier because of Jakkula's role as coordinator of the research program designed to find the cause of oyster mortality. While this program was in progress, Jakkula realized that there was a need in the region for a well-rounded oceanography department which could provide trained personnel and adequate facilities to conduct both pure and applied diversified research to solve a broad spectrum of problems. As noted earlier, there were only three institutions of oceanography in the country. At the time, they were too preoccupied with conducting research related to their own specific problems and did not have surplus staff to become involved effectively elsewhere.

Determining a curriculum of studies for students who might be interested in becoming professional oceanographers required a different approach than designing a curriculum for future chemists, for example, because oceanography is necessarily multidisciplinary. Oceanographers need a good grasp of many sciences. This means that a student must acquire a degree in a field of science, engineering, or mathematics as a basis for the study of the oceans, before proceeding to graduate studies. The graduate curriculum is unusual, as the interdisciplinary character of the subject militates against the ever-increasing specialization associated with training in unidisciplinary subjects. During the first phase of graduate studies leading to the Master of Science degree, the student should take a core curriculum in the basic sciences applicable to oceanography. Then, between the master's degree and the doctorate, the student should refocus on studies and research in a particular specialized subject of interest as it applies to oceanographic research.

The TAMU Department of Oceanography, established in 1949, was faced with the problem of designing a suitable curriculum. Dale Leipper, who served as head of the department for the following fifteen years effectively and with distinction, brought together a very competent staff and obtained the nucleus of facilities upon which to build and grow. During the early years its members taught both atmospheric and oceanographic sciences, while doing research in the area of their specialty. The department had the first series of sea-going oceanographic research vessels.[8] In 1956 the Department of Oceanography became the Department of Oceanography and Meteorology, resulting in a very rapid growth. By this date, the faculty had increased to ten members supported by a specialized staff of nearly one hundred people. The operating budget was of the order of one million dollars. From 1957 to 1958 the department served as the "World Data Center" for the International Geophysical Year. In 1964 oceanography and meteorology became separate departments and at the same time were combined with the geology, geography, and geophysics departments to form the College of Geosciences. Horace Byers, formerly with the University of Chicago, became the first dean of the college.

In 1966 the author, who had been director of oceanography for Texas Instruments for a number of years, was appointed head of the oceanography department at TAMU and served in that capacity for over ten years. During this period the faculty increased to thirty members, the supporting staff and the graduate enrollment to more than two hundred. There was a comparable expansion of pertinent facilities, both on the main campus and at the operations base on Pelican Island at Galveston. This included the completion of a new, ten-story building (fig. 5) on the campus to house the Departments of Oceanography and Meteorology, and the operations building at Galveston, which was necessary as logistic support for the newly acquired 186-foot research vessel *Gyre* (fig. 6) and the 21-foot, two-man submersible *Diaphus* (fig. 7). The former was built by the U.S. Navy and was then made

Figure 5. *Oceanography–Meteorology building, TAMU, College Station, Texas.*

Figure 7. Diaphus, *research submersible of the Department of Oceanography, TAMU, berthed at Galveston, Texas.*

Figure 6. Gyre, *oceanographic research vessel of the Department of Oceanography, TAMU, berthed at Galveston, Texas.*

available to the department on bailment. The department's annual budget to support these diversified activities had increased to nearly five million dollars.

The Department of Oceanography at TAMU was responsible for almost one quarter of all the master's and doctoral degrees granted in oceanography by the early 1970s—a peak fraction, for during the late 1960s institutions granting graduate degrees in oceanography had proliferated dramatically. Almost one half of this number remained in the academic community, one third went into governmental agencies, and the remainder into industry. Over 30 percent of the graduates remained in Texas after graduation.

From the late 1960s the geographic scope of research activities expanded well beyond the Gulf of Mexico into the Atlantic and Mediterranean as well as to the Antarctica. The most recent major achievement occurred in 1984, when TAMU was designated as the operating arm of the Ocean Drilling Program, sponsored by the National Science Foundation.[9] As part of the support services for this program, a $2,000,000 core laboratory is now (1986) under construction on the campus. Core samples taken from the Gulf of Mexico, Caribbean Sea, South Atlantic Ocean, and Indian Ocean will be stored there. They will be available for scientific study in the laboratory by qualified research personnel from other institutions as well as from TAMU.

For many years the department has been a member of domestic and international organizations such as the Joint Oceanographic Institutions, Inc. (JOI) and the University National Oceanographic Laboratory System (UNOLS). These memberships permit the oceanography department to assume a major active role in both planning and directing national and international oceanographic expeditions and programs.

Visits by distinguished members of the oceanographic community, from both the United States and abroad, have always been welcomed by the department because they facilitate and enhance the global interchange of scientific ideas and data. Many visitors have come for various periods of time and from all over the world: from Europe, Canada, Australia, New

Zealand, as well as Mexico and other parts of Latin and South America. In addition, many visiting scientists have been able to spend sabbaticals and more extended periods doing research at the department. These visitors have included, for example, Enrique Balech, Grethe R. Hasle, and G. A. Knox from Argentina, Norway, and New Zealand, respectively; R. Marumu, S. Fukase, and Y. Sugimura from Japan; Elzbieta Kopczynska from Poland; and Mao Xinghua and Zhang Kuncheng from the Peoples Republic of China.

The department was a pioneer in the use of submersibles by academic institutions in oceanographic research programs. As early as 1974, it had acquired its own two-man submersible, *Diaphus*. Since then it has been engaged in a wide variety of underwater activities. *Diaphus* is 21 feet long, cruises at 2 knots, and has a depth capability of 1200 feet. Many of its frequent dives were made to accumulate data from direct oceanographic observations in the study of a broad range of pollution problems. This included the study of off-shore reefs along the entire continental shelf of Texas and Louisiana, with emphasis on the ecological

aspects.[10] For the most part these dives were conducted under the auspices of the Bureau of Land Management of the Department of the Interior. Similarly, dives were made to study naturally occurring hydrocarbon seeps in the same general geographic area for a major research program conducted for a consortium of oil companies. The maiden voyage of *Diaphus* included a total of 60 hours of underwater dives off the Texas coast, varying in depth from 65 to 300 feet. Geological features, biotic communities, and natural gas seeps associated with five natural reefs were investigated and documented using still and motion pictures.

The Applied Research Laboratories of the University of Texas

The second phase in the development of oceanographic capabilities for UT–Austin began in 1965 with the merger of the Military Physics Research Laboratory, founded in 1942 as part of the Physics Department, and the Defense Research Laboratory, organized in

Figure 8. Applied Research Laboratories, UT-Austin.

Figure 9. Field Testing Facilities, ARL–UT-Austin.

1946, to form the Applied Research Laboratories of the University of Texas at Austin (ARL–UT–Austin) (figs. 8 and 9). The Defense Research Laboratory had been an outgrowth of a program begun at the Harvard Underwater Sound Laboratory (HUSL) during World War II. HUSL had lent support to the U.S. Navy by advancing our limited knowledge of acoustics and by getting the Navy to adopt acoustical equipment for its fleet. The importance of both of these roles was recognized, and the Navy made a strong declaration of its intention to continue its interaction with the universities. When C. P. Boner returned to UT–Austin from his position as deputy director at HUSL, he founded the Defense Research Laboratory and became its first director. Loyd Hampton is the current director.

At present (1986), ARL–UT–Austin has 140 professionals and about the same number of students working on a wide spectrum of applied problems. The laboratory has supported approximately 300 master's theses and 125 doctoral dissertations during its history. About 20 percent of the research programs are concerned with the use of satellites for navigation and

geodetic problems. The major effort is to establish the limits of accuracy for measurements made with the new geodetic positioning system (GPS). Of special interest to oceanographers is the system's potential for reconstructing ship motion in three dimensions to within a few centimeters.

The remainder of the program is devoted to underwater sound projects. Most of the tasks performed are supported by the Navy, but the technology spinoffs include a significant number of contributions to oceanography. In 1966, relationships between acoustics and oceanography were examined by Lindsay, who concluded that "a new field of acoustical research has been opened up as a branch of Physical Oceanography".[11] Kibblewhite has developed the usefulness of underwater sound in investigating the environment.[12]

ARL–UT–Austin has made many contributions to methods of data management, data analysis, and signal processing. Numerous developments in instrumentation have had direct application to oceanography. Placing instrumentation packages in the ocean for research programs in underwater sound (and getting them back!) has contributed to the development of ocean engineering techniques. ARL–UT–Austin has participated in many ocean acoustic measuring programs in which the goal of total characterization of the acoustic environment has increased our understanding of ocean properties and dynamics. Of special interest to oceanographers is the current study of acoustic properties of ocean sediments. It has now been recognized that information about the physical and geological properties of the sediments can be extracted from those acoustic studies. Knowledge of these properties is essential for the design and use of a wide range of acoustic systems.

The Marine Science Institute and the Institute for Geophysics of the University of Texas

The UT–Austin Marine Science Institute (fig. 10) was organized by combining the resources of three campuses of the university: the UT Marine Biomedical Institute in Galveston, the Marine Laboratory at Port Aransas, and several departments of UT–Austin. This new institute represented the third phase of the development of oceanographic capabilities at the university. The first step involved establishing a new laboratory in Galveston in 1972 as part of the Earth and Planetary Sciences Division of the Marine Biomedical Institute of the University of Texas Medical Branch. Maurice Ewing, who had been director of the Lamont-Doherty Geological Observatory of Columbia University, was chosen as the first director.[13] Ewing died soon after and was succeeded by one of his colleagues, Lamar Worzel. The laboratory adopted the new name, Galveston Marine Geophysical Laboratory (GMGL). In 1974 the programs at the three campuses were merged to form the Marine Science Institute. Creighton Burk, a geologist with Mobil Oil Corporation, became the first director of the new institute. In addition, he became a chairman of the Department of Marine Studies at Austin. Worzel continued as director of the GMGL, and Oswald Roels, also from the Lamont-Doherty Geological Observatory, was appointed director of the Marine Laboratory in Port

Figure 10. Laboratory of the Institute of Marine Science, University of Texas at Port Aransas, Texas, and the Lorene.

Aransas. The aquaculture research that he had conducted at St. Croix in the Virgin Islands was transferred to the University of Texas. When Burk resigned in 1978 because of illness, he was succeeded by Robert Moore from the University of Alaska, where he had been conducting an active program in marine mining and where he had been the editor of the *Marine Mining Journal.*

With the completion of yet another reorganization in 1982, the university entered a fourth phase of the development of its oceanographic capabilities. Robert Jones, a fisheries biologist from the Harbor Branch Laboratory in Florida, became director of the Marine Science Institute at Port Aransas and was also appointed chairman of the Department of Marine Studies in Austin. Arthur Maxwell, former associate director of the Woods Hole Oceanographic Institution, became the director of a separate Institute for Geophysics of the university, with faculty activities centered in the Department of Geological Sciences. When the center of research activities was moved from Galveston to Austin, the fledgling Institute for Geophysics benefitted from the stimulus of proximity to other major components of the university having interest in the earth sciences. These included the Department of Geological Sciences and its students, the Bureau of Economic Geology, and ARL–UT–Austin.

Virtually all the research activities and staff had moved from Galveston to Austin by the end of 1982. However, the GMGL, including the computerized vessel *Fred H. Moore* (fig. 11) and the 150-foot *Ida Green,* which had been donated in 1972 by Cecil and Ida Green of Dallas, remains an important component of

Figure 11. Research vessel Fred H. Moore, *Institute for Geophysics, UT-Austin.*

the institute. Besides serving as a base for ships and as a staging area for research cruises, it houses core and dredge sample collections as well as laboratories. As one result of an agreement between UT–Austin and TAMU signed by the presidents of both universities in the late summer of 1983, the use of the institute's Galveston facilities is shared with those of the Department of Oceanography at TAMU, which also operates its own oceanographic research vessels out of its marine facilities at Galveston.

The Institute for Geophysics is a nationally and internationally recognized research unit of UT–Austin. It was established to serve the research and graduate teaching needs of the university. The institute conducts geophysical investigations of the history, structure, and dynamics of the earth's crust and mantle, with emphasis on the ocean basins and margins, and on earthquakes. Development of new methods and instruments for these studies is an integral part of the institute's activities, as is the training of graduate students. Its research programs provide information fundamental to a better understanding of the physical evolution of the earth and the processes that shape it. Thus they also have a bearing on geologic exploration for natural resources, environmental problems associated with extraction of minerals, problems of earthquake prediction and the characteristics of strong earthquake motion, and the phenomena associated with acoustic transmission in the ocean and through the sea floor.

The interests of the staff and students at the institute are very broad, ranging from lunar seismology to paleobiogeography. In addition to oceanographic sample collections, the resources of the institute include an extensive collection of multichannel marine seismic data, worldwide seismograms on microfilm, and the entire collection of lunar and Martian seismic data obtained during the *Apollo* and *Viking* projects. The present research staff numbers about thirty scientists and engineers, of whom approximately one third hold joint appointments with the Department of Geological Sciences, and forty-five staff members who provide overall support. At this writing, more than twenty-five graduate students are associated with the institute.

Many of the institute's programs focus on the Gulf of Mexico and the Caribbean and Central American regions. However, recent projects have involved work off Morocco, Indonesia, Alaska, and in the South Atlantic. The institute encourages cooperative research with scientists from other departments within the university or from other institutions, both within the

Unitcd States and abroad. This provides important opportunities for the research staff to exchange data and ideas with colleagues on a worldwide basis. For example, the institute's scientists have been active in research off Morocco in conjunction with colleagues from TAMU and the Lamont-Doherty Geological Observatory; in the southwest Pacific Ocean as part of the internationally funded Ocean Drilling Program; and off eastern Canada in conjunction with scientists from the Woods Hole Oceanographic Institution. Through membership in organizations such as JOI and UNOLS, the UT–Austin Marine Science Institute plays an active role in the planning and direction of major national and international research-related activities.

The Role of Governmental Agencies in Oceanographic Research

Before World War II, governmental agencies such as the U.S. and Texas Fish Commissions, the Bureau of Commercial Fisheries, and the Coast and Geodetic Survey conducted much of their own research in the Gulf of Mexico, especially off the shore of Texas. Although it might be argued that the role of these agencies continued to be very important in the development of oceanography in the Gulf of Mexico, the format that was used differed markedly. For example, to an appreciable extent, data gathering and analysis activities were not performed directly by the agencies, but were carried out by the various oceanographic institutions through grants and contracts from these agencies. Among others added later were the Bureau of Land Management and, to a lesser extent, parts of the National Oceanographic and Atmospheric Administration (NOAA).

After the war, two very important new sources of funding for oceanographic research programs surfaced: the Office of Naval Research of the U.S. Navy, and NSF. They became the mainstay for support of oceanographic research in a variety of forms, including funding for the construction and operation of large, deep-water, oceanographic research ships, particularly during the period from 1946 to about 1970. Unfortunately, funding by the Office of Naval Research has decreased substantially since the 1970s, especially for ship operations. Though NSF support for most programs generally reached a plateau, the worldwide Ocean Drilling Program continues to be funded in a meaningful way to this day.

A part of the decline in individual support could be attributed to the nationwide proliferation of new oceanographic institutions. These were all seeking their share of an annual budget that had not even begun to expand commensurately nor to keep up with the inflation that was so rampant from the middle to late 1970s and early 1980s. To put it simply, a smaller pie was being cut into more pieces. Reduction in available funds has also decreased the number of students entering graduate school. Fewer scholarships and research programs are available, and there has been a marked decline in career opportunities.

This era of lack of adequate funding for oceanographic research might have been avoided if many of the major recommendations of the Commission on Marine Science, Engineering and Resources had been implemented. This Commission was appointed by President Johnson in 1967 and was known more generally as the "Stratton Commission" after its chairman, Julius A. Stratton, President Emeritus of the Massachusetts Institute of Technology. The author, then head of the Department of Oceanography at TAMU, was the vice-chairman of the Commission. The twenty-three members and the large staff were very active from 1967 to 1969. Hearings were held in all of the major coastal cities of the United States, including the Great Lakes cities. The results of these investigations appeared in January 1969 in the Stratton Report, a lengthy collection of documents describing in detail the methods used, the conclusions reached, and the recommendations made by the many subcommittees charged with studying the multifaceted problems associated with this broad task.[14]

Two major recommendations were made: that adequate funding for a system of UNOLS that would include existing oceanographic institutions be provided and that NOAA be established. Although the first recommendation was not implemented, the second one was. But because the prevalence of criteria based on jurisdictional, political, and territorial protection considerations excluded many government agencies that logically should have been a part of the NOAA administration, it never reached the critical mass needed to achieve the original objectives of the commission. As a result, it never had the political clout necessary to obtain the required overall funding. Furthermore, at least initially, the needs of the oceanographically oriented components included in NOAA became somewhat subordinated to those of the atmospheric components.

The Stratton Report had far-reaching repercussions for subsequent development of oceanography in Texas and elsewhere in the nation. Aside from the funding aspects, it had one tangible effect: immediately after the report was issued, a group of Texas state legislators convinced the sixty-first Legislature to form an Interim Study Commission of Oceanography.[15] For thirteen months until January 1971, this committee functioned in a manner quite similar to that of the Stratton Commission, except on a much more restricted scale financially and geographically. Moreover, the report was limited to twenty pages and the number of hearings to seven. They were held in various cities on a variety of topics. In Beaumont the focus was on offshore oil and gas production and the construction industry; in Galveston, on commercial fisheries and maritime industries; in Harlingen, on tourism and the water development industry; in Dallas, on legal, financial, and insurance aspects of marine resource development as well as on the chemical and mineral industry; in Corpus Christi, on state regulatory agencies and high technology industry; and in Bryan on academic interests in Texas.

The principal recommendation made by the commission was the establishment of a Texas Council on Marine Related Affairs to provide the legislature, the governor, and the people of Texas with a source of experienced judgment and expert advice. This council was subsequently established as a forum where lawmakers could join with experts in marine affairs to plan the state's future as the nation's leading coastal state. Two other recommendations were made: (1) "We do not completely reject the idea of an Institute of Oceanography, but we recognize that marine-oriented programs in existing institutions are still in their formative stage," and (2) "We believe that the administration of the state's marine-related programs should be handled, not by independent agencies, but through the office of the Chief Executive Officer of the State, the Governor."

The Role of Industry in Oceanographic Research

Although industry has been primarily a user—rather than a supplier—of data obtained through oceanographic research, there have been a few exceptions. For example, Texas Instruments Incorporated (TI) of Dallas pioneered in supplying information in the early 1950s for the oil industry as it turned to the sea, first on the continental shelf in the Gulf of Mexico, and subsequently on a worldwide basis. Its first marine geophysical ship, the *Sonic*, started operations at this time. In the beginning, TI concentrated on obtaining marine seismic data but later looked for

magnetic and gravity information as well. Its oceanographic base was broadened in the early 1960s by helping to develop and then field ocean-bottom seismometer systems. These instruments placed on the bottom of the ocean were retrieved after a period of some months by sending properly coded acoustic signals from a ship. The instruments were returned to the surface where the data obtained were analyzed and used to augment pure seismological data from land observations to study the earth's crustal structure and to monitor clandestine nuclear blasts.

During the middle 1960s, marine geophysical surveys were conducted by TI for the U.S. Navy. In addition to seismic and magnetic data, a variety of instruments were used to gather acoustic information from the ocean bottom and in the water column from various parts of the Atlantic Ocean. Subsequently, these data were analyzed in detail, and the results were used to help solve military as well as purely oceanographic problems.

As the need to study ecological problems increased in the middle 1970s, TI again broadened its oceanographic capabilities, this time conducting ecological baseline studies on the continental shelf along the east coast of the United States. These data were also subjected to sophisticated analyses. TI was not alone in its interest in ecological research. An earlier example was the support given by the oil industry to the Oyster Mortality Research Program, described in some detail earlier.

Other pioneers in marine geophysical surveys include the Western Geophysical Company, Digicon, United, and the Seismic Service Corporation (SSC). The Tracor Company in Austin has been very active in supplying oceanographic data to a number of U.S. governmental agencies. It also provides support vessels for this purpose and data analyses of marine acoustics surveys.

Industry also played a major role during this period in supporting oceanographic institutions with undergraduate and graduate fellowships as well as providing a significant amount of unrestricted operating and equipment funds through grants. These have been used to augment other sources of funding for faculty and staff engaged in pure research. In addition, major support in the form of donating research vessels has been provided from time to time. For example, in 1978 the Mobil Oil Corporation gave the 165-foot ocean-going research ship *Fred H. Moore* to the Galveston Geophysical Laboratory of the University of Texas.

Industrial concerns also support oceanographic institutions significantly by regularly underwriting long-term research programs that demand guaranteed

Figure 12. Computer Laboratory of the Fred H. Moore, *berthed at Galveston, Texas. This vessel belongs to the Institute for Geophysics, UT-Austin.*

funds for success. For example, in 1971 a consortium of sixteen oil companies made a long-term commitment—between 1971 and 1978—to a research group in the Department of Oceanography of TAMU to support a study on naturally occurring hydrocarbons in the Gulf of Mexico and the Caribbean Sea. At about the same time, similar grants were made to study the ecology of coral reefs in the Gulf of Mexico. These funds permitted extensive and frequent surveys at sea by ocean-going ships, as well as the use of the submersible *Diaphus* for continued underwater observations and sampling. Detailed and sophisticated analyses were made of various types of data obtained from the water column and on the bottom.

Oceanography in Scientific Literature

The interdisciplinary character of oceanography inevitably makes bibliographic searches difficult. There are many journals and periodicals dealing directly with the subject, but many more pertinent references in specialized literature treat the biological, chemical, geological, geophysical, mathematical, and engineering sciences. Then there are a myriad of other journals of broader scope, such as *Nature* and *Science,* as well as foreign language journals.

Of the numerous books and monographs on oceanography, few are restricted to the Gulf of Mexico, and especially Texas. Before World War II almost nothing had been written about the Gulf, largely because little had been done there. For example, there were only four expeditions to the Gulf of Mexico between 1800 and 1930, while there were over one hundred to the Arctic and Antarctic during the same period. Both

UT–Austin and TAMU rectified this situation after World War II by publishing research in several *Contributions* series, designed to provide the scientific community with a more comprehensive treatment of the current status of oceanographic research in this area.

Ecological oceanographic studies are multiplying. For example, a coordinated and detailed research program has been conducted for the last ten years on the coral reefs of the Gulf, under the auspices of the Bureau of Land Management of the U.S. Geological Survey by the TAMU Department of Oceanography.[16] Hydrocarbon pollution of the oceans has increased in recent years, which has given rise to an expanding literature.[17]

Finally, two comprehensive annotated bibliographies dealing specifically with the Gulf have been published,[18] but thirty-five years have elapsed since the most recent one, and a new bibliography would be of great benefit to researchers.

Notes

1. Until the beginning of World War II, the Woods Hole Oceanographic Institute operated only during the summer months and was staffed with university scientists who were interested in the ocean.

2. Agassiz, 1888.

3. Parr, 1935.

4. Report to Governor Hogg, 1892.

5. Red tide is a term used by oceanographers to describe a cause of mass mortality of marine organisms, especially of fish in the shallower waters of the continental shelves of much of the World Oceans. It is generally believed to be caused by overturning of the water column, bringing nutrient-rich waters toward the surface. This in turn permits microorganisms such as dinoflagellites to multiply in such numbers that the supply of dissolved oxygen becomes insufficient to support life for the macroorganisms, such as fish, in the immediate area. It is also believed by some scientists that certain of these microorganisms secrete into the water toxic substances which may also help to kill the fish.

6. These studies appeared in the first issue of *Publications of the Institute of Marine Science of the University of Texas.*

7. See acknowledgments for contributors to this section.

8. These research vessels included the *Jakkula, Hidalgo,* and *Alaminos.* In the mid-1950s the *Hidalgo* participated in a joint expedition off Puerto Rico involving vessels from the Lamont-Doherty

Geological Observatory and several governmental agencies.

9. The first vessel used for this purpose was the *Glomar Challenger*. It was built in a New Orleans shipyard, and as part of its shakedown cruise drilled several core holes in the Gulf of Mexico. It continued to serve in this capacity for nearly twenty years at many locations in the oceans of the world.

10. Rezak, et al., 1985. Bright, 1974.

11. Lindsay, 1966, p. 642. There is a good bibliography associated with the article.

12. Kibblewhite, 1974.

13. Maurice Ewing was born in Texas and received his doctorate from Rice University in Houston in the late 1903s. He spent World War II at the Woods Hole Oceanographic Institution in Massachusetts, conducting research into the military applications of marine acoustics and seismic surveys. Subsequently, he became the first director of the Lamont Doherty-Geological Observatory, a component of Columbia University in New York. There he conducted marine, seismic, gravity, and magnetic surveys on a global scale. The analysis of data obtained has led to a better understanding of the geology and geophysics of the oceans and continents. For this research, he and his staff received world-wide recognition.

14. Stratton, 1969. The report was supported by three volumes totaling about 1000 pages: Vol. 1. *Science and Environment*; Vol. 2, *Industry and Technology*; Vol. 3, *Marine Resources and Legal-Political Arrangements for their development*.

15. The Commission was formed in accordance with H.S.R. 381. Members were: Representatives Ray Lemmon (Chairman), Lauro Cruze, Forrest Harding, Menton Murray, and Bill Presnal as well as Richard Geyer, George Kozmetsky, Robert Bybee, Cecil Green, Jot Hodges, and William McIlhenny.

16. Rezak et al., 1985; Bright and Pequegnat, 1974.

17. For example, see Geyer, 1980 and 1981.

18. Galtsoff, 1940; Geyer, 1950.

Bibliography

Agassiz, Louis. *Cruises of the Blake, 1877–1880.* New York, Houghton Mifflin Co., 1888.

Bright, Thomas J., and Pequegnat, Linda H. *The Biota of the West Flower Garden Bank*, Gulf Publishing Co., Houston, 1974.

Capurro, Louis, and Reid, J. L., Eds. *Contributions on the Physical Oceanography of the Gulf of Mexico*, Houston, Gulf Publishing Co., 1972.

El Sayed, Z, et al. *Chemistry, Primary Productivity and Benthic Algae of the Gulf of Mexico.* New York, American Geographical Society, Serial Atlas, 1971.

Galtsoff, Paul. *Gulf of Mexico—its Origin, Waters and Marine Life.* Washington, D.C., U.S. Department of Interior, Fish and Wildlife Service, Fishery Bulletin #89, Vol. 55, 1940.

Geyer, Richard A. "Annotated Bibliography of the Gulf of Mexico." *Texas Journal of Science*, 2 (1950), 49–93.

Geyer, Richard. "Marine Environmental Pollution (Ocean Mining and Dumping)." *Oceanography Series*, Vol. 27B, Amsterdam, Elsevier Press, 1981.

Geyer, Richard, et al. "Marine Environmental Pollution (Hydrocarbons)." *Oceanography Series*, Vol. 27A, Amsterdam, Elsevier Press, 1980.

Graham, Joe, and Geyer, Richard A. "The Use of Meteorology in the Oil Industry." Preprint, American Petroleum Institute Proceedings, 1950.

Kibblewhite, A. C., "The Interaction of Underwater Acoustics and Marine Geophysics," in Hampton, L., Ed. *Physics of Sound in Marine Sediments.* Plenum Press, 1974.

Lindsay, R. Bruce. "The Story of Acoustics." *J. Acoust. Soc. Am.*, 5 (1966), 629–44.

Pequegnat, Willis and Chase, F. A., Jr., Eds. *Contributions on the Biological Oceanography of the Gulf of Mexico.* Houston, Gulf Publishing Co., 1970.

Pequegnat, Willis, et al. *Gulf of Mexico Deep Sea Fauna; Decapods and Euphausiasea.* New York, American Geographical Society, Serial Atlas, 1972.

Rezak, Richard, and Henry, Vernon J., Eds. *Contributions on the Geological and Geophysical Oceanography of the Gulf of Mexico.* Houston, Gulf Publishing Co., 1972.

Rezak, Richard, Bright, Thomas J., and McGrail, David W. *Reefs and Banks of the Northwestern Gulf of Mexico and their Geological, Biological and Physical Dynamics.* New York, John Wiley & Sons, 1985.

Stratton, Jay, et al. *Our Nation and the Sea.* Report of the Commission on Marine Science, Engineering and Resources, Washington, D.C., Government Printing Office, 1969.

Texas A&M University, Department of Oceanography. *Contributions in Oceanography.* College Station, Private Printing, Vols. 1–16, 1957–73.

University of Texas Institute of Marine Science, *Contributions to Marine Science*, Austin, Private Printing, 1945–Present.

3

Meteorology

John F. Griffiths and

James R. Scoggins

Sources of Weather Data

In a broad sense of the term, the science of meteorology had its beginnings in Texas around 1830, when a few temperature and precipitation measurements were made at isolated sites. By 1850 observations were being taken at about twenty stations, but it was not until 1886 that the number of stations in operation was sufficient to provide representative values for the whole state. In August of the same year, Indianola was wiped out by a hurricane and was never rebuilt, and in October floods in Jefferson County associated with a hurricane caused one hundred fifty deaths.

The U.S. government has operated weather stations in Texas since 1850. Between 1850 and 1876 the War Department made weather observations at El Paso; it started making weather observations at Galveston in 1871. Later, this station, located in the downtown area, was taken over by the Weather Bureau. It has the longest continuous record of weather observations of any station in Texas—from July 1881 to the present. Governmental weather stations in the state are listed in Table 1 according to the year in which they began operating. The station at Hondo is a weather radar facility, and those at Stephenville and Longview are combined radar and sounding facilities.

Originally, the Texas Weather Service acted in conjunction with the Signal Service of the U.S. Army. In 1891 it became part of the Weather Bureau, which was under the U.S. Department of Agriculture until 1940, when it came under the U.S. Department of Commerce.

A valuable source for weather observations in Texas has been a network of cooperative observers. These unpaid observers, who have performed a valuable service for Texans, and will continue to do so, receive little recognition. Some of those who served for long periods are listed in Table 2. Many others should be commended as well.

Anomalous Texas Weather

The 1890s saw some unique weather situations in Texas. In mid-February 1895, from ten to thirty inches of snow fell along the upper coast from Beaumont to Victoria. On February 12, 1899, the state recorded its coldest night ever, with the lowest reading being -23°F at Tulia, Swisher County. The next day the temperature plunged to 12°F at Brownsville. In 1913, floods of the Brazos River led to 177 deaths. The year 1917 gave the state its driest year on record, only 47 percent of

Table 1
Government Weather Stations in Texas

1850 El Paso	1898 Fort Worth	1946 Lubbock
1871 Galveston	1906 Austin	1947 San Angelo
1877 San Antonio	1909 Houston	1953 Midland
1885 Abilene	1922 Brownsville	1972 Hondo
1887 Corpus Christi	1944 Port Arthur	1973 Stephenville
1892 Amarillo	1944 Wichita Falls	1975 Longview

Table 2
Texas Cooperative Weather Observers

Location	Observer	Period
Brownwood	Pearl Smith	1905–1959
Cleburne	W. S. Ownsby	1913–1962
Crowell	Roy Lee and John Lee Black	1932–present
Dimmitt	Edwin Ramey	1923–present
Henderson	Michael Kangerga	1908–1962
Hewitt	Dr. Hallie Earle	1916–1963
Hondo	H. E. Haass	1899–1951
Honey Grove	W. G. and Richard M. McCleary	1916–present
Kaufman	Mr. and Mrs. J. E. Stevens; Mary A. Stringer; Melba A. Stevens; B. J., Bertha, F. V. and Lillian Hubbard	1904–1969
Matagorda	R. R. Traylor	1926–present
Memphis	John J. McMickin	1919–1966
Mexia	Josephine Newman	1909–1913; 1921–1974
Muleshoe	R. J. Klump	1921–1968
Runge	Paul and John Dickson and Addie L. Koenig	1918–present
Sarita	John G. Kenedy and Mrs. John G. Kenedy, Jr.	1899–present
Seymour	Mrs. Veda C. Daugherty	1925–1970

its average annual rainfall. In September 1919, a hurricane caused 234 deaths in and around Corpus Christi.

On September 8, 1900, a devastating hurricane hit Galveston. Although twelve thousand people had evacuated the city earlier, over six thousand deaths were attributed to the storm, and it is estimated that only a thousand people on the island survived. One of Edison's earliest movies gives a first-hand impression of the devastation. Isaac Monroe Cline was the senior meteorologist in Galveston and director of the Texas Section of the Weather Bureau when the storm struck the island. His wife was drowned, but he and other family members survived. Cline, who had earned three doctorates, also taught medical climatology at the University of Texas Medical Branch (UTMB) in Galveston and published numerous scientific articles and books, especially on tropical cyclones.

The 1930s were famous, or infamous, for the long drought. However, Texas fared better than most of the states of the Great Plains. The drought affected the Panhandle and northern counties, but overall, it was not as severe as the drought of the 1950s.

Any synopsis of the Texas weather since 1940 would have to note the state's wettest year ever, 1941, with

153 percent of the average annual rainfall, and the very severe drought that lasted from 1950 through early 1957. On May 11, 1953, Waco was hit by a tornado that caused 114 deaths and damage of over $40 million. Carla, an extreme hurricane, came ashore near Port O'Connor in September 1961, with wind gusts estimated at 175 mph. Because of the early warning, about half a million people evacuated coastal areas, thus keeping the death toll to a minimum. In September 1967, hurricane Beulah hit Brownsville, doing great damage and spawning a record 115 tornadoes. In August 1970, Celia, another extreme hurricane, struck the coast between Corpus Christi and Aransas Pass. Celia was the costliest storm in terms of dollar damage ever to hit the state; damages totaled around half a billion dollars. Tropical storm Claudette made a great impact in July 1979, dumping as much as forty-three inches of rain during twenty-four hours at an unofficial, but checked, site near Alvin.

The first "Tornado Watch" was issued by the U.S. Weather Bureau, now the National Weather Service, on March 17, 1952, and included portions of east Texas and southeast Oklahoma. The severe weather activity was expected to move into south Arkansas and north Louisiana before daybreak the next day. The watch was disseminated by phone to the forecast center serving the affected area. Two tornadoes did occur at that time in north-central Texas, but they were just outside of the watch area. Severe weather watches are now issued whenever necessary, and weather radar continues to be the principal tool for observing severe weather.

Meteorological Education and Research at Texas A&M University (TAMU)

The first recorded educational activity in meteorology, as distinct from climatology, in Texas occurred in 1918. In May and June of that year, three hundred enlisted men attended the School of Meteorology, organized and maintained under the supervision of the Chief Signal Office of the Army. The school was located on the campus of the Texas Agricultural and Mechanical College at College Station, now Texas A&M University. The Director, Oliver L. Fassig, was assisted by Charles F. Brooks and two instructors. The camaraderie that developed in this group led to the foundation in 1919 of the American Meteorological Society. In 1959 the Society celebrated its fortieth anniversary at a meeting on the TAMU campus, with Brooks in attendance.

The use of radar as a meteorological tool was first studied in Texas by Myron Ligda and his colleagues and students at TAMU in the 1950s. The U.S. Air Force installed the first collegiate production model radar, a 3.2 cm AN/CPS-9, at the university in 1957. Vance Moyer replaced Ligda in 1958 and promoted the development of dual-wavelength meteorological radar with the help of George L. Huebner and Jake Canglose. The 10 cm wavelength radar now in use evolved from an earlier SCR-585 radar. Current research led by Huebner at the College Station campus involves the use of Doppler radar data, obtained from the National Severe Storms Laboratory, Norman, Oklahoma. Important climatologies of radar echoes in two Texas areas have been developed by Dennis M. Driscoll.

In February 1952, John C. Freeman, encouraged by Dale F. Leipper, head of the Department of Oceanography, came to the TAMU oceanography department to found the meteorology program. In the summer of that year he was joined by Walter J. Saucier and Guy A. Franceschini. All of these individuals, who had come from the University of Chicago, participated in many research projects and began to teach a program in meteorology for the U.S. Air Force. In 1961, Franceschini received the first doctoral degree in meteorology conferred by TAMU.

In January 1953 an undergraduate curriculum in meteorology within the Department of Oceanography was approved for the fall semester. The courses were designated oceanography courses, and the degree would be an oceanography degree with a meteorology option. Saucier was appointed assistant professor of meteorology. Maurice Halstead, who had also become a member of the faculty, was involved in pioneering work on the use of analogue computers to follow microclimatic processes.

The first class of basic meteorology students sponsored by the U.S. Air Force Institute of Technology (AFIT) to attend TAMU arrived in October 1953. This one-year program has continued uninterrupted to the present with more than one thousand students completing it. The second class of basics and the first Air Force meteorology graduate student enrolled in 1954, along with four civilian undergraduate students. Student enrollment grew steadily and reached more than two hundred in 1975, when the Department of Meteorology was one of the largest in the nation. The present class consists of twenty-two students.

The Second Texas Tornado Conference was held on the TAMU campus in conjunction with the dedication of the Texas Radar Network on June 24 and 25, 1955. This was a significant event for meteorology at

Figure 1. Participants in the Second Texas Tornado Conference and dedication of the Texas Radar Network held at Texas A&M University on June 24 and 25, 1955.

the university because its SCR-585 radar set became part of the network. Many prominent meteorologists attended (see fig. 1). On April 5, 1956, a tornado struck neighboring Bryan with heavy damage but no human casualties because of the warning given. Stuart G. Bigler, radar research scientist who gave the warning, was awarded a special citation by the American Meteorological Society for his alertness. The weather radars and other facilities at TAMU have been used to provide monitoring services to area residents and will continue to fulfill that purpose. At present, these services are provided by Brazos County Civil Defense under the capable direction of Jake Canglose, senior meteorological engineer for the Department of Meteorology.

On September 1, 1956, the oceanography department at TAMU was renamed the Department of Oceanography and Meteorology. Faculty of the department in the early 1960s are shown in figure 2. In 1965 the Department of Meteorology became a separate entity. Vance E. Moyer served as department head from 1965 to 1975, Kenneth C. Brundidge from 1975 to 1980, and James R. Scoggins from 1980 to the present. During recent years there have been about twelve faculty members and around eighty undergraduate students and a similar number of graduate students enrolled in the program. Since its inception, the department has conferred 471 bachelor's degrees, 279 master's degrees, and 49 doctorates.

During the late 1960s, Bernice Ackerman, Dusan Djuric, Phanindramohan Das, Thomas Sanford, James R. Scoggins, and Kenneth Bergman joined the meteorology faculty. Ackerman is now a scientist at the Illinois State Water Survey, Bergman is with the National Science Foundation, Sanford entered private business, and the others remain on the faculty. Retirees include Horace R. Byers, founding dean of the College of Geosciences and later vice-president for academic affairs of the university, who now resides in Santa Barbara, California, Vance E. Moyer, Walter K. Henry, and Guy A. Franceschini, professors emeriti, all now living in the Bryan–College Station area.

Research interests have varied widely, and the following list of principal investigators and their areas of research is but a summary of recent activities: tropical and satellite meteorology (Aylmer H. Thompson and James P. McGuirk); modification of air masses (Thompson and Walter K. Henry); jet-stream modeling and theory (Kenneth Brundidge and Dusan Djuric); numerical modeling (Djuric); air pollution (Robert C. Runnels and T. Steven Yuen); trends and variation in precipitation in the U.S. (McGuirk and John F. Grif-

Figure 2. Faculty of the Department of Oceanography and Meterology, Texas A&M University, in the early 1960s.

First row, left to right:

Bryan Logan, Vance E. Moyer, Guy A. Franceschini, Robert O. Reid, Kenneth C. Brundidge, Walter K. Henry, and Robert A. Clark.

Second row, left to right:

Louis Capurro, John Cochrane, Hugh McLellan, Sam Hall, Thomas E. Sanford, Basil Williams, and Dale F. Leipper.

Third row, left to right:

Aylmer H. Thompson, Richard Adams, K. M. Rae, William H. Clayton, Donald Hood, and Sayed Z. ElSayed.

fiths); tropical climatology (Henry and Griffiths); human biometeorology (Dennis M. Driscoll); forecasting clear-air turbulence, mesoscale analyses, and weather modification (James R. Scoggins).

Personnel of the department participated in the High Plains Cooperative Experiment (HIPLEX). This was a scientific program whose objective was to develop the technology for increasing precipitation from summertime cumulus clouds. The program was conducted in the Big Spring, Texas, area during the 1970s and early 1980s.

The Department of Meteorology at TAMU, the only department in a Texas university which offers bachelor's, master's, and doctor's degrees in meteorology, has outstanding facilities. These include a Harris 500 computer system with color graphics, a satellite receiver with looping capabilities, extensive meteorological data archives, a digitized micrometeorological tower system with magnetic tape recording, dual-wave-length (3 and 10 cm) weather radars with co-axial beams, a walk-in freezer room, a satellite data-receiving system, and spacious faculty offices. The department is housed in the Oceanography and Meteorology Building.

TAMU was a charter member of the University Co-operation for Atmospheric Research (UCAR) formed in 1959. UCAR manages the National Center for Atmospheric Research (NCAR), which was formed in 1960. Meteorology and other university personnel interact regularly with UCAR and NCAR personnel and have participated in several large research programs involving NCAR scientists.

Graduates of the Department of Meteorology have served in many distinguished capacities. Robert A. Clark was director of the Office of Hydrology, National Oceanographic and Atmospheric Association; William H. Clayton has served for many years as president of TAMU at Galveston; Henry E. Fuelberg, Jessie J. Stephens, James J. O'Brien, and David R. Smith continue to serve as faculty members in other universities. George Fichtl, Archie Kahan, Kenneth Hadeen, Lynn LeBlanc, and others have distinguished themselves in military service and/or civilian government service. Many more have enjoyed distinguished careers in meteorology.

Meteorological Research at Other Universities

Research in radar meteorology in Texas was initiated during World War II when two young Air Force meteorologists, Captains John Gerhardt and William Gordon, were sent to the Electrical Engineering Research Laboratory of the University of Texas at Austin (UT–Austin). They joined a group, led by Archie Straiton, which had been collaborating with personnel of the National Bureau of Standards, Boulder, Colorado, in studying atmospheric effects on the propagation of radio waves. The group's objective was to determine how the atmosphere below the ionosphere interfered with idealized theory. Their work was aided significantly by Cullen Crain's invention of the airborne X-band refractometer. Kenneth Jehn, Raymond Staley, Norman Wagner, and Vance Moyer participated in this research in radio meteorology, as it was then called.

Research and academic interest have continued at UT–Austin. The Atmospheric Science Group undertook measurements of atmospheric and substrate vari-ables in fundamental studies of micrometeorological phenomena, research which was allied with the group's earlier work in radar. Later, interest in instrumentation and a need for accurate temperature measurements in the stratosphere led to a fruitful period of rocketsonde research. Other research projects involved facets of radio-wave propagation and attenuation by precipitation.

Initially, the group's academic contact was the aerospace engineering department. By 1965, it appeared that many opportunities for cooperative research also existed in the civil engineering department, and interests were combined as the Atmospheric Science Group formally joined that department. Since 1965 numerous cooperative and individual research and academic activities have been undertaken, including studies of air pollution, meteorological and oceanographic aspects of oil spills on the open ocean, climate resources of the Texas coastal zone, wind-power potential in the Texas coastal zone, models of the general circulation, and convection motions.

In 1955 Freeman left the Department of Oceanography at TAMU to found Gulf Consultants. He and Ledolf Baer discovered and developed the bathystropic storm tide. In 1957 Freeman began teaching meteorology for nonscience students at the University of St. Thomas (UST) in Houston and in 1966 initiated a full undergraduate degree program in meteorology there. The program continues today and has a student enrollment of about sixteen. Other faculty members who have assisted Freeman include Joseph Goldman, Leon Graves, Bernard Meisner, and William Hildreth. In 1962 and 1963, UST presented a refresher course to about thirty Weather Bureau employees. In 1981 the university added a weather-communications emphasis to its meteorology degree program to prepare graduates for meteorological positions with television, radio, and newspapers.

In 1966 Freeman started the Institute for Storm Research in Houston, the only nonprofit organization for the study of storms in the world. Weather forecasts and climatological studies of weather and storms are made, and professionals do research on storm tides, storm waves, and storm currents. For several years the Institute, under Joe Hasling, has jointly sponsored storm-awareness days with the Houston Astros Baseball Organization.

Texas Tech University has had faculty working in meteorological subjects since the 1970s. Some of the subjects investigated are summertime convective clouds and their potential for rainfall stimulation (Gerald M. Jurica and Colleen A. Leary); tornadoes, dust storms, and drylines (Richard E. Peterson); and numerical/observational studies of severe local storms (Chia-Bo Chang). Often, these studies have been initiated by Donald R. Haragan, who has conducted research on hydrometeorology and climatology.

Activities at Other Agencies

Although air pollution has figured in research at both TAMU and UT–Austin, the Texas Air Control Board (TACB), created in the mid-1960s, has also contributed in a number of areas of air pollution and atmospheric sciences research. Two atmospheric-dispersion models, the Texas Episodic Model and the Texas Climatological Model, were developed by the staff. These models became widely used and accepted by atmospheric-pollution scientists in the United States and around the world to predict ground-level concentrations of air pollution. The TACB has also documented urban and rural visibility trends throughout Texas. This recent research project is leading to more intensive studies of the causes of atmospheric visibility impairment in selected urban and rural areas of the state. In the area of acid rain, in 1979 the TACB began routine measurements of precipitation pH at several sites throughout Texas to establish baseline data. Currently the TACB operates its own event-monitoring network as well as one National Atmospheric Deposition Program (NADP) monitor near Longview and has standardized methods for taking valid measurements and analyses of precipitation. The TACB is also currently characterizing the weather patterns typically associated with high ozone concentrations in the Houston area to help determine pollution trends and to develop the ability to predict ozone levels on the basis of meteorological forecasts.

In the 1970s, the National Weather Service established four Agricultural Weather Service Centers (AWSCs) in cooperation with various Weather Service Forecast Offices (WSFOs) to serve the needs of agriculture in the South and Midwest. The first AWSC began operation at Auburn, Alabama, in 1973, followed by the second and third at Stoneville, Mississippi, and Lafayette, Indiana, respectively, in 1974, and the fourth at College Station, Texas, in 1975. The AWSC at College Station serves Texas, Oklahoma, and New Mexico. The WSFOs issue agricultural weather forecasts, which supplement the public forecasts with information on rainfall amounts, relative humidity, dew formation and dry off, and sunshine amounts. The AWSCs provide day-to-day farm-weather management

information to help producers increase profitability, either by cutting weather-related losses or by increasing the timeliness of operations. The management information is relayed mainly through agricultural weather advisories, which are written generally state by state. Dissemination is by commercial radio and television, the wire services, and NOAA weather radio. Advisory topics include soil-temperature forecasts for planting purposes, harvest-weather information, pest management, livestock and poultry heat- and cold-stress management, and many others. Outputs from computer crop models yield information that increases the management of timing for the production of a number of crops.

Damage from hurricanes Carla in 1961 and Camille in 1969 prompted Dow Chemical Company in Freeport to develop a computer model to predict hurricane effects along the coast in and around Freeport. The model was developed in 1969–70 and was used during the 1970s. In 1980 it was noted that the model did not adequately account for the effects from hurricane Allen, and efforts were initiated to revise the model. A successful revision was accomplished at TAMU by James R. Scoggins, Aylmer H. Thompson, and Chung-Chieng Lai during 1981–82. The revised model correctly predicted the effects of hurricane Alicia in 1983, which made landfall a few miles east of Freeport. Dow maintains close contact with TAMU when hurricanes approach the Texas coast, and together, both organizations evaluate hurricane effects.

In 1961, in response to a recognized need for meteorological expertise in water planning and development, the Texas Water Commission (TWC) employed its first professional meteorologist, John T. Carr, Jr. Another meteorologist, John Kane, was added in 1962. During the mid-1960s, Carr became especially interested in the then new and largely unproven field of weather modification. With Carr's encouragement, the TWC became involved in weather modification.

In 1967 the Texas legislature enacted the Texas Weather Modification Act, which charged the TWC with the task of regulating all weather modification activities within the state and promoting research in weather modification. The TWC established a Weather Modification and Technology Division, headed by Carr, which monitored both research and commercial weather modification operations within the state. Staff meteorologists within the division also collected, catalogued, and analyzed meteorological and climatological data in support of the weather modification programs as well as other water-related projects performed by the TWC and other state agencies. As a member of the governor's State Emergency Management Council, the TWC provided meteorological expertise to support the Governor's Office of Emergency Preparedness.

Today, meteorologists within the TWC include Robert F. Riggio, George W. Bomar, Thomas J. Larkin, and William H. Hanshaw, who continue to administer the Weather Modification Act by monitoring ongoing weather modification activities and by participating in cloud seeding research. The TWC's Weather and Climate Section (formerly the Weather Modification and Technology Division), headed by Riggio, also serves as counsel to the governor on weather-related emergencies and performs studies in meteorology and climatology. The group ensures quality control of all climatological data archived in the Texas Natural Resources Information System, the official state repository for weather and climate information.

State Climatologist

In early 1957 Richard W. Blood was made the first state climatologist of Texas, an appointment within the federal Weather Bureau. He was succeeded in early 1960 by Hoye S. Dunham, whose brief term ended when he was replaced by Robert W. Orton in October 1960. Orton prepared many useful studies concerned with the Texas climate before the federal state climatologist program was disbanded in early 1973. In May 1973, John F. Griffiths was named by the governor as the Texas state climatologist and was given an office on the TAMU campus. The office has published various items, including an agroclimatic atlas, an engineering climatic atlas, and *100 Years of Texas Weather*. Griffiths has also been active in many applications of climatology to other disciplines and has published several textbooks and chapters in books.

4

Astronomy

David S. Evans

ASTRONOMY CAME to Texas with a bang some fifty million years ago when a large meteorite struck the earth twenty miles south of Fort Stockton and made a crater eight miles across. The crater edges have long since eroded and the depression has been filled in, but the central uplift still remains as a prominent isolated hill, the Sierra Madera, just north of the Glass Mountains.

Events such as this present a problem to the chronicler of astronomical history. Meteorites in flight are astronomy; when they land they turn into geology. Even so, we must mention a much more recent astrobleme ten miles southwest of the present site of Odessa, where there is a principal crater ninety feet deep and ten acres in extent. From this, now almost filled with debris, and two smaller craters, numerous meteorite fragments consisting of 90 percent iron and 7 percent nickel have been recovered by geologists. Anything like a bombardment of the earth belongs to the distant past, but falls still do occur, and by 1966 a total of 128 meteorites had been catalogued in Texas. Some had even been seen to fall, including one that went into Pena Blanca Spring and two that landed in northeast Texas in 1961. The leading authority on Texas meteorites is Oscar Monnig of Forth Worth, an enthusiastic amateur astronomer, whose notable collection, comprising 6 percent of all known meteorites, he has donated to Texas Christian University.

In the late summer of 1837 a train of wagons moved into the Republic of Texas led by John Johnson, who brought his wife and ten of their eleven daughters to settle on the Red River. Later he brought his family into the little town now called Paris, where he opened an inn. There, as a regular visitor, came one of the few doctors of medicine in the area, Henry Graham McDonald, who fell in love with and later married one of Johnson's daughters, a widow named Sarah Turner with two young children. In due course they had three sons, William Johnson McDonald (fig. 1), born December 21, 1844; Henry Dearborn McDonald, born in 1847; and James Thomas McDonald, born in 1850. Dr. McDonald became a major landowner, but his wife and her new baby died at its birth in 1852. The boys were brought up by a stepmother with whom relations were not cordial, and so they spent much time with a favorite aunt. Their father died in 1860, and they were placed under the guardianship of a Scottish Methodist missionary and sent for their education to his school at Clarksville, Texas. William, a hefty redhead, was an outstanding student, though his studies were briefly interrupted by a short and almost uneventful period of service with the Confederate forces.

Figure 1. William Johnson McDonald.

After the war it was hard to get a job, and William turned to a variety of occupations, ending with apprenticeship to a law firm in the small town of Mount Pleasant.

He learned enough about the law to return to Clarksville and open a law office in partnership with Marshall L. Simms. Eventually he began to make loans and was to profit greatly in the end from his purchase during the depression of the 1870s of Red River County warrants at about ten cents on the dollar. When boom times returned, William and his two brothers founded the Citizens' Bank of Clarksville in 1885, the First National Bank of Paris in 1887, and what would become the First National Bank at Cooper in 1889. In 1889 his first bank was merged with the First National Bank of Clarksville.

In 1887 William moved to Paris, at first lodging with a local cabinetmaker and his wife. At this time William came across the book *Popular Astronomy*,

translated from the French of the celebrated astronomer and popularizer, Camille Flammarion. It is said that at this time William acquired a small telescope and that he and the cabinetmaker observed from the latter's backyard.

By now William had become wealthy and he was able to indulge a variety of interests. His library, which is now kept at McDonald Observatory, includes books on natural history, geography, botany, and history and contains works of Darwin and Huxley, with a number of astronomy texts. He was able to travel to Europe and to take summer courses in botany at Harvard. Botany indeed was his first love, and when asked to state his occupation he always wrote "farmer." After a disastrous fire in Paris in 1916, when William lost most of his possessions not stored in the bank, he retired to one of his farms, Yam Hill, about three miles out of town, where he spent the rest of his life. William remained a bachelor, and the end of his life was lonely and beset with sickness. He suffered mainly from a kidney infection and deterioration of his eyesight. Visits to various medical institutions failed to alleviate his condition, which was diagnosed as terminal in 1925, and he was thereafter confined to a sanitarium in Paris to end his days. His niece-in-law, Leila, would read to him there, and he was attended day and night by nurses, who would later say that his mind would wander a little. Leila McDonald was to say that his mind was "as clear as a bell." He died on February 6, 1926, at the age of eighty-one, and then all the stories about his physical and mental condition assumed great importance.

William had made the last of several wills on May 8, 1925, and when the document was read it proved a shock both to his numerous relatives and to the University of Texas, and it provoked one of the most famous and long-drawn-out legal battles in Texas history. When finally probated on March 21, 1929, his estate totaled about $1.26 million, a very considerable sum in those days. In his will the banker provided expenditure for his gravesite and, by the standards of the times, quite generous legacies to eight of his kin. The clause that set off five legal actions read in part:

All the rest, residue and remainder of my estate, I give devise and bequeath to the Regents of the University of Texas, in trust, to be used and devoted by said Regents for the purpose of aiding in erecting and equipping an Astronomical Observatory to be kept and used in connection with and as part of the University for the study and the promotion of the study of Astronomical Science. This bequest is to be known as the W. J. McDonald Observatory Fund.

The university authorities heard about this through a telephone call from a newspaper reporter. Harry Yandell Benedict, then dean of Science, described it as "like lightning out of a clear sky." The university immediately received congratulations and a host of suggestions as to where the observatory might be located.

However, seven of the eight family legatees, together with some of those who had been left out, immediately sued the executors of this fund of just over a million dollars so that the legal causes appear in the records as "Mrs. Florence Rodgers et al. vs Morris Fleming et al." The grounds of the suit were that W. J. McDonald was not "of sound mind and disposing memory" at the time of the drafting of the will. In consequence of this, no astronomers were called to testify concerning the virtues of astronomy and its endowment, though Dean Benedict did in fact secure letters to this effect from a number of prominent contemporary astronomers.

The case came up in the District Court of Paris on August 30, 1926, with one of the regents, Sam Neathery, sent to assist in the defense of the will. Neither President Splawn nor Dean Benedict attended.

Many witnesses were called who testified that McDonald was excited, irritable, and prone to eccentric opinions, that he feared one of his nephews would murder him, and that he suffered from loss of business capacity and forgetfulness. One of the strangest pieces of testimony came from the proprietor of the local barbershop, who said that on one occasion McDonald had said to him that astronomy was the coming science and that if one had a big enough telescope one could look past the gates of heaven and see who was there. There was also a great deal of conflicting medical testimony concerning the mental effects of the testator's last illness.

On the other hand, business associates testified that McDonald was always a shrewd and careful businessman in full possession of his faculties, and that most of the previous versions of his will, drafted at various times over the years, contained the astronomical clause. Presiding Judge Newman Phillips instructed the jury in the law relating to testamentary capacity, the attorney for the plaintiffs described how the estate would have been divided among the relatives had there been no will, and Judge Moore, appearing for the defense, ended with a description of the

benefits which would be derived from the original bequest, using arguments supplied no doubt by Benedict and his correspondents. After a short deliberation, on Saturday, September 11, 1926, the jury found McDonald to have been of sound mind and the will valid.

The congratulations which poured into the university were somewhat premature since the family petitioned for a new trial on the grounds of suppression of evidence and the refusal of the judge to accede to their request to have put to the jury a particular definition of insane delusion. The motion was denied. The case was then taken to the Sixth Court of Civil Appeals in Texarkana. There all the evidence submitted to the lower court was reviewed, with the decision, on April 21, 1927, by Presiding Associate Judge Richard B. Levy upholding the verdict of the district court. Even this was not the end, for the case was then taken to the Texas Supreme Court on a writ of error. Justice Ocie Speer gave judgment on February 29, 1928, with the concurrence of Chief Justice C. M. Cureton, taking into account the medical testimony, the stories of aberrant behavior, the allegations of bad family relations, and stories about communication with the dead. He remitted the case back to the district court for a new trial on the grounds that McDonald was of unsound mind and that the original trial judge had erred in his instructions.

So the whole legal caravan traipsed back to Paris, Texas, to start all over again on October 29, 1928. There was now a formidable array of legal talent, including Attorney General Claude Pollard and his men, for the will. One way and another the list of witnesses had swelled to 107, though what they said was very much the same mix. At the end, each side summed up for six and a half hours, producing some fine, if rather tendentious, oratory. Clyde Sweeton, for the plaintiff, thundered, "If the University of Texas does not believe W. J. McDonald suffered from an insane delusion about the gates of Heaven, then it does not believe in the Bible and is no fit place to send boys and girls." His colleague, named Touchstone, asked, "Don't you see why the Lord never meant for mortal man to see into the spiritual heaven?"

Finally, an anticlimax: a hung jury and remission to the docket for February 1929. A motion for a change of venue was denied. By this time everybody was heartily sick of the business; the university had spent close to $80,000 in legal costs, and the plaintiffs had presumably made an enormous hole in the legacies they would receive if the will were upheld. A proposed fifty-fifty compromise had already been rejected. The case was finally settled out of court with an award of about a quarter of a million dollars to the plaintiffs. When everything was settled in 1929, the university received about $840,000 with the obligation to build an observatory and not much idea of how to set about it.

Although they could make no final decisions before the legal battles had been won, the university authorities sent Professor John M. Kuehne on a fact-finding mission in July 1927. The sum of $200 was enough for him to visit astronomers at Lowell Observatory at Flagstaff, Arizona, Mount Wilson at Pasadena, California, Lick Observatory at San Jose, California, and the Dominion Astrophysical Observatory at Victoria, British Columbia. The advice he received was as abundant as the amount of travel one could then buy for $200, and most of it in retrospect is seen to be bad. The general tenor of the advice was to put the observatory somewhere handy for the students, not right in Austin but well outside it. If this advice had been taken, the observatory would now have been well inside the proliferating suburbs of the city. An even more serious problem was that Texas had no working astronomers who might operate such a telescope once built.

The news of the astronomical legacy was, of course, a matter of the keenest interest in the very small astronomical world of the time, especially at the University of Chicago. Although possessed of the largest refracting telescope in the world, the Yerkes Observatory of the University of Chicago, located in Green Bay, Wisconsin, did not have an ideal climate. Its director, Otto Struve, and some of his colleagues, especially the Belgian George van Biesbroeck, had even dreamed of a Chicago observatory, perhaps near Amarillo in Texas. Struve was of Russian birth, from a family of German origin, constituting a remarkable dynasty of astronomers and other scientists dating back to the early nineteenth century. This particular member had been born in Kharkov in 1897, where his father was a professor. He served in the Imperial Army during World War I and then with the anti-Bolshevik forces until they were driven out of southern Russia, when he was forced to find work as a laborer in Istanbul. His situation becoming known in the West, he was offered a position at Chicago by then director Edwin Frost, who subsequently became blind. Struve succeeded Frost in 1932. Exactly who devised a plan of cooperation between Chicago and Texas is not entirely clear, but it seems to have been Struve who formulated it in detail and caused Robert Hutchins, president of the University of Chicago, to propose it

to Benedict in Texas. That such a collaboration could be envisaged seems commonplace now, but in those days, before the advent of "big science," the idea of such an arrangement linking a prestigious northern private university with an obscure southern state college was positively revolutionary. To some it seemed even scandalous. The proposal was that Texas should use about half the money to build a telescope, and that for a term of thirty years Chicago should manage it and use it, while Texas developed its own corps of astronomers.

The text of the agreement, mostly drafted by Struve, who was to be the director, went into precise detail concerning the construction and budget for the instrument. (In response to criticism at the appointment of a foreign-born director one regent opined that this was better than having a Yankee.) The Texas regents were to provide $10,000 per annum toward running costs, to produce a series of publications (starting with a biography of W. J. McDonald), to promote the library, to pay for tests of possible observatory sites, and to allocate time to observers from Yerkes, Austin, and possibly elsewhere. Chicago would appoint and pay for an assistant director to live on the site, with two observing assistants, and an engineer and janitor, and meet sundry other expenses.

The agreement was ratified by the Texas regents on November 23, 1932, and the board then viewed models and drawings of the proposed observatory submitted by the Warner and Swasey Company of Cleveland, Ohio, the lowest bidder.

The telescope did not necessarily have to be sited in Texas, though clearly there was some implication to this effect. All sorts of communities suggested themselves, but even at a very early stage there was a preference for the clear skies and higher altitudes of West Texas. However, a systematic search was then begun under the leadership of Yerkes astronomer Christian T. Elvey, who began with a thorough report on what was known of the weather, topography, and geology of Texas. Starting on June 13, 1932, Elvey and another astronomer, T. G. Mehlen from Amherst, set out in a little Chevrolet van to discover where to put the observatory. They had a number of instruments designed to measure the image quality and atmospheric transparency of various sites. The former was studied by means of a 4-inch aperture telescope designed to look only at the pole star under very high magnification, allowing the observers to rate the quality and stability of its image on an agreed scale. The transparency was measured by photographing a low-dispersion spectrum of the bright star Vega, readily available at high altitude in the summer skies of Texas. The camera was fixed so that the image of the star trailed to make a broad spectrum and the plates developed with as much uniformity of chemicals, time, and temperature as could be attained under field conditions. Back at Chicago the response of the plates could be measured with an appropriate instrument, with special attention being paid to the strength of the spectrum in the blue and ultraviolet regions, which are liable to especially strong absorption if the atmosphere is not perfectly clear. Tests were carried out near Austin, and in West Texas near Alpine, El Paso, and in the Guadalupe Mountains on the New Mexico border. A side trip to the Lowell Observatory in Flagstaff, Arizona, and to the Mount Wilson Observatory near Pasadena, California, enabled the astronomers to calibrate their findings against the experience of long-established observatories.

They were impressed with several sites in the Davis Mountains, but access was a problem. However, they found one eminence which gave "unbelievably good" results and which did not have this problem. Struve came to confirm these impressions and liked a slightly higher hill on the U-Up-and-Down ranch, the property of Violet Locke McIvor. After some negotiations, she generously donated the hill, which soon after was officially renamed Mount Locke after the grandfather from whom she had inherited it. In addition, the trustees of Judge Fowlkes also donated neighboring Little Flat Top, and the local inhabitants turned to with a will to survey "the metes and bounds" of the two properties totaling some 400 acres, for which title was secured in 1933 (fig. 2).

When it came to making the telescope there could really be only two contending firms—the J. S. Fecker Company of Pittsburgh and the Warner and Swasey

Figure 2. McDonald Observatory today showing 107-inch, 82-inch, 36-inch, and 30-inch domes (photo Kathryn Gessas).

Company of Cleveland. Both had built the mechanical parts of major telescopes, and Struve was familiar with their performance. However, the International Astronomical Union General Assembly had met in 1932 in Cambridge, Massachusetts, and on a boat excursion Struve had met Edwin P. Burrell, Director of Engineering at Warner and Swasey. Burrell told Struve that the firm had started an optical shop with C. A. Robert Lundin in charge; he was the son of C. A. Lundin associated with the celebrated optician Alvan Clark, who had figured the lenses of the great refractors. Warner and Swasey were prepared to bid on the entire project from optics to building. This would thus be the first large telescope to be entirely American made.

The building plans called for a single structure. The two lower floors would consist of library, offices, darkrooms, and some living accommodation, capped by an observing floor beneath a rotating dome. The building, of steel frame construction, was subcontracted to the Patterson-Leitch Company of Cleveland, while the on-site work for foundations and piers to support the telescope, as well as the on-site assembly of the building, was contracted out to several local companies from San Antonio and El Paso. The university exercised supervision through its architect, W. W. Dornberger, and the university building inspector, Hugh Yantis, who at first seemed to have the prospect of shooting a deer with a crossbow more on his mind than the construction work in hand. Sand and gravel for the 62-foot diameter foundations and the 45-foot high piers to support the telescope were found on a local ranch. After a trial assembly in Cleveland, the first steel arrived on the site in July 1934, and the main frame was finished by September. The shutters for the dome opening were in place by October.

The site was the scene of intense activity. This was the time of the Great Depression, and a local historian, Barry Scobee, has left a moving account of its effects.

Tents were strewn all over Mount Locke, on any level place in the brush or in the open, wherever space could be found, with the smell of cooking rising at all hours. Many of the men had their wives with them. . . . some of the men were on their first jobs in two or three years. Nobody tried to put on any style. They were careful of their new curiosities—cents and dollars. Some men laughed like kids and kissed their first checks. One steel worker showed his first check [to Scobee] with a grin that was all but drowned in tears.

Several of these workers remained and later joined the Observatory staff and gave loyal service over many years. The 75-foot high steel dome was primed and coated with aluminum paint late in October. On the last day of the month a gas-powered DC generator was hooked up, and the dome turned with a group of Fort Davis citizens and company representatives taking a Halloween ride.

In spite of the delays over the telescope itself, Struve was eager to get some astronomy done on the mountain. He chose a married man, Franklin E. Roach, as the first resident astronomer, in preference to C. T. Elvey, a bachelor. Roach, assisted by a German engineer immigrant, Theodor Immega, began a long study of the light of the night sky using a small telescope and developing the resulting photographic films in Fort Davis, where a house was rented until mountain accommodation should be ready. In the late fall of 1934, a 12-inch reflecting telescope was installed on the mountain for the observation of variable stars using the new technique of photoelectric photometry. Elvey, having acquired a wife, was named resident astronomer in 1935. He and Roach, using a small camera intended as part of the spectoscope for the big telescope, soon discovered extensive clouds of luminous hydrogen in the Milky Way. Their report constituted the first scientific publication from McDonald Observatory.

The continued delays in the completion of the main telescope were most frustrating. To make quicker use of the existing facilities, a spectroscope designed for nebular work was installed. This made use of the fact that the south slope of the mountain pointed to the north pole. The spectroscope was installed on this slope, with a camera and a small guiding telescope 75 feet lower down, the light of the sky being fed into the instrument from a large plane mirror at the upper end of the slope. This ingenious design, due to van Biesbroeck, was later copied at the Commonwealth Observatory in Canberra, Australia. The nebular spectoscope was used for three years and produced important new data on the structure of the Milky Way.

When the telescope contract was signed in 1933 everybody expected that it would be in service within a couple of years. This was to be a reflecting telescope 80 inches in diameter, provided with a prime focus, to be reached by a system of carriages and ladders. There was also a Cassegrain focus to which the light would come by reflection from a secondary mirror, and passage through a hole in the primary to a point just at the back of the lower end of the tube. In addition there was a coudé focus at a fixed point below the south pier to which the light would come by three reflections to direct it down the hollow polar axis of the instrument. The construction of the mechanical parts by the Warner and Swasey Company presented few problems, and all the mechanical parts were installed by the end of 1936. The big problem was the main mirror. Struve had decided that the big glass disk should be fabricated of the new Pyrex low thermal-expansion glass from the Corning Glass Company of Bradford, Pennsylvania. This would be the first big American disk, all previous ones having come from France. Professor and Mrs. Struve, together with Elvey, went to Bradford in December 1933 to watch it being poured. Four months later, now cold, when it emerged from the annealing oven, it was found to be covered with fissures regarded by the glassmakers as unimportant, but Struve insisted on its being remelted. During this process the edges of the mold were pushed out and the disk stretched to 82 inches, which thereafter became the diameter of the McDonald telescope.

The optician, Lundin, arrived at the Warner and Swasey works in September 1933 and got to work on edging the smaller disks that had been successfully made for the telescope's secondary mirrors. The big 82-inch blank arrived on October 3, 1934.

Lundin's first task was to trim the disk to exact circularity and to work the back face to a flat surface. He was also working on a 60-inch disk on another machine, and in January 1935 the arm of this struck the 82-inch disk and chewed a three-inch chip out of its back. This was repaired by cementing in a suitable piece of glass. Lundin then turned his attention to the front face of the mirror, which first had to be ground roughly to a spherical concave form and polished. Then began the most difficult part, changing this surface into a paraboloidal form accurate to a fraction of a wavelength of light. This process involved polishing away minute amounts of glass and frequent testing of the surface by reflected light to see how closely it approximated the desired parabolic form. Working conditions at Warner and Swasey were far from ideal: the manufacture of machine tools nearby, the mainstay of the firm, caused vibrations, there were heating pipes in the area causing convection currents, and the support system used to hold the mirror vertical for testing was liable to introduce distortion. Much of Lundin's work was done on weekends when some of these problems were absent, but the chief difficulty turned out to be that Lundin, whose experience with his father had been in lenses, had an inadequate grasp of the techniques for large-scale mirror manufacture.

The records of the time showed increasing exasperation by Struve, and even a suggestion that Lundin should be dismissed. Things got a little better when John Stanley Plaskett, emeritus director of the Dominion Astrophysical Observatory at Victoria, British Columbia, who had successfully commissioned the 72-inch telescope there, was called in as a consultant. Struve also summoned the Yerkes optician, E. Lloyd McCarthy, and finally a satisfactory figure for the mirror was attained. The surface had to be provided with a reflective coating. Until then, the traditional procedure used was chemical deposition of silver. However, a new process of vacuum deposition of aluminum had been developed, which gave higher reflectivity and better resistance to tarnish. The mirror was aluminized by one of the developers of the process, Robley C. Williams, and Struve signed his acceptance of the 82-inch mirror on October 15, 1938, followed by a celebratory dinner at the University Club. J. S. Plaskett then conducted a final series of tests by the so-called Hartmann method, and pronounced it accurate to one-twentieth of a wavelength of light, the most nearly perfect mirror in the world. It weighed 5,600 pounds, was 82.3 inches in diameter, 11.63 inches thick at the edge, and had a central hole (for access to the Cassegrain focus) 13.53 inches in diameter. Regrettably, it would turn out that Plaskett's judgment was far too optimistic.

The mirror arrived at the railroad station at Alpine on February 22, 1939, and was, with as little publicity as possible, transported to the mountain. This precaution was taken because there was a lunatic fringe of the population who thought it amusing to take pot shots at things like big mirrors. On March 1 the mirror was installed in the tube in the presence of a distinguished audience, and some observations, which gave great satisfaction, were made at the prime focus on March 2. On succeeding days the secondary mirrors were installed and tested. On March 5 Struve used the Cassegrain spectrograph to observe the star 17 Leporis, whose ultraviolet spectrum formed the basis of the first scientific results from McDonald's telescope, published in McDonald Contribution No. 14.

Spectroscopy does not require perfect images. However, Struve was concerned with the problem of deformed images, possibly because of the mirror support system that had been adopted. However, the trustees of the McDonald Observatory Fund accepted the telescope on March 25, 1939 (fig. 3). Even though Warner and Swasey had performed well beyond the line of duty, having lost $85,000 on the deal, they were still ready to finance the formal dedication of the instrument. This was to take place on May 5, 1939, and

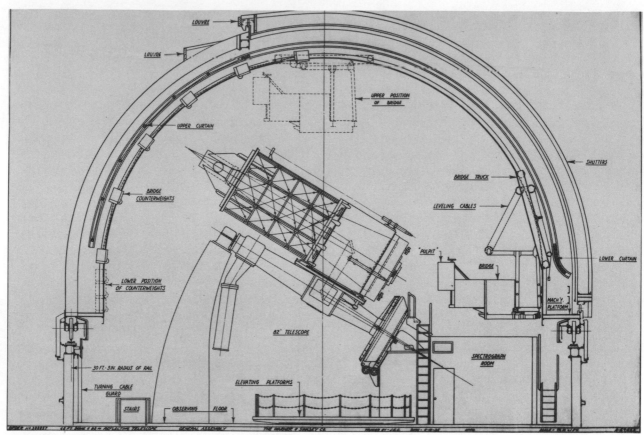

Figure 3. The placement and optical system of the 82-inch telescope.

Professor Morelock, president of Sul Ross State College at Alpine, arranged for it to be preceded by a regional meeting of the American Association for the Advancement of Science. The astronomical invitation list included nearly everybody of standing throughout the world and, except for a meeting of the General Assembly of the International Astronomical Union, was probably the most glittering array of astronomical talent ever assembled up to that time (fig. 4). Not everybody could come in those days of leisured travel, but an extraordinary number did to witness the dedication of the second largest telescope in the world. The entire Texas congressional delegation was invited, as well as the regents, and many local inhabitants attended the dedication itself. In addition, there were numerous Texas academics, while Chicago was represented by many of its distinguished personnel, and invitations were sent to its more prominent benefactors. Every bed that could be found in the area housed some guest. On the great day, Friday, May 5, 1939, ceremonies were held on the observing floor of the dome, presided over in the morning by Henry Norris Russell,

with Harlow Shapley as the first speaker, followed by J. Gallo of the National Observatory of Mexico. The morning ended with a description of the telescope by Plaskett. After a chuckwagon dinner, formal dedication ceremonies started at 3:00 P.M. along with the arrival of bad weather. Several of the most important contributors to the success of the project had died, including UT President H. Y. Benedict, Ambrose Swasey, and Edwin Burrell, as well as the company's president, Philip E. Bliss.

The observatory was formally tendered to the regents by Charles Stillwell for the contractor, and accepted, first by Struve in a speech emphasizing the value of large telescopes, and then for the regents by their chairman, Jubal Parten. A message from President Hutchins of Chicago, who was ill, was read on his behalf, and President-elect Homer P. Rainey of the University of Texas concluded his speech with the words that the observatory was now open for research—though, in fact, the telescope had been used for two months.

These formalities were followed by an astronomical

KEY TO PLATE

1. Dr. F. E. Roach, University of Arizona
2. Dr. Frederick Slocum, Van Vleck Obs.
3. Dr. Walter Baade, Mt. Wilson Observatory
4. Newspaper man
5. Dr. W. H. Wright, Lick Observatory
6. Dr. Joel Stebbins, Washburn Observatory
7. Dr. H. D. Curtis, University of Michigan Observatory
8. Dr. W. S. Adams, Mt. Wilson Observatory
9. Dr. Jan Schilt, Columbia University
10. Dr. R. J. Trumpler, Lick Observatory
11. Mr. Robert M. McMath, McMath Observatory
12. Dr. P. Van de Kamp, Sproul Observatory
13. Dr. Cecilia Payne-Gaposchkin, Harvard College Observatory
14. Dr. A. H. Compton, University of Chicago
15. Dr. Horace Babcock, Lick Observatory
16. Dr. Edwin Hubble, Mount Wilson Observatory
17. Dr. J. Gallo, National Observatory of Mexico
18. Dr. Jesse Greenstein, Yerkes Observatory
19. Dr. Bart J. Bok, Harvard College Observatory
20. Dr. N. T. Bobrovnikoff, Perkins Observatory
21. Dr. A. E. Whitford, University of Wisconsin

22. Dr. J. J. Nassau, Case School of Applied Science
23. Dr. J. H. Oort, University of Leiden Observatory (Holland)
24. Mr. Russell Porter, Calif. Institute of Technology
25. Dr. Henry Norris Russell, Princeton University Observatory
26. Prof. E. A. Milne, Oxford University (England)
27. Dr. J. S. Plaskett, Dominion Astrophysical Observatory (Victoria)
28. Dr. H. A. Wilson, Rice Institute
29. Dr. S. A. Mitchell, Leander McCormick Observatory
30. Dr. Bertil Lindblad, Stockholm Obs.
31. Dr. G. W. Moffitt, Perkin-Elmer-Moffitt Co.
32. Dr. F. E. Ross, Yerkes Observatory
33. Mr. Bradshaw Wood, Steward Observatory
34. Dr. Martin Schwarzschild, Harvard College Observatory
35. Dr. J. M. Kuehne, University of Texas
36. Dr. C. D. Shane, University of California
37. ?
38. Dr. E. G. Keller, University of Texas
39. Dr. J. A. Pearce, Dominion Astrophysical Obs. (Victoria)
40. Dr. Edwin Carpenter, Univ. of Arizona
41. Dr. C. E. Hesthal, Perkins Observatory

Figure 4. Astronomers present for the dedication on May 5, 1939, of the 82-inch telescope of the McDonald Observatory.

symposium that continued through the weekend, with contributions from sixteen of the world's most distinguished astronomers: they included J. H. Oort and G. P. Kuiper, both from Holland; E. A. Milne and Cecilia Payne-Gaposchkin from England; Walter Baade from Germany; S. Chandrasekhar from India; and Bertil Lindblad from Sweden. Several of them had already migrated to the United States and would become ornaments of the profession here. Added to this list were the names of such famous native Americans as Harlow Shapley, Edwin Hubble, Henry Norris Russell, and others. Regrettably, the texts of these talks were never published.

A glittering occasion it certainly was, but its timing was less than propitious. War broke out in Europe in September, and one of the German astronomers only made it back home on the last ship. A little later two Belgian astronomers who had been visiting the U.S. were cut off from their homeland, one of them being Pol Swings of Liège. From the astronomical point of view, this was a great gain since Struve and Swings wrote a long series of important papers, often in collaboration, on stellar spectroscopy.

The work with the telescope already begun included research on white dwarf stars by Kuiper, who had joined the Chicago staff; by Jesse H. Greenstein, who developed methods for the quantitative chemical analysis of stellar atmospheres; and a particularly important discovery by Swings of the so-called forbidden lines—that is, atomic transitions of which the probability is so small that they never take place except under very special conditions.

As the war situation developed, a certain amount of war and spy fever arose. Immega was suspected of Nazi propaganda, rightly or wrongly, and left. Some of the local ranchers of German ancestry came under suspicion, while Struve, a former military man with memories of World War I and German attempts to involve Mexico, even contemplated the possible necessity of burying the main mirror to save it from damage.

On April 7, 1940, there was an annular eclipse of the sun crossing Texas, and Elvey took a party to what is now Big Bend National Park to try to determine the way in which the surface brightness of the sun's disk falls off from its center toward its edge. The method used was in fact not a good one, and he was not successful. By 1941 members of the staff began to be called away for war duties, starting with Horace Babcock, who had conceived an instrument for observing the solar corona outside a solar eclipse. Struve, much perturbed about the possible future of McDonald in

those times of crisis, talked of moving the whole Yerkes operation to Texas and made a detailed proposal to UT comptroller Calhoun for a cooperation between many institutions, to be centered on McDonald. This overture came to nothing, but in it can be seen the seeds of what would become, after the war, the Kitt Peak National Observatory in Arizona. By the late 1940s big consortium science was less of a novelty than it had been when the Texas–Chicago agreement was signed. The one consequence of Struve's proposal was a compact with Indiana University, which is still in force. Elvey left to engage in rocket research, and Kuiper was called away intermittently for a variety of duties. At Yerkes an optical bureau was organized for war work, which took away van Biesbroeck, Greenstein, and others.

Even so, an astonishing amount of research was completed, helped by deferments of some of the support staff, and the appointment of a retired physicist, Elmer Dershem, to keep things going on Mount Locke. The observers included the well-known astronomers W. A. Hiltner, Armin Deutsch, W. W. Morgan, Daniel Popper, and from time to time Greenstein and Henyey. From neutral Argentina came Carlos Cesco and Jorge Sahade, and from Mexico, Guido Münch. One striking result was the discovery, by Kuiper, that Titan, the largest moon of Saturn, had an atmosphere, the first such case noted in the solar system.

During World War II there was an almost complete cessation of astronomical research in Europe and a sharp curtailment in the U.S. Possibly the most important exception to this trend was McDonald Observatory, strengthened not only by its association with the Yerkes Observatory and the Department of Astronomy at the University of Chicago but by the fact that the *Astrophysical Journal* was published from that institution. As a result, immediately after the war McDonald became a sort of mecca, not only for young Americans eager to resume civilian lives, but also for visitors from many other countries eager to restore their scientific resources.

During this postwar period a number of instrumental improvements were introduced. In August 1949 a ten-inch refractor was transported from Cook Observatory in Pennsylvania and used at McDonald for asteroid and Milky Way photography. Hiltner introduced the use of the new photomultiplier tubes for stellar photometry in 1946 and rebuilt the coudé spectrograph. Kuiper mounted one of the new image tubes at the Cassegrain focus to produce intensified images. Proposals for the installation of a Schmidt-type telescope proved abortive. George van Biesbroeck passed his sixty-fifth birthday in 1945, the official retirement age at the University of Chicago, though in his case retirement meant very little, and he continued active in astronomy for almost another thirty years. He was a tiny little man, absolutely fearless, who would terrify the night assistants by standing on the rails of the high prime focus observing carriage to reach the equipment he needed. He actually observed with the 82-inch on his eighty-second birthday and at the 90-inch Steward telescope on his ninetieth.

Dershem had to be replaced as resident astronomer, and Arthur Adel of Michigan was chosen, but he only stayed one night because his wife was dismayed by the evident isolation of McDonald. In the end, Paul D. Jose, who had attended the 1939 dedication unrecognized and become assistant director of the Steward Observatory by 1945, was chosen. Back in Chicago there were some internal rivalries, so Struve hit upon a plan whereby he retained the chairmanship and took on a new position as honorary director of the McDonald and Yerkes observatories. Kuiper became the second director of McDonald on July 1, 1947, with Hiltner as his assistant director, a situation which still left Struve in real control.

When Kuiper became director there was an influx of new young people, many of whom have become well known since, including Nancy Roman, John Philips, Arthur Code, Arne Slettebak, Marshal Wrubel, and Robert Hardie. In addition, Thornton Page, whose galaxy research had been interrupted by war service, Swings from Belgium, Bengt Strömgren and Mogens Rudkjöbing from Denmark, and Adriaan Blaauw and Jan Oort from Holland were also there. Kuiper, though a superb astronomer, was not very successful as an administrator, and his lack of authority, with Struve in the background, was frustrating. Jose left Mount Locke after three years, and at the end of the 1948–49 academic year Kuiper asked to be relieved of his administrative duties. Struve himself left to take up a post as professor and chairman of the astronomy department at the University of California at Berkeley. In retrospect, the period of Struve's directorship, though beset with difficulties, had brought the McDonald-Chicago-Yerkes organization, which he always saw as a single unit, to a peak of perfection. This is evidenced by the almost unique cluster of honors and medals awarded to him and his colleagues. Struve gained the vice-presidency and later presidency of the International Astronomical Union, the Gold Medal of the Royal Astronomical Society, the Draper Medal of the U.S. National Academy of Sciences, and the Janssen Medal of the Société Astronomique of France. Kuiper got his own Janssen Medal and the Rittenhouse Medal of the Franklin Institute. Chandrasekhar was awarded the Adams Prize from Cambridge University, the Russell Prize of the American Astronomical Society, and the gold medals of both the Royal Astronomical Society and of the Astronomical Society of the Pacific. Later he won the Nobel Prize. Aden Meincl received the Adolph Lomb Medal of the Optical Society of America.

The achievements which earned these awards can only be summarized. We have already mentioned Greenstein's work on the composition of stellar atmospheres and Thornton Page's work on planetary nebulae and on groups of galaxies. Popper became the leading authority on binary and multiple stars. Keenan and Morgan produced the standard modern system of spectroscopic classification. Herzberg, himself later a Nobel laureate, made infrared observations of stars related to isotope abundances in stellar atmospheres. Chandrasekhar, the theorist, as part of his massive contributions led the way in the theory of stellar evolution. Kuiper studied the population of stars close to the sun, emphasizing the high incidence of duplicity, and discussed the so-called subdwarf stars. He then went on to extensive studies of the planets, discovering the presence of carbon dioxide in the atmosphere of Mars and finding the new satellites Miranda of Uranus and Nereid of Neptune. He also produced a new lunar atlas in which the effects of projection were removed. All this time von Biesbroeck continued his massive studies of binary stars. Oort and Hiltner investigated the distribution of light and color in extragalactic nebulae, and it was Hiltner who found that the light of distant stars in the Milky Way was polarized by passage through the clouds of particulate matter which exist in the interstellar medium. As for Struve himself, he had an uncanny knack of picking out for study particular stars which would later prove to be the ideal type objects of new classes of stars, all of intense interest to later astronomy.

The resignations of Kuiper and Struve in 1949 led to the appointment of Bengt Strömgren of Chicago's astronomy department and director of the observatories. To succeed Jose, Marlyn Krebs, son of the long-time superintendent at Yerkes, was appointed mountain superintendent at McDonald. In the early 1950s a good deal of improvement work to houses and installations was undertaken at Mount Locke, and a new support system for the 82-inch mirror designed to cure the defects of image formation was installed.

In 1951 Hiltner installed an improved coudé spectograph. In 1957 a new 36-inch telescope was installed on Mount Locke with optics by Boller and Chivens and optical parts designed by Joseph Nunn and Associates, who also did the new 82-inch support system. The building was constructed out of local materials by the mountain staff. This telescope was to be used principally for photometry. The chief benefactor, Harold M. Johnson, began as an assistant professor at Chicago from 1950 to 1953, then went to Lowell Observatory, and returned to Chicago in 1957. Later he went to Austin. Johnson developed what has become the standard system of stellar photometry. With Morgan, he wrote a basic paper correlating the photometric work with the spectral and luminosity classifications of stars developed by Morgan and Keenan. The work was especially important in the study of clusters of stars, enabling ages to be assigned to them in the following years based to a considerable extent on the pioneering work of Chandrasekhar on the evolution of stars.

Strömgren, for his part, experimented with photometry using narrow band pass filters, which had advantages of their own. As an outgrowth of this work, Hiltner and Strömgren concluded that the general density of hydrogen in the Milky Way was of the order of 0.2 atoms per cubic centimeter, yet elsewhere this density might be as high as 50 atoms per cubic centimeter. These results were, of course, later confirmed in essence by the radio astronomers.

Meinel, who had become associate director of the observatories in 1953, was succeeded by Adriaan Blaauw in 1956, but Blaauw left a year later to return to Holland, and Strömgren resigned to return to Denmark. Effective September 1, 1957, Kuiper was invited to try again as director, this time with genuine power. One of his aims was to involve the University of Texas in the work of the observatory. Austin had, so far, gained little advantage from the possession of the observatory, while the University of Chicago, with its eye on the impending expiration of the original agreement in 1962, was reluctant to spend money on an institution they did not own.

In Austin, Benedict had had an astronomy degree, and Ervin Prouse, although officially a mathematician, had studied astrophysics. Efforts to start astronomy courses had been, as we have seen, abortive, and the only astronomical instrument available was an old nine-inch Brashear refractor in a dome on top of what is now the Painter building, erected in 1932.

One of the implications of the original Chicago-Texas pact was that an astronomy department should be started in Austin. In 1952 a recent graduate of Chicago, Frank N. Edmonds, Jr., was recommended to

UT's president Painter and duly appointed to the Department of Mathematics and Astronomy. He began making high dispersion spectroscopic studies of stars soon afterward. When Kuiper again became director of McDonald, he proposed that the two universities establish a joint department of astronomy. As a result, a separate department was started with Edmonds as associate professor, the first faculty member in Austin. Prouse remained in mathematics. In Chicago some internal difficulties finally caused Kuiper to resign his directorship again in 1959, and in his place W. W. Morgan, the first American-born, was appointed director, effective March 1, 1960, with Edmonds as associate director. Kuiper retained the Chicago chairmanship, and Harold Johnson was appointed professor of astronomy at Austin. Shortly afterward Kuiper left Chicago to found the lunar and planetary laboratory at the University of Arizona. Gerard de Vaucouleurs, who already had an international reputation for his studies of galaxies, especially while he was in Australia in the 1950s, was appointed associate professor at Austin on October 1, 1960. In Australia he had suggested the concept of a supergalaxy including all the nearby ones, for which he would later be awarded the Herschel Medal of the Royal Astronomical Society. Though the idea of a joint department did not work out, Harold Johnson was appointed chairman at Austin on September 1, 1960. When he did not receive the McDonald directorship, he left the next February to join Kuiper at Arizona.

Despite all these administrative maneuvers, a great deal of work was accomplished at McDonald. Kuiper's asteroid survey was published, as was his rectified atlas of the moon. Van Biesbroeck continued his studies of binary stars. Robert Kraft began his classical studies of the Cepheid variable stars, and Johnson at Austin introduced computer reductions of photoelectric observations, going on to extend his photometric system to other passbands in the infrared. Kuiper also studied Mars at the very close opposition of 1958. Margaret and Geoffrey Burbidge had arrived from England and began their studies of the rotation of galaxies, while de Vaucouleurs embarked on the first edition of his standard *Reference Catalogue of Bright Galaxies*. Morgan developed a new system of classification of galaxies. Robert G. Tull joined the faculty and introduced the technique of photoelectric scanning of spectra, which, ever more highly developed, would loom large in the later history of instrumental development at McDonald.

The new compact with Chicago was signed in 1962 with the proviso that Texas would now appoint the new director to succeed Morgan. On September 1, 1963, Harlan J. Smith was appointed and has held the post until the present time.

Smith felt that the first thing to do was to improve the optical performance of the big telescope, which had never functioned at the level of excellence claimed by Plaskett. The French optician Jean Texerau was called in, prompting the witticism that the collaborating university should have one called "Chicagerau." Texerau proposed to leave the main mirror alone but to refigure the secondaries, which had only been perfunctorily tested by Lundin, so as to remove the image-forming errors of each combination. He succeeded in doing this to a high degree of accuracy in a period of intense work by hand-polishing over many weeks.

During the initial period of Harlan Smith's directorate there was a paucity of contributions from McDonald partly because of the departure of some of the more assiduous observers, such as the Burbidges, whose studies of the rotation of galaxies had pointed the way to one of the prime problems of the 1980s, namely that there seemed to be far more mass in the galaxies than could be accounted for by the visible stars. Another great loss at this time was the departure of the mountain superintendent, Marlyn Krebs, who had become deeply concerned with the lack of facilities for the education of his children in the Fort Davis area. He was succeeded by John Weis, whose attempts to impose martinet discipline at the mountain met with no enthusiasm, so he departed to be succeeded by the present superintendent, Curtis Laughlin.

At Austin the infant department was fortunate in the selection of its earliest graduate students. Freddie Talbert studied the spectrum of Procyon, Harold Ables worked on the photometry of galaxies, and Rhodesian Anthony Fairall examined so-called compact galaxies. New Zealander Graham Hill earned the first doctorate in astronomy from UT–Austin for a study of the Beta Cephei variable stars, whose importance had been first realized by Struve. William Kunkel studied flare stars, and Ronald Angione demonstrated the nonperiodic variability of quasars. Harlan Smith and his student Edwin Barker showed that there were enormous height variations on the surface of Mars. Robert Roosen studied the gegenschein, that elusive patch of luminosity opposite to the sun in the zodiac, showing that it is a faint reflection from interplanetary dust. By far the most distinguished student was the British-born Beatrice Tinsley, who had been brought up in New Zealand. She took as her topic the evolution of galaxies resulting from the evolution of their component stars. She went on to gain an international repu-

tation and a professorship at Yale before her death in 1981 at the age of 40. In 1985 a memorial visiting professorship in her name was established at Austin.

In 1966 a symposium was held at Marfa associated with the renaming of the 82-inch as the Struve telescope. Again, unfortunately, the papers contributed were never published.

Once the 82-inch telescope had been refurbished, the first priority in the mid-1960s was the construction of a new and more modern instrument. Starting in 1964, Smith negotiated with NASA for the construction of a larger telescope with an especial eye on impending missions to Mars. A joint arrangement between NASA, the National Science Foundation, and the University of Texas led to agreement on the construction of a telescope of about 105 inches in diameter and a subsidiary one of 30 inches, the main mirror of which would come from the central disk cut out of the larger instrument to provide a Cassegrain focus. The main mirror was to be made by a new process out of fused silica by the Corning Glass works, and this was ready by the fall of 1965. When edged, the final blank was just short of 108 inches in diameter and was figured by new techniques in only thirty months by the firm of Davidson Optronics in California. The optical design was of the Ritchey-Chrétien form, in which the primary mirror does not by itself produce a perfect image but in combination with Cassegrain and coudé secondaries does produce good images at these foci. This requires the maintenance of a very exact mutual alignment of the mirrors, so the mechanical design adopted included a solid steel tube. The coudé spectroscope was the largest in the world and occupied one whole floor of the building beneath the observing floor. The principal designer was Robert Tull. For Texas, the project officer for the construction of the whole telescope was Charles H. Jenkins.

The formal dedication of the new telescope and facility took place on November 26, 1968, with VIPs from Austin flying out on an Electra aircraft, and the NSIs (not so important) going by bus on the previous day. The day dawned in a downpour, but the dedication went off well, attended even by a few who had been present at the ceremonies in 1939. When it was time to return to Austin, the weather was frightful, with rain, sleet, and snow. The heavy aircraft broke through the taxiway and ground to a stop, fortunately with no injuries to it or its passengers.

In spite of this inauspicious beginning, the new telescope proved a great asset to Texas astronomy. One of the first programs undertaken with it was mounted in an incredibly short time by the observatory engineers led by Johnny Floyd and a group of scientists mainly from the Northeast. This was the proposal to shoot a laser beam at reflectors to be placed on the moon by the Apollo astronauts. The purpose was not only to measure distances exactly but also, when several reflectors were in place, to measure the attitude of the moon, which, so to speak, both nods and shakes its head in its orbit in motions known as librations. These laser measurements eventually attained an accuracy of only a few centimeters largely due to the skill of the leader of the observational team, Eric Silverberg. For many years McDonald was the only source of this type of data, which were analyzed partly in house by Derral Mulholland and Peter Shelus, and in more detail by the group led by Carol Alley. After fifteen years of use the laser principally responsible was donated to the National Air and Space Museum in Washington. In the meantime, newer equipment was installed on a smaller dedicated telescope erected on Mount Locke.

An additional enterprise was the construction of laser-ranging equipment, mounted on trailers, for observation of earth satellites. It was intended to detect earth crustal movements. After five years of operation under Texas' control in the Western U.S. and Chile, this equipment was turned over to NASA.

Another lunar program begun in 1968 by Evans and Edward Nather was the observation of lunar occultations with high-speed photometric equipment. This project continued until 1985 and produced a large body of information having many applications in stellar astronomy. It also led to an important instrumental development in the application of high-speed techniques to observation of many kinds of stars, especially the so-called cataclysmic variables and to the eruptive objects known as flare stars.

Yet another discovery made in 1968, using high-speed techniques, was the precise determination of the form of radiation from a neutron star, a supernova remnant in the Crab nebula, which rotates thirty times a second, by Nather and Brian Warner.

In 1970 a much-publicized near-tragedy occurred when a disgruntled employee attacked the 107-inch mirror with hammer and pistol, fortunately not doing significant damage to its optical functioning.

In 1971 three expeditions were sent to Australia, India, and South Africa to observe, with a variant of high-speed technology, the occultation of the bright multiple star Beta Scorpii by Jupiter, a very rare type of event. The results analyzed by W. B. Hubbard proved most enlightening and were used in planning the later spacecraft missions to Jupiter. An additional expedition was sent to the Virgin Islands to observe the occultation of one component of Beta Scorpii by the Jovian satellite Io. This led to very exact determinations, in combination with results obtained elsewhere, of Io's dimensions and form.

In 1973 one of the six very long solar eclipses of the twentieth century took place, with a track crossing the African territories of the Sahara. The astronomy and physics departments at Austin collaborated with Princeton to send an expedition to Chinguetti in Mauritania to observe the so-called Einstein shift, the bending of light rays passing near the sun by its gravitational field, detectable by displacement of star images seen near the sun during a total solar eclipse. In spite of the unfavorable weather, the results from the eclipse photographs and from comparison photographs taken at night by a follow-up expedition using the same equipment in November confirmed the Einstein result, though not with the accuracy hoped for. Better accuracy would have made it possible to discriminate between Einstein's theory and variants of it.

Back at home, using over the years ever more sophisticated equipment designed by Tull, David Lambert and many students and visiting associates were making important contributions to the observational evidence of stellar evolution by studying the abundances of isotopes in stellar atmospheres. A vigorous program of planetary research was funded by NASA, while de Vaucouleurs and many associates from different parts of the world were advancing galaxy research and incorporating the results from Texas and elsewhere in later editions of the great galaxy catalog. A British and Australian husband and wife team, Derek and Beverly Wills, specialized in the observation of quasars and other sources of radio waves.

Many of these radio sources had been identified by surveys conducted at the University of Texas Radio Astronomy Observatory (UTRAO) south of the highway between Marfa and Alpine. This facility, designed by James N. Douglas who came to Texas about the same time as Smith, was built by him and his associates. It looked nothing like a telescope but consisted of a series of antennae, each of helical form, numbering 832, arranged in several east-west lines over a two mile square area of flat land (fig. 5). The antenna arrays could be tilted up to various angles so that they pointed to selected zones of the sky. The signals from all these arrays were fed to a trailer containing recording equipment.

The arrangement is a radio interferometer: because the angular resolution attainable on the sky by a telescope of given diameter depends on the ratio of the

Figure 5. Part of the University of Texas Radio Astronomy Observatory near Marfa, Texas.

diameter of the telescope to the wavelength of the radiation being received, a conventional telescope to operate in radio wavelengths would have to be miles across to match the visual resolution of a relatively small optical telescope. The interferometer principle, which combines signals from widely separated antennae, so to speak, deceives the sky into believing that it is being observed with a telescope of the diameter equal to the longest separation between the antennae. UTRAO was designed to survey the radio sky accessible from Texas. A catalog of some 70,000 sources, which may be quasars, galaxies, or even other objects, is in the course of publication. The positional accuracy of the catalog is sufficiently great that efforts can be made, for example in the Wills' program, to identify optical counterparts of those radio sources.

A second excursion into the longer wavelength regions of the electromagnetic spectrum is provided by the University of Texas Millimeter Wave Observatory, which consists of a 16-foot metal dish concentrating

radiation to a receiver at a focal ratio of f/0.5. This instrument, originally constructed for other purposes and installed at the Balcones Research Center near Austin, was moved to the slopes of Mount Locke in 1967. In cooperation with the electrical engineering department and Bell Laboratories, it was greatly improved. Under the direction of Paul Vanden Bout, now director of the National Radio Astronomy Observatory, began an important series of investigations of features of the interstellar medium in our own and other galaxies, especially those known as giant molecular clouds.

Back in Austin, the diversity of the Department of Astronomy was steadily increasing, especially at first with a strengthening of the theoretical side. David Arnett and David Schramm specialized in studies of the cosmic abundance of the elements arising from the Big Bang. After they left, Craig Wheeler, Gregory Shields, and others earned great reputations for their studies of the causes of the stellar outbursts known as supernovae. The department is strongly represented in the Space Telescope programs, the astronomic one being led by William H. Jefferys.

During recent years hopes for a new and larger telescope have led to extensive studies of the engineering and optical problems associated with the construction of a telescope with a diameter of the order of 300 inches.

During these later years other universities in Texas have embarked on astronomical programs. For some twenty years, beginning in 1956, Pan American University in Edinburg maintained a series of courses for astronomy majors that supplied quite a number of graduate students to more advanced courses elsewhere. However, this effort was terminated and a 41-inch mirror obtained in hopes of installing a telescope in South Texas was sold off to Stephen F. Austin State University in Nacogdoches (where the telescope was recently completed). Paul Engle, chief architect of the program at Pan American University, left for Arkansas.

At the University of Texas at Dallas, Beatrice Tinsley, before leaving for Yale, had an important effect on theoretical research, but the chief center for theoretical research had been at Rice University in Houston. To quote the newsletter announcing the fact that the Department of Space Physics and Astronomy was to act as host to the meeting of the American Astronomical Society in 1986:

> Since 1963 Rice has continuously expanded its programs in Space Physics and Astronomy. In the two decades following, approximately 100 students have received Ph.D.'s and about 50 have received the Master of Science. Today the Department consists of 24 faculty members, whose research activities are mainly concerned with large-scale phenomena ranging from Earth's atmosphere to the cosmos. The primary discipline running through Professor D. D. Clayton's research is nuclear astrophysics, focusing during the past few years on the abundance of heavy nuclei and the theory of nucleosynthesis through analysis of the results of gamma ray astronomy. Professor L. L. Dressel has used many observatory facilities to observe galaxies from radio to x-ray wavelengths to study phenomena such as the presence of neutral and ionized gases in elliptical galaxies and the "starbursts" in lenticular galaxies. Professor R. J. Dufour makes observational studies of gaseous nebulae and galaxies to determine the variations and nucleosynthetic origins of the CNO element group. Professor R. C. Haymes helped start gamma

ray astronomy 20 years ago and made the first detection of gamma rays from the central region of the galaxy. Professor F. C. Michel is interested in the physics of astrophysical magnetospheres, and has made important theoretical advances in the explanation of the behavior of neutron stars, and their associated pulsars. Professor C. R. O'Dell, having been project scientist for the Hubble Space Telescope for the ten years prior to 1982, when he went to Rice, proposes to use this to develop a new cosmic distance scale through studies of H II regions, as well as studying, in collaboration with Professor Lyman Spitzer of Princeton the abundance and ionization of the interstellar medium. He is a coinvestigator on the Astro Shuttle mission, which will conduct measurements of Halley's comet.

Some of the observational work done by the Rice faculty has used the balloon-launching facility at Palestine, Texas, where, among other experiments, telescopes with instruments sensitive to x-ray and cosmic radiation, which are absorbed by the earth's atmosphere, have been launched high into the stratosphere to make astronomical and other observations. Many of the users of this facility come from out-of-state institutions, and, although the launching is strictly a Texas activity, it is difficult to claim most of this for Texas astronomy any more than the Johnson Space Center (discussed elsewhere in this volume) can be claimed for Texas astronomy.

In every sense of the word "Texas" we are on surer ground in noting some of the state's amateur astronomers and societies that have been very active, especially since World War II, stimulated possibly by the presence of McDonald Observatory and by the development of the space program. One of the most colorful was Walter Woodford Myers (1908–85), who had in 1955 a 20-inch Cassegrain telescope on a truck (he claimed it was the second largest in Texas after McDonald). He was mainly interested in public education and reactivated the Houston Amateur Astronomy Club, which had had a brief life during the war. Myers was probably better known to the public as an official timer of boxing bouts, but he did make some variable star observations. So did J. Russell Smith (born 1908), who contributed an article on Mars to *Sky and Telescope* in 1942. After the war he wrote a book for high school students, founded the Association of Lunar and Planetary Observers, and established his 16-inch telescope at the Skyview Observatory in Eagle Pass. John Wesley Simpson (1914–77), an Antarctic explorer, pistol champion, fingerprint expert, and deputy sheriff as well as teacher of navigation who photographed the 1940 eclipse from a plane over Houston, wrote numerous articles on the libration clouds of dust that linger near the so-called Langrangian points in space ahead and astern of the moon. Thomas R. Williams, a senior chemist at the Shell Company in Houston, has been very active as an observer, as a writer of popular and other articles, and as an official of the Houston Astronomical Society with a keen interest in the history of astronomy in Texas. Prominent among the younger set is Paul D. Maley, now at Ford Aerospace, who has been an assiduous observer of comets, occultations, minor planets, and an organizer of astronomical activity. He joined a moon-watch team for artificial satellite observations in 1960 when he was only thirteen years old. In 1979 Maley went to Guyana to observe the occultation of a star by the asteroid Metis; he is currently president of the Johnson Space Center Astronomical Society.

These are only a few of the many names that might be mentioned since there are active amateur societies in several Texas cities, including Austin. Outside San Antonio, Curtis Vaughan, who has endowed a chair of astronomy at Austin, has erected a fully-equipped private observatory of professional quality. He has served for many years as a member of the Board of Visitors of the McDonald Observatory, a body of prominent Texans who have supported its work with generous endowments and many other kinds of help. One outcome of their efforts has been the establishment of the J. L. Moody Junior Visitor Center near the observatory containing exhibits illustrating astronomical topics of special relevance to its work. Another important outreach has been the effort, not supported by state funds, to produce a monthly *McDonald News* and an award-winning daily radio spot called "Star Date," carried by many stations around the U.S. Deborah Byrd has been the moving spirit in the prepa-

ration of the scripts for this and is also active in promoting the annual get-together of observers with their own telescopes, which is held at the Prude Ranch, not far from the foot of Mount Locke.

In composing this paper I have received a great deal of most generous assistance from many sources: they include the staffs of the Institute of Texan Cultures at San Antonio, of the Barker Historical Collection at the University of Texas, of the Austin Public Library, of the Library of Texas Christian University at Fort Worth, and of the U.S. Coast and Geodetic Survey. Among individuals I wish to thank especially Oscar Monnig, Dr. Virgil Barnes, Dr. Robert Harrington of the U.S. Naval Observatory, and Thomas R. Williams of Houston, who allowed me to use items from his astronomical history files, Janet Mattei of the American Association of Variable Star Observers, and Dr. Jean Dommanget of the Belgian Royal Observatory at Uccle. I have drawn extensively on the publication "Men of Science in Texas, 1820–1880" by S. W. Geiser in *Field and Laboratories*, Vols. 26 and 27, and on the manuscript of a history of McDonald Observatory, "Big and Bright," by Dr. Derral Mulholland and myself now in publication by the University of Texas Press.

Bibliography

American Astronomical Society (1985): Notice of January 1986 meeting.

Evans, D. S., and Mulholland, J. D. *Big and Bright: A History of McDonald Observatory*. Austin and London: University of Texas Press, 1986.

Mattei, J. Files of American Association of Variable Star Observers.

Williams, T. R. Private astronomical biographical files.

5

NASA and the Space Sciences

Wm. David Compton

"Houston, Tranquility Base here. The Eagle has landed."
— Neil Armstrong, commander of *Apollo 11*,
20 July 1969.

BY THE TIME those words were spoken from the moon's surface, radio and television audiences around the world had become accustomed to hearing transmissions from space begin with the name of Texas' largest city. Starting in June 1965, NASA's manned space missions were directed from the Mission Control Center at the Manned Spacecraft Center (MSC), principal focus of the United States' manned space flight program, twenty-five miles southeast of downtown Houston. For the next twenty years MSC—since 1973, the Lyndon B. Johnson Space Center (JSC)—charted the course for manned space flight (Fig. 1). Ten two-man Gemini earth-orbital missions; eleven Apollo missions, including six moon landings; three long-duration flights of Skylab; a cooperative mission with the Soviet Union; and the flight testing and operational flights of the world's first reusable manned spacecraft, the Shuttle Orbiter, were all directed from the Texas center.[1] In 1984 JSC was named to lead NASA's effort to build a permanent space station in earth orbit.

Manned space flight was certainly the most widely publicized aspect of the American space program, the aspect that brought worldwide attention to Texas as a center of space activity. The act creating the National Aeronautics and Space Administration (NASA) in 1958, however, gave the new agency a much broader mandate: to expand human knowledge of phenomena in the atmosphere and space. That mandate encompassed the scientific study of space phenomena as well as human exploration of space. Indeed, for its first two years NASA's principal activities in space were scientific: research in astronomy and space physics using instrumented (unmanned) probes and earth-orbiting spacecraft. NASA recognized from the outset that a sound program of space exploration must involve the nation's scientific research community, located for the most part in the universities. Hence, in its early days the new space agency established a program of grants to support space research, provide financial aid for students in space-related fields, and assist universities in upgrading their scientific research facilities.[2]

The flights of the Soviet spacecraft *Sputnik 1* and *2* in 1957 were widely perceived as a challenge to the supremacy of American technology and science. Among the consequences of *Sputnik* was a national soul-searching to discover the causes of this loss in world

Figure 1. NASA's Lyndon B. Johnson Space Center, Houston, Texas (photo courtesy National Aeronautics and Space Administration).

leadership. Attention quickly centered on education in the sciences and mathematics, and a thoroughgoing reappraisal of the effectiveness of the American educational system followed. Texas participated fully in a national effort to improve the quality of educational institutions and programs from the elementary level to graduate school. By the end of the lunar decade Texas could claim more than one center of excellence in academic research, and several Texas universities were actively pursuing projects in space-related sciences. NASA's support, in the form of research grants and stipends for promising graduate and undergraduate students, was an important stimulus to this development.

But it was manned space flight that drew the attention of the world to Texas, and the Johnson Space Center is the major focus of space activity in the Lone Star State. Perhaps it seems appropriate to the world at large that this outsized adventure is directed and con-

trolled from the state that has always liked to think of itself as larger than life.

Origins of Johnson Space Center

Space exploration came to Texas in 1962 when the first of nearly two thousand employees of NASA's Langley Research Center moved from Hampton, Virginia, to Houston to open a new Manned Spacecraft Center. Scarcely four years old as an organization, MSC had begun as the Space Task Group, organized at Langley Research Center shortly after the space agency began operations on October 1, 1958. At that time NASA had formulated no detailed plans for America's exploration of space, but two things were clear: the new frontier offered almost unlimited possibilities for scientific research, and humans would venture into space as soon as the technology could be developed to sustain them there. With the advent in mid-1961 of Apollo, the manned lunar landing project, manned space flight became NASA's largest single activity, and the need for a separate research and development installation to direct it was apparent. A search for a suitable location began that summer, and on September 19, 1961, NASA Headquarters announced that a 1,000-acre tract near Houston, to be donated to the government by Rice University,[3] had been picked as the site for the new development center. While their sixty-million-dollar complex was being built, MSC's engineers and managers transacted their business from rented offices in eleven locations scattered around southeast Houston.[4]

Houston and the smaller communities surrounding the new space center warmly welcomed NASA and its contractors. Within three years a score of new buildings arose on the featureless coastal plain. Together with the facilities put up by the major contractors involved in manned space flight, the center was the nucleus around which a residential and commercial complex began a period of growth which has not yet abated.

Johnson Space Center's Role in the Space Program

Since 1958 the Johnson Space Center has borne the primary responsibility within NASA for developing the spacecraft and techniques for manned operations in space.[5] JSC's engineers and scientists formulated and refined the concepts for the spacecraft that took astronauts to the moon, landed them there, and returned them to earth; selected and trained the crew members who flew the spacecraft; monitored and safeguarded the physical condition of the astronauts and investigated their physiological reactions to the space environment; developed the techniques for conducting flight operations; and provided the facilities for collecting, preserving, and distributing for scientific study the samples of lunar rock and soil returned by the lunar exploration missions.

SPACECRAFT DEVELOPMENT

When manned space flight began, data on the effects of that harsh environment on humans and machines were almost nonexistent. Test flights—one means whereby such data were customarily acquired—were hazardous, time-consuming, and expensive; hence, a major part of the development effort at Johnson Space

Center was an extensive developmental testing and preflight simulation program. Systems, spacecraft, and materials—and sometimes crew members as well—could be exposed to simulated mission conditions before lives were risked in actual flight. The test facilities built for this purpose support the center's ongoing research and development programs, contributing to improvements in existing technology and development of new technology for manned space flight. To date, they represent an investment of more than $200 million. Many of these facilities were unique when they were built. Some have later been duplicated elsewhere, but as a group, they are without equal in the United States.[6] In JSC's test laboratories complete spacecraft, major subsystems, components, and materials can be subjected to conditions approximating those of launch and ascent, free flight in space, and re-entry and landing. The center's major facilities are briefly described in the paragraphs that follow.

In the vibration and acoustic test facility entire spacecraft can be mechanically shaken over wide acceleration and frequency ranges and subjected to the acoustic pressures experienced during launch and ascent through the atmosphere. Thermal vacuum chambers with working space up to 55 feet in diameter and 90 feet high can be pumped down to pressures less than 10^{-6} torr. Chamber walls cooled to $-193°C$ by liquid nitrogen provide a heat sink similar to the blackness of space, and a battery of carbon-arc lamps simulates solar radiation. Some chambers are man-rated—provided with the safeguards necessary for tests involving humans—so that fully manned spacecraft can be tested. During Apollo these chambers were extensively used to work out problems of thermal control in the command and service modules and the lunar landing module.

Smaller thermal vacuum chambers, ranging in size from 3.6 feet in diameter and 6 feet high to 1.3 by 2 feet, are used in the space environment effects laboratory for development, evaluation, and qualification testing of spacecraft components, preflight conditioning of flight articles, development and calibration of instruments to be used in the large chambers, and evaluation of materials for seals, adhesives, and surface coatings. The larger two chambers are equipped with solar simulators and heat sinks. All can be evacuated to 10^{-6} torr or less.

Protection against re-entry heating, always a problem in manned space flight, has been studied in two arc-heated tunnels at JSC. These tunnels produce high-temperature gas streams at supersonic or hypersonic speeds, in which test panels of heat-protective material up to 2 feet square can be tested. Conditions of mass flow and temperature closely approximating those of spacecraft re-entry can be produced. Heat shields for Apollo and Shuttle were developed in these tunnels, and they are used for continuing study of materials for heat protection.

Among the more important requirements of the Apollo project were systems for communication, telemetry, and spacecraft tracking at distances up to 250,000 miles. To support development in these areas, JSC has a large anechoic chamber, an outdoor antenna range, a sophisticated electronic systems test laboratory, and radar and telemetry development systems laboratories. The anechoic chamber, like the thermal vacuum chambers, is large enough (50 by 50 by 60 feet) to contain an entire spacecraft, permitting interference-free measurement of antenna patterns for spacecraft transmitters. On the outdoor range similar measurements can be made at distances up to 2,000 feet. In the electronic systems test laboratory, JSC engineers can simulate the entire communications network that links a spacecraft in orbit to ground installations, including voice, television, and telemetry. The system can incorporate radio-frequency links to the orbiting tracking and data relay satellite used in mission communication. Controlled inputs injected into the system simulate the noise levels, signal attenuation, Doppler shifts, and antenna pattern effects experienced during actual flights. In this laboratory new and unproven designs for communications systems can be tested in the earliest stages of design to assess their performance and compatibility.

A 115-acre corner of Johnson Space Center accommodates the thermochemical test area, where spacecraft propulsion and auxiliary power systems are evaluated. Small rocket thrusters, fluid storage and transfer systems (including cryogenics), pyrotechnic devices, and the performance and reliability of fuel cells can be evaluated under space conditions.

CREW SYSTEMS

JSC's Crew Systems Division is responsible for life-support systems, environmental-control systems, and the space suits and mobility aids that allow astronauts to work outside the spacecraft. During Apollo and Skylab the division worked closely with the Medical Research and Operations Directorate to develop the sensors and monitoring systems required in the medical research program (see section entitled "Research in Space Medicine").

The division has its own test chambers in which crew systems technology can be tested. Environmental conditions within the chambers can be controlled to simulate many types of environment. Ranging in size from 9 to 6,500 cubic feet, these chambers allow testing of developmental hardware and conduct of procedures which may include fully suited crew members. The largest of these, the 20-foot chamber, was used before the Skylab missions as a mockup of the orbital workshop in which a complete simulation of a three-person, fifty-six-day mission was conducted.

Among the notable contributions of the Crew Systems Division are the space suits used during Apollo and subsequent programs. These suits must provide a closed, life-sustaining environment in space without unduly restricting the mobility and dexterity of the astronaut. For lunar surface exploration, an additional garment and equipment were added, protecting the explorers against thermal and cosmic radiation and meteoroids while supplying oxygen and water and dissipating metabolic heat. The lunar surface suit was sometimes called "the third spacecraft" because it provided virtually all of the life-support systems found in the command module and lunar module. Using the most advanced versions of these suits and recharging them with expendables between excursions, the astronauts on *Apollo 17* left their lunar module three times, staying more than seven hours on the moon's surface each time. Since then, working outside the spacecraft has become a normal part of space operations.

Mobility for astronauts outside their spacecraft in earth orbit has always been an objective of space flight, and one of the major experiments on Skylab was the evaluation of an astronaut maneuvering unit. The unit gives the astronaut control of translation and rotation on three axes, incorporates gyroscopic stabilization and control, and allows free use of the hands. Developed in cooperation with the Air Force and tested in orbit on Skylab, this "one-man spacecraft" has since been used on Shuttle missions for the repair and recovery of malfunctioning satellites.

ASTRONAUT SELECTION AND TRAINING

From Mercury through the Apollo era the astronauts were the celebrities of the manned space flight program. Mercury, Gemini, and the early Apollo missions were concerned largely with developing spacecraft systems and operational procedures; hence, the first three classes of astronauts, thirty members in all, came from the ranks of military test pilots experienced in aircraft development work. Later, partly because science was perceived to be of increasing importance to late Apollo and post-Apollo programs, astronaut candidates having professional scientific qualifications were chosen and trained as pilots so that they could competently operate spacecraft systems.

As space programs have evolved, so have the qualifications of spacefarers. One of the conclusions from Skylab was that persons of ordinary rather than exceptional physical condition could withstand the stresses of orbital flight, and plans for Shuttle were based on the fact that crews need not be composed entirely of pilots. Shuttle missions may involve three classes of crew members: pilot-astronauts, who are responsible for operation of the spacecraft; mission specialists, who may be scientists and whose prime responsibility is for conducting in-orbit experiments; and payload specialists, who are trained for the operation of specialized Shuttle payloads. Shuttle has also established another first for American manned space flight: the recruitment of women into the astronaut corps as mission and payload specialists.

Astronaut training has always been strongly spacecraft- and mission-oriented and has leaned heavily on simulations to duplicate as closely as possible the actual hardware and procedures to be used in flight. Astronauts spent hours in training simulators, kept up to date as changes were made in spacecraft, working on procedures for managing spacecraft systems, navigation, and operation of scientific equipment. JSC engineers developed high-fidelity simulators in which such critical mission operations as rendezvous and docking could be rehearsed. Earth- and lunar-orbital operations simulators were equipped with the most realistic views possible, using both photographs and three-dimensional models, of what the astronauts could expect to observe in flight. Procedures trainers coupled to computers allowed instructors to drill the crews in emergency and contingent procedures as well as normal spacecraft operations. Virtually every phase of a lunar mission, from launch through earth orbit to lunar flight, could be duplicated on the trainers at JSC.

A major problem in spacecraft development as well as training was the limited ability to simulate reduced gravity on the earth's surface. Short periods (less than one minute) of null gravity can be created in aircraft flying on parabolic paths such that centrifugal force offsets gravity. A modified Air Force KC-135 aircraft provides one of two major methods used to acclimate astronauts to weightlessness (null- or zero-g) as well as to verify in-flight procedures such as the operation of controls or experiments. The alternative method is to immerse the suited astronaut in water, carefully

weighting his body and limbs so that they are neutrally buoyant, neither floating nor sinking; this produces an effect closely resembling null gravity. Johnson Space Center built a large neutral-buoyancy training facility in the late 1970s; it is extensively used to train crews in extravehicular tasks and to work out procedures for zero-gravity operations.

MISSION PLANNING AND FLIGHT OPERATIONS

Johnson Space Center is responsible for the detailed planning of a manned space flight mission, an exercise in optimization involving dozens of factors. During Apollo the principal objective was to place the greatest useful payload on the moon at the spot where the most useful scientific information could be obtained, with minimum risk to the astronauts. Trajectory calculations, which involved extensive application of celestial mechanics, took uncounted man-hours and thousands of hours of computer time. Flight planning—the distribution of the essential tasks in the time available during the mission—required equally meticulous study.

The most visible phase of space missions to the public is mission control, the responsibility of the Mission Control Center at JSC. From liftoff to landing, flight control officers, mission planners, and scientists constantly monitored the condition of astronauts and spacecraft via telemetry and observed lunar surface activities via television, keeping track of essential systems and directing the activities of the lunar explorers. Mission planners provided many contingency plans in case of need. At almost any point in a mission, malfunction of a system could imperil crew safety or mission success, and flight directors were prepared to change the flight plan as necessary. The most conspicuous test of contingency planning occurred on *Apollo 13*, when explosion of an oxygen storage tank deprived the spacecraft of electrical power and primary propulsion. For four days mission planners worked with systems experts, improvising procedures to navigate the moribund spacecraft back to a successful re-entry.

JOHNSON SPACE CENTER AND ITS CONTRACTORS

Like NASA's other development centers, Johnson Space Center relies on contractors to build its space hardware. But development of a manned spacecraft has always been a collaborative venture—an operating mode that has been called "participative responsibility."[7] NASA has never been merely a customer, providing specifications to a contractor and accepting the finished product. From the beginning, the space agency based its planning on the premise that no single organization has all the resources necessary to carry out an entire space project and that the national space programs arc most successful when every source of talent, in government or outside, can be brought to bear on development. JSC engineers are involved in spacecraft production from start to finish, refining design concepts, evaluating new technology, conducting development tests and simulations to discover problems that might otherwise appear only during operations, and periodically subjecting systems and subsystems to the environmental tests previously described. When problems are uncovered, JSC's engineering staff works hand in glove with the contractor—sometimes at the contractor's plant, sometimes in JSC's own laboratories—to resolve them.

Contractors also support the research and development operations at JSC, staffing the test laboratories and other support functions and providing experienced personnel to conduct many of the operational functions of the center. Recently, as orbital flights of the Shuttle have become more frequent and the spacecraft's characteristics better understood, JSC delegated more responsibility for conducting Shuttle operations to contractors. The technical staff is thereby largely freed to concentrate on the center's primary tasks, research and development of more advanced projects.

The close cooperation between JSC and its contractors was typical of the 1960s and 1970s and led to the common description of the space program as a "team effort." Though the phrase is trite, it accurately represents the reality of the manned space flight program. In a project the size of Apollo, no individual could expect to win fame, perhaps not even recognition; but the satisfaction of participating in an achievement such as the lunar landing was reward enough for most participants. Motivation was seldom a problem. Much has changed since Apollo ended, in particular the sense of urgency imposed by President Kennedy's challenge; but the spirit of that era survives at Johnson Space Center, assuring that Texas will be in the forefront of space exploration for many years to come.

Scientific Activities at Johnson Space Center

For its first few years the Johnson Space Center had no significant program of purely scientific research. It was, after all, the engineering development center for manned space flight, and engineering and operational tasks came first. This situation reflected the near-total separation of manned space flight and space science in NASA; the problems of manned space flight were not problems that required scientific research, and the urgency of Apollo pushed scientific questions into the background until the lunar landing was reasonably assured.[8]

In 1966, however, looking ahead to manned space flight activity after the lunar landing, the Houston center created a Science and Applications Directorate and a Medical Research and Operations Directorate, both of which would support research programs related to manned space flight. An important role of scientists in these directorates was to provide competence within the center to work with researchers who were conducting investigations in the Apollo program. Sometimes this involved the JSC scientist as a co-investigator; more often the science staff assisted outside investigators in working through the problems that arose in the course of fitting a scientific experiment into spacecraft and flight operations.

The principal research activity at JSC grew out of two major responsibilities of the center: the biomedical problems of manned space flight and the collection and management of the lunar samples.

RESEARCH IN SPACE MEDICINE

Before people flew in space, medical opinion was divided as to the effects of the space environment on the human body and its ability to function normally in weightlessness. Optimists believed that the effects would be minimal; pessimists believed they could be catastrophic, and this view, espoused by some highly reputed scientists, was widely publicized. JSC's own medical experts were more sanguine, but in order to refute the pessimists, they had to proceed cautiously, collecting as much data as possible as the program progressed.[9]

During Project Mercury, JSC's medical staff primarily supported flight operations—monitoring the health of the astronauts before flight, certifying their fitness for flight, and monitoring critical physiological systems during the mission. (In theory at least, a flight surgeon had authority to terminate a mission if a life-threatening medical emergency arose; this was never tested in practice.) Pre- and postflight examination of the astronauts yielded information concerning the effects of stress on normal, healthy individuals—data necessary to evaluate the effects of space flight and not otherwise available.

Mercury proved the doomsayers wrong and showed that man could not only survive but could function normally in earth-orbital flight and withstand the multiple-g forces encountered during re-entry. On the longer missions, however, signs of incipient cardiovascular deconditioning and other changes appeared. These observed changes, along with other effects that were expected to occur on longer flights, led to more extensive medical investigations in the second manned space flight project, Gemini.

During Gemini, flight times were systematically extended as much as the medical experts were willing to allow—first to four, then to eight, finally to fourteen days. All the Gemini astronauts performed normally in flight, but physiological changes occurred which could have presented problems for really long stays in space. Besides the effects on the cardiovascular system, changes in body fluids and blood chemistry occurred, along with loss of calcium. Although all the pilots soon returned to their preflight norms after the missions, data from Gemini raised the question of how long the changes might continue. Man's ability to take long journeys in space—such as a trip to Mars or an extended stay in an earth-orbiting space station—might be limited by physiology. The Gemini missions also cast doubt on the feasibility of working outside the spacecraft in weightlessness. The first attempts at extravehicular activity seemed to show that minor tasks on the ground became vastly more difficult in the absence of gravity, exhausting the astronauts after only a few minutes of work. When adequate handholds and foot restraints were provided, however, most of the difficulty disappeared.

During Apollo, medical investigators could collect only such data as could be transmitted back to earth by telemetry, and they were constantly constrained by operational necessities, which normally took precedence over most of the medical experiments. The limited number of test subjects made it more difficult than usual to determine whether a given change was a normal result of space flight or an idiosyncratic response to the environment. One lesson learned from Apollo was that it was essential to establish individual norms for each astronaut so that changes during flight could be better interpreted; a statistical treatment of results was impossible. Still, enough reliable information was collected to confirm that space flight entailed significant physiological penalties and to show where additional research was needed.[10]

In general, the biomedical observations made on the Apollo missions substantiated and extended the tentative conclusions drawn from Gemini. Two additional problems surfaced, however, that had serious implications for long-term space flight. Motion sickness appeared on *Apollo 8*. Nausea and vomiting created transient problems on two flights, and milder episodes of vestibular (inner-ear) disturbance affected half the lunar missions. On *Apollo 15*, the mission commander's electrocardiogram showed marked anomalies after a period of strenuous exercise on the moon, causing considerable concern until a possible cause could be assigned to it. Both of these problems appeared to be individualistic responses to weightlessness. The cardiac anomalies never reappeared; the vestibular disturbances did, and they were serious enough to threaten future missions.

The opportunity to conduct systematic biomedical research in space came with the Apollo Applications Program (later called Skylab), conceived in 1965 to bridge the gap between Apollo and the next major manned program, which was at the time still undefined. Apollo Applications was planned around the use of a large "orbital workshop" in a long-lived earth orbit to extend the duration of man's stays in space. Missions lasting as long as three months would allow astronauts to conduct numerous scientific and technological experiments. Long-term medical investigations were among the project's primary justifications.[11]

Skylab was the first project in which man's responses to the space environment were measured in real time from the beginning of the mission, so that trends in adaptation could be followed day by day. The workshop contained a bicycle ergometer and instrumentation for measuring heart rate and metabolic rate during exercise, a lower-body negative-pressure device to follow the course of cardiovascular deconditioning, and a rotating chair to measure the response of the vestibular system to weightlessness. Blood samples were taken regularly during the missions and preserved for later analysis to assess the magnitude of hematological changes. Perhaps the most difficult of all the experiments was a calcium-balance study conducted on all the Skylab missions to assess the seriousness of calcium loss over the long term. After each mission medical results were evaluated so that plans for the next flight could be modified if it seemed advisable. Between May 1973 and February 1974, data were collected on nine crew members for periods of twenty-eight, fifty-nine, and eighty-four days.[12]

Skylab's results showed that entry into weightlessness triggers a sequence of changes in the body, an adaptation process that continues for several weeks before a new equilibrium state is reached. The shift in the distribution of body fluids from the lower to the upper body sets off a series of responses, including loss of fluids, reduction in blood volume and red-cell mass, and changes in electrolyte and hormone levels. None of these changes is disabling and all are reversed, more or less rapidly, on return to normal gravity. Potentially more serious was cardiovascular deconditioning, which continued throughout the first (twenty-eight-day) mission. Longer flights, however, showed that deconditioning was time-limited and that the effects could be delayed by in-flight physical exercise and reversed by repeated exposure to lower-body negative pressure.

Vestibular problems were evident on Skylab, most notably on the second mission, when all three crew members were affected for the first three days of the missions, but after a short period of adaptation no amount of stimulation of the vestibular system could produce motion sickness in orbit. Readaptation on return to earth was uneventful for all the Skylab astronauts. Space sickness (or "space-adaptation syndrome") was the most important of all the problems remaining unsolved after Skylab, the only one that resisted countermeasures and was not completely alleviated by treatment. The most troublesome aspect of space-adaptation syndrome is that the susceptibility of any particular individual cannot be predicted before flight, and investigation of the syndrome continues on Shuttle missions.

JSC's medical investigations on Skylab allayed practically all the remaining fears concerning human adaptability to the space environment and the ability to readapt to normal gravity after flight. The continuous loss of calcium (which never produced any overt ill effects) seems controllable by dietary supplements. If proper attention is paid to exercise, diet, work-rest cycles, and conditioning of the cardiovascular system during flight, human physiology seems not to limit the ability to live and work in space.[13]

With the advent of the Shuttle Orbiter and Spacelab—a self-contained Shuttle payload comprising a manned laboratory in orbit—JSC's role in the life sciences is expanding to more general investigations of living systems in the space environment. The first steps have been taken on Shuttle missions in working with experimental animals in space. When the American space station becomes functional, long-term investigation of many aspects of life science can be undertaken.

LUNAR SCIENCE AT JOHNSON SPACE CENTER

JSC's responsibility for the lunar spacecraft implied that the Houston center would have to work intimately with the scientists whose equipment was to be carried to the moon and with those who would investigate the samples brought back by the lunar explorers. With the establishment of JSC's Science and Applications Directorate, this collaboration with the outside scientific community was placed on a firm footing. In the summer of 1967 JSC's director of Science and Applications convoked a conference of lunar scientists to help in planning for the management of lunar exploration. At this conference, JSC and the academic scientists laid the groundwork for cooperation in planning Apollo's science missions and handling the lunar samples.

Three years earlier, geologists at JSC had perceived a requirement for a receiving laboratory to preserve the lunar material in as nearly pristine condition as possible, to conduct preliminary examination of the material, and to prepare samples for investigation by academic scientists. In 1965 a requirement for two-way biological containment was imposed on the laboratory—on the one hand because of the remote possibility that alien organisms might be brought back from the moon to infect the earth's biosphere, and on the other to protect the lunar samples from terrestrial contamination so that they could be examined for the presence of lunar organisms or the chemical relics of life on the moon. JSC and concerned agencies (principally the U.S. Public Health Service) set up an Interagency Committee on Back Contamination to establish the requirements for facilities and procedures to effect quarantine. The receiving laboratory was expanded to include living quarters, so that crews could be quarantined for three weeks while the biological hazard in the lunar samples was assessed, and crews were taken from the recovery ship to Houston in specially modified travel trailers biologically isolated from the environment.

When completed in 1968, JSC's Lunar Receiving Laboratory was a unique scientific facility: an earth sciences laboratory in which all operations could be conducted behind two-way biological barriers. Lunar sample return containers could be opened under a vacuum of 10^{-6} torr, examined and photographed, and then manipulated *in vacuo* or in an atmosphere of dry sterile nitrogen. Special facilities allowed packaging of some samples at 10^{-11} torr. Within the vacuum system the samples could be subdivided and parceled out to researchers around the world. The laboratory was equipped with instruments and laboratory equipment for physical, chemical, petrographic, and mineralogical analysis so that scientific investigations could begin at once. A state-of-the-art radiation-counting laboratory, fifty feet below ground level and elaborately shielded against radiation, was equipped for the analysis of short-lived radioisotopes produced on the lunar surface by cosmic radiation. Biological investigations in the Lunar Receiving Laboratory focused on the detection of living organisms, or traces of their former presence, in the lunar material. Samples were analyzed chemically for organic material and tested for pathogenicity and other effects on living systems ranging from unicellular organisms to small mammals and plants. The elaborate and costly quarantine procedure was discontinued when results from the first three lunar landing missions showed no trace of organisms or organic material in the lunar samples.

The first samples of lunar rocks and soil, collected by the crew of *Apollo 11*, arrived at the Lunar Receiving Laboratory early in the morning of July 25, 1969. After preliminary examination and analysis, samples were released from quarantine and sent to outside researchers on September 10, and the rest of the returned material was cataloged and stored.

During the next four years five more crews returned more than 800 pounds of lunar rocks, soil, and core samples. Less than one-fifth of this material has been studied; the rest is in storage, a unique scientific resource awaiting new analytical techniques and new theories of the moon's origin that may justify its use. Johnson Space Center's Solar System Exploration Division is responsible for maintaining the lunar samples and overseeing their distribution for use in research. The Lunar and Planetary Sample Team of university scientists evaluates requests for samples from the research community and advises the JSC curator on their distribution. Besides providing material for research, the lunar sample curator also prepares thin-section collections which are loaned to educators for use in the classroom.

So far, the lunar samples have not yielded their ultimate secret—the origin and detailed history of the moon. Vast amounts of interesting information have been accumulated on the lunar materials, and scientists are in substantial agreement concerning the processes that formed the crust and the sequence of events that have shaped major portions of the moon. The emplaced instruments have provided data that reveal the internal structure of the moon. But the processes by which the moon was formed, and its relation to the earth, remain almost as enigmatic as they were in 1969.[14]

The Solar System Exploration Division conducts a small but active program of research in planetology. In recent years the division has expanded its interests to include collection and study of meteorites found in Antarctica and cosmic dust particles collected periodically by high-altitude aircraft. Basic information on the specimens in the collection is regularly disseminated to the research community, and research on them is encouraged.

LUNAR SCIENCE INSTITUTE

In 1969 NASA and the National Academy of Sciences established a Lunar Science Institute adjacent to the Johnson Space Center to promote research on the lunar samples and encourage the use of the specialized facilities in the Lunar Receiving Laboratory. The Institute (now known as the Lunar and Planetary Institute) is operated by the Universities Space Research Association and occupies a lake-front mansion built by J. M. West, now owned by Rice University. It provides a library, office space, meeting rooms, a collection of lunar maps and photographs, computer facilities, and support for visiting researchers using the materials and specialized equipment available at JSC.

Besides facilitating research with lunar materials, the institute cosponsors an annual Lunar and Planetary Science Conference, which has come to be recognized as the principal international forum for the presentation of new results in lunar and planetary research. Through an information bulletin the institute disseminates information on conferences and workshops in planetology around the world.

From the first Mercury flights through the operation of the Shuttle Orbiter, Johnson Space Center has been the focal point for scientific activity in manned space flight programs. The center has acquired basic scientific competence in the disciplines appropriate to the missions flown and is building competency in other areas such as astronomy and the life sciences, which are likely to prove fruitful in future manned research in space. Whether supporting the research of others or conducting their own scientific projects, JSC scientists have contributed to most of the advances in manned space science. Especially noteworthy are the pioneering research efforts in aerospace medicine, which have opened new areas for the understanding of human physiology under stress.

A definitive assessment of Johnson Space Center's contributions to technology is premature at this point. While the Houston center clearly stimulated the development of most of the structures, materials, and equipment to sustain humans in space, the impact of these developments outside the restricted field of manned space flight—the "spinoff" from the space program—is more difficult to trace. Nonetheless, certain applications are already obvious. It can be persuasively argued, for example, that the requirements of manned space flight (and of space operations generally, both civilian and military) for high-speed, high-capacity computers were the primary driving force for advances in computer technology. Computations too laborious to be feasible before the space age became commonplace during Gemini and Apollo. Determination of the maneuvers necessary to bring two spacecraft together in orbit around the earth, or the calculation of earth–moon trajectories for the Apollo spacecraft under various operational constraints (a variation of the classical three-body problem of celestial mechanics), were everyday exercises during lunar exploration. Had there been no need for the compact, lightweight computers and guidance systems for spacecraft, the development of miniaturized electronics to their present state might have taken many years longer. Improvements in accuracy and reliability of inertial guidance and navigational systems would have been much slower without the stimulus of the space program. The sensors and telemetry developed to monitor the vital functions of astronauts in orbit and on the moon have already found a place in medical technology, to name only one other application of space-developed technology, and many more will doubtless become equally commonplace in the future.

NASA's Space Science Programs

The conduct of research in the space sciences has always been a primary function of NASA. When the new agency was formed in 1958, it acquired Project Vanguard and more than a hundred scientists from the Naval Research Laboratory who constituted the cadre around which NASA's space science program was built. The first new field center projected for the space program, Goddard Space Flight Center at Greenbelt, Maryland, was planned to house the space science programs.

Even if it had been so inclined, NASA could not have conducted in its own facilities all the worthwhile research in space sciences that was to be done, nor could it expect the universities, on their own, to develop space research programs and support the training of future space scientists and engineers. Hence, it established a number of programs to support academic participation in space exploration and space-related scientific fields.

Grants and contracts for basic and applied research were the most direct means of supporting the space science community. Besides these, however, NASA also initiated a "sustaining university program" under which it provided broader and longer-term support to develop and sustain academic programs, provide graduate fellowships and undergraduate training grants to foster education in the space sciences, and, in some circumstances, pay for the construction of laboratories at universities where space research was limited by inadequate facilities.

Funding for these programs was never as generous as either the universities or NASA would have liked. For ten years starting in 1961, manned space flight projects took a larger and larger share of NASA's research and development funds, to the chagrin of many scientists within NASA and outside. Still, while its total budget was growing tenfold, from $523 million to more than $5,000 million, NASA's subvention of academic science under the sustaining university program grew three times faster, from $5 million allocated in fiscal 1960 to $145.2 million in fiscal 1966. From 1964 to 1974 the university programs never fell below $100 million per year, more than half that total going to research grants and contracts.[15] NASA's support of science was never more than a small fraction of the total federal subsidy of research and development,[16] but it was nonetheless important to academic scientists.

Besides the sustaining university program, NASA made research grants to outside scientists from its various scientific program offices: lunar and planetary, space physics and astronomy, and bioscience. The agency retained responsibility for the launch vehicles used in these programs, and its own scientists participated extensively in developing the payloads that carried the scientific instrumentation. Outside scientists, however, were kept informed of the general direction that NASA's research programs were taking and were regularly invited to submit proposals for conducting research within these programs. The head of NASA's Office of Space Science and Applications estimated that over the years about 60 percent of the agency's scientific research was conducted by outside experimenters, most of them from the academic world.[17]

NASA's space science program has, in twenty-seven years, expanded man's knowledge of the solar system (and the universe) beyond anything that could have been expected even a few years before the space program began. Rocket- and balloon-borne instruments have explored the outer fringes of earth's atmosphere. Orbiting solar, astronomical, and geophysical observatories have carried out long-term studies of the sun, the stars, and the earth itself, contributing more to knowledge in twenty years than all the scientific activity in all the centuries before them.[18] Instruments placed on the lunar surface by the Apollo astronauts have made it possible to measure the earth to moon distance and variations in it with an accuracy of a few meters, to record the moon's seismic activity, and to monitor its atmosphere and the flow of heat from its interior over a period of years. Mercury, Venus, Mars, Jupiter, Saturn, and Uranus have been visited and photographed. Instruments have returned detailed information on magnetic fields and particle fluxes in space, the chemical composition of Mars' surface, and the environment of the giant planets, to mention only a few of NASA's unmanned projects.

SPACE SCIENCE IN TEXAS

Scientists in Texas universities participated in many of NASA's research programs from the very early days of space science. Between 1961 and 1985, thirty-nine colleges and universities[19] in Texas received more than $200 million from NASA to support research and education in the space sciences. About one-third of this funding came from NASA's Office of Space Science and Applications, one-fourth from Johnson Space Center, one-fifth from Goddard Space Flight Center, and the rest from the other NASA centers (Ames, Langley, Lewis, and Marshall). Over half of this total went for the support of basic research, more than a third to applied research and development programs, and most of the rest to physical plant and equipment and direct support of students.

In fiscal 1984 Texas ranked fourth among thirty-one states in which research institutions received NASA grants or contracts totaling $1 million or more. Seven Texas institutions received $20.5 million of the $321.2 million distributed by NASA in grants and contracts for research. Only California, Massachusetts, and Maryland received more. The 1984 totals included $23.1 million granted to nonprofit institutions by Johnson Space Center. Texas ranked third among the states in research funding by JSC. Twelve percent of JSC's research support went to eight Texas universities in grants and contracts ranging from $76,000 to $937,000; the balance was distributed among forty-two recipients in twenty-two other states.[20]

DISTRIBUTION AMONG INSTITUTIONS

Most of Texas' universities have, at one time or another, conducted research under NASA sponsorship. Only the largest, most research-oriented universities, however, have been long-term participants in NASA-funded programs. Over the years 90 percent of the NASA research money coming into Texas has gone to ten institutions,[21] 64 percent to five. Those five have received support averaging from just under a million to two million dollars per year from 1962 to 1985.

Facilities grants of substantial size went to three universities. Rice University was granted $1.6 million to build a space science building, which housed the first department of space sciences in the country; Texas A&M received $1.01 million for expansion of its activation-analysis laboratory; and the University of Texas was given $4.9 million for a new 84-inch telescope at the McDonald Observatory.

Training grants for the support of students were another important part of NASA's contribution to science education in Texas, and again five schools received most of the money. The University of Houston was the leader in this category; training grants of almost $3.5 million amounted to nearly 20 percent of its total NASA funding from 1961 to 1985. Texas A&M ($2.3 million) and Rice ($1.5 million) followed.

DISTRIBUTION AMONG DISCIPLINES

The field of "space science" includes the investigation of natural phenomena occurring in space and the investigation of terrestrial systems in the space environment. As usually conceived, space science comprises mainly the physical and environmental sciences (physics, astronomy, atmospheric science, and geology/planetology), with the life sciences receiving considerably less attention (except for aerospace medicine). Some 60 percent of the research money NASA awarded to Texas institutions went to investigations in the physical and environmental sciences. Life sciences and engineering projects, funded at roughly equal levels, together received about 30 percent. Research programs in physics, astronomy, atmospheric and geological sciences, and biological/medical sciences accounted for more than 75 percent of NASA's support of Texas investigators.

PARTICIPATION IN SPECIFIC PROJECTS

Through their participation in NASA projects, scientists in Texas have made their contributions to the incremental advance of knowledge about the solar system and the universe. The Apollo missions emplaced six sets of lunar surface instruments, among them experiments designed by researchers at Rice, the University of Texas at Austin, and the University of Texas at Dallas. University of Houston scientists participated extensively in the planning of lunar geology investigations and in the chemical and geological analysis of the samples returned from the moon. The McDonald Observatory was one of the primary installations making observations with the laser reflectors left by Apollo crews, which has enabled scientists to measure the earth to moon distance and instabilities with an accuracy of 4 meters. Baylor University College of Medicine worked closely with JSC's medical directorate to develop instrumentation for monitoring physiological parameters on Apollo and Skylab. Among the unmanned projects, Pioneer, Explorer, and Viking have carried instruments developed by Texas experimenters.

The long-lasting contribution made by NASA's investment in Texas science programs, however, is the assistance it has given to scientists and institutions in enhancing the quality of educational and research programs.

Notes

1. Anderson, 1981.
2. Newell, 1980.
3. NASA also purchased an adjoining tract of 660 acres to improve access to the center and allow for expansion.
4. Oates, 1964; Swenson, Grimwood, and Alexander, 1966, pp. 390–92.
5. Other NASA centers sharing the responsibility for the manned space flight programs were: Marshall Space Flight Center, Huntsville, Ala. (Saturn launch vehicles); Kennedy Space Center, Cape Canaveral, Fla. (launch facilities and launch operations); and Goddard Space Flight Center, Greenbelt, Md., and the Jet Propulsion Laboratory, Pasadena, Calif. (tracking, communication, and data-handling network).
6. In January of 1986 the Department of Interior designated the Space Environment Simulation Laboratory and the Mission Control Center at JSC to be national historic landmarks.
7. Mark and Levine, 1984. Editors' Note: The importance of the responsibility has been made evident by the Challenger Seven disaster.
8. Compton and Benson, 1983; Newell, 1980, pp. 245–56, 290–94.
9. Berry, 1973.
10. Ibid.
11. Compton and Benson, 1983, pp. 22–39.
12. Ibid., pp. 149–65, 279–338.
13. Berry, 1976; Compton and Benson, 1983, pp. 339–42.
14. Schmitt, 1977; Taylor, 1975.

15. Newell, 1980.
16. For example, in fiscal 1966 the National Science Foundation alone put $385 million into programs comparable to those funded by NASA, i.e., basic research, fellowships, facilities, and others.
17. Ibid.
18. Newell, 1975; Newell, 1980; Ezell and Ezell, 1984; Nicks, 1985.
19. Unless noted, figures do not include support of research in nonprofit research organizations or other government entities, e.g., the Southwest Research Institute in San Antonio, the Texas Institute for Rehabilitation and Research in Houston, the University Corporation for Atmospheric Research in Palestine, and the Air Force Aerospace Medical Laboratory in San Antonio.
20. These and subsequent statistics are from "NASA University Program Management Information System Report MA01, as of March 31, 1985," or from NASA Headquarters and JSC Annual Procurement Reports for fiscal 1984.
21. In decreasing order of amount of NASA funding received: University of Texas at Dallas, University of Texas at Austin, Rice University, Texas A&M University, University of Houston, Baylor University Medical College, UT Health Sciences Center at Dallas, UT Medical Branch, Southern Methodist University, and Texas Technological University.

Bibliography

Anderson, Frank W., Jr. *Orders of Magnitude: A History of NACA and NASA.* 2d ed. (NASA SP-4403). Washington, D.C.: National Aeronautics and Space Administration, 1981.

Benson, Charles D., and Faherty, William Barnaby. *Moonport: A History of Apollo Launch Facilities and Operations* (NASA SP-4204). Washington, D.C.: National Aeronautics and Space Administration, 1978.

Berry, Charles A. "View of Human Problems to be Addressed for Long-Duration Space Flights." *Aerospace Medicine* 44(10) (1973): pp. 1136–46.

Berry, Charles A. "Medical Legacy of Apollo." *Aerospace Medicine* 45(9) (1974): pp. 1046–57.

Berry, Charles A. "Medical Legacy of Skylab as of May 9, 1974: The Manned Skylab Missions." *Aviation, Space, and Environmental Medicine* 47(4) (1976): pp. 418–24.

Brooks, Courtney G., Grimwood, James M., and Swenson, Loyd S., Jr., *Chariots for Apollo: A History of Manned Lunar Spacecraft* (NASA SP-4205).

Washington, D.C.: National Aeronautics and Space Administration, 1979.

Compton, W. David, and Benson, Charles W. *Living and Working in Space: A History of Skylab* (NASA SP-4208). Washington, D.C.: National Aeronautics and Space Administration, 1983.

Ezell, Edward Clinton, and Ezell, Linda Neuman, *The Partnership: A History of the Apollo-Soyuz Test Project* (NASA SP-4209). Washington, D.C.: National Aeronautics and Space Administration, 1978.

Ezell, Edward Clinton, and Ezell, Linda Neuman. *On Mars: Exploration of the Red Planet, 1958–1978* (NASA SP-4212). Washington, D.C.: National Aeronautics and Space Administration, 1984.

Hacker, Barton C., and Grimwood, James M. *On The Shoulders of Titans: A History of Project Gemini* (NASA SP-4203). Washington, D.C.: National Aeronautics and Space Administration, 1977.

Hall, R. Cargill. *Lunar Impact: A History of Project Ranger* (NASA SP-4210). Washington, D.C.: National Aeronautics and Space Administration, 1977.

Johnston, Richard S., Dietlein, Lawrence F., and Berry, Charles A., eds. *Biomedical Results of Apollo* (NASA SP-368). Washington, D.C.: National Aeronautics and Space Administration, 1975.

Johnston, Richard S., and Dietlein, Lawrence F., eds. *Biomedical Results from Skylab* (NASA SP-377). Washington, D.C.: National Aeronautics and Space Administration, 1977.

Link, Mae Mills. *Space Medicine in Project Mercury* (NASA SP-4003). Washington, D.C.: National Aeronautics and Space Administration, 1965.

Mark, Hans, and Levine, Arnold. *The Management of Research Institutions: A Look at Government Laboratories* (NASA SP-481). Washington, D.C.: National Aeronautics and Space Administration, 1984.

Newell, Homer E., Jr. "The Legacy of Apollo." In *Apollo Expeditions to the Moon*, edited by Edgar M. Cortright. (NASA SP-350), pp. 289–302. Washington, D.C.: National Aeronautics and Space Administration, 1975.

Newell, Homer E., Jr. *Beyond the Atmosphere: Early Years of Space Science* (NASA SP-4211). Washington, D.C.: National Aeronautics and Space Administration, 1980.

Nicks, Oran W. *Far Travelers: The Exploring Machines* (NASA SP-480). Washington, D.C.: National Aeronautics and Space Administration, 1985.

Oates, Stephen B. "NASA's Manned Spacecraft Center at Houston, Texas." *Southwestern Historical Quarterly*, 67(3) (1964): p. 355.

Schmitt, Harrison H. "Evolution of the Moon: The 1974 Model." In *The Soviet-American Conference on Cosmochemistry of the Moon and Planets*, edited by John H. Pomeroy and Norman J. Hubbard (NASA SP-370). Washington, D.C.: National Aeronautics and Space Administration, 1977.

Swenson, Loyd S., Jr., Grimwood, James M., and Alexander, Charles C. *This New Ocean: A History of Project Mercury* (NASA SP-4201). Washington, D.C.: National Aeronautics and Space Administration, 1966.

Taylor, S. Ross. *Lunar Science: A Post-Apollo View.* Elmsford, N.Y.: Pergamon Press, Inc., 1975.

Physical Sciences

6

Mathematics

James C. Bradford

Introduction

The mathematical sciences research community has wide and varied interests. Its two broad divisions may be thought of as pure and applied mathematics. Algebra and number theory, analysis, geometry-topology and logic belong to pure mathematics. Applied mathematics has traditionally referred to the methods used in physical science and engineering, but has now grown to include statistics and operations research or management science together with their related problems of numerical analysis.

Mathematical research is almost always conducted in centers of intellectual and social activity, usually universities with doctoral programs. This would seem to be an obvious environment for the applied areas with their need for computing facilities and interaction with other scientific workers. It is, in fact, also the case for pure mathematics. For, even though research in pure mathematics is usually done by an individual working alone or with at most one collaborator, the climate of stimulation and support that is found in the universities is necessary for continued success. Furthermore, the guidance of doctoral students not only perpetuates the line of mathematicians but also provides the professor with continued examination of his or her own thinking. For these reasons, a history of mathematical research must concentrate its account around the work of the doctorate-granting universities. The body of mathematical knowledge is a mosaic of theorems, perpetually being put in place by numerous individuals. The history of this activity is not the record of a project or a task force but the continuing story of individuals. It is a history of professors, their personalities, their research, and their students.

The University of Texas at Austin

The University of Texas at Austin (UT–Austin) has the longest and most widely recognized tradition of mathematical research in the state. Indeed, a major area of mathematics, point set topology, was created mainly by the work of a UT–Austin professor, Robert L. Moore (Fig. 1), and his mathematical progeny. But research in mathematics at the university did not begin with Moore.

George Bruce Halsted came to the university in 1884, its second year of operation. He published several research articles and translated a Hungarian text on non-Euclidean geometry into English. One of his

Figure 1. R. L. Moore. Taken during registration in September 1939.

own books on geometry was translated into French. His main contribution to the history of mathematical research in Texas was the education of four outstanding students who with one exception received their master's degree from UT–Austin in the years indicated: Milton B. Porter (B.S. 1892), Harry Y. Benedict (1893), Leonard E. Dickson (1894) and Moore (1901). Dickson received a doctorate from the University of Chicago, where later, as professor, he was extremely prolific both in the production of students and publications: over three hundred research papers as well as treatises and texts. Benedict's doctorate was obtained from Harvard University. Eventually he became president of UT–Austin and his name was given to a mathematics building there.

After receiving a doctorate from Harvard University, Porter held an appointment at Yale before returning to Austin in 1902. Since Benedict already held the

title of Professor of Mathematics, and there could be only one full professor in each department at this time, separate departments of Pure and Applied Mathematics were set up so that Porter and Benedict could each hold the rank of professor; Benedict became professor of Applied Mathematics, and Porter became professor of Pure Mathematics. Porter discovered the first known example of over-convergence and made important contributions in comparing and contrasting the concepts of finite difference calculus and differential calculus. Like Halsted before him and others after, his greatest contribution was in preparing the department for the work of Edward L. Dodd, Hyman J. Ettlinger, Moore, and Harry S. Vandiver.

Dodd, brought to the university by Porter in 1907, was one of the pioneers who established mathematical statistics as a field of research. He was a fellow both of the Institute of Mathematical Statistics and the American Statistical Association. Through his publications, Texas became nationally known for the work done here in actuarial science.

Ettlinger came to the university in 1913. His brilliance is indicated by service on a doctoral committee before he left to finish his own doctorate at Harvard in 1920. His field of research was differential equations. Many of those who earned doctorates under his supervision are pillars in departments of mathematics in the colleges and universities of Texas, only one indication of his contribution to higher education and mathematics in the state.

Moore was Halsted's fourth outstanding student. By the time he returned to Austin as associate professor in 1920, Moore was a mature mathematician. He had received a doctorate under E. H. Moore at the University of Chicago and had served for ten years on the faculty of the University of Pennsylvania where he directed the doctoral work of J. R. Kline and G. H. Hallett. Anna Mullikin, whose work was in progress when Moore moved to Texas, obtained her doctorate from UT–Austin. By this time Moore had already served on the Council of the American Mathematical Society and was an associate editor of the *Transactions of the American Mathematical Society*. His research had produced a set of axioms for plane analysis situs, a precursor of topology which set an agenda for remarkable developments in point set topology for fifty more years.[1] Also in place when Moore returned to Austin was a method of teaching, which in time came to be known widely as "the Moore method." It proved to be amazingly effective in attracting and developing students of high caliber.

During the remainder of his professional career at

UT–Austin—almost 50 more years—Moore published many papers, but his own research became less important to him as he concentrated on his students. His teaching methods have been described by Wilder[2] and Traylor[3] and are recorded on a film titled *Challenge in the Classroom*, produced by the Mathematical Association of America. Moore customarily taught five courses: calculus and an intermediate level course such as advanced calculus, in which he found promising students, and three graduate courses in which the subject of topology was developed. The heart of his method was how these courses were taught. Moore gave only enough axioms to get things started; the rest consisted of proofs by students. Acquisition of knowledge was given small stress compared to developing the power to reason, prove, and create.

Three of Moore's students have been elected to the National Academy of Sciences, to which Moore himself was elected in 1931; three of his students served as presidents of the American Mathematical Society, as Moore did in 1938; and five of his students served as presidents of the Mathematical Association of America. Most of his doctoral students have been very prolific themselves, both in research and in directing doctoral candidates. More than five hundred mathematicians can be counted as "descendants" of R. L. Moore. Some of his offspring are currently contributing at UT–Austin. R. H. Bing, who was professor for many years at the University of Wisconsin, returned to UT–Austin as professor and for a time as department chairman. Cecil E. Burgess made important contributions to the development of the doctoral program at the University of Utah. One of his students who earned a doctorate at Utah, William T. Eaton, is currently a professor at UT–Austin and was the recipient of a mathematical prize established by Ettlinger in honor of Moore and H. S. Wall. Mary Ellen Estill Rudin has herself guided many students to the doctorate at Wisconsin. One of them, Michael P. Starbird, is an associate professor at UT–Austin. Moore was honored when the 17-level building which houses the departments of Mathematics, Physics, and Astronomy was dedicated in 1973 as Robert Lee Moore Hall.

Vandiver was brought to Austin by Porter in 1924 as an associate professor. He had neither graduated from high school nor had he received a diploma. He never enrolled in any undergraduate program, although he did take some graduate courses at the University of Pennsylvania. His only academic degree of any kind was an honorary doctorate from Pennsylvania awarded in his sixty-fourth year. Yet, by the time he had come to Austin, Vandiver had done significant research and

had taught for five years at Cornell University. His field was number theory. Many of his papers dealt with the celebrated "Fermat's last theorem," others with Bernoulli numbers, and others with various concepts of algebra. One of his doctoral students, Milo Weaver, later became a professor at UT–Austin.

In 1931, Vandiver was awarded the prestigious Cole Prize in Number Theory. Also in the 1930s he was elected to membership in the National Academy of Sciences. He was active in mathematics and mathematical research until late in his life. Several of his papers were published after he reached the age of seventy.

Homer V. Craig's first and only academic appointment after receiving his doctorate at the University of Wisconsin was at UT–Austin beginning in 1929. A dedicated research worker, his interests included relativity theory, vector analysis, and tensor analysis. Around 1939 he developed the concept of an extensor and spent the remainder of his mathematical life working on the problems of expressing physical laws in extensor form.

Hubert S. Wall was a senior mathematician when he came to the university in 1946. He had been on the faculty at Northwestern University for seventeen years and had spent a year at the Institute for Advanced Study. His research interests had been in continued fractions and the Hellinger integral. His treatise *Continued Fractions* is the standard work in that area.[4] After coming to UT–Austin, Wall continued his research, but he became more interested in guiding doctoral students. The environment in which "the Moore method" flourished seemed to meet a need which Wall had felt for some time. He began to teach his own classes in a similar way with results that were most fortunate both for his students and for mathematics as a profession, especially in the state. He directed eighty students to their master's degrees and fifty-seven to the doctorate at UT–Austin. Many of his students currently staff mathematics departments in the state and continue to be active in research and in teaching.

The careers of the above-named professors at UT–Austin are described in some detail because the effect they have had on mathematics and mathematicians in Texas is legendary. But others have made significant contributions and opened bridges to a new era, too. Robert E. Greenwood who came to the university in 1938 carried out research in probability, combinatorics, and numerical analysis. W. T. Guy, Jr., who arrived in 1951, worked in transforms and other methods of applied analysis. In addition to his research and doctoral guidance, Guy made a great contribution to the department as chairman for a number of years in the 1950s and 1960s. He has received significant recognition as a teacher, especially of engineering mathematics. Don Edmondson strengthened the department in lattice theory—the area of his research activity—and in modern algebra.

In 1958 the University Computation Center was established with David M. Young, Jr. as director. He served in that position until 1970. Growing out of that effort was the Center for Numerical Analysis, which Young heads at this time. The areas of research being conducted in this center include approximation theory, ordinary and partial differential equations, and large sparse systems of linear and nonlinear equations. Grants supporting this work include those from the National Science Foundation (NSF), the Department of Energy, and the Control Data Corporation. Through the work begun here, Texas has achieved international notice for its strength in approximation theory. George Lorentz and E. Ward Cheney continue that effort.

Leonard Gillman came to UT–Austin from the University of Rochester to serve as chairman of the mathematics department beginning in 1970. By this time Moore, Ettlinger, and Vandiver had retired. Craig and Wall were about to retire. During the 1970s and 1980s many new faculty were added, with major areas of mathematics represented by groups of researchers. Bing, Eaton, and Starbird in topology were joined by Cameron Gordon, Andrew Casson, James Vick, and Gary Hamrick. Edmondson and John Durbin in algebra were joined by Efraim Armendariz, Stephen McAdam, Ray Heitmann, Martha Smith, Frank Gerth, David Saltman, and W. F. Schelter. Peter John was joined in statistics by David V. Hinkley, Carl Morris, and Anthony Davison. At this writing analysis and functional analysis are presented by Sterling Berberian, Simon Bernau, John Gilbert, Leonard Gillman, Haskell Rosenthal, William Beckner, Edward Odell, and Peter Tomas. H. E. Lacey was active in this group until he became chairman at Texas A&M University (TAMU). Working in various areas of applied mathematics are John Dollard, Clifford Gardner, R. E. Showalter, Charles Friedman, and Charles Radin. W. W. Bledsoe, Robert Boyer, and J. Strother Moore are doing research in automatic theorem proving and artificial intelligence. Abraham Charnes, an eminent authority on linear programming, has an appointment in the College of Business, from which he adds strength to the mathematics effort.

The breadth and depth of this faculty will be increased. Creation of four endowed chairs was announced recently, and provision has been made for six faculty fellowships named in honor of R. H. Bing, insuring that additional research faculty of the highest quality will be added.

Rice University

Rice University has had a strong doctoral program in mathematics since its opening as the Rice Institute in 1912. The first president of Rice was Edgar Odell Lovett, a 38-year old mathematician from Princeton. The official opening of the Institute was celebrated with an academic convocation which was addressed by world-renowned scholars, including Emile Borel and Vita Volterra, who gave lectures. Henri Poincaré, who had agreed to be present, died shortly before the ceremony took place. G. C. Evans was recruited by Lovett to be the first professor of Mathematics. In the 1930s Evans went to the University of California at Berkeley. Evans Hall, which houses the Berkeley mathematics department, is named after him. It is perhaps appropriate to note in a volume that celebrates the Texas and Houston Sesquicentennial, as well as the Sigma Xi Centennial, that Evans and L. R. Ford, another Rice mathematician of that time, married sisters who were great-granddaughters of Sam Houston.

The first doctorate in mathematics from Rice was granted to Hubert Bray in the early years of Rice Institute. Bray, who published significant work on integration, was to continue on the Rice faculty for the rest of his career, which lasted fifty years. A number of prominent mathematicians spent time at Rice in the period between the world wars. These included C. B. Morrey, Percy Daniel, T. Rado, and others. The important French mathematician S. Mandelbrojt was associated with Rice for about twenty years. In the period before and after World War II, he spent one half of each year at Rice and the other half at the Collège de France in Paris. Gerald MacLane spent several postwar years at Rice before going to Purdue.

During the 1960s there was a great expansion of the faculty. Because of the research done by Evans, Bray, Mandelbrojt, and MacLane, Rice had become strong in the theory of functions of a single complex variable. But the university was also gaining strength in other fields such as numerical analysis, led by Jim Douglas and Henry Rachford, and topology, led by Morton Curtis, who had come with Eldon Dyer and Ed Connell. They were later joined by several younger topologists, including L. Glaser, John Hempel, and S. Gersten. Development in algebra got a boost for a time with the appointment of G. Baumslag, who along with Gersten, gave significant representation in this area. However, research in algebra at Rice was severely curtailed when both Gersten and Baumslag left in the 1970s. Rapid strides were made in the area of functions of several complex variables in the late 1960s, with R. O. Wells, Jr., Howard L. Resnikoff, Reese Harvey, John Polking, and others carrying out important research. The appointment of the distinguished mathematician Salomon Bochner, retired from Princeton in 1968, played a significant role in the development of the department. His mature vision and the enthusiasm of the younger faculty were important ingredients for the major developments that occurred in the department during the next two decades when Rice gained national attention. The appointment of W. Veech, who works in ergodic theory and related areas and had studied with Bochner at Princeton, was an important step taken soon after Bochner's arrival.

Despite the earlier departures of Dyer and Connell, topology continued to prosper at Rice in the 1970s with William Jaco and Peter Shalen joining Hempel in that area. Because both Jaco and Shalen left Rice in the mid-1980s, topology is not now in so strong a position in the department. There has been a recent surge in the area of differential geometry in the department. The appointment of Robert Bryant in 1979 has helped attract a strong contingent of young mathematicians in this field in the last few years. In 1983 Roger Penrose, whose field is mathematical physics, was appointed as a part-time professor jointly with Oxford University. Because of the roles of complex analysis and differential geometry in modern physics, his interests have meshed with those already in place to create a stimulating research group in that area.

When Rice received a University Science Development grant from the National Science Foundation in 1967, a number of the new faculty that were added had diverse backgrounds in systems and modeling which did not find an appropriate home in any of the existing departments, and so a new one was created.

In 1968 the university approved the establishment of the Department of Mathematical Sciences. Fritz Horn accepted the temporary chairmanship of the department. In 1969 Robert M. Thrall of the University of Michigan joined the faculty as professor and chairman. Under his leadership, the department moved aggressively to implement graduate research in five areas: numerical analysis, computer science, operations research, statistics, and physical mathematics (classical applied mathematics together with new developments in that area). Although computer science

has since become a separate department, the remaining areas continue to be heavily involved in computational methods as well as software development.

Thrall has been an eminent figure in operations research. He and Guillermo Owen were active in the application of game theory and related mathematical models to social and behavioral problems. Richard Young, whose specialty is integer programming, has held a joint appointment in the Department of Economics. Robert Bixby has specialized in combinatorial optimization, matroids, and large-scale linear programming. C. C. Wang, who currently serves as the department chairman, works in continuum mechanics.

Numerical analysis has grown under the leadership of Richard Tapia. Tapia and John Dennis are working on a new approach to solving nonlinear optimization problems subject to nonlinear constraints. Dennis is also much involved in developing an interactive computer graphics package. One of the early researchers of importance in numerical analysis is Henry Rachford. Working with people in the petroleum industries in the Houston area, Rachford, Donald Peaceman, and Jim Douglas pioneered in the numerical simulation of flow in oil reservoirs. Mary Fannet Wheeler continued the work of Rachford and is currently developing efficient numerical methods for super computers. Bill Symes works on inverse problems for hyperbolic differential equations, such as might arise in exploration geophysics, nondestructive testing, and ultrasonic biomedical tomography.

In the statistics group, Paul Pfeiffer works in applied probability while giving primary attention to the undergraduate program. James R. Thompson specializes in simulation, working jointly with Barry Brown and Neely Atkinson of the M. D. Anderson Hospital and Tumor Institute in modeling the growth and spread of cancer. David Scott, who is also an adjunct professor of the Baylor College of Medicine, has been using statistical methods to study the role of blood fats in coronary artery disease. Shean-Tsong Chiu is studying the analysis of signals emitted by a moving source. George Terrel specializes in the area of nonparametric statistics and its connection with classical methods.

Texas A&M University

In its early days, the Department of Mathematics at Texas A&M University (TAMU) had the traditional service role of an undergraduate mathematics department, but also included those courses necessary for the engineering program and whatever might be needed for support of the agricultural and mechanical mission of the college. Under W. L. Porter, who served as department head from 1932 until 1952, there was no mandate to do research; however, serious scholarship and publishing did exist, as did excellence in teaching. For example, in 1947–48, E. C. Klipple gave special attention to a group of twelve undergraduates, known locally as "Klipple's Whiz Kids." All twelve went on to get doctorates at universities including the Massachusetts Institute of Technology and the University of California at Berkeley. Among those doing some research during that era were B. W. Brewer in number theory, E. R. Keown in algebra, J. J. Hurt and N. Naugle in applied mathematics, W. S. McCulley in special functions, H. A. Luther in numerical analysis, and J. Bryant in analysis. R. V. McGee published a book in mathematics for agriculture, which, although it was clearly not a research treatise, did serve a need so widely recognized that it was translated into Spanish.[5]

In the decades of the 1960s and 1970s, the entire southwest was becoming increasingly oriented to high technology. As a result all the major state universities became much more involved in related scientific research. During this period, the mathematics department of TAMU recruited a research faculty and began a doctoral program. Among the faculty added were G. R. Blakely and I. Borosh in number theory; C. J. Maxson and K. C. Smith in algebra; F. Narcowich and S. A. Fulling in mathematical physics; G. D. Allen and R. R. Smith in operator theory; M. J. Stecher and D. G. Barrow in partial differential equations; J. R. Boone in topology; L. F. Guseman in pattern recognition; D. J. Hartfiel in linear analysis; C. Chui in approximation theory; A. Stroud in numerical integration; W. L. Perry in integral equations; J. Walton in applied mathematics; S. Milne in combinatorics; M. Rahe in ergodic theory; and O. G. Aberth in constructive analysis. In these two decades, twenty-two doctorates were granted, and over one hundred master's degrees were given.

There have been two major research programs at TAMU during the 1970s. L. F. Guseman, Jr. has been the director and principal investigator of a NASA-funded program in the areas of pattern recognition and image analysis. Over its 12-year life, the total funding for the project has exceeded three million dollars. Charles Chui has led a group in approximation theory since his arrival at TAMU in 1970. This group has included many visitors and a few permanent faculty, notably J. Ward and P. W. Smith, who has since resigned. With the addition of Larry L. Schumaker in 1980, a Center for Approximation Theory was established

H. Elton Lacey became department head in 1980. Since that time, there has been a vigorous expansion of the permanent faculty, especially senior faculty. I. Bakelman is doing research in partial differential equations; W. B. Johnson and D. R. Lewis in functional analysis; M. Marcus, J. Zinn, and G. Pisier in probability; J. Pitts, Sloan Fellow in geometric measure theory; L. L. Schumaker in approximation theory; and Sue Geller in algebra. The department now has strong research groups in linear analysis, geometric analysis, approximation theory, applied mathematics, algebra, and probability.

There are more than twenty-five federally funded grants in the department. The faculty of eighty-six has been producing almost three hundred manuscripts per year.

The Owen Chair in Mathematics has been established with an endowment of one-half million dollars given by M. E. Owen. At the present time, the chair is jointly held by W. B. Johnson and G. Pisier.

Prior to 1962, statistics at TAMU was taught in a number of different departments. Research in statistics was virtually unknown; statistical consulting and collaboration in support of other research areas were provided primarily by the local computer center and only occasionally by the faculty involved in teaching statistics. A decision was made to recommend the establishment of a Graduate Institute of Statistics in which would be organized all the coursework, research, and consulting in statistics and in which would be established a curriculum that would provide for master's and doctoral degrees in statistics.

This institute was approved in the spring of 1962. R. J. Freund was named associate director and was the institute's first faculty member. Shortly thereafter the eminent statistician H. O. Hartley was appointed as director. By the fall of 1964, three additional faculty had been appointed, and from that modest base a strong program in statistics began. The success of this institute became the crowning academic achievement of Hartley's distinguished career. His worldwide reputation as a research scholar was an essential element in the founding and early development of the institute.

In the early years of the institute, Hartley and the other faculty were able to secure underwriting of the program development through a National Science Foundation (NSF) Departmental Development Grant and a National Institute of Health (NIH) Training Grant. As the department grew, an additional NSF grant was obtained to assist in construction of a building which would house the institute and also take over some of the functions previously served by the campus computer center. By 1968, when the department moved to this facility, subsequently named the Teague Building, there were ten faculty members with approximately fifty graduate students, and the institute had been awarded more than 1.5 million dollars in research grants and contracts. By 1970, a U.S. Office of Naval Research (ONR) Project THEMIS Research Grant had been received that would continue for twelve more years. Also, research grants and contracts were under way with the National Aeronautics and Space Administration (NASA), the Army Research Office, and the National Center for Toxicological Research.

During the 1970s an undergraduate program in Applied Mathematical Science was developed jointly with the mathematics department. This program currently produces more than half of the mathematics graduates of the university. When Hartley retired as department head in 1977, he was replaced by W. B. Smith. In 1982 the institute, now officially called "department," moved to newer and more spacious quarters in the Blocker Building. Current faculty numbers twenty-five, teaching 5,500 students annually. There are forty-five full-time graduate students.

The research efforts of the department have covered a wide range of activities including sample survey methodology, optimization theory and methodology, multiple response studies, optimization of experimental designs and statistical quality control, applications of numerical analysis to simulation, data editing, ecological statistics, multivariate statistics, time series, and stochastic processes. Current research activity is funded by the Army Research Office, IBM, Digital Equipment Corporation, and NSF. The Department of Statistics, in its 25-year history, has become a significant part of the total TAMU research effort and that of the entire Southwest.

The Johnson Space Center Theory and Analysis Group

In 1962, while Patrick L. Odell was in the mathematics department of UT–Austin, he and Byron Tapley of the aeronautical engineering department began collaborating with various mathematical and engineering scientists at NASA's new Johnson Space Center in Houston. Their aim was to define and solve mathematical, statistical, and celestial mechanics problems necessary for the manned space flight program. During that period, Eugene Davis, a NASA electrical engineer, saw a need for the formation of a special group of research mathematicians to do theoretical work in mathematics and celestial mechanics, particularly research associated with spacecraft orbit determination and estimation methods. This group, which became known inside the Johnson Space Center as the Theory and Analysis Group, included mathematicians like Henry P. Decell, then an army lieutenant, currently teaching at the University of Houston–University Park (UH–University Park), and Larry Guseman, also an army lieutenant, now at TAMU. These men were later joined by others who did research on mathematics related to space flight.

Odell and Decell collaborated and extended the matrix theory of generalized inverses. Decell developed techniques for computing a Moore–Penrose pseudoinverse by using the Cayley–Hamilton polynomial representation of a matrix. He developed a theory for differentiating a generalized inverse. In addition, Odell and Decell formulated the original theory of applying generalized inverses to the theory of finite Markov Chains, which became the basis for considerable research by others across the nation and the world. Real-time computing of spacecraft trajectories required recursive methods for inverting ill-conditioned and singular systems of equations. These real-time computing requirements were the driving force in this research.

The University of Houston–University Park

Founded as a junior college in 1927, the University of Houston had no research program in mathematics until 1956 when Louis Silverman was appointed to the faculty. After he had received his doctorate from Harvard University in 1919, he had an extended career in research and teaching, including an appointment at the University of Tel Aviv. His field of research was divergent series.

Louis Brand joined the department in 1957 as the first holder of the M. D. Anderson Chair in Mathematics. His tenure at UH–University Park came at the end of a long and distinguished career of significant work in the areas of vector and tensor analysis, integral equations, vector mechanics, and differential equations.

David G. Bourgin, who had come in 1965, was appointed to the Anderson Chair after the death of Brand in 1972. Quite well known for his contributions in algebraic topology, he was equally important in the UH–University Park mathematics department for his leadership role among the faculty. Like Bochner at

Rice, Bourgin helped to build a community for mathematics and culture in Houston.

Among others who came during the years of the school's transition from a private college to a major public university were Richard Sinkhorn working in matrix analysis, Wm. T. Ingram and Reginald Traylor in topology, Paul Knopp in analysis, and James Malone and Paul Hill in algebra.

An indication of the level of mathematical scholarship that has been attained in the UH–University Park department is the publication of the *Houston Journal of Mathematics* initiated in 1965 by Gordon Johnson, Andrew Lelek, Jurgin Schmidt, and John MacNerney. Johnson has been the managing editor.

The research faculty of the department has broad interests. Among the areas represented by groups of researchers and notable individuals are: applied mathematics represented by Neal Amundson, Giles Auchmuty, Martin Golubitskey, Roland Glowinski, David Bao, Henry Decell, Barbara Keyfitz, Richard Sanders, Homer Walker, and others; algebra and related areas with Dennison Brown, Jutta Hausen, Matthew O'Malley, Vern Paulsen, among others; differential equations and associated numerical analysis represented by Peter Brown, Garret Etgen, William Fitzgibbon, and others.

Texas Tech University

The early years (1925–1960) at Texas Tech University (TTU) in Lubbock saw only scattered research efforts: Heineman in matrix algebra; Underwood in number theory and extended analytic geometry; Fuller in complex analysis; and Riggs in statistics. During that time, TTU mathematics professors were better known for textbooks in algebra, trigonometry, analytic geometry, and calculus.

In the 1960s the university set its sights on a doctoral program, and the long-time chairman, Emmett Hazelwood, began to recruit research-oriented faculty. It would seem that he had no plan to seek strength in a particular field, but chose to hire the best qualified people available, with their area of research interest being of secondary consideration. Among those added at that time were S. K. Hildebrand and H. R. Bennett working and publishing in topology, A. A. Gioia in number theory, W. Perel in algebra, and Tom Atchison in analysis. Ali Amir-Moez, who came during this period, had the longest and strongest record in research. This gentle linear algebraist, a man of diverse inter-

ests, had an international reputation when he arrived at TTU, and he has had a strong influence on the research program for twenty years.

By the late 1960s TTU had a new doctoral program, a new chairman, Patrick Odell, and a strong desire to enhance the research effort. The Odell years were marked by an emphasis on statistics and related applied areas centered around the concept of the generalized inverse of a matrix, which Odell originated. Odell, H. L. Gray, T. L. Boullion, and T. O. Lewis published extensively in these areas—including at least three books—and attracted many doctoral students.[6] In many ways their work characterized the department during this time. However, researchers continued to gather in other areas of investigation, too. Dalton Tarwater, in Abelian groups, came to the High Plains during this time. Groups of workers in topology, algebra, and analysis were forming distinct identities, setting the stage for a decade of growth.

The 1970s were indeed, a time of much change: five of the seven chairmen who have led the department over the years served at some time during this decade. The department hosted four significant research conferences. A visiting professor program was begun with the appointment of a number of two-year lectureships. A graduate-degree program in statistics was authorized. Computer science was attached to the mathematics department for several years. The quality and quantity of published research increased greatly, with funded research increasing from nil to around $500,000 per year.

Research in statistics was done by Boullion, K. Chanda, B. Duran, and T. O. Lewis. In the early 1970s, Gray's pioneering work on the jackknife statistic was beginning to receive the broad attention it now enjoys.[7]

L. R. "Bob" Hunt, a student of R. O. Wells, Jr. at Rice, was perhaps the dominant researcher in analysis throughout the 1970s. His research began in functions of several complex variables, changed to differential equations for several papers with M. J. Strauss, and finally ended the decade in control theory, for which he is best known. The analysts R. Barnard. G. Frederick, D. Gilliam, and G. Harris began their careers at TTU during this decade.

An applied mathematics group began to assemble during this time with W. T. Ford and R. M. Anderson in fluid flow problems; P. Nelson and H. D. Victory in transport theory; and T. G. Newman in computer optics. The Institute for Numerical Transport Theory was formed, and by the end of the 1970s, Newman, Hunt, and R. E. Saeks were involved heavily in defense-related research.

The topologists Hildebrand and Bennett were joined by D. J. Lutzer and I. W. Lewis. The logician T. G. McLaughlin and the ring theorist W. H. Gustafson were other important research persons added during the 1970s.

With the addition of Clyde Martin in the 1980s, TTU became a center of national importance in control theory. The best known discovery of this period was due to Hunt and Su who found the necessary and sufficient conditions for easily controlling a dynamic system.

During the 1980s a number of outstanding research people left TTU, partly over academic governance issues. Those who left included Boullion, B. Ebanks, Frederick, Hunt, Lutzer, and Saeks. Fortunately, they are being replaced by young aggressive mathematicians who are expected to build on the research traditions of the past quarter of a century.

North Texas State University

In 1901 Texas Normal College in Denton gained state support and became North Texas State Normal College; at the time there were thirteen professors on the faculty with doctorates. William H. Bruce, the head teacher of mathematics began publishing in 1904 with the short monograph *Some Noteworthy Properties of a Triangle and Its Circles*.[8] In addition to two textbooks, he authored another work in 1932: *The Nine Circles of the Triangle*. This drew a number of letters of praise, including an effusive one from the Dean of Engineering at UT–Austin.[9]

Graduate work began at North Texas in 1935 when the master's degree was offered in thirteen departments, mathematics among them. Eugene H. Hanson was brought in as director of the mathematics program, joining J. V. Cooke on the graduate faculty. He immediately began to accumulate for the university a good mathematics library, whose development has provided a very solid base for all graduate work and research. Hanson, whose area was real analysis, instituted a strong master's degree program requiring a thesis in which some original research was expected. Eleven had finished before the United States entered World War II in 1941, and a total of twenty-five by 1949.

The graduate faculty was augmented by Herbert C. Parrish, real analysis, in 1949 and George C. Copp, continued fractions, in 1951. The master's degree program continued to grow. In 1957, though Hanson had taken an industrial position and there were only three pro-

fessors on the graduate faculty, North Texas produced about 2 percent of all the master's degrees in mathematics in the United States. A survey[3] of the baccalaureate origins of students who received doctorates in mathematics for the decade 1952–1962 showed that North Texas was forty-eighth in the United States behind only UT–Austin and Rice in the state.[10]

During the late 1950s and early 1960s, professors who were active in research were being added to the faculty. Nick Vaughan in algebra came in 1958; John Mohat in point set topology and David Dawson in summability, in 1959; Russell Bilyeu in functional analysis, in 1960; David Appling in real-valued set functions, in 1963; and Melvin Hagan in topology, in 1965. David Cecil and John Ed Allen came in 1962 and 1963.

The school had already been named North Texas State University (NTSU) when the doctoral program was approved in 1968. As expected, members of the faculty began to emphasize research much more than they had done in the past. In 1970 Frank Connor was named department chairman and Paul Lewis was added, joining Bilyeu in a fruitful and continuing collaboration in functional analysis. Research gained additional momentum when, in 1977, two senior faculty members experienced in directing doctoral students were added: John Neuberger and Dan Mauldin. Neuberger's research interest is systems of partial differential equations and related numerical methods. Mauldin has a wide range of research interests including descriptive set theory, measure theory, and the mathematical analysis of chaos in dynamical systems. In May of 1979 Mauldin organized and directed a highly successful conference on the *Scottish Book*.[11] This book of unusually insightful mathematical problems was accumulated by Polish mathematicians as they met for "coffee" at the Scottish Cafe in Lwow prior to and during World War II. A number of the world's premier mathematicians came to the NTSU campus to review progress on these problems and the new areas of mathematics opened by them for study.

The present faculty now numbers twenty, with fifteen of them actively engaged in research. Recent additions not already noted are Robert Kallman working in group representations, harmonic analysis, and image processing, who has edited the *Collected Works of S. Kakutani*; Joseph Kung and Neal Brand, who have published significant work in combinatorics; Beth Bator, who joined Lewis and Bilyeu in their work on Banach spaces; A. Castro, who works in differential equations; and Eric van Douwen, a leading researcher in general topology with more than sixty publications.

Southern Methodist University

The Mathematics Department at Southern Methodist University (SMU) began with the founding of the university in 1911. The department's mission was the teaching of undergraduates and master's degree students until the early 1980s. Prior to 1945, Gerald B. Huff was probably the best known research mathematician on the faculty. He made important contributions in geometry and number theory, which appeared in the *Proceedings of the National Academy of Sciences* and the *American Journal of Mathematics*. Huff later served as Dean of the Graduate School at the University of Georgia.

In the 1960s William Ayres did important work in topology. He had earlier been dean at Purdue and provost at SMU. W. M. Whyburn, who served as C. F. Frensley Professor of Mathematics during the late 1960s, is well-known for his contributions in differential equations. Prior to coming to SMU, he was president of TTU and later dean at the University of North Carolina. During his years at SMU, he was supported by grants from NASA.

In the late 1970s it was decided that the department should concentrate on applied mathematics. The most notable appointment of that period was the highly successful applied mathematician Milton Wing, who came as professor and chairman of the department. Wing had served as a junior scientist on the Manhattan Project and had coauthored, with Richard Bellman, the book *An Introduction to Invariant Embedding.*[12]

With the introduction of the doctoral program in 1980, the department began a period of expansion which still continues. Approximately ten faculty appointments were made between 1980 and 1985. Among those were Richard Haberman, author of the books *Mathematical Modeling*[13] and *Elementary Applied Partial Differential Equations*,[14] and George Reddien, who has served as department chairman in the 1980s and who edits the *SIAM Journal on Numerical Analysis*. Five of the recently appointed faculty members receive support from the National Science Foundation for their research.

In 1985, former Texas Governor William P. Clements gave the department one million dollars to endow the Betty Clements Chair of Applied Mathematics in honor of his sister. The first holder of the chair, Larry F. Shampine, was appointed in the spring of 1986. Shampine is well known for his work on the numerical solution of the initial value problem for ordinary differential equations. He is the author of three books and more than one hundred research papers.

A Texas–Oklahoma chapter of the Society for Industrial and Applied Mathematics (SIAM) was established in 1981. Richard Haberman led the effort to start the chapter and was selected as its first president. The chapter has seventy-five members and holds a meeting every spring.

Statistics at SMU began with Paul Minton, a professor of mathematics, who in 1960 began recruiting research statisticians for the department. In 1961 Minton became the first chairman of the statistics department. The first additions to the department were V. Seshadri, J. T. Webster, C. H. Kapadia, R. P. Bland, D. B. Owen, and J. E. Walsh.

A crucial milestone for the department came in 1968 when a Department of Defense contract was awarded for the THEMIS project on signal analysis statistics. The project was directed by D. B. Owen and supported a total of seventeen senior investigators, including all of the above-named faculty, for almost a decade. It also supported fifty-two graduate students and three undergraduates. In its seven years of operation, 112 research reports were produced, 110 papers were published in professional journals and 46 papers were presented at scientific meetings.

After the THEMIS project ended in 1975, Owen obtained contracts—running through 1986—from the Office of Naval Research on the subject of screening variables. These contracts supported numerous graduate students while they were writing their dissertations. Those who benefited are now employed in industries and universities throughout Texas and, indeed, throughout the world.

In May 1974 a Symposium on the American Mathematical Heritage to Celebrate the Bicentennial of the United States was held at SMU. The symposium was organized around three individuals enjoying worldwide recognition for their research and writings: William G. Cochran, H. O. Hartley, and Jerzy Neyman. Each of these three was asked to invite others, so that the program consisted of a significant number of the world's most respected statisticians. Their contributions were collected and published under the editorship of D. B. Owen in *On the History of Statistics and Probability.*[15]

In 1973 Owen started the journal *Communications in Statistics*, with an innovative way of handling papers, which made it an instant success. The journal presently has two series: *Theory and Methods* and *Simulation and Computation*. The journal has an international editorial board and articles to be published come from all over the world.

The Department of Statistics at SMU was the first

graduate department of statistics in any college or university in Texas. Built on the work of and foundation laid by its earliest members, it remains one of the outstanding statistics departments in the Southwest, enjoying a worldwide reputation.

An Operations Research Program at SMU was begun in 1967 along with a computer science program. The first research emphases of the program were in linear and nonlinear optimization being studied by H. Greenberg and W. Pierskalla, queuing theory investigated by Narayan Bhat, and discrete event simulation studies by R. Nance. Out of this initial group, only Bhat has remained at SMU. He continues his research on stochastic processes underlying queuing, reliability, and computer systems.

The faculty members added since 1970 have emphasized optimization algorithms. The late Leon Cooper was a distinguished authority on location problems. Larry LeBlanc has carried out extensive investigations on transportation networks. Jeff Kennington and Richard Helgason have led research on logistics and distribution problems for General Motors, the U.S. Air Force Logistics Command and Military Airlift Command, the U.S. Forest Service, the U.S. Navy Personnel Research Center, and the U.S. Treasury. Advanced mathematical programming systems incorporating the new theory developed at SMU have been installed at many of these sites. The research group has the distinction of having solved the largest real world network problem ever attempted. Some of these network models have in excess of 13 million arcs.

During its lifetime, the Operations Research group at SMU has published several books including *Elements of Applied Stochastic Processes* (Editions 1 and 2) by N. Bhat,[16] *Introduction to Operations Research Models* by Cooper, Bhat, and LeBlanc, *Dynamic Programming* by Leon and Mary Cooper,[17] and *Algorithms for Network Programming* by Kennington and Helgason.[18]

The University of Texas at Arlington

Research in mathematics at The University of Texas at Arlington (UT–Arlington) started in the fall of 1967 with the beginning of graduate work in mathematics. At that time, Professor H. A. D. Dunsworth had finished twenty years as chairman of the mathematics department and had developed a very strong undergraduate program that provided the base for the graduate program.

The doctoral program in mathematical sciences began in 1973, the same year that V. Lakshmikantham joined the mathematics faculty as chairman of the department. "Dr. Lak" was the leader in the effort to raise mathematical research to a high level.

In 1975 the department started the Area Support Program which brought many eminent research mathematicians to the UT–Arlington campus for series of lectures. During the period from 1976 to 1984, the department sponsored or cosponsored six international conferences, all dealing with the topic of nonlinear analysis.[19] At each of these conferences, fifty to sixty-five mathematical research papers have been presented by mathematicians from many countries of the world. The Seventh International Conference on Nonlinear Analysis and Applications was held in the summer of 1986.

There is further evidence that UT–Arlington is a center of international importance in the area of nonlinear analysis. Lakshmikantham is editor of the international journal *Nonlinear Analysis: Theory, Methods, and Applications*, and together with his Arlington colleague, G. S. Ladde, he edits the journal *Stochastic Analysis and Applications*. He has also directed a program under a U.S. Army Research Grant of approximately $500,000 during the period from 1975 to 1983.

Although nonlinear analysis is the most visible area, other fields of mathematics are also being investigated by the researchers at UT–Arlington. Don Greenspan, R. Kannan, and Steve Bernfeld are working in differential equations. Danny Dyer and Chien-Pai Han work in statistics, and Bennie Williams and A. Gillespie in fixed point theory. Others include Constantin Corduneanu in integral equations, Marion Moore in algebra, Larry Heath in complex analysis, and J. Eisenfeld in biomathematics.

The University of Texas at Dallas

During the 1960s there was a great interest in scientific development in the Dallas–Fort Worth area. General Dynamics, Vought Aircraft, and Texas Instruments were only three, but perhaps the largest, of the local corporations breaking into what would later be called the "high-tech" age. A great demand for a broad range of scientific research was accompanied by an increasing need for graduate training for scientists and engineers. In this climate there was a great deal of cooperation among the existing colleges and universities. SMU and Texas Christian University (TCU) started several graduate programs. Arlington State

College, only recently a junior college, surged into university status with advanced technical-scientific programs.

Notable at this time were the efforts of Erik Jonsson, Cecil Green, and Eugene McDermott, resulting in the establishment of the Southwest Center for Advanced Study in Dallas in 1963. Lloyd V. Berkner, a nationally eminent scientist-administrator with broad interests, was named director. The principal areas of interest in this center were geosciences, space science, molecular biology, and relativity. In the late 1960s this center became, basically, the University of Texas at Dallas (UT–Dallas).

Patrick L. Odell, who was mentioned earlier for his roles in the Theory and Analysis Group at the Johnson Space Center, and as chairman at TTU, came to UT–Dallas in 1972 as graduate dean and acting chairman of the Graduate Program in Mathematical Sciences. The specialties of this program are relativity, statistics, and applied mathematics. The relativity group of the former center became the nucleus of the mathematical sciences in the new university. This group includes Ivor Robinson, Wolfgang Rindler, and Istvan Ozsvath—all researchers of international reputation in relativity. In 1963 Robinson had been instrumental in organizing in Dallas a symposium for research in relativistic astrophysics, which became known as the "first Texas symposium." This symposium continues and meets every two years somewhere in the world. Rindler has published eight books, including the two-volume treatise *Spinors and Space-Time* with Roger Penrose of Oxford (and currently also of Rice).[20]

John Van Ness, an expert in clustering and classification, came to UT–Dallas in 1973. He was joined later by Larry Ammonn and John Wiorkowski, both working in the statistical theory of estimation, and by George Kimmeldorf in probability. These, together with Odell, who had by then relinquished administrative duties, comprise the highly active group in statistics. Applied mathematics is represented by R. L. Hunt, formerly of TTU, in automatic control and Ali Hooshyr in mathematical physics.

Other Programs and Individuals

Texas Christian University (TCU), under the chairmanship of Landon Colquitt, offered a doctoral program in mathematics during the 1960s and 1970s. One of the most prolific mathematicians in that program was H. Tomano, who made important discoveries in topology relating to paracompactness. C. R. Deeter and Mort Slater directed research in analysis.

Ben Goldbeck and his students developed and extended the concept of a near-ring.

Baylor University in Waco, under the leadership of Howard Rolf, has been building up its research faculty, although not offering a doctorate program. Paul Hill, with extensive publications in Abelian groups, holds an endowed chair. Robert Piziak, Baxter Johns, and Ed Oxford are all involved in research in algebra. Danny Turner, Eugene Tidmore, and Tom Bratcher are working in statistics and Max Shauck in mathematical modeling related to air pollution. Ron Stanke is doing research in harmonic analysis, and Vivienne Mayes has published in summability.

Thomas Atchison at Stephen F. Austin State University (SFASU) in Nacogdoches chairs a department doing research in statistics, analysis, and algebra.

Among those involved in research at the University of Dallas is Charles Coppin in a department that emphasizes topology, analysis, algebraic geometry, and modeling.

The department at Pan American University in Edinburg has been developing in the area of differential equations and control theory, and has hosted special symposia on this subject.

Russell Cowan of Lamar University (LU) in Beaumont has been active over a number of years in summability, regularly presenting reports to the Texas meetings of the Mathematical Association.

Richard Alo of UH–Downtown has been active in developing the field of mathematical applications, although he is in administration at the time of this writing.

Mathematical Association of America

The mathematical community in Texas is highly diverse. It contains research professors, academic scholars who do not publish original research, professors and teachers whose mathematical work is entirely pedagogical, commercial/industrial practitioners of mathematics who may or may not do original research, and a great number of persons with a lay interest in mathematics. Many of these find a common ground in the Mathematical Association of America. The purpose of the association is advancement of mathematics at the university level. However, its publications and meetings have a broader appeal. With a national membership of approximately 20,000, the association has twenty-nine sections through which it acts on a local level. The Texas Section of the association has about 800 members.

From its beginning in 1922, the Texas Section has

been an important force in the stream of mathematics scholarship in Texas. In earlier times, when travel to out-of-state meetings was less common, research papers which today would be presented only at research conferences were presented at the section meetings. These meetings have been forums for expository and pedagogical papers, as well as for research. The Texas Section has often been cited as one of the most active and innovative sections of the association. In 1971 the section began a newsletter, setting a trend in the association. Now, more than twenty sections of the association have newsletters.

The strength of the Texas section has always been the wide and enthusiastic participation of its membership. Many of the members of the research community mentioned elsewhere in this chapter have been active members of the section. Some of the many persons not mentioned earlier who have made significant contributions to mathematics in Texas through the work of the association and who are often mentioned among the honored veterans of the section are: Floyd Ulrich of Rice, W. I. Layton of SFASU, Harlan Miller of Texas Women's University, David Starr and Ed Mouzon of SMU, C. B. Wright of East Texas State University, Don Cude of Southwest Texas State University, M. E. Mullings of Abilene Christian University (ACU), J. E. Burnam of Hardin-Simmons University, A. D. Stewart of Prairie View A&M University, June Wood of UH–Downtown, and Ralph Whitmore of Southwestern University.

William S. McCulley and James R. Boone, both of TAMU, have been the state directors of the high school mathematics contest. Robert Greenwood of UT–Austin and George Berzsenyi of LU have made significant contributions to the contest work of the association on a national level. Glen Mattingly of Sam Houston State University (SHSU) and Charles Benner of UH–University Park have each been editor of *College Mathematics in Texas,* a series of compilations of mathematics course offerings in colleges and universities in the state. Martin Wright of UH–University Park, C. R. Deeter of TCU, and C. J. Pipes of SMU are among those who have served as section governor. John Ed Allen of NTSU and Louie Huffman of Midwestern State University have been active over a number of years in representing college mathematics interests to the Texas Education Agency.

The elected officer most often credited with providing leadership and stability in the section is the secretary-treasurer. In the last thirty years, only four persons have held the office: Charles Scherer followed by Ben T. Goldbeck, both of TCU, Jim Bradford of ABU, and the present secretary, Glen Mattingly of SHSU.

Leonard Gillman of UT–Austin has been serving as the treasurer of the association and, at the time of this writing, has just been elected national president. R. H. Bing, also at UT–Austin, has been president at the national level.

The Texas Association of Academic Administrators in Mathematical Sciences is a state group of department heads in mathematics. This group, the first of its kind in the nation, was begun under the auspices of the Texas Section. Among the many mathematicians in the state who have been active in this organization, the services of Robert Northcutt of Southwest Texas State University and Joe Cude of Tarleton State University have been notable.

Notes

1. Moore, 1916.
2. Wilder, 1976.
3. Traylor, 1972.
4. Wall, 1948.
5. McGee, 1954.
6. Boullion and Odell, 1971; Duran and Odell, 1974; Lewis and Odell, 1971.
7. Gray and Schucany, 1972.
8. Bruce, 1904.
9. Bruce, 1932.
10. Siebring, 1965.
11. Mauldin, 1981.
12. Bellman and Wing, 1975.
13. Haberman, 1977.
14. Haberman, 1983.
15. Owen, 1975.
16. Bhat, 1972.
17. Cooper and Cooper, 1981.
18. Kennington and Helgason, 1980.
19. Lakshmikantham, 1982.
20. Rindler and Penrose, 1984–86.

Bibliography

Bellman, Richard, and Wing, Milton G. *An Introduction to Invariant Embedding.* New York: John Wiley and Sons, 1975.

Bhat, U. Narayan. *Elements of Applied Stochastic Processes.* New York: John Wiley and Sons, 1972.

Boullion, T. L., and Odell, P. L. *Generalized Inverse Matrices.* New York: John Wiley and Sons, 1971.

Bruce, W. H. *Some Noteworthy Properties of a Triangle and Its Circles.* New York: D. C. Heath and Co., 1904.

———. *The Nine Circles of a Triangle.* Denton: North Texas State Teachers College, 1932.

Cooper, Leon, and Cooper, Mary W. *Introduction to Dynamic Programming.* New York: Pergamon Press, 1981.

Dodd, E. L. *Lectures on Probability and Statistics.* Austin: The University of Texas Press, 1945.

Duran, B., and Odell, P. L. *Cluster Analysis.* New York: Springer-Verlag, 1974.

Frantz, Joe B. "The Moore Method." Chapter 10 of *The Forty Acre Follies,* pp. 111–122. Austin: The Texas Monthly Press, 1983.

Gray, H. L., and Schucany, W. R. *The Generalized Jackknife Statistic.* New York: Marcel Dekker, 1972.

Greenwood, Robert E. "Mathematics." In *Discovery: Research and Scholarship at the University of Texas at Austin* 7, no. 3 (1983): pp. 18–22.

Haberman, Richard. *Mathematical Models, Mechanical Vibrations, Population Dynamics, & Traffic Flow, An Introduction to Applied Mathematics.* Englewood Cliffs: Prentice-Hall, Inc., 1977.

———. *Elementary Applied Partial Differential Equations.* Englewood Cliffs: Prentice-Hall, Inc., 1983.

Kennington, Jeff L., and Helgason, Richard V. *Algorithms for Network Programming.* New York: John Wiley and Sons, 1980.

Lakshmikantham, V., ed. *Nonlinear Phenomena in Mathematical Science.* New York: Academic Press, 1982.

Lewis, T. O., and Odell, P. L. *Estimation in Linear Models.* Englewood Cliffs: Prentice-Hall, Inc., 1971.

McGee, R. V. *Mathematics in Agriculture,* 2d ed. New York: Prentice-Hall, Inc., 1954.

Mauldin, R. Daniel, ed. *The Scottish Book. Mathematics From The Scottish Café.* Boston: Birkhäuser, 1981.

Moore, Robert L. "On the Foundations of Plane Analysis Situs." *Proceedings of the National Academy of Sciences,* 2 (1916): pp. 131–164.

———. *Foundations of Point Set Theory,* 2d ed. Colloquium Publications, vol. 13. New York: American Mathematical Society, 1962.

Owen, D. B. *On the History of Statistics and Probability.* New York: Marcel Dekker, 1975.

Owen, Guillermo. *Game Theory.* Philadelphia: Saunders, 1968.

Pfeiffer, Paul E. *Concepts of Probability Theory.* New York: Dover, 1978.

Rindler, Wolfgang, and Penrose, R. *Spinors and Space-Time.* 2 vols. Cambridge: Cambridge University Press, 1984–86.

Siebring, Richard. "Institutional Influences in the Undergraduate Training of Ph.D. Mathematicians." *The American Mathematical Monthly* 72 (1965): pp. 66–72.

Thrall, Robert M., and Spivey, W. Allen. *Linear Optimization.* New York: Holt, Rinehart and Winston, 1970.

Traylor, D. R. *Creative Teaching: Heritage of R. L. Moore.* Houston: The University of Houston, 1972.

Vandiver, H. S., and Birkhoff, George David. "On the Integral Divisors of $a^n - b^n$." *Annals of Mathematics* 5 (1904): pp. 173–180.

Wall, H. S. *The Analytic Theory of Continued Fractions.* New York: D. van Nostrand & Co., 1948.

———. *Creative Mathematics.* Austin: The University of Texas Press, 1963.

Wilder, R. L. "Robert Lee Moore, 1882–1974." *Bulletin of the American Mathematical Society* 82 (1976): pp. 417–427.

7

Physics

Claude W. Horton, Sr.

Introduction

By the fall of 1945, at the end of World War II, the number of faculty and students in physics had been severely reduced because of the national emergency. But soon student enrollment rebounded vigorously due to the veterans' programs. Faculty returned from wartime research and other assignments with renewed enthusiasm, especially since they were viewed as heroes in the "physicist's war." These factors together with the emergence of government funds for research administered by the Office of Naval Research, Office of Scientific Research and Development, and the Atomic Energy Commission (AEC) led to a rapid growth of physics programs in Texas.

Currently there are twelve universities in Texas that offer programs leading to the doctorate in physics (Table 1). There are also several universities that offer excellent graduate programs some of which lead to the master's degree. A recent listing of the staffs of these departments has been prepared by the American Institute of Physics.[1] The department faculties involved in the doctoral programs vary from six to sixty-six members.

The names of many of the universities in Texas have been changed during the period since the war. Part of this change was due to the increased popularity of the word "university" to denote a school with a broad range of professional interests and the prestige associated with it. The older term "college" lost some of its attraction. Another major cause was the organizational change in the university systems in Texas. Now many state universities are designated University of Texas (UT), or Texas A&M University (TAMU), or University of Houston (UH), followed by a specific location. The independent universities, too, changed their names or began as universities. For example, the Rice Institute changed its name to Rice University in July 1960. Both old and new names will be used according to the context.[2]

University Research

Early in the history of modern science, research was done by wealthy amateurs or with the support of wealthy patrons. During the nineteenth century, the state increasingly accepted the role of patron, and research became associated with state-supported universities or well-endowed private universities. Initially, equipment used in physics research was as simple as Galileo's plank, parchment, and small, hard, round spheres. In the years between the seventeenth and twentieth centuries, it has generally become more complex, more sophisticated, and more expensive. Moreover, physicists often worked alone until the late nineteenth century, when they began to work in teams—usually a physicist and his doctoral students, but in recent years, even groups of physicists. Although discussion in this chapter will center around research associated with a few pieces of equipment, those pieces are only representative samples of what is available.[3]

In 1945 the Rice Institute had a Van de Graaff accelerator that had been used just before the war, and it could produce beams of charged particles with energies up to 5.6 MeV. In 1954 this acclerator was replaced by a new one, manufactured by the High Voltage Engineering Corporation and housed in the newly constructed T. W. Bonner Laboratory. This facility was named after Tom Wilkerson Bonner who was the leader in the construction of the first accelerator at Rice and who was chairman of the department from 1947 until his death in 1961. His contributions to physics were so significant that the American Physical Society (APS) established a Tom W. Bonner Prize that is awarded each year.

Emmett L. Hudspeth, who as a graduate student at Rice had helped with the construction of their first accelerator, joined the faculty of UT–Austin soon after the war. He immediately began the construction of a Van de Graaff accelerator in Austin. This unit was used for many years in teaching and research, before it was replaced by a larger accelerator that was housed in a special building on the university campus. Beams of charged particles with energies up to approximately 15 MeV were available for research.

The energy range of a Van de Graaff accelerator is low by modern standards and limits the kinds of nuclear studies that can be pursued successfully. When the range of available experiments in nuclear structure was exhausted, the accelerators were used to produce Coulomb excitation of large atoms, the production and study of very-highly-ionized atoms (beam-foil technique), and charged-particle activation analysis.

TAMU responded to the challenge for higher energies by establishing a Cyclotron Institute. This institute has a variable-energy cyclotron that produces beams of both polarized and unpolarized protons and deuterons of up to 60 MeV. Beams of ^{3}He and alpha particles of energies of up 130 MeV can be produced as well as heavy ion beams of mass from that of lithium to xenon. A scientific and technical staff of approximately thirty-five persons are currently involved in this program.

Low-temperature physics is another area of research that has been pursued actively in Texas. The modern phase of this work began in 1950 when C. F. Squire came to the Rice Institute from the Massachusetts Institute of Technology (MIT). He brought with him a helium liquefier that he had helped build at MIT. Later Rice replaced this experimental model with a new liquefier, an ADL Collins Helium Cryostat, manufactured by Arthur D. Little Incorporated. The new liquefier, the gift of a private donor, was installed in the low-temperature laboratory.

The University of Texas at Austin was able to develop its own research program in low-temperature physics when a helium liquefier was furnished to the university by the Air Force as part of a research grant. The technical skill to utilize this research facility was provided by James C. Thompson, who had been a graduate student of Squire. This first unit was later replaced by a commercial unit manufactured by Arthur D. Little Incorporated.

The developments just summarized for the accelerators and the liquefiers are typical of research in physics. Usually physicists develop their own research equipment because they wish to measure quantities that have not been measured before. After they develop the prototype machine and publish the results of their research, industrial companies produce commercial models. Generally these ready-made machines save research time and give better results.

Fusion research is another area in which a substantial investment in research equipment is necessary. UT–Austin has an ongoing program in this field. At the present time there is a large machine, designated the Texas Experimental Tokamak, which is a toroid that can confine plasmas at high temperature. The toroid is a doughnut-shaped cavity that has an inner radius of 0.3 meter and an outer radius of 1.0 meter. Plasma of density $2-5 \times 10^{13}$ particles/cm^3 can be heated to electron temperatures of $1-3$ kilovolts. These design parameters were chosen so that experimental studies of plasmas could be made which would be relevant to Tokomaks designed to deliver electrical power from nuclear fusion. This vigorous and continuing research program was developed under the guidance of William E. Drummond and other faculty members.

It is easy and impressive to list large pieces of equipment; however, this does not lessen the importance and value of the smaller items that are actively used for basic research and teaching throughout the state. North Texas State University (NTSU) has excellent facilities for research on a variety of lasers. Their equipment spans the wavelengths of 0.25 μm to 10.6 μm and develops power of more than 10^9 watts pulsed. Their physics group is also active in developing applications of small accelerators.

The University of Houston–University Park (UH–University Park) has programs in space physics, condensed matter, and intermediate and high-energy research. The subject of instabilities and chaotic behavior of dynamic systems is of great current interest and the applications are many and varied. This area of research is pursued actively at UH–University Park and by several groups at UT–Austin.

The large national research centers are available for research by the faculty members of Texas universities. For example, high-energy physicists from Texas have participated in ongoing research at the Fermilab in Batavia, Illinois. Some even work regularly at the Conseil Européen pour la Recherche Nucléaire (CERN) in Switzerland as well as at other international centers. Faculty and graduate students of UH–University Park have the opportunity to do research at the Oak Ridge and the Brookhaven National Laboratories and at the Linear Collider at the Stanford Linear Accelerator. Many faculty members of UT–Austin have participated in research at the Los Alamos National Laboratory throughout the postwar period.

Active programs in theoretical physics are as important as experimental ones. All of the experimental projects mentioned above have been associated with these groups of theorists, whose contributions are essential for a well-balanced program. In some departments the theorists are organized into formal groups such as the Center for Relativity Theory established at UT–Austin in 1962. This center was the forerunner of significant programs in relativity at both UT–Dallas and Rice.

It is invidious to name outstanding faculty appointments, but a few names will be mentioned to show the strengths of the faculties in Texas. William V. Houston was well-known for his research when he was appointed president of Rice University and professor of physics. Polykarp Kusch, a 1955 Nobel laureate in physics, has been the Eugene McDermott Professor of Physics at UT–Dallas since 1972. Ilya Prigogine, an Ashbel Smith Professor and Regental Professor at UT–Austin, is also professor and director of the Free University of Brussels, Belgium. He was a member of the physics department at UT–Austin when he received the Nobel Prize in chemistry in 1977. Stephen Weinberg, Regental Professor, holds the Jack S. Josey-Welch Foundation Chair in Science at UT–Austin. He was a Nobel laureate in physics in 1979.

Before World War II the profession of physics was relatively unknown in Texas. Not until students had taken courses in physics did they realize that here was a challenging and stimulating career. The scientific developments and wide publicity of sonar, radar, and nuclear power that resulted from wartime research changed this situation. In the 1950s many students entered college with the definite intention of becoming a "nuclear physicist." This interest could not have been sustained without the availability of professional opportunities in Texas.

The Acoustical Society of America has met frequently in Austin. That choice is a reflection of the prestige, influence, and leadership of Charles P. Boner, who developed a strong program in acoustics in the physics department of UT–Austin. Boner founded the Defense Research Laboratory on the university campus in 1945. Later the name was changed to the Applied Research Laboratories. The staff has performed extensive research in underwater acoustics and other areas of physics since its founding, and it is still growing in size and importance. A group of physicists and engineers left this laboratory to form Texas Research Associates, which later became Tracor.

Aided by contracts with the U.S. Air Force, Alfred Schild of the UT–Austin physics department initiated a program in relativity theory that has developed steadily and has stimulated other Texas universities to establish programs in that field. This active program was associated with a national resurgence of interest in relativity. It led to a series of symposia that began with the "First Texas Symposium on Relativistic Astrophysics" held at Dallas in December 1963.[4] A proposal made by John A. Wheeler (presently the Jane and Roland Blumberg Professor in Physics at UT–Austin) aroused so much interest that a half day was set aside to discuss his findings.[5]

Industrial Research

The rapid expansion of physics teaching and research is intimately related to the expansion and growth of industry in Texas. In the early 1950s the major employment opportunities for physicists were provided by the oil companies and especially by the geophysical programs. At that time relatively few universities offered formal programs in geophysics, and a training in physics provided the best approximation to the needs of the geophysical industry.

Many physicists solved the problem of employment by forming their own companies or by marketing their equipment designs. A well-known early example was the development of the LaCoste-Romberg gravity meter in the late 1930s by Arnold Romberg and Lucien LaCoste. A later example is the Worden gravity meter developed by Sam Worden, a Rice graduate.

The gravity meter is an instrument of great value to the oil industry and to geophysicists who wish to study the structure of the earth. The gravity meter enables the geologist and geophysicist to map minute variations in the earth's gravitational field. Careful analyses of these maps provide clues to structural features such as salt domes and anticlines that are favorable for the accumulation of oil. The French scientific community considered the LaCoste-Romberg gravity meter so important that they included it in a permanent exhibit in the Palais de la Découverte in Paris, France. The author had the pleasure of seeing this exhibit in 1964.

An interesting example of a resourceful solution to the unemployment problem is provided by the Texas Nuclear Corporation of Austin. In the late 1940s a group of graduates of the UT–Austin doctoral program who had done research on the Van de Graaff accelerator wanted to stay in Austin rather than seek employment elsewhere. Since there were no employment opportunities for nuclear physicists in Austin at that time, they organized the Texas Nuclear Corporation to develop and manufacture various accelerators and particle detectors for industrial applications. Under the leadership of Emmett Hudspeth, the group obtained the necessary financial backing, and the venture was a success.

Limited projects of this kind could not sustain a large number of graduates. Fortunately, a new industry was created in Dallas which gave a significant impetus to the development of technology and physics in Texas. Cecil H. Green, Erik Jonsson, and Eugene McDermott had formed the very successful Geophysical Service Incorporated (GSI) in Dallas. In the early 1950s, Bell Telephone Laboratories decided to make their recently-invented transistor available to other companies. As part of this program, Gordon K. Teal, who had helped to develop the transistor, came to Dallas in 1953 as assistant vice-president and director of materials and components research for Texas Instruments (TI), the company newly created by directors of GSI.

The vision of such businessmen as Green, Jonsson, and Ross Perot, combined with the knowledge and skill of Teal, soon provided an impressive research laboratory that expanded into all phases of the field of semiconductors. This development provided a great stimulus to the career opportunities in Texas for physicists.

Another consequence of the success of TI was the decision to offer educational opportunities for advanced technology in the Dallas area. They invited Lloyd V. Berkner to organize an educational facility, the Southwest Center for Research. In publicity statements regarding this venture, Berkner made many critical comments about the lack of advanced scientific training in Texas and claimed that the brightest college students left Texas to pursue their graduate education elsewhere. These remarks were unfortunate since they alienated many people who were involved in education in the state. After a few years, the founders realized that the center was not viable in its original form, and it was reorganized in 1969 as UT–Dallas, a part of the University of Texas System.

During the 1950s, employment opportunities in physics were rather limited in Texas. As mentioned before, the oil companies in Houston and Dallas provided the best opportunities. An aircraft company in Fort Worth received a government contract to study the feasibility of a nuclear-powered aircraft. At that time Robert N. Little had a group of doctoral candidates who had measured the cross section of various elements for neutron scattering. These data are important for the design of such aircraft; so Little took a year's leave of absence and, with those candidates who had completed their doctorate, he formed a team that went to Fort Worth to work on the program.

From 1950 to the present, the industry of Texas has shifted steadily towards high technology. Employment opportunities for physicists have increased correspondingly. TI of Dallas has pioneered this movement in various cities. The National Aeronautics and Space Administration followed suit at its facilities, the Johnson Space Center, near Houston. IBM, Motorola, and Lockheed have established large research and manufacturing plants in Austin. These are only a few of the high-technology companies that have moved to Texas. These new employment opportunities have led to an increased enrollment in physics in Texas colleges and universities, which in turn has created a need for science educators at all levels.

The problem of providing active cooperation between industrial and academic research has attracted considerable attention in the last few years. One innovative solution to this problem is provided by the Houston Area Research Center (HARC) located in The Woodlands, a new community twenty-seven miles north of Houston. HARC was established in 1982 to provide industry, business, government, and other institutions with the combined research capabilities available through four distinguished Texas research universities. Composed of TAMU, Rice, UH–

University Park, and UT–Austin, HARC is a non-profit research consortium and an independent institution, chartered by the State of Texas with its own board of directors.

Currently, HARC has twenty-five full-time employees including an interim president, contracts administrator, comptroller, and clerical staff. There are twenty full-time scientists and technicians on site involved with on-going research projects. In addition, it employs a number of part-time personnel and graduate students to assist in its research efforts. Funded by endowments, contracts, grants and gifts, the institution hopes to serve as a catalyst between the more fundamental research of the academic sector and the applied research needs of government and industry.

One of the research programs sponsored by HARC is the Texas Accelerator Center. This center has a contract with the U.S. Department of Energy to design components for a newly proposed, high-energy particle accelerator, the Superconducting Super Collider (SSC). The staff at the center has completed the design of powerful magnets that can be used to direct and control the particle beams.

Another research program at HARC is the Laser Application Research Center which is engaged in the development of commercial opportunities for laser applications in business. This center is also developing laser applications for the medical and biomedical engineering fields.

Although the funding of fundamental research in the nation seems likely to diminish, the prospects for future expansion in Texas are most promising. There is a good possibility that one of the new generation of accelerators, the SSC, may be located in Texas. Its construction will require an underground, circular path for the charged particles, which will have a diameter of between fifteen and thirty miles depending on the design, beam energy, and funding.

There are also good prospects that more companies developing satellites and space programs will locate in Texas. For example, the launch vehicle *Conestoga I* of Space Services Incorporated of America had a successful firing after several false starts, on Matagorda Island on September 9, 1982.[6] Another commercial venture, which plans to develop a celestial mausoleum or space cemetery, would provide few employment opportunities for physicists, however.

A more probable source of future opportunities for employment exists in the science of materials. Conventional aspects of solid state physics and the study of semiconducting compounds will continue, but the most exciting new developments are in the field of surface physics. Economic applications are not easily visualized at the moment, but the prospects are encouraging and much research in materials science can be expected. This area of physics is of great importance to modern high technology, which appears to have a bright future in Texas.[7]

The Welch Foundation and Research in Physics

Public awareness of and interest in physics was further stimulated by the Welch Foundation in Houston. On his death in 1952 Robert A. Welch left an estate to be used to develop chemical research in Texas. W. O. Milligan, a professor of chemistry at Rice University, was the first director of the foundation and did much to establish its policies. Milligan initiated a series of conferences in Houston and attracted eminent scientists to attend and present papers. Although Welch's primary goal was to further research in chemistry, the first two conferences were of special interest to physicists because of Milligan's plan. He thought that the logical way to approach chemistry was to start with the atomic nucleus and work outwards. Thus, the first conference in 1957 was devoted to the nucleus, and the second one to the structure of the atom. Welch stipulated that the early grants be restricted to chemical research but that after ten years the grants could be given in related scientific fields. His wishes were followed. For example, the Welch Foundation has contributed to the cost of upgrading the cyclotron at TAMU.

At the first Welch Conference, held at the Rice Hotel in Houston November 20–22, 1957,[8] Willard F. Libby gave a talk on nuclear techniques in chemistry. Libby, who was at that time a member of the AEC, spoke enthusiastically about the possibility of developing electrical energy from nuclear fusion. These remarks had a significant influence on the development of physics in Texas because they stimulated an interest that led ultimately to a substantial research program in fusion research at UT–Austin and undoubtedly had some influence in the formation of the Texas Atomic Energy Research Foundation (TAERF).

In the early 1960s the investor-owned electric power companies of Texas established TAERF to promote nuclear fusion as a practical source of electric power. As part of this program, they organized symposia and brought in distinguished national speakers. In a move that may have had an even greater impact on the universities, they organized meetings for high school students and promoted interest in physics as a career. These meetings are still held every spring and are attended by some five hundred students and their teachers.

Physics Societies

During the postwar period the national physical societies such as the APS, the Acoustical Society of America, and the American Association of Physics Teachers (AAPT) have held numerous meetings in Texas. Often these were joint meetings with Texas organizations such as the Physical Science Section of the Texas Academy of Science.

The APS held a national meeting at Rice in November 1947. The program of this meeting provides an excellent epitome of the state of physics research in Texas at that time.[9] Harold A. Wilson, who for many years was head of the Rice physics department, gave an after-dinner speech. Wilson provided a fascinating connecting link between Texas and British physicists. As a young man, Wilson had studied under Sir J. J. Thomson at the famous Cavendish Laboratory in Cambridge, England. He was able to tell many interesting stories about Thomson (who was the first to measure the charge on an electron), Lord Kelvin, and other famous scientists of the period.

Claude W. Heaps of Rice, who was well-known and liked by many students for his fascinating freshman course in physics, was chairman of the local committee of the APS. Squire of Rice gave an invited paper on the low-temperature physics program at the Rice Institute. Some twenty-three faculty and students from UT–Austin and fifteen faculty and students from Rice were authors or coauthors of papers presented at this meeting.

The Texas Section of the AAPT has held a series of meetings that has probably helped more than the national meetings to promote the exchange of ideas and information among physicists in Texas. The second annual meeting was held in December 1956 on the campus of Howard Payne College in Brownwood, and meetings have continued regularly since then. The latest AAPT meeting was held in November 1985 at TAMU.

These meetings played an important role in the development of physics teaching and research in Texas, especially in the 1950s and 1960s when departments were expanding rapidly. Today, the meetings are still frequent, and the faculty and graduate students from many Texas universities in addition to those listed in Table I take an active role in the meetings. The many scientists who have served as officers of the AAPT organization include L. F. Connell, North Texas State College, Coleman M. Loyd, TAMU, M. F. Coffman, Abilene Christian College, R. N. Little, UT–Austin, Donald A. Cowan, UT–Dallas, H. M. Moseley, Texas Christian University, and H. Kendall Reynolds, UH–University Park. J. G. Potter, TAMU, and H. D. Schwetman, Baylor, have served not only as officers of the Texas Section, but also as representatives from the Texas Section to the National Council of the AAPT. Professor Robert N. Little, UT–Austin, was elected president of the AAPT in 1970. Currently Joe Pizzo, Lamar University, is president of the Texas Section of the AAPT and Joe S. Ham, TAMU, is the president-elect. J. David Gavenda, UT–Austin, is chairperson of the Texas Section of the APS.

In summary, one can say that there has been steady, perhaps even spectacular growth in teaching and research in physics in Texas as well as in the industrial application of its research findings from 1945 to the present. These developments have occurred in essentially all fields of physics. However, there have been no spectacular discoveries made locally. These are usually associated with the large accelerators, none of which have been located in Texas as yet.

Notes

1. Graduate Programs, 1984.

2. Details of the various name changes and when they occurred, as well as other information about Texas universities, can be found in Branda, 1976, pp. 1039–50.

3. A very detailed description of equipment and research programs can be found in Graduate Programs, 1984.

4. The proceedings of this conference were published by the University of Chicago. Robinson, et al., 1964.

5. This discussion formed the basis of a publication by Harrison et al., 1965.

6. Marsh, 1984, a.

7. Marsh, 1984, b and c.

8. Horton, 1958.

9. Bulletin, 1948.

Bibliography

Branda, Eldon Stephen, Ed. *The Handbook of Texas, A Supplement.* Austin: The Texas State Historical Association, Vol. 3 (1976).

Table 1

Data on Texas Universities That Offer the Ph.D. in Physics

University,[a] location	Number of faculty[b]	Number of Doctorates Awarded		
		1949–54[c]	1979–84[b]	1983–84[b]
UT-Austin Austin	66	48	97	21
TAMU College Station	42	6	24	9
Rice Houston	23	32	37	9
UH-University Park Houston	22		27	6
NTSU Denton	22		9	2
UTGSBS Houston	20		9	0
UT-Dallas Richardson	19		17	7
UT-Arlington Arlington	16		3	1
TTU Lubbock	16		8	1
UT-El Paso El Paso	15		2	1
BU Waco	9		4	0
TCU Fort Worth	6		5	0

[a]For full names, see Appendix B.
[b]American Institute of Physics, 1984.
[c]Southern Regional Education Board, 1955. Data are given for three schools only.

Bulletin of the American Physical Society, 73 (1948), p. 644.

Doctoral Programs Offered by Southern Universities. Atlanta: Southern Regional Education Board, 1955.

Graduate Programs in Physics, Astronomy, and Related Fields, 1984–1985. New York: American Institute of Physics, 1984.

Harrison, B. K., Thorn, K. S., Wakano, M., and Wheeler, J. A. *Gravitation Theory and Gravitational Collapse.* Chicago: The University of Chicago Press, 1965.

Horton, C. W. "Structure of the Nucleus." *The Texas Quarterly*, 1 (1958), pp. 9–15.

———, "Physics," *Discovery*, 7 (1983), pp. 23–25. (Centennial Issue).

Kevles, Daniel J. *The Physicists: The History of a Scientific Community in Modern America.* New York: Knopf, 1978.

Marsh, Alton K. (a) "Space Services Pushing Conestoga Launch Vehicle." *Aviation Week and Space Technology*, 120 (June 25, 1984), pp. 163–65.

———, (b) "High Technology in Texas: State Seeks Technology Center Status." Ibid., 121 (August 6, 1984), pp. 68–69.

———, (c) "High Technology in Texas: Austin's Lead in Research Spurs Growth." Ibid., (August 13, 1984), pp. 73–78.

Robinson, I., Schild, A., and Schucking, E. L., Eds. *Quasi-Stellar Sources and Gravitational Collapse.* Chicago: The University of Chicago Press, 1964.

8

Chemistry

Joseph J. Lagowski

CHEMISTRY AS A theoretical as well as a laboratory science has always been deeply embedded in the practical arts. Histories of chemistry often begin with a description of the technical arts of the Egyptians, Greeks, and Romans, who had accumulated a practical knowledge of the use and manipulation of such materials as pottery, glazes, pigments, metals, alloys, and leather. Among the most important raw materials exploited in recent history have been salt, metalliferous ores, coal, molasses, fats and oils (of plant and animal origins), water, and air. Since the early part of this century, however, the most important resources have been petroleum and natural gas. Texas is a major source of supply for these fossil fuels as well as for lignite, a form of coal. The petroleum and petrochemical industries that have been created by the need to find and process oil and gas have been the mainstay of the state's economy.

The Prewar Chemical Industry

Although oil wells multiplied like rabbits after Spindletop came in, the petrochemical industry developed more slowly and more sporadically before World War II (part I). But in 1940, war needs led the Dow Chemical Company to locate a major plant in Freeport.[1] Other large chemical companies quickly followed. In the same year, the Shell Chemical Company opened a plant in Houston to produce chemicals from natural gas; later, Shell built another plant to make butadiene, the monomer for urgently needed synthetic rubber. Also in 1940 the Union Carbide and Carbon Corporation began producing ethyl and isopropyl alcohols at Texas City. Between 1944 and 1948 six more major plants were opened: Diamond Alkali in Dallas (silicates) in 1944 and in Houston (chlorine and caustic soda) in 1948; Celanese in Bishop (chemicals from gas) in 1945; Dupont at the Sabine River Works (nylon intermediates and polyethylene) and in LaPorte (agrichemicals), both in 1946; and Rohm and Haas (chemical intermediates) in 1948.

It was a time, too, when the classic entrepreneurial spirit found encouragement in the Lone Star State. Many small chemical companies were started, most with checkered histories. A typical example is Merichem, founded in 1945 by John Files and Edward Lewis, two young engineers with ideas and ambition but little cash. Merichem at first produced soap, but soon grew by providing services for the refinery industry. The company purchased caustic soda that had been used for refining petroleum and converted it to sodium sulfide and cresylic acid, both valuable for other purposes.

Eventually the young Merichem Company needed an infusion of capital, which was obtained from Jefferson Lake Sulfur Company in return for an option to purchase Merichem shares. When Occidental Petroleum Company purchased Jefferson in 1963, Merichem became a division of Occidental. Two years later, Files regained control of Merichem by purchasing it from Occidental with the aid of a venture capital partner, and Merichem was again independent, but in a better financial position.

Although new industries may have been attracted by the abundance of oil and gas, both as resources and fuels, the processes used almost always involved nonpetroleum mineral resources or chemicals obtained from them such as chlorine, sulfur, and caustic soda. These industries were able to flourish because of the abundance of raw materials available (table 1).[2]

Chemical Education

Chemical education on a professional level began in Texas at Austin College in Huntsville (now in Sherman) in 1853 under the guidance of Washington McCartney.[3] For thirty years Austin College was the only institution of higher learning in the state with a chemistry department. Little research was done, however, until the arrival of C. C. Scott, who had received a doctorate in science from the University of Heidelberg. Scott was head of the department from 1889 to 1924.

When the University of Texas opened its doors in Austin for the first time in 1883, J. W. Mallett, well known for his research in analytical chemistry, was invited to chair the department. Laboratory facilities were obtained by his successor, Edgar Everhart, an aggressive teacher whose research interests were in physiological chemistry. By 1911 a faculty of three professors and their students were publishing extensive research in organic, analytical, and physical chemistry. During the years before World War II, the department gradually expanded and research included all of the traditional divisions of chemistry.

In 1888 H. H. Harrington, state chemist and chemist of the Texas Agricultural Experimental Station (TAES), began teaching chemistry at the Texas Agricultural and Mechanical College. His research in agricultural chemistry set the pattern for similar research

Table 1

Summary of the Major Nonpetroleum Mineral Resources of Texas

Caliche (calcium carbonate)
Ceramic Clay
   kaolinite
   montmorillonite
Nonceramic Clay
   fullers earth
   bentonite
   pumicite
   zeolites
Copper minerals
   malachite (basic copper carbonate)
   azurite (basic copper carbonate)
   covellite (copper^{II} sulfide)
   chalcocite (copper^{I} sulfide)
Dolomite (calcium magnesium carbonate)
Glauconite
   (iron, magnesium, calcium, potassium, and aluminum silicates)
Gypsum (calcium sulfate)
Iron ores
   siderite (iron carbonate)
   limonite (iron oxide)
Limestone (calcium carbonate)
Phosphorite
Potash (potassium carbonate)
Salt (sodium chloride)
   beds
   domes
Sulfur
Talc (magnesium silicate)
Soapstone (magnesium silicate)

Adapted from a map of the mineral resources of Texas. From Garner, L. E., Ann E. St. Clair, and Thomas J. Evans. *Mineral Resources of Texas*, Austin: Bureau of Economic Geology, 1979.

at Texas A&M during the prewar years. One of its outstanding exponents was George S. Fraps, who succeeded Harrington as state and TAES chemist.

When the Rice Institute was founded in 1912, it became the twelfth university in Texas to have a chemistry department, and most of them were doing both pure and applied research.

Before World War II the need for chemists in Texas was modest, and so were the research programs. As the number of universities increased over the years, chemistry departments were able to supply industry's needs, but for the most part, the relatively few professors needed came from outside of Texas, from the old and established universities of the East and the Midwest. With the advent of war, all of this began to change.

In universities where chemical engineers were being prepared, instruction was given in the chemistry department. In 1919 the University of Texas created a separate department for a brief interval, but the move was premature as the demand was not yet great enough. The Rice Institute successfully established a separate department in 1926, but the needs of industry did not warrant further expansion until the nation was threatened with war. Then, separate chemical engineering departments were founded quickly at the University of Texas in 1939 and Texas A&M in 1940.

The influx of heavy chemical industry into the state and the accompanying proliferation of small industries produced a demand for trained chemists who could address the diverse research and development needs of a growing industry. Each of the plants that was established in the state required experienced personnel able to deal with the idiosyncratic chemical problems associated with the processes employed. The plants also needed people to improve processes and/or to develop new materials for as yet undeveloped markets. Initially such personnel was brought in from out of state, but the burgeoning need for more trained personnel, brought about by expansion of the industry and exacerbated by the war effort, began to be met by chemistry and chemical engineering programs at both undergraduate and graduate levels in the colleges and universities of Texas.

The Welch Foundation

Coincidentally with the rising industrial need for trained chemists was the establishment of The Robert A. Welch Foundation in 1954.[4] Robert Alonzo Welch (fig. 1) had been the epitome of the "self-made" man. Although he was not a chemist nor even a scientist, he greatly respected and appreciated the value of chemical research for the betterment of humanity. In his will he wrote

> I have been spared to live beyond the alloted span of three score years and ten, and, in that lifetime, by hard work and sacrifice, assisted to some extent by good fortune, have accumulated property of

Figure 1. Robert Alonzo Welch.

substantial value. My desire, now, is to make that disposition of it by will which will result in it being used in the way most beneficial to mankind. I have long been impressed with the great possibilities of the betterment of mankind that lay in the field of research in the domain of chemistry. This is a feeling that I think is widely held by others. It is a popular expression to say that we are living in a 'chemical world.' Day by day we see marvels wrought in that field. . . .[5]

In 1954, less than two years after his death, The Robert A. Welch Foundation was established with an endowment of $25 million from his estate. Its purpose is to fund and encourage fundamental research in chemistry in Texas. The Foundation is governed by a board of trustees assisted by a distinguished scientific advisory board (table 2).

The mainstay of the Foundation's effort since 1954 has been a program of research grants awarded to faculty at about fifty Texas colleges and universities. More than $150 million has been awarded to the research program since it started in 1954. About two

Table 2

Members of the Scientific Advisory Board, The Robert A. Welch Foundation

Name	Affiliation when appointed	
A. P. Beutel	The Dow Chemical Company	1954–57
Detlev W. Bronk	National Academy of Sciences	1954–55
Roger Adams	The University of Illinois	1955–71
Arthur C. Cope	Massachusetts Institute of Technology	1960–66
P. J. W. Debye	Cornell University	1954–66
Henry Eyring	University of Utah	1954–81
C. Glen King	The Nutrition Foundation, Inc.	1954–64
Glenn T. Seaborg	U.S. Atomic Energy Commission[a]	1957–pres.
Wendell M. Stanley	University of California, Berkeley	1964–71
W. O. Baker	Bell Telephone Laboratories	1968–pres.
E. J. Corey	Harvard University	1968–pres.
George W. Beadle	University of Chicago	1971–82
C. S. Marvel	University of Arizona	1971–pres.
Paul Berg	Stanford University School of Medicine	1980–pres.
Norman Hackerman[b]	Rice University[c]	1982–pres.
Emil Thomas Kaiser	Rockefeller University	1982–pres.
William N. Lipscomb, Jr.	Harvard University	1982–pres.

[a]Currently at the University of California, Berkeley
[b]Current board chairman
[c]Currently at UT–Austin.

thousand persons, faculty and students, in the state are currently involved in research under the program.[6] Recently the Foundation has undertaken a program of departmental grants to Texas colleges and universities which currently do not have extensive resources in their departments of chemistry; such grants are in place at Austin College, Lamar University, Midwestern State University, Prairie View A&M University, Stephen F. Austin State University, Southwestern University, Texas Agricultural and Industrial University, Texas Southern University, and Texas Wesleyan College.

The Foundation also encourages young people to pursue chemistry as a profession by providing scholarships for promising high school graduates who wish to continue their education in the chemical sciences. In 1984 the Foundation inaugurated a four-year pilot project to encourage high school students to study chemistry by providing a summer enrichment program conducted at UT–Austin. This program is designed to give bright high school students a chemical research experience in their formative years. At the undergraduate level, students studying chemistry can

become Welch scholars; and, of course, much of the support of research in the grants program is assigned (by professional principal investigators) to fellowships for graduate research assistants.

Thus, the Welch Foundation is engaged at all levels of education—pre-college, undergraduate, and graduate—to encourage young persons to become professionally involved in chemistry. Since the vast majority of chemistry graduates (roughly 90 percent) are employed by industry and most choose to remain in Texas, the Foundation is, in one sense indirectly, engaged in improving the chemical training of future employees of the Texas chemical industry.

The Foundation also enhances the state of chemistry in Texas by supporting an annual conference on chemistry each year and a lecture program in the universities and colleges of Texas. Both of these efforts attempt to bring chemists from outside of the state to Texas for mutual exposure, a process which can only benefit the intellectual life of Texas. Since they began in 1957, the annual Welch conferences have become important international forums for summaries of current chemical research. They have steadily attracted

Table 3
Subjects of the Proceedings of the Annual Welch Conferences

Year	Conference Number	Subject
1957	I	The Structure of the Nucleus
1958	II	Atomic Structure
1959	III	Molecular Structure
1960	IV	Molecular Structure and Organic Reactions
1961	V	Molecular Structure and Biochemical Reactions
1962	VI	Topics in Modern Inorganic Chemistry
1963	VII	Modern Developments in Analytical Chemistry
1964	VIII	Selected Topics in Modern Biochemistry
1965	IX	Organometallic Compounds
1966	X	Polymers
1967	XI	Radiation and The Structure of Matter
1968	XII	Organic Synthesis
1969	XIII	The Transuranium Elements–The Mendeleev Centennial
1970	XIV	Solid State Chemistry
1971	XV	Bio-Organic Chemistry and Mechanisms
1972	XVI	Theoretical Chemistry
1973	XVII	Organic-Inorganic Reagents in Synthetic Chemistry
1974	XVIII	Immunochemistry
1975	XIX	Photon Chemistry
1976	XX	American Chemistry–Bicentennial
1977	XXI	Cosmochemistry
1978	XXII	Chemistry of Future Energy Resources
1979	XXIII	Modern Structural Methods
1980	XXIV	The Synthesis, Structure, and Function of Biochemical Molecules
1981	XXV	Heterogeneous Catalysis
1982	XXVI	Synthetic Polymers
1983	XXVII	Stereospecificity in Chemistry and Biochemistry
1984	XXVIII	Chemistry in Texas: The Thirtieth Year of the Welch Foundation
1985	XXIX	Genetic Chemistry: The Molecular Basis of Heredity
1986	XXX	Electrochemistry

outstanding chemical researchers from around the world, as either speakers or discussion leaders. The broad spectrum of themes addressed at the annual Welch conferences is summarized in table 3. The proceedings of these conferences are published regularly and are available in most academic libraries in the state.

The Welch Foundation's influence in chemistry has been exerted outside of the state—indeed worldwide—by the establishment in 1972 of the Robert A. Welch Award in chemistry "to foster and encourage basic chemical research and to recognize in a substan-

tial manner the value of chemical research contributions for the betterment of mankind. . . ."[7] The recipient of the Welch Award is "the person deemed by the Board of Trustees and the Scientific Advisory Board to have made an important chemical research contribution which will have a significant, positive impact on man and his environment."[8] The Welch Award winner receives $150,000, a gold medallion, and a certificate. The recipients of the Welch Award are given in table 4.

Finally, the trustees of the Welch Foundation have established Robert A. Welch endowed chairs in chemistry at thirteen major institutions in Texas and three

Table 4
Welch Award Recipients

Year	Recipient	Affiliation	Citation
1972	Karl A. Folkers	University of Texas at Austin	"For his basic research in the area of life sciences."
1974	Albert Eschenmoser	Swiss Federal Institute of Technology	"For his profound and highly creative contributions to synthetic chemistry."
1976	Neil Bartlett	University of California, Berkeley	"For his synthesis of chemical compounds of noble gases and the consequent opening of broad new fields of research in inorganic chemistry."
1978	E. Bright Wilson	Harvard University	"For his pioneering theoretical and experimental contributions to molecular structure."
1980	Sune Bergstrom	Karolinska Institute	"For his pioneering studies of the prostaglandins."
1981	Paul D. Bartlett	Texas Christian University	"For his original investigations of the mechanisms of organic reactions."
1982	Frank H. Westheimer	Harvard University	"For his significant achievements in the field of bio-organic chemistry."
1983	Henry Taube	Stanford University	"For his contributions to the field of chemistry, particularly in inorganics."
1984	Kenneth S. Pitzer	University of California, Berkeley	"For his theory for the internal rotation of groups within molecules."
1985	Duilio Arigoni	Swiss Federal Institute of Technology	"For his contribution of founding the field of bio-organic stereochemistry, which involves interaction of organic chemicals and enzymes."

chairs in science at three universities. The Welch chemistry chair holders are listed in table 5; the Welch science chair holders (who are not limited to chemistry) are listed in table 6.

The Welch Foundation and the Texas chemical industry have come together, independently and essentially accidently, to spur the development of chemistry and chemical technology in the state. The industry developed a need for trained personnel and for basic science, and the Welch Foundation provided (and still does) the means for training chemists at all levels of education in the context of fundamental research. The years between the start of World War II and the early years of the Welch Foundation were critically important for the development of chemistry and chemical technology in Texas.

Chemical Science

Although research reports from chemical laboratories may seem to span a bewildering array of subjects, only a few basic issues are involved—structure, energetics, and kinetics. Since chemistry is a molecular science, these fundamental areas of interest can be expressed in terms of any subject that involves matter. Thus, a description of the progress of the science of chemistry is contained in a wide spectrum of research reports from laboratories as diverse as industrial research laboratories concerned with the development of materials to academic laboratories focused on biochemistry or physics. The current intellectual frontiers are expanding with the chemist's increasing ability to probe and understand the elemental steps of chemical

Table 5
The Welch Foundation Chairs in Chemistry

University	Chair, Year Established	Holders
The University of Texas at Austin	The Welch Chair, 1963	M. J. S. Dewar, 1963–pres.
	The Norman Hackerman/ Welch Chair, 1984	Alan J. Bard, 1984–pres.
	The Marvin K. Collie/ Welch Chair, 1984	Josef Michl, 1986–pres.
	The R. P. Doherty, Jr./ Welch Chair, 1984	Unfilled
	The Richard J. V. Johnson/ Welch Chair, 1984	Unfilled
The University of Texas Health Science Center, Houston	The Welch Chair, 1973	Finn Wold, 1981–pres.
The University of Texas Cancer Center, M. D. Anderson Hospital and Tumor Institute	The Welch Chair, 1973	W. J. Lennarz, 1983–pres.
Texas A&M University	The W. T. Doherty/Welch Chair, 1963	F. R. Duke, 1963–65 F. A. Cotton, 1972–pres.
Rice University	The Welch Chair, 1963	J. L. Franklin, 1963–76 M. J. Berry, 1979–pres.
University of Houston	The Welch Chair, 1965	Ernst Bayer, 1967–70 A. J. P. Martin, 1974–79 J. K. Kochi, 1984–pres.
Texas Tech University	The Welch Chair, 1965	C. W. Shoppee, 1970–75 G. W. Robinson, 1976–pres.
Baylor University	The Welch Chair, 1965	M. Dole, 1969–81 S. Claesson, 1981–84
Baylor College of Medicine	The Welch Chair, 1973	M. Z. Atassi, 1983–pres.
Texas Christian University	The Welch Chair, 1973	P. D. Bartlett, 1974–pres.

Table 6
The Welch Foundation Chairs in Science

University	Chair, Year Established	Holders
The University of Texas at Austin	Jack S. Josey/Welch Chair, 1981	Stephen Weinberg, 1981–pres.
Texas A&M University	Robert J. Wolfe/Welch Chair, 1981	Unfilled
Rice University	Daniel R. Bullard/Welch Chair, 1981	Unfilled
Baylor College of Medicine	R. P. Doherty, Jr./Welch Chair in Science, 1985	Unfilled

change as well as to deal with molecular complexity. New and powerful instrumental methods have been developed to assist in such studies.

Although chemists are still trained, more or less, in the traditional areas of chemistry, i.e., analytical chemistry, biochemistry, inorganic chemistry, organic chemistry, and physical chemistry, current research interests increasingly transcend such historical classifications and include chemical kinetics, chemical theory, catalysis, materials, synthesis, life processes, and analytical chemistry. Chemical research in Texas has contributed to the evolution of these intellectual frontiers in both specific and general ways. Such contributions can be measured by looking at various sources: for example, the research of the Nobel prize winners in chemistry who have worked in Texas, of the Texas members of the National Academy of Sciences (table 7), the holders of the Welch-supported chairs in chemistry (table 5), and members of the Texas chemical community who have won the Welch Award (table 4).

LIFE PROCESSES

It is generally agreed that the year 1953 ushered in the modern era of biochemistry that is currently described as molecular biology. This term recognizes—albeit only partially—that the processes of interest to biologists are fundamentally chemical processes and are governed by the basic principles of chemistry. It was in 1953 that James D. Watson and Francis Crick deduced the double helical structure of DNA and proposed a structural basis for the precise replication of DNA. Also in that same year, Fredrick Sanger worked out the amino acid sequence in the polypeptide chains of the hormone insulin. Both the Watson and Crick team and Sanger worked at Cambridge University. These two reports, coming in the same year, focused strongly on the molecularity of life processes and on the advantage gained by approaching such problems from a chemical point of view. Accordingly, any description of the advances of the discipline chemistry as extracted from a study of the chemistry associated with life process stands the strong possibility of ignoring apparently important contributions to the science of chemistry. We hope to minimize that possibility in this chapter.

The Clayton Foundation Biochemical Institute,[9] associated with the Department of Chemistry at UT–Austin, has been an important organized research unit in the state focused on fundamental biochemical problems and their relationship to human health and disease. The institute was organized in September 1940 and was supported by a grant from the Clayton Foundation for Research under the direction of Roger J.

Table 7

Texas Chemistry Members of The National Academy of Sciences

Name	Current Affiliation	Date Elected
A. J. Bard	University of Texas at Austin	1982
P. D. Bartlett	Texas Christian University	1947
F. A. Cotton	Texas A&M University	1967
M. J. S. Dewar	University of Texas at Austin	1983
K. Folkers	University of Texas at Austin	1948
J. L. Goldstein	The University of Texas Health Science Center, Dallas	1980
N. Hackerman	University of Texas at Austin	1971
J. K. Kochi	University of Houston	1982
J. L. Margrave	Rice University	1974
W. A. Noyes	University of Texas at Austin	1943–80
L. J. Reed	University of Texas at Austin	1973
E. E. Snell	University of Texas at Austin	1955
R. J. Williams	University of Texas at Austin	1946
J. D. Wilson	The University of Texas Health Science Center, Dallas	1983

Figure 2. Roger Williams

Williams (fig. 2). The initial research programs of the institute were concerned with the discovery, isolation, structure, and function of B-vitamins and related growth factors. Williams, who had earlier developed a quantitative microbial assay technique to follow yeast growth, had used the technique to discover and concentrate a new vitamin. With the cooperation of Merck and Company he completed, in the early years of the institute, the structure and synthesis of this new vitamin which he named pantothenic acid. Further development of assays for substances essential for microbial growth led to an assay for another new vitamin which was first made available to researchers all over the world by concentrating the vitamin from thirty tons of spinach. Williams gave this new vitamin its name, folic acid, because of its relative abundance in leaves.

Members of the institute have contributed to our chemical knowledge in a number of significant areas. Esmond E. Snell turned his attention to a new vitamin activity, which was tentatively termed "pseudo-pyridoxine" because of its enhanced activity in re-

placing pyridoxine. He discovered two new functional forms of the vitamin: pyridoxamine and pyridoxal. Work with these two new vitamins demonstrated that these simple functional forms of the vitamin would catalyze reactions in a manner similar to the enzymes in which they function naturally. This discovery allowed for the first time a simple demonstration of how enzymes function in catalyzing chemical changes. Snell extended his work on the vitamin B_6 group and provided the most extensive chemical mechanisms for the mode of action of the vitamin B_6 group in catalysis of reactions analogous to their role in enzymatic processes. In 1955 Snell was elected to membership in the National Academy of Sciences. Within a few years after the founding of the institute and following its spectacular initial successes, Williams was also elected to the National Academy of Sciences, was awarded the Chandler Medal of Columbia University, and received the Meade Johnson Award of the American Institute of Nutrition. Snell received the Eli Lilly Award in Microbiology in 1944 and the Meade Johnson Award of the American Institute of Nutrition in 1946. During this early period, a number of microbial assays were developed, not only for amino acids and many known nutrients but also for a number of unknown or unidentified factors such as the "acetate replacing factor" discovered by Beverly Guirard, Snell, and Williams.

Biotin was shown to be a vitamin not only for yeast but also for some bacteria. These assays for biotin led Robert E. Eakin, then a graduate student of Williams, to the discovery of the cause of (raw) "egg white injury" to mammals. A protein in egg white was found to bind biotin, an essential B-vitamin, forming a nondigestible complex. This protein was isolated in crystalline form and given the name avidin. Upon returning to UT–Austin as a faculty member in 1946, Eakin and his student, Jessie Ternberg, discovered that the "intrinsic factor," known to be missing in pernicious anemia patients, bound the antipernicious anemia principle of liver extracts (vitamin B_{12}). This demonstrated that it was a receptor protein essential for the transport of the vitamin from the digestive system into the blood stream.

During the first decade, research at the institute, especially by W. Shive (fig. 3), also contributed a new method (called inhibition analysis) for determining metabolic pathways. This method was used to develop an assay for the antipernicious anemia principle that resulted in methods for isolation of that principle on a commercial scale. It also led to the discovery of a group of active coenzyme forms of folic acid—for example,

Figure 3. W. Shive

folinic acid, N^{10}-formyl-folic acid, and $N^{5,\ 10}$-anhydrofolinic acid and their roles in transfer of single carbon units. Many steps of metabolic pathways, particularly those forming the precursors of deoxyribonucleic acid (DNA) and ribonucleic acid (RNA) were elucidated. Shive received the American Chemical Society Eli Lilly Award in biological chemistry in 1950 for this work.

A long list of significant contributions from the early years of the institute includes evidence that pantothenic acid supplements increase the life span of mice, the first evidence for pantothenic acid (B-alanine) in coenzyme A, and extensive studies on the distribution of B-vitamins in food and tissues, particularly in tumors which were found to have a higher content of folic acid than normal tissue. Also, pimelic acid was shown by R. E. and Esther A. Eakin to be a precursor of biotin. During this period Williams developed extensive evidence for biochemical individuality and proposed the genetotrophic principle that the nutritional requirements of any organism depend upon its genetic background. The concept of genetotrophic disease, which proposes that human individuals must have at least slightly different quantitative nutritional needs, followed. This concept has broad implications for the interrelationship of nutrition and health and disease. Williams' group collected extensive data concerning individual differences. Studies on alcoholism demonstrated the need for vitamin supplementation, and the factor in liver extract affecting alcohol con-

sumption in rats was identified as glutamine by Lorene Rogers, after microbial assays demonstrated its effect on the growth inhibition caused by alcohol. Glutamine was also shown to be effective in hastening the healing of peptic ulcers, and S-methylmethione was identified as a naturally-occurring amino acid in a search for anti-ulcer substances. Also, asparagine was found to prevent alcohol-induced development of fatty livers in animal studies. Williams' research and publications in this field have spanned more than thirty-five years. His remarkable insight into biochemical individuality is beginning to be of benefit to studies concerning the improvement of human health.

Contributions to understanding enzyme processes also came from work conducted at the biochemical institute. Lester J. Reed pursued the investigation of the "acetate-replacing factor," developed methods of concentrating it from liver and, in subsequent collaboration with Eli Lilly and Company, isolated the growth factor in crystalline form. The new factor was named lipoic acid, and the Reed group provided much of the structural studies and synthesis of the new vitamin-like factor.

In a series of elegant studies of the biological role of lipoic acid, Reed provided the first well-described organized complex of enzymes, the pyruvate dehydrogenase complex. For this work Reed received the American Chemical Society Eli Lilly Award in Biological Chemistry in 1958. Reed's work on the elucidation of the macromolecular organization, function, and regulation of the multienzyme pyruvate and α-ketoglutarate dehydrogenase complexes has continued to be in the forefront of our understanding of the nature of organization of enzyme complexes, how they catalyze sequences of reactions, and how they are metabolically controlled. Reed became director of the Clayton Foundation Biochemical Institute in 1973 and also was elected to the National Academy of Sciences in the same year.

Daniel Ziegler discovered a unique enzyme system that catalyzes the oxygenation of foreign compounds incorporating nitrogen, sulfur, or selenium. Virtually all clinically useful drugs containing either nitrogen or sulfur are metabolized to less active derivatives by this system. However, a significant number of environmental chemicals are converted to more reactive intermediates by this enzyme, and it is a major route for the bioactivation of a variety of toxic or carcinogenic chemicals. More recently, Ziegler and his associates have shown that this enzyme catalyzes the oxidation of the physiological aminothiol, cysteamine, to its disulfide, cystamine. This reaction may be a major source of disulfide required for maintaining the thiol:disulfide redox state of the cell. Changes in this potential can affect a number of complex metabolic processes, and an enzyme mechanism for generation of disulfide is a potentially important reaction involved in the regulation of some metabolic processes. R. A. Prough of the UT Health Sciences Center—Dallas, has also produced interesting results on the metabolism and bioactivation of hydrazines and other toxic carcinogenic foreign compounds.

By the early 1960s a considerable portion of the research at the institute was devoted to the mechanisms by which enzymes exert their catalytic functions and to the control of these life processes. Among contributions to end-product control of these processes was the discovery of multiple genes (in aromatic amino acid biosynthesis) with corresponding enzymes catalyzing the same reaction of pathways with multiple end products, each controlling the functions of its own corresponding enzyme and gene.

A number of significant contributions to an understanding of the synthesis of proteins have been made by members of the institute. Joanne M. Ravel identified two of the twenty amino-acid-activating enzymes, each of which is specific for one of the twenty amino acids that are the basic units of proteins. She also isolated and elucidated the mechanism of action of an enzyme that is required for the incorporation of the twenty activated amino acids into a growing protein chain. Her more recent work is concerned with the mode of action of enzymes that are required for the initiation of protein synthesis.

Boyd Hardesty has been interested in peptide chain initiation and elongation associated with the ribosomal synthesis of hemoglobin in reticulocytes. His work also provides insights into the control of ribosomal translation of the genetic message into the protein structure; this process includes characterization of the phosphorylation and dephosphorylation mechanism of an initiation factor that appears to have an important regulatory function in the control of translation. Important chemical and biochemical studies on the mode of action of the platelet-activating factor, a derivative of phosphocholine, which is a potent lipid chemical mediator formed during systematic anaphylaxis, have been reported by D. O. Hanahan, (UT Health Science Center, San Antonio).

G. B. Kitto, who joined the institute staff in 1966, has made important contributions in the areas of comparative enzymology and the evolution of protein structure. He and his students have carried out extensive structural and physico-chemical studies on invertebrate hemoglobins. Biochemical and immunological techniques have been applied to study selected enzymes from several insect pests, including screwworm flies, fruit flies, and mosquitos, to find biochemical differences that can be exploited for purposes of biological control. This approach has resulted in improving the effectiveness of the Sterile Screwworm Release Program. S. J. Wakel of the Baylor College of Medicine has also contributed to our knowledge of enzyme action from his studies on the dimension of fatty-acid synthesis.

By 1974, James Brown had elucidated the complex amino acid sequence of both bovine and human serum albumins, the largest polypeptide chain (580 amino acid residues) to be sequenced up to that time. He located the seventeen disulfide bonds in serum albumin and developed a model of the three-dimensional structure of this protein based wholly on sequence analysis, an outstanding achievement. This model explains many of the known binding properties of serum albumin for fatty acids, drugs, and so forth, which underlie several of its physiological functions.

Kuan Wang joined the institute staff in 1977, adding capability in the area of molecular and cellular biology. Wang discovered a group of very high molecular-weight proteins in skeletal muscle that had been overlooked by muscle biochemists. He has purified and characterized two of these proteins, titin and nebulin, and has made significant progress toward elucidating their ultrastructural localization and function. He discovered another high molecular-weight contractile protein that restricts the length of actin filaments, and he is carrying out a detailed characterization of this protein and its interaction with actin. A significant part of this research has been the development of techniques for detecting and handling these very high molecular-weight proteins. This is highly innovative and important work in the area of cell motility and the cytoskeleton.

Marvin Hackert and Jon Robertus have provided insight into structure-function relationships of enzymes and other important biological macromolecules through the use of X-ray crystallography. Hackert and his associates have made significant progress in understanding the organization of phycobiliproteins as it relates to their structures and ability to capture and transfer radiant energy. His group is also well on the way toward solving the structure of histidine decarboxylase and several invertebrate hemoglobins. Robertus made important contributions to elucidation of the structure and mechanism of action of two toxic plant proteins, PAP and ricin, which exhibit antiviral and antitumor activities, respectively. He has also undertaken the task of cloning the gene for histidine decarboxylase, using recombinant DNA technology.

The study of the chemistry of life processes in Texas received a major impetus in the establishment of the Institute of Biomedical Research (IBR) at UT–Austin in 1968 under the direction of Karl Folkers. This institute was created to "provide an organizational area for bringing together organic chemists, biochemists, enzymologists, biologists, pharmacologists, physicians, and other professional staff in life sciences as required to carry out multidisciplinary research on new therapy of disease." The broad mandate of the institute illustrates the difficulty in deciding where progress in "chemistry" stops and progress in other related areas starts. Research at IBR is conducted primarily in the fields of vitamins and hormones. Vitamin research is conducted on the use of vitamin B_6 for treatment of the carpal tunnel syndrome. Research on coenzyme Q emphasizes cardiovascular and periodontal disease. The research programs on hormones include inhibition of ovulation, the thyrotropin releasing hormone, Substance P, Gln^4-neurotensin, the human parathyroid hormone, and chorionic gonadotropin, and the new field of thymic humoral factors.[10] Folker's research in biomedicinal chemistry led to his selection as the first Welch Award recipient (Table 4).

ANALYTICAL METHODS

Analytical methods are the diagnostic tools and/or separation methods that are useful in structure elucidation. Separation methods are included here because the diagnostic tools are generally most reliable with pure substances.

Separation in industry is often synonymous with distillation, a process traditional in the chemical and petroleum industry. Van Winkle and his students in the chemical engineering department at UT–Austin, have reported extensively on the details of the vapor-liquid equilibrium as they apply to distillation processes. The Separations Research Institute at UT–Austin, under the direction of J. R. Fair, was organized recently to study separation processes systematically. This institute focuses not only on the elements of distillation processes, but also on those associated with liquid-liquid extraction, supercritical extraction, adsorption and related chromatographic processes, and membrane separations. Early work on membrane separations in the Department of Chemical Engineering at UT–Austin was done by D. R. Paul and his students, and more recently by D. R. Lloyd.

Diagnostic tools are generally developed to assist in the understanding of problems of fundamental interest that have wide applicability. For example, the enormous interest in the solid state derives from attempting to understand heterogeneous catalysis and from a need to characterize thin film materials used in the semiconductor industry. One of the more extensively investigated catalytic systems is the conversion of mixtures of carbon monoxide and hydrogen (so-called syngas) into chemicals and fuels.

$$CO + H_2 \rightarrow \text{chemicals and fuels}$$

Although the interest in such conversion processes waxes and wanes with economic conditions, there are unique fundamental questions to answer in such a process. R. Pettit and his students attempted an understanding of homogeneous conversions of syngas from a classical point of view, i.e., to study the distribution of products as the catalytic factors are controlled systematically.

A more direct approach to such problems involves the techniques associated with the growing discipline called surface science. Surface science employs (among others) secondary ion mass spectrometry, Auger electron spectroscopy, thermal decomposition spectroscopy, and vibrational spectroscopy to probe the structure of the species at surfaces. J. M. White (UT–Austin) has developed and used such methods to investigate the details of reactant molecule/substrate interactions while the reaction is occurring for a number of important systems. He showed how to use surface science techniques to measure the concentrations of adsorbed CO and adsorbed O at a surface during the oxidation of CO to CO_2 on a variety of transition metal surfaces. White was involved in the early studies of line shape analysis from Auger electron spectroscopy of chemisorbed species and showed that important chemical information can be extracted from the line shapes. Throughout White's work there are two consistent threads: the measurement of reaction rates under well-controlled conditions on well-characterized (but not necessarily single crystal) surfaces, and the measurement of reaction rates on a variety of systems including working catalysts, thin film catalyst models, polycrystalline substrates, and single crystal substrates. Through this route, White continues to provide intellectual connections between surface science and catalysis.

In the past twenty years the resurgence of electrochemistry has been hastened by the work of A. J. Bard (UT–Austin) and his students (especially L.

Falkner, now at the University of Illinois). Bard's research has led him to use and develop electrochemical techniques in the study of chemical problems as widely diverse as electro-organic chemistry, photoelectrochemistry, and electrogenerated chemiluminescence, as well as to develop general techniques for electroanalytical chemistry. Important contributions to our understanding of electrochemical processes also have been made by J. O'M. Bockris (TAMU) and N. Hackerman (first at UT–Austin, then at Rice, and then again at UT–Austin).

The field of electronic photochemistry is well established—the Texas component of this field dating back to 1963 when W. A. Noyes Jr. established his laboratory at UT–Austin, on the occasion of his "second retirement." However, the newly emerging field of vibrational photochemistry is characterized by an embryonic understanding of phenomena and their causes together with high uncertainty about the ultimate utility of these phenomena for real application. M. J. Berry at Rice has been in the forefront of these developments. Important uses of laser spectroscopy have been made by R. F. Curl at Rice and G. W. Robinson at TTU, who has developed probes to study rate theory as applied to liquid state chemical reactions on the picosecond time scale; W. H. Woodruff at UT–Austin, who recently went to Los Alamos National Laboratories, developed time-resolved laser spectroscopy techniques with the objective of elucidating the fundamental processes involved in electron transfer and energy transduction in solutions.

There are two groups of chemists interested in the solid state: one is interested in structures that are intrinsically interesting because of the chemistry and/or the species present, and the other is concerned with surfaces that exhibit useful characteristics, that is, for solid state devices or for catalysis. A. Clearfield and J. H. Lunsford, both at TAMU, and J. T. Richardson and A. Ignatiev at UH–University Park have investigated a number of solid supports for catalytic systems. J. L. McAtee Jr. at Baylor University has produced a detailed analysis of the physical and surface properties of smectite clays.

The collection of techniques described as X-ray crystallography is, in a sense, the ultimate analytical tool because the method provides information on the geometrical arrangement of the atoms in the sample of interest. X-ray crystallography has matured as a structural tool in the past twenty years, and the Texas contribution has been important. Progress in crystallography can be described from two points of view: refinement of the techniques used to produce structural information as well as the uses to which the

techniques have been put. Major activity in X-ray crystallography as a structural tool exists at TAMU, UT–Austin, and the UH–University Park.

While at Rice, Jurg Wasser, who made important contributions to the numerical methods of analysis of crystallographic data, was the president of the American Crystallographic Association in 1960. The development of interactive computer graphics for the modeling of macromolecules has been pioneered by E. F. Meyer, Jr. at TAMU. Crystallographic techniques have become sufficiently systematized and automated, and J. M. Troup has organized the Molecular Structure Corporation in College Station to provide services for structure determination from single crystal and powder diffraction data; the firm also has developed and provides useful computer software for structure calculations. A potentially very useful approach to questions involving the topology of molecules in solution has been provided by M. R. Willcott at UH–University Park and R. E. Davis at UT–Austin.[11] Willcott, whose interests are in NMR spectroscopy, and Davis, a crystallographer, have applied simplex methods to obtaining detailed structural information from NMR shift-reagent data on complex molecules in solution. The growing interest in the chemistry of life processes has led to the evolution of a number of laboratories doing important work on biologically significant molecules: W. H. Watson at Texas Christian University, E. F. Meyer, Jr. at TAMU, S.S.G. Chu at Southern Methodist University, and M. L. Hackert and J. D. Robertus, both at UT–Austin; the latter two workers have produced useful information on the structures of proteins.

In the nonbiological realm of structure, both F. A. Cotton at TAMU and I. Bernal at UH–University Park have made significant contributions to our understanding of metal-metal bonding; S. H. Simonsen and R. E. Davis, both at UT–Austin, have made important contributions in describing the structural relationships in organic and organometallic substances. The structural relationships among inorganic compounds have come primarily from the laboratories of H. Steinfink (transition metal oxysulfides) at UT–Austin, W. O. Milligan (amorphous phases and metal complexes) at Baylor University, A. Clearfield (the structure of intercalation compounds) at TAMU, and Simonsen, who has studied the stereochemistry of the $CuCl_4{}^{2-}$ chromophore.

CHEMICAL SYNTHESES

Synthesis has always represented an important component in the development of chemistry. New methods of synthesis provide the promise of preparing new substances or more efficient ways of preparing existing substances that are of interest. The interest in new substances generally concerns their properties or their structures.

An early incursion into unusual synthesis schemes was made by G. W. Watt at UT–Austin, when in 1936 he initiated a program of research involving liquid ammonia as a solvent medium. The stability of solutions of the alkali metals in this solvent and Watt's ability to handle these solutions quantitatively provided the key to his synthesis of a variety of low-valent transition metal compounds. The alkali metal/ammonia solutions are basically stable solutions of solvated electrons, which can be used to reduce transition species in the more conventional higher oxidation states.

$$M^{n+} (am) + me^- (am) \rightarrow M^{n+(-m)} (am)$$

With appropriate ligands, e.g., those carrying low-lying orbitals capable of accepting electron density from the low-valent transition metal ion, a number of interesting species have been identified and/or isolated that are of synthetic and theoretical interest. Watt's initial work with the ammonia solvent system was continued in the 1960s by J. J. Lagowski, whose students have investigated the physical and chemical properties of ammonia solutions containing a variety of solutes. Lagowski's studies led to the development of a quantitative acidity scale in the ammonia solvent system, and to the formation and characterization of stable solutions containing the first metal anion, Au^-.

F. A. Cotton at TAMU has synthesized and characterized, mostly by X-ray crystallography, a number of polynuclear transition metal species. In the course of these investigations, his group has identified systems containing metal-metal single, double ($M=M$, M = Nb, Ta, Mo, W), triple ($M\equiv M$, M = Sn, Mo, W), and quadruple ($M\equiv M$, M = Mo, W, Cr) bonds. A. H. Cowley at UT–Austin and his students have been actively engaged in similar studies with the representative elements, especially those in Group V.

A broad range of inorganic synthesis techniques have emerged from the laboratories of J. L. Margrave at Rice. The Margrave group has developed a series of synthetic approaches using extreme conditions—high temperatures, high pressures, low temperatures—and generally incorporating extremely reactive species. Margrave was early associated with the synthesis and characterization of SiF_2, a reactive carbene-like species; the development of practical techniques for carrying out controled fluorinations of pure materials, including plastics and polymers at both low and high temperatures; the mass-spectrometric characteriza-

tion of high-temperature gaseous species over a great number of metallic fluorides; and the development of techniques to investigate the reactions of matrix isolated species (metal atoms, metal clusters, F_2, etc.) with a variety of room-temperature and high-temperature molecules including CH_4, H_2O, NH_3, HF, etc. The latter experiments provided the first experimental evidence for the direct insertion of a metal atom into the CH bond of methane. This reaction has now been demonstrated for Mn, Fe, Co, Cu, Ag, and Au.

Margrave's student, R. J. Lagow at UT–Austin, has also developed interesting chemistries derived from high-energy and/or extremely reactive species. Reactions of lithium vapor with a variety of carbon-containing substrates produces interesting poly-lithium carbon compounds, illustrated by the species Li_2CH_2, Li_3CH, and $(Li_4C)_n$. Lagow and his students have employed low-energy plasmas such as glow discharges as a source of energetic species that can react with organic or inorganic substrates at the edge of the discharge zone. Low-energy plasma chemistry has been used to prepare graphite fluoride, thin films of $(SN)_n$, $Xe(CF_3)_2$, and a variety of trifluoromethyl substituted compounds. Similar synthetic approaches have produced reactions of hydrocarbon radicals (e.g., CH_3) with a variety of substrates including metal species.

The metal atom techniques initiated by Margrave and his students were used by Timms, another Margrave student, to produce dibenzenechromium through the direct action of chromium atoms (obtained by evaporation) on a matrix of frozen benzene. The reaction has been exploited by J. J. Lagowski and his students at UT–Austin in an attempt to produce pi-arene metal complexes as model compounds for studying pi-metal interactions. Synthetic organometallic chemistry has also been influenced by E. P. Kyba's (UT–Austin) synthetic scheme for the preparation of polyphosphino macrocyclic ligand systems. Kyba's work is important from the standpoint of the synthesis of the polyphosphine complexes as well as from the use of these ligands to form transition metal complexes with potentially useful catalytic properties. One of the more spectacular synthetic achievements in the field of organometallic chemistry is the synthesis of the iron tricarbonyl complex of benzocyclobutadiene and cyclobutodiene itself by R. Pettit of UT–Austin. Pettit made outstanding contributions to our understanding of organometallic compounds when he synthesized a variety of novel iron tricarbonyl complexes of olefins, dienes, trienes, and 2,2,bicycloheptadienes. In addition, he and his students were able to produce iron carbonyl derivatives coordinated to a carbonium ion, i.e., tropylium, alkyl, or a pentadienate ion. These complexes are of interest not only for their own contribution to structure theory, but also because of their involvement as catalysts for the isomerization of olefins and dienes. Pettit and his group also have made outstanding contributions to our knowledge of new aromatic systems. The new ring systems synthesized by them include perinaphthindenyliums, bicyclo[5,1,0]octadenylium, homotropone, thienopyrilium, and selenapyrilium.

Major new thrusts in synthetic organic chemistry occured in the synthesis of alkaloids (E. Wenkert and R. E. Stevens, formerly of Rice University; S. F. Martin, UT–Austin) and terpenes (K. E. Harding, TAMU; S. C. Welch, UH–University Park). J. E. Whitsell at UT–Austin and his students have addressed the synthesis of naturally-occuring molecules with particular emphasis on the development of novel methods for the control of stereochemistry. Often insights into the synthesis of organic compounds are obtained from mechanistic studies, and a number of these have occured in Texas. W. E. Billups at Rice has investigated the chemistry of small ring systems and other reactive intermediates with synthetic potential. Bergbreitter and Newcomb (both at TAMU), R. P. Thummel (UH–University Park), and Billups have produced important synthetic insights from their studies of organometallic compounds as have M. A. Fox (UT–Austin) and J. K. Kochi (UH–University Park) from their studies of photochemical and other processes producing radical species. Our understanding of biosynthetic processes has been markedly improved through the work of A. I. Scott at TAMU and R. Parry at Rice.

THEORY

The function of chemical theory is the prediction and/or the correlation of experimental observations. According to *the New York Times* Science Section,[12] chemistry is changing its identity; it no longer deals exclusively with test tubes, the periodic table and ball-and-stick models, but with abstract mathematics and computers as well. Theoretical chemists have been the agents of this important change through the introduction of theoretical material into conventional courses and in the development of purely theoretical chemistry courses. For example, at UT–Austin, a course called "modchem" teaches modern theories of matter and the attendant abstract mathematics and computer science to a freshman honors class. The theoretical chemist has also been instrumental in

bringing high-performance computing into Texas colleges and universities, a move which has benefited all segments of these institutions.

The local development of theoretical chemistry has been quite rapid, with the addition of theoretical chemists to many chemistry departments in the state. Two years ago, D. L. Yeager of TAMU organized and held the first Southwest Theoretical Chemistry Conference with over one hundred attendants. In 1985 the conference was hosted by J. S. Hutchinson at Rice University. The conference provides a forum for the exchange of research ideas and also provides research students with an opportunity to present their work to a larger audience. The conference has played and will continue to play an important role in the development of theoretical chemistry research in Texas. Most observers would agree that theoretical chemistry has three main divisions: molecular structure and properties, spectroscopy and dynamics, and statistical mechanics.

The early work in molecular structure and properties was started in 1945 by F. A. Matsen at UT–Austin. The members of this group included a number of Matsen's students who later became professors of theoretical chemistry at other institutions: M. L. Ellzey at UT–El Paso, R. M. Hedges and A. Ford, and W. Seitz and D. Klein at TAMU–Galveston. Among the early accomplishments of this group were the prediction of the dipole moment of LiH three years before its experimental determination and the prediction of the binding energy of the helium molecule ion, a prediction which permitted the final complete analysis of the helium high-pressure spectrum.

Of major importance in this area is the research of M. J. S. Dewar's group at UT–Austin, which has carried out extensive semiempirical calculations on organic and organometallic molecules. Of particular significance has been their detailed delineation of reaction mechanisms and their selection of promising paths for the synthesis of large molecules. W. Herndon at UT–El Paso and the Seitz and Klein group have used graph theory in a very sophisticated way to predict the properties of organic molecules.

J. E. Boggs at UT–Austin has made exceedingly precise predictions of the geometry and the rotational barriers of important organic molecules. Also, Dewar's and M. B. Hall's groups at TAMU have made important contributions to this area. Yeager, also at TAMU, has made very exact predictions of the electronic spectra of oxygen and nitrogen and other important atmospheric molecules.

Hutchinson at Rice and R. E. Wyatt at UT–Austin

have studied the dynamics of molecules under thermal and photo (laser) excitations and have contributed considerably to our understanding of these processes. In addition, Wyatt's group was among the first to obtain accurate results on the quantum dynamics of a chemical reaction. R. Friesner at UT–Austin has developed new methods for predicting spectral and dynamical properties of molecules, including those of biological significance. D. J. Kouri of UH–University Park has developed sophisticated methods for studying the dynamics of chemical reactions.

Illya Prigogine, the 1977 Nobel laureate in chemistry, won the prize for his theory of dissipative structures, an extension to the classical theories of thermodynamics. Prigogine's mathematical model predicts the existence of structures whose essence is change and interactions with their surroundings. The validity of the model has been expressed in the Belousov-Zhabotinskii reaction.[13]

P. Rossky at UT–Austin has used sophisticated statistical mechanical methods to predict the behavior of large molecules in pure liquids and in solutions, research that is of considerable significance in biological processes.

Journals

An important recognition of the state of chemistry in Texas is the fact that a number of nationally recognized, important chemistry journals are edited by chemists in this state. Proceeding in chronological order: since 1951 *The Journal of the Electrochemical Society* has been edited by N. Hackerman, first at UT–Austin, then at Rice, and then again at UT–Austin. In 1979 *The Journal of Chemical Education* came to UT–Austin under the editorship of J. J. Lagowski. Finally, A. J. Bard of UT–Austin has been the editor of *The Journal of the American Chemical Society* since 1982.

Notes

1. Whitehead, 1979, Chapter 12.
2. Garner, 1979.
3. Schock, 1949, p. 7.
4. Information on The Welch Foundation and its activities that has been given in this chapter was drawn from The Welch Foundation annual reports, The Welch Foundation newsletters, and direct contact with administrators of the Foundation where necessary.
5. Clark, 1963, pp. 139–40.
6. A list of principal investigators, their research institutions, and the title of their current investigations are given in the annual report. An abstract of the work and a bibliography of publications by grantees during the fiscal year of the report are included in a separate document: Supplemental Information, Annual Report.
7. Welch Foundation Annual Report, 1982, p. 11.
8. Ibid., 1983, p. 10.
9. Williams, 1966. ·
10. Folkers, 1984.
11. Wilcott, 1975.
12. Science Section, *New York Times*, December 3, 1985.
13. Winfree, 1984.

Bibliography

Clark, James A. *A Biography of Robert Alonzo Welch.* Houston, Texas: Clark Book Co., 1963.

Folkers, Karl. "Perspectives from Research on Vitamins and Hormones." *Journal of Chemical Education*, 61 (1984), pp. 747–756.

Garner, L. E., St. Clair, Anne E., and Evans, Thomas J. *Mineral Resources of Texas.* Austin, Texas: Bureau of Economic Geology, 1979.

Schock, E. P. "Professional Chemists in Texas Prior to 1920." *Texas Journal of Science*, 1 (1949), pp. 7–17.

The Welch Foundation, Annual Report. The latest available report is for the fiscal year ended August 31, 1985.

Whitehead, Don. *The Dow Story.* New York: McGraw-Hill, 1968.

Willcott, M. Robert, III, and Davies, Raymond E. "Determination of Molecular Configuration in Solution." *Science*, 190 (1975), pp. 850–57.

Williams, R. J. *The Clayton Foundation Biochemical Institute: A Short History.* Austin, Texas: Private Printing, 1966.

Winfree, A. T. "The Prehistory of the Belousov-Zhabotinsky Oscillator." *Journal of Chemical Education*, 61 (1984), pp. 661–63.

9

Petroleum and Petrochemical Technology

Michel T. Halbouty

Introduction

The state of Texas has played an essential role in the growth and development of not only the United States' petroleum industry but also of the world petroleum industry. Through its multifaceted petroleum-related businesses and industries, numerous scientific breakthroughs, creative designs, conceptual advances, and innovative applications of technology have proved their merit in making Texas an acclaimed world leader in the development and use of petroleum technology.

To chronicle the history of petroleum technology in Texas, which has made the state a home base for the worldwide oil industry, is a monumental task, for when speaking of Texas petroleum technology what is really meant is global technology. Whether or not new products or processes were designed in Texas is important, but equally important is the fact that Texas companies, universities, and other research agencies have utilized every advance to some degree. The study of petroleum technology involves investigation of all of the processes vital to the search for oil and gas. From prospecting with witch-hazel twigs, to using conceptually derived maps of the paleogeomorphology of a region, to using the most sophisticated seismics and computer-generated models and using remote sensing imagery from satellites and spacecraft, petroleum geoscientists have charted a fascinating course in the records of American innovation.

Engineers, scientists, and technologists have contributed a constantly improving flow of designs for drilling and production equipment. These engineering advances have provided ways to recover more of the petroleum we have already discovered. The petroleum industry has progressed from using drilling rigs made of wood to developing giant offshore drilling platforms using state-of-the-art materials and technology.

Refining and petrochemical technological advances have produced countless thousands of uses for oil and gas. From many areas of research and development have come new processes, new concepts, and new applications for all aspects of petroleum technology—from exploration to gas tank—and a host of new products generally seen as unrelated to the petroleum industry, but quite beneficial to mankind.

Petroleum (rock oil and gas), formed under the surface of the earth millions of years ago, and tar pits have long been known to man. Yet only since 1859, when the first well in the search for oil was drilled, have we come truly to recognize oil's value and usefulness. In this brief time span, the functioning of modern society has become almost totally dependent on petroleum and its by-products. Today there are thousands of uses for oil and gas—for transportation, heating, electricity, fertilizers, fabrics, medicines, plastic goods, pesticides, paints, and beverages, to name only a few. In essence, there would be little exaggeration in saying that from oil and gas and the technologies involved in their discovery, production, refining, and development of by-products have come the essential ingredients of modern civilization.

From its beginnings the petroleum industry, science, and technology have been interdependent. Energy research and development (R&D) have provided the impetus that has enabled Texas and the nation to stay abreast of the ever-changing needs of our society. R&D involves creating new facilities to supply energy, adapting existing technologies to changes in cost or regulation, and introducing new processes that incorporate advances in materials and technology. Whether conducted by industry, government agencies, or academia, energy R&D in Texas has played an integral part in the ever-expanding realm of petroleum technology.

"Petroleum technology" is a catch-all phrase. Anything and everything related to petroleum, from geological concept to gas tank, can be incorporated in this one term. For the present work a broad overview will be more valuable than a detailed but narrow study; hence this chapter focuses on the post–World War II developments in exploration for and production of oil, refining and petrochemicals, and the role of academia, industry, and government in furthering Texas' technology in this burgeoning field.

The Early Search for Oil

In its early years, petroleum exploration was beset by numerous problems. Many errors and misconceptions by petroleum geologists, including condemnation of areas which later were determined to be productive, caused the oil industry to be not only reluctant but also most hesitant to recognize the profession.

Fortunately, geological fundamentals espoused by the earliest petroleum geologists were accompanied by the application of common sense, courage, stubbornness, and intestinal fortitude in the search for oil from the nonprofessional, the wildcatter. Such men include Edwin L. Drake, the railroad conductor, and his associates who explored Oil Creek, Pennsylvania, experimented with well-drillers, and gave birth to the petroleum industry in 1859. Another is John Galey, an adventurer in the oil fields who was bold enough to

suggest and promote, in 1883, a practical application of the anticlinal theory promulgated by Israel C. White. Geologists of the day debated White's anticlinal theory and could reach no consensus. In 1885 White formalized the theory that oil and gas accumulate along anticlines. In papers published in 1885 and 1892 he gave petroleum geology its first status, and the anticlinal theory permanence.[1]

Three significant events have greatly influenced the course of the modern petroleum industry in the United States: (1) Edwin Drake's discovery of oil at Titusville, Pennyslvania, in 1859; (2) the discovery of the Spindletop field, near Beaumont, Texas, in 1901 by Patillo Higgins and Anthony F. Lucas; and (3) the discovery of oil in East Texas in 1931 by Columbus "Dad" Joiner. Each of these three events had a profound effect not only on the growth but on the scientific thinking of the industry.

The discovery of oil at Spindletop changed the thinking of geologists, engineers, chemists, and economists the world over because it proved that vast quantities of oil could be produced in a short time from a single source.[2] Before Spindletop, oil was used for lamps and lubrication. The famous Lucas gusher changed that. It initiated a new liquid fuel age, which gave birth to the automobile, the airplane, the network of highways, improved railroad and marine transportation, the era of mass production, and untold comforts and conveniences. It revived and gave growing impetus to competition in all fields, but particularly in oil. It was a crushing blow to all forms of monopoly, and it opened a thousand new frontiers, awakening the dormant pioneer spirit of the century.

Only a few years later Spindletop experienced its second "boom." In 1923 Marrs McLean conceived the idea that oil could be found on the flanks of salt domes. His concept was rejected by the most renowned petroleum geologists of his day. Nevertheless, McLean's theory became completely accepted in 1926 when Miles Frank Yount bought the idea and leases from McLean and was rewarded with a great new discovery at Spindletop—the opening of the vast reserves on the flanks of this historic salt dome. This second boom at Spindletop resulted in operators returning to the domes to drill and finding millions of barrels of new reserves off the immediate flanks of the known domes.[3]

Skeptics were also plentiful when Joiner began drilling for oil on a nonexistent geological feature which he termed "the Overton anticline" in East Texas. In reality the Overton anticline was a nondescript topographic feature devoid of subsurface expression. Learned professionals surmised and believed that oil was to be found only on anticlinal structural highs. Scientists accepted the anticlinal theory of accumulation as dogma, and they publicly stated that any deviation from its principle was not only foolish but destined for certain failure. Fortunately, Joiner did not heed the advice of the learned explorationists of his day. It is now evident that he did not have the correct geologic picture but he believed strongly that his efforts were right. This he proved by the discovery of the East Texas field in Rusk County, one of the largest purely stratigraphic oil accumulations yet found in the world.[4]

The Spindletop and East Texas discoveries led to Texas' rise as a leader in petroleum activities and as a home for the thriving industry. Countless thousands were drawn to the state, and hundreds of oil companies, and their related service companies, appeared. Each new field discovered was the result of intensive effort, and with each discovery came the need for new and better methods of exploration, drilling, production, and transportation. Eventually this oil field technology found world-wide applications.

Petroleum Exploration and Production

Petroleum exploration is a complex process that involves many technologies. Gravity, magnetometer, and geochemical surveys; remote sensing (from satellites, spacecraft, and aircraft); geologic field work; seismic surveys; and subsurface studies are all part of the exploration process. Exploring for petroleum was once a matter of good luck and guesswork. Today exploration is based on technical and scientific principles. In the late 1800s and early years of this century the most successful oil-finding method was to drill in areas of oil seeps where oil was actually present on the surface. This period of exploration should possibly be termed the "seepage years." Numerous discoveries were made as a result of surface indications (oil seeps) and random drilling. Especially in the Gulf Coast region, exploration was focused primarily on a search for surface mounds similar to that at Spindletop and for other surface indicators such as paraffin dirt, gas seepages, and sulphur water in wells.[5]

Between 1915 and 1920 subsurface geological studies and applications of micropaleontology to exploration had begun. Structure drilling started in 1919 and enabled petroleum geologists to map bedrock structures. The torsion balance was introduced in 1920, and in 1923 the seismograph was brought into the search. J. A. Udden, State Geologist of Texas, is credited with

one of the earliest discussions of the seismograph's use in structure mapping in a paper read in 1920. Geophysical instruments were widely in use between the late 1920s and the early 1940s.[6]

During and after World War II, the increased U.S. demand for petroleum products generated a tremendous surge in exploration and development. Research departments throughout the oil industry increased in number and size. Effectiveness in exploration increasingly depended on technical innovation. But during the late 1940s, geophysical methods for oil exploration underwent little change except for the increased use of the aerial magnetometer.[7] This device, which had been developed in 1939 by Gulf Research and Development Company, instead of being widely used for petroleum exploration, spent its first few years as a tool for locating enemy submarines.[8]

The technology to measure gravity and magnetism and to record electromagnetic waves in the earth established geophysics as a remarkably useful exploration tool. In 1955 W. Harry Mayne of Petty Geophysical Engineering Co. (San Antonio) received a patent for his common depth point (CDP) geophysical technique, and shortly thereafter Geophysical Service, Inc.'s (GSI) offspring, Texas Instruments, introduced its advanced playback technology. In 1963 Texas Instruments' first transistorized digital recording system was completed for commercial use. These developments spurred greater research throughout the geophysical services industry to perfect higher channel recording and computerized data handling technology.

Medium-range radionavigation, analog magnetic recording, Vibroseis recording, continuous velocity logging, movable magnetic heads, and central data processing were also developed in the 1950s. In the 1960s analog deconvolution and velocity filtering and digital data recording were established. Bright spot technology, seismic stratigraphy, three-dimensional (3-D) surveying, and vertical seismic profiling soon followed.[9]

Introduction in the early 1960s of digital computers and high speed digital seismic acquisition equipment resulted in additional imagery and data enhancement. Numerous geophysical service companies have put the new technologies to use and have continued the search for new and better applications of seismology to the exploration effort. In addition, today's computers have provided a major support technology for the petroleum industry. They operate pipelines and chemical plants, log data, interpret them, and print them out in any desired form. Designing new types of drill bits, performing structural analysis of offshore platforms, and plotting ice movements as functions of weather are other common applications. In addition, some oil companies are subjecting huge accumulations of geophysical records to new analyses in order to find "new" reserves in old or overlooked oil and gas fields and regions.[10,11]

In the 1960s another new tool was added to the oil finder's repertoire—remote sensing. Remotely sensed imagery from satellites gave the geoscientist a new view of the world and a new way of evaluating potential sites for petroleum exploration. Remote sensing from space, especially in the form of Landsat images, is one of the newest exploration tools the petroleum and minerals industries have. The data have many general applications, among which are: (1) detection of large-scale geologic structures that previously were unknown and that may be significant with respect to the localization of hydrocarbons; (2) the possible detection of very subtle tonal anomalies that may represent alteration of the soils resulting from miniseeps of gas from hydrocarbon reservoirs; and (3) the potential for detecting natural marine oil seeps with consequent improvement in efficiency of offshore exploration.[12]

In June of 1975, the National Aeronautics and Space Administration (NASA) held the first comprehensive symposium on the practical application of earth resources surveys. The NASA Earth Resources Survey Symposium held in Houston was a three-and-a-half-day meeting that combined the utilization and results from NASA programs involving Landsat, the Skylab Earth resources experiment package, and aircraft, as well as from other data acquisition programs.[13] Today, remotely sensed images for use in petroleum exploration are commercially available from numerous Texas companies.

The petroleum exploration and production methods used at present have developed gradually as improvements have been made to the technology used throughout the history of the industry. A summary of current industry operations illustrates the interrelated and interdependent functions involved in finding an oil field and producing what is found.

The time from the start of exploration until production begins may be from five to ten years, and the productive life of an oil or gas field can be twenty-five to fifty years or longer. The petroleum exploration effort begins with extensive geological and geophysical studies, and continues through drilling and evaluation of several wells. Confirmation and extension wells are drilled to determine if a reservoir is of commercial quality and size. After sufficient volumes of producible oil and/or gas have been found, production facilities are installed, development wells are drilled, transportation to markets is arranged, and petroleum production is begun (see Fig. 1).

During a field's productive life, it is often necessary to re-enter wells for repairs and modifications (production stimulation, control of produced waters, and control of formation sand intrusion). When the natural reservoir pressure declines as oil is extracted and a well no longer flows, artificial lift devices, such as beam-and-rod-supported subsurface pumps or gas lift facilities may be required, and compressors are frequently used to increase the rate of production and extend the producing life of gas wells. Well and reservoir performance are studied continuously, and remedial, stimulation, and recompletion work is performed. Fluid or gas may be injected to maintain production. Some wells may be deepened, or supplemental wells may be drilled.

Water flood or gas injection (secondary recovery) may extend the productive life of an oil field. Some oil reservoirs are revived for a third life (tertiary recovery) by steam, carbon dioxide, or chemicals (polymers, surfactants) injection. Maintenance work never ceases. Wells that become uneconomical to produce are plugged with cement; salvageable casing is pulled; surface equipment is removed; and the surface area is cleaned.[14]

Research and development programs of industry, academia, and government (both state and federal) have generated new concepts and better applications of existing methods of petroleum production. It is estimated that primary recovery (based on natural pressure) can recover only 10 percent to 30 percent of the oil from its natural reservoir; secondary recovery (using gas, steam or water injection) can raise recovery efficiency. Tertiary recovery utilizing surfactants and solution polymers can also aid the recovery effort. Enhanced oil recovery (EOR) projects now under development within the industry and through academic and government-sponsored research include micellar-polymer, caustic, and microemulsion flooding. The importance of all this research is that as much as 350 billion barrels of oil already discovered in the United States—but currently considered to be nonproducible—could be produced.[15]

The Texas petroleum industry has been very successful in applying the technology of petroleum exploration. Excluding service wells, the cumulative total of wells drilled in Texas from 1866 to the end of 1984 was an astounding 805,124 (471,997 oil wells, 69,974 gas wells, and 263,153 dry holes). From the oil and gas wells have come a grand total of 49.3 billion

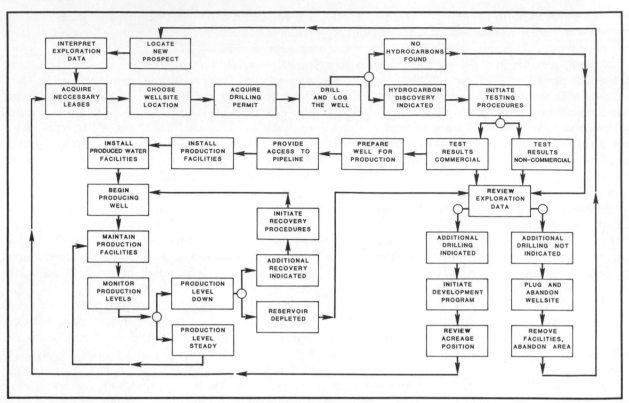

Figure 1. Simplified flow diagram of operations for exploration, discovery, production, and abandonment of an oil or gas field.

barrels of oil and almost 250 trillion cubic feet of natural gas. Texas became the leading oil-producing state in 1928, a position it has held ever since.

The late 1800s and early 1900s were a time of rapid technological development. The first patent for a rotary rock drill using diamonds and other hard materials was awarded in 1863 to J. R. Leschot; P. Sweeney received a patent in 1866 for a bit using rolling cutters, the forerunners of today's rock bit; and in 1899 M. T. Chapman received a patent on his rotary drilling machine. The Spindletop discovery in 1901 popularized rotary drilling, drilling mud, and the air lift pumping technique. In addition, the first "Christmas tree" (an assembly of valves and connectors that control the flow of oil or gas into the gathering pipeline) was used to harness the Lucas gusher at Spindletop.

In 1908 Howard R. Hughes designed the first tricone bit for drilling hard rock, and a year later Hughes Tool Co. was founded to manufacture rotary rock bits. Conrad Schlumberger began his studies of electrical surveying in 1912; in 1919 Erle Halliburton introduced cementing with the two-plug method in north Texas; and in 1926 Cameron Iron Works (Houston) was issued a patent for its first ram-type blowout preventor (BOP).

The 1940s, 1950s, and 1960s, brought advances in technology for offshore drilling: Texaco's use of the first submersible drilling barge off the Louisiana gulf coast in 1934,[16] the first pilot waterflood in Texas by Texaco in 1936, and gas lift commercialization by Camco, Inc. (Houston) in 1946. J. Ray McDermott & Co. (now McDermott International, Inc.), an industry leader before World War II, built the first template offshore platform in 1947, installed the first all-concrete platform in the Gulf of Mexico in 1950, built the first full revolving derrick barge for offshore use in 1955, and installed the first all-aluminum offshore platform in Lake Maracaibo, Venezuela, in 1956. Shell built the first semisubmersible rig in 1962, enabling drilling in water depths greater than 300 feet.[17]

It was during this period also that the downhole camera was introduced by Dowell (1947); the ball pump used for lifting oil was invented by Stanolind Oil and Gas Co. (1950); and Sun Oil Co. developed a drillstem electric logging tool that allowed for making logs without pulling drillpipe (1958).[18]

In the not too recent past, nine of every ten offshore drilling rigs came from the Texas operations of R. G. LeTourneau & Co. of Longview.[19] Recent technological innovations such as Exxon's Lena Guyed Tower and

Shell's Bullwinkle platform (the world's tallest) are significant achievements in the history of oil well drilling and production.

In 1964, in Cook Inlet, Alaska, Shell installed the first platform designed to resist the forces of ice sheets moving with strong tides. Shell also developed the first dynamic positioning system for drilling from a floating vessel. The system, which maintains a ship's station without the assistance of anchors, was first used in 1961 for core drilling off the California coast. The system was used to position the drillship off the mid-Atlantic coast where Shell established the world depth record of nearly 7,000 feet in 1984. From that start has arisen a worldwide fleet of about 150 semi-submersible vessels, some capable of drilling in 6,000 feet of water.[20]

Refining and Petrochemicals

Much of the technology with which today's oil refining is conducted was in place before World War II. In order to place Texas' role in the growth of the refining industry in perspective, a brief history of events in refining processes is required. The first refineries, which sprang up shortly after oil was discovered in Pennsylvania, used simple distillation units that resembled moonshine stills. Credit for the first commercial crude oil refinery goes to William Barnsdall and William J. Abbott, whose refinery at Oil Creek, Pennsylvania, was built in 1861. The gasoline and naptha produced, which formed about 45 percent of all the distilled products, were considered worthless. Kerosene was the product goal and all remaining residue went into making greases and lubricating oils.

John D. Rockefeller, then in the wholesale grocery business, and his partners decided to enter this new industry in the 1860s. In 1870 the partnership expended $4 million and established Standard Oil Co. of Ohio. The Standard name dominated refining for almost fifty years thereafter until the Supreme Court ordered the Standard trust split into thirty-eight competing companies.

The emergence of the internal combustion engine and its increasing use demanded that refining shift from kerosene production to gasoline and lubricating oils. The need for higher quality gasoline grew rapidly. In the 1920s the commercialization of the thermal cracking process occurred. The new method was patented by William M. Burton of Standard Oil of Indiana in 1913 and was later improved by others. In 1915 Universal Oil Products (UOP) patented and licensed to the industry the Dubbs thermal cracking

process, and in 1920 Texaco perfected the Holmes-Manley thermal cracking process.

By the end of the 1920s gasoline demand had quadrupled, and the railroad and aviation industries demanded new fuels. High quality gasoline to eliminate engine knocks was needed, and the General Motors Research Laboratory in Dayton, Ohio, through the work of Charles F. Kettering and Thomas Midgely, Jr., produced the first anti-knock compound, tetraethyl lead (TEL), in 1921.

Thermal cracking technology gradually gave way to catalytic cracking, pioneered by Eugene Houdry's fixed-bed catalytic cracking process. In 1936 the process was first tried out by Socony-Vacuum (now Mobil) at its Paulsboro, New Jersey, refinery. One year later, Sun Oil put the first commercial Houdry unit into operation at Marcus Hook, Pennsylvania. In 1939 Standard Oil of New Jersey (now Exxon) announced its invention of the fluidized catalytic cracking (FCC) method. Pre–World War II technology also generated oil-based TNT, and the first tankload of toluene for making TNT was produced with Exxon's hydroforming process.[21]

The refining and petrochemical industries steadily grew and matured during the Second World War and after. During the early days of World War II, the federal government established a policy of pooling refinery technology to speed up new developments. From industry cooperation came new techniques and improvements in refining processes—alkylation, polymerization, isomerization, Houdry's fixed-bed cracking, Thermofor cat cracking, and FCC. The HF-alkylation process, patented by Universal Oil Products (UOP), was first used by Phillips Petroleum Co. at its Borger, Texas, plant in 1942. The following year Phillips unveiled a number of refining accomplishments in Texas, including the Cycloversion process for the manufacture of high quality aviation gasoline, first used at the Borger facility, and the first shipment of carbon black for making tire-quality rubber, also produced and shipped out of Borger. The Thermofor catalytic cracker went on stream at Magnolia's Beaumont refinery, and Shell's Houston plant was producing butadiene, a feedstock used in the manufacture of synthetic rubber.[22] In 1948 the first plant for making alcohol by direct hydration of ethylene went into operation at Shell's Houston installation.[23]

By the 1960s refining technology began to move toward advanced heavy oil cracking.[24] In 1961 the Phillips Petroleum Co. installed the oil industry's first heavy oil cracking (HOC) unit, developed with the M. W. Kellogg Co., at Borger, Texas. Its second unit, at Sweeney, Texas, was finished in 1981.[25]

Table 1
Typical Petroleum Fractions

Fraction	Boiling range	Hydrocarbon molecules
Gas and liquefied gas	up to 25°C	C_1—C_4
Gasoline (petrol, naphtha)	$\approx$ 20–200°C	C_4—C_{12}
Kerosene	$\approx$ 175–275°C	C_9—C_{16}
Gas oil and Diesel oil	$\approx$ 200–400°C	C_{15}—C_{25}
Lubricating oil	———	C_{20}—C_{70}
Fuel oil	———	C_{10} upwards
Bitumen and coke	———	large molecules

Today's refining processes begin by separating crude oil into boiling range fractions that are then processed by "cracking" the large hydrocarbon molecules into smaller ones. (See Table 1.) During the process the structure of some molecules is rearranged, and others are joined in different combinations, to provide the desired components that are then blended into finished products. This activity occurs in several refinery process units, each having a specific purpose for integration into a processing sequence. Refining operations can be divided into seven steps:

1. Separating crude oil into its many components by atmospheric and vacuum distillation
2. Converting crude oil into products of higher value through cracking (thermal, catalytic, viscosity breaking, hydrocracking, and coking), combining (alkylation and polymerization), and rearranging (catalytic reforming and isomerization)
3. Treating crude oil fractions, often producing hydrogen sulfide, which can be separated and converted to elemental sulfur, and removing sulfur compounds through treating processes such as hydrodesulfurizing and chemical treating
4. Blending hydrocarbon products
5. Utilizing auxiliary operating facilities to maintain normal operating conditions and to support processes such as hydrotreating; to improve efficiency by allowing re-use of water and the use of sour gas as fuel; and to help the refinery meet environmental standards
6. Utilizing refinery offsite facilities (equipment and systems used to support refinery operations, including storage tanks, steam generating systems, flare and blowdown systems, cooling water systems, receiving and distribution systems, and refinery fire control systems)
7. Controlling emissions and effluents (air emissions, wastewater, solid waste, and noise, which must be controlled for efficient processing and environmental protection)[26]

Whether developed in Texas research laboratories or elsewhere around the country and the world, new refining processes have been tested or put into commercial use throughout the refining and petrochemical industries of Texas. The degree of change in refining technology from its early years has been tremendous. In 1935, from 100 barrels of crude oil, refiners could produce 44 barrels of gasoline and almost 27 barrels of residual fuel oil. At present, from 100 barrels, the yield is 7 barrels of jet fuel (unknown in 1935), 51 barrels of better-quality gasoline, 6 barrels of residual oil, and a wide range of products, from coke to gaseous petrochemical feedstocks and fuel for the refinery itself.[27] (See fig. 2.)

One of the most important aspects of Texas' rise to industrial significance has been the growth of the petrochemical industry. A central factor in its development was the increased production of industrial chemicals from oil and natural gas and, especially notable, the growing use of plastics and other synthetics requiring chemicals. Perhaps no area of the world has more of the raw materials needed by this industry than the Texas Gulf Coast region, and probably none was the site of more rapid expansion after World War II.

The history of the petrochemical industry, however, does not begin with petroleum. The first petrochemicals were derived from hydrocarbons and other compounds that occur naturally in coal. In the last half of the nineteenth century, Europe was a leader in coal-

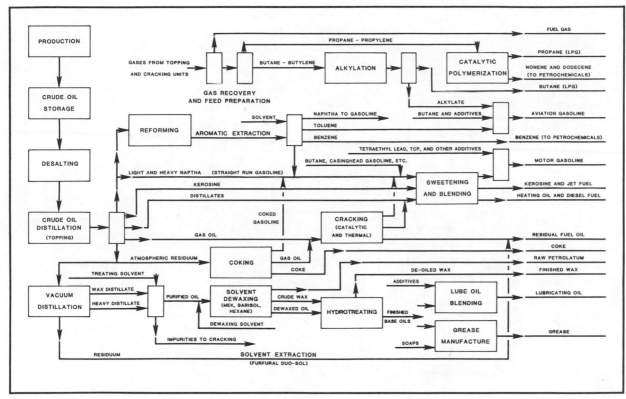

Figure 2. Simplified flow diagram of a complex refinery.

based chemistry. Based primarily on European discoveries, a parallel but definitely smaller coal-chemicals industry was growing in the U.S. The first true petrochemical deliberately synthesized from natural petroleum fractions was developed in 1920 by Standard Oil of New Jersey (now Exxon). The product was isopropyl alcohol produced by a new process involving hydration of propylene that was obtained from cracked refinery gases.[28]

Our modern petrochemical industry owes its beginnings to the development of the internal combustion engine. Refineries were required to produce higher performance fuels for automative and aircraft engines. As the value of gas by-products was recognized, propylene and butylene were recovered and converted to chemicals as well as to polymers that were added to gasoline to improve its efficiency (give it a higher octane number).

World War II brought increased demand for textiles, explosives, plastics, drugs, and synthetic rubber. The overabundance of refinery gases produced after catalytic cracking processes were introduced in the mid-1930s was put to good use in fulfilling these demands.

Although the petrochemical industry can produce almost an infinite variety of chemicals and finished products, it rests on a relative handful of basic building blocks—naptha, methane, ethane, propane, and butane. Next come the primary intermediates—ethylene, propylene, butadiene, benzene, paraxylene, ammonia, and methanol. Six basic processes are used to convert petroleum hydrocarbons into raw materials for the chemical industry: (1) removing hydrogen to produce unsaturated hydrocarbons, olefins, and aromatics; (2) adding oxygen to the molecule to produce oxygen-containing compounds; (3) adding chlorine to make chlorinated compounds; (4) adding sulphur; (5) removing all hydrogen to leave elemental carbon; and (6) removing all carbon to leave elemental hydrogen.[29] (See fig. 3.)

Today petrochemical companies outnumber oil companies. Innovation and process advances can be as simple as changing one step in an established process to arrive at a similar or different product. Already thousands of useful products have been developed by the petrochemical industry, and tens of thousands more await only a use or need.

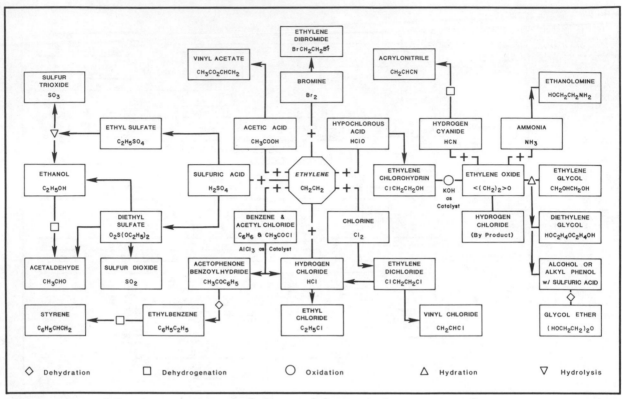

Figure 3. *Some of the numerous uses of ethylene and the types of processes used.*

Industry and Academic Research and Development

Much of the technology so readily available today in both the Texas and world petroleum industry was developed through cooperative efforts of companies and through their funding of academic research. Integrated oil companies and independents alike conduct research programs in various aspects of petroleum technology. More often than not the results derived from these studies are of a proprietary nature, and even an examination of patent literature tends to be vague. Concurrent research often results in legal contests for proof of patent and licensing rights. Decades may pass before final judgment is handed down. The following example, taken from a history of Standard Oil of Indiana, is but one illustration of the path research can take.

Standard filed its first significant patent application on crystalline polypropylene (as a composition of matter invention based on first production—not on the process of production) in early October, 1954. But research doesn't take place in a vacuum. By 1957, at least five companies in the

U.S. and abroad had applied for patents, and, as a result, in 1958 the U.S. Patent Office initiated what are called interference proceedings to determine which applicant was entitled to the U.S. patent rights for inventing crystalline polypropylene.

On November 29, 1971, the Board of Patent Interferences awarded priority to Montedison S.p.A. The legal marathon resumed when this decision was appealed early in 1972 by Standard, E.I. duPont de Nemours and Company, and Phillips Petroleum Company. The three cases were consolidated in the U.S. District Court in Delaware on May 15, 1975, and hearings resumed before Senior Judge Caleb Wright.

The District Court's opinion, delivered in January, 1980, affirmed the claim of Montedison that it was entitled to a June 8, 1954, priority date. But much to the surprise of all, the court held that Phillips was entitled to a priority date no later than January 27, 1953, instead of the January 11, 1956, date assigned to it by the Patent Office. Since the priority date awarded to Phillips predated the others, the remaining litigants promptly appealed.

The U.S. Supreme Court refused to review the case on April 5, 1982, with the result that Phillips was awarded the patent in the composition of matter interference, based on the lower court's determination for Phillips of the January 27, 1953, invention priority date.[30]

In addition to work conducted throughout the state by individual petroleum companies and engineering firms, a vast amount of the energy research conducted in Texas is accomplished in the state's universities. Because oil and gas are the traditional stronghold of Texas' energy base, research in petroleum fields must cover a wide diversity of areas connected with exploration, recovery, and environmental impact mitigation.

The University of Texas at Austin houses the joint offices (along with Texas A&M University) of the Texas Petroleum Research Committee. Also at UT-Austin are the Center for Energy Studies and the Bureau of Economic Geology (formerly the Geological Survey of Texas). These offices work in conjunction with the Department of Petroleum Engineering in research and development programs. TAMU's Engineering Experiment Station and the Center for Energy and Mineral Resources are that institution's research arms, and the Energy Laboratory serves in that capacity for the University of Houston–University Park. Research centers whose primary concern is in the other energy fields are located in Texas Tech University, West Texas State University, Stephen F. Austin State University, the University of Texas at El Paso, the University of Texas at Arlington, Tarleton State University, Texas A&I University, and Lamar University.

In 1982 the Houston Area Research Center (HARC), a contract and grant research institution located in The Woodlands, was formed. The Center is a nonprofit consortium of four universities: UT–Austin, TAMU, Rice University, and UH–University Park, designed to serve as a catalyst between the more fundamental research of the academic sectors and the applied research needs of industry and government.

In 1985 the Texas Legislature established a Geotechnology Research Institute (GTRI) as part of HARC to study energy and improved exploration and production techniques. The institute was provided with "seed money" from Mitchell Energy and Development Corp., which founded The Woodlands. Here eminent geoscientists will work on advanced, original research. GTRI is now launching an industry-sponsored program for research in processing seismic data, reservoir modeling, establishment of database systems for cooperative use in the energy industry, and original geological and geophysical research in remote areas such as Alaska and Antarctica.[31]

Another recent cooperative effort was the founding of the Petroleum Environmental Research Consortium of Houston. Chevron Corp. and Unocal Corp. are the industry leaders, and although these are major companies, the primary appeal of this consortium will be in the area of the nonmajor company. Cooperative research of this kind will help companies apply advanced technology throughout the industry. As recently as September 1985, twenty specific proposals for study had been submitted.[32]

Texas Petroleum Statistics

Texas is one of the world's major petroleum-producing areas, and although the state's economy is no longer so securely bound to the production of oil and other materials, petroleum continues to play a major role. Energy companies account for some 22 percent of the state's economic base. Nearly 88 percent of the crude oil produced in Texas is refined in the state itself, and petroleum and coal products rank second in importance only to the closely allied chemical industry. The Texas-Louisiana coast has been the largest refining district in the U.S. since the 1950s, with most of Texas' fifty-eight refineries grouped around Houston and the Beaumont–Port Arthur area and oil being brought by pipeline from all over Texas and other states as well. In 1984 there were 73 petrochemical plants, 9 carbon black plants, and 472 natural gasoline processing plants located in the state.

Ever since oil was discovered at Spindletop in 1901, energy has played an ever-increasing role in Texas' economy. The state's crude oil and natural gas production increased until 1972, peaking at 2.9 billion barrels of oil equivalent per year in 1972. Production has decreased since then, but it remains a major source of income in Texas and a crucial supply of energy to the U.S. Current proved reserves in Texas are 7.6 billion barrels of oil, 26.8 percent of the U.S. total, and 49.9 trillion cubic feet of gas, 25.3 percent of the U.S. total.[33] Texas also is the home of two of the Strategic Petroleum Reserve's (SPR) storage areas. Salt caverns at Bryan Mound, near Freeport, and at Big Hill, southwest of Nederland, hold portions of the emergency crude oil mandated by the Energy Policy and Conservation Act (EPCA) of 1975, which created the SPR.[34]

In the greater Houston area alone, there are some nineteen hundred petroleum and petroleum-related companies. The 1985 *Houston Oil Directory* lists fifty-four categories, from bits and tools to workovers and well services, from engineering and construction to rental tools and equipment. The largest group of companies, to no surprise, is comprised of geologists and geophysicists and seismograph service companies.[35]

Of the top 400 U.S. oil and gas companies, 136 are headquartered in Texas. In 1985, the top 10 companies, as listed in the *Oil and Gas Journal* (*OGJ*), were (in order of total assets) Exxon Corp., Mobil Corp., Texaco, Inc., Chevron Corp., Amoco Corp., Shell Oil Co., Atlantic Richfield Co., Tenneco, Inc., Standard Oil Co. (Ohio), and Phillips Petroleum Co. Of these 10, 2 are headquartered in Houston, Texas— Shell Oil Co. and Tenneco Inc.[36] But whether Texas is a home-base to various oil and gas companies, there are hardly any that do not maintain some operation in the state. Texas also leads the nation in the number of persons employed in the petroleum industry. In 1984, 393,703 employees worked in mining, manufacturing, transportation, wholesale, and retail activities.[37]

Also of great interest to petroleum scientists, engineers, and technologists in Texas and throughout the world is the Offshore Technology Conference (OTC), which has been held annually in Houston since 1969. It is the world's biggest trade and technical show. Simply put, it is the single largest gathering in the world for the display and dissemination of information on new technologies for all aspects of the petroleum industry, not just the offshore portion. Drawing crowds of over a hundred thousand in some years, the conference has been held in Houston's Astrodome complex, housing both the technical sessions and the displays, which have included complete drilling platforms that had to be airlifted into the parking lot by helicopters.

From the industrial, governmental, and academic laboratories of Texas have come numerous scientific and technical innovations and process advances that have fostered the growth of the oil and gas industry both domestically and worldwide. In essence, Texas has been a haven for the industry in the past, and there is no reason to believe the state will not continue its premier role for decades to come.

Research in science and technology is an ongoing and overlapping effort, and the boundaries of development are not often clear. Even a slight modification of an existing process may yield a new result. For every process advance or personal or corporate achievement cited in this brief overview, there are hundreds of others that, because of space contraints, could not be mentioned. Short of making an in-depth study of the histories of all of the petroleum and petroleum-related companies operating in the state of Texas, neither a complete nor a completely accurate accounting of scientific and technological developments can be made. The following remarks will lead the interested reader to more broad-range sources, and the bibliography will add special topics.

In his book, *The Chronological History of the Petroleum and Natural Gas Industries*, James A. Clark outlined in exemplary fashion the history of the industry. His book records pertinent facts about oil and gas discoveries worldwide and the technologies developed to make not only those discoveries possible, but the technology to produce, transport, refine, and distribute these valuable resources. Clark's chronology ends with 1962, and it is understandable that no one has chosen to revise his work. The task would be monumental.

Bates et al. provide an in-depth record of geophysical advancements, and *Geophysics'* fiftieth anniversary issue contains classic papers in the development of geophysics. Wayne Gard's account of oil and gas in Texas during the first one hundred years has been updated through the 1970s, and it is an excellent chronicle of Texas' discoveries and the economic growth of the petroleum industry in the state. Publications such as the *American Association of Petroleum Geologists Bulletin, Journal of Petroleum Technology, Oil and Gas Journal, The Oil Daily, Petroleum Engineer International, Texas Energy Reporter, Texas Energy Week,* and *World Oil* carry timely articles on new developments in virtually all aspects of petroleum technology.

Notes

1. Halbouty, 1967, p. 1180–81.
2. Halbouty, 1979, p. xiv.
3. Halbouty, 1967, p. 1181
4. Halbouty, 1979, p. xiv.
5. Halbouty, 1970, p. 92.
6. Landes, 1959, pp. 10–11.
7. Bates, 1982, p. 83.
8. Clark, 1963, p. 202.
9. Sheriff, 1985, p. 2409.
10. Anderson, 1984, p. 184.
11. Halbouty, 1980, p. 1216–17.
12. Halbouty, 1976, p. 745.
13. NASA, 1975, p. iii.
14. National Petroleum Council, 1981, p. 61–63.
15. National Research Council, 1985, p. 35–36.
16. Anderson, 1984, p. 148.
17. Shell Oil Company, 1985, private communication.
18. *The Oil Daily*, 1984, p. 43.
19. Wilborn, 1984, p. 5.
20. Shell Oil Company, 1985, private communication.

21. Murphy, 1984a, p. 35.
22. Murphy, 1984a, p. 35–37.
23. Clark, 1963, p. 226.
24. Murphy, 1984a, pp. 35–36.
25. Murphy, 1984b, p. 61.
26. National Petroleum Council, 1981, pp. 217–21.
27. Anderson, 1984, p. 218.
28. Anderson, 1984, p. 226.
29. Anderson, 1984, p. 230.
30. Dedmon, 1984, pp. 185–86.
31. *Texas Energy Reporter*, 1985, p. 2, 5.
32. Fanshier, 1985, p. 4.
33. Texas Mid-Continent Oil & Gas Association, 1985, p. 2.
34. National Petroleum Council, 1984, p. 3, 11.
35. *Houston Oil Directory*, 1985, p. A-9–A-46.
36. *Oil & Gas Journal*, 1985, pp. 102–24.
37. Petroleum Independent, 1985, p. 111.

Bibliography

American Gas Association, *Guide to New Natural Gas Utilization Technologies*, Nelson E. Hay, ed., Atlanta: Fairmont, 1985.

Anderson, Robert O., *Fundamentals of the Petroleum Industry*, Norman: Univ. of Oklahoma Press, 1984.

Bates, Charles A., Thomas G. Gaskell, and Robert B. Rice, *Geophysics in the Affairs of Man; A Personalized History of Exploration Geophysics and its Allied Sciences of Seismology and Oceanography*, New York: Pergamon, 1982.

Beaton, Kendall, *Enterprise in Oil*, New York: Appleton-Century-Crofts, 1957.

Brantley, J. E., *History of Oil Well Drilling*, Houston: Gulf Publishing, 1971.

Clark, James A., *The Chronological History of the Petroleum and Natural Gas Industries*, Houston: Clark Book Co., 1963.

Clark, James A., and Michel T. Halbouty, *Spindletop*, New York: Random House, 1952.

———. *The Last Boom*, New York: Random House, 1972.

Copp, E. Anthony, *Regulating Competition in Oil; Government intervention in the U.S. Refining Industry, 1948–1975*, 28–31, College Station: Texas A&M Univ. Press, 1976.

Dedmon, Emmett, *Challenge and Response; A Modern History of Standard Oil Company (Indiana)*, Chicago: Mobium, 1984.

Fanshier, Keith, "Cooperative Research Can Aid the Industry," *The Oil Daily*, September 11 (1985): 4.

Gard, Wayne, *The First One Hundred Years of Texas Oil and Gas*, Austin: Texas Mid-Continent Oil & Gas Association, 1966.

Halbouty, Michel T., "Heritage of the Petroleum Geologist," *American Association of Petroleum Geologists Bulletin*, 51(7):1179–84 (1967).

———. "Giant Oil and Gas Fields in the United States." In *Geology of Giant Petroleum Fields*, 91–127, Tulsa: AAPG, 1970.

———. "Application of LANDSAT Imagery to Petroleum and Mineral Exploration," *American Association of Petroleum Geologists Bulletin*, 60(5):745–93(1976).

———. *Salt Domes: Gulf Region, United States and Mexico*, 2d ed., Houston: Gulf Publishing, 1979.

———. "Methods Used, and Experience Gained, in Exploration for New Oil and Gas Fields in Highly Explored (Mature) Areas," *American Association of Petroleum Geologists Bulletin*, 64(8):1210–22(1980).

Houston Oil Directory, Houston: Resource Publications, 1985.

Landes, Kenneth K., *Petroleum Geology*, New York: John Wiley & Sons, 1959.

Murphy, Marvin, "Refining Rides Crest of New Technology," *The Oil Daily*, August 27 (1984a): 35–37.

———, "The '70s and '80s Brought New Processes to Refining," *The Oil Daily*, August 27 (1984b):61.

National Aeronautics and Space Administration, *Proceedings of the NASA Earth Resources Survey Symposium*, NASA TM X-58168, Houston, 1975.

National Petroleum Council, *Environmental Conservation; The Oil and Gas Industries*, Washington, D.C., 1981.

———. *Enhanced Oil Recovery*, Washington, D.C., 1984.

———. *The Strategic Petroleum Reserve*, Washington, D.C., 1984.

National Research Council, *Opportunities in Chemistry*, Washington, D.C., National Science Press, 1985.

Nicholson, Patrick J., *Mr. Jim; The Biography of James Smithers Abercrombie*, Houston: Gulf Publishing, 1983.

The Oil Daily, "Exploration and Production Highlights," August 27 (1984):43.

Oil & Gas Journal, "OGJ 400 Reflects Industry's Restructuring," September 9 (1985):102–24.

Owen, Edgar W., *Trek of the Oil Finders: A History of Exploration for Petroleum*, Tulsa: AAPG, 1975.

Petroleum Independent, *The Oil and Gas Producing Industry in Your State*. 55 (September 1985).

Sheriff, Robert E., "History of Geophysical Technology Through Advertisements in *Geophysics*," *Geophysics*, 50(12):2299–2408(1985).

Texas Energy and Natural Resources Advisory Council, *Texas Five Year Energy Research Plan; 1984–1988, Parts I and II: Background and Analysis of Future Needs*, Austin, 1983.

Texas Energy Reporter, "Houston Area Research Center: GTRI's Innovative Approach to Public/Private Cooperation," 3(6):2, 5 (1985).

Texas Mid-Continent Oil and Gas Association, *85 Facts About Texas Oil and Gas*, Austin, 1985.

Tinkle, Lon, *Mr. De; A Biography of Everette Lee DeGolyer*, Boston: Little, Brown & Co., 1970.

Wilborn, Gene, "Once U.S.-dominated, Offshore Rigbuilding Has Gone International," *The Oil Daily*, August 27 (1984):5.

10

Other Energy Technologies

Spencer R. Baen

Introduction

Energy is a very broad and important area of human concern. It impinges upon every aspect of physical endeavor. When there are shortages of available energy, the effects can be immediate, even startling. Who can forget the night the lights went out in New York City?

Energy resources involve the sun, oil and natural gas, geopressure and geotherm, nuclear fission and fusion, uranium, coal and lignite, energy from biomass, wind, ocean therm and currents, organic solid wastes, and conservation techniques (classified by many as a resource). Making energy available gives rise to many pursuits surrounding exploration and production. Energy use involves conversion to other forms of energy, conversion to base chemicals, electrical generation, transportation, manufacturing, construction, heating and cooling, lighting, cooking, regulation, law, economics, and taxation. Obviously, all aspects of energy cannot be treated in a few pages. Hence, in this chapter an attempt will be made to track both (1) important technological developments related to the various energy resources and (2) noteworthy contributions made by university and industry to these developments.

The consequences of the oil embargo imposed by the Organization of Petroleum Exporting Countries (OPEC) in 1973, including the subsequent price rise of oil from around $2 per 42-gallon standard barrel eventually to $34 per barrel, are well known.[1] The impact was immediate and affected the economies of people and nations throughout the world. The Texas legislature and the universities in Texas were spurred to create "centers" to coordinate and develop energy research programs to promote the growth of alternate energy resources, to investigate ways to better utilize energy, and to advise the state's industries and citizens of ways to reduce energy costs. Academic programs were also developed to better educate our future scientists, engineers, and graduates. The Texas legislature recognized the importance of adequate energy resources and trained people in the future economic development of the state, and it continues to provide special line-item appropriations for these activities.[2]

Energy research centers were established initially at the four large universities: the University of Texas at Austin (UT–Austin), Texas A&M University (TAMU), Texas Tech University (TTU), and the University of Houston (UH–University Park). The UT–Austin Center for Energy Studies began operation in January 1974. Herbert H. Woodson was named director and is still serving in that capacity. The Center for Energy and Mineral Resources at TAMU was established in

May 1975. Richard E. Wainerdi was named director; his successor, Spencer R. Baen, has served as director since September 1977. Initially at TTU the center was known as the Institute for Energy Research. Today it is designated as the Center for Energy Research; Marion O. Hagler served as director until September 1985, when Edgar A. O'Hair succeeded him. Two groups were formed at UH–University Park in 1973 to study energy issues: The Energy Institute, originally directed by Allen Commander and later by John R. Howell; and the UH Solar Energy Laboratory, directed by Alvin F. Hildebrandt and Lorin Vant-Hull. These two groups were merged in 1978 to form the current Energy Laboratory, directed by Hildebrandt. The Texas legislature added appropriations for the Alternate Energy Institute at West Texas State University, starting in 1977.[3] Vaughn Nelson is its director.

The centers have developed programs in special areas where facilities existed or could be developed and where faculty were capable of credible research to help solve Texas' and the nation's energy-related problems. The majority of the funding for the university energy research programs, four to seven times the state appropriations, has come from U.S. industries requiring research support and from federal and state sources. The larger research programs are interdisciplinary and involve scientists, engineers, economists, and other trained researchers as required.

The UT–Austin center has conducted more than 450 energy research projects, and published more than 120 research reports with major programs in energy conservation, electric power, energy policy, environmental studies, chemical separations, geothermal studies, nuclear studies, and solar energy. The center's activities now involve thirty to forty faculty a year from twenty-four departments—and easily twice that number of graduate students.

Programs of the center at TAMU address problems in the areas of coal and lignite, biomass conversion, petroleum and natural gas, alternate fuels (such as alcohol, vegetable oils, and hydrogen), nuclear energy, socioeconomic and environmental effects of energy development, energy conservation, mineral resources, and energy public service activities. During the 1982–83 academic year, this center conducted 109 projects involving 170 faculty and staff members, 195 graduate students, and fifty post-doctoral fellows. Approximately 250 publications and 300 oral presentations resulted from the center's research activities. The research involvement of the center has been increasing gradually over the past ten years.[4]

The Energy Laboratory at UH–University Park has made major progress in solar energy developments involving solar power towers; it also has programs concerned with conservation, oil and gas economic modeling, and coal and lignite.[5] Thirty-five faculty members and twenty graduate students are involved in these research areas.

At TTU in Lubbock, the Center for Energy Research is doing research in essentially all phases of alternate energy development and utilization. Major efforts have involved solar collection, energy conservation, and recently in pulsed power for the U.S. Strategic Defense Initiative. The 1984 Annual Report[6] summarizes research programs involving faculty and graduate students in each project. One of the most important research projects involves the largest known solar concentrating mirrored spherical bowl, located at Crosbyton, Texas.

The Alternate Energy Institute at West Texas State University (WTSU) received financial assistance from the state starting in 1977.[7] The Institute has concentrated mainly on wind energy and efficient location of wind generators and their utilization, because wind energy has been traditionally of great importance to settled life on the Great Plains.

Research in these centers and in the electrical and mechanical engineering departments of Texas colleges and universities has been directed toward the efficient use of the many energy sources available. Of particular interest in this chapter are fuels other than petroleum or natural gas. These include uranium for nuclear energy, fusionable substances, organic sources (lignite and biomass), geopressured–geothermal energy, solar energy, wind energy, and energy from the oxidation of hydrogen. The centers and departments also seek to be involved in research important to the transmission and use of electric power, as well as its generation, and to assist the electric utility systems in their task of supplying power to the public.

Electric Utility Systems Research

The Electric Power Institute at TAMU was formed in the early 1960s at the request of all of the investor-owned utilities headquartered in Texas together with the Dow Chemical Company. Under the leadership of Louis Haupt, the Institute was provided with a Westinghouse Analogue Circuit Analyzer, which was used to conduct fundamental power flow and stability studies for the benefit of all the utilities.[8] Today, these studies and research are vastly more complicated and more important to the control and reliability of our electric systems.[9] Other research at TAMU of near-term importance to utilities includes the location of high impedance faults, distribution systems, advanced load-leveling methods, use of high voltage direct current interconnects between systems, and energy storage systems. This research, using very powerful digital computers, has been carried out by many members of the faculty under the leadership of Haupt and his successors, Glenn Hallmark, John S. Denison, Robert Chenowith, and A. D. Patton.

Uranium for Nuclear Energy

Uranium suddenly became important as a source for electric power generation nationally and internationally after 1945. Deposits were discovered in the Texas coastal plain in 1954 when a radiometric anomaly was detected by an airborne survey. A flurry of exploration followed, particularly in Karnes, Live Oak, and Atascosa counties, and several shallow deposits were discovered. An early guide to uranium prospecting in the state was quickly assembled by Peter Flawn and published by the UT–Austin Bureau of Economic Geology (BEG) in 1955.[10] Mining commenced in 1960. Organized exploratory drilling resulted in the discovery of deeper deposits, which were first opened in 1963. Though cyclical, active mining has continued to the present. A technical milestone, the economical application of in-situ leach recovery of uranium, was begun in 1975.

The lull in mining and exploratory activity of the late 1960s was mirrored by a hiatus in active research. However, rapid expansion of the Gulf Coast district in the early 1970s led to a blossoming of research activity:

- Systematic studies in the Catahoula formation by W. Galloway and W. Kaiser began in 1975 and led to a number of Bureau reports of investigations.[11]
- C. D. Henry later published results of a study of the natural and mining-induced trace metals in soils.[12]
- A major grant from the U.S. Environmental Protection Agency funded a study of ore distribution and genesis, as well as mining impacts on the natural aquifer system in the Oakville Sandstone.[13]
- Working in collaboration with U.S. Geological

Survey scientists, Galloway completed a synthesis of the mineralization models applicable to the south Texas deposits and published results in 1982.[14]

At the same time, additional studies of known or potential uranium-bearing areas were being made in the Texas Panhandle and the Trans-Pecos region. J. McGowen and S. Seni examined the facies control of uranium in the Triassic Dockum formation. C. Henry and A. Walton examined the effects of high and low temperature alteration processes on the release of uranium from volanic rocks and glass.

Finally, the Bureau managed and compiled numerous quadrangle uranium resource valuation reports as a part of the U.S. Department of Energy's national uranium resource evaluation program.[15]

Thomas Tieh of the Geology Department at TAMU also investigated the potential for minable uranium in and adjacent to the Catahoula formation in shallow subsurfaces of central and east Texas.[16] The demand for uranium dropped, commercial mining was curtailed, and research was not continued. In-situ leaching recovery from uranium deposits was also the subject of geologic research for the industries involved.

Energy from Nuclear Fusion

Since the late 1950s UT–Austin has become one of the premier university centers for nuclear fusion research. Nuclear fusion occurs when nuclei with sufficient kinetic energy to overcome coulombic repulsion collide. Such energies are attained in a plasma heated to millions of degrees Celsius. Fusion energy holds great promise as a low-polluting, nearly limitless form of energy for the future. The physics and technology needed to achieve fusion power plants have been the subject of research around the world for decades. Basic physics research in the senior universities in the state of Texas is rapidly accelerating as facilities are expanded to meet new energy-related challenges.

The Fusion Research Center at UT–Austin began in 1966 as a cooperative effort with the Texas Atomic Energy Research Foundation, a consortium of ten Texas electric utilities, formed in 1957.[17] It was also backed by then-governor John Connally and the Texas congressional delegation. In the early years, a nucleus of about ten plasma scientists, led by William E. Drummond, concentrated on the basic physics of collisionless plasmas with emphasis on the study of plasma turbulence.

The program grew in the 1970s, attracting funding from the Edison Electric Institute and the federal government. In 1970 the Fusion Research Center had completed the construction of the state's first major fusion experimental device, the Texas Tokamak. A tokamak is an ingenious solution first suggested in the U.S.S.R. to the problem of how to contain the plasma in which fusion occurs—a plasma heated to millions of degrees Celsius. A tokamak uses powerful magnetic fields to hold the plasma inside a doughnut-shaped inner chamber. The Texas Tokamak was designed to study a new method of heating plasma, and heat plasma it did. In 1974 researchers achieved a spectacular world-record temperature of 200 million degrees Celsius—far exceeding the 50-to-100-million-degree range in which fusion begins to happen. That temperature was sustained for only a fraction of a second, however. Most fusion scientists believe that the temperature must be held for a full second or more to achieve self-sustaining fusion.

Another, smaller research device, the pre-TEXT Tokamak, was designed by UT–Austin physicist Roger D. Bengston and completed in 1979. It has been used in experiments on heating a plasma with low-frequency electromagnetic waves.

The Texas Tokamak was dismantled to be replaced by a successor, the Texas Experimental Tokamak (TEXT), completed in 1981, the brainchild of UT–Austin physicist Kenneth Gentle (fig. 1). The U.S. Department of Energy selected UT–Austin to be the home of TEXT and the national center for basic experimental research in tokamak fusion. Fusion devices at UT–Austin have all been research devices rather than test reactors. TEXT is located underground in the north part of the Austin campus and still operates today. It is used by fusion researchers from all over the world to conduct experiments and test new theories. TEXT was considered controversial at the time of its construction because of its structural features, designed to accommodate numerous instrumentation schemes at forty-six ports.

In 1980 another milestone for the UT–Austin fusion research effort occurred: the Department of Energy designated the university as a national center for

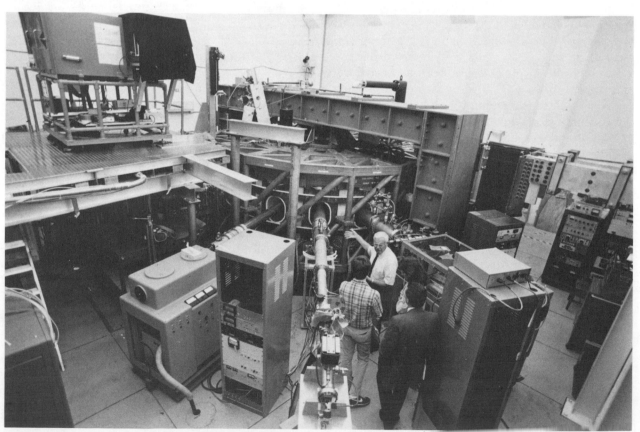

Figure 1. The Texas Experimental Tokamak (TEXT) at the University of Texas at Austin.

excellence in fusion theory and funded its new Institute for Fusion Studies, led by physicist Marshall Rosenbluth, one of the world's leading fusion scientists. The university founded a third fusion group, the Center for Fusion Engineering, in 1983.

In the 1970s fusion research became the largest research program in the history of UT–Austin and is still so today. Hundreds of graduate students, scientists, and engineers, including many from other countries, are involved in its fusion programs. A cherished, long-term goal of fusion researchers in Texas is that the first fusion power plant in the nation and perhaps in the world be built here.

Success of research into the basic physics of fusion conducted at UT–Austin led the Physics Department and Cyclotron Institute at TAMU to become more and more involved in fusion-related research. Contributions to basic knowledge include fundamental data and theories concerning ion collisions, atomic and molecular capture diameters of hydrogen and other elements, and the behavior of subatomic particles. Principal contributors to basic research in thermonuclear subjects in the Physics Department at TAMU include Hans Schuessler,[18] John F. Reading,[19] A. Louis Ford,[20] Edward S. Fry,[21] David A. Church,[22] Robert C. Webb,[23] and Peter McIntyre. The Cyclotron Institute operates as a department in the College of Science under the leadership of David Youngblood.

Recently Peter McIntyre has been instrumental in redirecting the construction of future U.S. high-energy research facilities. The Superconducting Super-Collider (SSC), originally designated in Texas as the Texatron, is now being proposed as a U.S. leadership program, with international participation, by the Department of Energy and Congress. A consortium of four Texas universities are as of this writing considering various aspects of the SSC construction. The Houston Area Research Center (HARC) at The Woodlands, Texas, is the contracting center for the SSC research efforts involving UT–Austin, TAMU, Rice, and UH–University Park. International aspects involve the Research Laboratory at CERN in Geneva, Switzerland, at which many Western European countries conduct research.

The TAMU Cyclotron Institute and the Nuclear Science Center both have made contributions to science and engineering related to energy as well as to medical science, biology, and other disciplines. Isotopes used as tracers, for example, have been used successfully to monitor the adverse effects of corrosion in drilling for oil in the deeper "sour gas" wells where hydrogen sulfide causes rapid corrosion and the need

for frequent parts replacement. Production pumps and components likewise may benefit from the use of tracers in oil wells, which also produce sour gas. Neutron radiography has proven to be effective in monitoring the soundness of fiberglass and other composite structural items used in automobiles and aircraft. The reduction of weight realized in the nation's transportation industries is, of course, producing increased efficiencies, thereby helping to reduce requirements for liquid fuels and the need to import great quantities of foreign oil.

The Cyclotron Institute began operating in 1967 and continues to be upgraded. It now offers a medium-energy range of versatile accelerator services to universities and researchers throughout the Southwest. It operates on a twenty-four-hour basis. The cyclotron is capable of accelerating protons to 50 MeV, deuterons to 65 MeV, alpha particles and ^{3}He ions to 130 MeV, and heavier ions (lithium to xenon) to the energy 147 (Q^2/A) MeV, where Q and A are the ion charge and mass (in atomic units). Some applications and contributions of the research institute go beyond physics to energy, medical science, biology, and other disciplines.

The Nuclear Science Center began operating in January 1962. It provides radioisotopes, irradiation services, and research facilities for TAMU, as well as for more than sixty other universities, medical research laboratories, government agencies, and industrial organizations. Isotopes for treatment of carcinoma are provided to hospitals on a continuous basis. The reactor core consists of highly enriched uranium-zirconium-hydride fuel elements positioned in a 33-foot-deep pool and has a maximum steady-state power output of one megawatt. In addition to providing isotopes, conducting neutron activation analyses, uranium analyses, and neutron radiography, the center provides industrial training courses and, of course, academic laboratory assistance.

Ron Hart at TAMU in cooperation with Hughes Research Laboratory, Malibu, California, is conducting research using neutron transmutation of the host atoms of semiconductor substrate materials—silicon, mercury-cadmium-telluride, and gallium arsenide wafers. Doping is obtained with phosphorus in the case of a silicon substrate, or with the next higher Z element in the periodic table in the case of other substrates. This innovative research in nuclear engineering indicates that high quality, uniform doping can be obtained.[24]

In 1972 engineers at UT–Austin took note that fusion researchers needed a less expensive, less bulky means to replace capacitors in supplying high-energy bursts of electricity to drive experiments. A research program on the subject started in 1972 under the leadership of H. Grady Rylander, Herbert H. Woodson, and William F. Weldon led to the construction of a pulsed power machine. The Energy Storage Group (renamed in 1977 as the Center for Electromechanics) designed and built a series of improved homopolar generators. The first was a 0.5-megajoule prototype, the second an advanced 5.0-megajoule unit that proved the most reliable homopolar generator of its time. It was later upgraded to 10-megajoule, and a 6-megajoule compact pulsed homopolar generator weighing only 3,400 pounds was also built. The compact unit was developed principally by the electrical engineer John Gully at UT–Austin.[25]

By 1978 the group had designed and patented a different type of pulsed-power machine, the compulsated pulsed alternator—"compulsator" for short. Weldon, Woodson, and Mircea D. Driga were its principal inventors.

The compulsator was built and first tested in 1979, and is now recognized as the first fundamentally new type of rotating electrical machine to be invented in the twentieth century. It uniquely combines a rotating flux compressor and a conventional alternator.

The compulsator and the homopolar generator are similar in that they each store energy and then discharge it in a huge split-second burst of electricity. The compulsator is capable of discharging multiple bursts of electricity.

None of the pulsed-power machines at UT–Austin has been applied in fusion research thus far. The compact pulsed homopolar generator was licensed in 1983 by the university to Parker Kinetic Designs, Inc., for commercial manufacture. The unit can resistance-weld two pipes in one tenth of a second, as opposed to the full hour or so needed using conventional arc welding applications.

Pulsed power has other promising future applications: improving magnetic recording tape, launching materials into space, spraying metal powders, heating metals to forging temperatures, and powering "Star-Wars"-type electric guns and laser weapons.

TTU has made considerable research progress in pulsed power technology since 1979.[26] Pulsed power technology is relevant to defense projects, to the successful development of magnetic and inertial confinement fusion reactors, and to laser systems used for isotope separation. A particularly difficult aspect of providing high power over a short time involves switching of the pulsed power at a high repetition rate and at high power and current over a long period of time. One project is aimed at a better understanding of the physics of conventional pulsed power switches so that engineering design equations can be formulated. A second project is aimed at improving control of these switches. A third project examines various novel approaches to high-power switching. One novel switching concept is to use electron beams and lasers to both close and open gas switches. To make these gas switches meet the requirements for a given application, the processes that lead to ionizations and the behavior of the gas in an ionized state must be better understood. A major accomplishment has been the development of a new theoretical model to explain how a gas changes from an insulator to a conductor under conditions of high electric stress. The theory gives a very different view from previous explanations, and experiments are under way to confirm it. A problem is that the breakdown often occurs in much less than one millionth of a second.

Development of reliable, long-life, repetitive switches is the key issue in many pulsed power applications. If research into opening switches for inductive energy storage pays off, it will lead to the development of energy storage devices of smaller size. Among the most significant research results to date is a more complete understanding of prefire processes in spark gaps, the breakdown initiation mechanism in high-power discharges, the formulation of several novel opening switch concepts, improved understanding of arc channel development, gas flow dynamics, development of a model for spark gap breakdown, improved understanding of electrode and insulator damage phenomena, improvements in insulator flashover strength, and the development of new diagnostic techniques.

Six departments are involved in the research; numerous national conferences and workshops have been conducted for industry and the federal government. Recently, TTU was awarded a $3.75 million research contract to continue this line of research in support of the U.S. Strategic Defense Initiative.

Another approach to fusion initiation involves RF plasma heating. A "plasma" is a gas that has been ionized by heating to extreme temperatures. Research at TTU is aimed toward development of nuclear fusion. The major emphasis has been on the development of new approaches to plasma heating and on the techniques for developing continuous reactors. Investigators are studying wave absorption mechanisms when RF waves are used to heat fusion plasmas and the use of RF waves to drive DC currents in toroidal plasmas.

A small tokamak device was built to provide a

toroidal plasma, and is being used to study low frequency plasma waves. Investigators are using probes covered with boron nitride, which survive very high temperatures, to measure the wave processes deep within the plasma.

At the present time the main research emphasis is on RF current drive experiments using a concept which differs fundamentally from the approach used at the national laboratory facilities and on various fundamental RF wave phenomena in toroidal plasmas. Researchers from many foreign countries have participated in this work.

Energy from Lignite

Of the organic fuels other than petroleum and natural gas, lignite is the most abundant in this region. The vast quantities of lignite coals in Texas, from the Mexican border (near Laredo) to the Arkansas and Louisiana state lines near Shreveport, are expected to be Texas' next major energy resource. Estimates of these resources, principally by the Bureau of Economic Geology at UT–Austin, have ranged from fifty billion tons surface-minable lignite at depths of 200 feet to 100 billion tons of deep-basin lignite. The lignite lies in two principal belts: in the Wilcox geologic formation and in the Jackson-Yegua formation. There are presently seven major electric generating plants operating on lignite—two in the Jackson-Yegua and five in the Wilcox. The net power produced by these plants totals 7,645 megawatts.[27]

Lignite found early use as a fuel in the power plants of TAMU and UT–Austin for producing steam and hot water as early as the 1910s and electric power in the 1920s. Lignite was mined at Rockdale, Texas, and transported by train to the power plant at TAMU in College Station until about 1936, when it was phased out in favor of natural gas with oil as a back-up fuel. At UT–Austin lignite continued to be used until the early 1950s.

At about the same time, the Texas Power and Light Company was busy building a power plant called Trinidad in Henderson County to use lignite as its fuel.[28] This decision was apparently based on unstable oil prices and costs associated with delivery and use of then distant gas supplies. In 1926 two units, each producing 20,000 kilowatts, at Trinidad went on line. In 1931 a third generating unit was added. But in the late 1930s natural gas was discovered in a nearby field and was offered at very low prices. Trinidad's fuel was converted to natural gas, and the lignite mine at Malakoff, Texas was closed in 1942.

The lignite mine at Rockdale, however, was reopened in the mid 1950s to provide the fuel for a large power plant that would meet the needs of the Aluminum Company of America (Alcoa) for the production of high-grade aluminum. The Sandow mine continues to meet the fuel needs for the Texas Power & Light Company and Alcoa today—some thirty years after its reopening.

During the early days of the Rockdale generating plant, problems involving combustion, control, and utilization of fly-ash were usually analyzed by faculty at UT–Austin and TAMU on an informal basis.

In 1972 the Texas Utilities Company began operating the first of a number of multi-megawatt modern lignite plants. The first of these plants was located at Fairfield, Texas.

In 1980 the Texas Utilities Company mined its 100 millionth ton of lignite. Since then, 38.5 million tons were mined by Texas utility companies and three other operators in 1983 alone. Projections are that quantities mined for electric power will continue to increase as additional power plants are brought on line. A second expected use of lignite is as a feedstock for the petrochemical industries of Texas and Louisiana. To date, efforts to upgrade the energy value of lignite economically and to remove sulfur to prevent air quality problems have been unsuccessful and remain challenges for future research. Briquetting of Texas lignites has also not been successful so far.

Lignite Research

Lignite research at UT–Austin has been conducted principally by the Bureau of Economic Geology. Headed by William L. Fisher since 1970, the Bureau has a long history of assessing the geology of the state and its geological resources. Established in July 1909, it has shown particular interest in assessing oil, gas, coal, lignite, uranium, hard minerals, and water resources. The first report of estimated lignite reserves was published in 1955.[29] In the 1960s regional lignite inventories were made in east and south Texas for a state atlas.[30] The atlas included available data on resources, chemistry, mining, and utilization of the mineral.

Since the publication of the first estimate of state lignite resources, the Bureau has expanded its program to include coring of the Wilcox and Jackson-Yegua formations, and is using these data and data made available by lignite leaseholders to refine its estimates. Modern statistical methods, depositional models, and reliability assessment techniques are being used to further refine estimates. Research currently is being expanded to include groundwater hydrology associated with lignite deposits and a characterization data base for the mineral. The Bureau currently estimates that production will climb to at least fifty million tons in 1990, and will possibly reach 100 million tons in the year 2000. These estimates are based on the results of extraction using the current method of mining shallow deposits. Recently Thomas Edgar, a chemical engineer at UT–Austin, has been studying the possibility of in-situ gasification of lignite.

Lignite research at TAMU has been extensive and it has been given a high research priority, since lignite is expected to be Texas' next major energy resource. Petrochemical industries in the state support this conclusion and have leased the majority of the higher quality surface minable deposits in Texas as well as some of the deep basin reserves. Lignite is expected to be used principally for the generation of electricity. However, if beneficiation is developed and it proves to be economical, it will also be used for cogeneration and as a petrochemical feedstock. Lignite-related research[31] at TAMU's Center for Energy and Mineral Resources (CEMR) involves:

• Gasification and Liquefaction. Several projects attempt to convert Texas lignite into a gas or into a liquid, such as gasoline, diesel, solvents, and chemical feedstocks. A low-Btu gas, which can be rather easily obtained from lignite, can be used as boiler fuel for turbines and diesel engines. A range of liquid hydrocarbons can be obtained by combining carbon monoxide and hydrogen, obtained from water, with coal over a catalyst. Efforts to improve this process have been undertaken by CEMR-supported researchers who are working to develop better catalysts with a higher specificity and a longer lifetime.[32]

• In-Situ Gasification. A major project of the Petroleum Engineering department involved a demonstration of in-situ gasification of deeper lignite deposits. Initially, gasification was attempted using a five-foot lignite stratum located under the campus of TAMU. A much larger demonstration was conducted at Rockdale, Texas, using land owned by Alcoa (see fig. 2). The latter project involved a twelve-foot stratum of Wilcox lignite. The project successfully demonstrated that low-Btu gas could be produced from a successive series of wells drilled into the lignite, using air as the source of oxygen for the in-situ lignite combustion. A number of production problems involving the formation of water, heat effects on piping, and control of combustion were demonstrated.[33] The project, concluded in 1982, was supported financially by six major

Figure 2. The In-Situ Lignite Gasification Project located on ALCOA property at Rockdale, Texas.

energy companies and with services and equipment by two additional companies.

Texas Utilities, using proprietary Russian technologies, conducted two demonstrations of in-situ lignite combustion to produce low Btu gases for power plant use in the same time period as the TAMU demonstration.[34] A further demonstration of procedures used by Texas utilities is currently planned to be conducted near Lexington, Texas, by Basic Resources, Inc., of Dallas, Texas.

• Characterization of Lignite. Lignite consists mainly of carbon, hydrogen, and oxygen, but like all coals it also contains many other elements, such as uranium, arsenic, selenium, and vanadium in minor amounts. Some of the elements might be valuable by-products, others are pollutants and poisons for the catalysts required in the upgrading of lignite-derived liquids and gases. Work is now in progress to determine trace element compounds in lignite deposits with special emphasis on deep-basin lignite.

• Lignite-Related Environmental Issues. Surface mining of lignite disturbs land, changes aquifers, and sets in motion particulate matter and soluble compounds. CEMR investigators are studying the effect of mining on groundwater quality, soil fertility, pollution of creeks and streams from runoff, and methods for successful reclamation of strip-mined land.

Lignite-related research at TTU has involved coal beneficiation, coal slurry pipelines, coal gasification and liquefaction, and analysis of mineral matter in coals. Most of this research is recent, beginning in the late 1970s and continuing into the 1980s. In most projects the fundamental mechanisms are the subject of such research.

UH–University Park has also been involved in research related to combustion of lignites and gasification of chars associated with the combustion. Neal R. Amundson and Stratis V. Sotirchos are the principal investigators.[35]

Energy From Biomass

Research concerning energy from biomass naturally has a high priority at TAMU and at TTU, principally because of the impacts of agriculture on the Texas economy and the adverse impacts of energy shortages and/or high costs on agriculture-related industries throughout this vast state.[36]

Biomass, a word coined in recent decades, is defined as all organic matter except fossil fuels: that is, all crop and forest materials, animal products, microbial cell mass, residues, and by-products that are renewable on a year-to-year basis. Biomass serves as food, feed, fiber, bedding, structural material, soil organic matter, and fuel. The entire food system in the U.S.—including production, processing, transportation, marketing, and final preparation—consumes about sixteen percent of the nation's total energy use, with about three percent used in production agriculture. Hence, extensive research and development programs have been undertaken during the past decade to improve energy use efficiency and develop alternate energy resources. Agricultural residues and waste products, by-products of forest utilization, and municipal solid wastes have the potential to serve as solid fuels and as precursors of liquid fuels. Cellulose, the most abundant organic compound on earth, is a very desirable feedstock for alcohol production. The following five topics summarize biomass research in the various parts of the TAMU system:

• Anaerobic Digestion of Manure and Biomass. Manure can be easily converted to biogas consisting of 60 to 65 percent methane and 35 to 40 percent carbon dioxide. A digester thermally controlled by solar collectors is operating as a demonstration unit at Tarleton State University. The system is now being refined and changed to a two-stage system for digestion of rice hulls, stover, and grass. An active project at TAMU involves the conversion of genetically altered high-energy sweet sorghum to methane gas.

• Thermal Biomass Conversion Processes. Thermal units capable of gasifying, combusting, and pyrolyzing biomass have been constructed and are operating at the TAMU campus. In one project, a fluidized-bed gasifier, fed by cotton gin trash, is coupled to a steam generator, which could supply all the energy needed

Figure 3. The Biomass Gasification plant at Texas A&M University.

by a cotton gin (see fig. 3). In another project, pyrolysis liquids are treated with hydrogen to produce a diesel-like fuel, which is now being tested in engines.[37]

• Alcohols as Fuels. Ethanol and methanol are attractive alternatives to current liquid fuels. A research and demonstration plant for small-scale ethanol production is operating on the TAMU campus to test various heat sources used in the distillation process, the performance of the equipment, and the uses for by-products. Sweet sorghum and hydrolyzed cellulose are yet to be tested as sugar sources. A dual-fuel system for alcohol-gasoline fueled vehicles has been developed and road-tested over thousands of miles and now is being refined. In addition, ethanol is being tested as a fuel for diesel engines, and for natural gas-fueled irrigation pump engines.[38]

• Ethanol from Wood and Other Feedstocks. Ethanol production from agricultural food products, such as corn and sugar cane, competes with the human food and animal feed market. Cellulose, a constituent of wood and a polymer formed from fermentable glucose, would be the ideal feedstock for ethanol production. However, cellulose is not fermentable unless it is changed to glucose. Attempts are being made at TAMU to make cellulose more accessible to conversion to glucose by the chemical treatment of wood and by extrusion pretreatment of cellulose.[39]

• Oils from Agricultural Plants and Animal Fats. These have been considered as possible substitutes for diesel fuels for many years. Vegetable oils, in fact, were first tested in the late 1800s by Rudolph Diesel. During and following the two World Wars, there was considerable research especially in Germany to find substitute diesel fuels, and this interest was revived with the OPEC oil embargo. Extensive research at

TAMU in the late 1970s and early 1980s on the history of "ersatz" fuels helped to improve the extraction and purification processes. Engine tests with refined oils indicated improved performance of plant oils as alternative fuels. However, tests concluded that none of these fuels should be used commercially unless the engines are warranted by the manufacturer for use with that fuel.[40]

Biomass-related energy research at TTU was greatly expanded in the 1970s. Research there focused on: conversion of cattle feedlot manures to petrochemical feedstocks and anhydrous ammonia, modeling of fixed-bed biomass gasifiers, alcohol production, and a joint project with TAMU regarding semi-arid native woody biomass crops.[41]

Biomass energy research at UH–University Park has been limited to a project to evaluate the growth and cultural conditions of the Chinese tallow tree, *Sapium sebiferum*. This "trash" tree was selected for intensive study since it is relatively fast growing, particularly in the Gulf Coast region of Texas, and because, in addition to producing woody biomass, it also produces an oilseed which could be the source of a useful oil. Growth of the Chinese tallow was begun in 1973 in experimental plots and was studied over a six-year period by Joe Cowles and H. W. Scheld.[42]

The economic feasibility of producing energy from biomass has yet to be demonstrated on a large scale basis. There are, however, examples of locally developed energy from biomass applications in the timber industries, in alcohol production, and there is current interest in producing electrical power from agricultural residues. In addition, anaerobic digesters are serving a useful purpose for heating and for food preparation in less-developed countries. They may find economical applications in domestic poultry and swine industries and for methane gas production, using sweet sorghum, for the gas industry.

Geopressured-Geothermal Energy

In the 1950s, the oil and gas industry along the Texas and Louisiana Gulf Coast became aware of an unwanted and expensive nuisance: highly pressurized geothermal zones that lay deep underground. When a drill bit punched into a 15,000-psi, geopressured-geothermal formation, catastrophe often raced up the drillstem—a blowout.

The industry learned it was wise to avoid geopressured zones until the blowout problem was surmounted. In the early 1970s others, including geologists and engineers, began to think of geopressured

formations in a new light: as a potential energy resource.

In 1975 UT–Austin began a research program investigating the energy potential of geopressured-geothermal energy, a program that is still in progress. The Bureau of Economic Geology at the university worked jointly with the Center for Energy Studies, particularly in defining regions with the highest potential for maximum benefits.

The Bureau of Economic Geology's initial assessment of hydrothermal and geopressured-geothermal energy in Texas focused on resource characteristics (aquifer depth and thickness, thermal and pressure gradients) that could be derived or inferred from electric logs, subsurface maps, and public records. After locating suitable exploration sites, research topics included water composition, lateral continuity and hydraulic conductivity (or permeability) of the aquifers, and diagenetic histories of the rocks that determine reservoir quality and help explain the origins of interstitial fluids.

Hydrothermal resources occur along major tectonic zones such as the Rio Grande Rift in Trans-Pecos and the Balcones-Ouachita structural trend in central Texas. Although ground waters are hotter (up to 70° C) in the former area, the latter area has more people and greater potential for economical utilization. School buildings and a hospital in central Texas are currently being heated by warm water produced from shallow (1,500 m) wells.

Deep geopressured sediments in the Gulf Coast Basin contain vast quantities of geothermal energy, but as shown by a deep (5,000 m) well in Brazoria County, drilling and production costs prohibit large-scale development of the resource. Hot (150° C) overpressured brines were originally located for potential electric power generation. Later, heat conversion inefficiencies and increased gas prices resulted in a greater interest in the solution methane and traces of liquid hydrocarbons recovered from the brines.

Researchers tackled the problems of characterizing the resource and pinpointing the best sites for test wells. They created behavior simulations of a geopressured-geothermal reservoir as it is produced. Several studies were done of above-ground systems for converting heat, pressure, and methane to useful energy, as well as studies of possible economic and regulatory incentives that would stimulate industries to venture into geopressured-geothermal production efforts. The groups at UT–Austin estimated that the geopressured formations contain natural gas equal in amount to a ten-year supply for the entire U.S.

Ten wells have been tested in Texas and Louisiana,

and UT–Austin researchers have analyzed the results, which have been mixed. The resource appears to be economical to produce, with natural gas prices of $2 to $6 per thousand cubic feet at the wellhead if capital investment and operating expences are kept at a minimum.

This program, led to date by Myron Dorfman, Don Bebout, and Robert A. Morton, has been carried out jointly by the UT–Austin Center for Energy Studies and the Bureau of Economic Geology, and has been funded by the U.S. Department of Energy and five Texas utility companies[43] (fig. 4).

Petroleum engineers at TAMU were not involved in the U.S. Department of Energy program at UT–Austin but previously had analyzed permeabilities associated with wells which were drilled into geopressured formations in south Texas. Because of the low permeabilities existing in a number of wells where data were available, Joe Esoba, of TAMU, in a cooperative project

Figure 4. The Pleasant Bayou No. 1 geopressured-geothermal well.

with Southwest Research Institute at San Antonio, concluded that flow rates from overpressured wells would be too low to make recovery of gas from these formations profitable.[44]

Solar Energy and Energy Conservation

Each of the four universities contributing to this chapter has conducted research involving solar energy and conservation. However, each of them concentrated their efforts on separate applications.

At UH–University Park major efforts were applied in the area of solar radiation to produce electric power from steam. In 1969 researchers there led by Alvin Hildebrandt and Lorin Vant-Hull began to develop a new approach for use of the solar resources. Their concept involved a solar tower or central receiver using a field of large steerable mirrors to reflect and concentrate many megawatts of direct beams of sunlight to an elevated central point. A tower-mounted receiver large enough to catch the reflected beams converts the sunlight to heat energy. The solar tower system simulates a large-scale parabola with the receiver atop the "power tower" at a focal point. A heat transfer fluid pumped through the receiver collects this heat and brings it to the ground. Here it may be used to power a steam generator, it may be stored for use during cloudy periods or at night, or it may be used as process heat. An important aspect of the original concept was that the operation of such a large-scale solar facility by public utility companies would make the benefits of solar energy taken from desert areas available to everyone on the electrical grid. The design of the heliostat mirrors spread throughout the field and the problem of adequate storage were first research priorities.

In 1973 the National Science Foundation (NSF) funded a UH–University Park solar power proposal under the Research Applied to National Needs program. The principals involved were well equipped to analyze the optical system and to carry out overall plant design but recruited McDonnell Douglas Astronautics Corporation (MDAC) to carry out component design, costing analysis, and detailed system design. In the initial two-year study extensive computer codes were developed to analyze the optics and interaction of a multitude of closely spaced heliostats (shadows move and contort as the heliostats rotate to reflect the moving sun onto the receiver throughout the day and year). Computer models were developed to evaluate the instantaneous direct beam insolation, the amount of heliostat sun shading and receiver blocking, and the intensity distribution on the receiver caused by one or a multiplicity of mirrors. In addition a 12 m² heliostat was designed, built, and tested in the California desert. Several receiver designs, working fluids, and storage concepts were evaluated by the contractor (MDAC) and their subcontractor (Rocketdyne). The result of all these studies was sufficiently favorable that NSF decided that the central receiver concept was a leading contender for large-scale solar applications (over parabolic dishes, parabolic troughs, and hemispheric bowls). In the ensuing competition for pilot plant design (1975–77) the UH–University Park/MDAC/Rocketdyne team (now headed by MDAC) produced the preferred design.[45]

By 1978, the UH–University Park Energy Laboratory team had developed extensive capabilities to design and optimize heliostat fields and to compute receiver power levels and flux distributions. These codes were used extensively in the final design of Solar One, the 10 MW electrical pilot plant constructed near Barstow, California, in 1980–81 (fig. 5). During a two-year start up and test phase, Solar One achieved all of its significant goals. Since August 1984, it has been operated by Southern California Edison as a regular component of its electrical grid.

UH–University Park has conducted numerous supporting studies of the solar tower, or solar power tower, for the U.S. Department of Energy, and it is continuing this research under a program entitled Solar Thermal Research Center. Research has involved use of alternate fluids (rather than steam), energy storage including thermal and chemical storage, heat pipes, alternate reflecting surfaces, and material studies for the collector, to name a few. Research reports are on file.[46]

Solar thermal research at UH–University Park has had considerable success in developing the solar tower or power tower concept. Four utility companies have

Figure 5. The solar power tower—Solar One—a 10 MW solar central receiver pilot plant located 10 miles east of Barstow, California. The center of the illuminated receiver is 260 feet above the ground, and there are 1,818 heliostats, each 430 ft². Photo credit: Southern California Edison.

requested that this power source be fully developed for future commercial application. The present oil glut, level economy, and regulations have all resulted in no extensive new capacity requirements in the utility area. Thus the present research is directed to meet the needs of the 1990s and beyond.

A considerable effort by UH–University Park was also put into energy conservation promotion for the petrochemical industry. This involved workshops with groups of industry and academic participants. Conservation is generally good business for industry and has resulted in greatly improved combustion efficiencies, greater use of cogeneration, and greatly improved process efficiencies. All these have contributed to a reduction in the energy required to produce a ton of product. On an average, the reduction has been approximately 30 percent over 1972 levels. Industry is now willing to insert more capital into a plant to make it more efficient.

Solar energy has not been extensively studied at TAMU. Early research involved water heating using floating deck heaters with heat absorption surfaces. These were installed on the roof of the Zachry Engineering Center by William Harris and Richard R. Davison, but were later abandoned because of plumbing leaks and a conclusion that economics could not justify this type of heater. Short-duration projects involved a comparison of commercially available solar collectors and the use of solar heaters for drying rice prior to storage. The current solar research of C. F. Kettleborough involves the modeling of solar air conditioners that would use either liquid or solid desiccants.

Storage of energy in underground aquifers in the form of thermally heated or refrigerated water was demonstrated by Donald Reddell, Richard R. Davison, and William B. Harris at TAMU. Under certain conditions aquifer storage of heated water—for example, from solar heaters or from industrial sources—can provide district heating of homes or commercial buildings during winter heating periods. Conversely, chilled water stored during winters can provide cooling during summer periods. The demonstration conducted on the TAMU campus stored winter-chilled water in an aquifer at a depth of fifty-five feet.

Conservation studies at TAMU have been extensive. Energy efficiency in large buildings, industries, fast food restaurants, and residences has been extensively modeled to show methods for load-leveling, proper siting of buildings, use of construction materials, effects of landscaping, and the use of computers to analyze proposed construction and to manage energy use. Part of the Center for Energy and Mineral Re-

sources' program has included the dissemination of conservation information to the public and to industries. The Energy Advisory Service for Texas (EAST) was the initial program (1976) for the U.S. Department of Energy; it was concerned with developing an energy extension program using existing institutions to disseminate energy conservation information to schools, hospitals, industries, and the public.

The Department of Energy then began a ten-state pilot Energy Extension Service (EES) program, and the Center administered the program for Texas. Participants in the Texas Energy Extension Service included UH–University Park, UT–San Antonio, UT–Arlington, UT–El Paso, TAMU, and the Texas Agricultural Extension Service (in the Lubbock area). The management of the program was transferred to the office of the governor about January 1, 1980, and now resides in the Energy Efficiency Division of the Texas Public Utility Commission. The TAMU center provides technical and publication support and operates an energy hotline for the Public Utility Commission. The Texas Engineering Extension Service operates energy audit offices in Arlington, Houston, and San Antonio, and the Texas Agricultural Extension Service provides conservation services in Lubbock as part of the Texas Energy Extension Program.

Gary C. Vliet from UT–Austin designed, built, and tested one of the first multifamily solar heating and cooling demonstration facilities in the country. The project, carried out from 1976 to 1979, was a retrofit of the Gateway married-student apartments in West Austin.[47] A hybrid solar desiccant-adsorption air conditioner, invented by John R. Howell at UT–Austin and graduate student Patrick Peng, was patented in 1981. In conservation, Jerold W. Jones led the development of the state's Home Energy Analysis Training (HEAT) Program in the late 1970s.[48] The HEAT materials were used in training many of the first utility-sponsored home energy auditors in Texas and several other states. All these projects were carried out through the Center for Energy Studies at the university.

The largest spherical surfaced solar collector ever built (a 65-foot bowl) and the first solar-thermal system to generate electricity was built at Crosbyton, Texas, by TTU in the late 1970s (fig. 6). The concept employs a huge fixed mirror to focus incident solar energy onto a tracking linear receiver. Under this intense heat, water pumped through the receiver's helically-wound boiler tubes is converted to superheated steam at 1,000°F and 1,000 psi.

In operation since January 1980, the system has been tested at various temperatures, pressure settings,

Figure 6. The Crosbyton solar collector.

and tracking modes under varying conditions and control schemes. It has proved to be very reliable under field test conditions, consistently producing steam for many days.

Performance data are in agreement with design predictions from a detailed computer model, and the boiler has performed better than anticipated. Output-performance predictions have been made for a 200-foot diameter collector. These predictions, along with costs estimated from engineering drawings, indicate that the solar bowl concept is cost-competitive with the other solar thermal concepts being investigated by the Department of Energy. A 5MW solar thermal electric power plant has been designed with ten 200-foot collectors that will meet about 28 percent of the annual electrical power demand in the city of Crosbyton. An interim goal is to construct a peaking power plant coupled with four 200-foot diameter solar bowls which can support irrigation and the ginning of cotton.[49]

Current research efforts are directed toward a new boiler design, mirror panel development, an automatic mirror cleaning system, lightweight mirror panel support structure, and advanced control algorithms. The new boiler design focus is on the use of oil as a heat transfer medium (water/steam has been used). Companion solar energy research has involved studies of improved collector materials, construction designed to withstand damage from hail and windborne projectiles, irrigation systems involving solar photovoltaics, and fundamental studies of other photo-conversion mechanisms. John D. Ruchert was the project director until 1982 and E. A. O'Hair is the current director. At any one time ten to twelve faculty and twenty to thirty students are working on solar bowl research.

Energy conservation activities have involved architectural design, earth-sheltered buildings, solar greenhouses, and computer modeling of the fundamentals of thermal factors in building siting and materials.

The practical aspects of wind energy generation and the integration of the electrical power generated into the local power system are being evaluated by Tarleton State University using a wind generator. Jimmy McCoy is the principal investigator of the project.[50] Information on additional wind energy research in Texas can be obtained from WTSU.

Energy from Hydrogen Oxidation

Hydrogen is a clean-burning, nonpolluting element that is part of water and of all hydrocarbon fuels; it is important to our space program; it can be used efficiently in fuel cells; and it is a major component of essential fertilizers and many of our industrial products. The only product of pure hydrogen combustion is water.

The Hydrogen Research Center at TAMU, under the leadership of John O. Bockris, was established on July 1, 1983, by a grant from the National Science Foundation and with the participation of industry. The research at the center dates from 1978, when experiments with solid state devices were begun using sunlight to produce hydrogen from water. Research has advanced to include catalysis and surface effects of various elements on hydrogen production, not only from water but also directly from coals. Considerable improvement in the efficiency of energy use in the production of hydrogen has been shown by research on the photoelectrochemical kinetics of various electrodes.

This energy resource has the potential of meeting a large portion of our energy needs because it can be produced using many low-level sources of power (energy). In addition, energy storage using hydrogen has many possibilities.[51]

The universities in Texas have been actively involved in energy-related research to help develop alternate energy technologies to supplement oil and gas resources and to educate their graduates in these technologies. The economic health of the state to date has been largely based on oil and gas resources and on its related industries; its future will lie in the scientific and technological development of its alternate resources.

Notes

1. Stobaugh and Yergin, 1979.
2. State of Texas, H.B. 20, 1985.
3. Ibid.
4. *Energy Projects*, 1985–1986.
5. Hildebrandt et al.
6. *Annual Reports*, 1979–1984.
7. State of Texas, H.B. 20, 1985.
8. Patton, 1970.
9. Patton et al., 1979.
10. Flawn and Anderson, 1955.
11. Galloway and Kaiser, 1980.
12. Henry and Kapadia, 1980.
13. Galloway et al., 1982.
14. Galloway, 1982.
15. Henry and Walton, 1978.
16. Ledger et al., 1984; Bomber et al., 1986.
17. *Fusion Research*, 1985.
18. O and Schuessler, 1981.
19. Ford et al., 1981.
20. Ibid.
21. Fry and Voss, 1984.
22. Church and Holzscheiter, 1982.
23. Webb, 1984.
24. Hart et al., 1979.
25. *Center for Electro Mechanics*, 1985.
26. *Annual Reports*, 1979–1984.
27. Kaiser, 1985.
28. *Lignite*, 1980.
29. Perkins and Lonsdale, 1985.
30. Maxwell, 1962; Fisher, 1963.
31. State of Texas, H.B. 20, 1985.
32. Ibid.; Clark, 1979.
33. Jennings et al., 1977; Jennings, 1980; Russell et al., 1985.
34. Grant and Fermbacher, 1979.
35. Sotirchos and Amundson, 1984.
36. State of Texas, H.B. 20, 1985; Hiler and Stout, 1985; Stout, 1979.
37. Hiler and Stout, 1985.
38. Ibid.
39. Ibid.
40. Ibid.
41. *Annual Reports*, 1979–1984.
42. Scheld et al., 1984.
43. Dorfman, 1982.

44. Osoba et al., 1976.
45. Hildebrandt et al.; *Annual Reports*, 1982–1983.
46. Hildebrandt and Vant-Hull, 1977; *Annual Reports*, 1982–1983.
47. Vliet, 1977.
48. Broughton, Jones, et al., 1980.
49. *Annual Reports*, 1979–1984.
50. *Energy Projects*, 1985–1986.
51. Bockris, 1980.

Bibliography

Annual Reports, 1979–1984, Center for Energy Research, Texas Tech University, Lubbock, Texas.

Annual Reports, 1982 and 1983, Contract No. DE-ACO3-81SF 11557; 1984, Solar Energy Research Contract No. XX-4-04006-7. UH–University Park, Solar Thermal Advanced Research Center. Available from NTIS.

Bockris, J. O. *Energy Options—Real Economics and the Solar-Hydrogen System.* Australia & New Zealand Book Co., 1980.

Bomber, B. J., E. B. Ledger, and T. T. Tieh. "Ore Petrography of a Sedimentary Uranium Deposit, Live Oak County, Texas." *Economic Geology*, 81 (1986), pp. 131–42.

Broughton, J. A., J. W. Jones, et al. *Home Energy Analysis Training Program for Existing Residences.* Texas Energy and Natural Resources Advisory Council, 1980.

Center for Electro Mechanics–History, Center for Electro Mechanics, UT–Austin, 1985.

Church, D. A., and H. M. Holzscheiter. "Charge Transfer from Atomic Hydrogen to O^{+2} and O^{+3} Ions with Electronvolt Energy." *Physical Review Letters*, 49 (1982), 643–46.

Clark, R. A., Jr. *A Study of Pyrolysis of Texas Lignites.* M.S. thesis, TAMU, 1979.

Dorfman, M. H. "The Outlook for Geopressured-Geothermal Energy and Associated Natural Gas." *Journal of Petroleum Technology*, 1982, pp. 1915–19.

Energy Bibliography & Index, Vols. I–V. Houston: Gulf Publishing Co. This source provides easy access to all energy-related publications held by the TAMU libraries.

Energy Projects Funded 1985–86, Center for Energy and Mineral Resources. College Station Texas: Texas A&M University, 1985.

Fisher, W. L. *Lignites of the Texas Coastal Plains.*

UT–Austin: Bureau of Economic Geology, Report of Investigation No. 50, 1963.

Flawn, P. P. and G. H. Anderson. *Prospectives for Uranium in Texas.* UT–Austin: Bureau of Economic Geology, Resources Circular No. 37, 1955.

Ford, A. L., J. F. Reading, and R. L. Becker. "Inter-shell Capture and Ionization in Collisions of He^+, HE^{2+}, and Li^{3+} Projectiles with Neon and Carbon." *Physical Review*, 23A (1981), 510–78.

Fry, E. S. and K. J. Voss. "Mueller Matrix Measurements of Ocean Waters." *Proceedings of SPEI—The International Society for Optical Engineering.* Vol. 489 (1984), Ocean Optics VII, pp. 127–29.

Fusion Research, The University of Texas at Austin. UT–Austin: Fusion Research Center, 1985.

Galloway, W. E. *Epigenetic Zonation and Fluid Flow History of Uranium-bearing Fluvial Aquifer Systems, South Texas Uranium Province.* UT–Austin: Bureau of Economic Geology, Report of Investigation No. 119, 1982.

Galloway, W. E. and W. R. Kaiser. *Catahoula Formation of The Texas Coastal Plain: Origin, Geochemical Evolution, and Characteristics of Uranium Deposits.* UT–Austin: Bureau of Economic Geology, Report of Investigation No. 100, 1980.

Galloway, W. E., C. D. Henry, and G. E. Smith. *Depositional Framework, Hydrostratigraphy, and Uranium Mineralization of the Oakville Sandstone (Miocene), Texas Coastal Plain.* UT–Austin: Bureau of Economic Geology, Report of Investigation No. 113, 1982.

Grant, J. F. and J. M. Fermbacher. "Tennessee Colony Steam-Oxygen In-Situ Gasification Test." *Proceedings of the Fifth Underground Coal Conversion Symposium.* Alexandria, Va.: Department of Energy, 1979.

Hart, R. R., et al. "Measurements of ^{31}P Concentrations Produced by Neutron Transmutation Doping of Silicon." In Meese, John M., ed. *Neutron Transmutation Doping in Semiconductors.* New York: Plenum Press, 1979, pp. 345–54.

Henry, C. D., and R. R. Kapadia. *Trace Elements in Soils of the Texas Uranium District: Concentration, Origin, and Environmental Significance.* UT–Austin: Bureau of Economic Geology, Report of Investigation No. 101, 1980.

Henry, C. D., and A. W. Walton, eds. *Formation of Uranium Ores by Diagenesis of Volcanic Sediments.* UT–Austin: Bureau of Economic Geology, Final Report, Department of Energy Contract No. GJBX-22-79, 1978.

Hildebrandt, A. F., et al. (UH–University Park), and the McDonnell Douglas Astronautics Co. *Solar Thermal Power Systems Based on Optical Transmission.* Final Report. National Science Foundation: NSF/RANN/SE/GI-39456 FR 75/3 NTIS ACCESSION No. PB 253 167/AS.

Hildebrandt, A. F., and L. L. Vant-Hull. "Power with Heliostats." *Science,* 198 (1977), 1139–46.

Hiler, E. A., and B. A. Stout, eds. *Biomass Energy: A Monograph.* College Station: Texas A&M University Press, 1985.

Jennings, J. W. "Underground Conversion of Texas Lignite." In *Proceedings of the Lignite Symposium,* TAMU Center for Energy and Mineral Resources, 1980, pp. 12.1–12.7.

Jennings, J. W., R. T. Strictland, and W. D. Von Gonten. "Texas A&M Project Status Underground Lignite Gasification." In *Proceedings of the Third Annual Underground Coal Conversion Symposium.* Fallen Leaf Lake, Cal.: Lawrence Livermore Laboratory, Conference 770652, 1977, pp. 83–91.

Kaiser, W. R. *Texas Lignite—Status and Outlook to 2000.* UT–Austin: Bureau of Economic Geology, Mineral Resources Circular No. 76, 1985.

Ledger, E. B., T. T. Tieh, and M. W. Rowe. "An Evaluation of the Catahoula Formation as a Uranium Source Rock in East Texas." *Transactions of the Gulf Coast Geological Societies,* 1984, 99–108.

Lignite: Texas Energy for Texans, A History of the Development of Lignite Coal by the Texas Utilities Company System, Texas Utilities Company, May 7, 1980.

Maxwell, R. A. *Mineral Resources of South Texas.* UT–Austin: Bureau of Economic Geology, Report of Investigation No. 43, 1962.

O, C. S., and H. A. Schuessler. "Confinement of Ions Injected into a Radio-Frequency Quadrapole Ion Trap: Pulsed Ion Beams of Different Energies." *International Journal of Mass Spectrometry and Ion Physics,* MASSPEC-1620, 1981.

Osoba, J. S., R. K. Swanson, P. Oetking, and R. C. Hagens. "Production of Water from Geopressure–Geothermal Reservoirs in South Texas."

Proceedings of the Second Geopressure–Geothermal Energy Conference, Austin, Texas, February 23–25, 1976.

Patton, A. D. *Methods of Bulk Power System Security Assessment (Probability Approach).* Final Report. Edison Electric Institute Project No. RP 90-6, 1970.

Patton, A. D., A. K. Ayoub, C. Singh, G. Hogg, and B. L. Deuermeyer. *Large Scale System Effectiveness Analysis.* Report, Department of Energy Contract EC-77-S-01-5104, November 1979.

Perkins, J. M., and J. T. Lonsdale. *Mineral Resources of the Texas Coastal Plains.* UT–Austin: Bureau of Economic Geology, Mineral Resources Circular No. 38, 1985.

Russell, J. E., E. R. Hoskins, D. Becker, C. Forster, and Y. J. Lang. *Geotechnical Studies Related to In-Situ Lignite Gasification Trials.* Final Report. Texas A&M Research Foundation, U.S. Department of Energy Grant, No. DE-FG22-80PC30221, 1985.

Scheld, H. W., et al. "Seed of the Chinese Tallow Tree as a Source of Chemicals and Fuels." In *Fuels and Chemicals from Oilseeds.* AAAS Selected Symposium 91, 1984, pp. 81–101.

Sotirchos, S. V., and N. R. Amundson. "Dynamic Behavior of a Porous Char Particle Burning in an Oxygen Containing Environment." *AICHE Journal,* 30 (1984), Part I, p. 537; Part II, p. 549.

State of Texas, H.B. 20. *General Appropriations Bill for the 1986–1987 Biennium,* 1985.

Stobaugh, R., and D. Yergin, eds. *Energy Future.* New York: Random House, 1979.

Stout, B. A. *Energy for World Agriculture.* Rome: Food and Agriculture Organization of the United Nations, 1979.

Vliet, G. C. *Multiple Family Residential Solar Heating and Cooling Project.* U.S. Department of Housing and Urban Development, Grant No. H-2272, April 1977.

Webb, R. C. "Status of the Texas A&M GUT Monopole Search." In Stone, J. L., ed. *Monopole '83.* New York: Plenum Press, 1984, pp. 581–88.

11

Civil and Mechanical Engineering

Joseph E. King

OPPORTUNITIES AS vast and varied as the state itself awaited Texas professional engineers at the close of World War II. Ahead lay challenges to build upon the rich mineral and agricultural base that had long sustained the Texas economy, but also to meet a future of rapid urban and industrial growth. In 1950 the Census reported for the first time that a majority of Texans lived in cities and towns. The 60-percent urban residency of 1950 leaped to more than 80 percent in the 1970s, ranking Texas among the most urbanized states in the nation. During the same period of time the industrial base steadily expanded, with value added by manufacturing reaching $33 billion in 1977. These urban, industrial trends fostered major technological changes and demanded the skills and resources of civil and mechanical engineers.

In the immediate postwar period, engineers and planners recognized the preeminent importance of water management to municipal, agricultural, and industrial development. While noting in 1947 the growing number of inquiries from manufacturers who sought building sites with an adequate water supply, the State Board of Water Engineers acknowledged the heavy drain on underground water to meet current needs. The Board reported that ground water use for industrial purposes alone had nearly doubled between 1935 and 1945.[1] Limitations on this source forced a reexamination of the state's rivers and streams for additional water supply. In several parts of the state the construction of dams and reservoirs promised multiple benefits, including flood control, irrigation, water supply, drainage, and recreation.

Between 1940 and 1980 Texas acquired more than 100 reservoirs and increased its water storage capacity more than ten-fold to 53,302,400 acre-feet. The greatest activity occurred between the late 1940s and the 1960s when state, federal, and local authorities built new dams that represented important engineering feats as well as better water management. The largest projects usually involved federal agencies such as the U.S. Army Corps of Engineers and the Bureau of Reclamation. An important example of international cooperation between the United States and Mexico, through a water treaty signed in 1944, made possible the completion of the 150-foot high, over 26,000-foot long Falcon Dam on the Rio Grande below Laredo. The International Boundary and Water Commission (IBWC) completed the rolled earthfill structure in 1958, using engineers and contractors from both countries. The dam's two hydroelectric plants, each housing three Francis-type turbines that develop over 14,000 horsepower each, were interconnected between Mex-

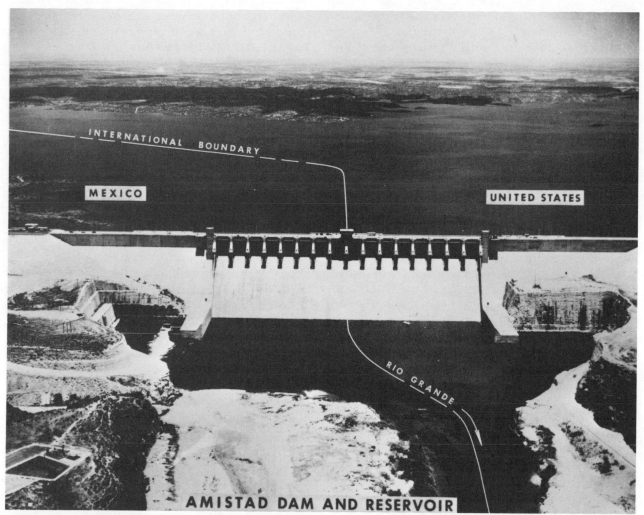

INTERNATIONAL BOUNDARY

MEXICO

UNITED STATES

RIO GRANDE

AMISTAD DAM AND RESERVOIR

Figure 1. Completed in 1969, the Amistad Dam is one of two international dams on the Rio Grande to provide flood control, water conservation, and power generation. (Photo courtesy of International Boundary and Water Commission, United States Section.)

ico and Texas. Success in this project prompted the IBWC to build a second multipurpose storage dam farther upstream.[2] The Amistad Dam (Fig. 1), built between 1964 and 1969 near Del Rio, is among the state's most impressive engineered structures. The concrete gravity dam, with its flanking earth embankments, stretches over six miles, and its hydroelectric plants can supply 323 million kilowatt-hours each year. Aside from flood control, these international dams have had an enormous impact on the economic development of the Rio Grande Valley and its communities on both sides of the river.[3]

Concerned with future needs and competing with irrigated farming for ground water from the Ogallala Aquifer, urban centers in the Panhandle–South Plains

tapped the Canadian River in the 1950s. The Bureau of Reclamation in conjunction with the Canadian River Municipal Water Authority built Sanford Dam, with a crest length of almost one and a quarter miles, creating Lake Meredith near Amarillo.[4] Bureau engineers D. L. Chappelear and Earnest L. Gloyna (later dean of engineering at the University of Texas at Austin) utilized innovative mass production techniques to lay 322 miles of pipe for the aqueduct system. Improved methods of excavating the trench and bedding the pipeline reduced costs and increased speeds; in one record day 3,200 feet of pipe were laid. Farmers, cities, and oil field developers benefited from the new Canadian River supply, but perhaps no more than water drinkers, who welcomed the end of brown tooth stain caused by the high fluoride content of the ground water.[5]

"Houston's difficulty," in the view of one of that city's historians, "was not so much in finding water, but in deciding which source to tap."[6] Yet, water management in southeast Texas posed more serious problems in the postwar years than that statement suggests. The population of Harris County exceeded one million in 1954, and Houston itself, not to speak of its suburbs, grew to more than one and one-half million people by 1980. Rapid development of the oil and petrochemical industries, which attracted many of the new residents, placed heavy demands on water supplies. With water consumption rising, planners had to confront the dual problems of destructive flooding by local rivers and streams and the almost total reliance on hundreds of artesian wells, which drained subsurface water and caused severe land subsidence in the Houston–Galveston area. The San Jacinto monument had sunk six feet between 1940 and 1964, and its reflecting pool disappeared. Houston area engineers, notably Mason Lockwood, Pliny Gale, and the Houston branch of the American Society of Civil Engineers (ASCE), alerted the public in the 1950s and 1960s to the sinking land level and helped develop some remedial measures.[7]

Ambitious programs began after World War II to provide Houston with flood control and to develop a supply of water from surface sources. From 1945 to 1946 the Galveston district of the Army Corps of Engineers constructed two of the world's largest earthfill dams west of Houston to regulate flood waters in Buffalo Bayou. Thirteen-mile long Barker Dam and twelve-mile long Addicks Dam afforded protection from catastrophic floods, such as the one which inundated two-thirds of Harris County in 1935. These new structures permitted the city to focus on water supply questions, resulting in the construction in 1953 of an Ambursen-type (slab and buttress), low concrete dam on the San Jacinto River. Engineers chose a lighter-weight dam because of the soft, sandy soil and designed a diffuser spillway that reduces erosion in overflows. During the 1960s Houston overcame opposition in Dallas and Fort Worth to tap the Trinity River for additional supplies of municipal water.[8]

Houston confronted equally serious problems in controlling water pollution. The city had been plagued since the 1890s with municipal and industrial waste flowing into its streams—particularly Buffalo Bayou, once a source of drinking water—and creating a health hazard. A 1945 study revealed that Buffalo Bayou was 80 percent sewage.[9] In 1951 the city built in east Houston an innovative sewage treatment plant, designed by the engineering firm of Freese, Nichols, and Turner and constructed by Brown & Root, another of Houston's large engineering companies. Planned to handle 200 million gallons of sewage a day, the plant took advantage of the mild climate to place many of the treatment facilities in the open air, saving on construction and operation costs.[10] The city also added a major sludge disposal plant in the early 1950s to dry sludge cake and sell the product as fertilizer to rice farmers in the region.[11] These facilities represented important progress in sanitary engineering, although, typical of rapidly expanding urban areas, Houston continued to experience water pollution.

Statewide efforts at better management of water resources included the construction of new hydroelectric plants as part of multiple-purpose projects on major rivers. Although not extensively developed in Texas due to low stream flow and an abundance of natural gas to power generators, hydroelectricity was feasible in some places. The initial project of the Brazos River Authority to develop water power on the Brazos was the construction of the Ambursen-type Possum Kingdom Dam (Morris Sheppard Dam) during the late 1930s near Mineral Wells. Its success in supplying power in high-demand periods led to the completion in 1953 of the Whitney Dam near Hillsboro by the Corps of Engineers. Whitney's powerhouse used highly efficient Francis-type waterwheels to drive its generators.[12] Buchanan Dam, completed in 1936 on the Lower Colorado in Burnet County and believed to be the world's largest multi-arch dam, became in 1950 one of the first facilities in the nation to utilize a reversible pump-turbine that allowed "pumped storage." Water is pumped back into Lake Buchanan during low demand periods in order to increase hydropower capacity at peak periods. A significant engineering advance, the pumped storage technology made hydroelectricity more flexible and economical.[13]

For other members of the state's engineering profession, the principal challenge of the postwar years was found in constructing a modern system of highways and bridges to accommodate the burgeoning number of automobiles. Motor vehicle registration in Texas rose from 1.7 million in 1945 to nearly 12 million by 1980. Continuous federal government financial aid to the states made possible an ambitious road building program that culminated in the Federal Aid Highway Act of 1956 which increased the national share of construction costs to 90 percent and launched a vast plan to construct an interstate highway system, including connecting roads into the cities. Eventually costing more than $114 billion, the Interstate program boosted the national economy and brought great benefits to the Southwest where imposing distances separated town and cities; Texas has more interstate highway mileage than any other state (3,215 miles). By 1980 the Texas Highway Department maintained over 70,000 miles of paved roads and thousands of bridges, and annually expended more than $1.5 billion on repairs and new construction. Building methods and materials steadily improved during the period, leading Texas to claim one of the finest highway systems in the nation.

Houston's boom, however, produced choking traffic jams that clogged thoroughfares in the central business district and arterial roads to the suburbs. In the late 1940s, transportation engineer Thomas Willies, formerly a Yale University professor, initiated numerous reforms, including one-way streets, that offered some relief. In 1952 the Texas Highway Department completed the Houston sector of the Gulf Freeway, a limited access highway to Galveston, which utilized a novel four-street interchange system to move traffic near the central Houston area.[14] This freeway, and other urban expressways that followed in the 1950s and 1960s, provided a temporary solution to Houston's congestion. However, each new freeway seemed in fact to invite greater use of private automobiles, meaning that roads reached peak volume during rush-hours far sooner than planners had anticipated.[15]

The Houston Ship Channel remained a barrier to north-south roadway traffic until the early 1950s when two tunnels replaced slow-moving ferry boats. Completed in 1950, the 3,000-foot long Washburn Tunnel was a recently devised, trench-type structure. The main units consisted of four welded, double steel tubes, each 385 feet long and 35 feet wide, fabricated in a Mississippi shipyard and floated 400 miles to the construction site. The units were fitted with concrete roadways and sunk, with a concrete jacket, into a trench 85 feet below the surface of the Channel.[16] Three years later the Baytown–La Porte Tunnel was completed near the Channel's outlet to Galveston Bay. Nine steel tubes, reinforced with concrete linings, formed the sunken portion of the tunnel. The New York engineering firm of Parsons, Brinckerhoff, Hall, and MacDonald designed the structure for the Texas Highway Department and the U.S. Bureau of Roads, and Houston engineers of Brown & Root constructed the sunken tube portion of the project.[17] At the time of their construction, the Washburn and Baytown tunnels employed the most modern techniques in building subaqueous tunnels and met the area's need for new roadways.

Although the Houston tunnels represented important technical achievements, they could not convey the power and wonder of the engineer's work like the construction of a major bridge. The journal *Texas Highways* captured this spirit in a "Ballad of the Bridge Designer":

There are poems of trees, of birds and bees,
There are poems of men and mice;
But to a bridge designer there's nothing finer
Than the poem he sees in a riveted splice.

· · · · · · · · · · ·

He may mildly thrill to a grassy hill
Bedecked with the flowers of May
But a graceful arch, be it May or March
Fair steals his heart away.[18]

Throughout the postwar years, Texas added striking examples of the bridge builder's art to its road network, occasionally replacing equally attractive but antiquated structures and modernizing the system to handle the rising volume of commercial and private traffic. By the mid–1960s the Texas Highway Department reportedly maintained over 19,000 bridges and was building new structures at the rate of nearly 400 a year.[19]

In one of its largest projects, the Texas Highway Department took nearly four years to complete the impressive Corpus Christi Harbor Bridge that opened in 1959. Designed by a team headed by bridge engineer Pat W. Clark, the mile-long steel, cantilever truss bridge towers 140 feet over the harbor entrance. Notable engineering features include a 400-foot long suspended steel arch in the central portion and extensive use of prestressed concrete in building the foundation. A major boost to the growth of Corpus Christi as a port city, the structure replaced an old bascule drawbridge that slowed vehicular traffic and obstructed the movement of large ships into the port.[20]

During the 1960s the Highway Department added several major bridges to its inventory. Among them, the E. H. Thornton Causeway, opened in 1961 to span Lavaca Bay between Port Lavaca and Point Comfort, ranked as the state's longest bridge (2.2 miles) and the first to be entirely prefabricated. The Houston engineering firm of Elmer C. Gardner cast 388 prestressed concrete slabs, which were then bolted into place to form the roadway. In a novel way of obtaining hydraulic fill for the job, Department engineers utilized sonar to locate suitable deposits of sand and shell.[21] In 1965 in West Texas the American Institute of Steel Construction awarded a prize for graceful design to the Devil's

River Bridge, completed in 1964 across the Amistad Reservoir near Del Rio. The steel, continuous plate girder span sits on a concrete substructure that conveys an appearance of strength and lightness.[22]

The requirements of moving increasing numbers of motor vehicles, while leaving sufficient clearance for the navigation of large oceangoing ships, particularly oil tankers, resulted in the building of huge, distinctive bridges all along the Gulf Coast from Beaumont to Brownsville, and especially over the Houston Ship Channel, during the 1970s and 1980s. Completed in 1972 as part of the East Loop, the Houston Ship Channel Bridge, described in *Texas Highways* as a "mammoth piece of engineering," became the first to span the channel and was then the biggest bridge in Texas.[23] The ten-lane structure, built on a strutted girder design, required 18 million pounds of structural steel and 14.5 million pounds of reinforced concrete. Reflecting the city's dynamic growth, a second bridge across the channel in 1982 set new records for size. The Jesse Jones Memorial Bridge (Fig. 2) on Beltway 8 was fitted with a wide and long (750 feet) main span that makes it one of the most massive concrete box girder bridges in the world. It rises nearly 200 feet above the channel. Engineers chose concrete because of its resistance to the area's humidity and to corrosion from neighboring petrochemical plants. The builders used special techniques to set the piers on soft, subsiding ground and also resorted to using ice in the concrete to avoid slumping by the mixture in the hot weather.[24] These bridge projects across the ship channel succeeded because of innovative thinking by Texas engineers who were able to adapt methods and materials to fit the task and location.

As might be expected after decades of experience in producing oil and gas, Texas had earned a reputation as a technical leader in the petroleum industry. After 1945 the state maintained this position, despite occasional economic setbacks. Oilmen steadily invested in exploration which brought into production rich, new fields in West Texas and in coastal waters, while they also extended the network of oil and gas pipelines and fostered the development of a petrochemical industry that had begun during World War II. The Houston area, with its access to raw materials and established refineries, became the center of a multibillion dollar petrochemical industry that produced synthetic rubber, butane, plastics, and other materials derived from petroleum and natural gas.[25] Great strides were also made in the transportation of oil and gas by pipeline. Old methods of laying pipe gave way to highly mechanized, assembly-line techniques that resulted in faster and more efficient construction of intrastate and interstate lines. Engineers and specially trained crews from Texas could be found across the country applying their expertise to the building of large diameter, long-distance pipelines.[26]

Texas engineers also made important contributions to the technical progress of offshore drilling. During the early 1950s, Texas and other littoral states were authorized to extend oil drilling operations into the underwater lands along their coastlines, an objective long sought after by oilmen. Thus, an active program of exploration of tidelands began.[27] Several engineering firms in the state, among them Brown & Root of Houston, designed and fabricated steel drilling platforms for use in the unprotected waters of the Gulf of Mexico. The structures had to withstand wave action, stormy seas, corrosion and high winds. What evolved is sometimes called a "Texas tower," a steel drilling platform erected on a tubular frame jacket (substructure) that is anchored to the sea floor. In 1968 Brown & Root designed a single-leg platform for use in Alaska's Cook Inlet where ice pressure threatened to crush conventional structures. As drilling moved into deeper waters, engineers employed heavier materials and new methods of construction, including welding together several sections of substructure underwater.[28] Union Oil Company achieved a milestone in 1982 when it launched the world's tallest platform, the Cerveza, on a single prefabricated jacket towed to the site about 100 miles south of Galveston.[29] Meanwhile, the Texas-based technology for offshore drilling became a major worldwide export.

Figure 2. The 1,500-foot main span of the Jesse Jones Memorial Bridge over the Houston Ship Channel places it among the longest concrete box girder bridges in the world. (Photo courtesy of the Texas Turnpike Authority.)

Pacesetting developments in the oil industry were matched by the vigorous growth of aviation-related activities. During World War II the military favored Texas for the building of training airfields because of the wide-open spaces and mild climate, and aircraft manufacturers located in the state for economic reasons. By the early 1950s Texas rated as a national leader in aircraft production with manufacturers such as General Dynamics, the Vought Corporation, and Bell Helicopter, all located in the vicinity of Dallas–Fort Worth, serving as major defense contractors. These north Texas communities came to possess exceptional technical resources, including skilled workers, trained engineers, and high-technology firms, notably Texas Instruments, which sustained the progress of the aviation and aerospace industries. Some of the world's most sophisticated combat aircraft, including Vought's A–7 Corsair and General Dynamic's F–16, have been largely engineered and assembled in Texas plants employing thousands of workers in research, development, and production.[30]

In the realm of commercial aviation, both Houston and Dallas–Fort Worth gained international repute for building large and innovative airports. Houston Intercontinental Airport, built between 1962 and 1969, was among the first designed to accommodate jet-powered airliners and to provide an automated system of "people-movers" for transporting passengers between terminals. When Dallas and Fort Worth, under federal government pressure, finally set aside their chronic rivalry over the location of a regional air terminal, they succeeded in building one of the world's largest and most impressive facilities at Grapevine, Texas, a mid-point between the cities. At its opening in 1973, Governor Dolph Briscoe proclaimed the Dallas–Fort Worth Regional Airport "one of the greatest technological achievements in the history of transportation."[31] Covering about thirty square miles, the huge airport was hailed for its innovative system-engineering to handle a high volume of passengers and jumbo jets, provide noise abatement, and leave room for future expansion. The extensiveness of the project necessitated cooperation between many Texas engineering firms and contractors, including Joe Rady and Associates, and Freese and Nichols who accepted major roles in constructing roads, bridges, and water systems at the airport.[32] Perhaps appropriately, the chairman of the airport board, former mayor of Dallas Erik Jonsson, was a mechanical engineer. One mechanism at the airport drew particular attention. A transportation system called Airtrans utilized a number of computer-controlled, rubber-tired vehicles moving along a concrete guideway to move people, luggage,

mail and supplies. Designed and built by Vought in Grand Prairie, the vehicles are fully automatic and pre-programmed to serve different routes and purposes at the sprawling facility. The large size, pioneering technology, and flexibility of Airtrans, despite lapses in reliability, have made it a principal prototype for the construction of automated ground transportation systems.[33] In an interesting counterpoint to the modernistic Airtrans, a Fort Worth department store introduced in 1963 a short-line streetcar system, using old PCC cars from Washington, D.C., to transport customers between the store and a fringe parking lot.

Houston, meanwhile, dramatically entered the space age in 1961 when the National Aeronautics and Space Administration (NASA) announced that it had selected a site on Clear Lake, southeast of the city, to build a new Manned Spacecraft Center (designated the Lyndon B. Johnson Space Center in 1973). An extraordinarily large and complex undertaking, the Center's main purpose was to test spacecraft vehicles, train astronauts, and supervise missions into outer space. Hundreds of architects and engineers, headed by the prime contractor Brown & Root, designed dozens of prefabricated buildings and laboratories and laid out a vast, interconnected system of tunnels and pipelines to support a community of scientists and technicians who played a vital role in the American space program.[34] Aside from its scientific impact, the Center gave a tremendous boost to Houston's urban and industrial growth. Aerospace firms and personnel relocated, stimulating new investment in housing and services, and federal dollars poured into the area for university research and technical programs geared to the Center. In the process of change, Houston shed its well-worn image of a boisterous cotton, cow, and oil town to don one more reflective of a modern, even futuristic, metropolis.

Between 1962 and 1965 the new image of Houston was bolstered by the construction of the Harris County Domed Stadium, popularly known as the Astrodome (Fig. 3) and variously described as the "Taj Mahal of stadia" and the "eighth wonder of the world." The idea of an air-conditioned domed stadium originated with civic leader Roy Hofheinz, president of the Houston major league baseball club and former mayor, who oversaw its building at a cost exceeding $45 million.[35] Upon completion, baseball sage Branch Rickey remarked: "The day the doors on this park open, every other park in the world will be antiquated."[36] A historic event in sports, the Astrodome brought the game of baseball inside, into an artificial environment away from the area's hot, humid weather and fierce mosquitos, and removed the fear that a tropical rainstorm

Figure 3. The complex steel work used in constructing the Houston Astrodome is an important part in its claim as the "eighth wonder of the world." (Photo courtesy of Houston Sports Association, Inc.)

might cancel the games. Ironically, the stadium achieved another first in 1976, when flooded grounds *outside* the park forced postponement of an Astros game.

Not only did the Astrodome make a significant impact on sports, it proved a major achievement in architecture and structural engineering. Designers planned a mammoth facility: 710 feet in diameter, 202 feet high, 642 feet of clear span (roughly twice the size of any other stadium), 250,000 square feet of floor space, and up to 66,000 seats for sporting events. A large and talented group of professionals, including structural engineer Walter P. Moore and the Houston firm of Lockwood, Andrews & Newnam, participated in the project and chose high-strength steel to build a lamella-type trussed roof that steelworkers considered a "geometric nightmare." A huge tension ring circles the stadium, while the complex framed dome sits on columns fitted with articulated joints which allow for movement without stressing the lower structure.[37] Furthermore, a model of the dome was wind-tested at McDonnell Aircraft Corporation in St. Louis and the structure rated to withstand hurricane winds of 165 miles per hour. Acrylic plastic, the kind developed for use in gunner domes on bombers, provided the material for thousands of skylights that let in sunlight but resisted condensation.[38]

Mechanical engineering in the Astrodome proved equally innovative. Viewing stands were mounted on rails and moved by electrical motors to create different seating arrangements for sporting events. A sophisticated computer center, nicknamed "The Brain," controlled more than 6,000 tons of cooling capacity

and automatically regulated temperature while circulating two and a half million cubic feet of air per minute; conditioned air can be projected 300 feet by powerful blowers. However, not all of the original system functioned as planned. A variety of Bermuda grass grown by the Texas A&M University Extension Service in a special greenhouse for use inside the dome had to be replaced when skylights were painted to eliminate glare on the playing field. The necessity for an artificial surface prompted Monsanto Chemical Company to produce a synthetic grass, AstroTurf, which was then zippered into place. A monument to technical ingenuity, the Astrodome became both a widely-recognized symbol of the city and a spur to experimental building methods.[39]

Houston possesses several examples of departures from traditional engineering design techniques in the construction of major buildings. The new Miller Memorial outdoor theater, designed by Walter P. Moore, Jr. and Associates and located on the same site in Hermann Park as the original structure, includes a folding plate roof framed by steel box members that span 195 feet. Basing his conclusions on an analysis of loading conditions, the engineer chose to support the structure on hollow steel balls, anchored into a concrete base and permitting freedom of revolution in all directions. Steel claws surround the balls to prevent an uplift in high winds.[40] Besides producing an attractive building, the design of the theater resulted in a larger, sheltered stage area, better acoustics, and improved visibility for amphitheater spectators.

The central business district of the Bayou City also attracted fresh approaches to construction design and methods. The city's bold skyline, shaped by 25- to 45-story conventional rigid frame office buildings, typified by the Humble building—now the Exxon building—and the Tenneco building, began to change in the late 1960s, according to Houston engineer Joe Colaco who helped bring about the new look. The demand for taller buildings was satisfied by newly-conceived skyscraper designs which replaced the rigid steel frame with a variety of structural systems that more efficiently used concrete and steel. This "menu" of designs is principally credited to Chicago engineer Fazlur Khan, who utilized a computer for a complex mathematical analysis of structural types. Khan and his associate Colaco recommended the use of belt trusses, trussed tube, and other designs as cheaper and better alternatives to rigid frame construction.[41] Houston real estate developer Gerald D. Hines, a mechanical engineer himself, brought the new style skyscrapers to the city in 1969 when he erected One Shell Plaza, the 50-story headquarters of the oil company.[42] The tallest lightweight concrete building in the world, Khan's design used a "tube-in-a-tube" structural system that resists wind forces, while permitting faster and lower cost construction. One Shell Plaza, like most high-rise buildings in the city, sits on a heavy floating concrete pad; the combination of a mat foundation and lightweight concrete structure demonstrated that taller buildings could be constructed in Houston despite the extreme depth of bedrock. Other skyscrapers followed, including the First International Bank Building and the Texas Commerce Tower, the latter having an exterior of steel columns and beams encased in concrete.[43]

Maybe the most striking example of recent additions to the Houston skyline in the early 1980s is the Transco Tower, designed by Philip Johnson and John Burgee and developed by Hines. The 64-story structure with mirrored glass siding rises almost 500 feet above any of the other buildings in the Galleria–Post Oak complex on the West Loop and is allegedly "the tallest building in the Southwest outside a central district."[44]

Structures with a special character highlighted San Antonio's 1968 world's fair; they became a permanent part of the community through efforts to revitalize the central business district. The city selected a slum area in downtown as the site for HemisFair 68, and over five years it planned the world exhibition with an added goal of urban renewal. The plan included construction of a civic center complex, diversion of the San Antonio River to the fair site, several concrete bridges, and a vaulted dome pavilion to house the Institute of Texan Cultures. These public projects in turn stimulated a considerable amount of private investment in the area. To meet the need for additional hotel rooms, San Antonio contractor H. B. Zachry Company, with consulting engineer Roy W. Gillette, built the 21-story Palacio del Rio Hotel in nine months by employing an unusual construction technique. Precast concrete modules, entirely assembled on the ground and equipped with furniture and carpeting, were lifted by a novel hoist that utilized a helicopter rotor blade to guide the 35-ton units into place. The speed and efficiency of the method permitted completion of the 496-room hotel in time for the opening of the fair.[45]

The fair's most spectacular building proved to be the 622-foot high Tower of the Americas whose design and construction as the tallest slip-formed structure in the western hemisphere exhibited considerable engineering skill. The structural engineering firm of Fieganspan and Pinnell of San Antonio created a hollow concrete stem in a complex geometric pattern that supports a 640-ton observation deck at the top. Employing an unusual technique, the engineers suspended the first through the fourth levels of the top-house from steel columns which float free from the concrete shaft.[46] The result of these efforts is a slender, soaring structure that has become a city landmark and a symbol for a rejuvenated downtown.

By giving more attention to comprehensive community and regional planning, Texas reflected national trends, which were often directed toward improving the quality of urban life, reducing air and water pollution, and showing a greater respect for the natural environment. Congress promoted some of these goals in 1970 by passing the Model Communities Act to make available low-interest loan guarantees from the U.S. Department of Housing and Urban Affairs for planners interested in constructing new towns. Oilman George Mitchell of Galveston, himself a petroleum engineer with a degree from Texas A&M University, responded with a plan to build a self-contained model community on 25,000 acres of heavily wooded land in southern Montgomery County, 27 miles north of downtown Houston.[47] Soliciting advice from city planner-environmentalist Ian McHarg and employing engineers Charles Everhart and Dick Browne, Mitchell chose to "humanize ecology and development" in The Woodlands community and undertook intensive study of the area's ecology to determine soil types, the variety of plant and animal life, and the natural drainage of water in the pinelands. As the project took shape in the mid–1970s, environmental experts and engineers cooperated to a considerable extent in planning a technologically modern city without disturbing the ecosystem.[48]

Hydrology studies showed that streets could be built without gutters or sewers, thus permitting much of the runoff to infiltrate the soil, recharge aquifers, and collect in holding ponds. To conserve precipitation in areas not subject to flooding, wide, shallow swales lined with natural vegetation were left to drain the runoff, rather than cut deep ditches. Lawn chemicals are restricted to avoid water pollution. While sewage water is treated and returned to recreational lakes, drinking water is supplied from underground sources. In addition to the novel drainage system, The Woodlands made use of soil studies to select those areas best suited for constructing roads, houses, and industries and those best left as open spaces. Soil erosion was reduced by preserving stands of the pine and hardwood forest and by leaving in a natural state much of the undergrowing vegetation.[49]

Original plans to keep large areas of land undeveloped are being changed to provide housing for a population which is expected, perhaps unrealistically, to reach 100,000 by the year 2000. In addition to residential growth, The Woodlands continues to attract commercial and industrial development. Among its most innovative features is an area set aside by Mitchell as The Research Forest to conduct high-technology and scientific research. The Houston Area Research Center (HARC) coordinates and integrates academic and corporate research in order to facilitate the rapid commercial adoption of new scientific discoveries and inventions.[50] The Center has emerged as a force in presenting the state with a set of dynamic alternatives to continued dependence on petroleum products as the basis for economic growth. Thus, The Woodlands represents both a significant experiment in comprehensive planning for urban development and a catalyst for scientific and technological progress. Mitchell's Woodlands Conferences since the mid–1970s have analyzed limits to growth and synthesized ideas for sustainable societies.

The support given HARC by several of the state's universities is indicative of the role higher education in science and technology has played in the growth of Texas since 1945. The training of civil and mechanical engineers responded to the needs of a rapidly changing society by offering research and teaching programs emphasizing preparation for professional practice.[51] Yet, while students need greater depth of knowledge in their specialized field of study as well as education in basic science, mathematics, and computer methodology, they are expected to become aware of the implications of their work on society and human values. In 1964 Dean Harvey Brooks of Harvard's College of Engineering reminded engineers of the necessity to "learn how to call on all the resources of the scientific community to help foresee the consequences of new technology and plan for its introduction."[52] The value of this wider scope of vision to engineers is convincingly demonstrated by the Texas experience; members of the profession have played a significant part in determining the social and economic development of the state.

Throughout the postwar period, faculty and advanced students in the engineering colleges have contributed their expertise to a wide range of public and private projects. For instance, Texas A&M, which had created the Texas Engineering Experiment Station in 1914, encouraged engineering faculty to accept research projects that were in the public interest. Similarly, in 1924, the University of Texas founded the Bureau of Engineering Research, which continued to function during World War II and afterward as a center for conducting scientific experiments and as a laboratory for testing new technology and processes.[53] During the early 1950s the Personal Aircraft Center at College Station participated in designing an improved crop-dusting airplane, called the Ag–1, which made an important contribution to both the general aviation and the agricultural industries. The 1950s also saw Texas A&M set up the Texas Transportation Institute (TTI) as the research arm of the state department of highways. TTI employed two distinguished engineers, Thomas H. McDonald, the former U.S. Commissioner of Public Roads, and Gibb Gilchrist, former head of the Texas Highway Department, to launch the program, now recognized around the world as leading in transportation research.[54] At Texas Tech University in the early 1970s the engineering college established an Institute for Disaster Research to study the effect of tornadic winds and wind-driven debris on structures. These few examples of many programs conducted at engineering colleges merely suggest the breadth of involvement by universities through research in engineering in the technical progress of the state.

Professional organizations, such as the local sections of the ASCE and the American Society of Mechanical Engineers (ASME), with steadily growing membership lists, provide engineers with a forum for the exchange of ideas, philosophy, and practice and with an outlet for the presentation of new research. Although their paramount purpose is keeping members abreast of recent trends and addressing public issues of concern to the membership, both the ASCE and ASME have formed history and heritage committees as a means to recognize engineering achievements of the past. Texas civil engineers are particularly active in identifying and documenting historic landmarks, such as the acequias of San Antonio, and providing a historical perspective on the development of the profession. Joe J. Rady stated in 1968 that the formation of the Texas Committee on History and Heritage, which he chaired, was both "a good sign that our profession has come of age" and a "realization that what we accomplish today is possible because of the work of those engineers who went before us."[55] Fellow members of the Texas ASCE seemed to share this point of view. Israel W. Santry, long a professor of civil engineering at Southern Methodist University and editor of the *Texas Civil Engineer*, compiled *The First Fifty Years: A History of the Texas Section*, published in 1964.[56] John A. Focht, who earned distinction as a professor of civil engineering at the University of Texas at Austin from 1926 to 1965, traced his career in *An Engineer Remembers* (1978) and today continues his active interest in the history of Texas engineering.[57]

To the great tradition and achievements of the past, the practice of civil and mechanical engineering in Texas since 1945 has added its own impressive list of accomplishments. The study of recent Texas history reveals the development of a modern urban, industrial state founded on the talents and resourcefulness of the professional engineer.

Notes

1. E. V. Spence, "Conservation and Development of Texas Ground Water," *Texas Engineer* 17, (May 1947): pp. 9–13.

2. C. M. Ainsworth, "International Irrigation Developments Along Rio Grande Started," *Civil Engineering* 21, (May 1951): pp. 38–41; "Building Falcon Dam—in Two Languages," *Engineering News-Record* 148, (May 15, 1952): pp. 62–67.

3. Armstrong et al., 1976, p. 283.

4. H. N. Roberts, "Water Supply in West Texas," *Texas Engineer* 19, (August 1949): pp. 6–15.

5. "New Lifeline for 12 Thirsty Texas Cities," *Engineering News-Record* 151, (July 16, 1953): pp. 43–50; D. L. Chappelear and E. L. Gloyna, "Innovations in the Laying and Bedding of Pipe," *Civil Engineering* 37, (December 1967): pp. 57–60.

6. David G. McComb, 1981, p. 145.

7. Mason G. Lockwood, "Ground Subsides in

Houston Area," *Civil Engineering* 24 (June 1954): pp. 48–50; Glenn W. Spencer, "The Fight to Keep Houston from Sinking," *Civil Engineering* 47, (September 1977): pp. 69–71.

8. "Extensive Earthfill Dams Remove Threat of Severe Floods at Houston, Tex.," *Civil Engineering* 18, (October 1948): pp. 67–68; "Lightweight Dam to Pass Heavyweight Flow Over New Diffuser Spillway," *Engineering News-Record* 151, (August 20, 1953): pp. 43–48; "More Water for Fast Growing Houston?" *Engineering News-Record* 152, (April 1, 1954): pp. 43–44.

9. McComb, 1981, pp. 147–149.

10. *Engineering News-Record* 147, (September 27, 1951): p. 62.

11. J. G. Turney, Samuel A. Greeley, and Paul E. Langdon, "Houston Sludge Disposal Plant Profits from Use of Existing Facilities," *Civil Engineering* 21, (May 1951): pp. 26–29.

12. Homer B. Pettit, "Federal Government Plays Important Role in Development of Hydroelectric Energy," *Civil Engineering* 18, (June 1948): pp. 34–38, 92; "Whitney Dam—Saddle on the Brazos," *Texas Professional Engineer* 8, (May 1949): pp. 4–5, 22.

13. G. E. Schmitt, "Pumped-Storage Hydro Plant in Texas Proves Economical," *Civil Engineering* 21, (May 1951): pp. 21–25.

14. McComb, 1981, pp. 123–125.

15. Robert H. Dodds, "Houston's Boom is a Steady Roar," *Engineering News-Record* 145, (July 27, 1950): pp. 33–37.

16. Marilyn M. Sibley, 1968, p. 196; "Houston Tunnel Opens for Business," *Engineering News-Record* 144, (June 8, 1950): pp. 32–33.

17. J. O. Bickel and M. P. Anderson, "New Ideas Mark Design and Construction of Baytown Tunnel," *Civil Engineering* 21, (March 1951): pp. 30–33; "Baytown Tunnel Ready for Traffic," *Texas Professional Engineer* 12, (September 1953): pp. 7–8.

18. *Texas Highways* 2, (May 1955): p. 123.

19. Tommie Pinkard, "Bridging Texas," Ibid. 12, (September 1965): p. 19.

20. Pat W. Clark, "Design of the Corpus Christi Bridge," *Texas Highways* 2, (May 1955): pp. 108–123; Duane Orr, "Corpus Christi Tackles Major Port Development Program," *Civil Engineering* 26, (March 1956): pp. 33–36, "A Bridge for Growth in Corpus Christi," *Engineering News-Record* 162, (April 23, 1959): pp. 44–47.

21. "Texas' Longest Bridge Dedicated," *Texas Highways* 8, (August 1961): pp. 2–5.

22. "Devil's River Bridge—Looking to the Future,"

Ibid 12, (March 1965): pp. 16–20; "Prize Bridge of 1965," Ibid., (December 1965): p. 9.

23. Frank G. Kelly, Jr., "Texas Giant," *Texas Highways* 17, (November 1970): pp. 28–30.

24. "Bridging the Gap," Ibid. 20 (May 1973): pp. 20–21; "Concrete Box Girder Span Establishes U.S. Record," *Engineering News-Record* 208, (January 7, 1982): pp. 22–24.

25. Gard, n.d., pp. 32–37.

26. T. A. Hester, "Assembly-Line Techniques Speed Construction of Cross-Country Oil and Gas Lines," *Civil Engineering* 19, (May 1949): pp. 22–24.

27. "Oil from the Tidelands," *Texas Professional Engineer* 12, (July 1953): pp. 7–8, 24; F. R. Hauber, "Design and Construction of Offshore Platforms," *Texas Engineer* 26, (January 1956): pp. 9–11.

28. Marshall P. Cloyd, "Monopod," *Civil Engineering* 38, (March 1968): pp. 55–57; Ibid. 49, (April 1979): pp. 53–56.

29. Raymond Teague, "Engineering Wonders of Texas," *Fort Worth Star-Telegram*, 13 August 1983, sec. E, pp. 1, 5.

30. Bilstein and Miller, 1985, pp. 230–235.

31. Scott and Davis, 1974, p. 66.

32. "Texas Airport Systems Planned to Last Parking Space," *Engineering News-Record* 183, (July 17, 1969): pp. 28–29; Nichols, 1983, p. 27.

33. Dennis M. Elliott, "Dallas-Fort Worth's Airtrans: Model for Future PRT Systems," *Civil Engineering* 44 (July 1974): pp. 70–73.

34. Bilstein and Miller, 1985, pp. 228–230; Paul C. Nail and William M. Rice, "NASA's Manned Spacecraft Center," *Texas Professional Engineer* 21, (December 1962): pp. 12–15.

35. McComb, 1981, pp. 187–189.

36. Reidenbaugh, 1983, p. 122.

37. Louis O. Bass, "Unusual Dome Awaits Baseball Season in Houston," *Civil Engineering* 35, (January 1965): pp. 63–65.

38. *Astrodome and the Astrodomain*, pp. 47–48.

39. Ibid., pp. 29, 32–33.

40. Walter P. Moore, Jr., "Houston Amphitheater Roof," *Civil Engineering* 39, (November 1969): pp. 70–72.

41. "The Quiet Revolution in Skyscraper Design," *Civil Engineering* 53, (May 1983): pp. 54–59.

42. "Gerald Hines: Houston's Biggest Space-Maker," *Engineering News-Record* 183, (September 25, 1969): pp. 31–32.

43. McComb, 1981, pp. 133–135.

44. "Johnson & Johnson," *Texas Monthly* (September 1983): pp. 152–225; "Architecture: Brazen Energy in 2 Powerful New Skyscrapers in Houston," *New York Times* (February 13, 1984): p. C-13.

45. Roy W. Gillette, "Precast Boxes Stacked to Build 496-Room Hotel in Nine Months for Hemis-Fair," *Civil Engineering* 38, (March 1968): pp. 44–47.

46. R. E. Portik, "Engineering Close-up of Hemis-Fair 68," Ibid., (April 1968): pp. 80–85.

47. *Southern Living*, (December 1985), Reprint article.

48. Ralph Everhart, "New Town Planned Around Environmental Effects," *Civil Engineering* 43, (September 1983): pp. 69–73.

49. "What's New in Dallas and Texas?" Ibid. 47, (March 1977): pp. 64–69.

50. Kuhn, 1985, Reprint article.

51. G. Brooks Earnest, "Civil Engineering Education—Some Vital Issues," *Civil Engineering* 33, (February 1963): pp. 52–53.

52. Harvey Brooks as quoted in: Waldo G. Bowman, "New Dimensions for Civil Engineering," Ibid. 34, (June 1964): pp. 39–41.

53. "UT Carries on National Research," *Texas Professional Engineer* 5, (March-April 1946): p. 9.

54. Crawford, 1976, pp. 66–97; *Texas Engineer* 35, (June 1965): pp. 9–10.

55. Joe J. Rady, "Our History—Our Heritage," *Texas Engineer* 38, (June 1968): pp. 15–17.

56. *Texas Civil Engineer* 55, (May 1985): p. 8.

57. *Texas Engineer* 34, (August 1964): p. 2.

Bibliography

Armstrong, Ellis L., Robinson, Michael C., and Hoy, Suellen M., eds. *History of Public Works in the United States, 1776–1976*. Chicago: American Public Works Association, 1976.

Astrodome and the Astrodomain. Undated souvenir booklet.

Bilstein, Roger, and Miller, Jay. *Aviation in Texas*. Austin: Texas Monthly Press and University of Texas Institute of Texan Cultures, 1985.

Civil Engineering, 1945–1983.

Crawford, C. W. *One Hundred Years of Engineering at Texas A&M, 1876–1976*. N.p.: Privately Printed, 1976.

Engineering News-Record, 1945–1983.

Focht, John A. *An Engineer Remembers*. Austin: Privately Printed, 1978.

Gard, Wayne. *The First 100 Years of Texas Oil and Gas, With Postscript*. Dallas: Texas Mid-Continent Oil and Gas Association, n.d.

Kuhn, Robert Lawrence. "Let George Do It," *Texas Business*, August, 1985. Reprint.

Lohr, Lenox R., ed. *Centennial of Engineering, 1852–1952*. Chicago: Museum of Science and Industry, 1953.

Lubove, Roy, "Urban Planning and Development." In Vol. 2 of *Technology in Western Civilization*, pp. 461–483. Edited by Melvin Kranzberg and Carrol W. Pursell, Jr. New York: Oxford University Press, 1967.

McComb, David G. *Houston: A History*. Austin: University of Texas Press, 1981.

Nichols, James R. *Freese and Nichols, Inc.: An Engineering Institution*. New York: Newcomen Society in North America, 1983.

Reidenbaugh, Lowell. *Take Me Out to the Ball Park*. St. Louis: *The Sporting News*, 1983.

Rotsch, Melvin M. "Building with Steel and Concrete." In Vol. 2 of *Technology in Western Civilization*, pp. 196–217. Edited by Melvin Kranzberg and Carroll W. Pursell, Jr. New York: Oxford University Press, 1967.

Santry, I. W., Jr. *The First Fifty Years: A History of the Texas Section*. N.p.: Texas Section, American Society of Civil Engineers, 1964.

Scott, Stanley H., and Davis, Levi H. *A Giant in Texas: A History of the Dallas–Ft. Worth Regional Airport Controversy, 1911–1974*. Quanah, TX: Nortex Press, 1974.

Sibley, Marilyn McAdams. *The Port of Houston: A History*. Austin: University of Texas Press, 1968.

Teague, Raymond. "Engineering Wonders of Texas," *Southern Living*, December 1985. Reprint. *Fort Worth Star Telegram*, 13 August 1983.

The Texas Almanac, 1984–1985.

Texas Civil Engineer (formerly *Texas Engineer*), 1945–1985.

Texas Highways, 1954–1982.

Texas Professional Engineer, 1946–1981.

12

Computers

Lewis Harris

Phillip Hopkins

Sue A. Krenek

THE CONCEPTS which led to the invention of the computer as we know it today can be traced to the time when the concept of counting became known to humankind. The idea of a mechanical device that could perform addition and subtraction was a milestone that cannot be attributed to a single person. Napier, the discoverer of logarithms, in the seventeenth century worked out a crude device for mechanical addition, as Blaise Pascal was to do later. These machines, while useful in reducing the amount of errors in computation, were limited by their design; it was Charles Babbage who in 1833 conceived the idea of a machine which would be designed to solve any type of problem—the analytical engine.

Babbage's analytical engine was never built, but he is credited as being the first man to envision the modern computer. Babbage received credit for the first computing machine, in part, due to the aid of the first programmer, Ada Lovelace Byron, the daughter of the famous poet Lord Byron. In the late nineteenth century, mechanical logic machines and tabulators began to appear, among them Herman Hollerith's statistical tabulator, the first data-processing machine. Mechanical tabulators such as Hollerith's, however, were general enough to solve a wide variety of problems.

In 1946, ENIAC (Electronic Numerical Integrator and Computer) was unveiled at the University of Pennsylvania's Moore School of Electrical Engineering. Invented by J. Presper Eckert and John W. Mauchly, it was the first general purpose electronic calculator. In 1945 John von Neumann had envisioned the concept of stored instructions, clearing the way for the modern computer. The first commercial computer, the UNIVAC, was completed in 1947.[1]

At the time of the latest of these developments, the state of Texas was completely occupied with its burgeoning oil industry. The company that was to become one of Texas' leading electronics firms was founded in Tulsa, Oklahoma, in 1924 as the Geophysical Research Corporation (GRC), a subsidiary of Amerada Petroleum. The company was founded by two physicists, Clarence "Doc" Karcher and Eugene McDermott, who discovered that a reflection-seismograph process which used sound waves to map faults could be applied to the finding of oil deposits. By 1930 GRC was the region's leading geophysical company. That year Karcher and McDermott, along with others, opened an independent company, Geophysical Service, Inc. (GSI), in Dallas. The company set up a research and development laboratory in Newark, New Jersey, and proceeded to find so much oil that the owners founded their own oil company, the Coronado Corporation, in 1938. When Coronado was sold in 1940, a group of employees bought GSI. J. Erik Jonsson, the head of the Newark laboratory, realized that the same echo-tracking techniques that found oil could also be used in searching for enemy ships, submarines, and planes. At his urging GSI entered the defense business; its wartime work with the Navy and the Signal Corps made it an important supplier of military electronics. In 1950 the company changed its name to General Instruments, Inc., and in 1951, due to a name conflict with another military supplier, the name was changed to Texas Instruments, Inc. (TI).[2]

Also in 1951 Bell Laboratories announced its licensing of the right to manufacture transistors, which had been invented in 1947 by Bell Laboratories scientists William Shockley, Walter Brattain, and John Bardeen using developments in semiconductor physics. Transistors, which achieved amplification and rapid on/off switching by moving electric charges along controlled paths in a solid block of semiconductor material, in theory provided an excellent alternative to the vacuum tubes then in use in electronic equipment. In practice, transistors could not yet be mass-produced and were therefore prohibitively expensive. TI was among the first companies to pay the $25,000 license fee, and Bell Labs scientist Gordon Teal was hired to make the transistor inexpensive, mass-producible, and reliable.

TI's decision to proceed with the commercial development of the transistor marked the take off of high-technology electronics in Texas. The development of the computer as we know it today would not have been possible without the concurrent advances in solid-state physics and electronics which produced the transistor, the integrated circuit, and the microprocessor. Consequently, the history of the computing industry in Texas is intertwined with the history of the electronics industry in general, and the eventful history of Texas Instruments in particular.

TI teamed with Regency, a radio manufacturer, to market an early application of transistor technology, the first portable transistor radio. Introduced on November 1, 1954, it was a huge hit, being smaller, lighter, and more reliable than any others on the market. In May of 1954, TI scientists Gordon Teal and Willis Adcock (a physical chemist) presented a new innovation: the silicon transistor, thought by most to be several years away from practicability. The early transistors had been manufactured from germanium, a semiconductor material that could not withstand high temperatures. Silicon, by increasing the range of temperatures at which transistors could operate, opened the door to new transistor applications.

Texas Instruments' greatest contribution was yet to come. The major problem in electronics was that resistors, capacitors, diodes, and transistors were each manufactured separately from different materials and assembled in different circuits for different functions. The circuits most needed by the industry were tremendously complicated, often involving hundreds of components; while components could be mass-produced, the wiring had to be done by hand, which drove up the cost of the circuit. Jack St. Clair Kilby came to TI in May of 1958, and that summer developed the concept of the integrated circuit. His idea was that if all components of a circuit could be made out of one material, they could probably be manufactured all at once from a single block of the material. No wiring would be needed as the connections would be laid down internally in the semiconductor chip. Without wiring, the chip's size could be decreased. Kilby knew that transistors and diodes made of silicon were common; silicon capacitors and resistors, while not as efficient as those of other materials, would work. Kilby's idea was first tested on September 12, 1958, and integrated circuits were unveiled in early 1959. Six months later Robert Noyce of Fairchild Semiconductor developed an improved integrated circuit process. Patents were awarded to both men, and TI and Fairchild battled over the rights to the invention all the way to the Supreme Court.

While TI was the most innovative company in the young Texas electronics industry, it certainly was not the only one. General Dynamics had located a plant in Fort Worth in 1942; firms such as Rockwell, LTV, Lockheed, E-Systems, and Bell Helicopter also located in Texas, in and around Dallas and Fort Worth. These installations were to provide the basic pool of talent for the industry, as employees later split off to form their own companies.

By 1959 Texas ranked eighth in the nation in electronics manufacturing. Texas Instruments' sales had jumped to $193 million, up from $92 million in one year. Also during 1959 the first applications of computer technology began to affect Texas. The Texaco plant at Port Arthur became the first in the nation to be run by a fully automated computer-based system for process control, and the banking industry adopted magnetic ink character recognition (MICR) as a method for speeding the processing of checks. By 1960 the Texas Highway Department was using an electronic digital computer in Austin to aid in solving land survey problems and determining bridge specifications, among other tasks.

The 1962 opening of NASA's Manned Spacecraft Center (MSC, now JSC) at Houston triggered a new influx of high-technology firms to the area. Many of them were aerospace-related. Companies such as Lockheed, Rockwell, and International Business Machines (IBM), already established in Texas, opened offices near the MSC for support services. By this time IBM had branches in a total of thirteen Texas cities, and Arthur Collins had made Texas the corporate headquarters of Collins Radio, which would soon become a leading manufacturer of electronics for commercial airlines. The year 1962 also saw the establishment of two of the mainstays of the Texas electronics industry: Frank McBee, a former engineering professor at the University of Texas, incorporated Tracor as a defense electronics company; and H. Ross Perot founded the phenomenally successful Electronic Data Systems Corporation, on the concept of handling development and operations for customers who did not have their own computer systems.[3]

The first generation of spinoff companies from Texas Instruments and Collins Radio were founded from roughly 1967 to 1971. In 1967 three former TI employees formed a company, Datapoint, to build computer terminals in San Antonio. Datapoint now brings in half a billion dollars a year. The year also saw the location of an IBM office products manufacturing plant at Austin. Texas Instruments' 1968 decision to open a division in Houston also led to spinoffs. In 1969, led by G. Ward Paxton, Jr., most of TI's Optoelectronics Department left, later to be reformed as Spectronics, Incorporated, of Richardson. Four other TI employees who did not want to move to Houston, L. J. Sevin, Louay Sharif, Berry Cash, and Vin Prothro, in 1969 formed Mostek. Other companies formed during this period were Action Communications Systems, makers of WATS-line equipment; Electrospace Systems, manufacturers of military electronics; and Danray, Inc., makers of digital switches, which was founded by Jim Donald of TI and John Israel of Collins Radio.[4] The 1967–71 period also saw the formation of Michael Corboy's Tocom, E. C. Karnavas' Textool Products, Inc., and Jay Rodney Reese's Recognition Equipment, Inc., all TI spinoffs. The Rolm Corporation was also founded in 1969 by four Rice University alumni.

The spinoffs did not keep TI from developing new technology; in 1971 the company released the Pocketronic, a pocket calculator developed by Jack Kilby, the inventor of the integrated circuit. Kilby had been asked by Pat Haggerty (president of TI) to invent a small electronic calculator as far back as 1964; the final version made use of a TI-developed single-chip microcomputer and sold for only $150, when standard electronic calculators cost $1,200. This development moved TI to the forefront of both the calculator and the semiconductor fields.

Computer technology in the 1970s was greatly affected by two developments: the invention of the microprocessor, or "computer on a chip," and the development of the transducer, which converts light, heat, pressure, and the sound of the human voice into electrical impulses. In Texas several changes occurred in the electronics industry. The Mexican government's decision to allow "twin plants" along the Texas–Mexico border provided an incentive for manufacturing plants to locate in south Texas. Under the agreement, companies could build a warehouse in Texas for parts storage and an assembly plant in Mexico; parts could then be transferred to the Mexican factory without the usual customs duties, providing significant savings in labor costs for the manufacturer. General Electric was one of many United States companies to build twin plants.

In 1974 TI introduced what was to become one of its most profitable products, the TMS 1000 microprocessor chip. This four-bit chip became one of the most widely used in the industry, and TI followed it up a year later with the TMS 9900. At sixteen bits, the 9900 was simply too far ahead of the current technology; other firms were just introducing eight-bit chips, and sales of the 9900 were disappointing. The mid-1970s also saw the location of several new plants in Texas. Between 1972 and 1975, Motorola opened new facilities in Seguin (radio manufacturer), Austin (semiconductors), and Fort Worth (communications products). In 1974 Xerox opened its first Texas plant at Dallas; it is now the headquarters for the Information Products Division. Texas experienced its largest increase in high-tech firms (those that are labor intensive with a highly skilled employee base) during the late 1970s.

In September of 1977 another Texas company, Tandy Corporation, introduced an innovative product. The Tandy Model 1 was the first home computer and was priced at $599; its success was largely due to Tandy's Radio Shack chain, which provided a network for instant market distribution of the computer among electronics enthusiasts.

By 1978 the Texas information technology industry had grown substantially. Sales of computer equipment alone brought in $781.9 million, while electronic components added $1,031 million, data-processing services contributed $830.5 million, measurement and control equipment sales were at $169.3 million, and engineering, laboratory, and research equipment sales stood at $95.2 million. The number of workers employed in the various areas of the industry was as follows: computer equipment, 15,100; electronics components, 31,600; data-processing services, 19,200; measurement and control equipment, 4,700; and engineering, laboratories, and research equipment, 1,900.[5]

The second generation of spinoffs from the major companies occurred from about 1978 to 1982. In 1978 Northern Telecom bought Danray, Inc. Danray founders Jim Donald and John Israel moved on to other ventures, Donald joining Digital Switch and Israel founding Advanced Business Communications. Mike Bowen, a Danray executive, formed Intecom. The state capital in Austin became something of a center for software firms. Among the companies there were BPI, which produced a popular accounting program, and Omega Software, a TI offspring which marketed a version of the Bible on diskette billed as "The Greatest User Friendly Story Ever Told." Several independent firms were grouped under Sam Wylie's University Computing Company. Larger corporations continued to migrate to Texas: Honeywell bought Action Communications and Spectronics, Advanced Micro Devices opened facilities in San Antonio and Austin, and in 1980 Apple Computer located its largest computer-manufacturing plant at Carrollton. After establishing a marketing support center at Las Colinas in 1979, IBM built a circuit-packaging plant in Austin three years later.

These changes had not gone unnoticed. By 1979 *Texas Business* magazine was able to label electronics in Texas a "huge, hidden industry," justifying the claim by quoting Fred Bertner, a financial analyst with Underwood, Neuhaus: "We are not just a semiconductor state anymore."[6] The magazine also noted an application of computer technology to another traditional Texas concern, agriculture. The Plains Cotton Cooperative Association in Lubbock used a computer network, Telcot, to link 150 cotton gins to forty buyers' offices.[7] The system provided sale and price recaps, which served to standardize prices, and was considered a model for farm commodity marketing by the United States Department of Agriculture. The number of computer installations had also increased. By 1979 the Houston area had 490 installations worth $725 million and the Dallas area had 998 worth $658 million, giving the state a ranking of tenth in the nation according to installation value.

The next year, 1980, saw the release of Tandy's Radio Shack Color Computer. In early 1980 TI released its own home computer, the 99/4. Originally envisioned as the low end of a three-computer series that would retail for $300–$400, the design was gradu-

ally changed until the release price was $1,150. It was doomed from the start by its price, its inadequate keyboard, and its lack of software. TI was determined not to open the architecture, which meant that outside companies could not produce 99/4 software; TI itself did not provide sufficient software. Within nine months the 99/4 was being redesigned.[8]

The electronics industry in Texas continued to grow; in 1980 Texas had 4.6 percent of the nation's high-technology employment in manufacturing, up from 3.3 percent in 1975. The state had the third largest share of national electronics manufacturing employment (behind California and Massachusetts) but had the greatest percentage growth in employment, 73.5 percent from 1975 to 1980. Employment in Texas high-tech manufacturing in 1980 reached 153,204 and was estimated to exceed 225,000 by the end of 1984.[9]

In the summer of 1981 the redesigned Texas Instruments home computer, the 99/4A, appeared in stores. TI's marketing manager for the Consumer Products Group, William J. Turner, realized that the home computer would not sell in a computer store and that it should go instead to general retailers. He also planned a price reduction to stimulate buying. By this time, however, Atari had introduced a home computer and in early 1982 Commodore introduced the VIC-20, retailing at $299. What ensued was a battle to control the market and a price war that TI would ultimately lose.

Meanwhile, other Texans were entering the computer business. In January 1982 Tim Shirley began CCS Incorporated. The company ran Sofsearch, a subscription-based service to "provide custom reports on software products available to meet user-specified requirements."[10] Honeywell came to CCS to procure software for their machines, and Burroughs had also used the service. The Radio Shack TRS-80 Sourcebook refers to Sofsearch for a fuller listing, and Apple has used information from the company in an advertising campaign. Also in 1982 three former TI employees—Rod Canion, Jim Harris, and Bill Murto—founded Compaq Computer Corporation in Houston. They began with the idea for an IBM-compatible personal computer and have profited handsomely.

By 1983 Texas was second only to the Far East in terms of production of computers for home use. The industry received a boost from the selection of Austin as the site for the Microelectronics and Computer Technology Corporation (MCC), headed by Admiral Bobby R. Inman, USN (Ret.).[11] The corporation, which was chartered in August of 1982, is a research and development cooperative of 21 major United States companies. Participating firms are Control Data, Mostek, RCA, Digital Equipment, Honeywell, Motorola, NCR, National Semiconductor, Advanced Micro Devices, Harris Corporation, Allied, and Sperry Corporation. It is designed to keep the United States out in front of Japan in the high-tech field by furthering research, especially into artificial intelligence. With 400 employees and an annual budget of $60 million, MCC will concentrate its research in four areas:

1. A ten-year program in advanced computer design to include artificial intelligence, database management, human interface, and parallel processing.
2. An eight-year program in computer-aided design and computer-aided manufacture.
3. A seven-year program in computer software technology.
4. A six-year program in packaging integrated circuits.

MCC should lead to even more growth in electronics in Texas and should be especially beneficial to the University of Texas at Austin.

The year 1983 also produced two milestones of sorts for Texas Instruments. It was the first year that Motorola outproduced TI in semiconductors, and it was the year that TI dropped out of the home computer market. TI's 99/4A price war cost it $500 million in corporate losses over two quarters, and in October the product was abandoned.

Computer usage had grown to the extent that Texans were founding companies to address problems they faced: Harold Nachimson of Irving found no software suitable for a family physician, so he founded CompuMed Corporation to market his CompuDoc software package.[12] Catherine DeMarco, a mother with thirteen years of computer experience, was unable to find adequate home educational software for her children; her dissatisfaction with available products led her to begin Software Town, a retail store in Dallas specializing in educational software.

In 1984 computers helped to solve a Texas political dilemma. During efforts to reform school finance, the Texas Education Agency made its computer available to legislators. Those who submitted formulas were provided with printouts detailing the effects of their formula on every district in the state, helping others to immediately see the advantages or disadvantages of a proposal.

Also in 1984 the U.S. Department of Defense conducted preparations for the awarding of a contract worth $103 million over five years for Software Engineering Institute (SEI). A consortium of universities from Texas is involved in the competition. It is headed by the Texas Engineering Experiment Station at Texas A&M and affiliate schools of the University of Texas at Austin, the University of Houston at Clear Lake City, Prairie View A&M University, the University of Southwestern Louisiana, and the University of Southern California.[13] Although the consortium failed to obtain the contract, the bid marked the first attempt by any Texas institution to gain major research funds in the area of software engineering.

Early in 1986 the Houston Area Research Council (HARC) announced that it had reached an agreement with NEC, a major Japanese electronic conglomerate to purchase a NEC SX2 supercomputer. This new machine is necessary for the Texas academic community to keep abreast of advances in research techniques. High speed and the ability to handle multiple computations make the supercomputers attractive to research projects which require massive computations. Applications envisioned for the SX2 include research activities in geotechnology, accelerator physics, laser development, materials science, space technology, and biomedical engineering. The members of HARC are the University of Texas, Texas A&M University, The University of Houston, and Rice University.

According to the records of the Comptroller of Public Accounts,[14] the number of high-technology businesses in Texas has grown from 1,638 in 1978 to 7,541 in 1984, an annual average increase of 29 percent. During the same period, the total number of businesses in Texas has grown by an average of 6 percent. Table 1 shows the distribution of high-technology employment in the state. Total sales of high-technology businesses in Texas now account for 3.6 percent of total sales in the state, up from 2.6 percent in 1978. Table 2 summarizes the distribution of these sales.

The Texas computer industry is still growing. There are approximately 1,500 high-tech firms in Texas and the industry continues to produce new spinoff companies. Trammell Crow was expected to finish construction in 1985 of the International Information Processing Market Center (Infomart), a permanent facility in Dallas where equipment manufacturers and resellers can buy and sell. Infomart expected to draw 350 companies to establish corporate showrooms.[15] It should provide still more impetus to the growth of the high-tech industries in Texas.

By 1984 roughly half of the state's 1,500 high-technology firms were located in the north and central regions of the state, which includes Austin, the Dallas–Fort Worth Metroplex area, and San Antonio.

These three areas had 31.8 percent of the state population in 1982 but 40.6 percent of manufacturing employment and over two-thirds of the high-technology employment.

In Austin 44 percent of all manufacturing occurs within high-tech industries. The industry is electronics-based, but many research and development firms are beginning to locate in the area. Manufacturing in the area accounts for 10.8 percent of the total wage and salary employment.

In the Dallas–Fort Worth area, manufacturing accounts for 18 percent of the total wage and salary employment, and 28 percent of that manufacturing is for the high-technology portion of the economy that revolves around producers of communication, electronics components and accessories, and aerospace and defense systems.

In San Antonio manufacturing makes up 10 percent of the total wage and salary employment, and 16.6 percent of this is high-technology manufacturing. The city's technological base is in electronic components and the manufacture of surgical, medical, and dental instruments.[16]

Houston, home of NASA's Johnson Space Center, accounted for 12.7 percent of high-technology employment in 1984. Houston's economy still has its

Table 1

High Tech Employment

HIGH-TECH EMPLOYMENT BY INDUSTRY*

Industry Type	Total Employed 1979	Total Employed 1984**	Average Annual Change
Guided Missiles and Space Vehicles	859	10,692	65.6%
Measuring and Controlling Instruments	5,427	9,151	11.0
Electronic Computing Equipment	12,725	28,197	17.3
Computer and Data Processing Services	20,648	38,306	13.2
Research and Development Laboratories	5,277	9,932	13.5
Scientific and Research Equipment	3,542	3,383	−0.9
Communications Equipment	21,323	23,450	1.9
Electronic Components	57,600	59,795	0.8
Aircraft and Parts	48,279	42,496	−2.5
Optical Instruments	876	658	−5.6
Computer Equipment Stores	NA	NA	
Total	176,556	226,060	5.1%

HIGH-TECH EMPLOYMENT BY SELECTED METROPOLITAN AREAS

	Total Employed 1979	Total Employed 1984	Average Annual Change
Austin	11,906	24,909	15.9%
Houston	21,468	28,620	5.9
San Antonio	9,079	11,896	5.6
Dallas–Fort Worth	105,599	129,788	4.2
Bryan–College Station	518	946	12.8
Rest of State	27,987	29,901	1.3
Total	176,557	226,060	5.1%

**The figures for 1984 are based on average employment during the first three quarters of the year.
*Source: Texas Employment Commission and Comptroller of Public Accounts.

Table 2
High-Tech Taxable Sales

BY INDUSTRY
(In Millions)

Industry Type*	Taxable Sales for 1974	Taxable Sales for 1984(e)	Percent of 1984 Total	Average Annual Increase
Guided Missiles and Space Vehicles	$ 0.1	$ 38.2	1.5%	81.2%
Computer Equipment Stores	0.8	352.9	14.2	83.8
Computer and Data Processing Equipment	8.7	445.1	17.9	48.2
Electronic Computing Equipment	12.4	217.7	8.7	33.2
Optical Instruments	0.4	6.5	0.3	32.2
Research and Development Laboratories	4.7	20.3	0.8	15.8%
Scientific and Research Equipment	5.9	39.2	1.6	20.9
Measuring and Controlling Instruments	25.7	176.3	7.1	21.2
Electronic Components	69.3	563.6	22.6	23.3
Aircraft and Parts	54.7	156.5	6.3	11.1
Communication Equipment	391.9	474.1	19.0	1.9
Total	$574.6	$2,490.4	100.0%	15.8%

BY SELECTED SMSA
(In Millions)

Standard Metropolitan Statistical Analysis (SMSA)	Taxable Sales for 1974	Taxable Sales for 1984(e)	Percent of 1984 Total	Average Annual Increase
Bryan–College Station	$ 0.0	$ 7.5	0.3%	79.7%
San Antonio	6.9	92.2	3.7	29.6
Austin	4.9	134.5	5.4	39.3
Dallas–Fort Worth	192.2	926.4	37.2	17.0
Houston	296.6	483.1	19.4	5.0
Rest of State	74.0	846.7	34.0	27.6
Total	$574.6	$2,491.1	100.0%	15.5%

(e) estimated
*Source: Comptroller of Public Accounts sales tax records

major roots in the energy-related industries, and taxable sales from high-technology businesses grew at a rate of only 5.0 percent per year from 1975 to 1984, considerably less than the growth rate for other metropolitan areas in the state. However, in 1984 those sales in the Houston area were 19.4 percent of the total for the state.

Texas, whose industrial base has traditionally been in oil and chemicals, has established a strong, growing position in the fields of electronics and computing. Fortuitously, the growth in the high-technology industries in Texas has coincided with a decline in the fortunes of the oil/petrochemical industry. This circumstance has helped Texas to avoid some of the economic woes besetting other less fortunate states during the late 1970s and early 1980s. In the future, the economy of the state, now more diversified and charged with the vigor of expanding technology, will continue to bring prosperity and stability to Texas.

Notes

1. Davis, 1977.
2. "Some Spin-Offs," 1978.
3. Ashton and Dalton, 1983.
4. "Some Spin-Offs," 1978.
5. Knight et al., 1981.
6. Hershberger, 1979.
7. "Agriculture," 1979.
8. Nocera, 1984.
9. Goodman and Arnold, 1983.
10. Benyon, 1982.
11. "Special Report," 1984.
12. "Computers," 1984.
13. "Universities Vie," 1984.
14. Comptroller, 1985.
15. Flournoy, 1984.
16. Goodman, 1984.

Bibliography

Abelson, Philip H., and Allen L. Hammond. "The Electronics Revolution," *Science*, Vol. 195 (March 18, 1977), pp. 1087–1090.

"Agriculture: Computer in Lubbock Aids Cotton Farmers," *Texas Business*, Vol. 4, No. 1 (January 1979), p. 15.

Arbingast, Stanley A. "Texas Industrial Expansion: 1962," *Texas Business Review*, Vol. 37, No. 2 (February 1963), pp. 24–27.

Ashton, Peter K., and James A. Dalton. "Strategic Behavior and Performance in the Semiconductor Industry," *Texas Business Review*, Vol. 57, No. 2 (March-April 1983), pp. 57–61.

Benyon, Roger. "In Search of Software," *Texas Business*, Vol. 7, No. 9 (September 1982), pp. 59–62.

"Chips and Money," *Texas Monthly*, Vol. 10, No. 7 (July 1982), pp. 104–105.

Clark, Dave. "Machines Take Over the Office," *Texas Business*, Vol. 3, No. 12 (December 1978), p. 61.

———. "Micro, Micro on the Desk," *Texas Business*, Vol. 8, No. 7 (July 1983), p. 38.

———. "Texas Instruments and Its Breakaway Offspring," *Texas Business*, Vol. 3, pp. 36–41.

"Computer Science 'Firsts,'" letter in "ACM Forum," *Communications of the ACM*, Vol. 24, No. 5 (May 1981).

"Computers: Just What the Doctor Ordered," *Texas Business*, Vol. 9, No. 2 (February 1984), p. 16.

Davis, Ruth M. "Evolution of Computers and Computing," *Science*, Vol. 195 (March 18, 1977), pp. 1096–1100.

Eames, Charles and Ray Eames. *A Computer Perspective*, ed. Glen Fleck. Cambridge: Harvard University Press, 1973.

Flournoy, Nina. "Mainframes, Modems and All that Jazz," *Texas Business*, Vol. 9, No. 2 (February 1984), pp. 24–27.

Goodman, Susan. "High Technology in North and Central Region," *Texas Business Review*, Vol. 58, No. 8 (August 1984).

Goodman, Susan, and Victor L. Arnold. "High Technology in Texas," *Texas Business Review*, Vol. 57, No. 6 (November-December 1983), pp. 290–295.

Hammond, Ray. "Understanding the Computer, Part 1," *Computers and People* (May-June 1984), pp. 15–20, 25.

———. "Understanding the Computer, Part 2," *Computers and People* (July-August 1984), pp. 17–20.

"Hardware/Software Center to Open at Boston Museum," *Publishers' Weekly*, Vol. 226 (September 21, 1984), p. 50.

Hershberger, Steven L. "Electronics in Texas: A Huge, Hidden Industry," *Texas Business*, Vol. 4, No. 5 (May 1979), pp. 60–65.

Howell, Susan L. "Computer 'Expert System' Supports Texas Power Plants," *Computers and People* (November-December 1984), p. 28.

Hurt III, Harry. "Birth of a New Frontier," *Texas Monthly*, Vol. 12, No. 4 (April 1984), pp. 132–135, 238–247.

"IBM Awards Computer Systems to 20 Universities," *Communications of the ACM*, Vol. 26, No. 9 (September 1983), pp. 642–645.

Kelly, James J. "Texas Industrial Expansion," *Texas Business Review*, Vol. 37, No. 2 (February 1962), pp. 28–32.

Knight, Kenneth E., et al. "The Information Technology Industry in Texas: Forecast to 1990," *Texas Business Review*, Vol. 55, No. 3 (May-June 1981), pp. 122–125.

Kramer, David. "It's a High-Tech Life," *Texas Monthly*, Vol. 12, No. 4 (April 1984), pp. 140–143.

Kristinat, R. A. "Sand, Glass, Quartz, and Silicon," *Computers and People* (July-August 1980), pp. 15, 22.

Kuhn, Robert Lawrence. "The Austin Coup," *Texas Business*, Vol. 8, No. 1 (July 1983), pp. 44–46.

Linvill, John G., and C. Lester Hogan. "Intellectual and Economic Fuel for the Electronics Revolution," *Science*, Vol. 195 (March 18, 1977), p. 1110.

Mace, Scott. "Texas Instruments in the Saddle," *Infoworld*, Vol. 5, No. 22, pp. 26–27.

Marsh, Alton K. "High Technology in Texas: Austin's Lead in Research Spurs Growth," *Aviation Week and Space Technology* (August 13, 1984), pp. 73–76.

———. "High Technology in Texas: States Seek Technology Center Status," *Aviation Week and Space Technology* (August 6, 1984), pp. 68–69.

"Microchip Problems Plague DOD," *Science*, Vol. 226 (October 5, 1984), pp. 24–26.

Nocera, Joseph. "Death of a Computer," *Texas Monthly*, Vol. 12, No. 4 (April 1984), pp. 136–139, 216–230.

Olsen, Jerome, Rita J. Wright and Bonnie M. Young. "The State Data Center Network as an Information Resource," *Texas Business Review*, Vol. 56, No. 3 (May-June 1982), pp. 148–152.

Pole, Joyce. "Texas Instruments Gives $115,000 Computer System to University of Texas at Austin," *Computers and People* (March-April 1981), p. 32.

Reid, T. R. "The Texas Edison," *Texas Monthly*, Vol. 10, No. 7 (July 1982), pp. 102–109+.

"Retailing: Radio Shack Launches 'Home Security' Chain," *Texas Business*, Vol. 3, No. 10 (October 1978).

Rice, Mitchell F., Ruth A. Alsobrook, and George M. Weinberger. "Computer Security in Small Local Governments in Texas," *Texas Business Review*, Vol. 56, No. 2 (March-April 1982), pp. 100–104.

Rodriguez, Louis J., and Robert Marchesini. "Impact of the NASA Johnson Space Center on the Houston Area Economy," *Texas Business Review*, Vol. 54, No. 6 (November-December 1980), pp. 325–326.

Simpson, Phil. "The Electronics Industry and Texas," *Texas Business Review*, Vol. 34, No. 8 (August 1960), pp. 6–8.

———. "The Electronics Industry and Texas," *Texas Business Review*, Vol. 34, No. 9 (September 1960), pp. 13–16. (Conclusion)

Smith, William G. "Ross Perot Runs the Tightest Ship in Texas," *Texas Business*, Vol. 3, No. 12 (December 1978), pp. 35–36.

"Some Spin-Offs Still do Business with TI," *Texas Business*, Vol. 3, p. 39.

"Special Report: An MCC Update," *Communications of the ACM*, Vol. 27, No. 7 (July 1984), pp. 636–637.

"Special Section: Computing in Space," *Communications of the ACM*, Vol. 27, No. 9 (September 1984).

Schneck, Paul B. "Introduction to the Special Section on Computing in Space," p. 901.

Trevathan, Charles E., et al. "Development and Application of NASA's First Standard Spacecraft Computer," pp. 902–913.

Madden, William A., and Kyle Y. Rone. "Design, Development, Integration: Space Shuttle Primary Flight Software System," pp. 914–925.

Carlow, Gene D. "Architecture of the Space Shuttle Primary Avionics Software System," pp. 926–936.

Spector, Alfred, and David Gifford. "The Space Shuttle Primary Computer System," *Communications of the ACM*, Vol. 27, No. 9 (September 1984), pp. 874–900.

Steier, Rosalie. "Cooperation is the Key: An Interview with B. R. Inman," *Communications of the ACM*, Vol. 26, No. 9 (September 1983), pp. 642–645.

"Through the Earth, Darkly," *Forbes*, Vol. 134 (December 17, 1984), pp. 182–183.

"Universities Vie for DOD Software Center," *Science*, Vol. 226 (October 5, 1984), p. 26.

"A Visit to Software Town," *Publishers' Weekly*, Vol. 226 (October 26, 1984), pp. 60–61.

West, Felton. "School Legislation by the Numbers," Houston *Post* (June 20, 1984), section B, page 2, column 3.

"You've Got to Keep on Inventing," *Texas Business*, Vol. 3, p. 41.

Zipper, Stuart. "How Does High-Tech Love Texas?" *Texas Business*, Vol. 8, No. 8 (August 1983), pp. 34–36.

Life Sciences

13

Ecology

Howard McCarley

Introduction

The history of ecology, environmental biology, and natural history in Texas since World War II revolves around institutions, organizations, people, and the responses they have made to the cultural and technological changes of the last forty years. To say there were no environmental studies prior to World War II is incorrect, but before the war ecological work in Texas lagged behind that in other parts of the U.S. There were relatively few ecologists in Texas at that time, and the production of graduates in the life sciences was low. During the period between 1930 and 1939, for example, only thirty-eight doctoral degrees in botany and zoology were granted by universities in the southwestern U.S., compared to eighty-eight in the middle states.[1]

Nevertheless, some natural history work was done in Texas before World War II. The very early studies were mostly concerned with plant collections.[2] The first known collection of Texas plants was made by Edwin James in 1820 in the Texas Panhandle as part of Major Long's expedition to the Rocky Mountains.[3] Berlandier made collections from 1826 to 1834, and Lindheimer, the "father of Texas botany," began his observations on plants and plant geography during the Texas revolution. Between 1899 and 1920 W. L. Bray of the University of Texas at Austin (UT–Austin) wrote on such diverse topics as ecological relations of west Texas vegetation, forest management, and distribution and adaptation of vegetation in Texas. Robert Runyon came to the Rio Grande Valley in 1909 and contributed to an understanding of the south Texas flora. His 8,750-item collection was given to UT–Austin, but his extensive botanical library went to Texas A&I University in 1970. In 1915 I. M. Lewis prepared the first guide to Texas trees,[4] and several years later Tharp described the structure of Texas vegetation east of the 98th meridian.[5] About the same time, S. R. Warner, later on the faculty of Sam Houston State University (SHSU), did a dissertation at the University of Chicago on the distribution of native plants of eastern Texas.[6] Later, Warner, along with H. B. Parks and V. L. Cory, provided the first biological survey of the east Texas Big Thicket area.[7] E. A. Clover did a vegetational survey of the Rio Grande Valley.[8]

Ecological studies on animals lagged behind botanical work. Collections of vertebrates, made in the 1800s by H. P. Attwater, were reported by J. A. Allen in the 1890s. In the late 1800s and early 1900s Frank B. Armstrong collected extensively in the Rio Grande Valley, depositing many of his bird specimens in the

Smithsonian Institution.[9] Vernon Bailey's biological survey of Texas was the first comprehensive study of both fauna and flora of the state[10] and set the stage for further studies in the distribution and taxonomy of vertebrates. During the period from 1910 to 1935, J. K. Strecker and others constructed faunal lists and published short observational notes on Texas animals. In 1935 J. K. G. Silvey came to North Texas State University and began his investigations of Texas lakes. Work in western Texas was popular in the thirties and forties.[11] Of the biologists involved, only W. B. Davis was connected with a Texas institution, Texas A&M University (TAMU). It was not until W. Frank Blair studied the mammals of the Davis Mountain region that a major zoological study was done by a native Texan,[12] but even in this case, Blair had not received his education in Texas. A. E. Borrell and M. D. Bryant worked on the mammals of the Big Bend Park while they were at the University of California in Berkeley,[13] but Bryant was a native Texan and later returned to Texas. During the late 1930s and into the 1940s W. P. Taylor and W. B. Davis led the Department of Wildlife Sciences at TAMU. Along with Hobart Smith, they developed strengths in wildlife management, mammalian taxonomy, and herpetology. Their graduates were to have great influence in applied ecology circles at both state and national levels.

The immediate post–World War II years were times of modest expansion of biology, botany, and zoology departments in Texas and a time for reorganizing existing resources after the war. Perhaps most important, the people who would later have the most influence on ecological thinking in Texas were finding their places. In 1946 W. Frank Blair was hired by UT–Austin, and Clark Hubbs joined him in 1949. Together and separately these two men influenced ecological research in zoology at the university in ways that would have far-reaching consequences. In the same period, Frank W. Gould came to TAMU and Lloyd Shinners to Southern Methodist University (SMU). Both men were to have major impact on plant systematics and ecology.

The years between 1946 and 1949 marked the time when research publications with Texas addresses began to appear in appreciable numbers. Important publications during the postwar years included cooperative papers between TAMU and Texas Parks and Wildlife Department in the *Journal of Wildlife Management*. SMU published a journal, *Field and Laboratory: Contributions from the Science Department at SMU*. Gordon Gunter at the University of Texas Marine Science Institute and Jack L. Baughman at Texas

Parks and Wildlife were publishing papers on bay and gulf ecology. In 1949 the first in a long series of papers on the biogeographic relationships of Texas vertebrates by W. Frank Blair and his students appeared. Blair and Clark Hubbs began to build the Texas Natural History Collection of Vertebrates. Papers on invertebrates were lacking during this period except those of H. A. Freeman of SMU on butterflies and T. E. Pully of the University of Houston–University Park on mollusks. Unfortunately, few papers on invertebrates have been published compared to those on vertebrates.[14] It is perhaps indicative of the quality and sophistication of ecological work in Texas that during the period between 1945 and 1949 only one paper with a Texas author appeared in the journal *Ecology*.[15]

From 1950 to the present, work in ecology, environmental biology, and natural history has been centered in academic institutions, related organizations, and a few governmental agencies. Advances, changes in thinking, new approaches, and consequent contributions have generally become more sophisticated, but in some cases merely prolific. During the 1950s federal funding for research through agencies such as the National Science Foundation, National Institutes of Health, and the Atomic Energy Commission became important, and grant funds for research began to flow. By the 1960s these funds together with the increase in undergraduate and graduate enrollments, the environmental movement, and the availability of jobs created a climate conducive to a growth of the general field of ecology that is unlikely to be equaled in the future. Federal budget-tightening in the early 1970s reduced funding, particularly to the smaller, less research-oriented institutions. At this time there was a coinciding leveling off and even decrease in undergraduate enrollments, which had a negative effect on the academic job market. By the late 1970s, graduate school enrollments in ecological specialties sagged. A countering effect to these negative influences, however, was the National Environmental Policy Act of 1970 and the subsequent need for environmental studies and impact statements. This thrust the business world into ecology and created federal and state agencies to review impact statements, to interpret environmental regulations, and to administer them. Environmental consulting became a new business that pushed the ecological sciences into an applied level to an unparalleled extent. The issues of economic development, land use, and environmental consequences became big business. Means of gathering and analyzing data were needed that were more efficient than the "old ways." The availability of computers and people who could use them led to ecological modeling, simulation studies, and more sophisticated statistical analyses. Consequently, the 1970s and early 1980s have been exciting and challenging times for environmental and ecological studies.

The Nature and Origins of Research in Texas

What sort of research has been done in ecology and related fields in Texas, and where was it done? To answer the first question, *The Southwestern Naturalist*—a journal that serves as a popular outlet for ecological and natural history papers—was chosen for analysis. Of the 2,170 articles published between 1956 and 1984, 765 (35 percent) carried a Texas address. Table 1 provides, by five-year periods, the numbers of somewhat arbitrary categories of articles by Texas ecologists. Far more papers on the fauna than on the flora have been published, probably an accurate reflection of the fact that there are more zoologists than botanists in Texas. Botanical and zoological work in the 1950s emphasized taxonomy and distribution; in the 1970s and 1980s there was a shift toward ecological (relationships) and evolutionary papers. Papers were from most of the institutions that will be mentioned in this chapter. A few universities have been singled out because their research in ecology, environmental biology, and natural history has been more extensive.

In an attempt to determine the sources of major ecological contributions in Texas, *Ecology* and *American Naturalist* were reviewed. These journals were chosen because they represent publications of high quality and because acceptance for publication is not based on the organism. Seventy-one articles bearing Texas addresses were published in *Ecology* from 1946 to 1980. These were from seventeen Texas institutions, including some nonacademic ones. Of the fourteen academic institutions, UT–Austin was responsible for twenty-eight papers, TTU for eleven, and TAMU for seven. Thus, 69 percent of the Texas papers came from only three universities. In the *American Naturalist* for the period from 1946 to 1984, forty papers carried Texas addresses and thirty-one of them originated at UT–Austin. The remaining contributions were from only five other places (TAMU, TTU, UH–University Park, SMU, and the U.S. Department of Agriculture). It is apparent that most of the ecological and natural history research in Texas has been and is being done at relatively few places. The titles of papers in these and other journals suggest that Texas ecologists and natural historians have been more concerned with constructing species lists and naming new taxa than they have with such topics as community structure, species diversity, predator-prey relations, competition, and behavioral ecology. Especially absent are reports of long-term studies.

Research at the University of Texas at Austin

Ecological work in botany at UT–Austin in the early 1950s was mainly done by B. C. Tharp. B. L. Turner was hired in 1954, and Tharp retired in 1956 after forty-one years of service to the university. Turner's undergraduate work was done at Sul Ross State University, where he was influenced by Barton Warnock (a

Table 1

Summary of Types and Numbers of Articles by Texas Ecologists Published in
The Southwestern Naturalist, *1956–84*

Articles Published	Total	BOTANICAL				Total	ZOOLOGICAL				
		Dist.	Tax.	Ecol.	Evol.		Dist.	Tax.	Ecol.	Evol.	Behav.
1956–60 (200)	50	6	40	4	0	56	19	8	16	5	8
1961–65 (277)	53	24	26	3	1	65	21	12	15	11	6
1966–70 (389)	44	8	27	8	1	78	31	15	12	13	7
1971–75 (391)	28	7	13	7	1	95	41	8	18	18	10
1976–80 (524)	33	10	7	14	2	129	27	14	50	20	19
1980–84[1] (389)	36	4	5	20	7	74	19	9	24	11	7

1. Only four years.

former student of Tharp), and he did his work on the master's degree at SMU with Lloyd Shinners. In 1958 Calvin McMillan (ecology) joined the botany faculty, followed in 1959 by Marshall C. Johnston (a student of Tharp and Turner and a former colleague of Barton Warnock). Johnston and McMillan began work on the phytogeography of northeastern Mexico. Turner was well into his cytotaxonomic study of Compositae, and Walter V. Brown, a long-time faculty member, was working on the genetics of the stomata of grasses and related survivability in arid and semi-arid conditions. In 1960 Ralph Alston (biochemical systematics) rejoined the botany faculty to collaborate with Turner on biochemical and cytotaxonomic studies. This was an important milestone in Texas botany because classification of living organisms according to chemical content provided new insights into evolutionary relationships.

New facilities were added in 1961 at the Balcones Research Center to provide a study site to investigate ecotypic variation of grassland vegetation. Turner became chairman of Botany in 1967 and during this period gained an international reputation while serving on the steering committee for systematic botany of the Eleventh International Botanical Congress. The 1970s were exciting times for botany at UT–Austin. New faculty were added, including Gary Cole (mycology), Donald Levin (population and co-evolutionary biology), and Beryl Simpson (biosystematics). The herbarium (with Johnston as acting director) acquired and integrated the C. L. Lundell Herbarium to create a 650,000-specimen research facility in newly renovated quarters. The herbarium supported expeditions to New Guinea, Mexico, and South America. Johnston and Turner were building the university's Rare Plant Study Center and its propagation facility. In the middle 1970s additional faculty with ecological leanings were hired: Daniel Kambouski (joint appointment in botany and marine science) and Verne Grant (evolution). Turner finished his work on Compositae.[16] He is also an authority on community structure. Johnston, with support from the Kleberg Foundation, was preparing his work on flora of the Chihuahuan desert and some semi-popular books on medicinal and edible plants of Texas. He had also worked on the very important *Manual of the Vascular Plants of Texas* with Donovan S. Correll.[17] By the late 1970s the botany department had developed a first-class graduate program and was rated in the top five programs in botany by a National Academy of Sciences survey. By 1983 UT–Austin's botany department was tied for top ranking with that of the University of California at Davis. The

doctoral program, with sixty students, was one of the largest in the world. Four members of the faculty (Harold Bold, Richard Starr, Verne Grant, and Jack Myers) had been elected to the National Academy of Sciences. The UT–Austin Plant Resources Center included the university and the Lundell herbaria containing about 900,000 specimens. In addition, seeds or propagules of threatened or endangered plant species are held in storage so that future generations of biologists might be able to restore them in garden or greenhouse environments. The Algae Culture Collection, under the direction of Starr, is one of the largest in the world.

Since about 1908 the UT–Austin Zoology Department had been strong in genetics and developmental biology. Long-time faculty members and Dana B. Casteel (entomology and invertebrate zoology) were naturalists, but it was not until the arrival of W. Frank Blair (fig. 1) in 1946 and Clark Hubbs in 1949 that ecological studies began to flourish. These two men

Figure 1. W. Frank Blair (1912–1985). Eminent ecologist, Professor of Zoology, The University of Texas at Austin, 1946–1985.

established a graduate program in ecological and evolutionary biology whose influence would be far-reaching. During the 1940s Blair and his students published biogeographic studies of vertebrates of Texas that culminated in Blair's paper, "The Biotic Provinces of Texas."[18] In the early 1950s Blair's research emphasis shifted from biogeographic studies to evolutionary processes, species concepts, and the "new systematics." For the next twenty years, Blair and his students used amphibians to study interbreeding, isolating mechanisms, and speciation processes. These studies were carried out in North and South America and resulted in the publication of *Evolution in the Genus Bufo.*[19] During this time Hubbs worked on the distribution of Texas fishes, and by the middle 1950s he had moved his research in an analytical direction, studying hybridization in fishes. In 1955 Robert K. Selander (ornithology) joined the faculty, and in 1957 Bassett Maguire (invertebrate ecology) was hired. By 1958 Maguire was studying "the ways small aquatic organisms are transported from one body of water to another across dry land."

The 1960s were years of progress and expansion in environmental studies. Blair and Hubbs continued their work on natural populations of vertebrates, particularly as related to basic eco-evolutionary questions. Blair assumed an expanding role, coordinating the International Biological Program on convergent and divergent evolution, particularly in South America. Hubbs established his expertise in the area of aquatic pollution, particularly in thermal pollution of lakes.[20] Marshall Wheeler and Osmond P. Breland were studying *Drosophila* taxonomy and ecology, and mosquito chromosome taxonomy. Maguire was investigating the genetics and ecology of cave animals. New additions to the faculty during the 1960s were Gray Merriam (mammalian ecology, telemetry, and animal behavior), Eric Pianka (evolutionary ecology), and Richard N. Richardson (behavior and ecological genetics).

Of great signficance to the ecology program at UT–Austin was the 1963 NSF grant to help establish Brackenridge Field Laboratory. This facility, adjacent to Lake Austin, provided a place to bridge the gap between controlled laboratory experiments and studies under natural circumstances. The Brackenridge laboratory was formally opened in 1967 with Blair as the first director. In 1980 Lawrence E. Gilbert, Jr., became director. The eighty-acre facility includes a natural area, a laboratory building and greenhouses, various population enclosures, eight ponds, and a rare plants area. In 1966 a two-year NSF grant provided support

for graduate teaching and research in systematic and environmental biology. The grant supported thirty-three graduate research assistantships, ten for eleven months, and twenty-three for three months. These grants freed students from teaching responsibilities so they could spend extensive lengths of time on field projects. During the 1970s David Crews (reproductive physiology), John Rawlins (entomology and systematics), Lawrence E. Gilbert, Jr. (animal-plant interactions, insect population biology), Mary A. Rankin (physiological ecology of insects), and Michael Singer (population biology, behavior, and evolution) were added to the ecology group. By the late 1970s Blair was nearing the end of a long career but was still active. He conducted (with Maguire) an international workshop in Juarez, Mexico, on "People and the Biosphere" and was the keynote speaker at an international conference in Saltillo, Mexico, on resources of the American deserts. Clark Hubbs became leader of the Department of the Interior's Rio Grande Fishes Recovery Team, responsible for endangered species. His work on reproductive biology and hybridization of fishes was extensive.[21] He served as president of the Southwestern Association of Naturalists, the Texas Academy of Science, and the American Society of Ichthyologists and Herpetologists. He was on numerous national committees concerned with ecology, preservation of resources, and endangered species and for thirteen years was managing editor of *Copeia.* Recently, Michael J. Ryan (neurobiology, behavioral ecology, and evolution) was added to the faculty. Maguire became involved in studies on the dynamics of closed ecological systems. The Texas natural history collection of vertebrate specimens amassed by Blair, Hubbs, and their students was transferred to Texas Memorial Museum. The collection also included seven hundred audiotapes of vertebrate vocalization. Blair became Emeritus Professor of Zoology in 1982. Rapidly declining health led to his death on February 9, 1985, after a long and distinguished career in ecology and evolutionary biology. Blair had been chairman of the U.S. Committee for the International Biological Program, editor for the IBP volumes, and the author of *Big Biology.*[22] He had also been president of the American Institute of Biological Science, the Ecological Society of America, the Society for the Study of Evolution, the Southwestern Association of Naturalists, and the Texas Herpetological Society. He had been a member of four National Academy of Science/National Research Council committees and chairman of an environmental advisory panel for the Interior Department.[23] Blair published more than one hundred and fifty papers and books on evolution, genetics, ecology, and population biology. Most of these publications were not coauthored. It was accepted and appreciated by his graduate students that he rarely allowed himself to be listed as a coauthor or junior author, thereby giving the graduate student the advantage. In 1977 he received the Joseph Priestley Award, given annually by Dickinson College at Carlisle, Pennsylvania, to scientists who have contributed to the welfare of humanity. During his tenure at UT–Austin he supervised forty-nine doctoral students and fifty-one students seeking the master's degree. He and his wife, Fern, who served as his companion and field assistant, left their Austin home, a ten-acre area with pond and cottage, to the Travis County Audubon Society as an ecological preserve. In 1983 the Department of Zoology was ranked seventh in the nation by a National Academy of Sciences survey. The work of the ecology group certainly contributed to this high ranking.

In the early 1950s Gordon Gunter (ichthyology) directed the University of Texas Marine Science Laboratory at Port Aransas. His work concentrated on fishes and bay ecology. Gunter was succeeded in 1956 by Howard Odum, who secured Rockefeller Foundation grants to work on productivity in Puerto Rican rain forests and NSF grants (with Louis S. Kornicker) to study ostracods of Texas bays. By 1958 there were five fulltime professional staff at the Port Aransas facility. In 1960 the Texas legislature authorized construction of additional buildings. Patrick Parker was added to the staff to study trace elements of radioactive substances in Texas bays. Odum resigned in 1961, and Parker served as acting director until Donald E. Wohlschlag became director in 1965. Christopher L. Kiting (foraging and competition among marine invertebrates and algae) and Davis M. Checkley, Jr. (ecology of plankton and fishes) joined the institute in 1978. In 1980 John J. Cullen (biological oceanography and phytoplankton ecology) was added to the staff.

Research at Texas A&M University

The Biology Department at Texas A&M University generally emphasized nonecological research. Nevertheless, the contributions and work of Sewell Hopkins in parasitology and marine biology must be acknowledged. Hopkins came to TAMU in 1935 and retired in 1972. He served on various NSF panels in the late 1950s, was a vice-president of the Texas Academy of Science, and supervised the work of about thirty master's and twenty doctoral students. William J. Clark's

work in aquatic biology over the three decades beginning in the 1960s and the efforts of Lawrence Dillon on insects have also made useful contributions to environmental biology.

Botanical work of an ecological nature at TAMU was mainly carried out in the Department of Range Science. Contributions varied from the pioneering work of Omer E. Sperry on brush control and the use of herbicides, to the McDougal and Sperry study of plants of Big Bend National Park.[24] Frank W. Gould's work on grasses spanned nearly four decades.[25] In addition to holding the title of Distinguished Professor of Range Science, he was also curator of the Tracy Herbarium from 1949 until his retirement in 1979. During this time he increased the holdings of the herbarium from 4,000 to 150,000 specimens. Gould was succeeded as curator by Stephen Hatch. At the time of his death in 1981, Gould was Distinguished Professor Emeritus of Range Science with an international reputation. He had participated in a 1958 project screening parts of plants for sources of oil and protein for the U.S. Department of Agriculture. Later he worked with the Smithsonian Institution on "Flora of Ceylon." In the year 1972–73, with NSF support, Gould studied North American and African species of grass (*Schizachyrium* sp. and *Digitaria* sp.) at the Royal Botanic Gardens in Kew, England. He was an authority on grama grasses (*Bouteloua* sp.). Besides writing or coauthoring five books, he was also the author—singly and with others—of seventy-eight shorter publications. Gould was more than a scientist, however; he loved nature, fishing, and hunting. He was extremely competitive in all of his endeavors. To Frank Gould a thunderstorm was a wonderful event and an opportunity to illustrate "nature" to his daughters, his students, or whomever else was his audience.[26]

At TAMU ecological work in the Department of Wildlife and Fisheries Sciences in the early 1950s was done by W. B. Davis, his colleagues, and students. Studies were frequently cooperative efforts with the Texas Parks and Wildlife Department. Aquatic studies were the responsibility of Frank Knapp (fish ecology), who was active until 1954. His successor, George K. Reid (aquatic ecology), resigned in 1956. Later in that decade Richard Baldauf (herpetology) and Jack Inglis (ecology and ornithology) came to TAMU, to be joined in the early 1960s by Kirk Strawn (ichthyology and fisheries management). During the next few years the department broadened its offerings and continued its research emphasis in applied ecology and the taxonomy and ecology of Mexican and Central American vertebrates. Davis and Dilford Carter worked on mammals, particularly bats, and Davis and James Dixon worked on amphibians and reptiles.[27] Keith Arnold (ornithology) came to College Station in 1966, and in the late 1960s comprehensive fisheries and ornithology programs under the direction of Strawn and Arnold were added to the curriculum. Davis retired in 1967 after forty years in the department, including more than twenty as its head. His work in mammalian taxonomy earned him a national reputation. Recognition of his accomplishments and contributions was noted by election to two terms as president of the American Society of Mammalogists. Later, Davis revised "The Mammals of Texas."[28] This semipopular, largely anecdotal, and sometimes criticized[29] discussion of Texas mammals was the only comprehensive treatment of this group in Texas at that time.

Faculty research productivity expanded in the late 1960s and early 1970s mainly because of the availability of grant funds and the spinoff from the "environmental movement" of the 1960s, which created an interest among college students in ecological studies. More faculty were added: Dale Caldwell (ichthyology), Fritz Walther (animal behavior), David Schmidly (mammalogy), and Fred Hendricks (ichthyology). Nova Silvy (wildlife management and population dynamics) and John Bickham (cytogenetic taxonomy) were added later. Before the early 1970s undergraduates had only two choices: fisheries or wildlife. In 1972 other options were wildlife ecology, natural history, aquaculture, fisheries ecology, museum science, and teaching. Work expanded to include crayfish and fish-farming projects along the Texas coast and studies of thermal enrichment of lakes by power-generating plants. Recent research at TAMU in wildlife and fisheries science has included work in Mexico and a continuation of classical taxonomic and distributional studies.[30]

The Department of Recreation and Parks at TAMU also worked with environmental problems, frequently in cooperation with the Texas Parks and Wildlife Department and the Nature Conservancy.[31]

Research at Southern Methodist University

Ecological and natural history contributions at Southern Methodist University (SMU) in the 1950s were mostly of a botanical nature and resulted from the work of Eula Whitehouse (cryptogamic botany) and Lloyd H. Shinners (systematic botany). Shinners was an intellectual leader in Texas and the nation with his contributions to systematics, ecology, and occasionally "philosophy." He built the SMU herbarium into a

major plant repository and—with grants from the Ford Foundation and NSF—produced numerous papers on taxonomy and plant distribution in Texas.[32] Born in Canada (Blue Sky, Alberta) in 1918, Shinners received his undergraduate and graduate degrees at the University of Wisconsin. His career in systematic botany was relatively brief but highly productive. He became director of the SMU herbarium in 1949 and full professor in 1960. His goal to make the herbarium in Dallas the largest and finest in the South was accomplished, for during his twenty-three years as director the number of specimens grew from about 20,000 to 340,000. SMU's taxonomic library is ranked between twelfth and fifteenth in the nation.[33] Shinners' knowledge of seven languages allowed him to use the international scientific literature very effectively. Some difficulty in publishing a lengthy and controversial manuscript led him to found his own botanical journal, *Sida, Contributions to Botany*. To Shinners, money was a necessity to be used to purchase private herbaria and literature and to subsidize authors. His ability to avoid busywork was well known; postcards were used to answer correspondence. One of Shinners' greatest contributions was his dedicated service as the first editor of the *Southwestern Naturalist*. His guidance and editorial talent were instrumental in the ultimate success of this journal. In a tribute written by his good friend Donovan S. Correll, his personality was captured by these comments:

His greatest handicap in his having to contend with his colleagues and fellowmen generally was the fact that he was far too intelligent for most of them. He could immediately spot a phony, and, unfortunately for his peace of mind, he could not use false diplomacy in dealing with stupidity. . . . Although some could not agree with him, there were very few who did not admire him. Lloyd frequently injected into his scientific writings not only pungent witticisms of his own but also those of historical figures in botany. His mind and that part of the Herbarium that could be housed were orderly and efficient, but he was basically a "packrat" and to the casual visitor his herbarium always appeared to be in total disarray. To some he was a "loner," but to those who were closest to him he was a soft-spoken, fascinating conversationalist, who always seemed apologetic for having to make any sort of criticism of that which should be criticized.[34]

Diabetes contributed to the gradual decline of his health and led to his death in February 1971. William F.

Mahler succeeded Shinners as director of the herbarium and editor of *Sida*, a position in which he was ably aided by Barney Lipscomb. Bob Slaughter's work at SMU was mostly in vertebrate paleontology, but his provocative thinking on natural history topics[35] represented a stimulating approach too seldom seen in academic circles. The biology department of SMU expanded its horizons in the 1970s with the addition of John E. Ubelaker (invertebrate zoology), John O. Mecom (ecology), Raymond P. Canham (biochemical systematics), and Kirkland Jones (competition ecology).

Research at Texas Tech University

In 1948 the biology department at Texas Tech University (TTU) consisted of only three professional-level faculty (including Russell W. Strandtmann) and three instructors. In the early 1950s faculty additions included Robert Mitchell (invertebrate zoology), Vernon Proctor (algology), Donald W. Tinkle (population biology and evolution of reptiles), and Chester Rowell (systematic and ecological botany). Proctor and Strandtmann had support for their separate projects on algae and mites from the National Institute of Health. In addition Strandtmann worked on the nesting habits and density of golden eagles in the Cap Rock area. Proctor and his students developed an active algology research program in the postwar decades. In 1954 the second annual meeting of the Southwestern Association of Naturalists was held at TTU in conjunction with the Southwestern Division of American Association for the Advancement of Science. This indicated the rising stature of the university.

The 1960s were a time of expansion and diversification for TTU. Robert L. Packard joined the faculty in 1962 and with Chester Rowell was instrumental in establishing a field research station at Kermit. In 1965 additional research space was created on campus, and in 1969 the biology department moved into a new six-story building. In 1965 John H. Mecham replaced Tinkle, who moved to the University of Michigan. Kent Rylander (ornithology), Eric Bolen (wildlife ecology), and Francis L. Rose (vertebrate zoology) joined the faculty in 1966, followed in 1967 by Robert Baker (cytotaxonomy of mammals). By that time active research programs were in progress in algology, herpetology, mammalogy, and invertebrates. The mammal work of Packard and Baker during this period established a base for TTU's growth as a center for taxonomic research on mammals. At about the same time, J. Knox Jones and Dilford Carter (mammalogists) came to the

university with appointments in biology and at the TTU museum. New faculty also included William Atchley (population biology), David Worthington (plant chemosystematics), and Hugh Genoways (mammalogy, the museum).

The museum of TTU was founded in 1935 with little or no connection to academic programs. The present museum building was dedicated in 1970, and the adjacent Natural Science Research Laboratory currently houses all the biological collections except for the herbarium. The museum publishes two serials, *Occasional Papers* and *Special Publications*, both started in 1972, with a cumulative publication of about 120 articles, mainly in mammalian taxonomy.

Research at Other Universities in Texas

Angelo State University began operating as a four-year institution in 1965 and almost immediately included environmental biology and natural history in its program. By the late 1960s Gordon Creel and W. A. Thornton were investigating isolation mechanisms in cottontail rabbits (*Sylvilagus* sp.) and foxes (*Vulpes* sp.). In the early 1970s Royce Ballinger (herpetology) and Chester Rowell (systematic botany) joined the faculty. A 4,600-acre instructional and research center was developed, and in 1972 the department began a master of science program including opportunities for ecologically oriented research. By the late 1970s the faculty expanded to include Terry Maxwell (ornithology), Crosby Jones (entomology), and Ned Strenth (invertebrate zoology).

The presence of M. D. Bryant (vertebrate ecology) on the faculty of Austin College in the early 1950s ensured attention to ecological matters there. Bryant privately funded a series of publications on geology, reptiles, birds, and vegetation of the Lake Texoma region. He was joined in 1961 by Howard McCarley (vertebrate ecology), who continued working on isolating mechanisms in white-footed mice (*Peromyscus* sp.) and later did population and behavioral studies on ground squirrels (*Spermophilus* sp.). During the 1970s McCarley and his students worked on vocalization in coyotes and red wolves and cooperated with the U.S. Fish and Wildlife Service red wolf recovery staff.[36] In 1967 Jack R. Pierce (herpetology) came to Sherman with his interest in hybridization processes in amphibians. The addition of George M. Diggs, Jr. (systematic botany) in 1980 expanded the opportunities in environmental biology at Austin College.

Ecological contributions at Baylor University in the 1950s centered around the work of Bryce Brown on amphibians and reptiles and around Floyd Davidson's work on algae. The addition of Thomas E. Kennerly (mammalian ecology) in 1955 and his interest in eastern pocket gopher (*Geomys* sp.) ecology and evolution added another dimension to Baylor's program. Summer field courses in biology and geology were added to the curriculum. The presence in the 1960s of Frederick R. Gehlbach, Owen T. Lind, and Julian F. Watkins, II, provided new research directions and possibilities for the biology department. Watkins' work on army ants was one of the few research programs on invertebrates in the state at that time.[37] In the late 1960s Watkins and Gehlbach collaborated on chemical communication in predator-prey coactions of snakes and arthropods. In 1971 Baylor initiated Master of Science programs in ecology and an interdisciplinary ecology program. Faculty additions (or replacements) during this time included Jerry Snider (bryophyte evolutionary biology), Anthony E. Echelle (ichthyology), and J. Spencer Johnston (*Drosophila* genetics and ecology). Owen T. Lind built a research group concerned with productivity of reservoirs. Gehlbach's work on the biomes of the Guadalupe Mountains and adjacent areas resulted in an analysis of the ecology of the U.S.—Mexico border.[38] His concern with species diversity and natural area conservation is reflected in his paper for resource managers,[39] in which he applied multivariate statistical analysis to the solving of ecological problems.

Environmental studies at Huston-Tillotson College included work by Exalton A. Delco in the early 1960s on sound production and discrimination in fishes.[40] C. S. Lin worked on the behavior and bionomics of some neotropical wasps.[41]

When Walter W. Dalquest came to Midwestern University in the early 1950s, he began his work on living and extinct mammals. By the mid-1960s Dalquest had built the university's vertebrate collection to a respectable size and was adding to it through expeditions to Mozambique, where he studied and collected fossil and recent mammals.

Ecological work at North Texas State University immediately after World War II concentrated on aquatic biology. J. K. G. Silvey and his students worked on the problem of odors and tastes in water. In the 1960s Harold E. Schlichting studied dispersal of algae and related organisms. Kenneth Stewart then collaborated with Schlichting and extended the study of dispersal mechanisms to insects. By the 1970s Lloyd C. Fitzpatrick (physiological ecology) was studying energetics in lizards and mammals, and Earl Zimmerman (cyto- and chemical taxonomy) was focusing on mammalian taxonomy.

Ecology and natural history at Pan American University began with Pauline James (ornithology and ecology) and Robert I. Lonard (plant taxonomy). In 1972 a master's-degree program was approved, and Lonard started two graduate courses in tropical biology. Frank Judd came to Pan American in 1972 and began publishing in physiological ecology, phytogeography, and hurricane ecology. By the mid-1970s N. L. Savage was studying the microbial ecology of the Rio Grande River; Lonard's studies of flowering plants and algae of South Padre Island and Pauline James' studies of cowbird-nest parasitism were continuing. By 1974 the university had established a marine biological laboratory on the south tip of Padre Island. NSF curriculum development grants to Lonard and Richard Ross (environmental and evolutionary biology) strengthened the environmental aspect of the department. The addition of Robert J. Edwards (ichthyology) in 1980 extended opportunities for fish studies in the lower Rio Grande Valley.

Biology at Rice University in the 1950s did not emphasize ecology or natural history. Asa Chandler's laboratory, however, was a productive unit for parasitology, and Roy Talmage and Dale Buchanan reviewed the natural history and ecology of the nine-banded armadillo (*Dasypus novemcinctus*).[42] In 1959 Clark P. Read (parasitology) joined the faculty and, until his untimely death in 1973, helped elucidate biochemical, physiological, and ecological mechanisms regulating the existence of parasites in the intestinal habitat.[43] In the 1960s Jack Hudson initiated studies in the physiological ecology of vertebrates, emphasizing temperature, moisture, and torpor relationships of mammals. At this time C. H. (Herb) Ward was publishing results of his work in aquatic ecology and related topics. Ward is currently principal editor of the international journal *Environmental Toxicology and Chemistry*. When Hudson left for Cornell in 1970, Richard Newman joined the Rice faculty as physiological ecologist. Two years later Paul A. Harcombe arrived. He has specialized in structure and dynamic studies of the forests of the Big Thicket. Frank Fisher, Jr., established the Wetland Studies Program in the early 1970s, emphasizing pollution effects on natural fauna in the wetlands. Joan E. Strassman, a population biologist who joined the faculty in 1980, has focused on the evolutionary biology of social wasps (*Polistes* sp.).

Ecological work at Sam Houston State University in the 1950s came from S. R. Warner (plant ecology), who was nearing retirement, W. A. Thornton (herpetology), and Claud McLeod. McLeod worked on the vegetation of east Texas until the early 1970s. In the 1960s and 1970s the graduate program expanded with an emphasis on aquatic biology.

Ecological studies at Southwest Texas State University began with Charles S. Smith, who taught a course in ecology in the 1940s. During the 1950s W. E. Norris, Jr., and W. K. Davis continued this part of the program. In 1966 the university acquired the property and buildings of the U.S. Fish Hatchery on the San Marcos River. This acquisition and the growing public concern in Texas over water quality and consumption provided the impetus to establish an aquatic station as a subdivision of the biology program. The completion of the H. M. Freeman building in 1983, equipped with modern instruments, allowed an expanded aquatic program. Current faculty include H. H. Hannan (limnology), W. C. Young (aquatic ecology), B. G. Whiteside (ichthyology and fisheries management), Glenn Longley (pollution biology), David Huffman (biometrics and parasitology), Robert Short (stream ecology and invertebrates), and Joseph Tomasso (toxicology). In 1979 the Edwards Aquifer Research and Data Center was formed as a state-supported agency on the Southwest Texas State campus to study the Edwards aquifer and provide information to the public.

Ecological contributions from Stephen F. Austin State University during the 1950s were from Howard McCarley (vertebrate ecology), who came in 1950, and Walter Lewis (systematic botany), who joined him in 1957. McCarley began a vertebrate collection, and Lewis added to a small herbarium begun in 1948 by Hugh B. Smith. McCarley was interested in the distribution of vertebrates in eastern Texas and ecological and evolutionary processes in white-footed mice (*Peromyscus* sp.). Nine years of data collection on east Texas mammals resulted in the first comprehensive paper on the subject since Bailey's work.[44] Lewis was one of the earliest users of cytotaxonomic techniques in Texas. In 1959 Robert Packard (mammalogy) succeeded McCarley, and in the early 1960s Packard and Lewis received grants to work on white-footed mice and bluets (*Heydotidae*), respectively. In 1964 Packard moved to Texas Tech University. New additions during this decade were Jack McCullough (aquatic ecology), Elray S. Nixon (plant ecology), and Victor Hoff (plant cytotaxonomy) in part replacing Lewis, who had moved to Washington University and the Missouri Botanical Garden at St. Louis in 1964. It was during this period that the department began offering graduate work leading to the master's degree. In 1967 William H. Gibson (entomology) joined the faculty. In the 1970s McCullough and his students studied productivity in a variety of aquatic circumstances, including those in which hot-water effluents were a factor. Nixon and his students conducted vegetational surveys and analyses, and under his directorship the herbarium grew to 60,000 specimens by 1985. Charles D. Fisher (ornithology) and Fred L. Rainwater (ichthyology, herpetology), worked with National Park Service support, studying birds, amphibians, and reptiles of the Big Thicket National Preserve.

In the early 1950s ecological work at Sul Ross University was done by Barton S. Warnock (plant systematics and ecology), who made the Sul Ross biology department a center for understanding Trans-Pecos vegetation.[45] In 1963 A. Michael Powell (systematic botany, cytotaxonomy), one of B. L. Turner's students, joined Warnock and continued the studies of Big Bend vegetation. In the succeeding decades James F. Scudday (vertebrate ecology) contributed distributional and ecological information on vertebrates of the area. When Warnock retired in 1979, John Miller (plant systematics and phytochemistry) was added to the faculty. In 1974 Powell was instrumental in organizing the Chihuahuan Desert Research Institute, and along with Scudday served on its original board of directors.

Ecological work at Texas A&I University (TAIU) during the 1950s was vested in E. R. Bogusch, who worked on mesquite and factors influencing its distribution. During the following decade George Williges and David Pratt studied African game mammals that were becoming an important part of the economy and ecology of south Texas ranches. Burrus McDaniel contributed data on the taxonomy and distribution of mealybugs (*Homoptera*). A boost to the TAIU ecological program was a 1967 grant from the Caeser Kleberg Foundation to establish a wildlife program. By 1968 nineteen graduate students were enrolled in this program. During the 1970s, work of varied emphases continued on wildlife ecology. Allan Chaney and Brian Chapman studied plant succession and avian uses of dredged material on offshore islands of the Texas coast.

Serious ecological work did not begin at Texas Christian University until the middle 1960s although John Forsyth had earlier been active in herpetological circles. Russell Faulkner, Dee Keeton, and Clifford Murphy began limnological investigations of Lake Benbrook, and their work carried over into the 1970s as it applied to the dispersal and biology of the Asiatic clam (*Corbicula*). During that decade Gary Ferguson (ecology), Glen Kroh (plant ecology), and Gail Doel (behavior) were added. Ray Drenner came to Fort Worth in the late 1970s, and his investigations of feeding selectivity and the ecological impact of planktivorous fish on aquatic systems gained international stature.

Warren M. Pulich at the University of Dallas contributed data on Texas birds. For over fifteen years, he studied the life history, distribution, and habitat requirements of the golden-cheeked warbler (*Dendroica chrysoparia*), an endangered species.[46] It was through the studies of Pulich and the efforts of many others that some nesting habitat for this species was preserved in Texas.

Serious ecological work at the University of Houston (UH–University Park) began about 1968 when over 900 acres in Galveston County were dedicated as the University of Houston Coastal Center. An environmental laboratory was built in the early 1970s, and 209 acres were dedicated for instruction, 539 acres for manipulative research, and 181 acres to study ecological succession. The center serves the university at large as well as Rice University, the University of Texas School of Public Health, and Welder Wildlife Foundation. David L. Jameson, who came to UH–University Park in 1967, directed the center from 1972 to 1976 and was largely responsible for its early success. He was succeeded by Glen D. Aumann in 1977. In addition to Jameson and Aumann, ecologists working out of the center and the main campuses include Guy N. Cameron (behavioral ecology and bioenergetics) and Edwin H. Bryant (ecological genetics). In 1978 the center established a data base for coastal weather records and cooperated with the Texas System of Natural Laboratories to produce a computer-based index system of Texas species providing data for environmental assessment studies. Published papers associated with the center grew from seventeen in 1974 to seventy-nine in 1983 and included studies on demographic responses to species manipulation,[47] habitat selection and trophic diversity,[48] anuran systematics,[49] and the effects of man-made structures on bird migration.[50] In 1976 a cooperative program in marine sciences was begun with the National Marine Fisheries Center in Galveston.

After becoming part of the University of Texas system in the 1960s, UT–El Paso established the Museum of Arid Land Biology. In 1976 this unit was reorganized into the Laboratory for Environmental Biology, with William H. Reid (plant biology) as coordinator. A. H. Harris (vertebrate ecology and mammalogy) supervised the collections, assisted by Richard Worthington and Robert Webb.

The University of Texas at San Antonio in its Division of Allied Health and Life Sciences (and later the Division of Life Sciences) chose not to emphasize natural history. Nevertheless, O. W. Van Auken (frequently working with A. L. Ford) made significant contributions to the understanding of the composition and diversity of upland vegetational communities,[51] floodplain forests,[52] and more recently vegetation of the Chihuahuan Desert.[53]

Research in Governmental and Private Sectors

The Chihuahuan Desert Research Institute was incorporated in 1974 as a nonprofit scientific and educational organization dedicated to understanding the Chihuahuan Desert region through research and publication. A. Michael Powell was the prime organizer. W. Grainger Hunt and Dwight E. Deal were successive unpaid general managers of the institute. In 1978 Dennis J. Miller became the first executive director and presently serves in that capacity. Projects that have been sponsored or conducted by the institute include studies on the ecology of the peregrine and aplomado falcons, plant foods of Texas Indians, endangered fish populations in Trans-Pecos Texas, the flora of the Guadalupe Mountains and Carlsbad Caverns national parks, and surveys of potentially endangered plant species. Additionally, the institute provides resources for precollege science education in Texas, maintains a visitor center (including a nature trail system), and provides scholarships to students at Texas colleges and universities. The visitor complex is located in the Davis Mountains, three miles south of Fort Davis on Highway 118, with headquarters on the campus of Sul Ross State University. Permanent staff include Alan G. Brenner, education director, and Allan D. Zimmerman, research director.

The Texas Committee on Natural Resources (TCONR) was founded in 1968 by Dallas attorney Edward C. (Ned) Fritz to educate the public on ecological issues. Over the years, TCONR has been active in advocating the Big Thicket Natural Preserve, opposing the 1976 Texas water plan, delaying clear-cutting practices in east Texas forests, and preserving five areas (35,000 acres) as east Texas wilderness areas. The guiding force behind these activities has been Fritz and his adversarial style. He received the 1970 National American Motors Conservation Award, the 1975 Oak Leaf Award of the Nature Conservancy, and in 1985 the Sierra Club Outstanding Service Award.

Concern about the preservation of rare and endangered species brought about the formation of the Texas Organization for Endangered Species in 1972. This group of professional and amateur biologists, conservationists, and other interested persons assumed the job of listing those species in need of preservation.[54] The organization has been active since its inception, serving as a clearinghouse and information center for groups and individuals studying taxa in danger of being lost.

The Texas Parks and Wildlife Department began as the Texas Game, Fish, and Oyster Commission but assumed its current name when it was combined with the Parks Division in 1963. Freshwater fisheries management received emphasis in 1939 when the first professional biologist was hired. Marion Toole became chief aquatic biologist in the 1940s and for many years supervised the freshwater surveys. The early 1970s began a new era of fisheries management when Robert J. Kemp was appointed director of fisheries. Kemp recognized the conflicts between recreational and commercial fishing interests in coastal waters and believed there was a need for more management of freshwater habitats. In 1983 legislation was passed regulating the taking of red drum and speckled trout. This was the first time in the United States that management of a marine fish species was directed at maintaining the sportfishing potential.[55] In fresh water, new species of nonnative fishes are introduced—for example, striped bass (*Morone saxatilis*)—to create diversity, rejuvenation of fishing success, and perhaps problems as yet unknown.

Wildlife management by the Texas Parks and Wildlife Department in the 1940s and early 1950s was very closely related to the Wildlife Science Department at TAMU. Students of Walter P. Taylor and W. B. Davis, including Daniel W. Lay, Phil Goodrum, Valgene W. Lehmann, John Singleton, Matt H. Whisenhunt, Jr., Gus A. Engeling, Wendell Swank, and many others, worked for the department as game biologists and were to have a lasting influence on the approach to management programs in the state. These programs were coordinated and directed in the 1940s and 1950s by W. C. Glazener and Eugene Walker. Terrestrial research programs aimed at improving habitat and understanding the concept of sustained yield have increased in the last thirty years. The creation of a nongame unit broadened the department. Wildlife management areas such as Black Gap, Engeling, J. D. Murphree, and others provide opportunities for studies in ecologically diverse areas. Publication of the monthly magazine *Texas Parks and Wildlife* has been a positive influence calling attention to environmental concerns with the help of beautiful color photographs taken in all parts of the state.

Aquatic pollution was not a public issue until the late 1950s and the early 1960s. Before that period, people such as J. L. Baughman, Gordon Gunter, Rudy Marek, and Clark Hubbs were reporting fish kills and pollution problems, but the responsibility for pollution investigation was not the assignment of any particular agency. In part, this problem was focused on when the Texas Water Quality Board was formed in 1967. This was a start toward curbing industrial waste polluters in Texas through a permit and enforcement process. In 1977 the Water Quality Board and the

Water Development Board were joined into the Department of Water Resources, which became the Texas Water Commission. Increasingly stringent restrictions were placed on industrial and municipal discharges, including the obtaining of Environmental Protection Agency permits for the discharge of pollutants. Toxic wastes and aquatic pollution are real problems, but at least a vehicle for problem-solving is in place.

The Research Foundation established immediately after World War II at Renner later became part of the Texas A&M University system. During its existence, however, Cyrus Lundell directed the development of an extensive herbarium, including the 35,000-specimen collection and library of the late S. F. Blake. Donovan S. Correll made significant contributions to the taxonomy and distribution of the vascular plants of Texas.[56]

The Texas System of Natural Laboratories was founded in 1967 as a nonprofit organization. A central aim was to secure the use of blocks of land in ecologically diverse and sensitive areas as natural laboratories where ecological research and teaching could occur. The information gained from these laboratories was to be shared among all interested parties and used by the people and industries of Texas in preserving and enhancing the natural resources and quality of life in the state. Laboratory lands are now in excess of one million acres and located in such varied ecological settings as the coastal prairie, pine-hardwood forests, Edwards plateau, blackland prairies, and the Trans-Pecos mountains and deserts. Included are not only private holdings but Texas public school lands and Texas state parks. Nevenna T. Travis, in Austin, has been secretary–treasurer and acting system coordinator since the laboratories were founded.

Ecological contributions from the U.S. Fish and Wildlife Service revolve mostly around the management and public relations programs of eleven refuges in Texas encompassing 204,500 acres. These refuges are primarily wintering sites for migratory waterfowl. The Aransas National Wildlife Refuge is the only wintering place for the endangered whooping crane, and the Attwater Prairie Chicken National Wildlife Refuge in Colorado County is the only locality in the state where this bird can be found. Santa Ana National Wildlife Refuge and the expanded Lower Rio Grande Valley National Wildlife Refuge provide shelter for tropical bird species not found elsewhere in Texas as well as a retreat for the endangered occlot.

The Rob and Bessie Welder Wildlife Foundation was established in 1953 at the death of Rob Welder. The general purpose of the foundation was "to further the education of the people of Texas in wildlife conservation, the habits of wild creatures and to understand the relationships of wildlife to domesticated livestock."[57] Welder state wildlife management area consists of a 7,800-acre working cattle ranch in San Patricio County. The refuge includes varied habitat types with high species richness. Since 1953 the main thrust of the program has been to fund students doing graduate work in wildlife ecology and natural history of vertebrates. Until 1985 about 250 students have been supported (in most of the major universities of the U.S.), and about 80 percent of these have done their research on the refuge. In addition to support of graduate students and independent investigators, the foundation supports a lecture tour and hosts classes from public schools and universities for instruction and experience with the natural world. Clarence Cottam was the first director (1955–1974) and was succeeded at his death by W. Caleb Glazener (1974–1978). Upon Glazener's retirement, James G. Teer became director and currently serves in that position. Offices of the foundation are at the refuge.

Scientific Associations

The Southwestern Association of Naturalists was probably the professional society that had the most influence on Texas ecologists, and, conversely, was the organization on which Texas ecologists and natural historians have had the most impact. That an organization of naturalists should be formed in the Southwest was first discussed in 1950 by a group led by W. Frank Blair. Reasons for forming such an organization included (1) the postwar expansion of natural history research and interest in the Southwest, (2) the need for a publication outlet for natural history research originating in the region, and (3) the need for an annual meeting of people with interests in natural history in this region. In February 1953 a committee was formed to promote an organizational meeting, which was held at the University of Oklahoma biological station on Lake Texoma in May. Texas ecologists W. Frank Blair, Clark Hubbs, and Lloyd Shinners were among the planners. The object of the association was to promote the field study of plants and animals, living and fossil, in the southwest United States and Mexico and to aid the scientific activities of its members. W. Frank Blair was elected the first president, with W. K. Clark, Clark Hubbs, and J. C. Elkins on the board of governors from Texas. Within three months membership stood at about one hundred and included thirty-seven naturalists/ecologists from Texas. By 1954, 100 of the 300 members were from Texas. The organization grew to about 800 in 1980, including approximately 225 with Texas addresses. Many Texas ecologists have served as officers in the organization, including fifteen of the thirty-two presidents. Publication of a quarterly journal, *The Southwestern Naturalist*, which began in 1956 under the able and skilled editorship of Lloyd Shinners, continues at this writing.

In February 1953, fifty-eight people met in Austin to organize the Texas Ornithological Society to promote the discovery and dissemination of knowledge of birds, particularly those of Texas. The annual meetings are held in the spring and include a field trip in addition to presentation of papers by invited speakers. The fall meetings are devoted to field trips.

Notes

1. Gruelach, 1946.
2. Winkler (1915) and Tharp (1926) provided accounts of early botanical investigations and field work.
3. Shinners, 1949.
4. Lewis, 1915.
5. Tharp, 1926.
6. Warner, 1925.
7. Parks and Cory, 1936.
8. Clover, 1937.
9. Oberholser, 1974.
10. Bailey, 1905.
11. Mosauer, 1932; Van Tyne and Sutton, 1937; Burleigh and Lowery, 1940; Davis, 1940; Davis and Robertson, 1944.
12. Blair, 1940.
13. Borrell and Bryant, 1942.
14. Neck, 1984. This is still true at present.
15. Potzger and Tharp, 1946.
16. Turner, 1976.
17. Correll and Johnston, 1970.
18. Blair, 1950.
19. Blair, 1972.
20. Hubbs, 1972.
21. Hubbs, 1971.
22. Blair, 1977.
23. *Austin American Statesman*, Feb. 12, 1985.
24. McDougal and Sperry, 1951.
25. Gould, 1951; 1968; 1978; Gould and Box, 1965.
26. Additional information about Gould and his work can be obtained from Sperry, 1972.
27. Dixon, 1966; 1969.
28. Davis, 1960. It was originally coauthored with Walter P. Taylor.

29. Blair, 1960.

30. Schmidly, 1977; 1983. Research and publications along different investigative lines were typified by such works as Horkel and Silvy, 1980; Gant et al., 1980.

31. Carls and Neal, 1984.

32. A guide to the 277 publications of Lloyd Shinners can be found in Flook, 1973.

33. Mahler, 1971.

34. Correll, 1971, pp. 101–104.

35. Slaughter, 1977.

36. McCarley and Carley, 1979.

37. Watkins, 1964.

38. Gehlbach, 1981.

39. Gehlbach, 1984.

40. Delco, 1960.

41. Lin, 1971.

42. Talmage and Buchanan, 1954.

43. Self, 1975.

44. Bailey, 1905; McCarley, 1959.

45. For example, Warnock, 1970.

46. Pulich, 1976.

47. Jameson and Green, 1974; Cameron and Kincaid, 1982.

48. Cameron, 1972.

49. Jameson, 1982.

50. Aumann, 1977.

51. Van Auken et al., 1981.

52. Ford and Van Auken, 1982.

53. Aide and Van Auken, 1985.

54. Publishers' lists are available from TOES, Box 12733, Austin, TX 78711.

55. Private communication: undated intra-agency memo.

56. Correll and Johnston, 1970.

57. From the bylaws of the Welder Foundation.

Bibliography

Aide, Mitch, and O. W. VanAuken. "Chihuahuan Desert Vegetation of Limestone and Basalt Slopes in West Texas." *Southwest. Nat.* 30(1985):533–542.

Aumann, Glen. "Environmental Assessment of an Active Oil Field in the Northwestern Gulf of Mexico. The Effect of Structures on Migratory and Local Birds." *Final Report* (1977), Southeast Fisheries Center, Galveston, Tex. Laboratory.

Bailey, Vernon. "Biological Survey of Texas," *N. Amer. Fauna* 25(1905):1–216.

Blair, W. Frank. "A Contribution to the Ecology and Faunal Relationships of the Mammals of the Davis Mountain Region, Southwestern Texas." *Misc. Publ., Mus. Zool.,* Univ. Mich. 46(1940):7–39.

———. "The Biotic Provinces of Texas." *Tex. J. Sci.* 2(1950):93–116.

———. "Review: The Mammals of Texas." *Southwest. Nat.* 5(1960):176.

———. *Evolution in the Genus Bufo.* Austin: Univ. of Texas Press, 1972.

———. *Big Biology: The U.S./IBP.* Dowden, Hutchinson and Ross, 1977.

Borrell, A. E., and M. D. Bryant. "Mammals of the Big Bend Area of Texas." *U. Cal. Publ. Zool.* 48(1942): 1–62.

Burleigh, Thomas, and G. H. Lowery, Jr. "Birds of the Guadalupe Mountains Region of Western Texas." *Occas. Pap. Mus. Zool.* Louisiana State Univ. (1940), No. 8.

Bush, J. K., and O. W. VanAuken. "Woody Species Composition of the Upper San Antonio River Gallery Forest." *Tex. J. Sci.* 36(1983):139–148.

Cameron, Guy. "Trophic Diversity Determination in Insects in Two Salt March Communities." *Ecol.* 53(1972):58–73.

———, and W. B. Kincaid. "Species Removal Effects on Movements of *Sigmodon hispidus* and *Reithrodontomys fulvescens.*" *Amer. Midl. Nat.* 108 (1982):60–67.

Carls, E. Glenn, and James Neal. "Protection of Texas Natural Diversity: An Introduction for Natural Resource Planners and Managers." *Tex. Agric. Exp. Sta.* Texas A&M Univ. (1984), M.P. 1557.

Clover, E. A. "Vegetational Survey of the Lower Rio Grande Valley, Texas." *Madroño* 4(1937):41–72.

Correll, Donovan S. "Lloyd Herbert Shinners—a Portrait." *Brittonia* 23(1971):101–104.

———, and M. C. Johnston. *Manual of the Vascular Plants of Texas.* Tex. Res. Found., Renner, 1970.

Davis. W. B. "The Mammals of Texas." *Tex. Game, Fish and Oyster Comm. Bull.* 41, 1940.

———, and J. L. Robertson, Jr. "The Mammals of Culberson County, Texas." *J. Mamm.* 25(1944): 254–273.

Delco, Exalton A. "Sound Discrimination by Males of Two Cyprinid Fishes." *Tex. J. Sci.* 12(1960):48–54.

Dixon, James R. "Speciation and Systematics of the Gekkonid Lizard Genus *Phyllodactylus* of the Islands of the Gulf of California." *Proc. Cal. Acad. Sci. 4th Ser.* 33(1966):415–452.

———. "Taxonomic Review of the Mexican Skinks of the *Eumeces brevirostris* Group." *Los Angeles County Mus. Contr. Sci.* 168(1969):1–30.

Flook, Jerry M. "Guide to the Botanical Contributions of Lloyd H. Shinners (1918–1971)." *Sida* 5(1973):137–179.

Ford, Allen L., and O. W. VanAuken. "The Distribution of Woody Species in the Guadalupe River Floodplain Forest in the Edwards Plateau of Texas." *Southwest. Nat.* 27(1982):383–392.

Gehlbach, Frederick R. *Mountain Islands and Desert Seas: A Natural History of the U.S.–Mexican Borderlands.* College Station: Texas A&M Univ. Press, 1981.

———. "Species Diversity and Natural Area Conservation: An Introduction." In *Protection of Texas Natural Diversity: An Introduction for Natural Resource Planners and Managers*, edited by E. G. Carls and James Neal. *Texas Agric. Exp. Sta.* Texas A&M Univ. (1984), M. P. 1557.

Gould, Frank W. "Grasses of the Southwestern United States." *Univ. Ariz. Biol. Sci. Bull.* (1951), No. 7.

———. *Grass Systematics.* New York: McGraw Hill, 1968.

———. *Common Texas Grasses.* W. L. Moody, Jr., Nat. Hist. Series No. 3. College Station: Texas A&M Univ. Press, 1978.

———, and T. W. Box. "Grasses of the Texas Coastal Bend." *Welder Wildlife Found. Contrib.* 34. College Station: Texas A&M Univ. Press, 1965.

Grant, W. E., N. R. French, and L. J. Folse. "Evaluation of the Role of Small Mammals in Grassland Ecosystems: A Modelling Approach." *Ecol. Modelling* 8(1980):15–37.

Gruelach, Victor A. "Botanical Education in Southwestern Colleges and Universities." *Proc. and Trans., Tex. Acad. Sci.* 30(1946):114–120.

Horkel, J. D., and N. J. Silvy. "Possible Evolutionary Consideration of Creating Artificial Leks for Attwater's Prairie Chicken." *N. Am. Prairie Grouse Conf.* 1(1980):42–47.

Hubbs, Clark. "Teleost Hybridization Studies." *Proc. Cal. Acad. Sci.* 38(1971):289–297.

———. "Some Thermal Consequences of Environmental Manipulation of Water." *Biol. Consv.* 4(1972):185–188.

Jameson, David L. "Non-Morphological Approaches to Anuran Systematics. Hybridization." *Bull. Ecol. Soc. Amer.* 62 (1982):167.

———, and A. Green. "Experimental Manipulation of Population Density in Rodents." *Trans. 1st Int. Therio. Cong.* 1(1974):240.

Lewis, I. M. "The Trees of Texas." *Univ. Tex. Bull.* (1915), 22.

Lin, C. S. "Bionomics of *Stritiea carobina* at Lake Texoma with Notes on some Neotropical Species (Hymenoptera: Sphecidae)." *Tex. J. Sci.* 23(1971): 275–286.

McCarley, Howard. "The Mammals of Eastern Texas." *Tex. J. Sci.* 11(1959):385–426.

———, and Curtis J. Carley. "Recent Changes in Distribution and Status of Wild Red Wolves (*Canis rufus*)." *U.S.F.&W. Albuquerque, Endangered Species Rep.* No. 4 (1979):1–38.

McDougal, W. B., and Omer E. Sperry. *Plants of Big Bend National Park.* Washington: U.S. Govt. Print. Office, 1951.

Mahler, Wm. F. "Lloyd Herbert Shinners 1918–1971." *Sida* 4(1971):228–231.

Marks, P. L., and P. A. Harcombe. "Community Diversity of East Texas Forests." *Ecol.* 56(1975): 1004–1008.

Mosauer, Walter. "The Amphibians and Reptiles of the Guadalupe Mountains of New Mexico and Texas." *Occas. Pap. Mus. Zool.* Univ. Mich. (1932), 246:1–18.

Neck, R. W. "Reflections on the Plight of Invertebrates in Texas with Thoughts on Their Conservation." In *Protection of Texas Natural Diversity: An Introduction for Natural Resource Planners and Managers*, edited by E. G. Carls and James Neal. *Tex. Agric. Exp. Sta.* Texas A&M Univ. (1984), M. P. 1557.

Oberholser, H. C. *The Bird Life of Texas*, edited by Edgar B. Kincaid, Jr., Vols. 1 and 2. Austin: Univ. of Texas Press, 1974.

Parks, H. B., V. L. Cory, et al. "Biological Survey of the East Texas Big Thicket Area." Privately published, 1936.

Potzger, J. E., and B. C. Tharp. "Pollen Profile from a Texas Bog." *Ecol.* 28(1946):274–280.

Pulich, Warren M. *The Golden Cheeked Warbler, a Bioecological Study.* Tex. Parks and Wildl. Dept., 1976.

Schmidly, David J. *The Mammals of Trans-Pecos Texas.* W. L. Moody, Jr., Nat. Hist. Series No. 2. College Station: Texas A&M Univ. Press, 1977.

———. *Texas Mammals East of the Balcones Fault Zone.* W. L. Moody, Jr., Nat. Hist. Series No. 6. College Station: Texas A&M Univ. Press, 1983.

Self, J. Teague. "The Contributions of Clark P. Read on Ecology of the Vertebrate Gut and Its Parasites." *Bios.* 46(1975):3–21.

Shinners, Lloyd H. "Early Plant Collections Return to Texas." *Tex. J. Sci.* 1(1949):69–70.

Slaughter, Bob. "Wolves, Coyotes, Ducks and Hybridization." *Tex. J. Sci.* 28(1977):351–354.

Sperry, O. E. "25 Years of Range Science at Texas A&M University." *Symposium of Proc., Silver Anniversary, Range Science.* College Station: Texas A&M Univ. Press, 1972.

Talmage, R. V., and G. D. Buchanan. "The Armadillo, a Review of its Natural History, Ecology, Anatomy and Reproductive Physiology." *Mono. in Biol., The Rice Inst. Pamph.* 41(1954):1–35.

Tharp, B. C. "Structure of Texas Vegetation East of the 98th Meridian." *Univ. Texas Bull.* (1926), 2606.

Turner, B. L. "Fossil History and Geography of Compositae." In Vol. I of *Biology and Chemistry of Compositae*, edited by J. B. Harborne, V. Heywood, and B. L. Turner. London: Academic Press, 1976.

VanAuken, O. W., A. L. Ford, and J. L. Allen. "An Ecological Comparison of Upland Deciduous and Evergreen Forests of Central Texas." *Amer. J. Botany* 68(1981):1249–1256.

VanTyne, J., and G. M. Sutton. "The Birds of Brewster Co., Texas." *Misc. Publ. Mus. Zool.* Univ. Michigan 37(1937):1–119.

Warner, S. R. "The Distribution of Native Plants and Weeds on Certain Soil Types in Eastern Texas." Ph.D. diss., University of Chicago, 1925.

Warnock, B. H. *Wildflowers of the Big Bend Country, Texas.* Alpine: Sul Ross State Univ., 1970.

Watkins, J. F., II. "Laboratory Experiments on the Trail Following of Army Ants of the genus *Neivamyrmex.*" *J. Kans. Ent. Soc.* 37(1964):22–28.

Winkler, Chas. H. "The Botany of Texas: An Account of the Botanical Investigations in Texas and Adjoining Territory." *Univ. Texas Bull.* (1925), 18.

14

Applied Biology: Agriculture, Animal Husbandry, Forestry, and Veterinary Medicine

H. O. Kunkel

THE 1950s and 1960s were bright times for publicly supported agricultural research systems in the United States. Agricultural, forestry, and veterinary scientists came to be viewed as "real" scientists—and this was a time when science enjoyed more respect than at any other time in American history. This popularity was capitalized on in Texas, first at the U.S. Department of Agriculture (USDA) Laboratories and at Texas A&M University (TAMU), then soon at other institutions.

At the end of World War II research in Texas in applied biology—agriculture, forestry, and veterinary medicine—had a history of some solid accomplishments, but research capabilities were geographically dispersed throughout the state and almost wholly separated from the academic scene. Thus, institutional changes and development over the next few years would be as important to applied biological sciences in Texas as developments in the sciences themselves.

The Institutions

The Texas Agricultural Experiment Station (TAES) was established in 1888 and research was immediately initiated within the Agricultural and Mechanical College of Texas (later TAMU). The USDA was established in 1862, principally as a research organization, and its people could be found working in Texas at the turn of the century. But the overriding need was for agricultural research that would be time- and location-specific. The long distances in Texas; its unique local and political interests; the enormous ranges of soils, topography, and climate; and the press for quick responses and practical prescriptions for farming under trying conditions forced dispersion of research capabilities. In 1946, applied biological research was being conducted at more than forty field units and farms throughout Texas. Research installations and personnel of the USDA were also located at the corners of Texas and at places in between—at Amarillo (Bushland), Beaumont, Weslaco, El Paso, Kerrville, Temple, Chillicothe, Lubbock, and Brownwood.

The desire for practical prescriptions also prompted the early postwar development of several privately supported research institutions and initiatives, notably, the Texas Research Foundation located at Renner (now north Dallas), the High Plains Research Foundation near Plainview, the Southwest Agricultural Institute at San Antonio, the M. G. and Johnnye D. Perry Foundation at Robstown, and the Rob and Bessie Welder Wildlife Foundation at Sinton. Inspired, perhaps, by the agricultural societies of the nineteenth century and the imperative to solve problems of South Texas agriculture, the King Ranch also carried out empirical research and tests relating to ranching and livestock.[1]

Nineteen forty-seven was a watershed year in the development of agricultural and other applied biological research in Texas. For several decades, though all was headquartered at College Station, the administration and activities at the School of Agriculture of the A&M College of Texas, the TAES, and the Texas Agricultural Extension Service flowed independently, and in 1946 little interrelationship, exchange, or mutual support existed among the academic, research, and extension functions. Less than a handful of agricultural and veterinary scientists held academic appointments. In 1947, however, these entities were integrated under the Vice President for Agriculture, D. W. Williams, and the leadership of Dean Charles W. Shepardson, Director Ide Peebles Trotter of the Texas Agricultural Extension Service, and Director R. D. Lewis of the TAES. These individuals implemented a strategy that placed academic, research, and extension personnel in a common subject area under a single department head. Two new departments were created: Biochemistry and Nutrition, and Plant Physiology and Pathology. Of equal importance was the creation of graduate research assistantships by Lewis of the TAES.

The effect was immediate and remarkable. The forced union simultaneously facilitated the first major, substantial integration of graduate study and students into the biological sciences in Texas, and led to an unprecedented concentration of research capacity, drawing support from public agencies and industry. It built complementarity between academic programs and agricultural research; it markedly increased the number of scientists working in the TAES; and it made research a mission of the departments of the College of Agriculture and Veterinary Medicine at TAMU. Over 150 persons received doctor's degrees in the departments of the College of Agriculture during the decade of 1949–58, compared to only 6 during the entire previous history of TAMU.

The imperative that research be integrated with an academic effort was implemented in time also at the College of Agricultural Sciences at Texas Tech University (TTU) at Lubbock, the College of Agriculture at Prairie View A&M University, Texas A&I University at Kingsville and its Citrus Training Center at Weslaco, and the College of Forestry at Stephen F. Austin State University at Nacogdoches. Established in 1925, TTU had laid a foundation for research in biology by

the end of World War II.[2] After struggling from inadequate funds and facilities during its first twenty-five years, a series of new buildings, which included facilities for research, was completed in the early 1950s. Using the argument that farmers of the region required local prescriptions, the TTU College of Agricultural Sciences gained public support for its active participation in research. Acquisition of the PanTex Farm near Amarillo from the federal government and a state appropriation to the TAES for research by TTU formed the basis for development of a research program. Beginning in 1967 TTU, under the leadership of Dean Gerald Thomas, received its own appropriated funds for agricultural research directed largely at removal of brushy plants from rangeland, grass reseeding and grazing practices, and the impacts of such practices on wildlife.[3] State appropriated institutional support was extended to research on swine in 1968, and to research on vegetable production in 1973. By the mid-1970s TTU could count a diversified research program ranging across the faculty spectrum of the College.

On June 13, 1946, the TAMU Board of Directors ordered the establishment of a branch station of the TAES at Prairie View A&M to help the College of Agriculture teach agriculture and conduct demonstrations and research as circumstances warranted. Prairie View then became the first experiment station in the nation for blacks. The men involved at Prairie View were Edward B. Evans, president; George L. Smith, dean; and a group of young scientists, J. C. Williams, John M. Coruthers, Oliver E. Smith, Johnie J. Woods, and Roscoe E. Lewis. The research program, however, remained a modest one until the Congress recognized the special existence of the colleges created by the Second Morrill Act in 1890, and with Public 89-106 in 1966 provided small amounts of funding. In 1975 the Congress provided for more substantial federal funding to the "1890 Institutions" for agricultural and related research and extension. The Cooperative Agricultural Research Center and the College of Agriculture at Prairie View A&M now conduct research in environmental quality, human resources, computer applications, soils and agronomy, and animal science. Prairie View A&M boasts research strength in toxic elements in the soil and an International Dairy Goat Research Center.[4]

The longest running of the private initiatives, the King Ranch effort had contributed substantially to the eradication of the fever tick in Texas. By the end of World War II, Robert J. Kleberg, Jr., and the ranch had created a new breed of cattle, the Santa Gertrudis. Cooperative efforts had demonstrated that the phosphorus content of forages was a severe limitation on cattle production in South Texas and could be overcome by dietary supplementation. After World War II, the King Ranch, Inc., and the foundations linked to the ranch (the Robert J. Kleberg, Jr., and Helen C. Kleberg Foundation, Caesar Kleberg Wildlife Foundation, King Ranch Family Trust, and R. M. Kleberg Foundation), turned increasingly to supporting research by grants to other institutions, both public and private. They remain to this time a substantial factor in supporting applied biological research in Texas.

Other privately run institutions for agricultural research were heroic in their efforts to fill the perceived gaps. An Institute of Technology and Plant Industry was launched under the leadership of C. L. Lundell by Southern Methodist University in 1944 to "carry on, supervise and integrate basic and applied research in scientific fields primarily related to agriculture and industry."[5] The Institute, located at Renner, was reorganized in 1946 as the Texas State Research Foundation (later the Texas Research Foundation) to be supported primarily by private subscriptions and grants. Land was acquired, and buildings were built. The herbarium was enlarged. Tests were carried out on soils, grasses, and farming systems, the latter a bold undertaking in light of the minimal understanding of agroecology at the time. The High Plains Station of the Texas Research Foundation was established near Plainview in 1957 to work on the problems peculiar to irrigated farming, and it was turned over to the new High Plains Research Foundation in 1959.

Following the early work on embryo transplantation at the Southwest Foundation for Research and Education, and growing out of the interest of benefactor Tom Slick in agricultural research, a nonprofit Southwest Agricultural Research Institute was chartered and organized also in 1957.[6] Its purpose was "to secure higher productivity of the rangelands of the semiarid Southwest and to increase their efficiency of operations." Judd Morrow, a range scientist, became the first director. Tests for genetic dwarfism in beef cattle, ultrasonic techniques to measure fatness of cattle, mechanical methods of brush control on rangeland, and methods of delivery of pesticides were the principal objects of the work.

For each of these institutions and foundations, however, dependence upon private funds and existence outside of the larger scientific networks became a burden. The facilities and personnel of the Texas Research Foundation at Renner were turned over to the University of Texas at Dallas and the TAMU System

in 1972, resulting in the establishment of the TAMU Research and Extension Center at Dallas. The facilities of the High Plains Research Foundation were leased in 1975 and subsequently granted, in part, to the TAES. The legacy from the estate of Tom Slick, intended for the Southwest Agricultural Research Institute, was divided between Texas Christian University to support training in ranch management and TAMU for the establishment of an endowment to support graduate research scholarships in the agricultural sciences that impact Southwest Texas.

The Rob and Bessie Welder Foundation, unlike others, has continued to thrive. It was set in place by an endowment of both land and funds in 1953 to carry out research and education in wildlife and allied resources, and it remains self-supporting. Under the successive leadership of Clarence Cottam, W. Caleb Glazener, and James G. Teer, the foundation has carried on its programs largely with graduate students from a number of universities across the United States rather than with a permanent research staff.[7] Over 225 graduate students have done their dissertation and thesis research under the auspices of the Foundation. Over four hundred research publications have been produced, largely on the ecology and management of wildlife and on wildlife habitats.

Research and Extension Centers

As the scientific capabilities of the TAES during the postwar years turned increasingly to work in the Colleges of Agriculture and of Veterinary Medicine at TAMU, it became evident in the early 1960s that the maintenance of more than forty small and dispersed sites of TAES research was no longer feasible. The multiplicity of locations came to be afflicted both by scientific and practical problems of operation, and by the coexisting feelings of farmers and ranchers that they were forgotten and their local research station was not well treated by a far-removed administration. By 1965 the imperative to consolidate and redefine the functions of the outlying units was accepted by both the administration of the TAMU system and the Legislature. Two circumstances shaped their thinking: (1) although continuation of the small, one-to-three-man research stations was no longer defensible, some of the remarkable agricultural research in Texas, for example, hybrid sorghum, had emanated from small stations because remarkable men did their work there; (2) models of the effectiveness of larger multidisciplinary research groups grew out of the co-locations of

USDA and TAES at substations at Bushland, Beaumont, and Lubbock. Also, extension specialists were co-located with research scientists at Weslaco in 1959.

A plan was initiated in 1965 to consolidate the off-campus complex of the TAES into twelve regional centers and six other stations having limited research activities.[8] The substations at Beaumont, Lubbock, and Weslaco were designated as "Research and Extension Centers," a term that was also to be applied to the Stephenville and El Paso substations. The locations at Temple and Bushland were being developed as USDA centers. New centers were established at Overton, Dallas, Amarillo, San Angelo, Vernon, Corpus Christi, and Uvalde. First round construction at all centers was completed in 1978.

The centers received defined responsibilities that related to the agricultures of the region. The regional agricultural research and extension center at Lubbock, located above the Ogallala underground water reserves, emphasized research on water usage, cotton, sorghum, vegetables, grapes, and farming systems. The center at Amarillo, 100 miles to the north, undertook research primarily on wheat, sugar beets, weed and insect control, and beef cattle diseases and nutrition. The center at Dallas turned to cropping systems and forage and foliage plants. Weslaco, in subtropical South Texas, was the center for investigation on citrus and vegetable culture and marketing, cotton, sugar cane, and forage. The center at Beaumont cradled work on soybeans as well as rice. Research on sheep and goats was concentrated at San Angelo.

The Center concept proved to be an effective institutional device for multidisciplinary research. The presence of scientists who were highly competent to do independent research resulted in networking of scientific efforts among centers and the departments at TAMU. The centers formed a powerful system that extended research beyond the modalities of academic departments, but maintained academic links through graduate education. This system is still unfolding, flexible, and perhaps unpredictable in its evolution.

The Agricultural Research Service of the USDA was strengthened in a similar multidisciplinary development of its research centers in Texas. New facilities and staff were added to provide additional capability in remote sensing and sugar crops at Weslaco, in forage and grassland research at Temple, and in soils and minimum tillage at Bushland. Additional scientists for work in rice quality, rice drying, and storage insects were placed at Beaumont. The USDA Veterinary Toxicology and Entomology Research Laboratory and the USDA National Cotton Pathology Research Laboratory were constructed in 1970 on the edge of the TAMU campus at College Station. A plant stress laboratory is on the drawing board for placement on the TTU campus at Lubbock.

Entomology

The warfare between the world of insects and that of man and his animals and crops set the stage for some of the finest science in Texas' history. Insect scourges were known and endured in Texas for decades, but only the control of the cattle tick and Texas fever (babesiosis) had been devised prior to World War II. The boll weevil (*Anthonomus grandis* Boheman), the pink bollworm (*Pectinophora gosypiella* Saunders), bollworm (*Heliothis Zea* Boddis), and tobacco budworm (*Heliothis viriscens* Fabricus) on cotton, the grasshoppers and locusts, and the screwworm (*Cochliomyia hominovorax*) on livestock and sometimes humans were the principal antagonists to man. Outbreaks of these insects were but part of the life of the farmer and rancher as infestations mounted and decreased year after year.

The tools for coping with insects prior to World War II were mostly cultural, with reliance being placed principally on sulfur preparations and calcium arsenate. For insects on cattle and sheep, periodic dipping was used. Control of cotton insects required early planting dates and stalk destruction, enabled only by mechanization. The battle against grasshoppers and locusts was carried on by means of laborious outlays of arsenic-laden baits. But a legacy of World War II was the organic insecticide, first DDT and then a passing array of pesticides: Benzene hexachloride, chlordane, toxaphene, aldrin, dieldrin, endrin, methyl parathion, tetraethylpyrophosphate, and so on. The age of agricultural chemicals exploded in the United States.

Under the leadership of J. C. Gaines and the Department of Entomology at TAMU, research in Texas immediately after World War II centered on adaptation of chemical controls to Texas crops and conditions. The airplane, modified in Texas, was adapted as a means of delivery and provided an ultimate in agricultural mechanization. Tests on the timings and methods of applications of insecticides yielded effective, though ephemeral technologies. For the most part, the techniques worked in ways that were marvelous to behold. Insects were held in check. But the euphoria was short-lived.

Doubts raised by Rachel Carson began to shape environmental policy in the 1960s.[9] But adapting heredities of insect populations also outran the usefulness of pesticide after pesticide, and the natural controlling enemies of the pests were often destroyed. For example, on cotton the development of resistance to pesticides, especially by the bollworm complex, cut through the enthusiastic promise of the economical and effective insecticides applied in multi-applications.[10] The strategies of insect pest control had to be rerouted.

It was then, in research on insects, that the distances between basic biology and technology were cut short. Entomologists bound together both scientific and technological knowledge.[11] Three trails of events are most notable: the eradication of the screwworm fly, the development of techniques to attack certain insects in the diapause stage, and the integration of pest control methods to ensure the viability of cotton north of the Rio Grande.

The screwworm fly, native to the tropical Western Hemisphere, overwintered only in the southernmost parts of Florida and Texas. During the months of April through November, flies from Florida would invade Georgia, Alabama, and sometimes the Carolinas, and from Texas would move into Oklahoma, Kansas, Missouri, and at times more northern states. Infested animals that were not treated frequently died. Treatments had to be of individual wounds by the application of a smear with diphenylamine the active agent, and hundreds of thousands of animals had to be treated each year. Yet, with the cold weather of fall, the fly was eliminated again except in the southernmost areas of the United States.

Edward F. Knipling (fig. 1), a USDA entomologist with academic credentials from TAMU and Iowa State University, returned to Texas in 1937 and originated the idea of controlling the screwworm flies with a technique of releasing sterile males in numbers overwhelming to the population of wild flies. Comparatively, the insect was not numerous, and it was possible to raise large numbers of flies on hamburger meat in the laboratory. Mathematical models for control were devised.

The final ingredient for the sterilization of the flies was added after 1950.[12] That element had its roots in the studies of Herman J. Muller in the late 1920s at the University of Texas at Austin on the effect of X-rays on genetic mutation of *Drosophila* and Muller's 1950 writings, which argued the genetic and sterilizing potential of nuclear explosions.[13] Realizing the possibilities, Knipling, now in Washington, D.C., persuaded his colleagues in Texas to undertake research on the sterilizing effects of radiation. Raymond C. Bushland, working in the USDA Bureau of Entomol-

Figure 1. Texan Edward F. Knipling of the USDA originated the concept of total population control of screwworm flies by releasing sterile males.

ogy's Livestock Insects Investigations Laboratory at Kerrville, handled the studies. He arranged to irradiate flies at Brook Army Medical Center, Fort Sam Houston, San Antonio. He was successful. Screwworms were irradiated and sterilized, and the sterile male could be mated competitively with normal females with resulting egg masses that were not fertile.[14] A Cobalt-60 source of radiation was found to be as effective as X-rays.[15]

The island of Curaçao in the Dutch West Indies became a successful testing ground in 1954–55. A program was subsequently initiated in Florida in 1957. The screwworm was eradicated in both areas. A massive population control effort followed in Texas in 1962. The USDA and the government of Mexico then moved to suppress the fly in all of Mexico north of the Isthmus of Tehuantepec. Today only an occasional screwworm fly is seen north of the Isthmus. So complete was the genocide, that entomology would never be the same.[16]

While the theory of total population control of the screwworm could be formulated out of knowledge of the biology of the fly, the susceptibility of the fly to the cold provided the key geographic factor for total population control. Other insects, however, have mechanisms for surviving ecological factors that are dangerous to them. One of them is the diapause, the enforced dormancy in the life cycle of insects.

Perry L. Adkisson (fig. 2) was employed in 1958 at TAMU by the TAES to do research on the pink bollworm. Recommendations for control of this insect were based on killing diapausing larvae that remained in the field after harvest. Adkisson sharpened his understandings of diapause physiology as a special postdoctoral fellow at Harvard University,[17] and re-

Figure 2. Entomologist Perry L. Adkisson, TAES and TAMU, led development of integrated pest control in the 1960s and 1970s.

turned to TAMU in 1964 to develop a line of basic biological research that would have major applications.

Adkisson and his colleagues ascertained that the growth, development, reproduction, and diapause of the pink bollworm are confined to appropriate seasons as a direct response to the photoperiod.[18] The response to the photoperiod provided the key for control, as the onset of diapause could be predicted for any given location with precision on the basis of the period of daylight as seasons changed. The timing of cultural practices—defoliation, harvesting, shredding, plowing under, irrigation, and planting new crops—during a period that allows for suicidal emergence was a technique devised to control the insect.[19]

Diapause also proved to be a key characteristic in the control of the boll weevil. The boll weevil, unlike the pink bollworm, diapauses as an adult and hibernates outside the cotton field. This phenomenon was exploited in extensive tests in 1964 and 1965 in the High and Rolling Plains of Texas in which insecticidal treatments of the last reproductive generation proved to be effective.[20] The procedures developed then are used today.

Public pressure mounted in the 1970s to reduce insecticides on cotton. But recurring development of insecticide-resistant strains of pests had already depleted the arsenal of effective insecticides for use on cotton. The threat had mounted in the late 1950s in South Texas when the tobacco budworm had proliferated for two reasons: it had developed resistance to the organophosphorous insecticides, and it was unleashed from natural control by the multiple insecticidal treatments of cotton for the boll weevil and cotton fleahopper. By the late 1960s, cotton was no longer a viable crop in northern Mexico. The new strategy applied to maintain cotton production north of the Rio Grande River was an integration of methods.

Integrated pest management grew out of fundamental studies on the life cycle of the insects.[21] The new system recognized three components: (1) an area-wide control program during the harvest season, combining destruction of stalks and insecticidal treatment of harvested cotton fields, to reduce greatly the number of weevils that overwinter; (2) control of over-wintered adults in the spring by insecticides before they can reproduce; and (3) the cultivation of rapid-fruiting, "short season" cotton varieties. The latter was fortuitously facilitated by parallel programs to develop cotton varieties whose seeds and seedlings tolerate cold and resist disease.[22]

The range of entomological science extended

Applied Plant Genetics

SORGHUM

Applied genetics, more than any other force, has re-shaped almost every crop and commercial plant in Texas during the years since World War II. Designing wheat, sorghum, and cotton for mechanization had been the work of many scientists in the United States during the 1930s and 1940s. But after the war, Texas researchers pursued their own genetic studies.

The effort in applied genetics that must be regarded as one of the most significant events in Texas science was the development of hybrid sorghum. The setting was the clapboard buildings and the red soils of the TAES Substation near Chillicothe; the model was the hybrid onion.

Hybrid vigor was produced in corn (*Zea Mays* L.) in the United States after inbred lines were developed and crossed. Producing crossed seeds was relatively easy in corn because staminate (male) and pistilate (female) flowers occur in different organs and emasculation could be accomplished by pulling the tassels from plants to be used as females. Sorghum, a monoecious plant, has stamens and pistils in the same spikelet.[28]

Hybrid vigor was introduced into corn twenty-five years before it could be produced in sorghum. But sorghum was a crop that had responded magnificently to genetic manipulation. Varieties of sorghum that could be harvested by mechanical combine appeared just prior to World War II, and sorghum acreage expanded throughout Texas.[29] J. C. Stephens, a USDA geneticist at the TAES Substation at Chillicothe, had been working on the possible use of induced male-sterility as a technique for achieving a hybrid sorghum. By the time hybrid vigor in sorghum was recognized, Stephens had already found genetic male steriles, and he was trying to devise a method of producing hybrid seed. But in 1943 H. A. Jones and A. E. Clark published their work on cytoplasmic male-sterility in onions. The search for genetic sterility residing in the cytoplasm of sorghum rather than in the nucleus was undertaken.[30]

Research toward economic production of hybrid sorghum seed was set in motion with approval of the project by Director R. D. Lewis in 1946. By 1952 Stephens and J. R. Quinby (fig. 4) had found cytoplasmic sterility in sorghum. Five years later, commercial hybrid sorghum went into production. Since that time, yields of sorghum per acre in Texas and the United States have more than quadrupled, due to a combi-

Figure 3. TAES and TAMU scientist Max Summers, in the new cohort of scientists, leads the applications of molecular biology into entomology and biological systems.

through the years from insects on every crop of commercial importance in Texas, to insects affecting man in urban areas, old pests and some new ones (such as the rice stem borer on sugarcane), forest tree pests, and insects helpful to man as well.

Entomological research in Texas has been buttressed by studies on the taxonomy[23] and life cycles of insects. The research arsenal now has strength in insect physiology,[24] insect pathology and applied molecular biology (Max Summers; fig. 3),[25] computer-aided decision making,[26] and simulation modeling of complex systems in biology.[27] But perhaps unlike other areas of applied biology, entomology in Texas has maintained a strong content of ecology, and as such, it is a likely model for future applications of biology in agriculture.

Figure 4. After the success of the hybridization of sorghum, TAES geneticist Roy Quinby and USDA geneticist J. C. Stephens set in motion to convert tropical sorghums to temperate varieties.

nation of application of hybrid vigor, inclusion of new genetic sources, irrigation, and improved plant nutrition.

A second surge in the momentum of sorghum breeding followed in the 1960s. The genetic bases of the height and the duration of growth had been determined in the 1940s. But the mass of genetic diversity resided in the tropical sorghums. It was apparent that a tropical variety could be converted to a temperate variety by a breeding program consisting of substituting a recessive maturity allele for a dominant one and two or three recessive height alleles for dominant ones through backcrossing and selection.[31] Stephens developed a proposal to undertake a tropical conversion program, and the project was approved in 1963.

The work was undertaken using the USDA facilities at Mayaguez, Puerto Rico, for the winter crops and the TAES field unit at Chillicothe for the summer crop. In the two decades that followed, hundreds of tropical varieties were converted. These converted varieties were distributed to plant breeders and are now being used in the production of commercial varieties. Moreover, the conversion program is producing parents for the entire sorghum-producing world. The short-statured temperate zone varieties that were converted are the bases of new hybrids and strains for the tropics.

WHEAT AND RICE: THE SYSTEMS APPROACH

Research in small grains in the 1940s and 1950s was largely on breeding lines adapted to Texas conditions: for resistance to disease, particularly rusts, which

Figure 5. Irvin M. Atkins, TAES and USDA, carried the small grain breeding program into the postwar years.

underwent periodic and unpredictable genetic change, and for use as a crop for the dual purposes of grazing and grain production. The breeding program adapted varieties of barley, oats, flax, and wheat. But small grains other than wheat eventually failed in their bid to be major crops in Texas.

Irvin M. Atkins (fig. 5), jointly employed by the Experiment Station and USDA, carried the breeding program of Elmer McFadden on small grains into the postwar years. Tascosa wheat, a variety that had resistance to hail, shattering, and lodging, was released from the USDA-TAES program in 1959.[32] It helped remove the prejudice of millers against Texas wheat, and it captured the farmers' loyalty, though other varieties were released, until a semidwarf wheat, Sturdy, was introduced.

Semidwarf or short wheat and rice varieties, to-

Figure 6. The first semi-dwarf wheats resulted from the skilled breeding efforts of Kenneth Porter at Bushland beginning in the early 1960s.

gether with a package of improved production inputs, formed the bases of what is popularly known as the "Green Revolution" in many developing nations. Despite a fairly extended history in Japan and Korea, semidwarf varieties are relatively new to U.S. agriculture. Breeding wheats of short stature was initiated in 1951 by Kenneth B. Porter (fig. 6), an Experiment Station researcher working at the USDA Southwestern Great Plains Research Center at Bushland. Crosses were made that involved the Norin 10 out of Japan, Norin 10 × Brevor strains, and Seu Seun 27 out of Korea; some of the new lines were being tested in the early 1960s.[33] Sturdy, a hard red winter wheat variety six to nine inches shorter than existing commercial varieties, was released in 1966.[34] Sturdy was followed by the release of a sister selection, Caprock, in 1969 and in 1972 by the release of TAM W-101. At the time, these were the only semidwarf hard red winter varieties available for commercial production in the U.S. Other improved semidwarf varieties followed with TAM 107 and TAM 108 being released in 1985.[35] Wheat varieties coming out of the Porter-led research program were grown on eight million acres of the United States' hard red winter wheat region in 1984. Texas now ranks as the state second in wheat acreage in the United States.

The infrastructure for rice research was already in place at the end of World War II: a USDA cooperative and comprehensive rice breeding program co-located with the Substation at Beaumont, a TAES program concerned with the agronomic features of rice production, and a producer-supported Texas Rice Improvement Association organized for the purpose of producing and distributing seed. The USDA Regional Rice Quality Laboratory was established in 1955 at the Beaumont Substation to determine the quality of rice varieties in milling and cooking. The USDA initiated studies on drying and storage in 1954 and on rice storage insects in 1967.[36]

Successive releases of new varieties of rice, from Texas Patna in 1942 to Lemont in 1983, set the bases for rice yields that increased from about two thousand pounds of rough rice per acre in 1950 to over six thousand pounds per acre in 1983. The rice plant was literally restructured such that an increasing portion of the photosynthate was partitioned into the rice grain, and the resultant shorter, stronger stalk was far less susceptible to falling over and lodging and the problems and costs that lodging created. The growing season was shortened with the Belle Patna, and later varieties beginning in 1961, so that a ratoon crop could be grown in the southern parts of the Texas rice belt. The scientists involved were Henry Beachell and Charles N. Bollich in rice breeding; L. E. Crane, Julian Craigmiles, and J. W. Stansel in leadership; B. D. Webb in food quality; J. G. Atkins in plant pathology; and N. S. Evatt, C. C. Bowling, D. G. Westphall, J. E. Scott, and E. F. Eastin in combining the agronomic package of inputs. The system concept remains dominant in rice research today.[37]

The research program on rice serves as a model for constructing agricultural systems. The Texas Rice Research Foundation has been added to the financial support network. Scientists of the TAES and the USDA work cooperatively in a multicomponent program on an agricultural system that must be revised with each successive variety. Such talents have been complementary, creating a multiplicative rather than a merely additive effect of their work.

COTTON AND OTHER CROPS

Basic genetics and cytology were the dominant thrusts in work with cotton in the 1950s. The team was also a cooperative one in which Experiment Station and USDA scientists worked together. Located at College Station and providing the national leadership in the research, the team was led by Thomas R. Richmond and included cotton breeders Charles Lewis and George Alva Niles and cytologists Meta Brown (fig. 7), Margaret Menzel, Thomas White, John Endrizzi, Safia Naqi, and Russell J. Kohel.[38] The team gathered, evaluated, and developed methods of using the genetic characters of primitive cottons that were collected in their natural habitats in Guatemala and southern Mexico. The team of cytologists systematized and mapped, largely by monosomic (aneuploidal) analyses, the linkage groups on all chromosomes of cotton.[39] As a result, the genetic diversity available for cotton breeding in the United States was greatly enhanced.

A dominant feature in genetics applied to agriculture in Texas was the plant breeding efforts directed toward resistance of the host plant to diseases and insects.[40] Luther S. Bird (fig. 8) spent a professional lifetime focusing on cotton for this purpose. Bird came to TAMU as a graduate student in 1948 and stayed on with the Agricultural Experiment Station. Successively, cotton was being bred at the Experiment Substation at Lubbock to be resistant to bacterial blight (late 1940s), verticillium wilt (early 1950s), nematodes, and fusarium wilt. The approach of Bird and his students was the simultaneous incorporation of resistances to several diseases and insects, the ability to

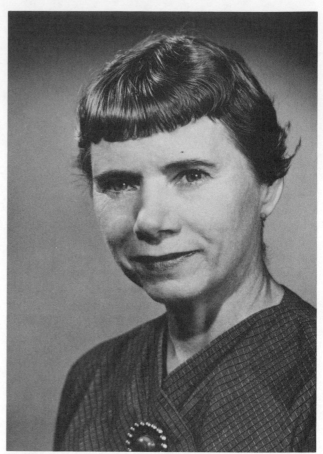

Figure 7. TAES geneticist Meta Brown led the team that mapped the linkage groups on the chromosomes of cotton in the 1950s and 1960s, enhancing the genetic diversity available for cotton breeding.

survive stress, and earliness.[41] His thinking was bold. By 1982 Bird's TAMCOT varieties, and the germ plasm that he developed and released, were grown on one-third of the Texas cotton acreage (2.5 million acres) and 18 percent of the U.S. cotton acreage.

The warm, sun-drenched irrigable farm environment, which was less challenged by disease and pests, allowed Paul Lyerly and his colleagues at the Experiment Station unit at El Paso to build the technology for long-staple cotton production in far West Texas. But Bird's short-season multiple adversity (MAR) cottons, which matured twenty to thirty days before conventional varieties, and other cultivars bred by G. A. Niles, Lavon Ray, John Gannaway, and other breeders of the Agricultural Experiment Station, formed the key elements in the short-season cotton production concept that gained prominence in the rest of Texas. Short-season plants are somewhat di-

Figure 8. Multiple resistance to adversity and disease was genetically captured in cotton by TAES scientist Luther S. Bird.

minutive in size and have accelerated fruiting and earlier maturity, which offers escape from damage by the boll weevil and other insects. Short-season production systems also reduce the inputs and energy requirements of the cropping system.

Breeding for insect resistance was also a thrust with sorghum. The greenbug unexpectedly emerged as a devastating pest on sorghum in 1968. But by 1976 resistant lines were released by the TAES.[42] The development of sorghum lines also resistant to sorghum midge has resulted in redefinition of the economic threshold of this insect.[43]

For two decades after World War II, soybeans were, at best, a minor crop in Texas, limited by lack of adapted varieties. The available varieties developed elsewhere grew well but would not always fruit, and they were highly susceptible to disease, particularly to the root rot that was endemic in central Texas. In the early 1960s, less than 60,000 acres of soybeans were grown in Texas. But by 1979 the acreage had grown to over 800,000 acres.[44]

Soybean research was undertaken first at the Texas Agricultural Experiment Substation at Lubbock and then at Beaumont. The first varietal trials and a breeding program at the Beaumont Center were established in 1967 by Julian Craigmiles and John R. Wood. The same team that provided multidisciplinary research support to revise the rice production system worked with J. W. Sij to build the package of inputs.[45] The warm, humid, subtropical climate of southeast Texas was ideal for disease, insect, and weed problems to

proliferate, and these had to be overcome. The first new variety of soybeans for Texas was released in 1972. The first full-time breeder was assigned to the Beaumont Center in 1978. A similar multidisciplinary approach was followed at the Center at Lubbock with Raymond Brigham as the focal agronomist working on soybeans and other oil seed crops. Soybeans are now a major, permanent crop in Texas.

In research on corn in the early 1950s, Texas had an illustrious scientist in John S. Rogers. With Rogers' discovery of the Texas male sterile cytoplasm and its restorer gene, corn hybrids were commercially created for Texas. But even hybrid corn in the fifties and sixties still required the best field conditions and cultural practice, and such conditions were rare in Texas. Corn lost out to hybrid sorghum. The TAES dropped corn research in the 1960s. The Texas cytoplasm would live on outside of Texas to be displaced in a certain infamy. T cytoplasm, as it was called, came to be widely used to produce corn hybrids throughout the United States, but it carried with it the susceptibility that set the stage for the devastating 1970 epidemic of southern corn leaf blight. Fortunately, T cytoplasm was replaced within two years, and agriculture then knew that it had the research and industrial mechanisms to react to biological disaster. Ironically, a substantial production of corn has since returned to the irrigated areas of northwest Texas without a significant research base in Texas. The technology this time was simply imported and provided by industry.

The procedures and technologies of plant breeding and culture have been applied to almost every conceivable crop in Texas. Breeding and experiments on the culture of peanuts have kept this crop viable in Texas.[46] The pecan breeding program at the USDA station at Brownwood, a program continuous for over fifty years, yielded sixteen new cultivars, each given the name of an Indian tribe.[47] Peaches have been fashioned to be grown in South Texas, where never grown before. Sunflowers were adapted to Texas conditions. Sugar crops—sugar beets in the Panhandle region and sugar cane in deep South Texas—have been returned to Texas.

Horticultural research in Texas was concentrated at the TAES Substation at Weslaco during the first two postwar decades. Elsewhere, horticulture received diminished support. In fact, the Department of Horticulture at TAMU was merged into a new Department of Soil and Crop Sciences in 1959 and did not re-emerge as an autonomous department until 1977. Again, it seems that the vitality of the academic program controlled the institutional bases for the research program. But at Weslaco, Paul Leeper, Rumaldo Correa, and Norman Maxwell focused a continuing productive program on vegetable breeding and citrus. They were joined in the early 1970s by geneticists Leonard Pike and J. Creighton Miller at TAMU. Varieties of tomatoes, cantaloupes, lettuce, carrots, hybrid cucumbers, potatoes, and onions were bred and released to provide varieties of high table quality that could be transported to distant urban markets.[48]

The re-emergence of a Department of Horticultural Sciences at TAMU, the growing expertise at TTU, and the interest in new horticultural crops for Texas, for example, blueberries and wine grapes, have surely signaled new vitality in horticulture and its sciences in Texas.

The scientific improvement of field and forage grasses came of age in the 1950s with the work of Ethan Holt of the Department of Soil and Crop Sciences at TAMU and E. C. Bashaw, a plant breeder with the USDA at College Station. Selections and introductions of grasses were generally made in cooperation with the USDA Soil Conservation Service. Kleingrass 75, Bell rhodesgrass, which was tolerant of rhodesgrass scale, common buffelgrass, and Abon and Israel clovers, for example, were developed and introduced into Texas rangelands and pastures. The notable scientific contribution of the work on grasses was that apomixis (asexual seed development) was identified to become an important tool for locking in the results of hybridization.[49] Two hybrid cultivars of buffelgrass were developed and released through the use of apomixis.

As a spin-off of the investigations on forage grasses, by 1956 the TAES had established a turf program. More oriented to the problems of people and their lifestyles, the program developed grasses for lawns, golf courses, football fields, parks, and roadways. Here, too, all of the biological parameters—fertilization; weed, insect and disease control; and tolerance to drought and cold—were applied in research.

Plant Molecular Genetics

It now appears that the techniques of molecular biology can and will be applied to plant agriculture. The scientific capability to make such applications has been and is being assembled in Texas, in TAMU's Colleges of Agriculture, Science and Veterinary Medicine and, obviously, in other institutions, particularly the several colleges of medicine. The approaches are varied, but the prospects surely demand attention.

Agricultural Experiment Station geneticists Gary E. Hart and Neal Tuleen set in place a program of aneuploidal analysis of the wide crosses that are easily accomplished between cultivated wheats and their relatives in the tribe *Triticeae*. The gene pools of wild relatives of crop species contain a large amount of genetic material that is potentially useful in restructuring crops for agriculture. Studies have suggested that alien chromosomes in wheat can be identified by the study of isozyme structural genes, by determining the zymogram phenotypes.[50]

Research in the laboratories at TAMU has now made extensive use of recombinant DNA strategies to understand molecular mechanisms of gene structure, function and regulation in higher plants. T_i plasmid vectors of *Agrobacterium tumefaciens* have been used to transfer a B-phaseolin gene to tobacco plants where it was fully expressed in the seed.[51] Study of the mechanism of gene expression in higher plants is under way in Timothy C. Hall's laboratory. The potato has been used by William D. Park as a system to study the molecular control of gene expression.[52] There are well established procedures for tissue culture of the potato, and it has been found to be an excellent host for DNA vectors based on the T_i plasmid. DNA technology has been extensively used by H. James Price in cytogenetics and developmental genetics of higher plants.[53]

Soil Science

The technological development that is responsible for both the largest employment of resources for agricultural science and the major increase in crop agricultural production since 1947 has been the use of fertilizers. The tonnage of fertilizer used in Texas in 1946–47 was less than 400,000; in the 1980s the usage has burgeoned to 2.5 to 3 million tons per year. As World War II ended, empirical tests of fertilizers were a common part of the research of every unit, Agricultural Experiment Station or USDA, in which crops were grown or tested.[54]

Chemical fertilizers were determined early to be a key ingredient for high yields. Fertilizers replaced the use of intergrown legumes and barnyard fertilizers as soon as war-caused shortages were alleviated. In 1960 research forcused principally on the various forms of phosphates in the soil and the soil factors related to availabilities of phosphorus. Nitrogen received increased interest in the mid-1960s as plant breeders began to incorporate increased genetic potential for productivity into crop plants and as the stalks of wheat and other crops were shortened and stiffened. By 1968 the TAES had published fertility and salinity data on over two hundred soils collected statewide by the Soil Conservation Service.

Research in the greenhouses and laboratories at TAMU increasingly turned to the fundamental soil sciences, soil classification, and management in the successive decades after the war. Identification of the important biological factors in agronomy was undertaken in efforts led by James E. Adams and Boyd Page, who were successive heads of the Department of Agronomy in the 1950s. Applied research then yielded improvements in management—weed control, fertilization, tillage, and soil conservation—but also included studies on soil morphology, crystallography, chemistry, microbiology, and ecology. The principals in these studies through the decades were Alex Pope, A. B. Onken, and Charles W. Wendt at Lubbock; C. J. Gerard and B. W. Hipp at Weslaco and later at Chillicothe and Overton, respectively; J. E. Matocha at Overton, L. B. Fenn at McGregor, D. E. Kissel, J. T. Ritchie, and Earl Burnett at Temple; and Curtis Godfrey, George Kunze, Jack Runkles, R. W. Weaver, J. B. Dixon, and L. R. Hossner at College Station. Research on soils and fertilizers over the years has been painstaking, productive, and increasingly sophisticated.[55]

Plant Physiology

With the 1947 integration of the activities of the TAES and the College of Agriculture at TAMU, plant physiology was established as an organized research discipline in Texas. Two principal thrusts evolved: the control of undesirable plants, and the regulation of the physiology of the plant for more efficient productivity.

Early postwar documents referred to injury to the crop, animal poisoning, problems of drift to neighboring fields, and susceptibility of desirable plants to the herbicide, as major problems with the chemical control of weeds.[56] The traditional hoe and plow might be better, but both farmer and scientist soon chose the easier, chemical way.

Most of the early postwar research in Texas involved the use of 2,4,5-trichlorophenoxyacetic acid (2,4,5-T) for the control of mesquite on rangelands and the use of 2,4-dichlorophenoxyacetic acid (2,4-D) for bindweed control on cropland. By 1965 much of the research had shifted to pre-emergence herbicides. Texas researchers were especially active in developing the use of triazine herbicides such as milogard and atrazine in sorghum fields.

By the late 1960s, emphasis changed again, with soil incorporation of herbicides such as treflan drawing attention. Researchers in Texas became interested in the incorporation of herbicides that were effective in the absence of rainfall. With the availability of herbicides such as Paraquat and Glyphosate (Roundup), limited tillage systems became possible.[57] Much of the research on weed science has been carried on by Allan Wiese at the USDA Center at Bushland, and so it is logical that that Center has also become the principal Texas site for research on limited tillage.

Other research on plant hormones and synthetic growth regulators pointed to the use of these substances to manipulate the behavior of crop plants to fit production environments and systems, as well as to increase yields. Through empirical testing programs in the early 1950s, TAMU's Wayne C. Hall contributed to developing defoliation of the cotton plant as a common preharvest practice.[58] The effort represented an early example of success in the empirical approach to agricultural chemistry, one of many successes that would follow. In this, technology preceded science.

Science followed in due time, however. Hall was interested in the role of ethylene in the abscission of the leaf. He and his young colleague Page Morgan (fig. 9) discovered that ethylene is a plant hormone, and any application of an exogenous auxin will promote ethylene production; the ethylene may cause a physiological response.[59] Against this background, industrial scientists created a synthetic source of ethylene, 2-chloro,1-ethylphosphonic acid, and the substance has become one of the most widely used plant growth regulators in agriculture.[60]

Plant physiology in Texas also contributed to management of fertility. Howard Joham developed the concept of testing plant tissues for nutrient status rather than the soils. Zinc was discovered to be a limiting factor in the production of some crops, including pecans. The study of the physiology of plant stress, under way in the laboratories at TAMU and by the USDA plant stress group at Lubbock will likely yield new technologies in improving the biological efficiency of water use.[61]

The Grasslands

The first academic department of range science in the United States, the Department of Range and Forestry, was established at TAMU in 1946. The first bachelor's and master's degrees were granted in 1948; the first

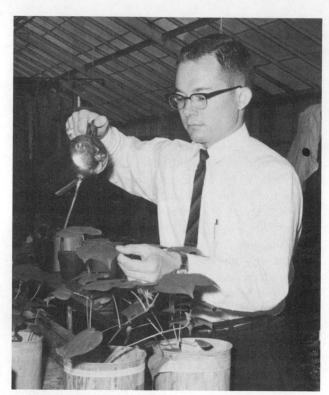

Figure 9. Young Page Morgan, working with Wayne Hall, elucidated the effects of ethylene on cotton in the early 1960s.

doctorate, which was also the first in the nation, was granted in 1950.[62] At present the department (now Range Science) shares a certain research expertise with TTU's Department of Range and Wildlife Management.[63] Vernon Young was the first head of the department at TAMU. His successors were Charles L. Leinweber (1960–71) and Joseph L. Schuster (1971–present).

The grasslands, savannahs, and forests of Texas have been rich sources of material for basic taxonomic study by D. S. Correll and C. L. Lundell at the Texas Research Foundation, Renner,[64] and Frank W. Gould at TAMU.[65] But range science in Texas was and is, in large measure, the application of ecology, although systematics and other biological sciences such as plant physiology, agronomy, animal nutrition, and biometrics surely contributed. It has been concerned with the most extensive use of land in Texas.

As a subject matter, range management was born just before the drought of the 1950s. Thus, the early concerns were the development of guidelines for stocking rates on West Texas rangelands. Since then, range science and technology has sought to optimize live-stock production while sustaining the vegetation and valuable populations of wildlife. Novel grazing systems, using rotations on fenced land, have been developed.[66] Patterns and nutrient compositions of diets selected by rangeland livestock have been detailed. A stronger data base has been created for empirical recommendations concerning range management and the supplemental feeding of livestock. Engineering technology has been applied in manipulating the vegetation on rangeland.

Aside from the vagaries of weather and patterns of rainfall and drought, no ecological phenomenon raises greater concern in Texas animal agriculture than does the persistence and invasion of brush on rangeland. The dominant species of brush on Texas rangeland is the mesquite (*Prosopis* spp.), which has spread over fifty-six million acres. Prior to the discovery of selective growth-regulators, most mesquite was controlled by oiling individual plants or by laborious mechanical methods. Application of the phenoxyacetic acid herbicides, particularly 2,4,5,-T, by Charles E. Fisher at the TAES Substation at Spur in 1951, resulted in a revolution in the approach to the control of mesquite and other rangeland brush. Significant technological advances, both in theory and practice, were made in this regard in the three decades that followed by scientists such as Henry A. Wright and Bill E. Dahl of TTU; R. W. Bovey, L. F. Bouse, and R. E. Meyer, USDA scientists located at TAMU; and Robert Darrow, R. H. Haas, H. T. Wiedemann, and Charles J. Scifres of the TAMU System. Other chemical substances included in subsequent studies in Texas and elsewhere were picloram or dicamba in combination with 2,4,5,-T; picloram alone; tebuthiron; hexazinone; 2,4-D; and 2,4-D plus picloram. A variety of mechanical controls were tested, and some have found practical use.

Prescribed burning was found to have some advantages not associated with other techniques—such as increased utilization of forage, use on rough terrain, absence of chemicals, compatibility with wildlife, suppressed parasites, and low cost—but it requires an amount of fine fuel not always present. The principal problems of cost, the inexorable and often unknown ecological forces that affect rangelands, and now the fear of adverse effects on human health resulting from minimal exposure to dioxin (2,3,7,8-tetrachlorodibenzo-p-dioxin, which was first recognized as a contaminant of 2,4,5-T,[67]) has left range management systems without a solution in which full confidence can be placed. Again, the suggested approach is the integration of methods.[68]

Engineering

Prior to World War II, mechanization—tractors and other power machinery, plows, planting equipment, harvesting machines, and gins—accounted for most of the increases in agricultural efficiency and productivity. After the war, science had its impact, but many of the biological elements of agriculture continued to be implemented through engineering.

A regional cooperative program between the USDA and the Experiment Station was located at Lubbock in 1947 with Rex Colwick as coordinator. Elmer Hudspeth joined the team in 1950. This program first involved restructuring the rotary hoe, and it led to the introduction of the seed press wheel in the early 1950s. Precision depth planters, mechanisms of metering the seed, redesigned harvesters to reduce the problem of bark in cotton lint, and a stripper elevator with a more efficient vertical pneumatic green boll separator resulted from the work. The first self-propelled harvester for narrow row cotton was constructed in 1963. The practice of furrow diking to capture rainfall and irrigation water was reintroduced in the Lubbock area in the late 1970s.

The design of irrigation systems that are efficient in the use of water and energy became an imperative in the 1970s, when the cost of energy soared and water tables were dropping. Trickle and mist irrigation were tested.[69] A low energy precision application (LEPA) system was devised. This was a low pressure system that also used furrow dikes and drop tubes fitted with special nozzles to place the water.[70] At TAMU, a day stress index was formulated to characterize the effects of water stress on crop yields and developed as a criterion for timing the irrigation.[71]

Engineering, too, has been employed in the past decade-and-a-half to manage the post-harvest: engineered systems for handling and storing cotton and grains, food engineering, and systems for managing the wastes of agriculture. The biological problems engendered by the pollution that may result from agricultural operations and forestry—sediment, nitrogen and phosphorus compounds, pesticides, biodegradable compounds, dissolved salts, and microorganisms—have truly challenged engineers. The four million cattle fattened annually in Texas feedlots posed a special problem, and considerable interest developed in the fate of heavy applications of cattle manure on land.[72] In the latter situation, deep plowing emerged as a useful technique of disposal.

Nutritional Sciences

Born in the 1947 "integration," the Department of Biochemistry and Nutrition at TAMU built programs of nutritional science in the traditions of biochemistry. Faculty for the new Department of Biochemistry and Nutrition was assembled out of the Department of Animal Husbandry (Paul B. Pearson, Bernard S. Schweigert), the Swine Division of the TAES (Carl M. Lyman, Kenneth Kuiken), and the Office of the State Chemist (Raymond Reiser, fig. 10; L. R. Richardson). Pearson was named both the head of the new department and dean of the Graduate School.

Pearson had brought research to Texas in the classical biochemical mode of the 1930s and 1940s, with

Figure 10. Contributions of biochemical nutritionist Raymond Reiser were many, but the synthetic diet for the pink bollworm may have had the greatest impact by facilitating studies for insect control.

emphasis on the requirement for vitamins and minerals in a range of animals. Pearson and his colleagues in the Department of Biochemistry and Nutrition can be credited for introducing the methods of scientific nutrition to Texas agricultural science.

Carl Lyman, and later Kenneth Kuiken and Bryant Holland, were employed by the TAES to fulfill the vision of Swine Division Chief Fred Hale that nutritional research on feedstuffs required chemical description. In the decades following World War II, Lyman first worked on methods of microbiological assay for the nutritionally essential amino acids in natural feedstuffs. After developing a reliable method for tryptophan, he built data on almost every type of feed material, for anyone interested in the "quality" of protein. The special complication for monogastric animals of gossypol and related pigments in cottonseed meal continued as a thrust of Lyman's laboratory until his untimely death in 1969.

Reiser's postwar career turned to the metabolism of fats when radioactive elements became available. For over twenty-five years Reiser produced an extensive literature on lipid biochemistry, the methodology of analyses, transformations within the body and within the rumen, and on metabolic diseases, metabolism of cholesterol, and atherosclerosis. The latter interests brought Reiser both distinction and occasion for debate.[73]

No history of research in applied biology in Texas would be complete without noting Reiser's successful development of a synthetic diet for the pink bollworm, which had been regarded as an insect entirely dependent nutritionally on plants belonging to the family Malvaceae.[74] Diets, refined later by Erma Vanderzant of the USDA Entomology Research Division working at TAMU, enabled the laboratory colonization of the pink bollworm and boll weevil, and out of that came prescriptions for insect control and the bases for the integrated management of pests.

Nutritional sciences were also applied by L. R. Richardson, who studied the effects of environmental factors on the nutritive quality of foods and feeds: the environment in which the crop is grown, the effects of sterilization of food by gamma-radiation, and the effects of mold growth on feeds.

These events and the department itself set the stage for substantial changes in practical nutritional science at TAMU, and these changes, in turn, led to massive changes in animal agriculture in Texas. Professor J. Russell Couch (fig. 11) exemplifies the new research impetus.

Self-confident, flamboyant, and inevitably controversial, Couch erupted on the nutrition scene in Texas

Figure 11. Modern high-tech poultry production began with J. Russell Couch's studies in poultry nutrition in the 1950s.

in 1948. Armed with the self-assurance of a student from the Wisconsin school, Couch inherited Paul Pearson's laboratory and launched over twenty-seven years of prodigious research activity, publishing over 300 papers, guiding nearly sixty students to doctor's degrees, and working as a consultant to the feed and poultry industries, which now wore the mantle of technology transfer.[75]

Prior to 1950 poultry and swine production was largely limited to the farmstead ecosystem. The feed industry, suspected of providing an unneeded service, relied heavily on "Big Five" formulas for both swine and poultry: one part each of meat scraps, corn, wheat bran, wheat middlings (a residue from wheat flour manufacture), and oats for poultry. Couch's tests, in which he attempted to replace the "Animal Protein Factor" with impure microbial sources of vitamin B_{12}, led to the discovery of growth stimulation that was verified by Lederle Laboratory's scientists to be an effect of antibiotics fed at a subtherapeutic level.[76]

Tests of other antimicrobials followed. Gerald Combs of the University of Maryland discovered the importance of the amino acid–energy relationship. He used the data base on productive energies put together by TAES scientist George S. Fraps over four decades of work (1904–47). Couch and his students extended the studies. The scientific bases for the formula feed industry and commercial poultry production was brought to Texas.

Couch and his students and colleagues R. L. Atkinson, Thomas Ferguson, and C. R. Creger studied intensively the roles of vitamins and minerals, always seeking to refine the poultry diet. John H. Quisenberry, who became head of the Department of Poultry Science in 1946, and his students developed a highly productive line of research on environmental aspects and nutrition that complemented and extended the work of nutritionists to the industrial production of poultry and eggs. The quarter century following World War II was by any measure auspicious for research on poultry in Texas. The legacy is a poultry industry in the state that is valued at over a half-billion dollars annually.

The mantle of responsibility for research in applied ruminant nutrition fell in the 1950s to John K. Riggs and H. O. Kunkel.[77] Their research was on the use of subtherapeutic levels of antimicrobials, mineral metabolism, and the use of Texas feedstuffs, primarily on sorghum. Riggs keyed on the productive significance of natural and varietal variability of the grain. He was able to confirm the notion that processing could increase the nutritional value of sorghum for cattle.

A massive, \$4 billion-plus, cattle feeding industry, developed on the back of hybrid sorghum production in Texas in the late 1960s and the 1970s, although corn production and usage by the industry has now replaced sorghum to some extent. Nutritional consultants and scientists in public institutions continued to refine the knowledge base. The players have changed, however, during the past decade. T. D. Tanksley and Darrell Knabe at TAMU and Leland Tribble at TTU worked to answer problems of swine producers, but also they have extended fundamental research on swine such as on the digestibilities of amino acids in feedstuffs.[78] Research on equine nutrition and management moved to the front burner at TAMU. Gary Potter led the work on understanding the digestive partitioning of nutrients and the nutritional requirements of mares, foals, and severely stressed exercising horses.[79] Fundamental and applied research on nutrition of cattle and sheep are now undertaken by Rodney Preston of TTU and David Hutcheson, Gerald Schelling, Floyd Byers, Wayne Greene, and Carl Coppock of the TAMU System. C. R. Creger leads continuing work on bio-availabilities of minerals in poul-

try. The nutritional requirements of fish and, hence, the technical base of aquaculture were pushed by Edwin Robinson and Robert Stickney at TAMU.[80]

Animal Genetics

Genetic selection of purebred beef cattle at the end of the 1940s was based on a visual evaluation system under empirical standards largely set by tradition and the cattlemen themselves. The animals that were selected then were those that exhibited the accepted hair coat color and pattern for the breed and were compact in body, straight of leg, and bright of eye. Little wonder that, by the early 1950s, this system of evaluating and selecting beef cattle for breeding purposes actually concentrated the recessive gene for genetic achondroplastic dwarfism in the registered beef cattle population in Texas and the United States.

A basis for genetic selection for productivity was first established with the discovery in the 1940s that groups of young bulls that were the progenies of different sires gained weight at different rates. Performance testing of beef cattle was first done at the TAES Substation at Balmorrhea in 1941; it was picked up at the station at McGregor in 1949 and at TTU's PanTex Farm in 1955.[81] Records accumulated by 1956 on some five thousand young breeding cattle tested showed that the ability to gain was highly heritable and that there was little relationship between the traditional selection standards for beef cattle and the ability of the animal to gain weight.[82] The long accepted importance of compactness of the body and short legs in beef cattle was invalidated.[83] Performance testing was soon extended to sheep at the Substation at Sonora.[84]

With the crack in the traditions of beef animal husbandry provided by the demonstration that the heritable propensity for weight gain would be important in future breeding of cattle, the day of a multicolored cattle culture in Texas was not far behind. Hybrid vigor was demonstrated in crosses between the English and Brahman breeds of cattle by T. C. Cartwright (fig. 12) and his colleagues in studies that would become the landmark of their time.[85] Crossbreeding in one form or another spread across South and East Texas and most of the Southern states as the principal ingredient of cattle production. A Basic Beef Cattle Genetics Laboratory was organized at TAMU in 1964, with fundamental work carried out in immunogenetics, cytogenetics, and developmental genetics of cattle.

Cartwright and his coworkers have centered their efforts during the past decade on application of the techniques of operations research to the study of breed-

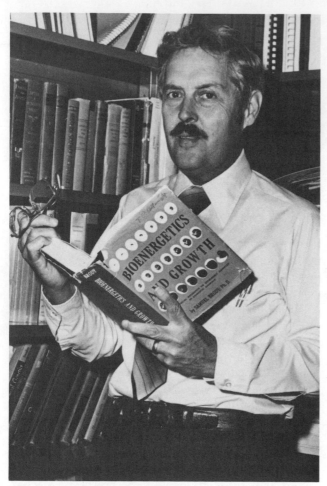

Figure 12. TAES animal scientist T. C. Cartwright and his colleagues reported hybrid vigor in cattle in 1964 and have since applied techniques of operations research.

ing and management of beef cattle.[86] Biologically based simulation models were developed to predict productivity of the cattle herd of a given genetic potential in a specified management-nutritional environment.

Muscle Biology

Inquiries into the quality and structure of meat products started with and proceeded in tandem with the genetics studies on the animals. Successively, over three decades, Silvia Cover, O. D. Butler, G. T. King, Zerle Carpenter, Gary Smith, and H. R. Cross carried out extensive studies to relate the quality and yield of meat to accepted methods of evaluation of the live cattle, sheep, and swine.[87] Efforts were made to identify the anatomical conformation and other measurable char-

acteristics of the animal that could be related to muscle-bone ratios, carcass yields, and palatability of meat products from beef cattle, swine, and sheep.[88] Long-honored concepts used in the selection of animals were tested with regard to meat quality. Here, too, many of the factors that tradition had related to quality and acceptability of beef were found to be wanting. Challenged also, in time, were the successive USDA systems of grading and evaluating meat products.[89] Through the years, a data base was accumulated that may permit manipulation of future production systems to provide meat products with stated qualities of taste and texture, and, perhaps, of nutrient content, for a consuming society increasingly conscious of diet and health.

Studies of the fine anatomy and the biology of postmortem muscle also brought basic science into application in animal agriculture. Long known was the fact that glycolysis is a principal source for regeneration of muscle adenosine triphosphate (ATP) for relaxation of muscle fibers after the animal dies. Rigor mortis or, if the muscle is chilled too quickly the potential for muscle shortening, sets in apparently when postmortem regeneration of ATP and creatine phosphate plays out. Tenderness is lost as a result of muscle contraction and cold shortening, but the loss can be offset, in time and in part, by subsequent catheptic proteolysis of the myofibrils as the carcass is "aged."

It was discovered that the loss of tenderness from rigor mortis could be diminished by the mechanical stretching of the muscle after slaughter and through the chilling period. This stretching could be achieved by hanging the carcass on the pelvic bone instead of the leg (TAMU Tenderstretch method), but the method resulted in cuts that were difficult to fit into the traditional beef marketing system. An alternative system was devised by the meats and muscle biology team at TAMU—Thayne R. Dutson, J. W. Savell, G. C. Smith, and Z. L. Carpenter—who adapted electrical stimulation of the fresh carcass to produce tenderness in those carcasses that would ordinarily be tough due to cold-shortening and the events of rigor mortis.[90] The biochemistry of the tenderizing effect of electrical shock is not clear. Out of these studies came an easily and now widely adapted and inexpensive new technology.[91]

Animal Physiology

Though physiology is an integral contributing discipline in the veterinary and medical sciences, certain aspects, particularly physiology of reproduction, have had extensive application in animal husbandry. Research in physiology of reproduction of animals in the decade following World War II was pursued by Raymond O. Berry and George L. Robertson in the Department of Animal Husbandry at TAMU. The emphasis then was on the effect of environmental factors, including nutrition, on ovulation and intrauterine survival of embryos of swine, sheep, and cattle. Reproductive efficiency also became one of the selection criteria in T. C. Cartwright's and Maurice Shelton's genetic studies on cattle and sheep in the 1960s. Synchronization of the occurrence of estrus in a group of cattle was studied by A. M. Sorensen and his students. Hatchabilities and embryo development were characteristics of concern for Thomas Ferguson, John Quisenberry, and W. F. Krueger in the Department of Poultry Science. Diseases of reproductive organs were monitored by John C. Ramge and his colleagues in the Department of Veterinary Large Animal Medicine and Surgery.[92]

In the early and mid-1970s the research team in reproductive physiology had its largest augmentation with the appointments of Paul G. Harms, Ronald D. Randel, Max S. Amoss, Jr., Duane C. Kraemer (fig. 13),

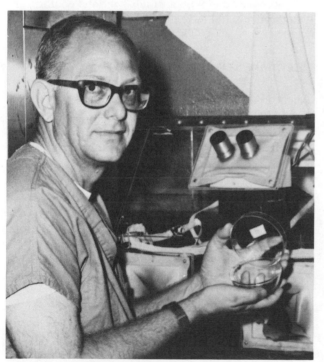

Figure 13. Duane Kraemer, whose experiment perfected the means of embryo transfer and cloning in cattle and other animals.

Gary D. Potter, and James N. Wiltbank to the faculty and staff of the Colleges of Agriculture and Veterinary Medicine and the Agricultural Experiment Station. Research at the Overton and Beeville locations was undertaken to decrease the age of puberty and the postpartum interval in cows by nutritional manipulation and treatment with hormones.[93] Postpartum anestrus, genetic differences such as between *Bos indicus* and *Bos taurus*, nutritional interactions, stress, and environment and management systems have been parameters for investigation.[94]

During the past decade, Experiment Station research at TAMU has looked at the endocrine mechanisms involved in regulating the estrous cycle during the prepubertal and postpartum periods. Attention also has turned to spermatogenesis in the horse and the specific hormonal factor that modulates the biosynthesis of testicular androgens. The methods employed have been cytochemical,[95] experimental,[96] and applied.[97]

Animal Biotechnology

The first studies attempting to link genetic factors expressed biochemically and physiologically to productive factors in animals was carried out in the 1950s. W. E. Briles and Roy Fanguy at TAMU sought genetic linkages to blood antigens in attempts to help commercial breeders select for superior birds. H. O. Kunkel also sought to relate measurable biochemical parameters with genetic differences in productive potential in beef cattle.[98] But applications of the results of these efforts never materialized, awaiting perhaps the development of the techniques of molecular biology for another attempt in the future.

The reach toward applied molecular biology (biotechnology) in animal agriculture was propelled by the development of nonsurgical embryo transfers by Duane Kraemer and his colleagues in research beginning at the Southwest Foundation for Research and Education, San Antonio, and, during the last decade, carried out in the Department of Animal Science and the College of Veterinary Medicine at TAMU.[99] These studies have evolved toward the determination of sex in the embryo, embryo splitting, and the injection of genetic material (DNA) into the developing embryo. Biotechnology that goes beyond sperm banks and impregnation has become industrial reality. Pronuclei of bovine embryos have been successfully injected with the herpes virus thymidine kinase gene, contributing perhaps to the beginnings of genetic engineering in agricultural animals.[100]

In other genetic studies, James E. Womack and his colleagues in the Department of Veterinary Pathology have applied recombinant DNA and molecular technology to cattle and laboratory animal models in order to identify, clone, and map host genes that respond in a pathogenic manner to infectious and xenobiotic agents. A major accomplishment has been the development of a bovine gene map that identifies major regions of homology with the well-defined genomes of mice and man.[101] These findings, too, set the stage for new applications of science in the future.

Wildlife and Fisheries

Opportunities also have been extensive for the applications of biological sciences in that arena in which ecology, zoology, and animal husbandry converge: wildlife biology and management. Applied wildlife biology has important economic and societal implications. Many ranchers gain more income from leasing hunting and fishing rights than from their livestock operations. Aquaculture is of growing interest in Texas. Commercial fishing in the Gulf must compete with the interests of sport fishermen. Predators trouble livestock farmers and ranchers.[102] Wild animals may be vectors of disease. Land and water that provide habitat needed by waterfowl are diverted into agricultural production. Some species are endangered.

Wildlife biology at TAMU during the first two postwar decades was largely directed toward systematics. Extensive collections were made of specimens of birds, fish, and other aquatic animals, mammals, amphibians and reptiles over Texas, Mexico, and the U.S. Southwest; they are now housed in the Texas Cooperative Wildlife Collections at TAMU. In the late 1960s attention turned increasingly to wildlife ecology and management. In the 1970s, activity emerged in fisheries ecology, animal behavior, environmental assessment and ecological evaluation, and wildlife in pest situations. TAMU was designated a Sea Grant College in 1971, and fisheries, both marine and freshwater, were added as serious research thrusts. Added in the late 1970s was the use of molecular genetic analysis and gene flows in wildlife and fish populations to address problems with management implications.

Aquaculture resembles animal husbandry in many respects, and the research problems have been similar: selection of species or breeds best suited to a location, rates of stocking and feeding, economic analyses, food technology, and losses from diseases, predators and drought.[103] The studies on shrimp culture also included the problems of maturation in captivity, spawning, fertilization, and larval development.[104]

Foundations have played an important role in the support of research on wildlife ecology. The Caesar Kleberg Foundation for Wildlife Conservation provided a grant to the College of Agriculture at TAMU in 1967, and support has been continuous since. In the program, big game, mostly ungulates, received the bulk of attention. Early in the program about half of the research was carried out in Africa, and about 40 percent was devoted to exotic animals introduced to Texas. Studies were made on axis deer, nilgai, blackbuck, and aoudad. Subsequent efforts turned to species indigenous to Texas. The Foundation extended its support in the 1970s to TAIU and TTU, each of which built an active program in wildlife biology. TTU's program has been concerned with waterfowl and agriculture and playa-lake management, fisheries management, nongame birds, and mountain lions.[105]

The contributions of the Rob and Bessie Welder Wildlife Foundation were noted above. Employing mainly graduate students, the Welder Foundation made significant contributions in interactions of predators with big game, integration of wildlife management and beef production, diseases and parasites that infect both domestic and wild animals, wetland ecology, and waterfowl and upland game management.[106]

Veterinary Sciences

Except for the work in toxicology, research in veterinary science in Texas historically has been concentrated within the TAMU System. As with research in agriculture, the early postwar period found veterinary research largely outside of the academic programs. In 1948 the staff of the Division of Veterinary Science of the TAES was incorporated into the School of Veterinary Medicine.[107] On September 1, 1948, I. B. Boughton, veterinarian at the TAES Substation at Sonora, was appointed dean of the School.

Although the prewar program in veterinary science was relatively small, it had left a substantial legacy. The work of Mark Francis had resulted in the practical elimination of "tick fever" (babesiosis). Investigations by Hubert Schmidt (fig. 14) had led to the discovery of the endemic deficiency of phosphorus in South Texas rangeland. Loin disease and "creeps" in cattle were brought under control. It was Schmidt who led veterinary science in Texas into the postwar period.

The Substation at Sonora was also a site of contri-

Figure 14. Hubert Schmidt, Texas Agricultural Experiment Station, led veterinary science in Texas into the postwar period.

butions to early postwar veterinary science. William Tyree Hardy concentrated on the life cycle of stomach worm in sheep and aided in the adaptation of its control with phenothiazine. The blue tongue virus was identified, and a living attenuated vaccine was developed for its control in adult sheep. Immunizations for enterotoxemia and contagious ecthyma (soremouth) were devised. A vaccine for pinkeye was developed at the TAES Substation at Angleton in 1954.[108]

Resources for research in the College of Veterinary Medicine remained small or modest during most of the decades following World War II. The early support was by the TAES, but in 1975 external support also began to be a substantial factor. Most of the funding prior to the last decade was devoted to programs that related to the prevention and control of diseases that affected food-producing animals. Considerable diversity and research strength have since emerged.[109]

Research on hemoparasitic diseases had a continuity that extended from continuing research on babesiosis to studies of tropical diseases. An Institute for Tropical Veterinary Medicine (now the Center for Tropical Animal Health) was organized in 1967 under the leadership of Fred Maurer.

Research on brucellosis was re-established in the mid-1970s when it became evident that the accepted methods of control were inadequate and that the unfettered marketing of Texas beef cattle was threatened by restrictions set by other states. Led by L. G. Adams, the study of the epidemiology of brucellosis was resumed. This work led to further definition of the usefulness of immunization of adult animals, to strategies for immunization of calves, to the development of an immunoabsorbent assay for *Brucella abortus* antibody, and to studies on the roles of wild animals in the spread of the disease.

Studies on equine diseases have been numerous since World War II. They have included equine infectious anemia and foal pneumonia. Charles Bridges has elucidated osteochondrosis in thoroughbred foals resulting from a metabolic copper deficiency induced by high levels of dietary zinc.[110] The steady movement of Venezuelan equine encephalomyelitis northward in 1971 was met and stopped by a vaccine first made for human use and tested on horses in South America.

Investigations in avian diseases have been concentrated on the immune system. So has the veterinary research on aquatic animals. Progress was made on an immunization procedure for shrimp through changes in the osmolarity of the water. The inventory of projects in veterinary science now includes work on respiratory diseases of cattle, cardiovascular diseases, disease in wildlife, and oncology.

Veterinary science today feeds on biotechnology. Monoclonal antibodies are moving to common use as diagnostic tools. The positive effect of interferon in bovine respiratory disease has been reported. The genes for the production and action of bovine interferon have been mapped with the thought that genetic (breeding) methods may be used to extend resistance to bovine respiratory disease.[111]

Animal Toxicology

Toxicology, particularly the toxins of plants, was a major concern of both veterinary and range sciences in Texas at the end of World War II. Toxicology is a particularly active focus of veterinary science today. The programs have become extensive and diverse with the contributions made by the TAES in the departments of Veterinary Physiology and Pharmacology, Veterinary Public Health, and Range Science at TAMU. Other active centers include the TAMU Agricultural Research and Extension Center at San Angelo, the USDA Veterinary Toxicology and Entomology Research Laboratory at College Station, and the Texas Veterinary Medical Diagnostic Laboratory also at College Station.[112] Identification of the toxic plants on Texas rangeland was an early cooperative effort.[113]

Characterization of the active agents in bitterweed toxicity for sheep and preparation of a concentrate from *Lobelia berlandieri*, an annual plant that causes occasionally heavy losses in cattle, were accomplished.[114] Photosensitization in lambs has been associated with kleingrass, and research is under way to characterize chemically the toxic substances in a wide range of native plants. Studies on the toxicities of pesticides and potential pesticides, natural toxicants in foods, and toxic effects of materials commonly found in the home and farmstead are programs that have received continuing attention through the past decades. The names of James W. Dollahite, Bennie J. Camp, Charles W. Livingston, M. C. Ivey, E. M. Bailey, Millard C. Calhoun, G. Wayne Ivie, and Stephen Safe thread through the papers that chronicle research in animal toxicology in Texas. New technological advances in the food industry's methods of inactivation of viruses and other disease-causing organisms, toxic elements and mycotoxins in feeds, and food hygiene have contributed to food science in the Department of Veterinary Public Health at TAMU.[115]

Figure 15. Leadership for the forest tree improvement program has resided in J. P. van Buijtenen since 1960.

Forestry

Biological science applied to forests was a postwar phenomenon, a relatively late entry into the scientific effort in Texas. The Texas Forest Service, cooperatively with the TAES, launched the tree improvement program in 1951, and that has been a continuing dominant facet of research in forest science. Stephen F. Austin State University initiated an academic program in forestry in 1946 and added the master's and doctor's degree in forestry programs in 1969 and 1973, respectively. TAMU was authorized to offer the doctoral program in forestry in 1965. A Department of Forest Science and the bachelor's and master's degree programs were added in 1969.

The Texas Forest Service seed orchard was established in 1951 under the technical leadership of Bruce J. Zobel.[116] This leadership of the tree improvement program has resided in J. P. van Buijtenen (fig. 15) since 1960. The selection theory that has evolved in the

program incorporates standards for rate of growth, volume and shape, resistance to insects and disease, hardiness in drought and cold, and characteristics of the wood.[117]

Research in forest resources has become diversified. Forest types and soil classifications were interpreted and mapped for all commercial forest lands by Robert D. Baker and David Moehring. A productive program of research on forest products has developed in the South, and Texas institutions contribute to the total. Perhaps, because of the relative youthfulness of the research programs related to forestry, research on forestry in Texas has been largely crisis driven: by insect and disease infestations and by the new needs (for example, to be able to appraise the tax valuations of commercial timberland on the basis of productivity and to set aside part of the "Big Thicket" as a National Park, a protected National Forest).

The central crises in Texas forests during the past twenty-five years seem to have occurred with insect infestations, mainly by the southern pine beetle (*Dendroctonus frontalis* Zimmermann), but also by the *Ips* species, pine and hardwood defoliaters, pine tip moth, and ants and other cone and seed insects, which mainly affect seed orchards and efforts toward reforestation. The southern pine beetle is reported to have killed more than 300 million board feet of timber in 1976 alone.[118] Losses in 1985, however, are reported to be the most extensive ever.

The response to peak outbreaks of the southern pine beetle was the establishment of the Southern Forest Research Institute at Sour Lake, under contract with the Boyce Thompson Institute, and the Pest Control Section by the Texas Forest Service, both in 1962. The Sour Lake effort was under the direction of J. P. Vite. The isolation and identification of the beetle attractant frontalin and the studies on the attack behavior of the southern pine beetle have led to novel control tactics such as the use of synthetic attractants and a cut-and-leave procedure. The research on southern pine beetle shifted to TAMU, Stephen F. Austin, the Texas Forest Service, and TAES in the 1970s.

Reliance on control of the southern pine beetle by insecticides only was abandoned early for many of the same reasons that it was given up for agricultural insects. The thrust of research has turned to biological, including ecological, phenomena: attractants, repellants, life processes of single and mixed species populations, behavior, population dynamics, and hazard ratings.[119] Again, integration of methods seems to be the eventual solution.

In Retrospect

Research in the biological systems of importance to Texas has been truly productive of both scientific knowledge and technology during the decades since World War II. It is dynamic and productive today not simply to provide food for humanity, but to provide for a healthy supply of food, a livelihood for many, and an efficient and vibrant economy, as well as for the benefit and welfare of Texas people. Research also moves in ways that are an increasingly exciting intellectual adventure.

Tribute should be paid to the research in applied biology in Texas which is *not* detailed here. Far more has been done than we can possibly include in this chapter. If one counts those who came and worked in Texas and then went elsewhere, as well as those who stayed and those who were graduate students in Texas universities, the men and women who have contributed to applied biological sciences in Texas since World War II number in the thousands.

Research in agriculture, animal science, forestry, and veterinary medicine has yielded a continuum of accomplishments, a few striking but most ordinary, that build to a significant understanding and improvement of the biological base and art of application. These ordinary accomplishments, which are not well marked in history or noted by awards or recognition, are the scientific infrastructure of the technical developments for agriculture, animal science, forestry, and veterinary medicine. Without the undergirding of persevering research, salient research would be of little consequence. Much hard and painstaking work, as well as the triumphs, have shaped the face and a substantial part of the economy of Texas.

Notes

1. Lea, 1957.
2. Green, 1977.
3. Green, 1977, 121.
4. Freeman, 1985.
5. Roddy, 1967.
6. Vagtborg, 1973, p. 417.
7. Teer, 1985.
8. Patterson, 1965.
9. Carson, 1962.
10. Parker et al., n.d.
11. Perkins, 1982, p. 161.
12. Knipling, 1959.
13. Scruggs, 1975.
14. Bushland and Hopkins, 1951.
15. Bushland and Hopkins, 1953.
16. Perkins, 1982.
17. Williams and Adkisson, 1964.
18. Adkisson, 1966.
19. Reynolds et al., 1982.
20. Adkisson et al., 1966.
21. Adkisson et al., 1982.
22. Bird, 1982.
23. Burke, 1972.
24. Keeley, 1981.
25. Summers, 1981.
26. Rykiel et al., 1984.
27. Curry, 1984.
28. Quinby, 1974.
29. Quinby, 1974.
30. Jones and Clarke, 1943.

31. Quinby, 1974, p. 76.
32. Atkins et al., 1960.
33. Porter et al., 1964.
34. Atkins, Porter, and Merkle, 1967.
35. Porter et al., 1985.
36. Craigmiles, 1975.
37. Stansel, 1984.
38. Richmond, 1975.
39. Menzel, 1955; Brown, 1980.
40. Maxwell, 1985.
41. Bird, 1982.
42. Dharmaratne et al., 1986.
43. Hallman, Teetes, and Johnson, 1984.
44. Craigmiles, 1981.
45. Craigmiles, 1981.
46. TAES, 1975.
47. Malstrom, Madden, and Romberg, 1978.
48. Correa, 1976; Leeper, 1976.
49. Bashaw, 1980, p. 45.
50. Hart and Tuleen, 1983, p. 339.
51. Sengupta-Gopalan et al., 1985.
52. Park et al., 1985.
53. Price et al., 1980.
54. TAES, 1950, p. 66.
55. Hipp, 1970; Fern and Kissel, 1973; Hipp and Gerard, 1973; Onken, Matheson, and Nesmith, 1985.
56. Rea, 1952.
57. Merkle, 1985.
58. Morgan, 1980, p. 374.
59. Hall and Morgan, 1964; Morgan, 1985.
60. Morgan, 1985.
61. Jordan, Newton, and Rains, 1982.
62. Sperry, 1972.
63. Britton and Smith, eds., 1984.
64. Correll and Johnston, 1970.
65. Gould, 1975.
66. Kothmann et al., 1970.
67. Tschirley, 1986.
68. Scrifres, 1985.
69. Hiler and Howell, 1973.
70. Lyle and Bordovsky, 1981.
71. Hiler et al., 1974.
72. Peters and Reddell, 1976.
73. Reiser, 1978.
74. Beckman, Bruckart, and Reiser, 1953.
75. Kunkel, 1985.
76. Couch and German, 1950.
77. Kunkel, 1985.
78. Tribble, 1984.
79. Potter, 1985.
80. Gatlin and Stickney, 1982.
81. Melton et al., 1966.

82. Warwick and Cartwright, 1955.
83. Patterson et al., 1955.
84. Shelton et al., 1954.
85. Cartwright et al., 1964.
86. Cartwright, 1979.
87. Cartwright, Butler, and Cover, 1958; Abraham et al., 1968; Cross, Carpenter, and Smith, 1973.
88. Abraham et al., 1980; Cross et al., 1975; Smith, Carpenter, and King, 1969.
89. Cross et al., 1980.
90. Savell, Smith, and Carpenter, 1978.
91. Savell, 1985.
92. TAES, 1979.
93. Smith et al., 1979.
94. Rhodes, Randel, and Long, 1982.
95. Culler et al., 1982.
96. Rahe, Fleeger, and Harms, 1982.
97. Rahe et al., 1980; Henneke, Potter, and Kreider, 1984.
98. Kunkel, 1985, p. 23.
99. Kraemer, 1984, p. 643.
100. Kraemer, Minhas, and Capehart, 1985, p. 221.
101. Womack, 1984.
102. Shelton and Klindt, 1974.
103. Klussmann, 1983; Stickney and Davis, 1981.
104. Lawrence, Chamberlain, and Hutchins, 1981.
105. Texas Tech University, 1984.
106. Teer, 1985.
107. Schmidt, 1958.
108. TAES, 1956, p. 49.
109. Loan, 1985.
110. Bridges et al., 1984.
111. Womack, 1984.
112. USDA-TAES, 1981.
113. Sperry et al., 1965.
114. Kim, Rowe, and Camp, 1975.
115. Childers et al., 1979, p. 1291.
116. Zobel and McElwee, 1964.
117. van Buijtenen et al., 1981.
118. Billings, 1984.
119. Payne et al., eds., 1984.

Bibliography

Abraham, H. C., Z. L. Carpenter, G. T. King, and O. D. Butler, "Relationships of Carcass Weight, Conformation and Carcass Measurements and Their Use in Predicting Beef Carcass Cutability," *Journal of Animal Science* 27(1968):604–10.
Abraham, H. C., C. E. Murphey, H. R. Cross, G. C. Smith, and W. J. Franks, Jr., "Factors Affecting Beef

Carcass Cutability: An Evaluation of the USDA Yield Grades for Beef," *Journal of Animal Science* 50(1980):841.

Adkisson, Perry L., "Internal Clocks and Insect Diapause," *Science* 154(1966):234–41.

Adkisson, Perry L., George A. Niles, J. Knox Walker, Luther S. Bird, and Helen B. Scott, "Controlling Cotton's Insect Pests: A New System," *Science* 216(1982):19–22.

Adkisson, Perry L., D. R. Rummel, W. L. Sterling, and W. L. Owen, Jr., *Diapause Boll Weevil Control: A Comparison of Two Methods*, Texas Agricultural Experiment Station Bulletin B-1054 (1966).

Atkins, I. M., K. B. Porter, Keith Lahr, Owen G. Merkle, and M. C. Futrell, *Wheat Production in Texas*, Texas Agricultural Experiment Station Bulletin 948 (1960).

Atkins, I. M., K. B. Porter, and O. G. Merkle, "Registration of Sturdy Wheat (Reg. No. 469)," *Crop Science* 7(1967):406.

Bashaw, E. C., "Aprmixis and Its Application in Crop Improvement." In *Hybridization of Crop Plants*, edited by W. R. Fehr and H. H. Hadley, 45–63, Madison, Wisconsin: ASA Press, 1980.

Beckman, H. F., Sara M. Bruckart, and Raymond Reiser, "Laboratory Culture of the Pink Bollworm," *Journal of Economic Entomology* 46(1953): 627–30.

Billings, Ronald F., "Forest Pests in East Texas: Past Approaches, Future Challenges." In *History, Status, and Future Needs for Entomology Research in Southern Forests*, edited by T. L. Payne, R. F. Billings, R. N. Coulson, and D. L. Kulhavy, Texas Agricultural Experiment Station, MP 1553 (1984).

Bird, L. S., "The MAR (Multi-Adversity Resistance) System for Genetic Improvement of Cotton," *Plant Disease* 66(1982):172–76.

Bollich, C. N., and J. E. Scott, "Past, Present and Future Varieties of Rice." In *Six Decades of Rice Research*, edited by Julian Craigmiles, Texas Agricultural Experiment Station Research Monograph 4 (1975).

Bridges, C. H., J. E. Womack, E. D. Harris, and W. L. Scrutchfield, "Considerations for Copper Metabolism in Osteochondrosis in Suckling Foals," *Journal of the American Veterinary Medical Association* 185(1984):173–78.

Britton, Carlton M., and Loren M. Smith, eds. *Research Highlights—1984: Noxious Brush and Weed Control; Range and Wildlife Management*, Lubbock: Texas Tech Univ. Press, 1984.

Brown, Meta S., "Identification of the Chromosomes of *Gossypium hirsutum* L. by Means of Translocations," *The Journal of Heredity* 71(1980):266–74.

Burke, Horace R., "The Insect Collection of the Department of Entomology, Texas A&M University," *Bulletin of the Entomological Society of America* 18(1972):174–75.

Bushland, Raymond C., and D. E. Hopkins, "Experiments with Screwworm Flies Sterilized by X-rays," *Journal of Economic Entomology* 44(1951):725–31.

———. "Sterilizations of Screwworm Flies with X-rays and Gamma Rays," *Journal of Economic Entomology* 46(1953):648–56.

Carson, Rachel, *Silent Spring*, Boston: Houghton Mifflin, 1962.

Cartwright, T. C., "The Use of Systems Analysis in Animal Science with Emphasis on Animal Breeding," *Journal of Animal Science* 49(1979):817–25.

Cartwright, T. C., O. D. Butler, and S. Cover, "The Relationship of Ration and Inheritance to Certain Production and Carcass Characteristics of Yearling Steers," *Journal of Animal Science* 17(1958):540.

Cartwright, T. C., G. F. Ellis, Jr., W. E. Kruse, and E. K. Crouch, *Hybrid Vigor in Brahman-Hereford Crosses*. Texas Agricultural Experiment Station Technical Monograph 1 (1964).

Childers, A. B., Norman D. Heidelbaugh, Z. L. Carpenter, G. C. Smith, and Scott White, "Technological Advances in the Food Industry: Their Influence in Public Health," *Journal of the American Veterinary Medical Association* 175 (1979):1291–96.

Correa, Rumaldo T., Oral history interview with Irvin M. May, December 15, 1976. Archives, Texas A&M University.

Correll, D. S., and M. C. Johnston, *Manual of the Vascular Plants in Texas*, Renner, Texas Research Foundation, 1970.

Couch, J. R., and H. L. German, "Vitamin B_{12}, APF Concentrates and Dried Whey in the Nutrition of the Growing Chick," *Poultry Science* 29 (1950):754.

Craigmiles, J. P., "Advances in Soybeans—History and Technology." In *Another Triumph of Research: Soybeans on the Texas Coastal Prairie*, 5–9, Texas Agricultural Experiment Station Research Monograph 11 (1981).

Craigmiles, J. P., *Six Decades of Rice Research in Texas*, Texas Agricultural Experiment Station Research Monograph 4 (1975).

Cross, H. R., Z. L. Carpenter, and G. C. Smith, "Equations for Estimating Boneless Retail Cut Yields from Beef Carcasses," *Journal of Animal Science* 37(1973): 1267–72.

Cross, H. R., L. W. Douglass, E. D. Linderman, C. E. Murphey, J. W. Savell, G. C. Smith, and D. M. Stiffler, *An Evaluation of the Accuracy of the USDA Beef Quality and Yield Grading System— A Report to the Inspector General, USDA*, Roman L. Hrusker Meat Animal Research Center, USDA, Clay Center, Nebraska, 1980.

Cross, H. R., G. C. Smith, Z. L. Carpenter, and A. W. Kotula, "Relationship of Carcass Scores and Measurements to Fine Endpoints for Lean Cut Yields in Barrow and Gilt Carcasses," *Journal of Animal Science* 41(1975): 1318–26.

Culler, Michael D., Newell H. McArthur, William L. Dees, Robert E. Owens, and Paul G. Harms, "Immunocytochemical Evidence that Suckling Inhibits the Postovariectomy Depletion of Median Eminence Luteinizing Hormone Releasing Hormone," *Neuroendocrinology* 34(1982): 258–64.

Curry, Guy L., "Mathematical Foundations of Modeling Poikilotherm Mortality," *Mathematical Bioscience* 71(1984): 81–104.

Dharmaratne, Gerard S., Ronald D. Lacewell, John R. Stoll, and George Teetes, *Economic Impact of Greenbug Resistant Grain Sorghum*, Texas Agricultural Experiment Station Miscellaneous Publication MP-1585 (1986).

Fenn, L. B., and D. E. Kissel, "Ammonia Volatization from Surface Applications of Ammonium Compounds on Calcareous Soils: I. General Theory," *Soil Science Society of America, Proceedings* 37(1973): 855–59.

Finer, J. J., and R. H. Smith, "Isolation and Culture of Protoplasts from Cotton (*Gossypium Klotzschianum* Andress.) Callus Cultures," *Plant Science Letters* 26(1982): 147–51.

Freeman, T. R., *Digest 85*, Prairie View, Texas, College of Agriculture and Cooperative Agricultural Research Center Annual Report, Prairie View A&M University, 1985.

Gatlin, Delbert M. III, and Robert R. Stickney, "Fall-Winter Growth of Young Channel Catfish in Response to Quality and Science of Dietary Lipid," *Transactions of the American Fisheries Society* 111(1982): 90–3.

Gould, Frank W., *The Grasses of Texas*, College Station: Texas A&M Univ. Press, 1975.

Green, Donald E., *Fifty Years of Service to West Texas Agriculture: A History of Texas Tech University's College of Agricultural Sciences, 1925–1975*, Lubbock: Texas Tech Univ. Press, 1977.

Hall, W. C., and P. W. Morgan, "Auxin-Ethylene Interrelationships," *Regulateurs Naturels de la Croissance Vegetale*, 727–45, Paris, Editions du Centre National de la Recherche Scientifique, 1964.

Hallman, G. J., George L. Teetes, and Jerry W. Johnson, "Relationship of Sorghum Midge (Diptera: Cecidomyiidae) Density to Damage to Resistant and Susceptible Sorghum Hybrids," *Journal of Economic Entomology* 77(1984): 83–7.

Hart, Gary E., and Neal A. Tuleen, "Introduction and Characterization of Alien Genetic Material." In *Isozymes in Plant Genetics and Breeding, Part A*, edited by S. D. Tanksley and T. J. Orton, Amsterdam: Elsevier Science, 1983.

Henneke, D. R., G. D. Potter, and J. L. Kreider, "Body Condition During Pregnancy and Lactation and Reproductive Efficiency of Mares," *Theriogenology* 21 (1984): 897–909.

Hiler, E. A., and T. A. Howell, "Grain Sorghum Response to Trickle and Subsurface Irrigation," *Transactions of the ASAE* 16(1973): 799–803.

Hiler, E. A., T. A. Howell, R. B. Lewis, and R. P. Boos, "Irrigation Timing by the Stress Day Index Method," *Transactions of the ASAE* 17 (1974): 393–98.

Hipp, Billy W., "Phosphorus Requirements for Tomatoes as Influenced by Placement," *Agronomy Journal* 62(1970): 203–6.

Hipp, Billy W., and C. J. Gerard, "Influence of Previous Crop on Nitrate Distribution in a Clay Soil Profile and Subsequent Response to Applied N," *Agronomy Journal* 65(1973): 712–14.

Jones, H. A., and A. C. Clarke, "Inheritance of Male Sterility in the Onion and the Production of Hybrid Seed," *Proceedings of the American Society of Horticultural Science* 43(1943): 189–94.

Jordan, W. R., R. J. Newton, and D. W. Rains, *Water-related Technologies for Sustaining Agriculture in U.S. Arid and Semi-arid Lands: II. Improving Biological Water-Use Efficiency for Dry Land Areas*, Washington, D.C., Office of Technology Assessment, Congress of the United States, 1982.

Keeley, L. L., "Neuroendocrine Regulation of Mitochondrial Development and Function in the Insect Fat Body." In *Energy Metabolism and Its Regulation in Insects*, edited by R. G. H. Downer, 207–37, New York: Plenum, 1981.

Kim, H. L., L. D. Rowe, and B. J. Camp, "Hymenoxon, A Poisonous Sesquiterpene Lactone from Hymenoxys odorata DC. (Bitterweed)," *Research Communications in Chemical Pathology and Pharmacology* 11(1975): 647.

Klussmann, Wallace, "Improving Fish Production," *Water Currents*, College Station, Texas Water Resources Institute, Texas A&M University, 1983.

Knipling, E. F., "Screwworm Eradication: Concepts and Research Leading to the Sterile-Male Method," *Smithsonian Report for 1958*, 409–18, Washington, D.C., Government Printing Office, 1959.

Kothmann, M. M., G. W. Mathis, P. T. Marion, and W. J. Waldrip, *Livestock Production and Economic Returns from Grazing Treatments on the Texas Experimental Ranch*, Texas Agricultural Experiment Station Bulletin B-1100 (1970).

Kraemer, D.C., "Contributions of Mammalian Embryo Transfer to Developmental Genetics," *American Journal of Medical Genetics* 18(1984):643–48.

Kraemer, D., B. Minhas, and J. Capehart, "Gene Transfer into Pronuclei of Cattle and Sheep Zygotes," *Banbury Report 20: Genetic Manipulation of the Early Embryo*, edited by Frank Constantini and Rudolf R. Jaenisch, 221–27. Cold Spring Harbor Laboratory, 1985.

Kunkel, H. O., *Nutritional Science at Texas A&M University, 1888–1984*. Texas Agricultural Experiment Station Bulletin 1490 (1985).

Lawrence, Addisen L., George W. Chamberlain, and David L. Hutchins, *Shrimp Mariculture, An Overview*, Texas A&M University Sea Grant College Program Publication TAMU-SG-82-503 (1981).

Lea, Tom, *The King Ranch*, vol. 2, Kingsville, Texas, King Ranch, 1957.

Loan, Raymond, to H. O. Kunkel, September 12, 1985.

Leeper, Paul T., Oral history interview with Irvin M. May, December 14, 1976. Archives, Texas A&M University.

Lyle, W. M., and J. P. Bordovsky, "Low Energy Precision Application (LEPA) Irrigation System," *Transactions of the ASAE*, 24 (1981):1241–45.

Malstrom, Howard L., George D. Madden, and Louis D. Romberg, "Evolution of the Pecan and Origin of Many Cultivars," *The Pecan Quarterly* 12(4):24–8 (1978).

Maxwell, F. G., "Utilization of Host Plant Resistance in Pest Management," *Insect Science Application* 6(1985):437–42.

Melton, A. A., L. A. Maddox, Jr., Walter E. Kruse, and R. E. Patterson, *The Evolution of Performance Testing of Beef Cattle in Texas*, Department of Animal Science, Texas Agricultural Experiment Station Departmental Information Report 10(1966).

Menzel, Margaret Y., "A Cytological Method for Genome Analysis in Gossypium," *Genetics* 40 (1955):214–23.

Merkle, M. G., to H. O. Kunkel, August 30, 1985.

Morgan, P. W., "Agricultural Uses of Plant Growth Substances: Historical Perspective." In *Plant Growth Substances 1979*, edited by F. Skoog, 373–76. Berlin and Heidelberg: Springer-Verlag, 1980.

———. "Chemical Manipulation of Abscission and Dessication." In *Agricultural Chemicals of the Future*, edited by James L. Hilton, 61–74, Rowman & Allanheld, 1985.

Onken, A. B., R. L. Matheson, and D. E. Nesmith, "Fertilizer Nitrogen and Residual Nitrate-Nitrogen Effects on Irrigated Corn Yield," *Soil Science Society of America Journal* 49(1985):134–39.

Park, W. D., D. J. Hannapel, G. A. Mignery, and C. S. Pikaard, "Molecular Approaches to the Study of the Major Tubes Proteins." In *Potato Physiology*, edited by H. L. Paul, New York: Academic, 1985.

Parker, R. D., J. K. Walker, G. A. Niles, and J. R. Mulkey, *The "Short-Season Effect" in Cotton and Escape from the Boll Weevil*, Texas Agricultural Experiment Station Bulletin B-1315, College Station, n.d.

Patterson, R. E., *Classification of Texas Agricultural Experiment Station Units According to Proposed Use, 1 October 1965*, Director's Files, Texas Agricultural Experiment Station, 1965.

Patterson, R. E., T. C. Cartwright, J. H. Jones, and J. J. Bayles, "Performance Testing of Beef Breeding Stock," *Journal of Animal Science* 14(1955):1034–41.

Payne, T. L., R. F. Billings, R. N. Coulson, and D. L. Kulhavy, eds., *History, Status, and Future Needs for Entomology Research in Southern Forests*, Texas Agricultural Experiment Station Miscellaneous Publication MP 1553 (1984).

Perkins, John H., *Insects, Experts, and the Insecticide Crisis: The Quest for New Pest Management Strategies*, New York and London: Plenum, 1982.

Peters, Robert E., and Donald L. Reddell, "Ammonia Volatilization and Nitrogen Transformations in Soils Used for Beef Manure Disposal," *Transactions of the ASAE* 19(1976):945–52.

Porter, K. B., I. M. Atkins, Earl C. Gilmore, Keith A. Lahr, and Pascal Scottino, "Evaluation of Short Stature Winter Wheats (Triticum Aestivum L.) for Production under Texas Conditions," *Agronomy Journal* 56(1964):393–96.

Porter, K. B., W. D. Worrall, J. H. Gardenhire, E. C. Gilmore, M. E. McDaniel, and N. A. Tuleen, *TAM 107 and TAM 108: New Short Wheats*, Texas Agricultural Experiment Station, 1985.

Potter, Gary D., "Equine Research Accomplishments, 1975–1985," Unpublished mss., Texas A&M University, 1985.

Price, H. J., K. Bachmann, K. L. Chambers, and J. Riggs, "Detection of Intraspecific Variation in DNA Content in *Microseris douglasii*," *Botanical Gazette* 141(1980): 195–98.

Quinby, J. Roy, *Sorghum Improvement and the Genetics of Growth*, College Station, Texas A&M Univ. Press, 1974.

Rahe, C. H., J. L. Fleeger, and P. G. Harms, "Evidence for an Inherent Rhythm in Pulsatile LH Release in Ovariectomized Cows," *Theriogenology* 18 (1982): 573–81.

Rahe, C. H., R. E. Owens, J. L. Fleeger, H. J. Newton, and P. G. Harms, "Pattern of Plasma Luteinizing Hormone in the Cyclic Cow: Dependence upon the Period of the Cycle," *Endocrinology* 107 (1980): 498–503.

Rea, H. E., to Director R. D. Lewis, November 24, 1952. Director's Files, Texas Agricultural Experiment Station.

Reiser, Raymond, "Oversimplification of Diet: Coronary Heart Disease Relationships and Exaggerated Diet Recommendations," *American Journal of Clinical Nutrition* 31(1978): 865–75.

Reynolds, H. T., P. L. Adkisson, Ray F. Smith, and R. E. Frisbie, "Cotton Insect Pest Management." In *Introduction to Insect Pest Management*, edited by R. Metcalf and W. Luckmann, 375–441, New York: John Wiley & Sons, 1982.

Rhodes, R. C. III, R. D. Randel, and C. R. Long, "Corpus Luteum Function in the Bovine *in vivo* and *in vitro* Evidence for Both a Seasonal and Breedtype Effect," *Journal of Animal Science* 55(1982): 159–67.

Richmond, Thomas R., Oral History interview with Irvin M. Mays and R. D. Lewis, December 19 and 22, 1975, Archives, Texas A&M University.

Roddy, Roy, *Texas Research Foundation, Its Historical Background Through 1966*, Renner, Texas Research Foundation, 1967.

Rykiel, E. J., M. C. Saunders, T. L. Wagner, D. K. Loh, R. H. Turnbow, L. C. Hu, P. E. Pulley, and R. N. Coulson, "Computer-aided Decision Making and Information Accessing in Pest Management Systems, with Emphasis on the Southern Pine Beetle," *Journal of Economic Entomology* 77 (1984): 475–87.

Savell, J. W., "Industrial Applications of Electrical Stimulation." In *Advances in Meat Research*, Vol. 1, edited by A. M. Pearson and T. R. Dutson, Westport, Conn.: AVI, 1985.

Savell, J. W., G. C. Smith, and Z. L. Carpenter, "Beef Quality and Palatability as Affected by Electrical Stimulation and Cooler Aging," *Journal of Food Science* 43(1978): 1666.

Schmidt, Hubert, *Eighty Years of Veterinary Medicine at the Agricultural and Mechanical College of Texas*, College Station, Archives, Texas A&M University, 1958.

Scifres, C. J., "IBMS: Ecological Basis and Evolution of Concepts." In *Integrated Brush Management Systems for South Texas: Development and Implementation*, 5–8, Texas Agricultural Experiment Station Bulletin B-1493 (1985).

Scruggs, Charles G., *The Peaceful Atom and the Deadly Fly*, Austin, Texas: Pemberton, 1975.

Sengupta-Gopalan, C., N. A. Reichert, R. F. Barker, T. C. Hall, and J. F. Kemp, "Developmentally Regulated Expression of the Bean B-phaseolin Gene in Tobacco Seed," *Proceedings of the Natural Academy of Sciences, U.S.A.* 82(1985): 3320–24.

Shelton, Maurice, and John Klindt, *The Interrelationships of Coyote Density and Certain Livestock and Game Species in Texas*, Texas Agricultural Experiment Station Miscellaneous Publication MP-1148 (1974).

Shelton, Maurice, J. C. Miller, W. T. Magee, and W. T. Hardy, "A Summary of Four Years' Work in Ram Progeny and Performance Testing," *Journal of Animal Science* 13(1954): 215.

Smith, G. C., Z. L. Carpenter, and G. T. King, "Ovine Carcass Cutability," *Journal of Animal Science* 29(1969): 272–82.

Smith, M. F., W. C. Burrell, L. D. Shipp, L. R. Sprott, W. N. Songster, and J. N. Wiltbanks, "Hormone Treatments and Use of Calf Removal in Postpartum Beef Cows," *Journal of Animal Science* 48(1979): 1285.

Smith, R. H., S. Bahaskaran, and K. Schertz, "Sorghum Plant Regeneration from Aluminum Selection Media," *Plant Cell Reports* 2(1983): 129–32.

Sperry, O. E., "25 Years of Range Science at Texas A&M University." In *Proceedings of the Symposium Commemorating 25 Years*, 12–15, Department of Range Science, Texas A&M University, 1972.

Sperry, O. E., G. O. Hoffmann, B. J. Camp, and J. W. Dollahite, *Texas Plants Poisonous to Livestock*, Texas Agricultural Experiment Station Bulletin 1028 (1965).

Stansel, J. W., *The Semidwarfs—A New Era in Rice Production*, Texas Agricultural Experiment Station Bulletin B-1462 (1984).

Stickney, R. R., and J. T. Davis, *Aquaculture in Texas: A Status Report and Development Plan*, Texas A&M University Marine Information Service Publication TAMU-SG-81-119 (1981).

Summers, M. D., "Viral Controls of Insects." In *Proceedings of Symposia IX International Congress of Plant Protection*, vol. 1, 152–55, College Park, Maryland, Entomological Society of America, 1981.

Swank, Wendell G., "Wild Ungulates as Competitives of Livestock." In *Parasites, Pests and Predators*, edited by S. M. Gafaar, W. E. Howard, and R. E. Marsh, 457–69, Amsterdam: Elsevier Science: 1985.

Teer, James G., to H. O. Kunkel, 1985.

Texas Agricultural Experiment Station, *Agricultural Research in Texas, 1950*, Annual Report, 1950.

———. *Agricultural Research in Texas Since 1888*, Miscellaneous Publication MP-177 (1956).

———. *Peanut Production in Texas*, Research Monograph RM-3 (1975).

———. "Review of Reproductive Physiology," College Station, Texas A&M University, unpublished mss., 1979.

Texas Tech University, *Fifth Annual Report to the Caesar Kleberg Foundation for Wildlife Conservation*, Lubbock, Department of Range and Wildlife Management, Texas Tech University, 1984.

Tribble, Leland F., *Proceedings of the 32nd Annual Swine Short Course*, Texas Tech University Agricultural Sciences Technical Report T-5-179(1984).

Tschirley, Fred H., "Dioxin," *Scientific American* 254(2):29–35(1986).

United States Department of Agriculture, Agricultural Research Service, and Texas Agricultural Experiment Station, "USDA/TAES Toxicology Program Review," mss., College Station, 1981.

Vagtborg, Harold, *The Story of Southwest Research Center*, Austin: Univ. of Texas Press, 1973.

van Buijtenen, J. P., G. A. Donovan, E. M. Long, W. J. Lowe, C. R. McKinley, J. F. Robinson, and R. A. Woessner, *Introduction to Practical Forest Tree Improvement*, Texas Forest Service Circular 207, Rev. 1981.

Warwick, B. L., and T. C. Cartwright, "Heritability of Rate of Gain in Young Growing Beef Cattle," *Journal of Animal Science* 14(1955):363–71.

Williams, Carroll M., and Perry L. Adkisson, "Physiology of Insect Diapause. XIV. An Endocrine Mechanism for the Photoperiodic Control of Pupal Diapause in the Oak Silkworm, Antheraea Pernyi," *Biological Bulletin* 127(1964):511–25.

Womack, J. E., "A Gene Map of the Cow," *Genetic Maps*, 3(1984):402.

Zobel, Bruce, and R. L. McElwee, "Seed Orchards for Production of Genetically Improved Seed," *Silvae Genetica* 13(1964):4–11.

15

Genetics

Thomas S. Matney

Introduction

Genetic research in Texas began shortly after the turn of the century with the development of a very productive group in the zoology department of the University of Texas at Austin and Edgar Altenburg (fig. 1) in the biology department of Rice Institute in Houston. Five members of the Austin group later became members of the National Academy of Sciences, and one of them received the Nobel prize. Collectively their research included the genetics and embryology of multiple births, reproduction in marsupials, the proof of genetic linkage groups in plants, genetic recombination mechanisms, a first understanding of the concept of chromosomal translocation, mammalian and human cytogenetics, and the discovery of mutagenesis by X-rays and ultraviolet light. Two members of the group compared genetic linkage maps with visual chromosome structures in Drosophila. Another two laid the foundation for population genetics with studies on Drosophila populations.

During the 1950s and 1960s a second group of geneticists assembled in the biology department of the University of Texas M. D. Anderson Hospital and Tumor Institute in Houston. Their research centered around the genetics of mammalian cell cultures. During the 1970s two new centers were added as part of the Graduate School of Biomedical Sciences in the University of Texas Health Science Center at Houston: the Medical Genetics Center, concerned with studies on the genetics of cancer, and the Center for Population Genetics and Demography, where research focused on human population studies and inherited diseases. During the same time period, the Baylor College of Medicine also developed considerable strength in genetics, especially in the Department of Cell Biology, which has made contributions toward understanding the basic structure, function, and regulation of eukaryotic genes.

During the 1960s the Research Institute for Radiation Biology was established in Dallas, which would later become incorporated into the University of Texas at Dallas. Genetic studies there involved the repair of radiation-induced DNA damage. A decade later, a separate component of the University of Texas, the Health Science Center at Dallas, initiated research for which a Nobel prize was awarded. The research identified novel genetic mechanisms involved in the regulation of cholesterol biosynthesis.

Figure 1. Edgar Altenburg

Early Research and the Austin Geneticists

John Thomas Patterson (fig. 1 in the History of Sigma Xi) was primarily responsible for the development of a strong group of geneticists within the zoology department of the University of Texas in Austin.[1] Patterson had been brought to Texas in 1908 by the new departmental chairman, Horatio Hackett Newman. Newman was interested in multiple births and later became well-known for his use of twins to study human inherited traits. Together with Newman, Patterson initiated studies on multiple births in the nine-banded Texas armadillo, *Dasypus novemcintus*, which normally gave birth to quadruplets. After Newman left Austin in 1911, Patterson concluded the experiments alone. These studies showed that the armadillo bred in late summer but that the attachment of the egg to the uterine wall did not take place for some two to three months, a delay during which the fertilized egg divided. The resulting multicellular form became implanted in the uterine wall, and growth began around four centers, thus creating genetically identical quadruplets. The series of papers on this work established Patterson as a leading embryologist of the time. He

was also able to organize people in a sizable project and enlisted the aid of a small army of ranchers with their dogs in the hills west of Austin to procure the live specimens. Armadillos are not so easy to find—especially the number of pregnant females needed in his studies—as current Texas beer commercials imply.

As soon as Patterson replaced Newman as chairman in 1911, he began to look for outstanding biologists who would fill certain gaps. The most pressing was perhaps that of a physiologist, since Newman had forced him to play that unwanted role. He enticed Carl G. Hartman back to Austin to resume graduate studies. Hartman, who had received an M.A. in zoology from the University of Texas in 1904 and had been teaching at Sam Houston State Teachers College, received the first doctorate awarded by the University of Texas in 1915.[2] Hartman remained in the department until he accepted a position at the Carnegie Institute in 1925. He later became a member of the National Academy of Sciences.[3]

In 1916 Patterson succeeded in drawing Theophilus Shickel Painter (fig. 2) to the faculty as an adjunct professor of zoology. Painter had obtained his doctorate in

Figure 2. Theophilus Shickel Painter

Figure 3. Herman Joseph Muller

cytology from Yale University in 1913. After a post-doctoral year with the famous Theodor Boveri at Würzburg, he returned to Yale as an instructor in zoology for two years. During the summers he was an instructor in the invertebrate zoology course at the Marine Biological Laboratory, Woods Hole, Massachusetts. His arrival in Texas began a long and fruitful association with the University of Texas, during which he was elected a member of the National Academy of Sciences. In 1944 he became acting president of the university and in 1946 he began a six-year period as president.

By 1920, when he succeeded in attracting Herman Joseph Muller (fig. 3) to the faculty of the University of Texas at Austin, Patterson had formed a genetics group of considerable strength within the zoology department. One of the graduates of the department, Clarence P. Oliver, was able to say later: "What a quadrumvirate! Patterson, Hartman, Painter, and Muller, all to be elected to the National Academy of Sciences and one, Muller, to become a Nobel laureate for work done at Texas. And this in an institution only five years beyond its first Ph.D."[4]

In addition to Hartman, three other graduates of the department played major roles in the Austin genetics group of the University of Texas. Clarence P. Oliver became a graduate assistant for Muller in the Drosophila laboratory where he first developed an interest in population genetics. He completed his doctorate in 1931, the last student to do so under Muller's supervision. After a brief stay at Washington University, he accepted a faculty position at the University of

Minnesota, where he remained until he rejoined the Austin group in 1946. While in Minnesota, he organized and directed the Dight Institute of Human Genetics, the first of its kind in the world. Upon his return to the University of Texas, he served as chairman of the zoology department from 1947 until 1959.

Wilson S. Stone, with interests in genetic mechanisms of crossing-over and population genetics, began his graduate studies under Muller and completed them under Patterson in 1935, after Muller's departure. Patterson and Stone laid much of the groundwork which resulted in an understanding of Drosophila evolution. Stone's productive scientific career led to his election as a member of the National Academy of Sciences. He became chairman of the zoology department and later the vice-chancellor for graduate affairs for the University of Texas system.

Robert Wagner, another one of Patterson's students, became an outstanding teacher with research interests in elucidating biochemical pathways in microorganisms, especially (*Neurospora crassa*).

Muller and Altenburg

Herman J. Muller and Edgar Altenburg were lifelong friends, and both attended Columbia College in New York City. Muller was accepted as a graduate student by Thomas Hunt Morgan to study Drosophila genetics in 1912. Altenburg also did his graduate work in Morgan's department, but in plant genetics. However, he was familiar with every detail of the famous "fly room." As a graduate student, Muller quickly established himself as a creator of ingenious experimental designs. His strain constructions and crosses are still used in Drosophila mutagen testing today, some seventy years later. Muller's dissertation was on crossing-over between homologous chromosomes. It introduced the new concepts of coincidence and interference which permitted the resolution of mapping problems and firmly established the law of genetic linkage. As we shall see, Altenburg obtained similar results with plants. Altenburg received his doctorate in 1915 and accepted a position at the University of Chicago. Muller finished a year later and accepted an invitation by Julian Huxley to take an instructorship at Rice Institute (later Rice University) in Houston. Muller soon convinced Altenburg that he should join him in Houston.

Shortly after his arrival at Rice Institute, Altenburg submitted for publication the results of an extensive plant study on the linkage in *Primula sinensis*, which he had begun when he was a graduate student at Columbia University.[5] At that time, genetic linkage had just been established in Drosophila in Morgan's "fly room." All Drosophila genes resided on one of four linkage groups, which in turn equated with the four types of visible structures called chromosomes. These were seen as four pairs of chromosomes in dividing Drosophila cells. One chromosome of each pair was maternal and came from the egg, while the other chromosome was paternal. Each inherited characteristic therefore was determined by two genes, called alleles, which mapped at the same locus on each of the two chromosomes constituting an homologous pair. Mendel, in the first recorded genetic study, had reported on the inheritance of seven sets of alleles in the common garden pea. In each set one allele had undergone a mutation while the other remained normal. As examples, dwarf-height contrasted with normal-height plants and wrinkled-coat contrasted with smooth-coated peas. In Mendel's data, none of the seven characters were linked with the other six; they had segregated randomly. Altenburg provided convincing evidence of linkage in plants. Mendel had evidently selected data for publication which involved seven genetic characters in the garden pea, each residing on a separate linkage group. The garden pea has seven chromosome pairs.

In an article published on the fiftieth anniversary of the occasion, Muller credits Altenburg with having diagnosed the first case of a chromosomal translocation, *Pale* in Drosophila. The event occurred in 1916, when a postal card arrived at Rice Institute from Alfred H. Sturtevant and Calvin B. Bridges bearing the news of an unusual inheritance in Drosophila. Muller described the scene:

> It is clear in my memory that after looking at this card for a short time, Altenburg (still standing) exclaimed as follows (or to this effect): "Why, this means that a piece of one chromosome has been broken off and attached to a non-homologous one—it has transposed!"[6]

They designed genetic tests of the "transposition," as Altenburg had called it, and sent them on an equally small one-cent postal card to Bridges and Sturtevant. Bridges conducted the experiments at once and confirmed the "transposition." Some six years later Bridges published an abstract on the case, coining for it the term "translocation."[7]

Mutagenesis and Environmental Factors

Muller and Altenburg designed and initiated a series of studies to determine whether environmental factors were mutagenic. The first experiments involved heat and revealed that mutation rates in Drosophila were essentially doubled for each ten-degree rise in temperature. It was through this work that they realized the nature of mutations: a change in a unit, the gene, which then replicated faithfully and was passed on in its changed form to future generations. It was also clear that every cellular component and activity must be controlled by a gene or genes. But what caused the spontaneous mutations? Were there environmental factors that induced mutations? Muller and Altenburg were about to test ionizing radiation as a possible mutagenic agent when the United States entered World War I. Huxley returned to England and Muller returned to Columbia, but Altenburg remained at Rice. Though Muller and Altenburg were never again at the same institution, they collaborated on several studies and corresponded frequently.[8]

In 1920 Muller went from Columbia to the University of Texas. His investigation into the mutagenesis of X-rays was initiated when he obtained the use of a dental X-ray machine.[9] This work was published in 1927 and earned him the Nobel prize.[10] Meanwhile, Altenburg attempted to test the mutagenic effects of gamma radiation from radium and then X-rays. Both efforts were plagued by mechanical failures.[11] Finally, about 1930, Altenburg initiated tests with ultraviolet (UV) light and found it to be highly mutagenic in Drosophila.[12] This discovery was important for the development of genetics on both the practical and conceptual levels. It provided laboratories with a relatively safe and inexpensive apparatus to generate a mutagen.

Cytogenetics

T. S. Painter was perhaps most famous for his studies of the giant chromosomes in the salivary glands of Drosophila, published in a series of papers starting in 1933.[13] Painter's early work involved mammalian cytogenetics. During his studies on human spermatogenesis, he arrived at a diploid chromosome count of forty-six in 1922, although he incorrectly revised it to forty-eight a year later.[14] This was quite a change from the prevailing opinion that the chromosome count in man was in the twenties. It was a value that would

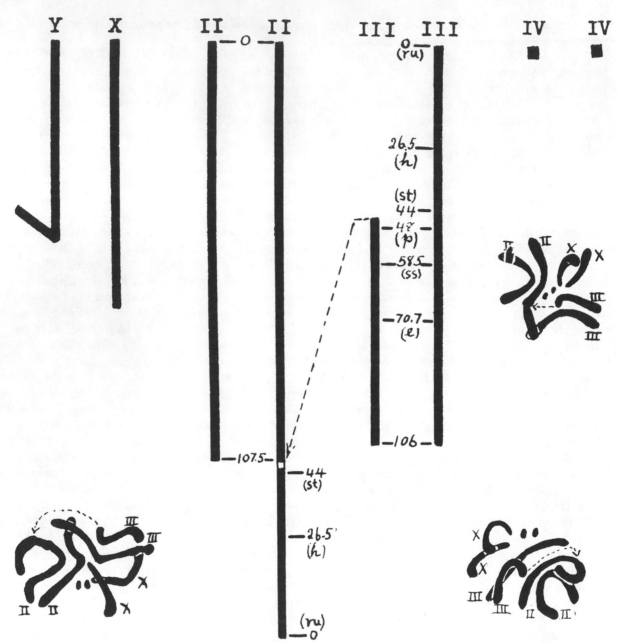

Figure 4. A figure from the original article by Painter and Muller showing the Star-Curly translocation in Drosophila.

stand for some thirty years and lends credit to Painter's ability to extract the most from the methods available to him. The studies published in 1929 with Muller[15] satisfied the need to join functional genetic maps with visual chromosome structures and remain among the classics in genetic literature. As Muller had predicted, the correspondences were not one to one. There were indeed regions in the chromosomes where crossing-

over occurred infrequently while other regions had an excessive frequency of such events. Figure 4 depicts Muller's genetic analysis of the "Star-Curly" translocation and Painter's visualization of the affected chromosomes structures taken from ovarian tissue following a technique he had devised.[16]

The needed technical breakthrough in mammalian cell culture cytogenetics was the result of a fortuitous

Figure 5. T. C. Hsu

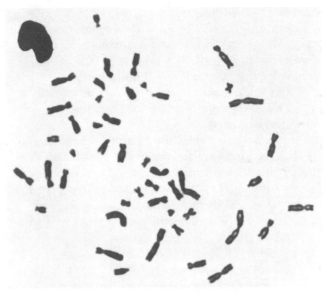

Figure 6. Picture made recently by Hsu of a metaphase spread from the lymphocyte culture of a male patient. It illustrates the scattering of the metaphase chromosomes, which he first saw in 1953.

accident. In 1951, Tao-Chiuh Hsu (fig. 5) was in the process of completing his graduate studies under Patterson in Drosophila genetics. Post-doctoral training positions in genetics were extremely hard to obtain, and neither Patterson nor Stone had been able to find a position for Hsu. Finally M. J. D. White told Hsu of a position with Charles M. Pomerat in Galveston. Pomerat had been trained as a cytologist and had spent some time in England learning methods for culturing mammalian cells. Upon returning he had set up a laboratory to study cells in culture and wanted someone to examine their nuclear phenomena. Hsu had no qualifications for the position and it meant a complete change in research interests, but he interviewed with Pomerat, found the research—particularly the time-lapse motion pictures of cellular activities—most fascinating, and accepted the position.

Hsu spent the first six months simply learning the many techniques needed. One day he set up some skin and spleen cultures taken from tissues that had been obtained from a therapeutic abortion. He had no particular experiment in mind, but when the cultures were ready he fixed them and stained them with hematoxylin. Imagine his surprise when instead of typical metaphase cells with clumped chromosomes

showing spindle orientations, he saw cells with beautifully scattered chromosomes (fig. 6). Efforts to repeat the experiment failed; but in April 1952, after three months of vigorous research, he discovered the answer. The balanced salt solution used by everyone in the laboratory to wash cells before fixation was too concentrated to allow spreading. When he diluted the balanced salt solution with distilled water, the chromosomes were again scattered in metaphase cells. Presumably a technician had erroneously made up a bottle of balanced salt solution with perhaps one-tenth the concentration normally used in the laboratory.[17] The hypotonic technique soon produced chromosome spreads in all kinds of mammalian cells.[18] Pomerat was so delighted that he raised Hsu's stipend and wrote a letter of recommendation to the U.S. Immigration and Naturalization Service in support of Hsu's application for permanent residence. Hsu's future in this new field of cell culture genetics was assured.[19]

Radiation-damaged DNA Repair Mechanisms

Felix L. Haas accepted a position as head of the new Department of Biology at the University of Texas M. D. Anderson Hospital and Tumor Institute in Houston in the early 1950s. He was responsible, like

Patterson before him, for developing another strong group of geneticists within a department. Haas had his graduate training at the University of Texas in Austin under the joint supervision of Wilson Stone in the zoology department and Orville Wyss in the bacteriology department. Part of his research concerned one of the earliest descriptions of a radiation-sensitive mutation in bacteria.

Evelyn Witkin at the Cold Spring Harbor Laboratories had isolated a resistant mutant, designated B/r, of the naturally occurring sensitive strain B of *Escherichia coli* (*E. coli*). Haas found that the defect in strain B involved the formation of cross-septa, since irradiated *E. coli* B cells formed long filaments while similarly irradiated B/r cells did not. The gene in *E. coli* genetics is called *fil*, for filamentous.

Haas was also involved with Wyss and Stone in the experiments which demonstrated the indirect mutagenic effects of ultraviolet light.[20] A growth medium which was first heavily irradiated with ultraviolet light could then effect mutations in bacteria which were added later. The effect was shown to be due to the production of peroxides in the medium which persisted long enough to effect mutations in the bacteria.

Walter Harm was one of several renowned scientists who were brought to Dallas in the 1960s to form a radiation biology research center. The center subsequently became a part of the University of Texas at Dallas. Harm was the first person to isolate an ultraviolet-sensitive mutant from a resistant strain of *E. coli*.[21] Viruses which use bacteria as hosts are called bacteriophages. He irradiated a suspension of virulent phage with ultraviolet light and used it to infect non-irradiated host bacteria. Most of the bacteria would repair the damaged phage DNA, whereupon the virus would replicate in the cell, killing it in the process. Rare mutant bacteria with defective DNA repair systems would not repair the phage DNA and would survive the attack and produce colonies when plated on a suitable agar medium. When these colonies were tested, they were found to be quite sensitive to ultraviolet light. Since the mutations had prevented the reactivation of the irradiated viruses, Harm called them host cell reactivation (*hcr*) mutants. Subsequent studies revealed these mutants to affect the DNA excision repair pathway—the major repair process in bacteria and most living things, including man—which recognizes physical distortions in DNA and removes them. Since they were initially characterized as ultraviolet light sensitive mutations, the genetic symbol became *uvr*.

A second scientist in the Dallas group, Claude S.

Rupert, was interested in a different DNA repair system in bacteria called photoreactivation, in which the exposure to white light reverses the mutagenic and lethal effects of a prior dose of ultraviolet light. Rupert succeeded in isolating the photoreactivating enzyme from *E. coli*.[22]

At about the same time, the Altenburgs, Edgar and his wife Luolin S., at Rice University, demonstrated photoreactivation in Drosophila.[23] That meant, of course, that this procedure for DNA repair was not confined to bacteria.

Several more Texas scientists have been involved in the elucidation of DNA repair mechanisms in both bacteria and mammalian cells, including Roger R. Hewitt, Raymond E. Meyn, and Ronald M. Humphrey of the M. D. Anderson Hospital and Tumor Institute and Rob Moses of the Baylor College of Medicine.[24] Hewitt's laboratory has carried the investigation to *in vitro* levels where repair enzymes are detected in gels when they react with damaged viral DNA.[25] Humphrey's group includes Gerald M. Adair and Rodney S. Nairn. They have contributed to our understanding of excision repair of DNA in mammalian cells through the isolation and characterization of repair defective mutants.

Mutation and Carcinogenesis

Light of wavelengths similar to that involved in photoreactivation was found by A. Clark Griffin to have an almost opposite effect: it activated 8-methoxy psoralen to become an active skin carcinogen. Unlike the previously discussed indirect effects of germicidal wavelengths of ultraviolet light, this activation occurred only when both chemical agents and illumination were applied to the organism simultaneously.[26] This work was initiated while Griffin was at Stanford University in California. He moved to the Baylor College of Medicine in the 1950s and then to the M. D. Anderson Hospital and Tumor Institute in the early 1960s where he held an American Cancer Society Research chair for the rest of his productive career.

Edgar Altenburg applied the same treatment described above to Drosophila and found it to be highly mutagenic.[27] This discovery provided one of the early experimental links between mutagenesis and carcinogenesis; the relationship was not understood for more than thirty years.

Griffin pioneered many investigations on the metabolic process which caused chemicals to become active carcinogens in animals. He was also one of the first investigators to recognize the importance of anti-mutagens and anticarcinogens in the environment with a study on selenium performed by Marice M. Jacobs and the author.[28]

DNA Base Compositions and Repeated Sequences

Among the first people Haas attracted into his new biology department at the University of Texas M. D. Anderson Hospital was T. C. Hsu, who in turn brought Frances E. Arrighi from Galveston. Another newcomer to the department, Manley Mandel, became a world authority on the base composition of bacterial DNA. Different bacterial species had DNAs with unique percentages of guanine-cytosine (G-C) base pairs versus adenine-thymine (A-T) base pairs, a fact which proved useful in their identification and classification. The favorite method to determine the percentage of G-C pairs employed ultracentrifugation in a neutral cesium chloride (CsCl) density gradient. DNA from a given bacterium would form a band in the centrifuge tube at a specific concentration of salt. On the other hand, DNA from all higher organisms appeared to form a broad band over the same range of CsCl concentrations.

Saul Kit at Baylor College of Medicine in Houston was one of the first investigators to identify a band of "satellite" DNA, a discrete band separate from the main DNA band.[29] He found it in preparations from the common laboratory mouse. It turned out that his satellite band, comprising some 10 percent of the total mouse DNA, was A-T rich. The base sequences within this DNA were short, but repeated many times. This was an interesting discovery. The cell was known to have too much DNA for all of it to be involved in the coding of proteins. But among several mammalian species examined, why did only the mouse exhibit satellite DNA?

Several investigators, including Grady Saunders in the biology department at M. D. Anderson, reasoned that other species had satellite DNA but that its base composition was so near that of the bulk of the DNA that it was not being separated by neutral CsCl gradient ultracentrifugation.[30] After several technical modifications, satellite DNA was found.

Chromosome Banding

Saunders encouraged Hsu and Arrighi to attempt to map the highly repeated sequences on chromosomes.

While performing *in situ* nucleic acid hybridizations with satellite DNA, they noticed a differential Giemsa staining along human metaphase chromosomes. The densely stained areas were all in regions known to be rich in heterochromatin. Consequently the technique became known as C-banding, for constitutive heterochromatin.[31] An additional step was taken by Maximo Drets, who was also working in Margery Shaw's laboratory. He applied the C-banding technique to flame-dried preparations and discovered far more dark banding patterns than in the ordinary C-banded material. These darkly stained regions were found to correspond to intensely fluorescent bands generated by quinacrine, a procedure that had been developed a short time before. The dark bands corresponded to A-T rich regions of DNA while the lightly stained areas of chromosome corresponded to G-C rich regions. It replaced the more expensive Q-banding procedure. Banding has proven of the utmost importance in cytogenetics. Since each pair of chromosomes exhibits a unique banding pattern, this means that chromosome pairs of identical size and gross structure could be distinguished from one another. Thus, the exact pair or pairs of chromosomes involved in a specific translocation or trisomy could be recognized.

Hsu, Arrighi, and San Pathak have used chromosome banding to trace the evolution of chromosomes in animals, especially in mammals. These sophisticated techniques have been used to identify several specific chromosome translocations which accompany the formation of certain cancers in man. Since other researchers have discovered that oncogenes map in or near such transposed chromosomal regions, these events are certain to play a critical role in initiating carcinogenesis (fig. 7).

These studies led Hsu and his coworkers to suspect that some individuals might inherit brittle chromosome sites which would make them more susceptible to chromosome translocation events and hence to specific types of cancer. This type of inherited predisposition to cancer was revealed in a study of patients with medulary carcinoma.[32] It triggered great interest in this area of cancer research.

Two other Texas scientists have made significant contributions toward our understanding of the mitotic apparatus. Bill Brinkley of the Baylor College of Medicine in Houston has provided insight into the structure and function of the spindle apparatus. Elton Stubblefield, a colleague of T. C. Hsu, worked with Brinkley in elucidating the structure of the centriole.[33] Stubblefield has also provided an understanding of the molecular structure of mammalian chromosomes.[34]

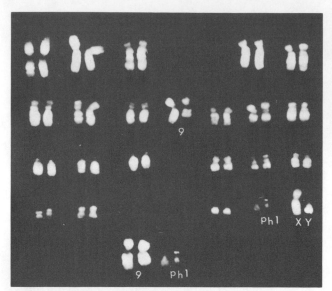

Figure 7. *A Q-banded karyotype from the bone marrow sample of a male patient with chronic myelogenous leukemia. The karyotype is arranged by cutting the chromosomes out of a print and pasting them on a page with the largest pair in the upper left (#1) and the smallest in the lower right (#22), with the sex hormones last. The exchange of genetic material has occurred between chromosomes 9 and 22 to form the Philadelphia chromosome PhI. The oncogene* abl *is translocated to 22. Additional pairs of chromosomes 9 and 22 from another leukemic cell from the same patient are shown at the bottom. The photograph of current clinical material was provided by Pathak.*

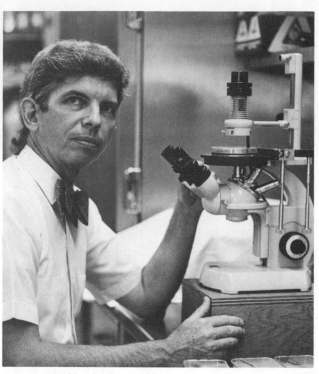

Figure 8. *Alfred G. Knudson, Jr.*

Alfred G. Knudson, Jr. (fig. 8) advanced a two-step mutational model for the origin of retinoblastoma in man, a concept in 1971 that was to shape a great deal of later research.[35] Knudson was dean of the University of Texas Graduate School of Biomedical Sciences in Houston. He was responsible for developing two genetic centers: the Medical Genetics Center, which he directed, and the Population Genetics and Demography Center, which William J. Schull (fig. 9) has directed since its inception. Schull's studies have involved human populations all over the world. He has made significant contributions to the Radiation Effects Research Foundation in Japan and to its predecessor organization, the Atomic Bomb Casualty Commission. His last tour was as vice-chairman and chief of the Department of Epidemiology and Statics from 1978 to 1980.[36] Schull was soon joined by Masatoshi Nei (fig. 10), a population geneticist. Nei had made theoretical advances of major importance at the interface of molecular evolution and population genetics.

Figure 9. *William J. Schull*

Figure 10. Masatoshi Nei

Isozymes and Electrophoretic Shift Mutants

Charles R. Shaw's research interests at the M. D. Anderson Hospital were concerned with isozymes, which are electrophoretically identifiable, discrete forms of enzymes having the same enzyme activity. With James N. Baptist, David A. Wright, and the author, he initiated research which resulted in the development of a new class of mutants. They developed techniques to treat populations of *E. coli* bacteria with chemical mutagens and to isolate mutants that had eletrophoretically distinct enzymes, distinct from the parental form of enzyme. The mutants came about by the substitution of one amino acid in the enzyme's peptide chain for another one which carried a different electrical charge. With the new net charge, the mutant enzyme would move to a different place in an electrical field during gel electrophoresis. Thus the mutant proten retained full enzyme activity but was recognized through gel electrophoresis tests.[37]

While the bacterial experiments were interesting, they were mainly important as stepping stones from which Michael J. Siciliano and Ronald M. Humphrey would succeed in isolating electrophoretic mutants in mammalian cell cultures.[38] Not only were these mammalian cell mutants (of Chinese hamster ovary [CHO] cells) useful as genetic markers in cell culture studies,

but they gave information about the complexity of the enzyme involved and confirmed that the cell culture was still diploid for the particular gene being studied. There was considerable question at the time as to whether CHO cell cultures retained two functional alleles. The detection of an electrophoretic shift mutant in a CHO cell involving the enzyme malatedehydrogenase (MDH) is shown in figure 11. CHO cells were treated with a chemical mutagen and cloned. Extracts were prepared from the resulting cultures and applied to wells in the gel. After a suitable time of electrophoresis, the gel was stained for MDH activity (fig. 11). The panel on the left in figure 11 shows the banding patterns obtained from four isolates. The first three from the left displayed single spots, wild-type bands, of MDH activity while the fourth formed three bands, indicating that one of its two MDH alleles had undergone an electrophoretic shift mutation and that the active form of the enzyme was a dimer containing two identical subunits. One form contained both mutant subunits, one contained both parental subunits, and one was a hybrid containing one mutant subunit and one parent subunit. In addition, this experiment proved that both MDH alleles were present and functioning in the CHO cell line. The panel on the right in figure 11 contains the results obtained from subclones of the original mutant culture and indicates that the mutation is passed on to progeny cells.

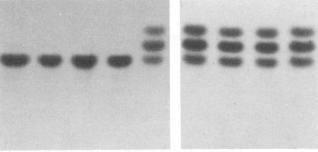

Figure 11. The two panels show the banding patterns of the malate-dehydrogenase isozymes from Chinese hamster ovary cells. The panel on the left depicts extracts prepared from five clones of cells and added to slots which were located below the picture. During electrophoresis the proteins were drawn upward by an electric current. The first four bands from the left are typical of the nonmutant or wild type. The fifth sample displays three bands and indicates the presence of a mutant isozyme. The panel on the right shows the testing of four subclones of the new mutant. Photo courtesy of The University of Texas Health Science Center at Dallas.

Siciliano and Humphrey were also able to use the electrophoretic shift techniques to detect regulatory mutants. For example, the Chinese hamster has five electrophoretically distinct forms of the enzyme esterase. Five separate genes are responsible for producing these enzymes. A pooled extract from all hamster tissues would yield five bands on the appropriate gel. The CHO cell line Siciliano and Humphrey were using displayed only two bands. The other three esterase genes had been turned off at some time during the early fetal development of the female Chinese hamster from which the ovarian cell line was obtained. Regulatory mutants were isolated in CHO cells in which all five esterase bands reappeared. These techniques made it possible to obtain a large number of genetic markers for use in cell culture genetics.

Genetic Control Systems and Cholesterol Biosynthesis Regulation

In 1972 Michael S. Brown and Joseph L. Goldstein (fig. 12) began work at the University of Texas Southwestern Medical School in Dallas for which they received the Nobel prize in physiology and medicine in 1985.[39] They were interested in understanding a human genetic disease called familial hypercholesterolemia (FH), which is characterized by very high levels of cholesterol in the blood. This results in heart attacks early in life. They felt that this dominantly inherited disease might be the result of failure of the cholesterol synthesis to be regulated by a process called end-product inhibition. Synthetic pathways are often shut down by the accumulation of the final end-product, through a regulatory process called feedback inhibition.

Cell culture studies led Brown and Goldstein to the conclusion that the defect that caused FH involved a cell surface receptor for a plasma cholesterol transport protein called low density lipoprotein (LDL). FH was shown to be caused by mutations in the gene which coded for LDL receptor. The discovery that the receptor-mediated control was effected by the highly organized movement of these membrane-embedded proteins from one cell organelle to another and that indeed many of the mutations for the LDL receptor occurring in FH patients blocked these sophisticated movements, provided an entirely new dimension in genetic control of cellular physiology. These findings will have profound impact on future genetic research.

Figure 12. Michael S. Brown and Joseph L. Goldstein

Intervening DNA Sequences in Eukaryotic Genes

The general question in molecular genetics as to the large surplus of DNA base sequences for the coding of a relatively small number of proteins has been alluded to in the sections on satellite DNA and highly repetitive sequences. Along this same line, perhaps one of the most important discoveries in molecular genetics was the finding that, unlike prokaryotic genes—genes from bacteria—in which essentially the entire DNA base sequence codes for amino acids, the majority of base sequences in eukaryotic genes do not code for amino acids but constitute intervening sequences. Within a year, four laboratories, including Bert O'Malley's laboratory at the Baylor College of Medicine in Houston, had cloned and sequenced eukaryotic genes using different systems and had reported on the phenomenon.[40] They studied the ovalbumin gene from the chicken in which some 80 percent of the base sequences within the gene were shown to be intervening or noncoding sequences whose function remains obscure.

This discovery has already had dramatic effects on the direction of research, especially genetic engineering. It meant that eukaryotic cells had a way of maturing messenger RNA (m-RNA) by removing the segments representing the intervening sequences and splicing the remaining coding sequences together. It meant that cloning such a gene in a bacterial host would do little good because the bacterial cell would not know how to process the m-RNA. If one wished to clone and produce a gene product in quantity, one would have to start with a mature m-RNA, use reverse transcriptase to produce a double-stranded DNA copy, insert it into a vector molecule with an appropriate promoter, and introduce it into the host bacterium.

In this chapter I have endeavored to select some highlights of genetics in Texas which represent contributions toward the conceptual appreciation of the subject. Any such effort must contain personal biases and omit areas with which the author has limited familiarity.

Notes

1. See Oliver, 1983, for further information on the early history of the zoology department, UT–Austin.

2. His dissertation was entitled, "Studies on the Development of the Opossum (*Didelphys virginiana*): I. The History of the Early Cleavage. II. The Formation of the Blastocyst."

3. Carl G. Hartman is the father of Philip E. Hartman, a well-known microbial geneticist at the Johns Hopkins University in Baltimore.

4. Oliver, 1983, p. 14.

5. Altenburg, E., 1916.

6. Muller, 1967, p. 202.

7. Ibid.

8. One of the great tragedies affecting the recorded history of genetics occurred in the early 1970s. Edgar Altenburg, then Professor Emeritus at Rice University, was assisting his colleague Luolin S. Browning to conduct some contract research with NASA on the effects of weightlessness on genetic mechanisms in Drosophila. The research was conducted in rental space in the second story of a building not far from the Rice campus. One night, a disgruntled former employee came back and set a fire which destroyed a carefully catalogued collection of over 15,000 pieces

of artifacts and correspondence mostly between Altenburg and Herman J. Muller.

9. The old machine is now enshrined as an exhibit in the first floor hallway of the Experimental Science Building.

10. Muller, 1927 and 1928.

11. The following sequence of events was told to the author by Luolin S. Browning: As per agreement, Altenburg purchased radium (with $600 of personal savings, an enormous amount of money in those days) and set out to Woods Hole Biological Laboratories for the summer to do some additional mutagenesis testing. Certainly the northeast would be a more comfortable environment in which to perform Drosophila experiments than the hot and humid Houston. Unfortunately, Woods Hole was so cold that summer that the lead shield shrank, breaking the vial and the radium was lost. Altenburg returned home quite depressed but managed to borrow an X-ray machine from the physics department. He hired an assistant and began some Drosophila experiments. Murphy's Law was still in effect for Altenburg: the machine burned up when the assistant left it unattended. Muller wrote that he had accumulated sufficient data to prove the mutagenicity of ionizing radiation, and it was agreed that it might be more profitable for Altenburg to examine non-ionizing radiation for mutagenic effects. Altenburg was delighted when the physics stock room clerk disregarded instructions from the department chairman and provided him with a modern ultraviolet lamp. This machine proved rather indestructible and its output highly mutagenic.

12. Altenburg, E., 1934.

13. Painter, 1933.

14. Painter, 1922 and 1923.

15. Painter and Muller, 1929; Muller and Painter, 1929.

16. Permission was obtained from the *Journal of Heredity* to reproduce the data in fig. 4.

17. The technician, whose mistake had been most fortunate, was never identified although a serious attempt was made to do so.

18. Hsu and Pomerat (1953).

19. For additional information, see Hsu, 1979, page 16.

20. Wyss et al., 1948.

21. Harm, 1959.

22. Rupert et al., 1958.

23. Altenburg and Altenburg, 1952.

24. Hewitt and Meyn, 1978.

25. Harless et al., 1983.

26. Griffin et al., 1958.
27. Altenburg, 1956.
28. Jacobs et al., 1976.
29. Kit, 1961.
30. Saunders, 1974.
31. Arrighi and Hsu, 1971.
32. Hsu et al., 1981.
33. Brinkley and Stubblefield, 1970.
34. Stubblefield, 1980.
35. Knudson, 1971.
36. It is of interest that Grant H. Taylor, the first and longtime head of pediatrics at the University of Texas M. D. Anderson Hospital in Houston, came from a position with the Atomic Bomb Casualty Commission.
37. Shaw et al., 1973.
38. Siciliano et al., 1978.
39. Brown and Goldstein, 1986.
40. Dugaiczk et al., 1978.

Bibliography

Altenburg, Edgar. Linkage in *Primula sinensis. Genetics* 1(1916): pp. 354–366.

———. The artificial production of mutations by ultra-violet light. *The Am. Naturalist* 68 (1934): pp. 491–507.

———. Studies on the enhancement of the mutation rate by carcinogens, *Texas Reports Biol. Med.* 14 (1956): p. 481.

Altenburg, Luolin S., and Altenburg, Edgar. The lowering of the mutagenic effectiveness of ultra-violet by photoreactivating light in Drosophila, *Genetics* 37 (1952): pp. 545–553.

Arrighi, Frances, and Hsu, T. C. Localization of heterochromatin in human chromosomes. *Cytogenetics,* 10 (1971): pp. 81–86.

Brinkley, Bill R., and Stubblefield, Elton. "Ultrastructure and Interaction of the Kinetochore and Centriole in Mitosis and Meiosis." In Volume 1, *Advances in Cell Biology,* edited by D. M. Prescott, L. Goldstein, and Edwin McConkey, pp. 119–186. Appleton-Century-Crofts, New York, 1970.

Brown, Michael S., and Goldstein, Joseph L. A receptor-mediated pathway for cholesterol homeostasis. *Science* 232 (1986): pp. 34–47.

Drets, Maximo E., and Shaw, Margery W. Specific banding patterns of human chromosomes. *Proc. Nat. Acad. Sci. U.S.* 68 (1971): pp. 2073–2077.

Dugaiczk, A. S., Woo, L. C., Lai, E. C., Mace, M. L., McReynolds, L., and O'Malley, Bert W. The natural ovalbumin gene contains seven intervening sequences. *Nature* 274 (1978): pp. 328–333.

Griffin, Clark A., Hakim, R. E., and Knox, J. *Journal of Investigative Dermatology* 31 (1958): p. 289.

Harless, Julie, Hittelman, Walter, Meyn, Raymond, and Hewitt, Roger. "Chromatin Factors Affecting DNA Repair in Mammalian Cell Nuclei." In *Cellular Responses to DNA Damage: Proceedings of the 1983 Cetus-UCLA Symposia on Molecular and Cellular Biology.* pp. 183–193. Alan R. Liss, Inc., New York, 1983.

Harm, Walter. Untersuchungen zur Wirkungsweise eines die UV-Empfindlichkeit bestimmenden Gens der Bakteriophagen T2 und T4. *Z. Vererbungsl.* 90 (1959): p. 428.

Hewitt, Roger R., and Meyn, Raymond E. "Applicability of Bacterial Models of DNA Repair and Recovery to UV-Irradiated Mammalian Cells." In *Advances in Radiation Biology,* Vol. 7, pp. 153–179. Edited by J. T. Lett and H. Adler. Academic Press, New York, 1978.

Hsu, T. C. Mammalian chromosomes *in vitro.* I. The karyotype of man. *J. Hered.* 43 (1952): p. 172.

———. *Human and Mammalian Cytogenetics: An Historical Perspective.* Springer-Verlag, New York, 1979.

Hsu, T. C., and Pomerat, C. M. Mammalian chromosomes *in vitro.* II. A method for spreading the chromosomes of cells in tissue culture. *J. Hered.* 44 (1953): pp. 23–29.

Hsu, T. C., Pathak, Sen, Saman, Nagib A., and Hickey, Robert C. Chromosome instability in patients with medulary carcinoma of the thyroid. *Journal of the American Medical Association* 246 (1981): pp. 2046–2048.

Jacobs, Marice M., Matney, Thomas S., and Griffin, A. Clark. Inhibitory effects of selenium on the mutagenecity of 2-Acetylaminofluorene (AAF) and AAF derivatives. *Cancer Letters* 2 (1976): pp. 319–322.

Kit, Saul. Equilibrium sedimentation in density gradients of DNA preparations from animal tissues. *J. Mol. Biol.* 3 (1961): pp. 711–716.

Knudson, Alfred G., Jr. Mutation and Cancer: Statistical Study of Retinoblastoma. *Proc. Natl. Acad. Sci., U.S.A.* 68 (1971): pp. 820–823.

Morgan, Thomas H. An attempt to analyze the constitution of the chromosomes on the basis of sex-limited inheritance in Drosophila. *J. Exptl. Zool.* 11 (1911): pp. 365–414.

Muller, Herman J. Artificial transmutation of the gene. *Science* 66 (1927): pp. 84–87.

————. The production of mutations by X-rays. *Proc. Natl. Acad. Sci. Wash.* 14 (1928): pp. 714–726.

————. Translocational *Pale* Drosophilae and Snaker mice, a semicentennial parallel. *Mutation Res.* 4 (1967): pp. 201–205.

Muller, Herman J., and Altenburg, Edgar. The frequency of translocations produced by X-rays in Drosophila. *Genetics* 15 (1938): pp. 283–311.

Muller, Herman J., and Painter, Theophilus S. The cytological expression of changes in gene alignment produced by X-rays in Drosophila. *Amer. Nat.* 63 (1929): pp. 193–200.

Oliver, Clarence P. "Zoology" in *Discovery: Research and Scholarship at the University of Texas at Austin* Vol. 7 (1983) pp. 13–17.

Painter, Theophilus S. The spermatogenesis of man. *Anat. Res.* 23 (1922): p. 129.

————. Studies in mammalian spermatogenesis. II. The spermatogenesis of man. *J. Exp. Zool* 37 (1923): pp. 291–336.

————. A new method for the study of chromosome rearrangements and the plotting of chromosome maps. *Science* 22 (1939): pp. 585–586.

Painter, Theophilus S., and Muller, Herman J. The parallel cytology and genetics of induced translocations and deletions in Drosophila. *J. Hered.* 20 (1929): pp. 287–298.

Pathak, San, Hsu, T. C., and Arrighi, Frances E. Chromosomes of *Peromyscus* (Rodentia, Cricetidae) IV. The role of heterochromatin in karyotypic evolution. *Cytogenet. Cell Genet.* 12 (1973): pp. 315–326.

Rupert, Claude S., Goodgal, Sol. H., and Herriot, Roger M. Photoreactivation *in vitro* of ultraviolet inactivated *Hemophilus influenzae* transforming factor. *J. Gen. Physiol.* 41 (1958): pp. 451–471.

Saunders, Grady F. Human repetitious DNA. *Adv. Biol. Med. Phys.* 15 (1974): pp. 19–46.

Shaw, Charles R., Baptist, James N., Wright, David A., and Matney, Thomas S. Isolation of induced mutations in *E. coli* affecting the electrophoretic mobility of enzymes. *Mut. Res.* 18 (1973): pp. 247–250.

Siciliano, Michael J., Siciliano, Jeanette, and Humphrey, Ronald M. Electrophoretic shift mutants in Chinese Hamster Ovary cells: evidence for genetic diploidy. *Proc. Natl. Acad. Science, U.S.* 75 (1978): pp. 1919–1923.

Stubblefield, Elton. The molecular organization of mammalian metaphase chromosomes. In *Genes, Chromosomes, and Neoplasia*, edited by Frances E. Arrighi, Patu N. Rao, and Elton Stubblefield, Raven Press, New York, 1980.

White, M. J. D. *Animal Cytology and Evolution.* Cambridge University Press, Cambridge, England, 1973.

Wyss, Orville, Clark, J. B., Haas, Felix, and Stone, Wilson S. The role of peroxide in the mutagenic effects of irradiated broth. *J. Bacteriol.,* 56 (1948): pp. 51–57.

16

The Health Sciences

Chester R. Burns

CHAUNCEY LEAKE'S SELECTION, in 1942, as the administrative head of the University of Texas Medical Branch at Galveston (UTMB) symbolized a major change in attitude toward the biomedical sciences in Texas. Leake was an experimental pharmacologist, not a physician. He had discovered divinyl ether and carbarsone, a drug used in treating patients with amoebic dysentery. He had established and guided the pharmacology department at the University of California School of Medicine in San Francisco between 1928 and 1942. Leake continued as the dean at UTMB for thirteen years.[1]

Cancer

On February 17, 1944, Chauncey Leake participated in the ceremonies dedicating the newly established M. D. Anderson Hospital for Cancer Research in Houston (now a part of The University of Texas System Cancer Center). Speaking as president of The University of Texas, Homer P. Rainey noted that the hospital would emphasize "basic scientific medical research."[2] Leake, as did other speakers, hoped that this emphasis on research would always remain the central feature of this hospital.[3]

Research had not been a hallmark of hospital activities in Texas. Texans entered hospitals as patients seeking cures, not as subjects for experimental investigation. Less than twenty years earlier, an anonymous newspaper reporter had noted that UTMB's John Sealy Hospital in Galveston had never been a "hospital of research."[4] But fears about death from cancer steadily replaced such fears about medical research.

By the 1920s and 1930s, cancer had become the second leading cause of death in the United States.[5] Texans were as alarmed as others. In 1929 the state legislature authorized the establishment of a cancer hospital in Dallas, but no funds were available. Fifteen more years elapsed before the M. D. Anderson hospital became a reality. That legislators would finally appropriate $500,000 of public monies for such an endeavor heralded a new day for biomedical research in the state.

In late December of 1942, four research scientists and a business manager began work in the main residence of the Baker Estate, properties designated for the new hospital by the M. D. Anderson Foundation.[6] The scientists included three biochemists and one microbiologist, all of whom had been members of the staff at UTMB. Believing that rapid protein synthesis was necessary for the growth of cancerous cells, these scientists focused on carbohydrate and protein metabolism at the cellular level, especially that involving transaminase systems.[7]

During the next two decades, many basic scientists explored the frontiers of biochemistry, biology, and physics in the laboratories of The University of Texas M. D. Anderson Hospital and Tumor Institute, its official name. Jorge Awapara discovered gamma-aminobutyric acid in mammalian brain tissue, and he devised a partition paper chromatographic technique for measuring transaminases.[8] Bruno Jirgensons studied the colloidal chemistry of proteins.[9] Saul Kit explored the amino acid pathways central to the formation of liver glycogen.[10]

Studies in embryology, cytology, genetics, and virology were conducted by experimental biologists. In 1957 Leon Dmochowski, then chief of the section of virology and electron microscopy, became the first scientist to observe viruslike particles in lymphoid tissue taken from a patient afflicted with acute lymphatic leukemia.[11] T. C. Hsu ardently investigated the chromosomes of cancer cells.[12] Warren K. Sinclair and others in the department of physics made comparisons of the effects of X-rays and cobalt gamma-rays on different biological structures.[13] The above exemplify some of the activities of research scientists who were employed by the hospital and institute.

Clinical research had not been ignored during the 1940s, but facilities for its implementation were significantly improved after all personnel and programs were transferred to a new building in the Texas Medical Center in Houston during February and March of 1954. Physicians and basic scientists collaborated on research projects, especially those involving diagnosis and treatment. This collaborative work was especially important to R. Lee Clark, the enterprising director of the hospital.[14] Confronted daily with patients suffering from thyroid carcinoma, carcinoma of the uterine cervix, primary lung tumors, malignant melanoma, and other forms of cancer, Clark and his colleagues were eager to devise more effective surgical techniques and to develop more effective protocols for radiotherapy and chemotherapy.

In addition to Clark, key physicians involved in the clinical research of the 1950s were John S. Stehlin, Jr., John E. Healey, Jr., and E. C. White. Antileukemic agents were intensively studied by C. L. Spurr, Clifton D. Howe, and H. Grant Taylor. Several staff members summarized their research efforts in a volume entitled *Cancer Chemotherapy* that was published in 1961.[15]

In June of that year, the National Institutes of Health acknowledged the outstanding work of this institution by awarding a multi-year grant of more than four million dollars for the purpose of establishing a twenty-bed clinical research center. These federal dollars were to be used for research studies with patients in nine general areas: enzymes, amino acids, hematology, and virology; breast cancer; thyroid and parathyroid metabolism; leukemia in adults; toxohormone; cancer in children; pathological effects of nuclear medical techniques; postsurgical physiology; and chemotherapy. By August 31 of 1961, 184 research programs comprising 242 projects were actively proceeding at the hospital and institute.

In 1948 the institution began publishing *The Texas Cancer Bulletin*. One year later it was renamed *The Cancer Bulletin of The University of Texas M. D. Anderson Hospital and Tumor Institute at Houston*. This journal is still published bimonthly. Just a glance at its pages will reveal the dramatic escalation of research projects at this hospital during the last twenty-five years. Its physicians and scientists have displayed an extraordinary devotion to the ideals espoused by Leake and others at the dedication ceremonies in 1944.

Cardiovascular Diseases

In 1948, just four years after the M. D. Anderson Hospital was dedicated, Michael E. DeBakey assumed the role of professor and chairman of the department of surgery at the Baylor University College of Medicine in Houston. This medical school had moved from Dallas in 1943.[16] DeBakey quickly transformed the fortunes of the school.[17] He was a dynamo. Even as a medical student at Tulane, he had invented a roller pump that significantly improved blood transfusions. During those student days, DeBakey was profoundly influenced by Rudolph Matas and Alton Ochsner, both outstanding surgeons. Matas was regarded as the "father of vascular surgery," and Ochsner had been his pupil and successor as surgeon-in-chief at Charity Hospital in New Orleans.[18] These physicians were tackling those diseases that had become the leading causes of death in the United States.[19]

In 1951 Denton Cooley became one of DeBakey's principal assistants. Cooley began his medical studies at UTMB, then transferred to the Johns Hopkins University School of Medicine, graduating in 1944. Cooley had participated in the first operation for tetralogy of Fallot that had been performed by Alfred Blalock at Johns Hopkins in November of 1944. The excitement of seeing chronically cyanotic children become pink after surgery and the rewards of working with Blalock encouraged Cooley to make a lifelong commitment to the newly emerging specialty of cardiovascular surgery.[20] After six years of postgraduate training at Johns Hopkins and one year at the Brompton Hospital for Chest Diseases in London, Cooley assumed a professorial position with the Baylor University College of Medicine, a position he held until 1969.

During the 1950s and 1960s, DeBakey, Cooley, and their colleagues in Houston focused on the treatment of obstructive vascular lesions, aneurysms, and congenital anomalies. Their accomplishments were extraordinary.

DeBakey and colleagues performed a successful carotid endarterectomy for cerebrovascular insufficiency on August 7, 1953. The patient survived for nineteen years without any recurrence of cerebrovascular insufficiency.[21] Cooley and colleagues performed a successful carotid endarterectomy on March 8, 1956.[22] By 1962, these surgeons could report, quite favorably, on similar treatment for 435 patients.[23] These accomplishments encouraged all physicians to recognize that stroke and stroke symptoms could be caused by extracranial vascular occlusive diseases that were surgically treatable.

Aneurysms located in different parts of the body were removed and replaced with knitted Dacron and Dacron-velour tubes.[24] The first successful resection and replacement of a fusiform aneurysm of the descending thoracic aorta occurred on January 3, 1953.[25] Other successful resections and replacements followed: of an aneurysm of the distal aortic arch on February 5, 1954;[26] of a dissecting aneurysm of the thoracic aorta on July 7, 1954;[27] of an aneurysm of the thoracoabdominal aorta on October 19, 1955;[28] of an aneurysm of the ascending aorta on August 24, 1956;[29] and of a fusiform aneurysm of the entire aortic arch on March 21, 1957.[30] The first successful patch-graft angioplasty occurred in 1958.[31] These were all path-breaking operations that revolutionized the surgical treatment of aneurysms.[32]

By the mid-1950s Cooley and his associates were repairing numerous congenital anomalies in patients at the Texas Children's Hospital located in the Texas Medical Center. Both atrial[33] and ventricular[34] defects were repaired. By the early 1960s it was possible to report on the surgical treatment of anomalies in three hundred infants younger than one year of age.[35] A year later there was a report on cardiac operations in 450 neonates.[36] During the next year 500 consecutive operations were reviewed.[37] Before these operative techniques were developed, most of these infants would have died at birth, or soon thereafter.

In the summer of 1962 the directors of Saint Luke's Episcopal Hospital and Texas Children's Hospital announced plans to construct a joint facility, to be called the Texas Heart Institute (THI). The institute would be directed by Denton Cooley. Raising funds was a chore, and construction of the new building proceeded slowly. Eventually the Cullen Cardiovascular Surgical Research Laboratories became a reality in February of 1972, and the Clayton Foundation for Research Invasive Laboratory was opened in May of 1974.[38] Meanwhile, the operating rooms of THI had become the busiest in the world. The surgeons of THI performed their 50,000th open-heart operation on February 16, 1983.

The surgeons in Houston had been able to accomplish so much because of the development of mechanical heart-lung devices that enabled them to open the heart directly for repairs. Their operations with such equipment began in Houston on April 5, 1956.[39] Within a year temporary cardiopulmonary bypass had been used in 95 patients.[40] Work by C. William Hall, Domingo Liotto, and E. Stanley Crawford enabled the implantation of an artificial ventricle in a patient on July 19, 1963.[41] An improved left ventricular bypass pump was successfully used for the first time on August 8, 1966.[42] Extracorporeal circulatory equipment was improved considerably during the following years, and a blood substitute was developed so that fresh blood was not needed for the procedure.[43]

A major clinical problem was that associated with blockage of the coronary arteries, those vessels which nourish the heart. Such blockage could cause intractable pain or sudden death of the heart itself. To handle this problem, surgeons had to develop procedures for bypassing normal cardiac function during surgery, and they had to determine if other vessels in the body could be effective substitutes for the diseased coronaries. On November 23, 1964, the first successful aorto-coronary bypass took place at the Methodist Hospital in Houston. DeBakey's team bypassed the patient's blocked coronary artery with a portion of a vein that had been taken from the patient's leg.[44] By the early 1980s, DeBakey's group at the Methodist Hospital was performing more than 1,700 bypass operations each year.[45] At the Texas Heart Institute almost 19,000 operations for myocardial revascularization had occurred by January of 1980. Mortality rates were quite low, and long-term results were gratifying.[46]

In May of 1968 Cooley and associates at the Texas Heart Institute performed the first successful cardiac transplantation in the United States.[47] Twenty-one additional transplants were performed during the ensuing two years, but the long term results were disappointing.[48] On April 4, 1969, a mechanical heart, designed with four chambers like a natural heart, was implanted in a dying patient at the Texas Heart Institute.[49] The device worked for sixty-four hours until a cardiac transplant was done. Although the patient died of overwhelming pneumonia, the mechanical heart had performed quite satisfactorily. Using cyclosporine and steroids for immunosuppression, a new program of cardiac transplants was begun at THI in July of 1982.[50] Forty patients had received donor hearts by November of 1984. The results have been far more satisfactory than those with the original series.

In 1950 there was no heart surgery in newborn infants, no open-heart surgery, no replacement of diseased heart valves with artificial ones, and no replacement of diseased vessels with artificial grafts. By 1970 these were standard operating procedures in surgical suites throughout the world. Michael E. DeBakey, Denton A. Cooley, and their surgeon colleagues in Houston had set the standards.

Burn Trauma

Accidents and injuries became leading causes of morbidity and mortality during the twentieth century. By the 1970s only cardiovascular diseases and cancer caused more deaths than accidents. Accidents were the leading causes of death for children. In 1973 alone, children in the United States under the age of seventeen experienced 25 million accidental injuries.[51]

A decade or so earlier, physicians and others realized that burn traumas constituted a major group of these injuries, but no hospital in the United States specialized in the care of burned children. At their convention in 1962, the Shriners of North America allocated ten million dollars for the establishment of three such hospitals, each to be affiliated with a university medical school. After reviewing the requests of seventy-one schools, the Shriners selected Harvard, Cincinnati, and UTMB. The latter was chosen because of the outstanding plastic surgery service that had been established at John Sealy Hospital by Truman G. Blocker, Jr., and associates.

Blocker had received his medical degree from UTMB in 1933. After further training he became a member of the faculty at UTMB, and he received certification from the American Board of Surgery in 1940 and the American Board of Plastic Surgery in 1942. After extensive military service, he returned to UTMB in 1946 as professor and chief of a new division of plastic and maxillofacial surgery. Between 1946 and 1974 he

held numerous administrative offices, eventually becoming the chief administrator at UTMB for ten years (1964–1974). He was chairman of the department of surgery when the Shriners first consulted him about their desire to establish a hospital for the care of burned children. The affiliation agreement between the Shriners and the University of Texas was signed on July 24, 1963.

Curtis Artz, who had been director of a surgical research unit at the Brooke Army Medical Center in San Antonio, was invited to be the medical director for the new hospital in Galveston. While a new building was being constructed, a seven-bed unit in John Sealy Hospital was opened on November 1, 1963. During the next two and one-half years, more than one hundred children were treated there by Artz's team.[52]

The new building for the Shriners Burns Institute (SBI) was opened on March 20, 1966. The three-story, thirty-bed facility was completed at a cost of 2.5 million dollars. There were 143 fulltime employees. The medical staff included a fulltime chief surgeon, three residents from the plastic surgery division of UTMB, two fellows in plastic surgery, an anesthesiologist, a nurse anesthetic technician, and a part-time anesthetic physiologist. The department of pediatrics at UTMB provided a staff pediatrician and pediatric residents. The hospital employed 43 staff nurses. During its first year, the budget for SBI was 1.2 million dollars.[53]

The care given to burned children at SBI has been extraordinary, and the outcomes have been most gratifying. In September of 1967 Duane Larson, then chief of staff, reported that the SBI mortality rate was 14 percent, considerably lower than the national average of 20 to 25 percent. By 1978 the mortality rate at SBI had decreased by almost three-fold, giving the hospital the lowest mortality rate of any burn center in the world. By 1985 more than five thousand patients had been treated at SBI. These patients had come from forty-three of the fifty states, and from thirty foreign countries.

Therapy for acutely burned children involves debridement and excision of the burn wound followed by skin grafting. Until 1979 the protocol at SBI was to allow the dead tissue to separate at its own pace, a process usually taking several weeks. The patient was bathed daily to remove loose skin and surface bacteria. The burn wounds were covered with antibacterial cream-saturated gauze, which was held in place with surgical mesh knit. Baths, debridements, and surgical dressings continued until the wound had granulated. Traction, splints, and neck conformers were used to prevent contractures during this phase of treatment.

After the burned tissue had been completely removed and granulation had occurred, live skin could then be grafted onto the site of the wound. Beginning in 1979 surgeons at SBI decided to be more aggressive in removing the dead tissue because it reduces the patient's risk of overwhelming infection. This removal is usually accomplished in about seven days.

SBI-UTMB teams have designed special equipment and have developed special therapeutic approaches. In 1966, for example, a burn tub was designed to facilitate the thorough and frequent cleansing of burn wounds. The easily mobile fiberglass tub has a dependent sink, drain, and outlet hose for disposal of necrotic tissue and debris. Stainless steel water hoses provide an aerated stream of water for the debriding bath. This tub is advantageous for three reasons: it enables thorough cleansing; it can be used in the patient's room; and it is easily cleaned so that contamination can be reduced and delays in usage can be avoided.

Managing the problem of fluid replacement encouraged SBI physicians to discover a more effective therapeutic approach. Burned patients may lose as much as four quarts of fluid a day. Replacement of fluids is essential, traditionally accomplished with intravenous solutions. In 1968 SBI staff began giving hourly doses of cow's milk to their young patients. After studies with various feeding formulas, milk was chosen because it was better tolerated by the children and because its antacid properties helped to alleviate the gastric ulcerations that often accompanied burn injury. In addition to the milk, therapeutic doses of diazepam were given every six hours, and intensive psychological support was provided. This approach was remarkably successful. Of the 582 children admitted to SBI between September of 1968 and December of 1974, only two required blood transfusion and only three required surgery for the management of gastric ulcer.[54]

Because of these and other innovations, more and more children have survived the acute burn injury, thereby becoming candidates for various kinds of reconstructive surgery. This surgery is intended to restore function and to improve the appearance of scarred areas. Such surgery not infrequently involves the reconstruction of a nose, or ears, or eyebrows, or other facial components. For many years Joseph Paderewski has sculptured numerous prostheses that have been used in these operations.

SBI staff have also developed effective ways to decrease hypertrophic scar formation and contracture. This has been a major challenge for burn treatment specialists because contractures and scarring cause such disability and disfigurement. In 1967 Barbara Willis and her associates in the occupational therapy department at SBI began experimenting with thermoplastic materials that would allow rapid production of individually fitted hand and wrist splints. Orthoplast isoprene was finally selected because it is firm, yet molds and cuts easily. Though pliable in hot water, it cools rapidly and is easily shaped into a form that can meet the needs of a particular patient. Within two years or so, over four hundred of these splints and braces had been used successfully with SBI patients.[55]

Another innovation in the management of scarring has involved the use of pressure bandages. Although the benefits of such bandages had been known since World War II, their use with burned children had not been studied systematically. After such studies SBI physicians and scientists concluded that sustained pressure on healing burn wounds significantly decreased hypertrophic scarring. This led to the development of elastic garments which patients wear for several months to provide the needed pressure.[56]

Physical and occupational therapy, psychological counseling for patients and their families, biofeedback to deal with pain and stress, and play activities have also been important features of the care of patients at SBI.

When the SBI staff occupied its new building in 1966, McChesney Goodall guided a research staff of some twenty-three scientists and technicians. Twelve projects were initiated, involving such concerns as prevention of infection, excision of burned tissue, homografting, and tissue perfusion. However, the research program was stymied because of inadequate space in the new building. By 1971, 12,000 square feet of new space had been added, mostly for research. Support from the Shriners, from UTMB departments, and from federal grants has enabled physicians and scientists at SBI to conduct numerous clinical and laboratory investigations of various problems associated with thermal injury and treatment.

Some of these studies, such as those with milk, have already been mentioned. Another early research breakthrough involved the use of hexachlorophene, a powerful antibacterial agent, which was being used in the debridement baths. During 1966, SBI physicians observed that several patients experienced convulsions shortly after their baths. Several hypotheses were suggested to explain the convulsions, but the crucial clue was provided when a local Shriner mentioned to Larson that a method of draft evasion during World War I had been to self-induce convulsions by swallowing soap suds just before induction physicals.

Laboratory tests of the convulsive children at SBI revealed abnormal serum levels of hexachlorophene. Subsequent laboratory experiments with rats confirmed the hypothesis that hexachlorophene passed readily into the bloodstream through burn wounds and that sufficiently high serum levels could cause convulsions.[57]

Currently there are ten research laboratories and approximately twenty scientists and technicians employed at SBI. They are investigating several problems associated with the care of burn patients. These include the prevention of bacterial infection in burn wounds, the development of skin culture techniques that will allow more extensive grafts of the patient's undamaged skin, the pathological consequences of smoke inhalation and how they can be managed, the effects of heat on the fibrinolytic enzyme system, and ways of dealing with metabolic abnormalities that are so common in burn victims.

University of Texas Medical Branch

When Chauncey Leake assumed his leadership role at the University of Texas Medical Branch in Galveston in September of 1942, he fully realized that research had not been emphasized at the oldest and most prestigious university medical center in Texas. But research had not been completely ignored during the fifty years that UTMB had been a training center for practitioners.

A small cadre of biomedical scientists with doctorates had been hired as departmental chairmen during the 1920s. William Sharp, chairman of microbiology, had earned a medical degree from Rush Medical College and a doctorate from the University of Chicago. Byron Hendrix, who had earned a doctoral degree from Yale, was chairman of biochemistry. The chairman of physiology was Eugene Porter, who had earned his doctorate at Harvard. Each of these individuals exhibited some active interest in research, but they were remunerated for their skills as teachers and administrators, not as researchers. These scientists were still chairmen when Leake arrived.

However, UTMB's most distinguished biochemist, Meyer Bodansky, had died suddenly in June of 1941. As professor of pathological chemistry and director of the laboratories at John Sealy Hospital for more than a decade, Bodansky had published almost one hundred scientific papers dealing with various problems in heart, endocrine, and muscle metabolism. Sharp, Hendrix, Porter, Bodansky, and a few others had tilled the

experimental soil at UTMB during the 1920s and 1930s. Yet, the institution as a whole still lacked tangible evidence of a genuine commitment to experimental science. This change was forthcoming with the employment of world-class basic scientists, the establishment of *Texas Reports on Biology and Medicine*, and the creation of a Sigma Xi chapter.

Charles Marc Pomerat became professor of anatomy at UTMB in 1943.[58] Pomerat had earned a doctorate from Harvard and had continued his studies at Cambridge and with Houssay in Buenos Aires. He established a tissue culture laboratory at UTMB that attracted scientists from all over the world. In 1946 Pomerat encouraged Wiktor W. Nowinski to affiliate with UTMB. Nowinski had earned doctorate degrees from the University of Berne and from the University of Cambridge. He was chief of biochemistry at the University of Buenos Aires when he decided to come to Galveston. Nowinski then directed the Tissue Metabolism Research Laboratory and the Cell Biology Laboratory. He was coauthor of *Cell Biology*, a text that was translated and published in several languages, including Japanese, Russian, and Spanish.[59] UTMB supported Pomerat and Nowinski as basic scientists and researchers, not as clinicians or administrators.

Texas Reports on Biology and Medicine was Chauncey Leake's brainchild. It was launched in the spring of 1943. Leake announced that "the main idea was to set up a medium of publication which would handle our own contributions and those of any other men of science which might be submitted, and to distribute this material to the libraries and medical institutions all over the world without charge."[60] It was remarkably successful. During its heyday in the 1960s, the journal was received by approximately 1,300 libraries in some ninety countries, and some 1,200 medical and scientific journals were received at UTMB in exchange with *Texas Reports*.

Many of the research contributions of UTMB faculty and their scientific colleagues in Texas were first published in this journal. Note, for example, the items in this chapter's bibliography that came from the M. D. Anderson Hospital and Tumor Institute during the 1940s and 1950s. *Texas Reports* ceased publication in 1982. The contents of its forty-one volumes reveal many contributions to multiple areas of investigative concern in both the basic and the clinical sciences of medicine.

The third symbol of a change in institutionalized values about research at UTMB was the founding of a Sigma Xi chapter. The initial efforts, spearheaded by John Sinclair, professor of anatomy, were met with considerable resistance. The national society believed that the scientists in Galveston should register with the chapter at The University of Texas in Austin. It was claimed that members of a medical school separated from a main university could not be expected to make significant research contributions.[61] But, with perseverance and the strong support of Chauncey Leake, thirty-three faculty members chartered a Sigma Xi "club" in 1949. Sinclair was elected president, and the group grew rapidly, accepting fifteen additional members by the end of that year. Beginning in April of 1950, the club sponsored visiting lecturers, usually distinguished biomedical scientists.

In the fall of 1953, fifty-three members of the club petitioned the national society for establishment of a chapter at UTMB. Some 235 research projects in both basic science and clinical departments were identified in the petition. Fifteen organized research laboratories were named. Among the supporting documents was a letter (dated July 31, 1953) from Donald Duncan, professor of anatomy. Duncan noted that there were thirty graduate students registered at UTMB. Eleven were working on their doctorates and the remainder were studying for master's degrees. Duncan argued that the creation of a Sigma Xi chapter would be a special encouragement to these graduate students and to the faculty who were participating in their education. The petition was approved, and the club was installed as a chapter on June 3, 1954.

The chapter prospered. In 1955 it recommended the creation of an Honors Convocation that would occur during commencement festivities. This convocation would recognize outstanding students, especially those who had engaged in meritorious research. The establishment of this ceremony marked a profound institutionalization of the scientific ideals that had been cherished so much by Chauncey Leake. The convocation has now become so large that it is scheduled as a separate event on the day of UTMB's commencement.

In 1960 the Sigma Xi chapter agreed to sponsor a forum that would provide an opportunity for students to present the results of their research efforts. The National Student Research Forum has occurred annually during the last twenty-six years. In 1985, 265 students from fifty-seven medical schools in the United States and Canada participated in the three-day event in Galveston.

The creation of the Sigma Xi chapter at UTMB did provide considerable encouragement to those students enrolled in graduate programs. Graduate degree studies in the biomedical sciences had been formally established between the Graduate School of The University of Texas at Austin and UTMB in 1952. Donald Duncan was the first director of this program. By 1966, ninety-seven master's degrees and forty-eight Ph.D. degrees had been awarded (UTMB 75 Year History, 1967, p. 223). In 1969 the Graduate School of the Biomedical Sciences at Galveston became an autonomous unit within the University of Texas System. Another boost to basic science research occurred with the establishment of the Marine Biomedical Institute in 1969. Most members of this institute have joint appointments in the basic science departments at UTMB.

Other events also signaled the institutionalization of experimental science at UTMB. Research labs were established in some clinical departments during the 1940s. Edgar Poth directed a research laboratory in the Department of Surgery, and William Levin, the current president of UTMB, established a hematology research lab in the Department of Medicine in 1946. Among the earliest projects in Levin's lab were collaborative studies with Rose Schneider involving sickle cell anemia.[62] Schneider, who had earned her doctorate in pathology from Cornell in 1938, had worked as a research assistant with both Pomerat and Nowinski. Schneider and her colleagues eventually discovered some three dozen new hemoglobins.[63] Her research activities were supported primarily by a National Institutes of Health grant that was renewed for thirty-one years (1950–1981).

A significant increase in federal funds for biomedical research began to be available in the late 1940s and early 1950s. In 1956 UTMB scientists attracted $395,000 of federal monies. That amount had increased to slightly more than two million dollars by 1963. An office of sponsored research was established in the dean's office in 1968. Spencer Thompson was appointed associate dean and coordinator of sponsored programs. By 1976 federal support for research at UTMB had increased to almost ten million dollars; by 1983 to almost fifteen million dollars.

Clinical research was formally institutionalized at UTMB with the establishment of a Clinical Study Center in June of 1963. Supported by a National Institutes of Health grant, the original twelve-bed unit was located on the fourth floor of John Sealy Hospital. Levin was the director of this project, and George Bryan, current dean at UTMB, came to Galveston at that time to be the assistant director of this new clinical research unit.

The foregoing review of highlights in the evolution of the health sciences in Texas since World War II is but a sketch. Texans, like other Americans, confronted the conditions of disease existing at mid-century. Cardiovascular derangements, cancer, and accidents had become the leading causes of death and disability. Texans responded to this situation with noteworthy boldness and courage. Their enterprise and creativity have been exemplified by certain accomplishments in cancer research and therapy at the M. D. Anderson Hospital in Houston, some of the surgical advancements in the treatment of cardiovascular diseases spearheaded by Michael DeBakey and Denton Cooley in Houston, and some of the progress made in the treatment of burned children at the Shriners Burns Institute in Galveston.

These extraordinary accomplishments, and the many ordinary ones too numerous to mention in this chapter, have been made possible by the steady growth of complex institutions—hospitals, medical schools, health science centers—and by the economic support afforded by governing groups and private foundations. Because it is the oldest health science center in the state of Texas, UTMB was used to exemplify the institutionalization of medical research in Texas during the last forty years. Equally instructive stories can be told about similar developments at the health science centers in Dallas and San Antonio.[64] The results have been astounding. The 1985 Nobel Prize in Physiology and Medicine was awarded to Joseph L. Goldstein and Michael S. Brown, both faculty members at the University of Texas Health Science Center in Dallas.

Considerably more historical research is needed before the growth of medical science in Texas can be viewed comprehensively. I hope that this brief sketch will encourage such research and writing.

Notes

1. UTMB 75 Year History, 1967, p. 170.
2. Proc., 1944, p. 22.
3. Proc., 1944, p. 45.
4. John Sealy II Scrapbook, 1926.
5. Bordley and Harvey, 1976.
6. *The First Twenty Years*, 1964, p. 24.
7. Schlenk, 1944.
8. Awapara, 1950.
9. Jirgensons, 1954.
10. Kit, 1953.
11. Dmochowski and Grey, 1957.
12. Hsu, 1957.
13. Sinclair, 1957.
14. Macon, 1976.
15. Clark, 1961.
16. Henderson, 1978, p. 106.
17. Thompson, 1971, p. 11.
18. Horwitz, 1980.
19. Bordley and Harvey, 1976.
20. Kneipp, p. 93.
21. DeBakey, 1975.
22. Cooley, Naaman, and Carton, 1956.
23. DeBakey et al., 1962.
24. DeBakey et al., 1958.
25. DeBakey and Cooley, 1953.
26. DeBakey and Cooley, 1954.
27. DeBakey, Cooley, and Creech, 1955.
28. DeBakey, Creech, and Morris, 1956.
29. Cooley and DeBakey, 1956.
30. DeBakey et al., 1957.
31. DeBakey et al., 1962.
32. DeBakey, 1979.
33. Cooley, 1955.
34. Cooley, McNamara, and Latson 1957.
35. Cooley and Ochsner, 1962.
36. Hallman and Cooley, 1963.
37. Cooley and Hallman, 1964.
38. Kneipp, p. 148.
39. Ibid., p. 188.
40. Cooley et al., 1957.
41. *Handbook of Texas*, p. 382.
42. Ross et al., 1971.
43. Kneipp, pp. 191–192.
44. Garrett, Dennis, and DeBakey, 1973.
45. Horwitz, p. 8.
46. Kneipp, pp. 111–112.
47. Cooley et al., 1968.
48. Kneipp, p. 37.
49. Cooley et al., 1969.
50. Frazier et al., 1985.
51. Lawrence, 1976, p. 25.
52. SBI Scrapbook.
53. SBI Files.
54. Watson and Abston, 1976.
55. Willis, 1970.
56. Larson et al., 1971.
57. Larson, 1968.
58. Supplement, Texas Reports, 1965.
59. UTMB 75 Year History, 1967, p. 221.
60. Ibid., p. 173.
61. Russell, 1974, p. 34.
62. Schneider, Levin, and Haggard, 1949.
63. Schneider, Charache, and Schroeder, 1980–81.
64. Chapman, 1976.

Bibliography

Awapara, J. "Application of Partition Chromatography to Problems of Amino Acid Metabolism." *Texas Reports on Biology and Medicine* 8 (1950): 117–122.

Bordley, James III, and A. McGehee Harvey. *Two Centuries of American Medicine 1776–1976.* Philadelphia: W. B. Saunders, 1976, pp. 667–704 for cancer; pp. 481–524 for cardiovascular diseases.

Burns, Chester R. "Medicine in Texas: the Historical Literature." *Texas Medicine* 82 (1986): 60–63.

Chapman, John S. *The University of Texas Southwestern Medical School: Medical Education in Dallas, 1900–1975.* Dallas: Southern Methodist University Press, 1976.

Clark, R. Lee, Jr. (ed.) *Cancer Chemotherapy.* Springfield, Illinois: Charles C. Thomas, 1961.

Cooley, D. A. "Surgical Closure of Atrial Septal Defects." *Surgery, Gynecology & Obstetrics* 100 (1955): 268–276.

Cooley, D. A., B. A. Belmonte, M. E. DeBakey, and J. R. Latson. "Mechanical Heart Lung for Temporary Cardiopulmonary Bypass: Report of 95 Cases." *Texas Journal of Medicine* 53 (1957): 397–400.

Cooley, D. A., D. G. McNamara, and J. R. Latson. "Surgical Treatment of Atrial and Ventricular Septal Defects: Results in 63 Patients." *Southern Medical Journal* 50 (1957): 1044–1047.

Cooley, D. A., D. Liotta, G. L. Hallman, R. D. Bloodwell, R. D. Leachman, and J. D. Milam. "Orthoptic Cardiac Prosthesis for Two-Staged Cardiac Replacement." *American Journal of Cardiology* 24 (1969): 723–730.

Cooley, D. A., and G. L. Hallman. "Surgery During the First Year of Life for Cardiovascular Anomalies: A Review of 500 Consecutive Operations." *Journal of Cardiovascular Surgery* 5 (1964): 584–590.

Cooley, D. A., and J. L. Ochsner, "Surgical Treatment of Cardiovascular Anomalies in Infants less than One Year of Age." *Heart Bulletin* 11 (1962): 12–17.

Cooley, D. A., and M. E. DeBakey, "Resection of Entire Ascending Aorta in Fusiform Aneurysm Using Cardiac Bypass." *Journal of the American Medical Association* 162 (1956): 1158–1159.

Cooley, D. A., R. D. Bloodwell, G. L. Hallman, and J. J. Nora. "Transplantation of the Human Heart: Report of Four Cases." *Journal of the American Medical Association* 205 (1968): 479–486.

Cooley, D. A., Y. D. Naaman, and A. C. Carton. "Surgical Treatment of Arteriosclerotic Occlusion of Common Carotid Artery." *Journal of Neurosurgery* 13 (1956): 500–506.

DeBakey, Michael E. "The Development of Vascular Surgery." *American Journal of Surgery* 137 (1979): 697–738.

DeBakey, M. E. "Successful Carotid Endarterectomy for Cerebrovascular Insufficiency: Nineteen-Year Follow-Up." *Journal of the American Medical Association* 233 (1975): 1083–1085.

DeBakey, M. E., and D. A. Cooley. "Successful Resection of Aneurysm of Thoracic Aorta and Replacement by Graft." *Journal of the American Medical Association* 152 (1953): 673–676.

DeBakey, M. E., and D. A. Cooley. "Successful Resection of Aneurysm of Distal Aortic Arch and Replacement by Graft." *Journal of the American Medical Association* 155 (1954): 1398–1403.

DeBakey, M. E., D. A. Cooley, E. S. Crawford, and G. C. Morris, Jr. "Clinical Application of a New Flexible Knitted Dacron Arterial Substitute." *American Surgeon,* 24 (1958): 862–869.

DeBakey, M. E., D. A. Cooley, and O. Creech, Jr. "Surgical Considerations of Dissecting Aneurysm of the Aorta." *Annals of Surgery* 142 (1955): 586–612.

DeBakey, M. E., E. S. Crawford, D. A. Cooley, and G. C. Morris, Jr. "Successful Resection of Fusiform Aneurysm of Aortic Arch with Replacement by Homograft." *Surgery, Gynecology & Obstetrics* 105 (1957): 657–664.

DeBakey, M. E., E. S. Crawford, D. A. Cooley, G. C. Morris, Jr., and W. S. Fields. "Surgical Treatment of Cerebrovascular Insufficiency." *Modern Medicine* 30 (1962): 110–123.

DeBakey, M. E., E. S. Crawford, G. C. Morris, Jr., and D. A. Cooley. "Patch Graft Angioplasty in Vascular Surgery." *Journal of Cardiovascular Surgery* 3 (1962): 106–141.

DeBakey, M. E., O. Creech, Jr., and G. C. Morris, Jr. "Aneurysm of Thoracoabdominal Aorta Involving the Celiac, Superior Mesenteric, and Renal Arteries. Report of Four Cases Treated by Resection and Homograft Replacement." *Annals of Surgery* 144 (1956): 549–573.

Dmochowski, L., and C. E. Grey. "Electron Microscopy of Tumors of Known and Suspected Viral Etiology." *Texas Reports on Biology and Medicine* 15 (1957): 704–753.

Doty, M. "Heart Transplants in Texas." *Handbook of Texas,* vol. 3, 1976.

The First Twenty Years of The University of Texas M. D. Anderson Hospital and Tumor Institute. Houston: The University of Texas M. D. Anderson Hospital and Tumor Institute, 1964.

Frazier, O. H., D. A. Cooley, O. U. J. Okereke, C. T. VanBuren, and B. D. Kahan. "Cardiac Transplantation at the Texas Heart Institute: Recent Experience." *Texas Medicine* 81 (1985): 48–52.

Garrett, H. E., E. W. Dennis, and M. E. DeBakey. "Aortocoronary Bypass with Saphenous Vein Graft: Seven-Year Follow-Up." *Journal of the American Medical Association* 223 (1973): 792–794.

Handbook of Texas, Walter Prescott Webb (ed.). Austin: Texas State Historical Association, 1952–76.

Hallman, G. L., and D. A. Cooley. "Surgery of the Heart and Great Vessels in the Newborn Period: Review of 450 Cases." *Postgraduate Medicine* 34 (1963): 48–52.

Henderson, Lana. *Baylor University Medical Center: Yesterday, Today and Tomorrow.* Waco: Baylor University Press, 1978.

Horwitz, Nathan. "Bringing Vascular Surgery into the 20th Century—Michael E. DeBakey, M.D." *Therapaeia,* Supplement to the *Medical Tribune,* September 24, 1980, pp. 4–8.

Hsu, T. C., C. M. Pomerat, and P. S. Moorhead. "Mammalian Chromosomes *in vitro,* VIII. Heteroploid Transformation in the Human Cell Strains." *Journal of the National Cancer Institute* 18 (1957): 463–471.

Jirgensons, B., and S. Sirotzky. "The Optical Rotation of Human Serum Albumin and Gamma-Globulin." *Journal of the American Chemical Society* 76 (1954): 1367–1370.

John Sealy II Scrapbook, unpaged clipping of article from unidentified newspaper entitled, "Bequest of Millions Will Make Galveston Great Medical Center," dated May 1, 1926. The scrapbook is located in The Galveston and Texas History Center of the Rosenberg Library in Galveston.

Kit, S. "Amino Acid Metabolism of Neoplastic Tissues and Regulatory Mechanisms." *Texas Reports on Biology and Medicine* 11 (1953): 685–692.

Kniepp, Marianne (ed.) *Reflections and Observations: Essays of Denton A. Cooley.* Austin: Eakin Press, 1984.

Larson, Duane L. "Studies Show Hexachlorophene Causes Burn Syndrome." *Hospitals* 42 (Dec. 16, 1968): 63–64.

Larson, D. L., Sally Abston, E. B. Evans, M. Dobrkovsky, and H. A. Linares. "Techniques for Decreasing Scar Formation and Contractures in the Burned Patient." *Journal of Trauma* 11 (1971)

Lawrence, Philip S. "The Health Record of the American People," in *Health in America: 1776–1976,* 17–36. Washington, D.C.: U.S. Department of Health, Education, and Welfare, 1976.

Macon, N. Don. *Clark and the Anderson: A Personal Profile,* Houston: The Texas Medical Center, 1976.

Minetree, Harry. *Cooley, The Amazing Career of the World's Greatest Heart Surgeon.* New York: Harper & Row, 1973.

Proceedings at the Dedication of the M. D. Anderson Hospital for Cancer Research. Houston: The M. D. Anderson Foundation, 1944.

Redding, Stan. "DeBakey—A Day with the Fabled Surgeon." *Texas: Houston Chronicle Magazine,* October 12, 1980.

Ross, J. N., Jr., D. W. Wieting, C. W. Hall, J. H. Kennedy, H. E. Garner, and M. E. DeBakey. "Use of a Paracorporeal Left Ventricular Bypass Pump in Experimental Heart Failure." *American Journal of Cardiology* 27 (1971): 12–19.

Russell, Glenn. "History of Galveston Sigma Xi 1949–1974." This unpublished manuscript is among the papers of the UTMB chapter of Sigma Xi, which are located in the archival collections of the Moody Medical Library in Galveston.

SBI Files. These are located in the office of the director of the Shriners Burns Institute in Galveston. Especially valuable in providing information were the volumes of minutes of the Coordinating Committee. I am grateful to Jack Hoard for permission to examine these files.

SBI Scrapbook. This has been faithfully arranged for many years by Sara Bolieu, who is the director of public relations for SBI. The scrapbook is in her office. Especially valuable are the many newspaper clippings about SBI activities.

Schlenk, F., "Whither Enzyme Chemistry." *Texas Reports on Biology and Medicine* 2 (1944): 183–205.

Schneider, Rose G., Samuel Charache, and Walter A. Schroeder (eds.). "Human Hemoglobins and Hemoglobinopathies: A Review to 1981." *Texas Reports on Biology and Medicine* 40 (1980–1981): 1–504.

Schneider, R. G., W. C. Levin, and M. E. Haggard. "Carbonic Anhydrase Activity in Sickle Cell Anemia, Sickle Cell Trait and Pernicious Anemia." *Journal of Laboratory and Clinical Medicine* 34 (1949): 1249–1253.

Sinclair, W. K. "The Relative Biological Effectiveness of 200 KV X-Rays, Cobalt-60 Gamma-Rays and 22 MV X-Rays." *Texas Reports on Biology and Medicine* 15 (1957): 443–444.

Supplement, *Texas Reports on Biology and Medicine* 23 (1965): 151–419.

Thompson, Thomas. *Hearts.* New York: McCall, 1971.

The University of Texas Medical Branch at Galveston, A Seventy-Five Year History. Austin: University of Texas Press, 1967.

Watson, Larry C., and Sally Abston. "Prevention of Upper Gastrointestinal Hemorrhage in 582 Burned Children." *American Journal of Surgery* 132 (1976): 790–793.

Willis, Barbara. "The Use of Orthoplast Isoprene Splints in the Treatment of the Acutely Burned Child." *American Journal of Occupational Therapy* 24 (1970): 187–191.

Social Sciences

17

Archaeology and Anthropology

E. Mott Davis

THIS CHAPTER is concerned initially with the history of archaeology in Texas since the end of World War II. The last section deals with the postwar history of Texas anthropology as a whole.[1]

Because of its anthropological orientation, archaeology in this state—as elsewhere—has fared best in well-rounded departments of anthropology. The position of Texas archaeology with relation to the other fields of anthropology can be stated briefly. Cultural anthropology, which provides the principal theoretical base for anthropological studies in general, has affected Texas archaeology especially through studies of ethnohistory and cultural ecology. Archaeology, in turn, has provided cultural studies with long-range views of processes of cultural change—in some parts of Texas the pageant is ten thousand years long—and a wide perspective of the variety of cultural adaptations in the diverse environments found within the borders of the state. Physical anthropology, through skeletal studies in the specialty now called bioarchaeology, has been illuminating the biological side of human prehistory, although only a beginning has been made in this particular line of research in Texas. Linguistic anthropology, through its historical reconstructions, has suggested directions for archaeology to explore concerning the prehistory of such peoples as the ancestral Caddo and Wichita. On a more mundane level, archaeology, as the field of anthropology that attracts the most public attention, has often provided the initial rationale for support of anthropology in general in Texas educational institutions.

We begin our history—before further narrowing our focus to archaeology—in 1945, at the end of World War II, when only two Texas institutions had anthropologists of any sort on their staffs. Those anthropologists were only four in number: two cultural anthropologists, one archaeologist, and one person doing research in both fields. At the University of Texas (today the University of Texas at Austin, and referred to hereafter as UT-Austin) J. Gilbert McAllister and George C. Engerrand, cultural anthropologists and inspired teachers, were no longer carrying on research but were stimulating students with the excitement of the anthropological approach. Alex D. Krieger, research archaeologist, had spent the war years analyzing records and collections in the archaeology laboratory. At Texas Technological College in Lubbock (now Texas Tech University, hereafter referred to as Texas Tech) W. C. Holden, trained as a historian, continued his pre-war interest in cultural anthropology in Sonora, Mexico, and the archaeology of the High Plains and environs, as well as in West Texas history.

Archaeology in Texas Since World War II

With the end of the war, archaeological research in Texas resumed on a greatly increased scale. The River Basin Surveys program of the Smithsonian Institution, founded to carry on archaeological salvage in river basins that were to be flooded by federal reservoirs, established an office at UT-Austin, with Robert L. Stephenson in charge. This program eventually came to dominate archaeological activity in the state. Back from the war to the Department of Anthropology at UT-Austin came archaeologists T. N. Campbell and J. Charles Kelley to join Krieger in the training of a new generation of students. In 1946 Krieger, bringing together his wartime research, published *Culture Complexes and Chronology in Northern Texas*, the second major scholarly study in anthropological archaeology to come out of the state.[2] In this work Krieger reviewed in detail all of the information on archaeological complexes from the Panhandle to East Texas, and used cross-dating to carry dendrochronological dates from the Pueblo Southwest across the southern Plains and into the southeastern Woodlands.

Three years later Krieger completed a second major study, *The George C. Davis Site, Cherokee County, Texas*, reporting excavations just before the war by H. Perry Newell in one of the most important sites in the state, a large prehistoric Caddo religious and village center on the Neches River near Alto, now called Caddo Mounds State Historic Site.[3] A work of pottery analysis, stratigraphic reconstruction, and culture-historical synthesis, this report put Texas archaeology on par with research in the rest of the country. It remains one of the classic monographs in North American archaeology, although later research has altered many of its conclusions.

At the same time, Campbell and Kelley were, like Krieger, pulling together and publishing information gathered from excavations in the 1930s, Campbell on Gulf coastal materials and Kelley on Central Texas.[4,5] At the Texas Memorial Museum of UT-Austin, E. H. Sellards—a geologist with a lifelong interest in the earliest human occupation of the continent, the Paleo-Indian stage—was publishing research on very early High Plains sites.[6]

One of the strengths of archaeology in Texas has been the collaboration that has always gone on between professionals and avocational archaeologists, united in the Texas Archaeological Society. Avocational groups began to play an increasing role in Texas archaeology after the war, often stimulated by the reservoir salvage work of the River Basin Surveys. An archaeological society was formed in Houston as the result of interest in Joe Ben Wheat's work in the Addicks Reservoir basin west of the city.[7] The Dallas Archaeological Society and the Central Texas Archaeological Society in Waco were cooperating with Stephenson in reservoir salvage work in Central and North Texas

These societies and other avocational archaeologists contributed to the progress of scientific archaeology through volunteer help in the field and through surface reconnaissance and recording of sites, at a time when site destruction by engineering activities and pot hunting (the random digging for relics by hobbyists) was accelerating. Excavations carried out by these groups also often served to salvage information that would otherwise be lost. Like the work of professionals, the work of avocationals varied in scientific rigor and degree of documentation, but in many cases the data have been essential in providing a base for further work.[8]

How was archaeology being advanced by this postwar resurgence? Most importantly, in two ways. First, order was being brought to a welter of hitherto unorganized information. Archaeological complexes were being defined, usually in terms of the components, foci, and aspects of the Midwestern Taxonomic System, and these units were being arranged into chronological sequences. In short, a history was being roughed out. It was, to be sure, a history of formal units—artifact types and artifact complexes—rather than of people, cultures, or adaptations, but the important first steps were being taken in building systematic bodies of information, especially in Central and East Texas.

Second, field work by trained persons was expanding into areas—as in the Houston area and parts of Central and East Texas—that had hitherto known at best only well-documented collecting (a preliminary contribution in itself), and at worst only pot hunting. As time went on, the expanding reservoir salvage program brought more of the prehistory of the state under skilled examination.

In the 1950s, the *Bulletin of the Texas Archaeological Society* continued to be the principal outlet for archaeological publication, and the annual meetings of the Society provided the main opportunity for archaeologists to assemble and exchange information. Full-time professionals with graduate degrees in anthropological archaeology, who in mid-decade numbered no more than eight, were at only UT-Austin (which had most of them), Texas Tech, and West Texas State University.

A landmark in the history of Texas archaeology, and

to some degree in North American archaeology, was the appearance in 1955 of "An Introductory Handbook of Texas Archeology," authored by Dee Ann Suhm (now Dee Ann Story), a graduate student at UT-Austin, Edward B. Jelks, a UT-Austin graduate who had succeeded Stephenson as head of the River Basin Surveys office in Austin, and Alex D. Krieger.[9] The first half of this work, initially assembled by Suhm and Jelks, presented in uniform outline fashion the information available on archaeological complexes throughout the state, mostly organized according to the Midwestern Taxonomic System. Since many of the complexes were defined in terms of diagnostic artifacts—which, for practical purposes, meant pottery vessels and projectile points—the last half of the "Handbook," inspired mainly by Krieger, was an illustrated guide to projectile-point and pottery types, described according to a uniform outline and conforming to Krieger's concept of type, which did not depend on an ideal static form, but involved variation and change. The "Handbook" provided a chronological and descriptive framework in terms of which artifacts, sites, and complexes could be identified and into which they might fit.

A measure of the importance of the "Handbook" was to be seen in the immediate adoption of most of its concepts by workers throughout the state. Ironically, its success also had negative effects. As research tools, the classificatory units worked so well that many researchers thereafter let the "Handbook" do their thinking for them: projectile points were fitted into the "Handbook" types whether the fit was Procrustean or not; dates in the "Handbook" continued to be cited after radiocarbon dating had made them obsolete; and the necessarily (for the time) relatively mechanical classificatory approach of the "Handbook" set the pattern for much of the analytical work in the decade to follow. Fortunately, not all archaeologists succumbed to this temptation. A few, Edward Jelks notable among them, were developing methods of putting flesh on the dry archaeological bones by seeking to define behavioral and other cultural correlates—such as ecological adaptations—of the material evidence they were recovering.

In the 1950s and early 1960s archaeological work, mostly reservoir salvage, was under way in most parts of the state. If primary importance is given to substantive advances in exploring prehistory, the most important projects were in Central and East Texas and on the Lower Pecos. In East Texas the work of Jelks and his colleagues, in a series of reservoir projects, shed much new light on the late prehistory of rural Caddo Indians (as contrasted with those at large ceremonial centers);[10] found the first evidence in Texas of Hopewellian burial-mound peoples of the early Christian era;[11] made the first intensive studies of the pre-ceramic Archaic horizon in East Texas;[12] and, at Lake Tawakoni, began the systematic exploration of the historic archaeology of the Wichita Indians.[13]

In Central Texas, at stratified sites, a sequence of projectile-point types was being defined that permitted ordering components in a chronological scheme.[14] At the Kyle site on Lake Whitney in the early 1960s, Jelks for the first time discussed complexes and their history in terms of environmental and technological changes.[15]

In the Lower Pecos area, engineering work began on the Amistad Dam on the Rio Grande above Del Rio. Consequently, archaeological work in the basin of the Amistad Reservoir was initiated in 1958 and continued through the 1960s under Jelks and his successors.[16] Especially notable here was the introduction of intensive paleo-environmental work—palynology, paleontology, geomorphology, and hydrology—and the construction of a cultural and environmental sequence spanning more than ten thousand years.[17] Unfortunately, much of the work of the Amistad project did not go beyond trait and sequence studies.[18]

There were other archaeological developments of importance in the 1950s and early 1960s. UT-Austin set up the Texas Archaeological Research Laboratory at the Balcones Research Center. Eventually, under the guiding hand of Dee Ann Story, it was to become one of the leading archaeological research facilities in the country, and for many years, it was the principal center for coordination of statewide archaeological information. In the Monahans Sandhills, southwest of Midland, the Scharbauer site produced Paleo-Indian skeletal material, "Midland Man" (actually a woman), the subject of a deservedly noted monograph.[19] In the Lewisville Reservoir basin northwest of Dallas, avocational archaeologists of the Dallas Archaeological Society found puzzling evidence of a Clovis-point occupation, puzzling because radiocarbon dates on charcoal from the site were beyond the dating range of the radiocarbon method—more than 38,000 years old.[20] All Clovis dates elsewhere were (and have been since) in the 11,000-plus range, and no validated evidences of human activity in the Western Hemisphere had yet been found with a date as early as the radiocarbon date suggested. After the initial sensation, the find was largely discounted or ignored because of the apparent contradiction in evidence. A quarter of a century later the Clovis-point association at Lewisville was validated, and the date discounted, when it was found that the supposed charcoal was in fact lignite that was being used by the Clovis people in their campfires.[21]

At the same time, W. C. Holden, a historian and one of the pioneer Texas anthropologists, was continuing archaeological work for Texas Tech in southeastern New Mexico, aided by his daughter Jane Holden (later Jane Holden Kelley) and F. Earl Green.[22] Rex Gerald joined the staff of the Centennial Museum of Texas Western College (now the University of Texas at El Paso) where he was doing extensive survey work.

The revolutionary effects of radiocarbon dating began to be felt throughout the world of archaeology in the 1950s. In Texas three oil companies, Humble, Shell, and Magnolia, set up radiocarbon laboratories for geologic research and dated a few samples for archaeologists without charge. In particular the Humble laboratory in Houston ran archaeological samples on weekends, at a time when few other laboratories in the country existed, and thereby made a significant contribution to American archaeology. In the 1960s these laboratories completed their research and closed, but meanwhile, in the early 1960s, UT-Austin and Texas A&M University (TAMU) had collaborated in the development of a new technique for radiocarbon dating, using liquid scintillation spectrometry, and the Austin laboratory was in full operation with this technique by 1962. Southern Methodist University (SMU) set up a laboratory some years later, and a commercial laboratory to serve archaeologists, Radiocarbon, Ltd., was established at Lampasas.

In 1962 the Texas Archaeological Society held a summer field school for amateurs at the Gilbert site near Emory, east of Dallas.[23] This was a volunteer effort to help the Texas Archaeological Salvage Project of UT-Austin (the successor to the River Basin Surveys office), which needed comparative information on protohistoric Wichita sites to supplement its work at Lake Tawakoni. The field school was so successful that it was repeated the next summer at Canyon Lake on the Guadalupe River. It has taken place every June since that time in different parts of the state.[24] The importance of this field school to anthropological archaeology in the state lies, first, in the creation of a network of avocational and paraprofessional archaeologists throughout the state who monitor what is happening to cultural resources, and, second, in the research that is accomplished under the supervision of a professional archaeologist.

Indeed, it came to be realized that cultural resources— historical and archaeological sites—were

being destroyed at an increasing rate by the alteration of the land through a multitude of construction and other activities, as well as by pot hunting. By the 1950s there was a clear need for the state to acknowledge that it had a stake in its antiquities. The Texas Archaeological Society passed a resolution in 1956 urging creation of the position of State Archeologist, but it was not until 1965 that such a position came into being.[25] In 1969, as a result of public outcry at the private plundering of an early Spanish shipwreck at Padre Island on the Gulf Coast, a state antiquities code was passed, protecting all antiquities on public land in the state. Although the destruction continues today at a discouraging rate, the Antiquities Code of Texas and an increased public awareness of the need for conservation of cultural resources have in some instances diminished the speed and severity of the damage.

In the 1960s American archaeology was shaken by an intellectual movement usually called the New Archaeology. This approach emphasized a concern with processes of cultural change, an evolutionary point of view, systems theory and the concept of the ecosystem, deductive reasoning and hypothesis testing, statistics and sampling, and the use of computers. A clarion call to the new orientation was sounded in 1962 by its principal protagonist Lewis R. Binford, then at the University of Chicago, in an article that appeared in the national journal *American Antiquity* while it was under the editorship of T. N. Campbell at UT-Austin.[26] No Texas archaeologists became members of what elsewhere came to be almost a Binford cult, but many features of the New Archaeology soon became implicit in Texas research, particularly in the form of statistics and ecosystems study.[27] They continue to be reflected in Texas archaeology today. Unfortunately, as Shafer has pointed out, the old culture-historical normative approach still plays too large a role and has resulted, through its effect on retrieval methods in the field, in the loss of an unconscionable amount of irreplaceable information on past human behavior.[28]

Historical sites archaeology, the meeting of the disciplines of archaeological and documentary research, is a logical field of activity to be pursued in a state with a rich and varied cultural heritage. In 1962 a group of citizens in the upper Nueces Valley joined with UT-Austin to sponsor an archaeological excavation at the site of the eighteenth-century Mission San Lorenzo de la Santa Cruz in Real County.[29] Interestingly, this was the first postwar archaeological project in the state that was supported entirely by state and private funds rather than being federally funded, in itself a sign that local interest was rising. From this successful beginning historical archaeology grew to become a major field of activity.

Contract archaeology, the successor to the reservoir salvage of earlier years, was responsible for an explosive increase in archaeologial activity in Texas in the 1970s. In this expansion the state reflected the wider picture: concern over environmental degradation had become nationwide, and archaeological sites were seen as part of the environment. A series of congressional and executive actions in Washington, D.C., had created a body of law that made archaeological survey, and excavation when necessary, mandatory in every federally related activity that might have an impact on the landscape. The planning and establishment of policy in the conservation of archaeological and historic sites came to be called the profession of cultural resource management.

Texas was in the vanguard of states that set up an effective body of state law to complement federal legislation in the field of archaeological and historic preservation. As we have seen, the office of Texas State Archaeologist was established in 1965, and a rigorous state antiquities code was passed in 1969.

The result of this state and federal legislation was that anyone whose activities came under these laws needed archaeologists to do the required surveys and excavations. The list of Texas institutions that in 1980 had well-established contract organizations to carry on legally mandated archaeological field work is long: SMU, Texas Tech (which had set up a Cultural Resources Institute with a special graduate training program), TAMU, UT-Austin, UT-San Antonio, UT-El Paso, North Texas State University, West Texas State University, and Stephen F. Austin State University. Archaeologists at a few other institutions, such as the University of Houston (UH), were doing contract work on an individual basis. A number of archaeologists set up private companies to do contract work, and several environmental engineering firms established archaeological laboratories for the same purpose.

What effect did all this activity have on the progress of archaeology as a scientific pursuit and as a body of knowledge? We must reemphasize here the crucial factor precipitating this flood of conservation archaeology, as contract work is often called. The data base on which archaeological research depends—artifacts (in the broadest sense) with their contexts—constitutes a nonrenewable resource that is destroyed by activities that disturb the earth. Patterns in the ground, once disturbed, cannot be brought back. The most desirable way to conserve archaeological information is

to leave sites alone; but if that is impossible, the loss of information can be diminished (the legal phrase is "mitigating the impact") through disciplined survey and excavation. Such work, carried out to satisfy legal requirements, suffers from pressures different from those of pure research. Obviously, it is appropriate to ask how well contract archaeology has met the standards of scientific research.

The scientific record of contract archaeology is, not surprisingly, widely varied in quality and significance, but a number of projects in Texas have made substantial contributions in terms of planning, field techniques, methods of analysis, and substantive results. A few examples are the Richland-Chambers Creek project of SMU,[30] the Choke Canyon project of UT-San Antonio with the collaboration of Texas Tech and TAMU,[31] the San Gabriel Project of North Texas with TAMU and UT-Austin,[32] the Allens Creek project of UT-Austin,[33] and the Hueco Bolson project of UT-El Paso.[34]

Although conservation archaeology is like other archaeology in its scientific aims, it differs in the deadlines involved, the amount of taxpayers' money invested, and the fact that some of it is carried out commercially for profit.[35] A special public responsibility for quality control (to use the industrial term) must be discharged. In Texas the legal responsibility for monitoring compliance—that is, overseeing the quality of the work—is in the hands of the Texas Historical Commission, including the Texas Antiquities Committee. In addition, professional archaeologists in the state, after several preliminary meetings, formed in 1977 the Council of Texas Archeologists (taking its name from a similar organization that functioned briefly just before World War II) to set up standards of field performance, reporting, and curation, following the precedent of the Society of Professional Archeologists, a national body founded in 1975.

Thus, the means exist for enforcing satisfactory scientific standards in legally mandated archaeological field work. The success of the enforcement has depended not only on the abilities of the persons given the responsibility, but also on the degree of support for monitoring compliance provided by legislative appropriations. Currently, this support is diminishing while site destruction continues unabated. One wonders how long scientific archaeology in the state will have a data base to which our increasingly sophisticated methods of collection and analysis can be applied.

However, archaeological field work in Texas in the last two decades has not been solely in the form of contract archaeology. Many institutions have run summer field schools, sometimes in connection with contract work, that have produced contributions to research (for example, Joel Gunn's project in archaeology and ecology at the Hop Hill site in Central Texas, for UT-San Antonio).[36] Often the field schools have been part of larger research projects, as with the continuing project of Eileen Johnson and Vance Holliday at Lubbock Lake for The Museum at Texas Tech,[37] the work of TAMU, under Harry Shafer and Vaughn Bryant, at Hines Cave in the Lower Pecos country;[38] and the research of Dee Ann Story of UT-Austin at the George C. Davis site in East Texas.[39] The last-named project was a renewed investigation of an already famous site that was the subject of Krieger's famous report of 1949, cited earlier in this article.

By this time most institutions in the state that had archaeological programs were including historical archaeology in their activities,[40] but only UT-San Antonio had set up an academic program in the specialty, eventually offering the master's degree. In 1967 an International Conference on Historical Archaeology took place at SMU, chaired by Edward Jelks. At this meeting the Society for Historical Archaeology, the national body concerned with these studies, was organized.[41]

Texas also has participated in the development of nautical, or marine, archaeology, a branch of the field that brings together the anthropological, classical, and historical aspects of the field. The public outcry that led to the passage of the Texas Antiquities Code and the creation of the Texas Antiquities Committee, led also to a program in marine archaeology administered by that committee. During the 1970s extensive survey and publication of investigations in coastal waters took place.[42] Even more important, in the middle 1970s George F. Bass—who, more than anyone else, merits the title of Father of Nautical Archaeology—joined the staff of TAMU and moved the Institute of Nautical Archaeology from the Mediterranean island of Cyprus to College Station. TAMU is now a world center for graduate training and research in that subject.[43]

The anthropological study of prehistoric rock art is another facet of archaeological work in Texas worthy of mention. Prehistoric sites in the desert area of the Lower Pecos and Trans-Pecos are famous for their pictographs and petroglyphs, the study of which has benefited from the precedent of meticulous recording established in the 1930s by Forrest and Lula Kirkland and carried on in recent decades in far West Texas by UT-El Paso and the El Paso Archaeological Society.[44,45] A basis for the anthropological approach to analysis of this art has been established by William Newcomb and Solveig Turpin.[46,47]

Summarizing the archaeological situation in Texas forty years after the end of World War II, nearly all parts of the state have seen archaeological work, and in many areas a cultural sequence covering more than ten thousand years has been roughed out. Despite this impressive record, the gaps, not surprisingly, remain larger than the areas of knowledge. Three examples will suffice. In most of the state little is known of the earliest human occupants, those we call Paleo-Indians, other than that they were here, possibly as early as eleven thousand years ago. Second, only a bare beginning, albeit an encouraging one, has been made in understanding the dynamics of hunter-gatherer adaptations and their changes over the millennia. With its varied environments, Texas is an ideal laboratory for this study. Third, the reasons for the appearance—and in some cases disappearance—of native economies based on horticulture are still obscure. Clearly, much remains to be done. It is heartening that methods of archaeological data collection and analysis are constantly being improved, although the culture-historical approach of the 1950s, with its emphasis on traits and chronology as ends in themselves, is still more prevalent than it should be. Unfortunately, the continuing site destruction by pot hunting and alterations of the land make it uncertain how much longer any information will be available in the ground for study.

Because our emphasis is on Texas, we have not noted the work of Texas archaeologists outside the state and the nation. It is not possible here to enumerate even a representative sample of this work or to discuss its substantive results, but Texas archaeologists who have been particularly prominent in areas outside the United States can be mentioned: Fred Wendorf of SMU in Egypt, Sudan, and Ethiopia; Frank Hole of Rice University (now at Yale) in Iran; Richard P. Schaedel of UT-Austin in the Andes; and Richard E. W. Adams of UT-San Antonio in the Maya area.

Anthropology in Texas after World War II

Although archaeology was the most visible aspect of anthropological research in Texas for more than a decade after World War II, cultural anthropology also had a new beginning. Oscar Lewis, later to become famous for his Latin American studies, was in Bell County, Central Texas, in 1945, comparing the culture of the people on the Blackland Prairie to that of the people in the nearby hills.[48] In 1947 three cultural anthropologists were added to the staff of UT-Austin (where J. G. McAllister and George Engerrand were still teaching): Wilfred Bailey, Charles Lange, and William Newcomb. Bailey made two community studies in the state, the first of a town in the Panhandle[49] and the second of a community displaced by the filling of the Falcón Reservoir on the Rio Grande.[50] Newcomb began a long career of research on Texas Indians.[51] Lange's work, in both archaeology and cultural anthropology, was in New Mexico.

Wilfred Bailey was succeeded in 1955 by William Madsen, who in the late 1950s organized a cultural anthropological study of Mexican-Americans in the Lower Rio Grande Valley.[52] UT-Austin also established a faculty position in physical anthropology in 1958, filled by Thomas W. McKern, an osteologist. McKern's coming signaled the permanent establishment of this subfield of anthropology in the state, although he was not the first physical anthropologist to work in Texas, as in the 1930s UT-Austin had an osteology laboratory in connection with WPA-sponsored archaeology.

Anthropology programs began their major growth in Texas in the 1960s. A convenient measure of the growth, starting in 1962, is available in the annual *Guide to Departments of Anthropology*, published by the American Anthropological Association.[53] The *Guide* lists faculty and staff members at each institution and their research interests. Listings are voluntary, and only graduate programs appeared until the 1969–70 *Guide*, so that an institution might be at work in anthropology and not send in an entry. (Texas Tech, for instance, does not appear in the *Guide* until 1970, some forty years after the beginning of anthropological activity there.) However, submitting or not submitting an entry reflects to some degree the extent of support for anthropology at the institution. A record based on entries in the *Guide* provides a rough chronicle of the fortunes of anthropology in academic institutions.

When the *Guide* began publication with its 1962–63 edition, the only Texas institution listed as having an anthropology program was UT-Austin, with a staff of thirteen. Six were cultural anthropologists, of whom two, William Madsen and William Newcomb, were doing research in Texas. Six staff members were archaeologists (those without graduate degrees are not counted here), all but one doing work in Texas; the exception was J. F. Epstein, who was working in northern Mexico. T. W. McKern, physical anthropologist, was continuing his work on the skeletal prehistory of the state.

Institutions of higher learning were expanding almost explosively throughout the United States in the 1950s and 1960s, and within them new anthropology programs were being established and old ones were growing. Texas was no exception to the trend. In 1964 SMU hired Fred Wendorf, an archaeologist, to establish an anthropology program; in the same year Richard N. Adams was appointed Chairman of the Department of Anthropology at UT-Austin and given an administrative mandate to build a large and strong department. Accordingly, in 1964 UT-Austin noted in the *Guide* that it had instituted a doctoral program in anthropology and in 1965 that it had awarded the doctorate to archaeologist Edward Jelks, the first such degree awarded in the state.

Until 1967 UT-Austin was still the only department listed in the *Guide*. The listing in 1966–67 shows that the staff had increased to twenty persons: eleven cultural anthropologists (three of whom had research interests in Texas), eight archaeologists (five doing research in the state), and still one physical anthropologist.

At last, in 1967–68 SMU appears in the *Guide* and is joined by Rice. SMU had established the Institute for the Study of Earth and Man in 1966 to sponsor graduate research in geology, anthropology, and statistics. The academic program was at first part of a Department of Sociology and Anthropology, with a doctoral program, but became a separate Department of Anthropology in 1968, at which time it had two cultural anthropologists, four archaeologists (a contract program was established), two physical anthropologists, and a linguistic anthropologist, George Trager, the first specialist in that field to be employed in the state. The program had seventeen graduate students in 1967–68 and thirty in 1968–69. Three of the four archaeologists, those in the contract program, were doing research in Texas. Wendorf instituted archaeological research on the prehistory of the Nile Valley in the Aswan Reservoir in Nubia. SMU was to become the preeminent Texas institution in Old World archaeology.

Rice also would build a reputation in Old World archaeology as part of its anthropology program. First appearing in the 1967–68 *Guide*, anthropology at Rice, in a department with sociology, had four cultural anthropologists and one archaeologist on the staff, none of them working on problems in Texas. Seventeen graduate students were in the program, which led to the master's and the doctor's degrees. Frank Hole, the archaeologist, was carrying on pioneering work on the origins of pastoralism and farming in western Iran.

The growth continued. By 1970–71 Rice had added one archaeologist to the staff, and had awarded one master's degree. The faculty at SMU had increased to fourteen, with the addition of two cultural anthropologists, one archaeologist, one physical anthropologist, one linguist, and one geoarchaeologist. The graduate student body had increased to forty-two. Two doctor's degrees had been awarded in 1969–70. UT-Austin had received a large development grant from the National Science Foundation that included physical anthropology and linguistics, with the result that the staff there now numbered twenty-seven: twelve cultural anthropologists (two with research interests in Texas), six archaeologists (three with Texas concerns), four physical anthropologists (two with Texas concerns), and five linguists. The graduate student body numbered sixty; it eventually grew to over 150. Nine doctor's degrees were awarded in 1970–71.

In the 1970s four new master's programs were established in the state, some of them complemented by contract archaeology units that were important not only in research but also as training programs. Texas Tech finally appeared in the *Guide* in 1970–71 with two cultural anthropologists and three archaeologists, in a Department of Sociology and Anthropology. A master's program, a contract archaeology unit with special training in cultural resources, and a separate Department of Anthropology with William J. Mayer-Oakes as Chairman, were in place by 1973.

TAMU also joined the trend in 1971, hiring Vaughn M. Bryant, Jr., a paleobotanist and archaeologist trained at UT-Austin, to set up anthropology at that institution. TAMU does not appear in the *Guide* until 1974, by which time Bryant had already set up a laboratory of palynological, coprolite, and other ecological research in archaeology that was to become world famous.[54] Contract archaeology also became important at TAMU, as did nautical archaeology.

UT-San Antonio, a newly established school, was not far behind. Thomas R. Hester, trained at UT-Austin and the University of California at Berkeley, arrived to create an anthropology program in 1973 and establish the Center for Archaeological Research in 1974. The Center quickly became one of the most productive archaeological programs in the state, conducting contract investigations throughout South Texas—hitherto almost untouched archaeologically—and pursuing a program in historical archaeology, centering on investigations in the San Antonio missions (succeeding earlier work by Mardith Schuetz, of the Witte Museum of San Antonio), and urban archaeology within the city.[55]

In 1977 UH, which had been offering anthropology courses for many years, appeared in the *Guide* with a master's degree program, emphasizing cultural anthropology. On the faculty were eight cultural anthropologists, two physical anthropologists, and one archaeologist. This was the most recent graduate program in anthropology to be added to the Texas listings in the *Guide*. In recent years the UH program has included projects in urban archaeology.

At present, the emphases in the various programs in the state are quite varied, a reflection of the heterogeneity of interests among anthropologists. Cultural anthropology is especially diverse; for instance, a number of Texas schools have instituted anthropologically oriented programs in folklore, Mexican-American studies, and anthropology in education, and museum studies have been affiliated with anthropology to a greater or lesser degree at Texas Tech and UT-Austin. In terms of geographical interests, one may find cultural anthropologists from Texas institutions in such widely scattered parts of the world as the Middle East, New Guinea, India, and Japan. Examples are the work of Pauline Kolenda of UH on caste and family in India and that of Edward Norbeck of Rice on Japan.[56,57] Both of these scholars have made substantial contributions in other aspects of cultural anthropology as well.

However, the principal focus of Texas research in cultural anthropology has been on Latin America and on Texas itself. The study of the cultures of our home state is currently a particularly lively area of research. Traditional cultural anthropologists are integrating their work with those of persons in closely related fields, notably folklore and sociolinguistics, in examining Chicano culture, Afro-American life, rural Anglo-American culture, and the effects of urbanization.[58]

Brief mention must be made of the innovative approach to cultural analysis of Richard N. Adams of UT-Austin. Hitherto best known for his studies of Latin American societies, Adams is now treating societies as energy systems, an approach that is attracting attention within and outside of anthropology. He sees the use of the thermodynamics of structures in non-equilibrium and the dissipative structure of Ilya Prigogine as a method for studying society as a self-organizing energy process.[59]

A new anthropological organization came into being in April 1975 when Adams and Annette B. Weiner initiated the Cibola Anthropological Association at a meeting in Austin, to bring together Mexican and North American anthropologists both in and out of academic institutions.[60] The first full meeting of the Association, with symposia and presentation of research papers, took place in San Antonio in 1977. Since then the Association has met annually at cities in the southwestern United States and northern Mexico.

Physical anthropology, which began in Texas in the form of osteology—the study of skeletal material, principally from archaeological sites—is now directed mainly toward research on the biology of the living. D. Gentry Steele of TAMU is an exception, being especially well known for his work in osteology.[61] His more recent research, however, has been mostly in zoo-archaeology, the analysis of animal bones in archaeological sites. Elsewhere in Texas, physical anthropologists are to be found in many institutions, many of them teaching in medical schools. Two anthropology departments, those at SMU and UT-Austin, have always had strong representation in this field, but the major center of research today is at the independent Southwest Foundation for Biomedical Research in San Antonio, where teams are working in primatology and human population genetics. UT-Austin also is active in primatology—often in collaboration with the Southwest Foundation.[62] It is additionally well known for the work of Robert M. Malina in human growth and development.

Linguistic anthropology has for some years been represented by more persons at UT-Austin than elsewhere in the state, because the university was able to build on a foundation provided by a development grant from the National Science Foundation in 1969, which enabled the creation of a number of positions in that field of study. The focus of research by a group in the Departments of Anthropology and Linguistics—Joel Sherzer, Brian Stross, Greg Urban, and Anthony Woodbury—is in the field of discourse—the use and contexts of language—as the expression of the relation between language and culture, especially as seen in the languages and cultures of indigenous peoples in the Americas.[63]

The fortunes of anthropology in Texas over the years are reflected in the number of doctor's degrees awarded. The first Texas doctorate in anthropology was awarded at UT-Austin in 1965, and SMU and Rice established doctoral programs soon thereafter. These three remain today the only doctoral programs in the state. In the decade from 1965 to 1975 approximately thirty-five doctor's degrees were awarded in Texas by these schools, mainly by SMU and UT-Austin. In the following decade the degrees awarded increased threefold, to approximately one hundred, even though this was a time when the market for academic employment in anthropology was shrinking dramatically:

in the United States the academic expansion of the 1950s and 1960s ended not long after 1970, leaving anthropology departments staffed mostly by persons in their thirties and forties, so that normal turnover created by retirements was not expected to begin until the 1990s. Although opportunities have been increasing for nonacademic employment of anthropologists, most of the careers are still in academia. But students continue to apply to graduate programs because they feel that the stimulation and challenge of anthropological research compensate for the risks.

Similar growth has taken place in master's programs. At the beginning of the 1970s less than five persons were receiving master's degrees in anthropology in Texas each year. In the mid-1980s, with master's programs at UH, TAMU, Texas Tech, and UT-San Antonio, added to those at Rice, SMU, and UT-Austin, between thirty and forty master's degrees are awarded each year.

On the undergraduate level, eight Texas institutions are currently listed in the *Guide* as offering an anthropology major, without having graduate students. Thus, including the schools having graduate programs, a total of fifteen schools offer undergraduate majors. Many of the faculty members in the undergraduate programs carry on research. At other colleges persons in related fields, such as sociology, give basic anthropology courses. We may add that anthropology is an accredited subject in the Texas high school curriculum, although few schools offer it.

In 1945 only four persons with graduate degrees were being employed as anthropologists in Texas. Forty years later there are approximately 170 in Texas colleges and universities. How many are employed outside academia is not known. These simple figures express graphically the growth in importance of anthropology in Texas in the past four decades, indicating that this field, once regarded as only esoteric and romantic, is now perceived as contributing significant insights to our understanding of the nature and history of humankind.

Notes

1. The term *archaeology* as used here refers to anthropological archaeology as distinguished from classical or art-historical archaeology, which, as traditionally practiced, are humanistic rather than scientific studies.

It must be pointed out that while many persons significant in Texas anthropology are mentioned in the text of this article, and therefore appear in the index, others equally significant are not named directly in the text but are cited in the references; their names appear in the bibliography.

The alternative spellings *archaeology* and *archeology* are both standard in the United States. In this article *archaeology* is used except in citing titles of organizations and publications that use the *e* spelling, such as the Texas Archeological Society.

2. The first was Kelley, Campbell, and Lehmer, 1940, a pre-war study of Big Bend archaeology. Certain other early studies, such as Jackson, 1938, were major works of consequence, but were not representative of anthropological archaeology as it had developed by that time.

3. Newell and Krieger, 1949.

4. Campbell, 1947, 1960a.

5. Kelley, 1947.

6. Sellards et al., 1947; Sellards, 1952.

7. Wheat, 1953.

8. An example is Crook and Harris, 1952.

9. Suhm, Krieger, and Jelks, 1954.

10. Jelks and Tunnell, 1959; Jelks, 1961.

11. Jelks, 1965.

12. Davis and Davis, 1960; L. Johnson, 1962.

13. Duffield and Jelks, 1961.

14. Suhm, 1957; L. Johnson, Suhm, and Tunnell, 1962; Sorrow, Shafer, and Ross, 1967.

15. Jelks, 1962.

16. A particularly well-known report is Dibble and Lorrain, 1968.

17. Story and Bryant, eds., 1966.

18. Shafer, 1986, pp. 2–3, points out serious shortcomings in the Amistad project.

19. Wendorf, Krieger, and Albritton, 1955.

20. Crook and Harris, 1957.

21. Stanford, 1982; pp. 208–9.

22. Holden, 1952.

23. Jelks, 1967.

24. Richmond, Richmond, and Greer, 1985.

25. Word, 1979.

26. Binford, 1962.

27. Stimulating examples are L. Johnson, 1967, and Weir, 1976.

28. Shafer, 1986.

29. Tunnell and Newcomb, 1969.

30. Raab, 1982.

31. Hall, Black, and Graves, 1982.

32. Hayes, ed., 1982.

33. Hall, 1981.

34. Whalen, 1978.

35. A series of conferences at Texas Tech examined these problems on the national level (Portnoy, ed., 1978; Mayer-Oakes and Portnoy, eds., 1979).

36. Gunn and Mahula, 1977.

37. E. Johnson, 1983.

38. Shafer and Bryant, 1977.

39. Story, ed., 1981.

40. Humphreys and Singleton, 1978, and Fox, 1983, provide reviews of historical archaeology in Texas.

41. Society for Historical Archaeology, 1967.

42. Arnold, 1978.

43. A recent report is Smith, Keith, and Lakey, 1985.

44. Kirkland, 1939.

45. A representative report is J. V. Davis and Toness, 1974.

46. Kirkland and Newcomb, 1967.

47. Turpin, 1982.

48. Lewis, 1948.

49. Bailey, 1953.

50. Bailey, 1955.

51. Newcomb, 1961.

52. Madsen, 1965.

53. American Anthropological Association, *Guide*.

54. Bryant, 1974.

55. An example is Fox, Bass, and Hester, 1976.

56. Kolenda, 1976.

57. Norbeck, 1970.

58. For example, Foley, 1978.

59. Adams, n.d.

60. Cibola Anthropological Association, 1983, pp. 3–4.

61. Steele, 1970.

62. Bramblett and Coelho, 1985.

63. A recent example is Sherzer, 1983.

Bibliography

Adams, Richard Newbold, "The Eighth Day: Human Society as the Self Organization of Energy Process." Submitted for publication, n.d.

American Anthropological Association, *Guide to Departments of Anthropology*. Published annually, beginning in 1962, by the Association, Washington, D.C.

Arnold, J. Barto III, *1977 Underwater Site Test Excavations Off Padre Island, Texas*, Texas Antiquities Committee Publication 5, 1978.

Aten, Lawrence E., *Indians of the Upper Texas Coast*, New York: Academic, 1983.

Bailey, Wilfred C., "The Status System of a Texas Panhandle Community," *Texas Journal of Science* 5 (1953): 326–31.

———. "Problems in Relocating The People of Zapata, Texas," *Texas Journal of Science* 7 (1955): 20–37.

Binford, Lewis R., "Archaeology as Anthropology," *American Antiquity* 28 (1962): 217–25.

Bramblett, Claud A., and Anthony M. Coelho, "Age Changes in Affinitive Behavior of Baboons," *American Journal of Primatology* 9 (1985): 259–71.

Bryant, Vaughn M., "Prehistoric Diet in Southwest Texas: The Coprolite Evidence," *American Antiquity* 39 (1974): 407–420.

Campbell, T. N., "The Johnson Site: Type Site of the Aransas Focus of the Texas Coast," *Bulletin of the Texas Archeological and Paleontological Society* 18 (1947): 40–75.

———. "Archeology of the Central and Southern Sections of the Texas Gulf Coast," *Bulletin of the Texas Archeological Society* 29 (1960a): 145–75.

———. "Texas Archeology: A Guide To The Literature," *Bulletin of the Texas Archeological Society* 29 (1960b): 177–254.

Cibola Anthropological Association, *Journal*, February (1983): 3–4.

Crook, Wilson W., Jr., and R. K. Harris, "Trinity Aspect of the Archaic Horizon," *Bulletin of the Texas Archeological and Paleontological Society* 23 (1952): 7–38.

———. "Hearths and Artifacts of Early Man Near Lewisville, Texas, and Associated Faunal Material," *Bulletin of the Texas Archeological Society* 28 (1957): 7–97.

Davis, E. Mott, "The First Twenty-Five Years of the Texas Archeological Society," *Bulletin of the Texas Archeological Society* 50 (1979): 159–94.

Davis, John V., and Kay Toness, *A Rock Art Inventory at Hueco Tanks State Park, Texas*, El Paso Archaeological Society, Special Report 12 (1974).

Davis, W. A., and E. Mott Davis, *The Jake Martin Site*, Department of Anthropology, University of Texas, Archaeology Series 3 (1960).

Dibble, David S., and Dessamae Lorrain, *Bonfire Shelter: A Stratified Bison Kill Site, Val Verde County, Texas*, Texas Memorial Museum, University of Texas at Austin, Miscellaneous Papers 1 (1968).

Duffield, Lathel F., and Edward B. Jelks, *The Pearson Site*, Department of Anthropology, University of Texas, Archaeology Series 4 (1961).

Foley, Douglas E., *From Peones to Politicos: Ethnic Relations in A South Texas Town From 1900 to 1977*, Austin: Univ. of Texas Press, 1978.

Fox, Anne A., Feris A. Bass, Jr., and Thomas R. Hester, *The Archaeology and History of Alamo Plaza*, Center for Archaeological Research, University of Texas at San Antonio, Archaeological Survey Report 16 (1976).

Fox, Daniel E., *Traces of Texas History: Archeological Evidence of The Past 450 Years*, San Antonio: Corona, 1983.

Gunn, Joel, and Royce Mahula, *Hop Hill: Culture and Climatic Change in Central Texas*, Center for Archaeological Research, University of Texas at San Antonio, Special Report 5 (1977).

Hall, Grant D., *Allens Creek*, Texas Archeological Survey, University of Texas at Austin, Research Report 61 (1981).

Hall, Grant D., Stephen L. Black, and Carol Graves, *Archaeological Investigations at Choke Canyon Reservoir, South Texas: The Phase I Findings*, Center for Archaeological Research, University of Texas at San Antonio, Choke Canyon Series 5 (1982).

Hays, T. R., ed., *Archaeological Investigations at The San Gabriel Reservoir Districts, Central Texas*, vols. 1–4. Institute of Applied Sciences, North Texas State University, 1982.

Hester, Thomas R., *Digging into South Texas Prehistory*, San Antonio: Corona, 1980.

Holden, Jane, "The Bonnell Site," *Bulletin of the Texas Archeological and Paleontological Society* 23 (1952): 78–132.

House, Kurt D., ed., *Texas Archeology: Essays Honoring R. King Harris*, Institute for the Study of Earth and Man, Southern Methodist University, Reports of Investigations 3 (1978).

Humphreys, Gerald, and W. Singleton, "Historic Archeology in Texas." In *Texas Archeology: Essays Honoring R. King Harris*, edited by Kurt D. House, 69–92. Institute for the Study of Earth and Man, Southern Methodist University, Reports for Investigations 3 (1978).

Jackson, A. T., *Picture Writing of Texas Indians*, University of Texas Publication 3809 (1938).

Jelks, Edward B., "Excavations at Texarkana Reservoir, Sulphur River, Texas," *Bureau of American Ethnology Bulletin* 179 (1961): 1–78.

———. *The Kyle Site*, Department of Anthropology, University of Texas, Archaeology Series 5 (1962).

———. "The Archeology of McGee Bend Reservoir,

Texas," Ph.D. diss. (Anthropology), University of Texas, 1965.

———, ed., "The Gilbert Site," *Bulletin of the Texas Archeological Society* 37 (1967).

Jelks, Edward B., E. Mott Davis, and Henry B. Sturgis, eds., "A Review of Texas Archeology, Part One," *Bulletin of the Texas Archeological Society* 29 (1960).

Jelks, Edward B., and Curtis D. Tunnell, *The Harroun Site: A Fulton Aspect Component of The Caddoan Area, Upshur County, Texas*, Department of Anthropology, University of Texas, Archaeological Series 2 (1959).

Johnson, Eileen, *Lubbock Landmark, Master Plan*, 3 vols. The Museum, Texas Tech University, 1983.

Johnson, LeRoy, Jr., "The Yarbrough and Miller Sites of Northeastern Texas, With a Preliminary Definition of The LaHarpe Aspect," *Bulletin of the Texas Archeological Society* 32 (1962): 141–284.

———. *Toward a Statistical Overview of the Archaic Cultures of Central and Southwest Texas*, Texas Memorial Museum, University of Texas, Bulletin 12 (1967).

Johnson, LeRoy, Jr., Dee Ann Suhm, and Curtis D. Tunnell, *Salvage Archeology of Canyon Reservoir: The Wunderlich, Footbridge and Oblate Sites*, Texas Memorial Museum, University of Texas, Bulletin 5 (1962).

Kelley, J. Charles, "The Lehmann Rock Shelter: A Stratified Site of the Toyah, Uvalde, and Round Rock Foci," *Bulletin of the Texas Archeological and Paleontological Society* 18 (1947): 115–28.

Kelley, J. Charles, T. N. Campbell, and Donald J. Lehmer, *The Association of Archaeological Materials with Geological Deposits in The Big Bend Region of Texas*, West Texas Historical and Scientific Society 10 (1940).

Kingston, Mike, "Archaeology: A Slow Start in Texas." In *The Texas Almanac, 1984–85*, edited by Mike Kingston, 51–55. Dallas: A. H. Belo, 1983.

Kirkland, Forrest, "Indian Pictures in The Dry Shelters of Val Verde County, Texas," *Bulletin of the Texas Archaeological and Paleontological Society* 11 (1939): 47–76.

Kirkland, Forrest, and W. W. Newcomb, *The Rock Art of Texas Indians*, Austin: Univ. of Texas Press, 1967.

Kolenda, Pauline M., *Caste in Contemporary India: Beyond Organic Solidarity*, Menlo Park, Calif.: Benjamin Cummings, 1976.

Krieger, Alex D., "Archaeological Horizons in the Caddo Area." In *El Norte de México y el Sur de Estados Unidos: Tercera Reunión de Mesa Redonda de la Sociedad Mexicana de Antropologia*, México, D. F., 1943.

———. *Culture Complexes and Chronology in Northern Texas*, University of Texas Publication 4640 (1946).

Lewis, Oscar, *On The Edge of The Black Waxy: A Cultural Survey of Bell County, Texas*, Washington University Studies, n.s., Social and Philosophical Sciences 7 (1948). St. Louis.

Madsen, William, *The Mexican-Americans of South Texas*, New York: Holt, Rinehart, and Winston, 1965.

Mayer-Oakes, William J., and Alice W. Portnoy, eds., *Scholars as Contractors*, Washington, D.C.: U.S. Department of the Interior, Heritage Conservation and Recreation Service, 1979.

Newcomb, William W., *The Indians of Texas*, Austin: Univ. of Texas Press, 1961.

Newell, H. Perry, and Alex D. Krieger, *The George C. Davis Site, Cherokee County, Texas*, Memoirs of the Society for American Archaeology 5 (1949).

Norbeck, Edward, *Religion and Society in Modern Japan: Continuity and Change*, Rice University Studies 56 (1), 1970.

Portnoy, Alice W., ed., *Scholars as Managers*, Washington, D.C.: U.S. Department of the Interior, Heritage Conservation and Recreation Service, 1978.

Raab, L. Mark, *Settlement of the Prairie Margin: Archaeology of the Richland Creek Reservoir, Navarro and Freestone Counties, Texas, 1980–81*, Archaeology Research Program, Southern Methodist University, Archaeological Monographs 1 (1982).

Richmond, Jean A., W. L. Richmond, and John W. Greer, "Texas Archeological Society Field Schools 1962–1982," *Bulletin of the Texas Archeological Society* 54 (1985, for 1983): 105–84.

Sellards, E. H., *Early Man in America: A Study in Prehistory*, Austin: Univ. of Texas Press, 1952.

Sellards, E. H., Glen L. Evans, Grayson E. Meade, and Alex D. Krieger, "Fossil Bison and Associated Artifacts from Plainview, Texas," *Bulletin of the Geological Society of America* 58 (1947): 927–54.

Shafer, Harry J., "The Future of Texas Archeology," *Texas Archeology* (Newsletter of the Texas Archeological Society) 30 (2): 1–6 (1986).

Shafer, Harry J., and Vaughn M. Bryant, Jr., *Archeological and Botanical Studies at Hinds Cave, Val Verde County, Texas*, Texas A&M University, Anthropology Laboratories, Special Series 1 (1977).

Sherzer, Joel, *Kuna Ways of Speaking,* Austin: Univ. of Texas Press, 1983.

Smith, Roger C., Donald H. Keith, and Denise Lakey, "The Highborn Cay Wreck: Further Exploration of a 16th-Century Bahaman Shipwreck," *International Journal of Nautical Archaeology and Underwater Exploration* 14 (1985): 63–72.

Society for Historical Archaeology, "Beginnings," *Historical Archaeology 1967.*

Sorrow, William M., Harry J. Shafer, and Richard E. Ross, *Excavations at Stillhouse Hollow Reservoir,* Papers of the Texas Archeological Salvage Project, University of Texas at Austin, 11 (1967).

Stanford, Dennis J., "A Critical Review of Archeological Evidence Relating to the Antiquity of Human Occupation of the New World," *Smithsonian Contributions to Anthropology* 30 (1982): 202–18.

Steele, D. Gentry, "Estimation of Stature from Fragments of Long-Limbed Bones." In *Personal Identification in Mass Disasters,* edited by T. Dale Stewart, 85–97. Washington, D.C.: Smithsonian Institution, 1970.

Story, Dee Ann, ed., *Archeological Investigations at the George C. Davis Site, Cherokee County, Texas,* Texas Archeological Research Laboratory, University of Texas, Occasional Papers 1 (1981).

Story, Dee Ann, and Vaughn M. Bryant, Jr., eds., *A Preliminary Study of the Paleoecology of the Amistad Reservoir Area,* Final report of research under the auspices of the National Science Foundation (GS-667), 1966. [Texas Archeological Salvage Project, University of Texas at Austin.]

Suhm, Dee Ann, "Excavations at the Smith Rockshelter, Travis County, Texas," *Texas Journal of Science* 9 (1957): 26–58.

Suhm, Dee Ann, Alex D. Krieger, and Edward B. Jelks, "An Introductory Handbook of Texas Archeology," *Bulletin of the Texas Archeological Society* 25 (1954).

Tunnell, Curtis D., and William W. Newcomb, Jr., *A Lipan Apache Mission: San Lorenzo de la Santa Cruz, 1762–1771,* Texas Memorial Museum, University of Texas, Bulletin 14 (1969).

Turner, Ellen Sue, and Thomas R. Hester, *A Field Guide to Stone Artifacts of Texas Indians,* Austin: Texas Monthly, 1985.

Turpin, Solveig A., *Seminole Canyon: The Art and The Archeology,* Texas Archeological Survey, University of Texas, Research Report 83 (1982).

Weir, Frank A., "The Central Texas Archaic," Ph.D. diss. (Anthropology), Washington State University, Pullman, 1976.

Wendorf, Fred, Alex D. Krieger, and Claude C. Albritton, *The Midland Discovery: A Report on the Pleistocene Human Remains from Midland Texas,* Austin: Univ. of Texas Press, 1955.

Whalen, Michael E., *Settlement Patterns of the Western Hueco Bolson,* Publications in Anthropology, El Paso Centennial Museum, University of Texas at El Paso, 6 (1978).

Wheat, Joe Ben, "An Archeological Survey of the Addicks Dam Basin, Southeast Texas," *Bulletin of the Bureau of American Ethnology* 154 (1953): 143–252.

Word, James H., "A History of The Texas Archeological Society and The Establishment of a State Archeologist," *Bulletin of the Texas Archeological Society* 50 (1979): 153–58.

18

Psychology

Rand B. Evans

ANY ATTEMPT to trace the history of psychology is complicated by the fact that psychology is really not just one discipline. It is, in fact, a collection of loosely related disciplines. One of psychology's difficulties over the past century of its existence as a formal discipline is that its constituents share neither a single methodological approach nor even a consistent disciplinary attitude. Some constituents of psychology are theoretically oriented, following the basic tenets of pure science. Others emphasize the application of theory to practical situations and follow the model of technological disciplines such as engineering. Yet others follow the model of medical arts more than either science or technology. The locations of psychologists in modern society are even more varied than their points of view. Some are found in academic settings, others in industrial and commercial settings, others in hospitals and in private practice. Within each of these settings and many others that could be named, the various attitudes and approaches are often intermixed.

One of the reasons for this apparent confusion is the subject matter of psychology itself. The problems psychologists consider as part of their subject matter include the physiological processes that underlie experience and behavior. Psychologists study sensation and perception: what we sense or fail to sense and how this affects our awareness in and involvement with the world around us. This includes not only theoretical and scientific work in psychophysics, the relationship between stimuli in the environment and our experience of them, but also work on sensory disabilities such as hearing loss, blindness, and the like. Psychologists work on sleep and dreaming, again in both scientific and clinical settings. Psychologists are involved in learning and conditioning, attempting not only to build theories of those subjects but also to apply those facts in education and in the therapeutic manipulation of behaviors. Educational psychology, usually found in colleges of education, often overlaps much of the subject material found in departments of psychology, which predominate in colleges of liberal arts. Psychologists study motivation and emotion. They study psychological development, not only in infants and children but through the life span, ending with the psychology of aging and finally the psychology of death and the impact of death on families. Psychology deals not only with normal experience and behavior but also with the abnormal side. The converse of normal personality and adjustment are neuroses and psychoses. Psychologists study intelligence and adaptability as well, dealing with the gifted individual and the psychologically retarded. The subject matter of psychology involves individuals and the way in which individuals function in society. Though lengthy, this list is still selective because the study of psychology is so wide-ranging. I have included it here to make the point that it is impossible to relate the history of "psychology" in Texas or anywhere else, at least not comprehensively. What this article attempts to do is to introduce the reader to some major subject areas of psychology and some major locations of psychological endeavor in Texas over the past century, and particularly over the past fifty years, that have affected our society.

Psychology in Academia

The problem of defining psychology is just as difficult in academia as outside of it. It is even difficult to date the beginning of the discipline in Texas. One usually dates the beginning of an academic discipline with its establishment as an independent department of study. In Texas, just as in many other parts of the country, however, psychology long existed in a shared status with other departments before reaching independence. In older institutions the dependent relationship was with philosophy. The University of Texas at Austin (UT–Austin) and Rice University are examples of this kind of relationship. In newer institutions or those with special mandates such as "normal" schools or teachers colleges, the dependent relationship was with education. In most cases, independent status for psychology was not obtained until after World War II, and in some cases only very recently. Some departments, usually in smaller institutions, still retain joint status, such as the joint Philosophy/Psychology Department at Sam Houston State University and at Southwestern University or the psychology program within the College of Education at Southwest Texas State University.

Experimental Psychology

To determine the beginning of experimental psychology, however, is somewhat simpler. Experimental psychology patterns itself on the scientific theoretical model, and its data are typically derived from laboratory settings. One can date the beginning of an experimental psychology program with the founding of its laboratory. The first such laboratory in Texas was founded at the University of Texas at Austin in 1898, less than twenty years after the founding of what is usually referred to as the world's first laboratory in psychology at Leipzig, Germany, by Wilhelm Wundt. UT–Austin has the oldest consistent program in experimental psychology and the most highly ranked nationally. Since its development at UT–Austin in many ways epitomizes its development elsewhere, a brief history of that program is not out of order. The reader should understand that the meaning of "experimental psychology" in this case involves the gathering of psychological data through experimental means. Whether the data are eventually used for theory-building or for practical application is not discriminated. Experimental psychology is often thought to deal only with theories of sensation, perception, learning, and similar "natural science" aspects of psychology. However, researchers can legitimately conduct experimental psychological work in clinical and industrial settings.

While the psychology program at the University of Texas has always had a strong scientific/theoretical component, it has developed over the years all the major subsets found in well-rounded psychology programs, including the technological/applied and clinical/medical arts approaches.

Although the psychology laboratory was founded in 1898, it was created in a joint philosophy/psychology curriculum. Psychology was a new discipline in those days, even in older universities in the East. A major turning point for psychology at the University of Texas, and in Texas as a whole, was the arrival at UT of Clarence S. Yoakum. He came to UT in 1908 as professor and head of the Department of Philosophy and Psychology. Typically the head of joint philosophy/psychology departments was a philosopher, since psychology usually represented only a very limited portion of the curriculum. Yoakum, however, was a psychologist who had taken his doctoral training at the University of Chicago. He was part of the Chicago functionalist movement begun by John Dewey and James Rowland Angell. An important aspect of that movement was that it studied not only consciousness but also behavior. The many research projects Yoakum and his students conducted during his years at UT ranged from studies on fatigue to experiments on the behavior of squirrels to problems of human motor dexterity behavior. By the time he left for World War I to work in the early psychological testing, Yoakum had established a tradition for research at Texas and had produced some students who would later become famous in their own right. One student who had been an undergraduate just before Yoakum came to Texas was Walter Hunter. Hunter graduated from UT in

1906 and did his graduate work at Chicago while Yoakum was there working on his degree. Joining the faculty at UT in 1912 and staying until 1916, Hunter went on to become one of the leaders of American experimental psychology, particularly the early development of behaviorism. He was elected in 1932 as president of the American Psychological Association. He carried out in the Texas laboratory his pioneering studies on delayed reaction in learning tasks in animals and children. Another student of Yoakum was Fleming Allen Clay Perrin, who came to Texas in 1914 and helped establish psychology as the study of behavior in his work on learning. In 1926 Perrin published with D. B. Klein an early, highly successful introductory textbook in psychology. This text introduced psychology as "the science of adaptive behavior" because the authors felt that behavior provided a "more effective introduction to psychological science than the study of consciousness as such."

Promising young faculty members were added to the philosophy/psychology program in the 1920s. O. R. Chambers came from Indiana University in 1926, along with Lloyd A. Jeffress from the University of California at Berkeley. Hugh Blodgett, also from Berkeley, but coming via Lehigh University, arrived in 1928. A specialist in the area of psychological testing, Chambers continued the line of research that had been strong from the time of Yoakum at the University of Texas. Blodgett had done pioneering work on the effect of reward on maze learning in the rat and he retained an interest in animal learning. Jeffress had worked with Warner Brown at Berkeley and was particularly interested in psychophysics and in sensation and perception.

In 1927, psychology separated from philosophy at UT to form an independent department which was housed in Sutton Hall for many years along with education. The subsequent development of the department is typical of what took place in most larger institutions of higher learning. Psychology was usually associated with Colleges of Liberal Arts and linked to the social sciences. Normally housed in attics or basements, along with the other psychologists, experimentalists either lacked the necessary laboratory facilities, or found themselves in makeshift affairs. Funding for the instrumentation required to study sensation and perception, physiological psychology, animal learning, and similar research topics was sparse. At UT, for example, the budget in the 1920s for maintenance, equipment, and services such as typing and duplication, came to $200. Even in 1920 dollars this made instrumental research virtually impossible. Researchers

experimenting with psychological tests were more fortunate since they were not so dependent on apparatus. It is not surprising to find so much of the early research activity in the area of psychological tests. Lloyd Jeffress was able to do some research work in psychoacoustics, the psychology of hearing, but only through the use of laboratories in the department of physics. Hugh Blodgett's students often did their learning research with simple, homemade instruments and mazes.

It was only after World War II that the surge of students and of funding allowed psychology to begin to realize its potential at the University of Texas. In 1948, Karl M. Dallenbach of Cornell was brought in to be department chairman of psychology. He came with the agreement that psychology would have a new building and sufficient facilities for research. The result was the construction of Mezes Hall and its outfitting for a full range of psychological investigation. Dallenbach's design of Mezes Hall was a classic and became the prototype for the construction of psychology laboratories all around the country. With the increased facilities came a massive influx of doctoral students and research. Jeffress was now able to conduct his experiments in psychoacoustics in one of the best sound rooms in the country. The facility, known to generations of students as "Room 9" long after the numbering system was changed, allowed much of the research that would become the basis for Jeffress's stimulus-oriented approach to the theory of signal detection.

Animal facilities were also provided in the move, although they were kept in structures away from the main building. It was only later that the animal learning facilities were constructed as part of Mezes Hall. Dallenbach's plan also included a psychological clinic to allow for the expansion of the clinical and personality research and training programs.

The new facilities and better funding drew well-known psychologists from around the nation. Harry Helson came for a number of years and did some of his classic work on adaptation theory, the effect of stimulus "anchors" on the ability to judge other stimuli. M. E. Bitterman arrived to do a tremendous amount of research on comparative psychology and animal learning. E. John Capaldi, a graduate of the department, became a faculty member in 1956 and published widely in the literature on animal learning during his years at Texas.

Not only did experimental psychology flourish, but clinical psychology and testing expanded as well. Ira Iscoe came to Texas in 1951 from UCLA and developed a large and productive program in clinical psychology and personality. Between 1953 and 1959, Harold Stevenson was at UT-Austin, organizing research activities in child development. In 1959 Donn Byrne joined the faculty, not long after leaving Stanford. His research on personality theory done during his ten years in Texas made significant contributions to the field. This list includes only a few of the individuals who distinguished themselves in the period of expansion from 1948 to 1960.

Another period of accelerated development at the University of Texas came during the administration of Gardiner Lindzey. Lindzey came to Texas in 1964 and did for the psychology program in the 1960s what Dallenbach's term had done in the 1950s. More major psychologists joined the faculty. There was Quinn McNemar in statistics, Clifford Morgan in physiological psychology, and especially Kenneth Spence in animal learning theory and Janet Taylor Spence in personality. Lindzey was a social psychologist with interest in the newly developing field of behavior genetics, a subject that flourished during his time at Texas.

After Gardner Lindzey, Janet Spence became department chair and carried on the development and strengthening of psychology programs into the 1970s. The Department of Psychology at the University of Texas has continued to be ranked highly in terms of research, often as high as sixth in the nation.

While not so spectacular as the growth of the psychology program at UT, other Texas colleges and universities showed a similar pattern. In general the beginnings of psychology were small and usually part of some other program. It was customary for the research that was most commonly conducted to be that which required the least apparatus. For this reason, the natural science side of psychology has always developed somewhat more slowly than the social science, paper-and-pencil type.

A second major center of experimental psychology in Texas is at the University of Houston (UH). The story of its development is not unlike that of the University of Texas. The University of Houston was founded in 1934 by the Cullen family of Houston as a Junior College. The psychology program did not develop at UH as an independent department until 1948, however. Richard I. Evans came to Houston in 1950 to start up the program in social psychology. His interests have been primarily in various aspects of social psychology. He was influential in developing projects in personality theory and group behavior and did some particularly important work on the social impact of educational television, being one of the leaders in the

establishment of the first educational television station in the nation at UH. His later work on the psychology of persuasion, particularly as it is applied to anti-smoking campaigns, has been a noteworthy addition to the literature of applied psychology. Evans was also largely responsible for the establishment of a program in what has become known as behavioral medicine. Evans' series of television interviews with famous psychologist-philosophers all over the world also made him a celebrity. His was the first such program in Texas and one of the first in the nation. Daniel Sheer also came in the early 1950s and established a highly influential program in physiological psychology. As with UT, the program at UH was constrained in its early days by insufficient funding. Originally a privately endowed university, UH was only able to develop into a major center for psychological research after 1963, when it became incorporated into the state-funded system of higher education.

One research area that never developed in psychology at UT was that of industrial/organizational psychology. Most of that line of work at the University of Texas was carried out in the College of Business. (Robert Blake and Jane Mouton had done some of their early work on the "managerial grid" at Texas, mostly outside of their department.) The University of Houston developed the first really substantial program in industrial psychology in the state. John F. MacNaughton and Hobart G. Osburn at UH were influential in the creation of the program, which in its early days was primarily personnel-industrial psychology. In recent years the study of group interaction within organizations has also received attention.

Another program in Texas known for its industrial/organizational research as well as its human-factors work is the program at Rice University. The graduate program in psychology at Rice is of fairly recent origin, but undergraduate psychology at Rice has been active for many years. In 1920, Radoslav Tsanoff, head of the Department of Philosophy at Rice Institute, as it was then known, brought to Texas one of E. B. Titchener's students from Cornell. The student, F. L. Bixby, was trained in the structuralist, introspective psychology then identified with Cornell University. Tsanoff had arranged for the establishment of an experimental laboratory at Rice, which easily rivaled that at the University of Texas in the 1920s, particularly in the study of sensation and perception. The purchase in the late 1920s of Titchener's unparalleled private library in psychology gave Rice the possibility of being a leader in psychology in Texas. Unfortunately, Bixby left before those possibilities were realized. Like UT, the Rice program waited out the Depression for better times.

A problem at Rice was the fact that psychology was entirely undergraduate in those days and the mandate of the department was primarily instructional rather than experimental. Psychology was joined not only to philosophy at Rice, but also with education into something of an all-in-one social science/philosophy department. Only in the 1960s when a graduate program emerged did the somewhat cognitive/phenomenological psychology traditions in the department give way to more behavioral influences. The graduate program there consisted of emphases in cognitive, engineering, and industrial/organizational psychology.

Clinical Psychology in Academia

In academic psychology, theoretical and applied disciplines exist side by side, but not always comfortably. Still, it is possible to do theoretical and experimental research on topics that will be of benefit to society as well. Clinical psychology is an example of this. Clinical programs, that is, those studying adjustment and maladjustment of human beings, developed out of the psychological testing work begun by Yoakum and people like him during World War I. Major stimulus to the study of clinical psychology in academic settings came during and after World War II, however. The rise of clinical and counseling psychology in Texas was one of the major impacts of the war on Texas psychology. The GI Bill, set up at the end of World War II, provided tremendous numbers of veterans the wherewithall to attend college. Many of them chose psychology and particularly clinical psychology. On the negative side, the war produced many thousands of veterans with severe psychological problems requiring treatment. This, in turn, produced an increased demand for qualified clinical and counseling psychologists. Colleges received large training grants to produce doctoral-level clinical psychologists. The result of this combination of increased students, funding for advanced degrees, and job opportunities in Veterans Administration hospitals led to rapid growth in clinical and counseling programs in Texas universities. The Korean War led to a second surge in available training money, this time not only for clinical psychologists but also for counseling psychologists.

Clinical and counseling programs were not always located in psychology departments in Liberal Arts. Education programs, particularly educational psychology programs, also produced doctoral-level counselors.

It is often difficult to tell the difference between the practitioners coming out of educational psychology programs and those from psychology programs. In some institutions, like Texas A&M, the educational psychology program was much older and more developed than psychology and had doctoral programs in counseling and clinically oriented subjects long before the Psychology Department developed its own doctoral programs.

A recent development in Texas psychology programs is that of the Doctor of Psychology degree, a degree primarily intended for clinical practitioners rather than academic psychologists. At present the only such program exists at Baylor University.

In the 1960s, with the arrival of the "baby boom" generation at college age, Texas saw an explosion of local colleges and universities. Two-year colleges became four-year and four-year colleges changed their names to universities and added graduate programs. Whole new institutions were founded and older ones were greatly expanded. With this expansion psychology departments separated from joint associations and developed their own unique programs. Most of them are still either four-year programs or programs with some limited graduate offerings, but several, such as the one at Texas A&M, are adding doctoral programs in psychology.

Industrial Psychology in Applied Settings

Some of the most significant achievements in the development of psychology in Texas have occurred outside of academia, however. This is particularly true in the areas of industrial psychology and engineering psychology, sometimes called human factors, or the study of man-machine relationships. Much of this trend came about because of the outbreak of World War II and the problems involving the training of pilots. Texas had been a center for military pilot training from the early days of military aviation. In 1931, Randolph and Kelly fields in San Antonio were particularly active in pilot instruction. Originally the training of pilots required a full twelve months. When the advent of war was apparent in 1939, the amount of time for training dropped from twelve to nine months, then to seven months by 1940. After Pearl Harbor, with the declaration of U.S. involvement in the conflict, the schedule had to be further reduced to nine weeks. Such a tremendous reduction in training time required a revolution in pilot selection and training techniques.

Most of the research done on aptitude tests for pilots was carried out by flight surgeons of the School of Aviation Medicine at Randolph Air Force Base in San Antonio. For this purpose and others, a large number of psychologists became involved in developing and evaluating aptitude tests. At first the intent of the work was only research, but as the war escalated, psychologists became involved in implementing training practices as well as studying them.

The psychologists who were brought from all over the country to Texas first attempted to devise tests to decide what abilities or aptitudes would predict success in each of the types of aircrew training. They performed job analyses for each of the crew specialties, analyzing just what skills were necessary to carry out a particular duty. Tests were then constructed to measure the degree to which each cadet had the needed abilities. Each person who took the battery was given three scores, each of which was a predictor of success in one of three crew positions. The resulting final test scores were summarized as a single number ranging from one to nine. The score was called the Standard Nine score, contracted to the "stanine" still referred to in testing literature.

Psychologists were involved not only in aptitude testing but also in the design of training devices to shorten training time. The results of this work were significant man-machine studies resulting in early flight simulators to allow cadets to learn flight conditions without getting into the air.

San Antonio was not the only location of psychological involvement in the war effort. The Office of the Flight Surgeon of the Army Air Force Training Command in Fort Worth was responsible for developing tests on alertness, observation, and perceptual speed, much of it resulting in literature later called "vigilance" research.

Many young psychologists who were involved in this applied psychological research during the war went on to develop the fields of industrial and engineering psychology when they went back to their home institutions after the war.

During the Korean War the Air Force carried out another major research project, centered in Fort Worth and San Antonio. Perhaps the best known of these centers was the one directed by Arthur Melton at Randolph AFB, the Air Force Personnel Training and Research Center, lasting from 1951 through 1957. Melton had been involved in much of the pilot training research during World War II. As a result of this operation, many experimental and applied psychologists were employed during those years. Their work was devoted not only to military research but also to nonmilitary work, since many of the psychologists were involved in unclassified, traditional experimental work in learning and in sensory and motor research as well.

Other applied research facilities were established after World War II in Texas, often loosely connected with universities. One of the most significant to psychology was the Defense Research Laboratory at the University of Texas, presently called the Applied Research Laboratory. Founded after World War II and headed for many years by physicist Paul Boner, the Defense Research Laboratory provided research facilities and funding for generations of graduate students in psychology who were interested in the psychology of hearing. While research of a classified nature was often conducted by psychologists, most of the work funded through Navy programs was for basic research on the processes of hearing. Lloyd Jeffress was, until his retirement, director of the psychoacoustics division.

Another important facility was the Balcones Research Station, also established after World War II. Some of the research carried out there dealt with the effects of radiation on behavior. Also, some of the early research on space flight was conducted there, including work on Ham, the first monkey in space.

Another example of a somewhat more broadly based applied research operation was the Institute of Behavioral Research (IBR) founded in the 1960s in Fort Worth at Texas Christian University and directed until recently by Saul Sells. Operating on research contracts from various industrial and governmental sources, the IBR's psychological research ranged from drug abuse studies to measurements of human judgments.

In the 1960s, with the establishment of NASA, psychologists were deeply involved in all aspects of manned space flight training. The same kinds of training and aptitude measuring activities that were devised for pilots in World War II and Korea were expanded for the new frontier of space. Much of this research and application took place at NASA's Manned Spacecraft Center, which later became the Johnson Space Center, under the direction of Robert Voas. Many Texas colleges and universities shared in the research work, however. Through NASA grants, Malcom Arnolt at Texas Christian University, for instance, did a large number of perceptual studies involving the localization of objects such as space capsules in outer space.

Industry has become a primary employer of applied psychologists, particularly those with industrial/organizational (I/O) backgrounds. Personnel selection and personnel management specialists are currently in high demand in Texas corporations. These professionals are not only trained in psychology programs but also in departments of management. Psychologists with I/O specialties are found in management departments as often as they are in psychology departments, training those I/O psychologists at both the master and doctoral levels.

Professionalization

Psychology became professionalized in Texas in 1948 with the establishment of the Texas Psychological Association (TPA), a statewide organization for psychologists. The TPA was founded by a small group of psychologists, fewer than a hundred in number. The purpose of the organization was to encourage communication among the diverse psychologists and programs in Texas. Originally, the group was made up largely of experimental psychologists, but over the years the group has become more of an association of practitioner/psychologists, particularly clinical psychologists. It remains the primary statewide organization of psychologists. There are many local psychological organizations as well, typically oriented toward clinical and counseling psychology but in some cases being made up of industrial/organizational psychologists and human-factors psychologists.

Licensing laws were passed in Texas during the early 1970s establishing the Board of Examiners of Psychologists, which attempts to set standards for ethical practice and screening by examining individuals who want to identify themselves as practicing psychologists. Currently, licensing is used primarily for those setting up clinical and counseling practices.

Psychology still has much room for development in Texas institutions both inside and outside of the academic environment. Psychology programs have historically responded to the needs of the society they serve in Texas, and they will continue to do so.

Selected Bibliography

Dallenbach, Karl M. "The Psychological Laboratory of the University of Texas." *American Journal of Psychology*, vol. 66, 1953, 90–104.

Jeffress, Lloyd. "Psychology." *Discovery*, vol. 7, No. 3. Austin, 1983, 31–34.

Melton, Arthur W. "Military Psychology in the United States of America." *American Psychologist*, vol. 12, 1957, 740–746.

Reisman, John R. *A History of Clinical Psychology.* New York: John Wiley, 2nd ed., 1976.

19

Psychiatry

Alex D. Pokorny

SINCE RESEARCH IN psychiatry frequently overlaps with that done by psychologists, social scientists, neurologists, neuroscientists, pharmacologists, and others, this review will be confined to research done primarily by psychiatrists or with major participation by psychiatrists.[1]

Centers of Research

As one might expect, research in psychiatry has been centered in the medical schools, along with their affiliated hospitals, institutes, and clinical programs. Other areas of activity have included the state mental hospital system, the Veterans Administration Hospital in Waco, the Public Health Services Hospital for addictive disorders in Fort Worth, and the School of Aerospace Medicine in San Antonio.

At the end of World War II, there were only three medical schools in Texas (Galveston, Dallas, and Houston), so these were naturally the most active psychiatric research centers in the 1940s and 1950s. The University of Texas Medical Branch (UTMB) at Galveston was established in 1881 and accepted its first class in 1891. A Department of Neurology and Psychiatry was established there in 1926. Titus Harris was appointed chairman and remained in the post for thirty-six years, during which the school became a major center of training and clinical innovation. Harris founded and edited a national neuropsychiatric journal (*Diseases of the Nervous System*), and his department trained a large proportion of the psychiatrists who were in practice in Texas in the 1940s and 1950s. The principal hospitals affiliated with UTMB have been the John Sealy and St. Mary's hospitals. The University of Texas Medical Branch pioneered in the clinical trials of somatic therapies such as insulin coma therapy and electroconvulsive therapy. It also introduced to Texas the application of electroencephalography into studies of neuropsychiatric disorders. One of Harris's earliest papers, published in 1928, was on the toxic effects of bromides, reflecting his early interest in what would later become the field of psychopharmacology.[2]

Baylor College of Medicine began in 1900 in Dallas, as the University of Dallas Medical Department, and in 1903 allied itself with Baylor University. The medical school moved to Houston in 1943, and in 1969 it became an independent institution. Baylor Medical School has been closely affiliated with psychiatric programs at Jefferson Davis Hospital, the Houston Veterans Administration (VA) Hospital, The Method-

have been done by Neil Burch, using evoked potential techniques.[14]

Texas psychiatrists played a leading role in the introduction of the benzodiazepines into clinical medicine.[15] In a 1970 report, Irvin Cohen gave a history of the development of the first benzodiazepine, namely chlordiazepoxide, introduced in 1958. At that point, the drug had been given to only a few human subjects, geriatric patients, and appeared to be a simple sedative. Later, this compound was offered to Cohen in Houston and Harris in Galveston for broader clinical trials. The results were very encouraging, leading to a clinical note in the *Journal of the American Medical Association* (JAMA) on March 12, 1960, the first published announcement that this drug was therapeutically effective. At a meeting of investigators from across the country at the University of Texas Medical Branch in Galveston in November 1959, a number of clinical reports on chlordiazepoxide were given. Later this compound was released under the trade name "Librium." Cohen, Harris, and their associates thus played a key role in opening up this class of drugs for human use.

Another category of useful psychopharmacological agents is represented by the antimanic drug lithium. Some of the early U.S. trials were in Galveston. George Schlagenhauf, Joseph Tupin, and Robert White[16] reported on the use of lithium carbonate in the treatment of manic psychosis, in a paper read at the 1965 American Psychiatric Association annual meeting. In 1968, Tupin, Schlagenhauf, and Creson[17] published a report on lithium's effects on electrolyte excretion.

Among the earliest definitive clinical trials of lithium were the cooperative studies of the VA and the National Institute of Mental Health (NIMH). The Houston VA Medical Center played a prominent part in them. A. Pokorny was a member of the group which planned and supervised the studies. During this same period, investigators at TRIMS, led by J. Claghorn, did a series of investigations comparing lithium levels in plasma, red cells, and salivary secretions.

One of the pioneers in applications of psychopharmacology to child psychiatry practice was Irvin Kraft of Baylor College of Medicine and Texas Childrens' Hospital. In April 1968 Kraft published a description of the use of outpatient psychoactive drugs in the treatment of children. In subsequent years he and his associates published numerous clinical papers on the pharmacotherapy of children in the context of psychiatric aspects of general medical treatment.

The very useful psychopharmacological agents unfortunately have many side effects, some persistent and serious. William E. Fann, of the Baylor College of Medicine and the VA Hospital in Houston, has conducted a major research program for more than a decade on these phenomena, their etiology or mechanisms, their course, attempts at treatment, and more recently attempts to detect their onset in the earliest stages, before they become clinically evident.

Community and Administrative Psychiatry

The state mental hospital system has been a principal source of information about the epidemiology of mental illness in Texas. A succession of mental health commissioners or directors has issued regular reports summarizing this data in ways useful to researchers (as well as to planners and administrators). In addition, there have been a number of expert reviews of the state's public mental health system, usually done by outside consultants. Moreover, in-state advisory groups and panels, supported by the Hogg Foundation and other private groups, have periodically reviewed the state's programs and have made recommendations.

The development of truly effective psychopharmacological agents in the 1950s made it possible to release patients who would otherwise have remained chronically hospitalized. This coincided with trends that had been underway since World War II to decentralize psychiatric treatment, to "open up" mental hospitals, and to develop innovative alternatives to hospitalization. This national "movement" was clearly felt in Texas, and was reflected in the establishment of an Office of Mental Health Planning within the state government, under the leadership of Spencer Bayles and later Moody Bettis. After a year of planning by a large group of the state's psychiatric and mental health leaders, a report, or "Texas Plan," was produced, one of the consequences of which was the passage of HB 3, creating the new Texas Department of Mental Health and Mental Retardation in 1965. The first Commissioner of Mental Health and Mental Retardation, Shervert H. Frazier, Jr., was appointed on December 1, 1965.

One of Frazier's first concerns was to assess the existing resident patient body in the state's public mental hospitals, more than 15,000 patients. From the standpoint of the newer thinking about community care, least restrictive alternatives, and so forth, what was the status of this very large group of resident patients? The existing reporting channels provided good information about patients being admitted and released but less about continuing patients. To remedy this, Frazier obtained grant funding for and led in the execution of what must have been one of the largest cross-sectional, descriptive, and correlative studies in the history of psychiatry, the 1966 "Administrative Survey of Texas State Mental Hospitals." The study was designed by Frazier, Robert Stubblefield, Bettis, Pokorny, and Louis DeMoll from Texas and by Morton Kramer, Earl Pollock, and Carl Taube from the NIMH in Washington. The survey essentially consisted of three parts:

1. A new and current census of all patients, with verification of all demographic and administrative data, plus an individual assessment of the nursing needs and characteristics of all 15,284 patients resident on July 1, 1966.

2. An intensive examination of a 10 percent sample of this patient group (1,537 patients), which included a review of the case record, a psychiatric examination, a physical examination, psychological testing, social worker interview, contact with family members, a battery of laboratory and X-ray tests, and a neurological examination if indicated. These examinations were all performed by teams of examiners brought in from the state's medical schools and larger cities, and required a massive logistical operation.

3. An individual review, assessment, and integration of data on each patient in the 10 percent sample.

This survey resulted in a series of reports[18] and research publications. Many of the findings and recommendations became incorporated into subsequent changes and practices in the state's mental health system, particularly the development of a system of community mental health centers and various alternatives to hospitalization. It may, however, have contributed to the problem of deinstitutionalization, in that centralized hospital facilities have been reduced without corresponding increase in capacity and diversity of local treatment programs.

In Galveston, Tupin and John Overall did a major project in John Sealy Hospital, exploring the value and uses of careful documentation of clinical practice in a natural treatment setting. This evolved into a clinical monitoring program applicable to hospital patients; this work is being continued by Overall, Faillace, and associates at the UT Medical School in Houston. The Galveston data base was also used in epidemiological studies.

A group of Beaumont psychiatrists, led by Winston Cochran, reported on a successful development of a community mental health center built around a private practice. They began by contracting to provide care for medically indigent in the county. They then expanded through contracts with the Texas Department of Mental Health and Mental Retardation, and the operation grew to include an inpatient facility and programs in two catchment areas. Cochran and his group studied the effects of this system on admissions to state hospitals, the effects on the private patients of the group (who were intermingled with the others), and the effects on the practice volume of the participating psychiatrists. In all these respects this proved to be a very satisfactory model.

Other studies in the community psychiatry area have come from the Baylor group. George Adams and associates have published a series of studies on quality-of-care evaluation in psychiatry. A. Pokorny and associates published a paper on prediction of chronicity in mental patients, based on a five-year follow-up of the patients examined in the 1966 Administrative Survey of Texas State Mental Hospitals. Pedro Ruiz published a description of the role of folk healers in community mental health services.

Members of the faculty of the University of Texas Medical School at San Antonio, including Robert Leon and Cervando Martinez, have published a series of studies on Mexican-American folk medicine, special cultural influences, and the effects of ethnicity on psychiatric disorder, its course, and its management. Martinez is continuing studies of hallucinations in bilinguals.

Suicide and Self-Destructive Behavior

This important area of human behavior, which is largely symptomatic of psychiatric disorder, has been the topic of considerable study by Texas investigators. One of those most active has been the author of this review, A. Pokorny, who with numerous associates, particularly his sociologist colleague, Howard Kaplan, has done a series of studies on suicide during the past twenty-five years. They have used as subjects primarily the psychiatric patients of the Houston VA Hospital; in other studies they have used the population of the City of Houston, the entire State of Texas, or other identified groups. Among them a series of studies on patients is included, which could be described as clinical epidemiology, aimed at case identification or prediction and (ultimately) prevention. They have also done a series of studies, with uniformly negative results, on alleged external influences on suicide and related behaviors, looking at such purported influences as weather, moon phases, sunspots, and numerous similar factors which keep cropping up in the literature. They have also studied the factors associated with suicide following psychiatric hospitalization, focusing on the interaction between defenselessness and adverse life events. A major publication[19] from this program has been a report on a five-year follow-up of a group of 4,800 consecutively admitted psychiatric patients; while numerous positive relationships were found or confirmed, it was concluded that these did not make it possible to identify the particular individuals who would commit suicide, largely because this is a relatively rare behavior even in this high-risk group.

Betsy Comstock, of Baylor College of Medicine, has studied suicidal behavior in another aspect, focusing on attempted suicide, particularly as encountered in an emergency-room setting. This study has overlapped with Comstock's other studies on drug abuse and drug overdose and on psychiatric emergencies and crises in general. Comstock and associates have also published results of clinical studies of group psychotherapy as a treatment technique for those who attempt suicide.

In San Antonio, Martin Giffen with his associates, Alvin Burstein and Russell Adams, did a study comparing how well psychiatry trainees compared to psychology trainees in their ability to judge suicide risk correctly.

Alcoholism and Drug Abuse

Among the earliest research studies in this topic area were two by Warren Brown and Jackson Smith of Baylor University College of Medicine. In 1952 these two psychiatrists reported a study of the physiological effects of the anti-alcohol drug disulfiram (Antabuse), using dogs as subjects. In the same year, Smith and Brown reported on the results of a treatment trial in a series of patients with alcoholism, using adrenocortical extract and pantothenic acid.

The staff of the United States Public Health Service (USPHS) Hospital in Fort Worth reported on a series of clinical investigations during the 1950s and 1960s. W. P. Jurgensen published a paper on problems of inpatient treatment of addiction. James Fred Maddux published a general description of treatment of narcotic addiction and related issues and problems in a book by Saul Sells[20] on rehabilitation of the narcotic addict. Maddux and associates also presented the results of a prerelease program for narcotic addicts. Later Maddux, Berliner, and Bates published a book describing

their trials of engaging opioid addicts in a continuum of services.

After moving to the University of Texas Medical School in San Antonio, Maddux continued his studies in which he followed the life course of opioid addicts. The principal findings of this study were published as a book in 1981.[21] Maddux and David Desmond have also published papers on a comparison of the childhood and adult life experiences of fifty heroin addicts with those of their nonaddicted brothers. An important finding was that addicts showed early deviant behavior, preceding heroin use, in contrast to the socially conforming behavior of the brothers. Desmond and Maddux[22] have also published a study of Mexican-American heroin addicts, stressing that next to blacks Mexican-Americans are the largest ethnic minority group among the visible opioid addict population in the U.S.A. Although these are frequently grouped with others under the title "Hispanic," the authors consider that Mexican-Americans have a unique culture and ethnic history, and they present supporting data from studies of Mexican-American opioid users in San Antonio. In another paper Desmond and Maddux report on the place of religion as a factor in recovery from chronic opioid dependency; it appears that programs of the Pentecostal type may be particularly effective among Hispanic drug users. They report on their own observations of religious program participation among 248 San Antonio addicts, 87 percent of whom were Mexican-American; affiliation with a religious group appeared to lead to a marked increase in abstinence. Maddux and Desmond also studied the effect of resident relocation on opioid drug use. They found that the frequency of one-year abstinence after relocation was nearly three times greater than at other times (17 percent versus 6 percent). They consider possible explanations to be drug availability, conditioned abstinence, and peer modeling.

The group of investigators at the Texas Research Institute of Mental Sciences has placed particular stress on studies of drug abuse and dependency. Among the early studies were many on LSD and the various "psychedelic" or hallucinogenic drugs. Louis Fabre and associates[23] did a series of basic studies on metabolic effects of alcohol. Schoolar and his associates did early work on the addictive properties of the drugs Darvon and Talwin. The TRIMS group also did extensive clinical studies with methadone in the treatment of opiate addiction.

The Houston VA began clinical trials of treating drug abuse patients with methadone and group therapy in 1970. In January 1971 the VA established substance-abuse treatment programs for inpatients at five hospitals (Houston, Sepulveda, Battle Creek, New York City, and New Orleans). The Houston program has been the site of numerous clinical studies.

The Medical School at Texas Tech has stressed teaching and clinical investigations on alcoholism since it opened in the early 1970s. George S. Tyner was one of the innovators in this, along with Robert Barnes and Dan Croy. The Department established facilities for alcoholism treatment and drug abuse treatment, and they have remained strong features of the department since. Texas Tech has also put on a series of annual continuing-education meetings on research and practice in the area of alcoholism, some of which have resulted in publications in book form.[24]

At the Houston VA Hospital, Pokorny and his associates did a series of follow-up and outcome studies in patients treated for alcoholism. This included comparisons of results of different or contrasting treatment programs, and comparison of the future adjustments of dropouts, with those who had completed treatment programs. He and associates also did several studies of rating scales and diagnostic criteria for alcoholism, studying particularly the differences between self-acknowledged alcoholics and those who were denying their alcoholism.[25] They also published studies on stages in the development of alcoholism.[26]

At Baylor College of Medicine, Charalampous published studies evaluating the usefulness of alcoholism counselors as compared to traditional therapists. He also published results of court-directed treatment and/or educational programs with driving-while-intoxicated offenders. Betsy Comstock reported on a medical evaluation of a series of inhalant abusers. Norman Decker, W. Fann, and their associates[27] published a survey of the incidence of alcoholism in a general hospital population. Martin Keeler published a controlled study[28] on the effects of disulfiram. David Kay and associates published results[29] of investigations into how much of the antisocial behavior associated with drug abuse was primary and how much was secondary.

Psychosocial Research

One of the nation's leading investigators into eating disorders, Hilde Bruch, moved to Baylor College of Medicine in Houston in 1964 and continued her investigations and publications until her death in 1984.

Her studies centered first on obesity and later on anorexia nervosa, and she continued her clinical investigations into these areas throughout her stay at Baylor. Bruch received a great many awards and recognitions, including the prestigious Joseph B. Goldberger Award in Clinical Nutrition of the American Medical Association in 1981. She also became a pioneer in the study of families while working with obese children. Later she continued and extended this approach to her work with patients having anorexia nervosa.

At the Scott & White Hospital in Temple, Harry Wilmer, Robert Rynearson, and their associates conducted investigations into the usefulness of videotaping in psychotherapy and in psychiatric education.[30]

High-quality research of national significance has been characteristic of the School of Aerospace Medicine in San Antonio. This group has done extensive basic work on the stressful, emotional, and adaptational aspects of flying and space flight. A long series of psychiatrists has participated in these research studies, including Don Flinn, Carlos Perry, John Mebane, Charles Sarnoff, Terry McGuire, James Boydstun, William Sledge, Richard Levy, Robert Brusano, Royden Marsh, and David Jones.[31] Many of the early studies are summarized in a 1967 book, *Psychiatry in Aerospace Medicine.*[32] Studies on astronauts began at the School of Aviation Medicine in the 1950s, years before Sputnik and the first manned flight. These initial studies were aimed at determining the effects of isolation, confinement, fatigue, and altered work-rest cycles on proficiency and interpersonal communication.[33] Other prominent research areas of this group have included airsickness and fear of flying (as a newly developed symptom). It is of interest that in preparation for the early manned space flights there was great concern about the stressful effects, but with increased experience these concerns have waned. More recent work has focused on responses of former prisoners of war, on the mechanisms and prevention of syncope, on the emotional aspects of disasters, and on relationships of mitral valve prolapse to development of panic attacks.[34]

At the University of Texas Medical Branch in Galveston, a new type of brief, intensive psychotherapy called multiple impact therapy, for families with disturbed adolescents, was developed. It was described in 1964 by Robert MacGregor (psychologist); Agnes M. Ritchie (social worker); Franklin P. Schuster, Jr., Albert C. Serrano, and Eugene C. McDanald, Jr. (psychiatrists); and Harold Goolishian (psychologist).[35] This interdisciplinary achievement had significant impact on psychiatric practice nationally; many features have been incorporated into the rapidly-growing field of family therapy. Other features have been adapted to "marathon" therapy sessions or to the general area of brief psychotherapy.

Robert Leon of the UT Southwestern Medical School in Dallas, with his associate Harry Martin, did a number of field studies on mental health, adjustment, and problems of American Indians. They later extended these studies to Alaskan natives.

Robert Rose came to the UT Medical Branch in Galveston as Chairman of the Department of Psychiatry in 1977. Here he continued his studies of one group of subjects working under high stress, namely air-traffic controllers.

At Baylor College of Medicine, James Lomax did a study comparing the differential utility of two different types of human relations training laboratories for a group of psychiatric residents.

One of the most productive research groups in the psychosocial area has been the group of investigators associated with the Timberlawn Foundation in Dallas. This has been well presented in a series of books from this group. In a 1976 book,[36] *No Single Thread: Psychological Help in Family Systems*, Jerry M. Lewis, W. Robert Beavers, John Gossett, and Virginia Phillips presented the results of a long-term study of the functioning of healthy families. They developed a concept of family systems as an outgrowth of general systems theory. They sought to identify the qualities which produced capable adaptive and healthy families. The authors introduced family system rating scales, including scales for characteristics such as structure, coalition, and closeness.

In 1978 Lewis described his methods of teaching psychotherapy.[37] His program involves educational research, the systematic exploration of different and presumably more effective and more efficient techniques to teach this intricate and complex skill.

Recently Gossett, Lewis, and F. David Barnhart have written on the outcome of hospital treatment of disturbed adolescents.[38] It is the final report of the Timberlawn Adolescent Treatment Assessment Project, a long-term follow-up study of disturbed adolescents after completion of hospital treatment. It presents a model for multivariate prediction of treatment outcome.

A study of well-functioning, working-class black families by Lewis and John Looney[39] repeated their earlier comparative study of normal families with another group of normal families, in a very different economic and social context, namely working-class black families in the inner city. The authors present a detailed comparison of the findings from these families with the findings from the earlier study.

Geriatric Psychiatry

Research in this area has been relatively delayed in starting, but this situation has now changed, as will be described later in the section on "Biologic Basis of Psychiatric Disorders."

One of the pioneer researchers in this area has been C. Gaitz, primarily associated with the Texas Research Institute for Mental Sciences in Houston, but also a participant in numerous other educational, research, and service organizations and institutions in the state (and nation). Gaitz and his associates have published numerous studies on the psychological aspects of aging, the role of social supports, the effects of disability, retirement, and others. They have also published pharmacological studies, such as one on the effectiveness of Hydergine in the treatment of dementia.

W. Fann has published numerous papers and a book on the differences and special features of pharmacological treatment with aging patients, with special emphasis on psychopharmacology.

Sleep Disorders

Several laboratories and centers have conducted studies of sleep physiology and sleep disorders since this field came into prominence in the 1950s: among the early psychiatrists active in this were N. Burch and Robert Roessler at TRIMS, Kenneth Gaarder and Augustin de la Pena at San Antonio, and Harold Roffwarg, who is now at the UT Medical School at Dallas.

The Baylor Sleep Disorders Center was established relatively late, in 1972, when the core group of researchers moved to Houston from Florida. It is now the largest sleep laboratory in the world.[40] This laboratory has made numerous and varied contributions, including the establishment of norms for various population groups and subgroups as a result of the very large number of records available in the laboratory. Major areas of focus have included sex disorders, sleep patterns as diagnostic tools in study of depression, sleep apnea and its treatment, including studies of respiratory physiology, and male sex physiology and dysfunction (initially related to work on evaluation of subjects for penile prosthesis implantation). The Center has broadened these studies into male sex physiology in general, including anatomy, physiology, endocrinology, psychology, and other aspects; more recently, the Center has begun similar studies of female sexual physiology.

The Center has also done numerous pharmacologic studies centered on side effects of drugs, notably sleep impairment, sleep disturbances, and sex dysfunction secondary to medications. The laboratory has also done major technical work on instrumentation and automated analysis.

More recent publications from this group have included diagnostic advances in impotence, various aspects of male sex physiology, and the etiology and mechanisms of impotence. Ismet Karacan, Betsy Comstock, and their associates have reported on disturbed sleep patterns during withdrawal from sedative drugs. Karacan and Robert Williams published a book reviewing sleep disorders, their diagnosis, and their treatment.[41] Karacan and Keeler reported on the effects of disulfiram on sleep patterns of alcoholics. Karacan and his associates from Endocrinology published a study on the relationship between Servin testosterone and prolactin levels in nocturnal penile tumescence.

Psychophysiology

During the late 1950s, William T. Lhamon and Sanford Goldstone at Baylor did a series of studies on the perception of time,[42] relating this to many physiological variables, fatigue, psychiatric diagnosis and severity of symptoms, and effects of medications.

In 1959, J. Shawver and associates from the Waco VA Hospital published a study reporting EKG findings and the prevalence of medical disorders in psychiatric hospital patients.

A similar but much more complete and elaborate study of this type was done in the 1970s by Richard Hall while he was affiliated with the UT Medical School in Houston and TRIMS.

In the late 1950s N. Burch, Ted Greiner, and a group of associates at Baylor and what was then the Houston State Psychiatric Institute did a large series of interrelated psychophysiological studies, including automated analyses of the electroencephalogram, studies of the galvanic skin responses, and later studies on evoked brain potentials. Burch began this work in 1953 while with the Air Force, with one of the early developments being a system for automatic analysis of the electroencephalogram. A practical problem

which this group addressed was measuring the state of consciousness of an individual, and also differentiating between effects of stress and fatigue (as in long-range flight). Greiner was studying possible pharmacological reversal in these states. This entire research team moved to Baylor College of Medicine and the Houston State Psychiatric Institute in 1956, where these studies were continued and expanded. Burch and his group later continued this work in relation to effects of therapeutic drugs, hallucinogens, and cocaine.

Psychophysiological studies have been prominent in the work at the UT Medical School in San Antonio. Gaarder has been one of the primary investigators.

At Baylor, Roessler and associates continued psychophysiological studies. One of these was on voice parameters as an indicator of affect during psychotherapy. Roessler and his group also studied relationships of physiological measures to emotional state.

At TRIMS, Claghorn, Roy Mathew, and their associates did a series of studies of catecholamines in relation to cerebral blood flow. Mathew later extended these studies of cerebral blood flow to numerous other psychiatric disorders and manifestations.

Since 1977 R. Rose and his associates at the UT Medical Branch in Galveston have continued their studies of air traffic controllers, which include as a prominent component studies of psychophysiological changes in persons undergoing stress.

Biologic Basis of Psychiatric Disorders

The development of effective psychopharmacological treatment in the 1950s initiated a shift in research focus of psychiatry toward the biological, and this trend has continued. The early focus was on efficacy of drugs, but rather quickly concern shifted to side effects and toxicity, and then to possible mechanisms of action. This has led to greatly increased collaboration with scientists from related basic and clinical sciences. It has also led to a renewed emphasis on exact description, identification, and classification of psychiatric disorders. As a result, it is no longer easy to separate much of recent psychiatric research into "psychophysiology," "psychopharmacology," "sleep disorders," etc., as attempted heretofore. Therefore, the broad heading of "biologic basis of psychiatric disorders" has been chosen to describe some of these more recent complex research programs.

As an example, at the UT Medical School in Houston there is an ongoing project on dementia of the

Alzheimer type being conducted by Suha Beller, Alan Swann, John Overall, and their associates.[43] The focus is on treatment of the memory impairment in this common form of dementia, using placebo and three-dose levels of physostigmine in a complex crossover design. The results are encouraging in that response parallels the dose levels. Other medications are also being studied, with the focus on longer-acting compounds. A project of this type involves not only psychiatry but numerous other disciplines.

The UT Medical School in San Antonio is one of seven institutions from across the country which are working with the National Institute of Mental Health as members of the NIMH-Clinical Research Branch Collaborative Program on the Psychobiology of Depression. James Maas of San Antonio is the chairman of this entire project, and Charles Bowden is the head of the San Antonio unit.[44] The group has gathered a vast amount of psychosocial and biological data on a large number of patients with affective disorders, and conducted many complex laboratory studies. This body of data, almost certainly unmatched anywhere else in the world, has already led to many significant publications.[45]

This major continuing project has stimulated numerous other related research projects at the San Antonio Center, by these and other investigators. One example is a project on biological markers for emotionally disturbed children being conducted by Graham Rogeness.

At the UT Medical Branch in Galveston, R. Rose and associates have developed a broad program of biological and psychosocial psychiatric research.[46] To follow up their opening of the newly built Mary Moody Northen Psychiatry Pavilion in 1983, members of the department are just completing a new Clinical Research Center scheduled to open for patients in January 1986. Rose is continuing his studies on the psychophysiology of stress, using as subjects air traffic controllers; this includes studies of endocrine activity in various situations. The laboratory also studies the endocrinology of stress generally, including endocrine influences on aggressive behavior. There is extensive collaboration with other disciplines, particularly in a major study of monoamineoxidase distribution patterns in the brain. Marco Amadeo is conducting studies of depression in aging, focusing on the relationship to lateralized brain decline with aging. Jordan Finkelstein is conducting studies of the physical, hormonal, physiological, and behavioral changes during adolescence.

An outstanding example of a broadly based biolog-

ical approach to mental illness is the program that has been developed at the UT Medical School in Dallas, under the leadership of Kenneth Altshuler. A major component is a study of cholinergic dysfunction in affective disorders by A. John Rush, Carl Fulton, and H. Roffwarg. Major research is being done on sleep abnormalities in those at risk for depression. There is another on the psychobiological assessment of unipolar depression, and still another, with numerous collaborators, on regional brain activity in schizophrenia. Other ongoing areas of research include EEG and xenon scan studies in normal persons and in patients with epilepsy; xenon brain-flow studies in affective illness, schizophrenia, and in stroke and vascular disease; sleep laboratory studies in affective disorders and bulimia; sleep laboratory studies of regional activation of cortex and REM sleep; and three-dimensional computer reconstruction of human brain regions. To conduct this research program, the department has recruited specialists in affective disorders; sleep disorders; the role of endorphins and enkephalins in pain, mental illness, schizophrenia, and related disorders; and specialists in cognitive therapy. Rush directs an Affective Disorders unit. Recently a new psychiatric laboratory has been installed at the affiliated Dallas Veterans Administration Center.[47]

Looking back at the period since World War II, Texas investigators in psychiatry have a great deal to be proud of. They have made several significant and pioneering contributions to psychopharmacology. They have produced outstanding research in many other areas, including alcoholism and substance abuse, family interactions, sleep physiology, and psychophysiology. As research in this field has become increasingly biological and much more complex, centers have been developed which remain at the forefront of psychiatric research.

Notes

1. Space limitations make it necessary for this review to be selective, and inevitably my personal contacts and experiences will influence my decisions on what may have been the most significant contributions. However, I have lived and worked in Texas in 1946–47 and continuously since 1949, and I have known personally most of those persons active in psychiatric research since then; I hope that these factors will make me somewhat more objective.

2. Personal communication, E. Ahmed Zein-Eldin, 1985.

3. Personal communication, Perry Talkington, 1985.

4. The research division in Lexington was the Addiction Research Center.

5. Personal communication, David Jones, 1985.

6. Personal communication, Patricia Santy, 1985.

7. Kinross-Wright, 1954.

8. Kinross-Wright, 1955.

9. Moyer, Kinross-Wright, and Finney, 1955.

10. Kinross-Wright and Charalampous, 1963a.

11. Gottlieb, Kline, Lhamon, et al., 1955.

12. Veterans Administration, 1975.

13. Kinross-Wright and Charalampous, 1963b.

14. Personal communication, Joseph Schoolar, 1985.

15. Cohen, 1970.

16. Schlagenhauf, Tupin, and White, 1966.

17. Tupin, Schlagenhauf, and Creson 1968.

18. Pokorny and Frazier, 1967.

19. Pokorny, 1983.

20. Sells, 1966.

21. Maddux and Desmond, 1981.

22. Desmond and Maddux, 1984.

23. Fabre, Farmer, and Davis, 1970.

24. Messiha and Tyner, 1980.

25. Kaplan, Pokorny, Kanas, et al., 1974.

26. Pokorny, Kanas, and Overall, 1981.

27. Decker, Fann, Girardin, et al., 1979.

28. Keeler, 1979.

29. Kay, 1980.

30. Personal communication, Robert Rynearson, 1985.

31. Personal communication, D. Jones, 1985.

32. Perry, 1967.

33. Personal communication, Don Flinn, 1985.

34. Personal communication, D. Jones, 1985.

35. MacGregor, Ritchie, Serrano, et al., 1964.

36. Lewis, Beavers, Gossett, et al., 1976.

37. Lewis, 1978.

38. Gossett, Lewis, and Barnhart, 1983.

39. Lewis and Looney, 1983.

40. Personal communication, Robert L. Williams, 1985.

41. Williams and Karacan, 1978.

42. Lhamon and Goldstone, 1956.

43. Personal communication, John Overall, 1985.

44. Personal communication, Robert Leon, 1985.

45. Koslow, Maas, Bowden, et al., 1983.

46. Personal communication, Robert Rose, 1985.

47. Personal communication, Kenneth Altshuler, 1985.

Bibliography

Cohen, I. 1970. Benzodiazpines. Chapter 10, pp. 130–140. In Ayd, F., and Blackwell, B., eds. *Discoveries in Biological Psychiatry.* Philadelphia: Lippincott.

Decker, N., Fann, W., Girardin, P., Miller, D., and Kanas, T. 1979. Alcoholism in a general hospital population. *Currents in Alcoholism* 6:33–39.

Desmond, D. P., and Maddux, J. F. 1984. Mexican-American heroin addicts. *Am. J. Drug Alcohol Abuse* 10:317–346.

Fabre, L. F., Farmer, R. W., Davis, H. W. 1970. Effect of ethanol on adrenocortical steroid secretion. In *Advances in Mental Science III, Biological Aspects of Alcohol*, Roack, M. K., McIsaac, W. M., and Creaven, P. J., eds. Austin: University of Texas Press.

Gossett, J., Lewis, J., and Barnhart, F. 1983. *To Find a Way: The Outcome of Hospital Treatment of Disturbed Adolescents.* New York: Brunner/Mazel.

Gottlieb, J., Kline, N., Lhamon, W., Moll, A., Himwich, H., and Saslow, G. 1955. *Psychiatric Research Reports I: Pharmacologic Products Recently Introduced in the Treatment of Psychiatric Disorders.* Washington: American Psychiatric Association.

Kaplan, H., Pokorny, A., Kanas, T., and Lively, G. 1974. Screening tests and self-identification in the detection of alcoholism. *J. Health Soc. Behav.* 15:51–56.

Kay, D. 1980. The Search for Psychopathic States in Alcoholism and Drug Abusers. In Fann, W., Karacan, I., Pokorny, A., and Williams, R., eds. *Phenomenology and Treatment of Alcoholism.* New York: Spectrum.

Keeler, M. 1979. Controlled study of disulfiram effects. *Alcoholism, Clinical and Experimental Research* 3:182, 1979.

Kinross-Wright, V. 1954. Chlorpromazine—A major advance in psychiatric treatment. *Postgraduate Medicine* 16:297–299.

Kinross-Wright, V. 1955. Chlorpromazine treatment of mental disorders. *Am. J. Psychiat.* 111:907–912.

Kinross-Wright, V., and Charalampous, K. 1963a. A psychopharmacology research unit. *Diseases of the Nervous System* 24:229–231.

Kinross-Wright, V., Vogt, A., and Charalampous, K. 1963b. A new method of drug therapy. *Am. J. Psychiat.* 119:779–780.

Koslow, S., Maas, J., Bowden, C., Davis, J., Hanin, I.,

and Javaid, J. 1983. CSF and urinary biogenic amines and metabolites in depression and mania. *Arch. Gen. Psychiatry* 40:999–1010.

Lewis, J. 1978. *To Be a Therapist.* New York: Brunner/Mazel.

Lewis, J., Beavers, W., Gossett, J., and Phillips, V. 1976. *No Single Thread: Psychological Health in Family Systems.* New York: Brunner/Mazel.

Lewis, J. and Looney, J. 1983. *The Long Struggle: Well-Functioning Working-Class Black Families.* New York: Brunner/Mazel.

Lhamon, W. and Goldstone, S. 1956. The time sense: estimation of one second durations by schizophrenic patients. AMA *Archives of Neurology and Psychiatry* 76:625–629.

MacGregor, R., Ritchie, A., Serrano, A., Schuster, F., McDanald, E., and Goolishian, H. 1964. *Multiple Impact Therapy With Families.* New York: McGraw-Hill.

Maddux, J. F., and Desmond, D. P. 1981. *Careers of Opioid Users.* New York: Praeger.

Messiha, F., and Tyner, G., eds. 1980. *Alcoholism: A Perspective.* Westbury, NY: PJD Publications, Ltd.

Moyer, J., Kinross-Wright, V., and Finney, R. 1955. Chlorpromazine as a therapeutic agent in clinical medicine. *Arch. Int. Med.* 95:202–218.

Perry, C., ed. 1967. *Psychiatry in Aerospace Medicine.* Boston: Little Brown.

Pokorny, A. 1983. Prediction of suicide in psychiatric patients. *Arch. Gen. Psychiatry* 40:249–257.

Pokorny, A., Kanas, T., Overall, J. 1981. Order of appearance of alcoholic symptoms. *Alcoholism: Clinical and Experimental Research* 5:216–220.

Pokorny, A., and Frazier, S. 1967. *Report of the Administrative Survey of Texas State Mental Hospitals 1966.* Austin: Texas Department of Mental Health and Mental Retardation.

Schlagenhauf, G., Tupin, J., and White, R. 1966. The use of lithium carbonate in the treatment of manic psychosis. *Am. J. Psychiatry* 123:201–207.

Sells, H., ed. 1966. *Rehabilitating the Narcotic Addict.* Washington, DC: U.S. Department of Health, Education and Welfare.

Tupin, J., Schlagenhauf, G., and Creson, D. 1968. Lithium effects on electrolyte excretion. *Am. J. Psychiatry* 125:536–543.

Veterans Administration. 1975. *Cooperative Studies in Mental Health and Behavioral Sciences,* 1B 11-49, Department of Medicine and Surgery. Washington, D.C.: Veterans Administration.

Williams, R., and Karacan, I. 1978. *Sleep Disorders: Diagnosis and Treatment.* New York: John Wiley & Sons.

20

Scientific Foundations, Societies, and Museums

Sylvia W. McGrath

DURING THE ERA of the American Revolution, when Americans severed political ties with England, American scientist-philosophers lost the support of the major institution encouraging colonial science, The Royal Society of London. The level of political and cultural maturity which helped shape the revolution also permitted Americans to create the first successful intercolonial scientific society, the American Philosophical Society. In the two centuries that followed, as American science became increasingly complex and professionalized, Americans interested in science created new institutions to encourage the advancement and the dissemination of scientific knowledge. Texans played a part in that process.

By the 1980s scientists working in Texas had received support from many varied institutions. Texas universities often provided facilities and the environment necessary for research, but other institutions also played a role in stimulating scientific research and development in Texas. Many such institutions were national in scope, but some Texas organizations, often in cooperation with universities, played significant roles in funding and encouraging research and in disseminating the results of that research. The number of Texas institutions supporting science increased significantly in the post-World War II period, but as early as the 1800s some Texans promoted institutions which sponsored scientific research and/or played important roles in educating other Texans about science.

As in many other frontier areas or new states, the earliest scientific studies in Texas concerned the natural resources of the area; scientists both in and outside of Texas sought support for such studies. Explorers working for the Spanish, Mexican, or American governments or sponsored by European patrons or societies made most of the early natural history and geological studies in Texas. In the colonial and republic years most Texans were preoccupied with survival, not with seeking support for science. However, when Texas became a state, those interested in scientific exploration worked to secure and eventually received state government help.[1]

Early in the 1800s East Coast states set a pattern of using state-sponsored geological and natural history surveys to locate, map, and prepare for exploitation of the states' natural resources. Individuals interested in scientific study could often convince legislatures to fund exploratory surveys by emphasizing the economic benefits of such surveys. Those surveys were usually the first state institutions to sponsor science, and many became permanent or semipermanent state organizations. In Texas that process occurred after mid-century.

In 1851 Governor Peter Bell tried to convince the legislature to fund a state survey to identify precious minerals, aid farmers, and increase the value of state lands. He failed, but in 1858, following an 1856 drought, the legislature authorized a survey, headed by B. F. Schumard, who became the first state geologist of Texas, to locate artesian wells in South Texas as well as conduct general geological studies. The Civil War ended funding for that survey, but from 1870 to 1875 J. W. Glenn and Samuel Botsford Buckley ran a second state survey. Then in 1888 chemist Edwin T. Dumble became state geologist heading a third survey funded as part of a land-reform program because legislators recognized the need for major reclassification of state lands. Funding for the Dumble Survey ended in 1896, in part because of economic depression and in part because East Texans saw little value in studying West Texas soil and water problems. In 1901 the legislature funded a new organization, the University Mineral Survey, to evaluate the mineral potential of state lands. That project continued until 1905, and in 1909 the state created the Bureau of Economic Geology as an organized research branch of the University of Texas charged with investigating Texas geology and mineral resources. In 1986 that bureau, a part of University of Texas at Austin, still functioned as the state geological survey providing information for Texans about Texas minerals.[2] Thus, Texas acquired a permanent state-sponsored scientific organization.

In the late nineteenth and early twentieth centuries, Texas also established other permanent research institutions, usually connected with state universities. In 1888 the state took a major step toward helping Texas farmers by creating the Texas Agricultural Experiment Station System at College Station as part of the Agricultural and Mechanical College of Texas. In 1915 the legislature created the position of state forester, which led to the development of the Texas Forest Service as a part of the Texas A&M University system. Thus, the state of Texas moved toward supporting science through state agencies if that support would bring practical benefits to state citizens. In the twentieth century the legislature created other state scientific agencies, many concerned with the natural resources of wildlife, land, water, and forests. By the 1980s the state supported science through several state universities and many specialized state agencies. Meanwhile, scientists in Texas had found additional means of support, especially for studies state officials did not consider immediately practical.

Foundations

In the late 1800s those who had made fortunes through industry began to use some of their wealth for philanthropic purposes. Ingenious scientists convinced some industrialists to perpetuate their names through the support of science; in the early twentieth century patterns and directions for new institutions, the philanthropic research foundations, became clear. Foundations began to support their own subagencies and departments, universities, independent research laboratories, and individual scholars. Most foundations were national in scope, but some concentrated on programs within the home states of the founders.[3]

Texas fortunes, often built on the discovery and exploitation of petroleum resources, permitted the creation of Texas foundations. By the mid-1980s there were more than two hundred major Texas foundations with endowments of one million dollars or more and/or providing annual grants of $100,000 or more. Yet, with the exception of medicine, only a few included in their purposes specific support for scientific research. Texas had become a leader in medical research, and many Texas foundations reflected that fact. More than one hundred major foundations provided support for hospitals, mostly in the local area. Around thirty of the large foundations granted funds for medical research with some specifying particular areas such as cancer research, heart disease, human growth, ophthalmology, or allergies. Some promoted health in general, and at least one sponsored a health camp.[4]

Small foundations also emphasized medical care and medical research. By the late 1970s there were over one thousand foundations in Texas with assets of $20,000 and/or making grants of $1,000. Of those, almost four hundred gave some support to medical research, not necessarily in Texas, and almost three hundred provided some help to hospitals and health care centers. At least twenty-four provided support either only or primarily for medical uses, including hospitals. Several emphasized cancer research, others heart disease.[5]

Most of the major foundations supporting medical research were organized in the two decades after World War II. However, the M. D. Anderson Foundation, built on the fortune of Monroe Dunaway Anderson, was established in 1936. Anderson, a Tennessee banker, moved first to Oklahoma and then to Texas in the early 1900s. With his brothers he created a profitable cotton business, opening a Houston headquarters in 1916. He gave much of his fortune to the University of Texas for cancer research. Anderson's goals also included promoting health, science, and education. Trustees used some of the funds he provided to establish the Texas Medical Center in Houston, and the foundation continued to help fund that center and related projects primarily in the Houston area.

Thomas Baker Slick, who earned a premedical biology degree from Yale in 1938 and made a fortune in oil, land, mineral, and cattle enterprises, provided funds and direction for another major foundation, established in the 1940s in San Antonio. He planned and financed the creation of the Southwest Research Center consisting of the Southwest Foundation for Research and Education which emphasized biomedical research, and the Southwest Research Institute for basic and applied research in engineering and physical sciences.

Another Texas oil millionaire, less formally educated than Slick, who also created a foundation to aid medicine and education, was Hugh Roy Cullen. In addition to giving over $11 million each to the University of Houston and to Houston area hospitals, he provided $160 million in 1947 to create the Cullen Foundation, located in Houston, which by the mid-1980s had provided grants for many areas of research.

As the cost of medical research became increasingly expensive, officials of the Robert J. Kleberg, Jr., and Helen C. Kleberg Foundation devoted an increasing proportion of foundation funding to that research. Robert J. Kleberg, Jr., grandson of Captain Richard King, the founder of the King Ranch, and his wife, Helen Mary Campbell Kleberg, promoted agricultural research, wildlife conservation, and varied cultural and civic activities. They established the Kleberg Foundation in 1950 as a general purpose foundation, and foundation directors supported a variety of projects, including medical research, veterinary and animal sciences, wildlife research, education, arts, and humanities. However, from the early 1970s on an ever larger percentage of the funding went to medical research, so that by 1984, 55 percent of all funds granted since 1950 had been for medical research, a trend foundation directors expected would continue.[6]

Other examples of foundations established in the post-World War II period that provided important support for medical research included: the Biological Humanics Foundation, established in 1950 in Dallas, which provided grants for research in human growth and development with an emphasis on the medical aspects of symmetry and asymmetry; the DeBakey Medical Foundation, established in 1961 in Houston to encourage education and research in medicine; the Sarah Campbell Blaffer Foundation, established in 1964 in Houston to encourage fine arts but also included an emphasis on ophthalmology; and the Harry S. Moss Heart Trust, established in 1973 in Dallas, which provided funds, in Texas only, for prevention and cure of heart disease.

Another Texas Foundation that provided significant grants for research in medically related areas was the Hogg Foundation. Created by a bequest of Will Hogg and strengthened by grants from Ima Hogg and other members of the Hogg family, the foundation began operations as a part of the University of Texas in 1940, emphasizing mental hygiene. The program in the 1940s and 1950s encouraged public education, mental hygiene clinics, and in-service training, but in the 1950s the foundation expanded its research programs and began to promote research in psychiatry and psychology, as well as continuing public education projects.

The Moody Foundation, whose purposes included increasing the scope of knowledge in the life, physical, and social sciences, supported medical, including psychiatric, research among its many programs. William Lewis Moody, Jr., and his wife, Libbie Shearn Moody, native Texans and longtime residents of Galveston who built a fortune in cotton, banking, insurance, and ranching, established the foundation in 1942. By 1980 the foundation had given over one hundred million dollars in grants to a wide variety of educational projects. About one-quarter of the grants had been used for health, physical, life, or social science projects.

Texas-based foundations have, therefore, since the 1930s, played a significant role in supporting medical research, in providing hospitals and other health care services, and in promoting public education in medical areas. Often foundation officials worked in close connection, officially and unofficially, with Texas universities. Foundation aid to medical schools often supported research projects. For example, the Hoblitzelle Foundation, established in 1942, provided funding for the Southwestern Medical School which Karl Hoblitzelle had helped found and which became part of the U.T. Health Science Center at Dallas. In the 1980s the foundation helped support projects at the center, searching for causes and cures for peptic ulcers and

Type I Diabetes, and a Bio-Behavioral Brain Science Program. Often foundations made grants to other foundations for medical research and equipment. For example, in 1984 the R. J. and H. C. Kleberg Foundation provided the Southwest Foundation for Biomedical Research funds for virology and immunology research laboratory equipment.

Though not as many foundations provided support for nonmedical sciences as for medicine, support for the nonmedical sciences also played a significant role in shaping science in Texas. Among the major foundations, at least eight have provided funds for wildlife, conservation, and/or ecology; five for agriculture, and one each for chemistry, engineering, and physiology. A few other foundations included research and/or science in their purposes but did not specify a particular science. Several major foundations provided aid to museums but not specifically to scientific museums. Smaller foundations also supported some nonmedical sciences; over forty included conservation and environmental programs among their varied projects in the late 1970s. However, only four listed conservation or ecology as the major projects funded. Nine foundations supported agriculture; two, the Vaughn Foundation of Houston and the James M. Vaughn, Jr. Foundation Fund of Temple, supported mathematical research; and one, the Copano Research Foundation of Victoria, devoted all its income to meteorology. Eight other minor foundations supported various aspects of scientific research, usually not specific.

Of the foundations supporting nonmedical sciences, the Welch Foundation is unique. It played a highly significant role in shaping the work of Texas chemists and became internationally recognized as a major force in chemistry. Robert Alonzo Welch, a teenager in the 1880s, came to Texas using $50 of borrowed money. He invested in oil lands in the early 1900s and made a fortune in oil, sulphur, banking, and real estate. When he died in 1952, he left $25 million to a trust fund to support chemical research. The foundation started functioning officially in 1954 and followed a general policy of supporting fundamental research in chemistry in Texas only. Most of the money went to researchers in university chemistry departments for flexible, and often long-range, research projects. Grantees were free to make changes in project design as the research progressed, so that the grants were basically unrestricted. When the foundation began its operations in 1954, officials had difficulty finding enough qualified chemists in Texas to make adequate use of the foundation's income. They awarded seventeen grants. By the mid-1980s the situation had changed;

not only did Texas have many qualified chemists competing for the Welch Foundation awards, but the original endowment had grown to assets of $180 million. The foundation income provided $10 million to $15 million annually for chemical research and other foundation programs, but the foundation was able to fund only about one in five qualified applicants for new grants. In 1983 alone, 1,825 people participated in Welch Foundation-sponsored research as principal investigators, post-doctoral fellows, graduate fellows or undergraduate scholars. By 1985 the foundation had awarded and administered more than $150 million in grants to scientists at fifty Texas colleges and universities.

In 1957 the foundation began a series of annual conferences on chemical research. Participants and speakers attended from all over the world. The 1976 conference, in the U.S. bicentennial year, focused on the history of chemistry. In 1984 the foundation's thirtieth anniversary, the conference theme was "Chemistry in Texas: The 30th Year of the Welch Foundation." The foundation program also created a lectureship program bringing outstanding scientists to speak at Texas universities. By 1985 the foundation had also established eighteen Welch Chairs in chemistry and three chairs in allied sciences at thirteen Texas universities, and had published *Research Bulletins* and the *Proceedings* of the conferences. The foundation had also awarded the Robert A. Welch award "for important chemical research contributions which will have a significant positive influence on mankind" to ten outstanding researchers. The first award, made in 1972, was $75,000. By 1983 that award had increased to $150,000. In 1985 the foundation awarded the tenth Welch Award to a Swiss chemist, Duilio Arigoni. In addition, the Welch Foundation provided undergraduate scholarships at many Texas universities and special grants designed to help small colleges develop research in chemistry departments.[7] Thus, in the three decades between 1954 and the mid-1980s the Welch Foundation had indeed shaped chemical research in Texas.

With the establishment of agricultural experiment stations, usually closely connected with state universities, scientists worked to help solve the problems of American farmers. In Texas the Agricultural Experiment Station System, a part of Texas A&M and other state and federal agencies, provided primary support for agricultural scientists, but some foundations also played a role in stimulating agricultural research.

A major agricultural foundation, created in 1927, was a gift of Edgar B. Davis. A multimillionaire by the early twentieth century, Davis made his first million in the shoe business in Massachusetts, made another $3 million investing in foreign rubber plantations, and moved to Texas in the 1920s to invest in and manage oil leases. He found oil in the Luling area and reinvested much of the fortune he made from it in that area, including establishing the Luling Foundation to teach improved agricultural methods. The foundation ran an experimental farm as a research and educational base, working closely with Texas A&M and supporting activities based primarily on the needs of farmers in Caldwell, Guadalupe, and Gonzales counties. Farm projects included experiments in soil and water conservation; growing varied crops including animal feeds; producing cattle, sheep, hogs, and poultry; and sharing information with area farmers through field days and demonstrations. Managers tested new farming techniques and equipment, seeking to help area farmers develop profitable operations. During the 1930s the Luling Foundation Farm ran a training school teaching young men from the area improved farming methods; after World War II the foundation operated a successful farm school for veterans. In the 1980s the foundation continued youth education through strong support of FFA and 4-H projects. Foundation officials also continued to work in cooperation with the Texas Agricultural Extension Service and to serve as a link between industry, experiment station and the farm and ranch user.[8]

Another important agricultural foundation, the Texas Research Foundation, established in 1944 at Renner, Texas as an outgrowth of the Institute of Technology and Plant Industry at Southern Methodist University, sponsored research on depleted Texas soils, searching for new crops for old cotton lands. Beginning in 1946, with Karl Hoblitzelle as president and Cyrus L. Lundell as director, the foundation built laboratories and created test fields north of Dallas. By 1966 the foundation owned 860 acres of test plots, fields, and pastures and had provided substantial aid to farmers and ranchers in Texas, helping to increase yields and upgrade soils. From 1944 to 1972 the foundation operated as a privately supported, nonprofit institution, but in 1972 it was liquidated and Texas A&M, UT-Austin, and UT-Dallas took over the lands, assets, and collections of the foundation.

Another foundation sponsoring agricultural research, the M. G. and Johnnye D. Perry Foundation, was created in 1946 at Robstown to support the economic development of agriculture in South Texas. The foundation established an experimental farm for studying varieties of grain, forage, and cotton crops;

set up a feed mill and feed lots; and provided area farmers with information on agricultural issues. One of the most successful projects which the foundation helped support was a program to eradicate the screwworm in the Southwest. In 1962, the foundation provided $100,000 seed money to help get such a program started in Texas; that program became a federally-funded program in the 1960s and a cooperative international program with Mexico in the 1970s. By the early 1980s screwworm, a serious threat to livestock production, appeared to be eradicated in the American Southwest. Another successful program, undertaken in cooperation with the Texas Agricultural Experiment Station System and the USDA, led to the development of a new variety of winter wheat, named for M. G. Perry, which could be grown successfully in South Texas.[9] Other foundations sponsoring agricultural research included the E. Paul and Helen Buck Waggoner Foundation, Inc., established in 1966 at Vernon; and the High Plains Research Foundation at Plainview.

Other Texas foundations have stimulated conservation and ecology research. Robert Hughes Welder, a western rancher who was interested in wildlife and land management, provided funds through his will for the establishment, in 1954, of the Rob and Bessie Welder Wildlife Foundation. The foundation created and operated a wildlife refuge in San Patricio County which served as a research station and headquarters for education in wildlife conservation. The foundation provided fellowship and research aid and facilities for both students and established scholars, sponsored publications, and offered teacher training programs, as well as public tours and lectures. The graduate student research program acquired an international reputation; more than 200 Welder Fellows had received graduate degrees from many colleges and universities by the mid-1980s. Welder Foundation supported research had led to more than 400 publications, including significant studies on predators, wildlife diseases, ecology, and game bird and wildlife management.

By the mid-1980s management of wildlife had become economically important to Texas ranchers because income from sport-hunting rights exceeded income from production of livestock on many ranches in South and South Central Texas. Thus, interest in research relating to wildlife management on rangeland increased, and the Welder Foundation sponsored research on game species on rangeland used for livestock production as well as research on nongame species. The foundation remained unique in that no other land management research organization conducted wildlife research in the midst of a ranching operation and an active oil field. The Welder Foundation in its varied activities played an important role in wildlife research and dissemination of knowledge.[10]

The Caesar Kleberg Foundation for Wildlife Conservation, established in 1951 at King Ranch, Kingsville, with funds exclusively for wildlife research, operated primarily by supporting such research at Texas A&I and Texas A&M. Projects at those universities included studies of wildlife habits and habitat, management techniques, wildlife and livestock diseases, and attempts to develop strategies that improved food and cover for wildlife population, thus increasing economic returns to landowners from wildlife and their habitat.

Other major foundations sponsoring scientific research in Texas included the Wacker Foundation, established in 1975 to provide grants for research and research dissemination on physiological aspects of learning and behavior, and the Schlumberger Foundation, established in 1954 in Sugarland to provide scholarships, fellowships, and endowed professorships in scientific fields, primarily engineering. The foundation funded the Schlumberger Chair of Advanced Studies and Research at Rice University and the Schlumberger Centennial Chair in Electrical Engineering at UT-Austin. Schlumberger Foundation funding was never limited to Texas, and, in the early 1980s, New York City became foundation headquarters, though the foundation continued to provide scholarships at several Texas schools.

Texas foundations have played important supplementary and, in the case of chemistry, wildlife management, and some medical areas, primary roles in strengthening science in Texas. Most Texas foundations provide important services in cooperative ventures linking public service and private industry. The agricultural foundations work closely with state and federal agricultural agencies and with farm organizations. For example, the Texas Swine Test Center, the only facility in the state for evaluating boars and thus improving breeding stock, became a reality in the mid-1980s through joint efforts of the Luling Foundation, the Texas Agricultural Extension Service, and the Texas Pork Producers. Many foundations support science indirectly through grants to public and private universities for buildings, equipment, operating funds, and scholarships. Though it is difficult to assess the direct impact of such funding in terms of specific scientific achievements, that funding has been and remains crucial for advancing science. State support for science is usually in areas seen by the legislature

as immediately beneficial; foundation funding from Texas as well as national foundations provides some of the additional resources needed for scientific research. Often it is difficult to distinguish the contributions of foundations from those of universities and state agencies; yet, Texas foundations are part of a significant support system for science. If Texans hope to be leaders in scientific and technological advancement, they must continue to support scientific research through both government and private sectors, including philanthropic foundations. Texas foundations supplement national foundations, the national government, state and private universities, other state agencies, and industry as patrons of scientific research and in disseminating scientific information.

Societies

As Texas communities grew, those people interested in promoting science banded together for mutual support, and, as scientific activities became increasingly professionalized, some scientists formed organizations principally for professionals. By the 1980s, Texas scientific societies included both those for professionals and those designed to bring together professionals and laymen. Some had as a primary purpose the encouragement of research and promotion of professional growth. Others primarily disseminated knowledge and encouraged public interest in scientific topics.

The earliest attempt to create a scientific society in Anglo-Texas was the organization, in December 1837, of the Philosophical Society of Texas. Founded by twenty-six leaders of the new republic, the society's purpose was to collect information about all aspects of Texas, including natural history. The society met during the annual sessions of the Texas congress but ceased functioning in the 1840s. In the mid-1930s new leaders revived the organization and received a state charter, but the new society became an honorary one with literary aims and no longer included natural history.

Other early attempts at scientific societies floundered, often due to lack of an adequate base of support. There were several agricultural clubs in the German communities in the 1800s. The Texas Agricultural Society, founded in 1853 to promote improved agricultural methods, published at least one journal before disappearing. The Texas Archeological Society existed briefly in Austin in 1876. The Texas State Horticultural Society, founded in Houston in

1875, existed until 1922; several horticultural papers and journals appeared briefly between the 1860s and World War I. Edwin T. Dumble organized the Texas State Geological and Scientific Association of Houston in 1884; but the societies of the late 1800s no longer existed in the 1980s.

In the mid-1980s the major scientific society in Texas, embracing many disciplines, was the Texas Academy of Science. That academy was actually the third Texas Academy of Science.

In 1880 Samuel Botsford Buckley, a geologist and botanist, Quintius Cincinnatus Smith, a physician with wide-ranging scientific interests, and Franklin L. Yoakum, a physician, minister, and educator, also with wide-ranging scientific interests, founded at Austin the Texas Academy of Science (also called the Academy of Science of Texas). Members included many state officials and the state governor, O. M. Roberts, who became president. Buckley replaced Governor Roberts as president in 1881. The academy accomplished almost nothing in its first two years; and in 1882 Yoakum and Buckley moved the academy from Austin to Yoakum's home in Palestine. There the academy prospered, growing to about one hundred members from various parts of the state. It began a museum collection, building on a collection Yoakum had started earlier, and planned to publish an annual journal. Buckley died in 1883, and the academy declined thereafter, ending activities in 1886 or 1887. It was one of the scientific societies to which the Smithsonian sent publications in 1885; and one of Yoakum's publications in 1889 mentioned the Academy of Science of Tyler. The museum collections remained, however. Yoakum took the collection to Tyler when he moved there about 1886, along with the academy's library. He exhibited the collection containing minerals, birds, fish, crustaceans, and botanical specimens at the state fair in Dallas in 1886. The collection also included fifty boxes of insects, but the entomologist working with the exhibits became ill and did not unpack the insect collection. Yoakum died in 1891; the collection may have remained part of the state fair exhibits. There was a collection of birds, shells, and minerals exhibited at the fair until 1916, when the manager of the fair threw it out. The president of Southern Methodist University, Robert Stewart, salvaged that collection and added it to SMU's geological and natural history collections.[11]

In 1892 fourteen scientists at the University of Texas organized the second Texas Academy of Science in Austin. They hoped to promote the natural and exact sciences. Edgar Everhart, professor of chemistry at the University, was the major organizer and first president of the new academy, but several other professors including George B. Halsted, mathematics, Alexander Macfarlane, physics, Frederick W. Simonds, geology, and Thomas U. Taylor, applied mathematics, helped form the academy. Edwin T. Dumble, the state geologist, became the second president, 1893–94. Several members of the new group had been members of the older academy of science. The new academy prospered for about twenty years, holding monthly meetings in Austin and general meetings in other parts of the state. The academy published twelve volumes of *Transactions* and then in 1912 ceased to function.

In 1929 scholars at the University of Texas reorganized and revitalized the academy, creating what was actually the third Texas Academy of Science; it was designed to stimulate scientific research and promote fraternal relationships among scientists. The academy received a state charter and resumed publication of the *Proceedings and Transactions*. However, the journals appeared irregularly. In 1949 the academy replaced the *Transactions* with the *Texas Journal of Science*, designed to promote prompt publication of papers and to keep members aware of, and interested in, the academy. By that year, the academy had approximately one thousand members, and academy leaders hoped to encourage and coordinate research in Texas through meetings and publication, to advise the government on scientific matters, and to assemble a scientific library and museum. The academy consisted of a senior academy divided into five sections: physical science, biological science, social science, geological science, and conservation; a collegiate academy, designed to promote the organization of science clubs in colleges and universities; and a junior academy, to encourage scientific activities in secondary schools. The academy had three regional groups: East Texas; South Texas; and West Texas. By 1985 the senior academy had grown to ten sections: mathematical sciences; physics; earth sciences; biological sciences; social sciences; environmental sciences; chemistry; science education; computer sciences; and aquatic sciences. The society listed as affiliated organizations the Texas sections of the American Association of Physics Teachers, the Mathematical Association of America, and the National Association of Geology Teachers, as well as the American Association for the Advancement of Science. The collegiate and junior academies remained parts of the organization, and in 1985 the academy had 1,100 members.

By the mid-1980s most scientists in Texas belonged

to the national professional societies of their particular specialty. Many of those national organizations had state or regional groups in which Texans participated and took leadership roles; for example, the Southeast Texas Section of the American Chemical Society had over 2,500 members in 1985, primarily because of the large number of industrial chemists in the Houston area. The American Society of Civil Engineers and the American Society of Mechanical Engineers had Texas sections. The Society of Petroleum Engineers of the American Institute of Mechanical Engineers, founded in 1922, had its headquarters in Dallas. Biologists also organized Texas groups, including the Southwest Entomological Society, which emphasized the study of insects of Texas.

Texans played leading roles in geological societies, primarily because of the importance of petroleum industries in the state. Texas and Oklahoma geologists organized the parent organization of the American Association of Petroleum Geologists (AAPG). In 1915, in Tulsa, Oklahoma, geologists at the University of Oklahoma began planning a meeting for Oklahoma and Texas geologists who felt isolated from the then existing geological societies, most of which held meetings in the East. They sent invitations to all known geologists in the Southwest area, inviting them to attend a meeting at Norman, Oklahoma, in 1916. About fifty geologists, plus those from Norman, attended. They held a second meeting in Tulsa in 1917 and formally organized as the Southwestern Association of Petroleum Geologists with 87 active members.[12] By 1985, the organization, with headquarters still at Tulsa, had become the American Association of Petroleum Geologists with 40,000 members. The association's goals were to advance geology—especially studies of petroleum, natural gas, and energy minerals; to promote research and better technology; and to disseminate information. Most of the members were Texans. The organization included subsections with Texans in the Gulf Coast and Southwest sections, and with affiliated societies in various areas of the country.

Many Texas geological societies had affiliated with the AAPG by the mid-1980s. Within the Gulf Coast section those societies were the Austin Geological Society, affiliated in 1969; the Corpus Christi Geological Society, affiliated in 1943; the East Texas Geological Society (at Tyler), affiliated in 1932; the Houston Geological Society, affiliated in 1932; the Lamar University Geological Society, affiliated in 1971; and the South Texas Geological Society, affiliated in 1949. In the Southwest section the Texas societies were the Abilene Geological Society, affiliated in 1947; the Dallas Geological Society, affiliated in 1935; the El

Paso Geological Society, affiliated in 1971; the Fort Worth Geological Society affiliated in 1931; the Graham Geological Society, affiliated in 1984; the North Texas Geological Society (at Wichita Falls), affiliated in 1938; the San Angelo Geological Society, affiliated in 1954; and the West Texas Geological Society (at Midland), affiliated in 1938. The Panhandle Geological Society at Amarillo, affiliated in 1932, was part of the Mid-Continent section of the AAPG. The affiliated societies met regularly and had publication programs. For example, the Houston Geological Society, founded in 1923 and incorporated in 1975 to stimulate interest in and promote study of geology in the area, published ten bulletins per year. National offshoots of the AAPG included the Society of Economic Paleontologists and Mineralogists and the Society of Exploration Geophysicists; those groups also had local affiliate societies. Other specialized Texas societies in energy-related industries included the Texas Solar Energy Society in Austin, and the Mid-Continent Oil and Gas Association, also in Austin.

Medical professionals in Texas created strong state organizations as well as joining the appropriate national societies. In January 1853 physicians in Austin, including Ashbel Smith and J. W. Throckmorton, organized a Texas Medical Association. The group elected officers and drafted a constitution and by-laws. The physicians held one more 1853 meeting, received legislative permission to incorporate as the Medical Association of Texas, and then stopped meeting until after the Civil War. In the 1870s the organization began publishing the transactions of the meetings; the early publications were the forerunners of the *Journal of the Texas State Medical Association* which began appearing in 1905. After various reorganizations and name changes, the organization became once again, in 1951, the Medical Association of Texas. By the 1980s members had organized county and regional affiliates throughout the state; the association had a large library in Austin, and it continued to publish a journal containing scientific articles and advice for professionals.

Another medical professional society began in 1879 when pharmacists organized the Texas State Pharmaceutical Association. The founders hoped to professionalize pharmacy in Texas, push for the passage of legal standards, and improve pharmaceutical education. The organization began a publishing program in the 1890s, and in the 1980s continued to publish *Texas Pharmacy*. Other medical professional state organizations active in the mid-1980s included The Texas Nurses Association, the Texas Osteopathic Medical Association, which began its journal in the

1940s, the Texas Psychiatric Foundation, the Texas Association for Mental Health, and the Texas Psychological Association. Many of the state organizations were concerned primarily with professional problems, especially licensing, and the dissemination of information. Several national medical professional organizations, such as the American Orthodontic Society, founded in 1975, had Texas headquarters. One group, the American Heart Association, founded in Dallas in 1924, was designed to bring together laymen and professionals and was to be financed by voluntary public contributions.

Some Texas scientific societies represented the recent development of new disciplines. Texas biologists created the Texas Society of Microscopy in the 1960s to provide a forum for the exchange of ideas, knowledge, techniques, and the dissemination of research done with the electron microscope. By the 1980s the organization had about five hundred members and was the best of the local or state groups promoting research with the electron microscope. Another group, organized in the early 1970s, reflecting increasing concern with ecological problems, was the Texas Organization for Endangered Species. The group brought together university scientists and those in state and federal conservation and resource use agencies who were professionals in biology concerned with endangered species. They put together lists of Texas' rare, threatened, and endangered species for the use of agencies developing and administering protection programs. By the mid-1980s, the group had about two hundred members, was holding yearly meetings, and was encouraging its members to promote public awareness of endangered species. In the 1980s, as the cost of attending national meetings became prohibitive for many scientists, local scientific societies played an increasingly important role for Texas professionals, improving scientific communication and research, at least regionally.

Another type of scientific society that organized for both professionals and amateurs has also been important in Texas. The avocational societies, uniting diverse groups, often sponsored meetings and publications to encourage the professional growth of members and to advance knowledge within the profession as well as encourage general interest and promote educational projects for the nonprofessional. Such societies were especially important in areas where well-qualified amateurs could play important roles in the observation and collection of data and artifacts, thus providing raw material for scientific study.

As was true throughout the United States, many of the early regional and local historical societies en-

couraged members to collect natural history specimens and Indian artifacts. Some of those societies became long-lasting organizations and their members made important contributions in various fields. In Texas, for example, the West Texas Historical and Scientific Society, organized at Alpine in 1925 in cooperation with Sul Ross State Teachers College, promoted research in archaeology in cooperation with the Peabody Museum and the WPA in the 1930s. Also in the 1930s, with money from the Centennial Commission, the society organized a museum which it turned over to the college in the late 1960s.

The Texas Archeological Society became one of the largest scientific societies in Texas to include both amateurs and professionals. The oldest and perhaps most prestigious of the avocational archaeological societies in the United States, the organization began in Alpine in 1928, first as the West Texas Archeological Society and then as the Texas Archeological and Paleontological Society. By 1929, it had over one hundred members. The society's goals included study of the history, prehistory, and major artifacts of man and fossils representing the past flora and fauna of Texas; encouraging the collecting and preservation of artifacts and fossils; and the publication of research results. Any person interested in the preservation of archaeological resources of Texas could join; the society worked in cooperation with universities and museums, and it published newsletters, an annual bulletin of scientific papers, and occasional special publications. In 1962 the society began sponsoring an annual archaeological field school to train members in field techniques and to conduct excavations of valuable archaeological sites. Sometimes entire families participated in field schools. By the mid-1980s the field school excavations had provided significant data for scientific studies and had become excellent training schools for avocational archaeologists. The society also published a highly respected journal.

Another avocational society organized in 1939 for the discovery and distribution of knowledge about amphibians and reptiles in Texas and to encourage fellowship among members was the Texas Herpetological Society. By the 1980s the society included almost all professional herpetologists in Texas and a significant number of nonprofessionals. The society united university professors, zoo curators, and knowledgeable amateurs. Many members joined as families. The society sponsored yearly field meetings to look for interesting species and help fill in gaps in the distribution maps for the state. Beginning in the early 1970s the society also held a second more formal yearly meeting to promote the dissemination of knowledge. The society retained a strong commitment to unite the various components of the society, young and old, avocational and professional, to maintain interest in herpetology. The society sponsored a newsletter to provide information to members.

Another large society uniting amateurs and professionals is the Texas Ornithological Society, founded in 1953 and dedicated to the observation, study, and conservation of birdlife in Texas. In 1967 the group began publishing an annual *Bulletin* of scientific papers to supplement its newsletters. Members conducted annual Christmas counts and other observations which provided necessary raw material for scientific studies and encouraged the work of the many local Audubon societies and other bird clubs in the state, thus playing a major role in data collecting and in disseminating information.

Many other groups also united professionals and amateurs in studying the state's resources. Examples included the Texas Speleological Association, which sponsored both cave trips and scientific studies and had several local affiliate caving societies that conducted speleological studies. A meteoritical society in Houston, founded in 1933, brought together professional and amateur meteoriticists to promote the study of meteorites and other samples of extraterrestrial matter. One local group, the Odessa Meteoritical Society, developed a museum and promoted the study of and educational programs about the Odessa Meteor Crater. Many local astronomical societies encouraged members to study and observe stars; the societies also promoted educational programs.

Some scientists also worked with groups promoting ecology in Texas. Most of those groups were national organizations such as the Sierra Club, with regional affiliates in Texas. One group, the Nature Conservancy, began acquiring land in Texas in the 1960s, opened a San Antonio office in 1979, and by 1985 had a Texas membership of 6,000, managed 16 sanctuaries and had acquired 158,145 acres of land in 30 separate projects in Texas attempting to help preserve the ecological balance and natural diversity of Texas lands. Other ecologically-oriented societies included the Big Thicket Association, founded in 1964, which united conservationists and others interested in preserving the Big Thicket, maintained a museum and sponsored environmental educational programs, tours, seminars, and nature retreats.

Thus, Texas societies, either as independent professional organizations or as affiliates of national groups, encouraged professional growth, sponsored research in many areas, promoted cooperation between scientists and interested knowledgeable amateurs, and disseminated scientific information.

Museums

The Texas scientific institutions directly affecting most individuals were museums. Texas museums, either including or specializing in scientific displays, helped countless Texans become familiar with scientific topics. Museums played a major public education role. New modern museums, with "hands-on" exhibits, introduced, often excitingly, schoolchildren and their elders to new science and technology. Several museums had both educational and research functions, a dual role that went back to Charles Willson Peale's museum in Philadelphia in the late 1700s, but became clearly important with the creation of national research museums such as the Smithsonian Institution in the mid-to-late 1800s.

In Texas some of the earliest science "museums" were its zoological gardens (zoos), which have provided education and recreation for Texans since the early 1900s. Many of the largest and oldest zoos in the state, built in urban areas, also provided opportunities for research: the Dallas Zoo opened in 1904; the Fort Worth Zoological Park in 1909; the San Antonio Zoological Garden and Aquarium in 1914; and the Houston Zoological Gardens in 1920. By the mid-1980s most had large collections of mammals, reptiles, birds, amphibians, and fish displayed in a variety of habitats. In the 1930s the San Antonio Zoo officials built a monkey island for their colony of gelada baboons and herd of Barbary sheep; by the 1980s many zoos had primate buildings and specialized collections of other animals in aviaries, herpetariums, and aquariums as well as the traditional outdoor exhibits. Most provided educational programs and guided tours, often in conjunction with local school systems. The Fort Worth Zoo provided summer classes in zoology and zoo art, as well as a regular schedule of films at its education center. Most zoos distributed newsletters and occasionally other publications.[13]

The early zoos and those organized in mid-century, such as the El Paso Zoological Park (1941) and the Central Texas Zoo at Waco (1955), had general and often wide-ranging collections, including animals from all over the world. The San Antonio Zoo, for example, had a worldwide waterfowl and antelope collection; in the mid-1980s the Houston Zoo included 520 species of reptiles, 261 species of birds, and 128 species of mammals. The Fort Worth Zoo's herpetarium and aquarium contained over 2,000 fresh- and saltwater creatures. Some of the zoos built in the 1960s and 1970s were a response to changing conditions in modern society. The Gladys Porter Zoo in Brownsville, founded in 1971 and created because of concern about vanishing wildlife, had major exhibit areas for African, Asian, Indo-Australian, and tropical American species. Zoo officials specialized in breeding rare and endangered species, and in the early 1980s the zoo had two species of antelope found at no other zoo in the world. The Texas Zoo at Victoria, founded in 1976, was a response to a different problem, an urbanized Texas in which many citizens had little familiarity with native species. The zoo collections stressed wildlife indigenous to Texas, and by the mid-1980s included 93 native Texas species. Urbanized Texans also welcomed children's zoos, which provided opportunities for city children to become familiar with the farm animals that previous generations of children had known.

Throughout the state, Texas zoos, both large and small, provided significant educational services, both formal and informal. Some zoos also promoted scientific research. By the 1980s many zoos had reference libraries available to local researchers, and some sponsored biological research programs. At the Houston Zoo, for example, researchers worked in herpetology, parasitology, and artificial insemination projects as well as in other areas. Some zoos, including the Abilene Zoological Gardens (founded in 1965), promoted research on capture reproduction; several had research projects on animal health and behavior as well as on reproduction. The Fort Worth Zoo conducted a zoo/ranch breeding research program. Most of the zoos were municipal, supported by city governments and entrance fees and/or voluntary contributions. Some were organized and run by nonprofit societies. Others, like Clifton's "Texas Safari," were commercial, although subsidized in part by philanthropy. Texas zoos provided living collections for enjoyment and study.

By the mid-1980s Texas had several museums specializing in science and technology collections and many others which included scientific displays. Some were municipal, some privately owned (usually by nonprofit societies or foundations), and some associated with universities. Many early science museum displays were simply collections of local specimens, Indian artifacts, and/or specimens travelers had collected in other parts of the world. In 1881 Albert Friedrich opened the Buckhorn Saloon in San Antonio and began collecting horns there. The collection grew steadily as cowboys and others traded horns for drinks. That collection, taken over by the Lone Star Brewery in 1956, became the basis of a natural history museum featuring wildlife, marine life, and birds. In the 1890s the Medical Branch of the University of Texas included a Museum of Human Anatomy. The John K. Strecker Museum of Baylor University at Waco, founded in 1893, included natural science specimens from the college's teaching collections. By the mid-1980s the Strecker Museum, accredited by the American Association of Museums in 1973, featured both natural science and general collections. The museum included a 6,000-volume science library, a nature center, and classrooms. Baylor's museum provided an extensive education program in cooperation with area schools, a museum studies program that led to a B.A. degree, publications, and permanent, temporary, and traveling exhibits. The museum had become an important research center for university faculty, especially in archaeology, herpetology, natural history, and zoology.

By the mid-1980s, in addition to Baylor, several Texas universities operated science museums or museums including science collections and exhibits. Some began in the 1920s and early 1930s, including the John E. Conner Museum, founded in 1925 at Texas A&I University in Kingsville, a general museum with varied collections including the King Ranch Natural History Collection. A geology museum at the University of Houston geology department opened in 1927 and provided a research library and research collections in geology, petrology, mineralogy, and paleontology; the North Texas State University Historical Collections created at Denton in 1930 included technology, ethnology, regional archaeology and anthropology exhibits.

The Panhandle Plains Historical Museum also began in the 1920s. The Panhandle-Plains Historical Society, organized and incorporated in the early 1920s in order to preserve in a museum materials relating to the history and the natural history of West Texas, began to raise funds for a museum in 1929. The museum, built with state funds as well as private contributions, opened in 1933 at Canyon on the campus of West Texas State Teachers College. The collections eventually included anthropology, geology, paleontology, and natural history as well as historical materials. The museum, with a research program emphasizing archaeology, became the oldest state-supported museum in Texas.

The celebration of the Texas Centennial in 1936 led to the creation of several major museums, many associated with universities. Though many who raised money for centennial museums were primarily concerned with preserving historic documents and artifacts, some of the museums built or strengthened science exhibits using already existing collections and new specimens. One of the most important for natural history research was the Museum of Texas Tech at Lubbock. In the late 1920s and 1930s the Plains Museum Society (later the West Texas Museum Association) made plans for a major museum; funding became available for part of those plans when, as a part of the Centennial celebrations, sixty-seven counties agreed to allocate funds for such a museum. The museum opened in a basement in 1937. After World War II the museum association was able to raise additional funds and the completed museum formally opened in 1950. In 1970 the museum, officially renamed the Museum of Texas Tech University, moved into a new facility which included a research wing with offices for university faculty; faculty continued to use and enlarge the museum collection and to do significant research in natural history. The museum complex also included the Ranching Heritage Center, an outdoor exhibit illustrating the history and development of ranching; and the Moody Planetarium offering regular public programs in astronomy. The museum published results of museum staff research and of other scholars using its collections. The museum and university cooperated in the International Center for Arid and Semi-Arid Land Studies. In 1974 Texas Tech began offering a Master of Arts degree in museum science. In addition the museum had extensive public education programs, including contracts with regional school districts for a comprehensive K-12 program which brought students to the museum several times during their school careers.

Another museum, also made possible by Centennial funding, is the Texas Memorial Museum at the University of Texas at Austin. In the mid-1920s faculty members at the university organized the Texas Museum Association to promote the establishment of a major museum. Attempts to get state funding failed in the 1920s, but in the mid-1930s the state legislature appropriated $250,000 for the museum. With the addition of federal money and private contributions, the museum became a reality, opening in 1939. The museum contained four major divisions: anthropology; botany-zoology; geology and paleontology; and Texas history; with exhibits from each collection displayed on a different floor of the building. The Texas Memorial Museum collections formed a basic research collection used by University of Texas faculty and others for major research programs in natural history. The museum facilities included several laboratories, research space, archives, and a reference library. Educational programs included a museum studies program; programs for area schools; and in the summer, children's workshops.

Still another university-related museum with important research programs that began in the 1930s with Centennial funding is the El Paso Centennial Museum, founded in 1936. The museum featured exhibits of history and nature collections, especially from the American Southwest and northern Mexico. Scholars used the natural history collections for research in archaeology, ethnology, geology, and paleontology. The museum also had a publication program. Another museum, the Stone Fort Museum in Nacogdoches, operated by the state, founded in 1936 as a local history museum with Centennial funds, included some archaeology and technology collections in the 1980s.

In the 1960s and 1970s, as Texas universities underwent a period of growth, several other universities opened museums. Most were primarily for public education, but some had potentially significant research collections. The Winedale Historical Center at Round Top, administered by the University of Texas at Austin, a 190-acre outdoor museum, opened in 1967; it included exhibits relating to Texas agricultural and farm technology history. The Museum of the Big Bend at Alpine, founded in 1969, affiliated with Sul Ross University, emphasized regional history including archaeological artifacts and collections for researchers. The A. M. and Alma Fiedler Memorial Museum, founded in 1973, in Seguin, operated by Texas Lutheran College, included geological and archaeological exhibits and a research collection for geologists. The Llano-Estacado Museum at Plainview, founded in 1976, operated by Wayland University, had geological, archaeological, and natural history collections as part of its historical collections. The Nuevo Santander Museum complex, also founded in 1976 and operated by Laredo State College, included archaeology and botany collections in the general collection related to the history of the Rio Grande Valley area. The Texas Forestry Museum in Lufkin, operated by the Texas Forest Service, a branch of Texas A&M, opened in 1976 with exhibits relating to the timber history of East Texas. Though not actually display museums, Midwestern State University at Wichita Falls and Texas A&M housed excellent research collections open to qualified researchers, the A&M collection was particularly good on recent invertebrates. SMU,

TCU, A&M, and the University of Texas also had excellent archaeological collections by the mid-1980s.

Two other museums connected with higher education dealt with a crucially important Texas resource: Spindletop Museum, founded at Beaumont in 1971 and operated by Lamar University; and the East Texas Oil Museum, opened in 1981 at Kilgore and operated by Kilgore College. Both museums had exhibits which recreated for visitors the history, technology and cultural impact of the petroleum industry. The East Texas Oil Museum averaged 75,000 visitors a year in its first four years. It included innovative exhibits and an educational program for teachers and students. Several nonuniversity museums also featured displays showing the history and impact of the petroleum industry. They included the Permian Basin Petroleum Museum, Library and Hall of Fame at Midland founded in 1976,

and the Western Company Museum at Fort Worth, founded in 1979. The latter featured learning experiences for adults and children using multimedia techniques.

By the 1980s the major scientific research museums in Texas were those connected with universities and founded as a result of the Texas centennial celebration in 1936. Directors of those museums had acquired good study collections over the course of a half century. Directors of new museums, created in recent years, found building similar broad research collections expensive and often impossible. Thus, most new museums tended to emphasize public display and education rather than research functions.

In addition to university museums, Texas had several museums operated by municipalities or private nonprofit museum agencies which specialized in sci-

Figure 1. The 70-foot long Diplodocus at the Houston Museum of Natural Science attracts numerous visitors. The museum plays an important role in the dissemination of scientific knowledge.

*Figure 2. A diorama in the Farrish Hall of Texas Wildlife in the Houston Museum of Natural Science.
This technique featuring wildlife in natural habitats was used by Charles W. Peale in the early 1800s and
is used extensively in twentieth-century museums.*

ence and/or technology. Many other general museums included scientific displays, usually natural history or archaeology. Most of the specialized museums were created in the era of rapid expansion in the 1960s and the 1970s. A few were older.

In 1909 a group of Houston citizens formed a Houston Museum and Scientific Society; the society persuaded city officials to buy part of a natural history collection which H. P. Attwater had assembled; in 1922 S. J. Westheimer purchased, and turned over to the city, the rest of the collection. The city managed the museum until 1946 when officials created a non-profit corporation to do so. In the 1960s the corporation built, and then enlarged, a new museum building and opened a first-class planetarium. By the mid-1980s the Houston Museum of Natural Science had become one of the largest natural science museums in the Southwest with extensive collections, a library, classrooms, and a large auditorium. Exhibits included a 70-foot long skeleton of a *Diplodocus*, Texas wildlife dis-

played in habital groups, African animals, Indian artifacts, a petroleum science and technology section, a Welch Foundation exhibit on the history of chemistry, a space science section, and geology displays. The second floor contained a separately organized health education museum, the Museum of Medical Sciences. Located in Hermann Park near a complex of other museums and gardens, the Houston museum offered a variety of organized educational programs for adults and children.

Another major museum organized early in the century was the Witte Memorial Museum in San Antonio. A general museum founded in 1923 with a gift from the will of Alfred Witte, it opened in 1926. Natural history became a significant part of the museum, which specialized in Texas wildlife, ecology, and archaeology. Many of the exhibits were participatory exhibits, designed to encourage children (and adults) to test and improve their scientific knowledge.

The Dallas Museum of Natural History/Dallas

Figure 3. Steve McDonald of The Museum setting traplines for mammal research. Photo by Nick Olson, The Museum, Texas Tech University.

Aquarium was organized as part of the Texas Centennial celebration and housed in a building in Fair Park in Dallas in the mid-1930s. By the 1980s the museum and aquarium contained large collections, with exhibits interpreting the plants, animals, rocks, minerals, and fossils of Texas and the Southwest. Fifty dioramas showed Texas wildlife in natural environments; the aquarium featured displays of more than three hundred species. The museum included a library, nature center, a field research station, classrooms and an auditorium. Officials offered a wide range of educational programs for children through adults, including college programs. Nearby science museums were the Dallas Civic Garden Center, founded in 1941, with landscaped grounds, a botanical garden, a library, classrooms, auditorium, and a variety of educational programs, and the Southwest Museum of Science and Technology, the Science Place, founded in 1946. The latter, called at first the Dallas Health Museum, became a learning center with inno-

vative hands-on exhibits dealing with energy, human environment, computers, engineering, and communications as well as health and anatomy. A nearby "Age of Steam" museum, founded in 1963, featured exhibits relating to the history and technology of railroads. All the science-oriented museums in Fair Park featured educational programs for adults and children.

Several science museums were organized as learning aids for local school systems. The Fort Worth Museum of Science and History began as The Fort Worth Children's Museum in an elementary school classroom in 1939, organized by a group of school teachers. Moved first to an old house and then to its own new building in 1953, the museum grew with support from both private gifts and public funds. In 1969 the museum acquired its new title. By the mid-1980s the museum centered around exhibits organized for family participation, including use of live animals. The museum included a planetarium, an Omnitheater, a research department, and a museum school; the staff

Figure 4. Museum research collections provide crucial material for scientific study. Liz Jones installing specimens of Peromyscus leucopus *into the collection of mammals, Texas Tech University. Photo by Nick Olson, The Museum, Texas Tech University.*

provided demonstrations, lectures, films, workshops, TV programs, a loan service for schools, and formal education programs including training for professional museum workers. The Corpus Christi Museum, established in 1957, had the strong support and leadership of the local Association for Childhood Education. Though a general museum, the Corpus Christi Museum did include natural history, marine science, and geology exhibits. By the mid-1980s that museum offered educational programs for children and for undergraduate students. The Environmental Science Center in Houston, founded in 1968, organized and operated by the Spring Branch Independent School District is a natural science museum with educational collections and connections to several nature parks and preserves, such as the Houston Arboretum in Memorial Park.

The science museums founded in the post-World War II era included the Austin Nature Center, a municipal natural science center and pioneer farm organized in 1960. The nature center exhibited displays, featuring the flora and fauna of the Central Texas area, a "touch-table," and other participatory exhibits. The museum also offered a wide variety of environmental education programs, interpretive nature trails, and

several education publications. Other natural science museums of note included the Brazosport Museum of Natural Science, founded in 1962, which specialized in interpreting the Texas Gulf Coast area; the Brazos Valley Museum at Bryan, founded in 1961 by the American Association of University Women, featured local exhibits, a "discovery room" with live animals, nature trails, programs for schools, special programs for the handicapped, and a summer daycamp. The Heard Natural Science Museum and Wildlife Sanctuary, founded in 1964 at McKinney, concentrated on the natural history of North Central Texas and provided a collection and setting for research in ornithology.

Several cities had botanical gardens, some with research collections. The Fort Worth Botanical Garden, founded in 1933, had a herbarium and educational programs; the San Antonio Botanical Center, founded in 1977, included plant material from East Texas, South Texas, and the Edwards Plateau. The Dallas Arboretum and Botanical Gardens, founded in 1978, had displays and research collections in horticulture, botany, and ecology, and sponsored a newsletter and educational programs.

Some of the postwar museums featured physical science exhibits. The Don Harrington Discovery Center, founded at Amarillo in 1968, had medical and physical science exhibits, a planetarium, and a solar telescope. Museum staff conducted research projects relating to solar activity. The San Antonio Museum of Science, Technology, and Transportation, founded in 1968, featured primarily transportation exhibits, as did the Pate Museum of Transportation, founded in Fort Worth in 1969. The Insights—El Paso Science Center, founded in 1979, had participatory science exhibits on perception and energy, using sight, smell, touch, and hearing exhibits. Discovery Hall, a Physics Museum for All Ages, incorporated in 1984 in Austin, featured hands-on demonstrations for both children and adults designed to improve public understanding of science and technology. Scientists from the University of Texas and other universities cooperated with museum staff in running the program. In 1985 William Greggs, director of the Harris County Heritage Society, was raising funds for a new museum to include Texas history and technology.

At least twenty other museums, mostly built in the post-World War II era, included science exhibits in their general displays, and several others included Indian artifacts in their collections and some archaeology exhibits.

One major museum in Texas, though not strictly a Texas museum, which had significant educational impact was the NASA Museum, founded in 1964 at the Lyndon B. Johnson Space Center in Houston. From its inception the museum has offered guided tours of the Space Center, including training and control areas, educational programs for children, and artifacts and exhibits pertaining to the U.S. manned space program. Displays included many of the spacecraft actually used and replicas of others, trainers, space suits—showing changes in suit technology—flags carried into space, moon rocks, films, and numerous photographs. More than one million visitors have toured the museum each year since its opening. In 1985 almost 1.5 million people visited the NASA museum. The federal government also operated museums with displays and research projects related to military technology on many of the armed services bases located in Texas.

By the mid-1980s Texas had more than five hundred museums. Though most were historical museums, a growing number featured natural history, physical science, or technology exhibits, and several functioned primarily as science museums. Most of the science museums had strong educational programs. Many coordinated those programs with the public schools, trying to raise the level of science understanding for future generations. Several science museums, some almost a half century old, associated with universities, had strong research programs leading to the advancement of knowledge as well as the dissemination of scientific information. In Texas, foundations, societies, and museums have strengthened scientific research and became important educational tools for those who will shape the future of Texas and the world.

Notes

1. Kingston, 1985, pp. 527–529.
2. Ibid., pp. 529–530; Webb, Vol. I, p. 680; Branda, 1976, p. 333.
3. Kohlstedt, 1985 has a good discussion of national science institutions; Miller, 1970 discusses the early history of American foundations.
4. Renz, 1983 includes some information on major Texas foundations.
5. Hooper, 1978 treats most Texas foundations briefly; other information sources include the annual reports of specific foundations and the *Handbook of Texas*.
6. *Annual Report*, Kleberg Foundation, 1984.
7. *Annual Report*, Welch Foundation, 1982, 1983.

For further information on the Welch Foundation consult Chapter 8.
8. Withers, 1982.
9. *South Texas Agriculture*, 1979–1980, pp. 2–7; 1981–1982, pp. 40–41; letter from Thomas E. Perry to the author, Feb. 10, 1986.
10. *Biennial Report*, 1984–1985; letter from James G. Treer to the author, February 11, 1986.
11. Geiser, 1945; the three volumes of the *Handbook of Texas* provide additional information on the academy and a few other Texas societies.
12. *Bulletin*, 1917.
13. Tyler and Tyler, 1983 and *The Official Museum Directory*, 1985 are the major sources of information about the history of a few museums. The *Handbook of Texas* contains information about the history of a few museums.

Bibliography

Alexander, Edward P. *Museum Masters: Their Museums and Their Influence.* Nashville: American Association for State and Local History, 1983.

Berliner, Howard S. *A System of Scientific Medicine, Philanthropic Foundations in the Flexner Era.* San Diego: Tavistock Books, 1985.

Branda, Eldon Stephen, ed. *The Handbook of Texas, A Supplement.* Austin: Texas State Historical Association, 1976.

Bulletin of the Southwestern Association of Petroleum Geologists, I:6, 1917.

Cavnar-Johnson, John, ed. *The 1984 Hooper Directory of Texas Foundations.* San Antonio: Funding Information Center, 1984.

Ferguson, W. Keene. *A History of the Bureau of Economic Geology, 1909–1960.* Austin: The University of Texas Press, 1981.

Froh, Riley. *Wildcatter Extraordinary.* Austin: Clearstream Press, 1984.

Geiser, S. W. "The First Texas Academy of Science." *Field and Laboratory.* January (1945), 13:34–39.

Hooper, William T., Jr. *Directory of Texas Foundations.* Austin: Texas Foundation Research Center, 1978.

Kingston, Mike. "Science in Early Texas," in *Texas Almanac.* Dallas: The Dallas Morning News, 1985.

The Robert J. Kleberg, Jr. and Helen C. Kleberg Foundation. *Annual Report,* 1984.

Kohlstedt, Sally Gregory. "Institutional History." *Osiris* (1985), 1:17–36.

Miller, Howard S. *Dollars for Research, Science and Its Patrons in Nineteenth-Century America.* Seattle and London: University of Washington Press, 1970.

The Official Museum Directory, 1985. Wilmette: National Register Publishing Company, 1984.

Oleson, Alexandra, and Sanborn C. Brown, eds. *The Pursuit of Knowledge in the Early American Republic, American Scientific and Learned Societies from Colonial Times to the Civil War.* Baltimore and London: The Johns Hopkins University Press, 1976.

Oleson, Alexandra, and John Voss, eds. *The Organization of Knowledge in Modern America, 1860–1920.* Baltimore and London: The Johns Hopkins University Press, 1979.

The Perry Foundation. *South Texas Agriculture, A Progress Report form the Perry Foundation,* Robstown: 1979–1980; 1981–1982.

Renz, Loren, ed. *The Foundations Directory.* New York: The Foundation Center, 1983.

Tyler, Paula Eyrich, and Ron Tyler. *Texas Museums, A Guidebook.* Austin: University of Texas Press, 1983.

Webb, Walter Prescott, ed. *Handbook of Texas.* 2 volumes. Austin: The Texas State Historical Association, 1952.

The Robert A. Welch Foundation. *Annual Report,* 1983, 1984.

The Rob and Bessie Welder Wildlife Foundation. *Biennial Report, 1984–1985.*

Withers, Zona Adams. *A History of the Luling Foundation, 1927–1982.* Luling: The Luling Foundation, 1982.

Wittlin, Alma S. *The Museum: Its History and Its Tasks in Education.* London: Routledge and Kegan Paul, 1949.

Appendix A

Texas Timeline for the History of Science and Technology

1836 The Republic of Texas gains independence

1846 First scientific report on Texas geology is given by Frederick von Roemer.

1848 First geodetic survey point is established astronomically at Dollar Point, near Galveston.

1849 First book on Texas geology is published.

1850 First government weather station is established in Texas.

1853 Texas Medical Association is organized.

- First professional chemistry program in Texas is initiated at Austin College.

1858 B. F. Shumard identifies Permian fossils from Osage Plains and Guadalupe Mountains, establishing presence of the Permian System in North America.

1876 Agricultural and Mechanical College of Texas (TAMC) opens near Bryan; will become Texas A&M University (TAMU) in 1963.

1878 Transit of Mercury is observed by William Harkness of the U.S. Naval Observatory from the grounds of the Land Office, Austin, on May 6.

- Total eclipse of the sun is observed from Fort Worth on July 29 by a party led by Leonard Waldo of Harvard University.

- Permian red beds yield new forms of vertebrate fossils, described by Edward D. Cope.

1880 Texas Academy of Science is established for the first time. It will be resurrected in 1892 and again in 1928.

1882 Transit of Venus is observed from San Antonio on December 6 by U.S. Naval astronomers led by Asaph Hall and a Belgian expedition led by J. C. Houzeau.

- A bright comet is widely observed in Texas; interest is so high in Waco that church bells are rung at 4:00 A.M. to awaken the public to view it.

1883 The University of Texas (UT) opens at Austin; will become UT-Austin in 1967.

1884 George B. Halsted comes to UT, marking the beginning of the serious study of mathematics in the state.

- First graduate program in chemistry in Texas begins at UT.

1886 FOUNDING OF SIGMA XI

- Petroleum Prospecting Company drills first commercially successful oil well in Texas (Nacogdoches County).

1887 Hatch Act of 1887 provides federal funds to establish the Agricultural Experiment Station at TAMC.

- Agricultural Bureau of the Texas Department of Agriculture, Fisheries, Statistics, and History is created.
1888 Legislature establishes third Texas Geological Survey, directed by Edwin T. Dumble.
- Natural gas in commercial quantities is found in Washington County.
1891 The University of Texas Medical Branch (UTMB) opens at Galveston.
1893 John K. Strecker Museum is founded at Baylor College at Waco.
1895 Texas Fish and Oyster Commission is organized.
1898 First experimental psychology laboratory in Texas is founded at UT.
- Joseph S. Cullinan opens his refinery on Christmas Day; within a year the value of Texas oil will double.
1901 Spindletop oil field is opened by Anthony Lucas on January 10 when the first gusher comes in.
- First oil from the Southwest exported by tanker from Port Arthur, Texas, by the Guffey Oil Company (later the Gulf Oil Corporation) in November.
- Refinery opens in Port Arthur; will be acquired in 1902 by the Gulf Refining Company.
- Robert T. Hill publishes *Geology and Geography of the Black and Grand Prairies.*
- The UT Mineral Survey is established.
1903 Legislature passes effective laws for the conservation of wild game.
- Agricultural extension work originates in Texas under Seaman A. Knapp.
1905 First comprehensive study of Texas fauna and flora made by Vernon Bailey.
1907 Legislature requires that courses on agriculture be taught in all public schools in the state.
- Governor Thomas N. Campbell signs One Board Medical Practice Act.
1909 Bureau of Economic Geology and Technology is organized in association with UT.
- Houston Museum and Scientific Society is formed, leading eventually to the foundation of the Houston Museum of Natural Science.
1912 Rice Institute opens; will become Rice University in 1963.
1913 Study detailing the production of genetically identical quadruplets in the nine-banded armadillo is completed by J. T. Patterson of UT.
- Texas lumber companies report a third annual production of over two billion board feet.
1914 Engineering Experiment Station is created at TAMC.

1915 First Sigma Xi chapter in Texas is founded at UT on May 17.
- Texas Department of Forestry is established.
- Bureau of Economic Geology and Technology is reorganized; separate divisions are formed for Engineering Research, Industrial Chemistry, and Economic Geology.
1916 TAMC organizes School of Veterinary Medicine.
- Comprehensive study of genetic linkage in plants is published by Edgar Altenburg of Rice Institute; first chromosomal translocation in Drosophila is conceptualized by Altenburg from data provided by C. B. Bridges and A. H. Sturtevant at Columbia University.
1917 Southwestern Association of Petroleum Geologists is organized; later becomes the American Association of Petroleum Geologists.
- Last large sawmill opens in East Texas.
- Legislature creates Texas Highway Department.
1918 American Medical Association accredits Baylor University College of Medicine.
- Texas offshore production begins at Goose Creek.
1919 Gas is discovered in the Texas Panhandle.
- Micropaleontology laboratories established in Houston.
- Proration is invoked for the first time in Burkburnett oil field.
1920 R. L. Moore joins the faculty of UT, initiating a unique period in American mathematics by introducing a new method of teaching.
- Modest gusher in Mitchell County signals the first production of oil in the Permian Basin.
1921 Total annual value of manufactures in Texas exceeds agricultural production for the first time.
1922 Texas section of the Mathematical Association of America is formed.
- Houston Museum of Natural Science opens.
- First natural gasoline plant opens in Mitchell County.
- Commercial aviation in Texas begins with air-mail service from Dallas to Chicago.
1923 T. S. Painter of UT–Austin correctly estimates the chromosome number of man to be 46, double the number accepted at the time.
1924 Geophysical Research Corporation is founded; will become Texas Instruments Incorporated in 1951.
- First state forest established; later will be named in honor of Eric O. Sieke.

1925 Texas Technological College (TTC) opens; will become Texas Tech University (TTU) in 1969.
- Legislature authorizes state wildlife reserve system.

1926 B. C. Tharp's "Structure of Texas Vegetation East of the 98th Meridian" is published.

1927 Herman J. Muller at UT discovers that X-rays cause mutations in Drosophila.
- First independent department of psychology in Texas is initiated at UT.
- Luling Foundation is established to fund research directed toward the improvement of agricultural methods.

1928 Texas becomes leading state in oil-well drilling and petroleum production.
- The Texas Archaeological and Paleontological Society is organized.

1929 T. S. Painter at UT uses giant salivary gland chromosomes of the Drosophila to confirm visually the large chromosomal mutations isolated by H. J. Muller.
- Settlement of claims on William J. McDonald's will favors the UT Department of Astronomy.

1930 Columbus M. "Dad" Joiner brings in largest oil well known at that time, near Henderson in East Texas, thus opening the East Texas oil field, a classic stratigraphic type.
- Railroads in Texas peak at 16,900 miles of track.
- Houston becomes the largest city in Texas.

1931 First Sigma Xi club in Texas is organized at TTC on May 26.

1932 Agreement between UT and the University of Chicago to jointly establish and operate the McDonald Observatory is ratified on November 23.
- Lumber production bottoms at less than four million board feet, the lowest annual figure since 1880, when the lumber boom began.

1934 Mutagenic effects of ultraviolet light are discovered by Edgar Altenburg of Rice Institute.
- Federal government begins purchasing land for national forests in Texas.

1936 Herman J. Muller of UT wins Nobel prize for his work in genetics.
- Submarine canyons are detected directly on the continental shelf of the Gulf of Mexico using electronic depth recorders.
- Magnesium and bromine are produced from the waters of the Gulf of Mexico for the first time by the Dow Chemical Company, near Freeport, Texas.

- M. D. Anderson Foundation is established.

1937 Pre-World War II Texas oil production peaks at 5.1 billion barrels, 25.7 percent of the total United States production.
- Museum of TTC opens.

1939 World War II begins in Europe.
- Formal dedication of the McDonald Observatory is held at Mount Locke in the Davis Mountains on May 5.
- Texas Memorial Museum at UT opens.

1940 Board of Directors of the Dow Chemical Company decides in January to build the company's first Texas plant at Freeport.
- Roger J. Williams announces elucidation of the molecular structure of pantothenic acid in the March 8 issue of *Science.*
- The Clayton Foundation Biochemical Institute is established at UT on September 13.

1941 First billet of magnesium from sea water is poured in the Dow Chemical Company plant at Freeport on January 21.
- UT Marine Science Laboratory is opened at Port Aransas, Texas.

1943 UTMB begins publication of *Texas Reports on Biology and Medicine.*

1944 M. D. Anderson Hospital and Tumor Institute (UT) is founded in Houston.

1945 World War II ends with nuclear explosions over Japan. Nuclear age begins.

1946 River basin salvage archaeology begins in Texas.

1947 Sigma Xi founds the Scientific Research Society for members working in industrial research laboratories.
- Activities of the Texas Agriculture Experiment Station are integrated into the departments of the TAMC schools of agriculture and veterinary medicine.

1948 Michael E. DeBakey, M.D., becomes professor and chairman of the Department of Surgery at the Baylor College of Medicine in Houston.
- Psychology program is initiated at the University of Houston (UH).
- Texas Psychological Association is founded.
- Era of oil, gas, and sulfur production from the deep-water sections of the continental shelf of the Gulf of Mexico begins.

1949 The genetotropic principle, first recognized by Roger Williams, is announced on April 27.
- Department of Oceanography is established at TAMC in College Station.

1950 W. Frank Blair's synthesis, "The Biotic Provinces of Texas," appears.

- The growth-producing effects of antibiotics in poultry are discovered and "above normal" growth in chickens is described.
- The concept of pumping water to a higher level during low peak, then storing it so that it will be available to produce hydroelectric power during high peak, is employed for the first time at Buchanan Dam.

1950s Severe weather radar network is installed in Texas; pioneering research on weather radar is carried out, including a dual-wavelength facility at TAMC.

1951 X-ray sterilization of male screwworm flies is reported by Raymond C. Bushland and D. E. Hopkins in the *Journal of Economic Entomology*.
- Forest tree genetics program is initiated.
- Denton Cooley, M.D., becomes a colleague of DeBakey at the Baylor College of Medicine.
- The Geophysical Research Corporation becomes Texas Instruments Incorporated.
- Roger Williams describes the interplay between hereditary and environmental influences based on nutrition and the genetotropic principle, in *Nutrition and Alcoholism*.

1952 First tornado watch is issued.
- Mezes Hall at UT opens; it is the first laboratory in Texas built specifically for psychology.

1953 DeBakey and Cooley perform the first successful resection and replacement of an aneurysm of the descending thoracic aorta on January 3.
- The Southwest Research Institute in San Antonio becomes the first Texas branch of the Scientific Research Society, an offspring of Sigma Xi.
- On August 7 DeBakey and colleagues perform a successful carotid endartarectomy for cerebrovascular insufficiency.
- A technique is developed by T. C. Hsu to spread metaphase chromosomes in mammalian cell cultures.
- First class of USAF Basic Meteorology students is enrolled at TAMC.
- Gordon K. Teal joins Texas Instruments Incorporated in Dallas.
- Texas Transportation Institute is founded at TAMC.
- Southwestern Association of Naturalists is founded.
- Rob and Bessie Welder Wildlife Foundation is established.

1954 Silicon transistor is invented by Gordon Teal and Willis Adcock of Texas Instruments Incorporated.
- First United States publication on neuroleptics (chlorpromazine) appears, written by V. J. Kinross-Wright of the Baylor College of Medicine at Houston.
- The Robert A. Welch Foundation is established.
- New Van de Graaf accelerator is installed at Rice Institute.
- *An Introductory Handbook of Texas Archaeology* is published.

1955 Heritability of the ability of beef cattle to gain weight is confirmed and reported.
- First national conference on psychopharmacology is held at UTMB in Galveston.
- Texas Weather Radar Network is dedicated.
- Sandow lignite mine reopens.

1956 Mechanical heart-lung devices are used for the first time on April 5 by DeBakey and colleagues in Houston.
- First commercial sorghum hybrid is released.
- First section of the interstate highway system opens.

1957 American space effort is mobilized by Sputnik 1, the first artificial satellite, sent aloft by the U.S.S.R.
- First Welch Conference is held in Houston.
- W. Harry Mayne of the Petty Geophysical Engineering Company receives a patent for his common-depth-point geophysical technique, a new tool for petroleum exploration.
- Department of Astronomy is established at UT.

1957–58 International Geophysical Year is held.

1958 First broad clinical trials of benzodiazepines to treat psychiatric disorders are conducted by I. Cohen of Houston and T. Harris of Galveston.
- First automated refinery in Texas is put on-line at Port Arthur.
- Space Task Group is formed by NASA to manage Project Mercury.
- Jack St. Clair Kilby of Texas Instruments Incorporated conceives the idea of an integrated printed circuit; he makes it a reality in 1959.

1959 First regional agricultural research and extension center is established at Weslaco by the TAMU System.
- Corpus Christi Harbor Bridge is completed.

1960 L. J. Reed and his coworkers report in the *Journal of Biochemistry* on July 7 the initial phases of what will become an elegant elucidation of the structure of the pyruvate dehydrogenase complex.

- NASA awards contracts on October 25 to study the feasibility of manned flight to the moon (Project Apollo).
- Mining of uranium, needed in nuclear reactors, begins in Texas.

1961 First American manned suborbital space flight is made on May 5 (Project Mercury).

- President Kennedy sets goal on May 25 of lunar landing by 1970.
- Houston is chosen on September 16 as the site for a Manned Spacecraft Center to manage all NASA manned space-flight projects.
- Definitive studies of the Loop and other currents in the Gulf of Mexico begin.

1962 Center for Relativity Theory is established at UT.

- Electronic Data Systems Corporation is founded.
- Construction of Houston Astrodome begins; it will be completed in 1965.
- Agreement between UT and the University of Chicago concerning the McDonald Observatory is renegotiated.

1963 First transistorized digital recording system for application in petroleum exploration is completed by Texas Instruments Incorporated for commercial use.

- First Texas Symposium on Relativistic Astrophysics is held in Dallas.
- Conversion of tropical sorghums to temperate varieties is begun.
- Harlan J. Smith is appointed director of the McDonald Observatory.

1964 DeBakey's team performs first successful aortocoronary bypass on November 23 at Methodist Hospital in Houston.

- Texas Instruments Incorporated produces the TMS1000 microprocessor chip.
- Diapause control of the boll weevil is applied on the High Plains of Texas.
- Heterosis (hybrid vigor) is described in beef cattle.
- Construction of U.S.–Mexico Amistad Dam begins on the Rio Grande; it will be completed in 1969.

1965 R. Pettit announces preparation of the iron tricarbonyl complex of cyclobutadiene, the first of many such compounds, making a significant contribution to the understanding of the structure of organometallic compounds.

- College of Geosciences is organized at TAMU; it includes the newly separated departments of meteorology and oceanography.

1966 New hospital opens on March 20 to house the Shriners' Burn Institute in Galveston.

- First semidwarf variety of hard red winter wheat (Sturdy) is released.
- Fusion Research Center is established at UT.
- Institute for Storm Research is founded at Houston.
- With Project Gemini, controlled from Houston, the U.S. achieves parity with the U.S.S.R. in space flight.

1967 The University of Texas system is organized; it will grow to fourteen components by 1979.

- Cyclotron Institute at TAMU begins versatile accelerator services for southwest U.S.
- Datapoint Incorporated is formed as a spinoff from Texas Instruments Incorporated.
- Texas Water Quality Board is organized to begin curbing industrial and municipal pollution of Texas waters.

1968 Cooley and his associates at the Texas Heart Institute perform the first successful cardiac transplantation in the U.S.

- The 107-inch telescope at the McDonald Observatory is formally dedicated on November 26.
- The Texas Committee on Natural Resources is founded to educate the public on ecological issues.
- First circumlunar manned space flight (Apollo 8) is completed in December.

1969 A mechanical heart is implanted in a dying patient at the Texas Heart Institute on April 4.

- First men land on the moon in July (Apollo 11); second crew visits moon in November (Apollo 12).
- First confirmed laser-return is received from a lunar reflector at the McDonald Observatory on August 2.
- First Offshore Technology Conference is held in Houston, bringing the latest scientific and technological developments in all aspects of petroleum technology to a worldwide audience.
- New skyscraper design (One Shell Plaza in Houston) is introduced by Fazlur Kahn and Gerald D. Hines.
- An era in mathematics ends with the retirement of R. L. Moore from UT-Austin.

1970 Texas Tokamak is completed at UT-Austin to be used for fusion research.

- First Annual Lunar Science Conference is held from January 5 to 8 in Houston for the Lunar Science Institute.
- First multiple-adversity-resistant varieties of cotton are released.
- National Environment Policy Act moves ecological science into the business world.

1971 UT-Austin astronomical expeditions to Australia, India, South Africa, and the Virgin Islands are organized to observe occultation of Beta Scorpii by Jupiter and its satellite, Io, on May 13.

1972 Studies initiated by M. S. Brown and J. L. Goldstein lead to an understanding of the receptor-mediated pathway for cholesterol homeostasis.
- Texas Utilities Company begins operating first modern multi-megawatt lignite power plant.
- Active oil and gas seeps are directly detected on the continental shelf of the Gulf of Mexico using seismic sub-bottom profiler techniques.
- Division of Earth and Planetary Sciences of the Marine Biomedical Institute of UTMB is established; it will become the Institute of Geophysics in 1983.

1973 Skylab, the first U.S. spacecraft designed for long-term occupancy, is launched on May 7. (Three 3-person missions, lasting a total of 171 days, will be flown in the next eight months.)
- Manned Spacecraft Center is rededicated on August 27 as the Lyndon B. Johnson Space Center.
- Dallas-Fort Worth (DFW) Regional Airport and its people-moving Airtrans system are completed.
- Office of State Climatologist moves from Austin to TAMU in College Station.
- Development of the Woodlands model community begins.
- UT-Austin expedition is organized to be in the Sahara on June 30 to observe the solar eclipse and the Einstein deflection of light; there will be a followup expedition in November.
- The Department of Oceanography of TAMU acquires the 186-foot, seagoing oceanographic research vessel *Gyre* from the U.S. Navy and purchases the research submersible *Diaphus*.

1974 The Scientific Research Society, an offspring of Sigma Xi, ceases to exist on January 1. Branches and clubs are integrated into Sigma Xi as chapters or clubs or are disbanded.
- Basic norms of sleep are given in *EEG of Human Sleep* by Robert Williams, Ismet Karacan, and Carolyn Hursch of the Baylor College of Medicine.
- Xerox Corporation opens its first Texas plant in Dallas.

1975 First cooperative manned space mission with a foreign country, the Apollo–Soyuz Test Project, takes place from July 15 to 24.
- Active gas seeps on the continental shelf of the Gulf of Mexico are observed and photographed directly from the submersible *Diaphus*.
- Agricultural Weather Service Center is established in College Station.

1976 Landsat images become available to the public for the study of whole-earth resources.

1977 Ilya Prigogine is awarded the Nobel prize in chemistry for his theory of dissipative structures, an extension of the classical theory of thermodynamics.
- Tandy Corporation introduces the home computer.

1978 Procedures are developed by Michael and Jeanette Siciliano and Ronald Humphrey to isolate electrophoretic shift mutants in cell cultures.
- Experiments are reported on the use of electrical stimulation to increase the tenderness of beef carcasses.

1980 Apple Computer locates a plant in Carrolton, Texas.

1981 In situ gasification of lignite is demonstrated.
- First of four orbital flights is made by Shuttle Orbiter 102 (*Columbia*), a seven-day mission beginning from Cape Canaveral on April 12 and ending with a normal shuttle landing at Edwards Air Force Base in California.

1982 *Columbia* carries first nonpilot astronauts (mission specialists) into orbit.
- The Houston Area Research Center (HARC) is established in the Woodlands to serve as a catalyst effecting interaction between fundamental research being done in the academic sector and applied research being carried out by industry and the government.
- Jesse Jones Memorial Bridge is completed in Houston.
- Compaq Computer Corporation is formed in Houston.

1983 National Academy of Sciences survey ranks the UT-Austin botany department first in the nation and the zoology department seventh.

- Lemont, a semidwarf rice system, is released.
- Microelectronics and Computer Technology Corporation (MCC) is founded in Austin.

1984 Southeast Texas Sigma Xi Council (SETSXC) is organized.

- On January 25 President Reagan advocates that a permanent earth-orbiting space station be NASA's major manned effort for the next ten years.
- Responsibility for the operation of the Ocean Drilling Program is transferred from the Scripps Institute of Oceanography in San Diego to the College of Geosciences of TAMU-Galveston; authorization is given to construct the associated Deep Sea Core Laboratory.

1985 Michael S. Brown and Joseph L. Goldstein of the University of Texas Health Science Center at Dallas win the Nobel prize for physiology or medicine for their research on cholesterol homeostasis.

- Fourth and last of the first-generation shuttle orbiter spacecraft (*Atlantis*) is launched on a mission for the U.S. Air Force.

- On December 11 R. E. Smalley of Rice announces discovery of the first spherical molecule, a 60-carbon molecule with a structure like a truncated icosahedron (a geodesic sphere with a hollow center). It has been called Buckminsterfullerene, after the originator of geodesic domes, Buckminster Fuller.
- The Geotechnology Research Institute is established by the Texas legislature as part of HARC to study energy sources and their characteristics and to improve exploration and production techniques.

1986 Explosion of the launch vehicle minutes after launch on January 29 costs the lives of the *Challenger* seven who had intended to do scientific research in space.

- Under the leadership of SETSXC, members of Sigma Xi in southeast Texas celebrate the centennial of Sigma Xi with a commemorative volume and many activities.

Appendix B

Senior Colleges and
Universities in Texas
by System

East Texas State University	ETSU
East Texas State University Center at Texarkana	ETSU-Texarkana
Lamar University System	
Lamar University at Beaumont	LU-Beaumont
Lamar University at Orange	LU-Orange
Lamar University at Port Arthur	LU-Port Author
Midwestern State University	MSU
North Texas State University	NTSU
Pan American University	PAU
Pan American University at Brownsville	PAU-Brownsville
Stephen F. Austin State University	SFASU
Texas A&M University System	
Prairie View A&M University	PVAMU
Tarleton State University	TStU
Texas A&M University	TAMU
Texas A&M University at Galveston	TAMU-Galveston
Texas Southern University	TSU
Texas State University System	
Angelo State University	ASU
Sam Houston State University	SHSU
Southwest Texas State University	STSU
Sul Ross State University	SRSU
Uvalde Study Center	USC
Texas Tech University	TTU
Texas Woman's University	TWU
Texas Woman's University Dallas Center	
Parkland Campus	TWU-Dallas Parkland
Presbyterian Campus	TWU-Dallas Presbyterian
Texas Woman's University Houston Center	TWU-Houston
The University of Texas System	
The University of Texas at Arlington	UT-Arlington
The University of Texas at Austin	UT-Austin
The University of Texas at Dallas	UT-Dallas
The University of Texas at El Paso	UT El Paso

The University of Texas of the Permian Basin	UT-Permian Basin	INDEPENDENT SENIOR COLLEGES AND UNIVERSITIES	
The University of Texas at San Antonio	UT-San Antonio	Abilene Christian University	ACU
		Amber University	AU
The University of Texas at Tyler	UT-Tyler	American Technological University	ATU
University of Houston System		Austin College	AC
University of Houston-Clear Lake	UH-Clear Lake	Baylor University	BU
		Bishop College	BC
University of Houston-Downtown	UH-Downtown	Concordia Lutheran College	CLC
		Dallas Baptist University	DBU
University of Houston-University Park	UH-University Park	East Texas Baptist University	ETBU
		Hardin-Simmons University	HSU
University of Houston-Victoria	UH-Victoria	Houston Baptist University	HBU
		Howard Payne University	HPU
University System of South Texas		Huston-Tillotson College	HTC
		Incarnate Word College	IWC
Corpus Christi State University	CCSU	Jarvis Christian College	JCC
		LeTourneau College	LTC
Laredo State University	LStU	Lubbock Christian College	LCC
Texas A&I University	TAIU	McMurry College	MC
West Texas State University	WTSU	Our Lady of the Lake University of San Antonio	OLLU
		Paul Quinn College	PQC
PUBLIC MEDICAL SCHOOLS AND HEALTH SCIENCE CENTERS		Rice University	Rice
Texas A&M University College of Medicine	TAMU-Med	Saint Edward's University Incorporated	SEU
Texas College of Osteopathic Medicine	TCOM	Saint Mary's University of San Antonio	StMU
Texas Tech University Health Sciences Center	TTU-HSC	Schreiner College	SC
		Southern Methodist University	SMU
The University of Texas Health Science Center at Dallas	UTHSC-Dallas	Southwestern Adventist College	SAC
		Southwestern Christian College	SCC
The University of Texas Health Science Center at Houston	UTHSC-Houston	Southwestern University	SWU
		Texas Christian University	TCU
The University of Texas Health Science Center at San Antonio	UTHSC-San Antonio	Texas College	TC
		Texas Lutheran College	TLC
The University of Texas Medical Branch at Galveston	UTMB	Texas Wesleyan College	TWC
		Trinity University	TU
		University of Dallas	UD
INDEPENDENT MEDICAL AND DENTAL SCHOOLS		University of Mary Hardin-Baylor	UMHB
Baylor College of Dentistry	BCD	University of St. Thomas	UST
Baylor College of Medicine	BCM	Wayland Baptist University	WBU
		Wylie College	WC

Senior Colleges and Universities of Texas

Abilene Christian University	ACU
Amber University	AU
American Technological University	ATU
Angelo State University	ASU
Austin College	AC
Baylor College of Dentistry	BCD
Baylor College of Medicine	BCM
Baylor University	BU
Bishop College	BC
Concordia Lutheran College	CLC
Corpus Christi State University	CCSU
Dallas Baptist University	DBU
East Texas Baptist University	ETBU
East Texas State University	ETSU
East Texas State University Center at Texarkana	ETSU-Texarkana
Hardin-Simmons University	HSU
Houston Baptist University	HBU
Howard Payne University	HPU
Huston-Tillotson College	HTC
Incarnate Word College	IWC
Jarvis Christian College	JCC
Lamar University at Beaumont	LU-Beaumont
Lamar University at Orange	LU-Orange
Lamar University at Port Arthur	LU-Port Arthur
Laredo State University	LStU
LeTourneau College	LTC
Lubbock Christian College	LCC
McMurry College	MC
Midwestern State University	MSU
North Texas State University	NTSU
Our Lady of the Lake University of San Antonio	OLLU
Pan American University	PAU
Pan American University at Brownsville	PAU-Brownsville
Paul Quinn College	PQC
Prairie View A&M University	PVAMU
Rice University	Rice
Saint Edward's University	SEU
Saint Mary's University of San Antonio	StMU
Sam Houston State University	SHSU
Schreiner College	SC
Southern Methodist University	SMU
Southwest Texas State University	STSU
Southwestern Adventist College	SAC
Southwestern Christian College	SCC
Southwestern University	SWU
Stephen F. Austin State University	SFASU

Sul Ross State University	SRSU	The University of Texas Medical	
Tarleton State University	TStU	Branch at Galveston	UTMB
Texas A&I University	TAIU	The University of Texas at	
Texas A&M University	TAMU	Arlington	UT-Arlington
Texas A&M University College		The University of Texas at	
of Medicine	TAMU-Med	Austin	UT-Austin
Texas A&M University at		The University of Texas at Dallas	UT-Dallas
Galveston	TAMU-Galveston	The University of Texas at El	
Texas Christian University	TCU	Paso	UT-El Paso
Texas College	TC	The University of Texas at San	
Texas College of Osteopathic		Antonio	UT-San Antonio
Medicine	TCOM	The University of Texas at Tyler	UT-Tyler
Texas Lutheran College	TLC	The University of Texas of the	
Texas Southern University	TSU	Permian Basin	UT-Permian
Texas Tech University	TTU		Basin
Texas Tech University Health		Trinity University	TU
Sciences Center	TTU-HSC	University of Dallas	UD
Texas Wesleyan College	TWC	University of Houston-Clear	
Texas Woman's University	TWU	Lake	UH-Clear Lake
Texas Woman's University		University of Houston-	
Houston Center	TWU-Houston	Downtown	UH-Downtown
Texas Woman's University		University of Houston-	
Parkland Campus	TWU-Dallas	University Park	UH-University
	Parkland		Park
Texas Woman's University		University of Houston-Victoria	UH-Victoria
Presbyterian Campus	TWU-Dallas	University of Mary Hardin-	
	Presbyterian	Baylor	UMHB
		University of St. Thomas	UST
The University of Texas Health		Uvalde Study Center	USC
Science Center		Wayland Baptist University	WBU
at Dallas	UTHSC-Dallas	West Texas State University	WTSU
at Houston	UTHSC-	Wylie College	WC
	Houston		
at San Antonio	UTHSC-San		
	Antonio		

Senior Colleges and Universities in Texas by Acronym

AC	Austin College
ACU	Abilene Christian University
ASU	Angelo State University
ATU	American Technological University
AU	Amber University
BC	Bishop College
BCD	Baylor College of Dentistry
BCM	Baylor College of Medicine
BU	Baylor University
CCSU	Corpus Christi State University
CLC	Concordia Lutheran College
DBU	Dallas Baptist University
ETBU	East Texas Baptist University
ETSU	East Texas State University
ETSU-Texarkana	East Texas State University Center at Texarkana
HBU	Houston Baptist University
HPU	Howard Payne University
HSU	Hardin-Simmons University
HTC	Huston-Tillotson College
IWC	Incarnate Word College
JCC	Jarvis Christian College
LCC	Lubbock Christian College
LStU	Laredo State University
LTC	LeTourneau College
LU-Beaumont	Lamar University at Beaumont
LU-Orange	Lamar University at Orange
LU-Port Arthur	Lamar University at Port Arthur
MC	McMurry College
MSU	Midwestern State University
NTSU	North Texas State University
OLLU	Our Lady of the Lake University of San Antonio

PAU	Pan American University	TWU-Dallas Parkland	Texas Woman's University Parkland Campus
PAU-Brownsville	Pan American University at Brownsville		
PQC	Paul Quinn College	TWU-Dallas Presbyterian	Texas Woman's University Presbyterian Campus
PVAMU	Prairie View A&M University		
Rice	Rice University	UD	University of Dallas
SAC	Southwestern Adventist College	UH-Clear Lake	University of Houston-Clear Lake
SC	Schreiner College	UH-Downtown	University of Houston-Downtown
SCC	Southwestern Christian College	UH-University Park	University of Houston-University Park
SEU	Saint Edward's University Incorporated	UH-Victoria	University of Houston-Victoria
SFASU	Stephen F. Austin State University	UMHB	University of Mary Hardin-Baylor
SHSU	Sam Houston State University	USC	Uvalde Study Center
		UST	University of St. Thomas
SMU	Southern Methodist University	UT-Arlington	The University of Texas at Arlington
SRSU	Sul Ross State University	UT-Austin	The University of Texas at Austin
STSU	Southwest Texas State University	UT-Dallas	The University of Texas at Dallas
SWU	Southwestern University	UT-El Paso	The University of Texas at El Paso
StMU	Saint Mary's University of San Antonio		
TAIU	Texas A&I University	UTHSC-Dallas	The University of Texas Health Science Center at Dallas
TAMU	Texas A&M University		
TAMU-Galveston	Texas A&M University at Galveston	UTHSC-Houston	The University of Texas Health Science Center at Houston
TAMU-Med	Texas A&M University College of Medicine		
TC	Texas College	UTHSC-San Antonio	The University of Texas Health Science Center at San Antonio
TCOM	Texas College of Osteopathic Medicine		
TCU	Texas Christian University	UTMB	The University of Texas Medical Branch at Galveston
TLC	Texas Lutheran College		
TSU	Texas Southern University	UT-Permian Basin	The University of Texas of the Permian Basin
TStU	Tarleton State University	UT-San Antonio	The University of Texas at San Antonio
TTU	Texas Tech University		
TTU-HSC	Texas Tech University Health Sciences Center	UT-Tyler	The University of Texas at Tyler
TU	Trinity University	WBU	Wayland Baptist University
TWC	Texas Wesleyan College		
TWU	Texas Woman's University	WC	Wylie College
		WTSU	West Texas State University
TWU-Houston	Texas Woman's University Houston Center		

About the Authors

Spencer R. Baen is director of the Texas A&M University Center for Energy and Mineral Resources and assistant director of the Texas Engineering Experiment Station. He is a native of San Antonio, Texas, and a graduate of Texas A&M University, where he received his Bachelor's degree in Engineering in 1943 for studies in petroleum and mechanical engineering. He received a M.S. degree in mechanical engineering in 1946 and a Ph.D. in mechanical and electrical engineering in 1950 from the California Institute of Technology. Following twenty years in the U.S. Army's missile research and development program, he returned to Texas A&M University in 1970 as head of the Space Technology Division; head of the Mechanical Engineering Research Division; and assistant director, Texas Engineering Experiment Station. He is a registered professional engineer and a past board member of the Brazos Chapter, Texas Society of Professional Engineers. As director of the Center for Energy and Mineral Resources since 1977, his principal responsibilities have been to help coordinate and develop engineering research in the College of Engineering and energy and mineral research throughout the Texas A&M University system.

Margaret S. Bishop has been professor emerita of the University of Houston–University Park since 1971. Born in Lewiston, Michigan, she received the A.B., M.S., and Ph.D. (1933) degrees from the University of Michigan. After graduation she worked for the Pure Oil Company as geologist until 1938, when she and her husband opened the consulting office of Bishop and Bishop. In 1953 she became a professor in the University of Houston geology department, where she taught until retirement. Honors include election to Phi Beta Kappa, Sigma Xi, and Phi Kappa Phi. Her publications include the textbooks *Subsurface Mapping* and *Focus on Earth Science*, in its fifth edition.

James C. Bradford is professor of mathematics at Abilene Christian University. He received B.S. and M.S. degrees from North Texas State University and the Ph.D. from the University of Oklahoma (1957), all with majors in mathematics. Except for the years 1961–65, he has been at Abilene Christian University since 1956 and served as department head from 1966 to 1979. He has participated in post-doctoral teaching activities at Texas Christian University and the American University in Washington, D.C. Industrial experience includes operations research at Vought Corporation and research on the detection of underground nuclear explosions while with Teledyne. He has served the Texas section of the Mathematical Association of America as secretary, governor, and public information officer. He also served as president of the Texas Association of Academic Administrators in Mathematical Sciences. He has been vice-president of the Texas Academy of Science and a member of its Visiting Scientist Program.

Chester R. Burns has been a faculty member at the University of Texas Medical Branch since July of 1969. He currently serves that institution as the James Wade Rockwell Professor of the history of Medicine, a professor in the department of preventive medicine and community health, a member of the Institute for the Medical Humanities, and a member of the University of Texas Graduate School of the Biomedical Sciences. He received baccalaureate and medical degrees from Vanderbilt University and a Ph.D. in the history of medicine from the Johns Hopkins University School of Medicine. He is coordinating the preparation of entries on medicine and health care that will appear in the revised edition of the *Handbook of Texas*, and he is overseeing the preparation of a centennial history of UTMB.

Wm. David Compton is currently under contract to Johnson Space Center, working on a history of the Apollo lunar exploration missions. He holds B.S. and M.S. degrees from North Texas State University, a Ph.D. from the University of Texas, and a M.Sc. from the University of London (Imperial College of Science and Technology). He has worked in NASA's history program since 1974; he is coauthor of the official NASA history of Skylab, *Living and Working in Space* (published in 1983). Compton was the 1984 winner of the annual Robert H. Goddard historical essay competition sponsored by the National Space Club. He is a member of Sigma Xi and the Society for the History of Technology.

E. Mott Davis is professor of anthropology, director of the Radiocarbon Laboratory, and director of Archaeological Studies at the University of Texas at Austin. Born in Shirley, Massachusetts, he obtained all of his academic training at Harvard (Ph.D. 1954). He was on the staff of the University of Nebraska, Lincoln, from 1948 until 1956, when he came to the University of Texas at Austin. His principal areas of archaeological field research are the Central Great Plains (especially the earliest occupants—the Paleo-Indian horizon), northeast Texas (prehistoric Caddo Indians and their precursors), Central Texas, and Balkans. His principal emphases are paleoenvironmental studies, radiocarbon dating, and the history of archaeological research.

David S. Evans has been professor of astronomy at the University of Texas at Austin since 1968. He is currently Jack S. Josey Centennial Professor. Born in Cardiff, Wales, he became Foundation Scholar at Cambridge University, England, where he received his B.A., M.A., Ph.D., and Sc. D. His list of awards is long, including the McIntyre Award for Astronomical History in 1972, and he has been active in several astronomical societies. In 1965–66 he was NSF Senior Visiting Scientist Fellow at UT-Austin. He is past president of the Astronomical Society of Southern Africa and of Commission 30, the International Astronomical Union. From 1968 to 1981 he was associate director for research at the McDonald Observatory. He has written or edited nine books and more than two hundred papers on astronomy, medical physics, and astronomical history. His recent research interests include stellar occultations and flare stars.

Born February 20, 1942, in Baytown, Texas, **Rand B. Evans** received his B.A., M.A., and Ph.D. degrees from the University of Texas at Austin. From 1972 to 1976 he served as co-director of the history of psychology program in the department of psychology at the University of New Hampshire. He has also been the history/theory editor of the *American Journal of Psychology*. From 1978 through 1983 he was head of the department of psychology at Texas A&M University, where he is currently teaching. His primary areas of research are the history and theory of psychology, with special emphasis on Edward Bradford Titchener and the beginnings of American experimental psychology.

Richard A. Geyer has been professor emeritus of oceanography at Texas A&M University since 1980. He received a B.S. in geology from New York University, then a Ph.D. in geology and geophysics from Princeton University. He subsequently pursued a diversified professional and academic career teaching geophysics and oceanography at Princeton University, the University of Houston, and Texas A&M University. At Texas A&M he was head of the oceanography department from 1966 to 1977. His professional activities included management of the Gravity and Magnetic Division of Texas Instruments, Inc., Dallas. He later became technical director of oceanography there.

He was awarded an honorary membership in the Society of Exploration Geophysicists in 1982. He has edited several books in geophysics and oceanography and published more than thirty papers. He was vice-chairman of the President's Commission on Marine Science and Engineering in Washington, D.C., from 1968 to 1970 and has served on numerous national and international geophysical and oceanographic committees. He has been president of Geophysics Associates, Inc., Bryan, Texas, since 1980.

John F. Griffiths is professor of meteorology at Texas A&M University and Texas state climatologist. Born in England, he received a B.Sc. in Mathematics, A.K.C. in Theology, D.I.C. in Physics, and a M.Sc. in Meteorology (1949), all from London University. His research interests include problems in which atmospheric conditions play an important role, especially in application to agriculture, architecture, and water resources.

From 1958 to 1962 he was principal scientific officer in charge of the research section of the East African Meteorological Department. From 1956 to 1958 he was bioclimatologist with the East African Veterinary Research Organization. From 1950 to 1956 he worked for British Colonial Scientific Research Service and served with the Desert Locust Survey in Ethiopia, Somalia, and Arabia. He has done research in Senegal, Mali, and Mauretania as an agrometeorologist advising the Greek and Spanish governments. Author of more than a hundred publications and eight books, he was elected to the World Academy of Art and Science.

Michel T. Halbouty is chairman of the board and chief executive officer of Michel T. Halbouty Energy Co., Houston, Texas. A graduate of Texas A&M University, he holds Bachelor's and Master's degrees in both geology and petroleum engineering, a Professional Geological Engineering degree, and a Doctor of Engineering (HC) degree from the Montana College of Mineral Science and Technology.

Halbouty has authored and coauthored several books and more than 280 articles and papers, primarily on petroleum geology and petroleum engineering, and has lectured throughout the world to geoscientists and engineers on the philosophy of petroleum exploration, development, production, new techniques, and concepts.

He is a member of numerous scientific organizations, is a past-president of the American Association of Petroleum Geologists, and is a member of the National Academy of Engineering. Two of his most recent awards include the Hoover Medal, presented by the American Association of Engineering Societies, and the designation by the Texas Academy of Science as the Distinguished Texas Scientist of the Year for 1983.

Lewis Harris is manager of the computer systems engineering department of Lockheed Engineering and Management Services Company, Inc., in Houston, Texas. The department he manages provides computer system engineering (hardware and software) for NASA Johnson Space Center. He has been responsible for development projects utilizing computers, microprocessors, and computer networks.

A native of Mexia, Texas, he is a graduate of the University of Houston (B.S. mathematics) and University of Houston–Clear Lake (M.S. computer science). He is a teaching lecturer of computer technology at the University of Houston–Clear Lake and has published papers on data-communication networks.

Phillip Hopkins is manager of the tracking and communication systems department of the Lockheed Engineering and Management Services Company, Inc., in Houston, Texas. The department he heads develops electronic devices for flight aboard the space shuttle and operates major electronic test facilities for the Johnson Space Center. He has been responsible for many development projects during his sixteen years at the NASA center.

A native of Trinity, Texas, he is a graduate of Tri-State College (BSEE), the Johns Hopkins University (MSEE), and the University of Houston (Ph.D. EE). He is a registered professional engineer in Texas and is an adjunct associate professor of technologies at the University of Houston–Clear Lake. In addition to his teaching at UH and for Lockheed, he has presented technical short courses in Europe. In 1982 he was an invited lecturer at the Swiss Federal Institute of Technology and at the University of Bern, Switzerland. He has published many papers on advanced communications theory.

Claude W. Horton, Sr., is professor emeritus of physics and of geological sciences at the University of Texas at Austin. He received the B.A., honors in physics, and the M.A. from the Rice Institute. He was awarded the Ph.D. in physics by the University of Texas at Austin in 1948. He has been a member of the UT–Austin faculty since 1946 and was chairman of the department of physics from 1957 to 1962. He was a research associate at the Harvard Underwater Sound Laboratory, Harvard University, from 1943 to 1945. He is a member of the corporation, Woods Hole Oceanographic Institution, and is currently an associate editor for underwater sound for the *Journal of the Acoustical Society of America.*

Joseph E. King is associate professor of history and director of the Center for History of Engineering and Technology at Texas Tech University. A graduate of Fordham University and the University of Illinois at Champaign-Urbana, he is the author of *A Mine to Make a Mine: Financing the Colorado Mining Industry, 1859–1902* (College Station: 1977) and numerous articles and research papers in history and historical preservation. He is currently advisory editor for engineering and technology in the preparation of a revised *Handbook of Texas.* At the Center he is conducting a research program to document historic engineering and architectural resources in the Southwest and maintains an extensive data base on this subject. He is an active member in many professional societies and historical organizations.

Leo J. Klosterman, C.S.B., is a Roman Catholic priest, member of the Congregation of St. Basil, and associate professor of the history of science at the University of St. Thomas in Houston.

Born in Windsor, Ontario, Canada, he received a B.A. from the University of Western Ontario in Windsor (Assumption College), 1949, a M.S. in chemistry from the University of Detroit, 1963, and a Ph.D. in the history of science from the University of Kent at Canterbury, England. He came to UST in 1976 after teaching chemistry at Catholic Central High School in Detroit from 1955 to 1973. In 1970 he received the James Bryant Conant Award of the American Chemical Society and in 1967 the Metropolitan Detroit Science Teachers' Association Distinguished Service Award. His research interest is the history of chemistry, with emphasis on the nineteenth century.

Sue A. Krenek is a journalism major at Texas A&M University, where she is a President's Endowed Scholar and a dean's list student. A native of LaMarque, Texas, Ms. Krenek graduated with honors from LaPorte High School in 1984. She is a National Merit Scholar and winner of the 1983 Achievement Award in Writing from the National Council of Teachers of English.

She is on the staff of *The Battalion,* the student daily newspaper, and is a member of other student organizations. She has been chosen for the Lambda Sigma, Phi Eta Sigma, and Alpha Lambda Delta honor societies.

H. O. Kunkel is dean of the College of Agriculture and professor of animal science, biochemistry and nutrition at Texas A&M University. He is a native Texan, with the B.S. and M.S. degrees from Texas A&M University and the Ph.D. in biochemistry from Cornell University, where he worked with Nobel laureate James B. Sumner. A faculty member at Texas A&M since 1951, he has served as associate director and director of the Texas Agricultural Experiment Station from 1962 to 1972, and as dean since 1967. He has published more than forty papers in nutrition and nutritional biochemistry and has recently written on ethics and the history of agricultural science. He holds elected membership in the American Society of Biological Chemists, the American Institute of Nutrition, and the Society for Experimental Biology and Medicine. He is a Fellow of the American Society of Animal Science and of AAAS.

Joseph J. Lagowski is professor of chemistry and professor of education at the University of Texas at Austin. Born in Chicago, he obtained a bachelor's degree from the University of Illinois at Champaign-Urbana. As a DuPont Fellow at Michigan State University, he received his Ph.D. in 1957. Lagowski spent the next two years in the Cambridge Laboratories of Professor H. J. Emeleus doing research on perfluoroalkylmercurials, for which he was awarded the degree of Ph.D. (Cantab.) in 1959. During the time at Cambridge he was a Marshall Scholar, a member of Sidney Sussex College, an assistant demonstrator at the Lensfield Road Laboratories, and a supervisor in inorganic chemistry for undergraduate tutorials. He joined the faculty of the University of Texas at Austin in 1959, where he supervises a research group of about twelve students working on a wide spectrum of chemical and educational problems. He is also currently the editor of the *Journal of Chemical Education.*

Thomas S. Matney is professor of medical genetics and professor of environmental sciences at the University of Texas Health Science Center at Houston. Born in Kansas City, Missouri, he received the B.A., B.S., and M.S. degrees from Trinity University in San Antonio, Texas. His Ph.D. (1958) in microbiology is from the University of Texas at Austin. He was associate dean of the UTHSCH Graduate School of Biomedical Sciences from 1969 to 1978. His research interests are fetal carbohydrate metabolism in cattle; ultraviolet mutagenesis in bacteria; genetics of bacterial thermophilism; genomic structure and evolution in bacteria; recognition of recombinant hetero-duplexes by bacterial DNA excision repair; and use of bacterial excision repair to estimate genotoxic risk of anticancer drugs.

Howard McCarley has been a professor of biology at Austin College since 1961. Born in Oklahoma, he received the B.A. from Austin College. His M.A. and Ph.D. (1953) were completed at the University of Texas at Austin. Professional experience includes appointments at Stephen F. Austin State University (1950–59), Southeastern Oklahoma State University (1959–61); and, since his arrival at Austin College in Sherman, he has been chairman of the biology department and dean of the Division of Sciences. Currently he is MacGregor Professor of Biology and is also visiting professor of zoology at the University of Oklahoma Biological Station. His publications and professional interests range from evolutionary processes to behavioral ecology.

Richard B. McCaslin is a doctoral candidate in history at the University of Texas in Austin. He holds a B.A. from Delta State

University in Cleveland, Mississippi, and a M.A. in Latin American history from Louisiana State University in Baton Rouge. He has published previously in *Delta Scene, Louisiana Business Review, Texas Professional Engineer,* and *Southwestern Historical Review.* His forthcoming works include a history of the College of Engineering at the University of Texas and a dissertation on the "Great Hanging at Gainesville, Texas, October 1862." He received the Clara Driscoll Fellowship in Texas History in 1986, and is a member of Phi Eta Sigma, Phi Alpha Theta, Phi Kappa Phi, and Pi Gamma Mu honor societies.

Sylvia Wallace McGrath is associate professor of history at Stephen F. Austin State University. She received her B.A. from Michigan State University, M.A. from Radcliffe College, and Ph.D. from the University of Wisconsin (Madison). Her major interest is American history, with specialization in science and the role of women. Her publications include *Charles Kenneth Leith, Scientific Adviser,* University of Wisconsin Press, 1971; encyclopedia articles; and book reviews.

Alex D. Pokorny, M.D., is professor of psychiatry and vice-chairman of the department of psychiatry at Baylor College of Medicine, Houston, Texas. Born in Taylor, Texas, he graduated from the University of Texas in Austin and from the University of Texas Medical Branch in Galveston in 1942. After military service in World War II, which included an assignment at Brooke Army Hospital in San Antonio, he was a resident in psychiatry at Southwestern Medical School in Dallas from 1946 to 1947 and at the Menninger Foundation and the VA Hospital in Topeka, Kansas, from 1947 to 1949. A member of the faculty of Baylor College of Medicine in Houston since 1949, he was chief of psy-chiatry service at the VA Hospital in Houston from 1955 to 1973. He has published extensively on research in the areas of suicide and self-destructive behavior, alcoholism, drug abuse, psychiatric epidemiology, and course and outcome of psychiatric illness.

James R. Scoggins has been professor of meteorology at Texas A&M University since 1969 and head of the department since 1980. He holds a B.S. degree in mathematics and physics from Berry College, Rome, Georgia, and B.S., M.S., and Ph.D. degrees in meteorology from Pennsylvania State University. Prior to joining the faculty at Texas A&M University in September 1967, he was employed by NASA for seven years as a meteorologist, and Lockheed Aircraft Corporation for three years as a meteorologist and mathematician. He spent almost five years in the Air Force as a weather officer. He currently serves as vice-chairman of the Texas Weather Modification Advisory Committee.

Loyd S. Swenson, Jr., is professor of history of science and technology at the University of Houston—University Park. A native Texan from Waco who obtained his A.B. degree in history at Rice Institute in 1954, he served the U.S. Navy as a gunnery officer before acquiring his Ph.D. in history in 1962 from Claremont graduate school. He is senior coauthor of two official NASA histories for manned spaceflight, *This New Ocean: A History of Project Mercury* (1966) and *Chariots for Apollo: A History of Manned Lunar Spacecraft* (1979). He has also written two books on the history of physics: *The Ethereal Aether: A History of the Michelson-Morley-Miller Aether-Drift Experiments* (Austin, 1972) and *Genesis of Relativity: Einstein in Context* (New York, 1979).

Name Index

Subject Index